THE COURT-MARTIAL OF
CAPTAIN JOHN ARMSTRONG

The Court-Martial of Captain John Armstrong

Life, Death, and Politics in America's First Regiment

Ellen Denning Smith

To order additional copies of this book, contact:
Xlibris
844-714-8691
www.Xlibris.com
Orders@Xlibris.com
832240

CONTENTS

To David, Courtney, Cara and Declan
And to the many John Armstrong descendants

ACKNOWLEDGMENTS

Relating the story of my fourth great-grandfather would have been impossible without the efforts of a kinsman, Charles F. Cochran (1876–1963), who gathered documents from family sources, organized Armstrong's many papers, researched our common ancestor's life through published and unpublished sources of the time, interviewed family members, and visited places of significance to the colonel's life with the apparent objective of someday publishing his biography. I am equally grateful to another distant relative, Mrs. Ruth Coffman, who had the foresight to entrust her cousin's papers to the William H. Smith Memorial Library, Indiana Historical Society, Indianapolis, Indiana, in the early 1970s where they remain today. These papers provided the framework for my work.

Many individuals have helped me throughout my writing journey. I am grateful to the helpful staff of the William H. Smith Memorial Library where I spent uncounted hours over a multiyear period researching Armstrong's papers. Special thanks go to Mr. Robert L. Greene Jr. of the Hunterdon County, New Jersey, Records Management Office whose help was invaluable in tracing the early history of the Armstrong family in the American colonies and to the staff of the Northumberland County, Pennsylvania, Records Office and the Northumberland County Historical Society in Sunbury who provided assistance in locating information concerning the family's Pennsylvania years. Anthony Wayne's papers were accessed at the Historical Society of Pennsylvania in Philadelphia. Staff at the US Army Heritage and Education Center in Carlisle, Pennsylvania; and the Allen County Public Library, Fort Wayne, Indiana, guided me toward finding extensive material concerning the First Regiment and its officers and men.

The staff at the Valley Forge National Historical Park; the Brandywine Battle Historic Site at Chadds Ford, Pennsylvania; the New Windsor Cantonment State Historic Park near Newburgh, New York; and the Morristown, New Jersey, National Historical Park added necessary dimensions to Armstrong's Revolutionary War experiences. A special thank-you goes to David Hospador of the Third Pennsylvania Regiment of reenactors for sharing the history of the unit's formation during its participation in the commemoration of the Battle of Monmouth Courthouse at the Monmouth Battlefield State Park, Freehold, New Jersey. Additional information on the Third Pennsylvania was accessed at the Robert Hutchings Goddard Library at Clark University, Worchester, Massachusetts. Visits to the Yorktown Battlefield Visitors Center were essential in understanding the siege. Information on the southern campaign and James Armstrong was found in Georgia at that state's archives in Morrow, the Reese Library at the University of Augusta, the Augusta Genealogical Society, and the Georgia Historical Society in Savannah. North Carolina's Guilford Courthouse National Military Park and the South Carolina Historical Society at Charleston also provided essential information regarding James's military career.

Information regarding John Armstrong's postarmy years was gleaned at the Cincinnati History Library and Archives at the Cincinnati Museum Center. Jeffersonville, Indiana, has been a particular source of enlightenment and inspiration. I owe special thanks to Nancy New Hemphill and Jeanne Burke of the Clark County Museum for their leadership in rehabilitating John Armstrong's gravesite and apprising me of his connections with the county. My sincere thanks also goes to Dr. Daniel T. Brown of St. Charles, Missouri, for lending his insights into conditions of the Missouri/ Mississippi River region during Spanish administration of the territory.

Trips to the Scottish Borders were invaluable in learning about both the Armstrong clan and the reiver culture. I am especially grateful to Ian Martin, project manager of the recently restored Gilnockie Tower and overseer of its current operation, for his availability in meeting with us multiple times and in relating family lore and regional information. Our trip to Ulster was also serendipitous. My heartfelt thanks goes to Dr. William Roulston of the Ulster Historical Foundation in Belfast who took the time to share information with his unexpected visitors regarding the Scots-Irish diaspora and answered questions about eighteenth-century life in Donagheady Parish. Lastly, our trip to County Tyrone would not have been complete without encountering James Kee at the Sollus Centre at the Bready and District Ulster-Scots Development Association who not only generously gave his time to two Americans who happened to drop in to find out about the region but also took us about the countryside in search of pertinent Armstrong landmarks.

I owe a huge thanks to friends who have supported both my husband and me in our quests to learn more about the Armstrongs. Longtime friend Jane Horenkamp guided me to the Indiana Historical Society on my initial visit, and I was a frequent visitor to the Horenkamp home where sharing my research with husband Vince and nearby sister Charlotte Schwendeman helped me put my findings into proper perspective. Hilde and John Holsonback ensured that we saw necessary Revolutionary War sites in and around Charleston. My brother Richard Denning and sister Susan Hinton have seen me through the long years of pulling this project together and have both encouraged and housed me along the way. I also owe a thank-you to Declan Corcoran who tutored me on the mysteries of computer graphics.

Finally, I thank my husband, traveling companion, and forever best friend David O. Smith for his encouragement and his seemingly endless knowledge of both the American Revolution and the United States Army. He also provided the basis for this book's two chapters detailing Armstrong's experiences during the American Revolution and outlined information concerning the United States Army's use of militia forces during later periods of armed conflict in Appendix 2.

Prologue

Fort Hamilton, Northwest Territory
February 13, 1793

He stood alone before the jury. His six-foot frame honed by life on the nation's frontier and its harsh and physically demanding conditions of clearing, living, and fighting in the wilderness, he was an impressive figure. Now thirty-seven, he had spent nearly half of his life in the army, and his career was on the line. After four frustrating months following his arrest based on nebulous charges, he had been apprised of specified indictments only four days before. He would be not only the defendant but also his own defense attorney.[1]

To the court of the thirteen men who were handpicked by his immediate commander and principal accuser, Cpt. John Armstrong was a colleague to the senior officers who had served with him in peacetime and in battle, but four members were new to the command and potentially biased against him. The judge advocate was an avowed enemy with his own agenda. No stranger to court-martial procedures, Armstrong had successfully argued several cases as a young lieutenant in the Revolution and served on countless boards of officers or as a witness in courts-martial over a seventeen-year period. He knew his rights as outlined by the Articles of War and recognized the glaring improprieties of his own case.

---

[1] Armstrong was six feet tall and weighed 195 pounds according to his grandson, William Goforth Armstrong II, in an interview appearing in a Jeffersonville, Indiana, newspaper. Reuben Dailey, ed., "A Sleeping Hero," *National Democrat*, January 2, 1885.

Physically absent from the room but whose shadow was omnipresent was the officer who had initiated the charges against him, Brig. Gen. James Wilkinson. In Wilkinson, Armstrong met no ordinary foe. Although specific details of Wilkinson's treachery and his dealings with the Spanish government as a paid spy were uncovered only after his death, rumors of collusion with New Orleans authorities abounded. With a history of vengeance toward those from whom he perceived slights to his honor, he later channeled his efforts toward ridding his path of individuals whom he felt stood in the way of his business or career advancements. In his wake stood both powerful friends whom he had courted and bitter enemies whom he had wronged. A would-be eighteenth-century Macbeth, Wilkinson now sought the ruin of the army's commander, Maj. Gen. Anthony Wayne. Armstrong's elimination presented one step toward clearing the way to replace him.

Armstrong entered the court-martial with the deck stacked firmly against him. Following an army career that was defined by physical bravery, resourcefulness, loyalty to his commanders and his subordinates, and determination to define his conduct with honor and dignity, he had reached a crossroads in his career.

John Armstrong's story and that of many of his fellow Revolutionary officers begins centuries before on the turbulent Scottish Borders. As a collective people, their character was forged in a society rewarding physical bravery and loyalty to clan and laird and later molded in Ireland into individuals with new respect for personal and group rights defined by law. Armstrong's ancestors and those of his compatriots had been both granted and denied civic freedoms by England's crown and Parliament. They had arrived in British colonial America seeking increased personal opportunities and were inherently sympathetic toward the colony's eventual cause for independence. Armstrong's choice of a military career was the logical extension of his ancestors' experiences.

At the Revolution's end, Armstrong jumped at the chance to continue military life in a proposed "Peace Establishment," becoming one of only fourteen commissioned officers in its initial Pennsylvania unit. He saw its eventual growth to an army of 5,120 officers and men and witnessed its accompanying growing pains resulting from congressional indecision, multiple changes in mission, and mounting territorial unrest as settlers flooded into the homelands and hunting grounds of the region's indiginous peoples. This is not his story alone but also that shared by his comrades in arms, as well as that of Native American nations affected by the nation's expansion into the Northwest Territory.

Armstrong needed every bit of savvy gained from his army years, his Scots-Irish reliance upon his rights under the law, and his Scottish-bred personal courage to survive the challenge that he now faced.

1

On the Border and Outside the Pale

On the border was the Armstrangs, able men;
Somewhat unruly, and very ill to tame.[2]

The lonely B6357 road skirts the border between Scotland and England, paralleling the Liddel Water for much of the way from the Cheviot Hills southwest toward Canonbie, the River Esk, and the Irish Sea. Barren hills, dotted white with sheep left treeless from centuries of grazing, are balanced by densely wooded rises managed by the forestry commission and by the vivid green foliage along the paths of streams cutting through the valley. Farms and villages present a picture of tranquility in this sparsely populated corner of the country that increases on weekends and holidays with the arrival of tourists hiking and biking along the valley's winding roads.

The quiet beauty of today's Liddesdale belies its turbulent history. Over the centuries, John Armstrong's forebearers and their neighbors found themselves in the midst of the chaos and devastation resulting from the collisions between two kingdoms. From 1040 to 1745, every English monarch but three either invaded Scotland or experienced the onslaught of its army. Scotland's first king, Duncan (1034–1040), was murdered by Macbeth after losing a war to the Northumbrians. Macbeth was in turn

---

2   From Satchell's *History of the Name of Scott*, cited in Robert Bruce Armstrong's *The History of Liddesdale, Eskdale, Ewesdale, Wauchopedale and the Debateable Land* (Edinburgh: David Douglas, 1883), 67.

slain after his defeat by another army from England. Malcolm "Canmore" (1058–1093) led his troops to England five times in hopes of conquering its northern provinces and was killed during his last attempt to do so. The Normans then attacked northward, taking their turn to initiate battle. After an interval of peace, Scotland's King David took his army into England in 1136, and the fighting began again. During the next century, most towns on both sides of the border were brutally sacked and burned, the countryside ravaged from Newcastle to Edinburgh. Churches and monasteries became favorite targets; one Scottish army struggled home so laden with loot that soldiers drowned in the river beneath the weight of plundered chalices and crucifixes.[3]

By the late thirteenth century, England decided it was time to put Scotland firmly under its control. Thus began the Wars of Independence, which would ebb and flow for nearly a century. England's Edward I, enraged by two Scottish leaders, William Wallace and Robert the Bruce, ravaged the country so fiercely that he became known as the "Hammer of Scots."

Following Bruce's victory at Bannockburn over Edward II in 1314, Scottish forces looted, burned, and raped the northern counties of England as well as part of Ireland. Fighting between armies of successive English and Scottish kings, as well as infighting and intrigue between warlords affecting monarchy on both sides of the border, continued for over the next centuries. Caught in the middle were the borderlands of England and Scotland, counties of present-day Northumberland and Cumbria to the south, and the Scottish Borders and portions of Dumfries and Galloway to the north. Battles were won and lost; once forested areas were razed and the country laid waste on both sides of the divide, a meandering artificial line defined in various places by rivers and at others by desolate treeless hilltops with small valleys and gullies running from them. At places only deforested, windy landscapes existed to suggest where one political entity ended and another began.[4]

★

---

[3] David Hackett Fischer, *Albion's Seed: Four British Folkways in America* (New York: Oxford University Press, 1989), 623.

[4] James Webb, *Born Fighting: How the Scots-Irish Shaped America* (New York: Broadway Books, 2004), 47, 55–63; Fischer, *Albion's Seed*, 624.

Within the three hundred years following Bannockburn, the Borders became a geographic and political entity with its own set of rules and understood laws, a society that successfully and persistently ignored royal or central government while keeping its own ancient culture intact. Alistair Moffat, in his comprehensive work *The Borders: A History of the Borders from the Earliest Times*, notes that besides contributing often-told ballads of its own infamous citizens and generating descriptive words to the language of crime, it created little except trouble. This was reiver country, and Armstrongs were well in the middle of all the felonious activities that it harbored. Family clans with their allies and retainers preyed upon each other's property, committed murder, engaged in multigenerational feuds, extracted blackmail, and fought for whichever country they preferred. Present day's peaceful, lonesome stretches of land were once the gathering place of clansmen on horseback, at times in numbers of over a thousand, riding at night, raiding rival clans on both sides of the border, stealing cattle and anything of value, and leaving mayhem in their wake.[5]

Common folk lived in hovels of stone and turf that could be constructed within three to four hours' time. To put up anything better would have been futile since they could well be destroyed again the next day. In places where wood was scarce, roof beams were removable so that at times of impending raids, they could be carried to the safety of the nearby laird's house for safekeeping.[6]

The residence of a laird was commonly a large square tower, placed within a landscape that discouraged invasion, ideally upon a precipice, on

---

[5] Among the seventy-eight names of known riding families, George McDonald Fraser lists twenty-one on both sides of the border that were most troublesome to authorities. Listed along with the Armstrongs in Scotland were the names Maxwell, Johnstone (Johnston), Bell, Irvine, Croser (Crozier), Nixon, Elliot, Scott, Kerr, Hall, Burns, and Hume. Charlton, Fenwick, Forster, Graham, Hetherington, Musgrave, Robson, and Storey were noted English families. Many occupied places on both sides of the border. George MacDonald Fraser, *The Steel Bonnets: The Story of Anglo-Scottish Border Reivers* (New York: The Akadine Press, 2001), 29–30, 55–64; Usage of the terms "blackmail," "red-handed," "gang," and "gear" originated in the Borders. "Bereaved" and "bereft" share a common root with "reiver." Alistair Moffat, *The Borders: A History of the Borders from Earliest Times* (Edinburgh: Birlinn Limited, 2002), 315, 320.

[6] Godfrey Watson, *The Border Reivers* (London: Robert Hale & Company, 1974), 97–98.

the banks of a river rapids, or surrounded by marshland, heavy woods, rock, or perhaps a moat. Generally built in view of that of a laird of an associated clan in order to signal oncoming raids, some were surrounded by barnekins, enclosures of stone, the walls of which, according to a statute of 1535, were a yard thick and six yards high. When an alarm was sounded, surrounding village residents dismantled their dwellings; and the women, children, and livestock retreated to safety within their chieftain's walls.[7]

Border clans had no formal councils, tartans, sporrans, bonnets, or septs, but were united in the most fundamental sense; they were groups of related families who lived near one another, were conscious of a common identity, carried the same surname, claimed descent from common ancestors, and banded together when danger threatened. Loyalty to the laird was paramount. In this reciprocal arrangement, the tenant rendered service to the laird as he worked on his estate, harvesting his grain, cutting and carrying peat, or thatching his buildings. His loyalty was manifested by his readiness to defend his laird's property when raided and to avenge slights to his honor. The laird's wealth consisted chiefly of cattle. He needed his kinsmen to acquire, guard, and transport these herds to market. In return, the laird assumed the responsibility for his kinsmen's protection. Without his tenants, the laird could not exist; without the laird's protection, his tenants could not survive.[8]

In the Border society, a man considered himself first and foremost as his surname. Names not only stood for family, they were the binding agent amid all the disorder and chaos inherent within the reiver system. Nationality was a distant second. In the absence of law and order and the

---

[7] James Lewis Armstrong, *Chronicles of the Armstrongs* (Jamaica, New York: The Marion Press, 1902), 69–70. Armstrong presents much of the information concerning Border life and the Armstrong clan from Sir Walter Scott's *The Minstrelsy of the Scottish Border*, Vols. 1–4 (numerous publications) and *The Border Antiquities of England and Scotland*, Vol. 1 (London: Longman, et al., 1814). Scott, in turn, appears to have referenced many of the observations made by John Leslie (Lesley), Scottish Roman Catholic bishop and historian, who published a history of Scotland in 1578 and those of medieval French author and historian Jean Froissart whose *Chronicles* was translated by Lord Berners in 1525.

[8] James G. Leyburn, *The Scotch-Irish: A Social History* (Chapel Hill: University of North Carolina Press, 1962), 6, 9; Fischer, *Albion's Seed*, 663; James Lewis Armstrong, *Chronicles*, 71–72; see also Scott, *Border Antiquities*, I: xl–xlvi.

---

ineffectual presence of a weak or remote central government, clan loyalty was all the security that most people had. With this relationship also came the observance of alliances, bloody interfamily and at times intrafamily feuds, and readiness to defend his laird and, by extension, himself in times of danger. Borderers were a martial breed whose descendants would someday provide the backbone of the Continental Army's resistance to Britain.[9]

In the agrarian society, Borderers grew corn, barley, oats, and rye in sufficient quantities to feed themselves, at least on the Scottish side where conditions were generally less rugged and the soil more fertile. They raised cattle for food, as well as draught purposes, and sheep, mainly for wool. Both activities, while requiring little in the way of manpower, needed comparatively large areas of land to support a family in any degree of comfort. This was not easily achieved. The increase in the birthrate since the days of the Black Death in the mid-1300s had led to a degree of overpopulation that centuries of warfare had not succeeded in abating. In contrast to the sparsely populated region today, the Border valleys were actually overcrowded. The custom of dividing one's inheritance equally between male heirs led to endless subdivision of lands with each successive generation receiving property so small that its size became uneconomical, providing neither a fair living for those who farmed nor a reasonable amount of food to supply a growing population.[10]

The shortage of usable farmland further complicated in some areas by the presence of bogs and nonarable land, led clansmen on both sides of the border to find their source of subsistence by armed plunder that reached its peak in the sixteenth century. While both governments officially deplored its existence, they exploited the practice to meet their own ends. The Borders provided an ever-ready source of fighting men, a permanent mobile task force to be used when war broke out. George MacDonald Fraser, in his book *The Steel Bonnets: The Story of the Anglo-Scottish Border Reivers*, notes

---

[9] Moffatt, *The Borders*, 331, 333.

[10] Godfrey Watson, *The Border Reivers*, 21–22; Keeping track of individuals within the numerous reiving families presents a formidable task. Citing Armstrong branches alone, the repetition of commonly used first names within clans often led to a combination of father and son's names ("Will's Christie", "Christie's Will", "the Laird's Jock".) Place names further identified members ("Old Sim of Mangerton", "Lance of Whithaugh", "Dick of Dryhope,") and some individuals were known by their nicknames ("Ill Will", "Black Jock", "Lang Sandy").

that the Borders provided a bloody buffer state that absorbed the horrors of war; its social chaos was almost a political necessity.[11]

The Borderers were "reivers" and "raiders," or thieves and riders. Their collective wealth revolved around the acquisition of cattle; but they also targeted oxen, milking cows, sheep, goats, and pigs, as well as whatever household or monetary goods they might plunder during their raids. Horses too were prime for lifting, essential not only in plying the raiders' mode of income but also for supplementing oxen in working the land. Reivers might even be inclined to steal the dogs that had been trained to track them, hence completely turning the tables on their victims. Nobody on either side of the border was safe. In the morning, a man might be rich in flocks and herds and by evening be without anything, not even a roof over his head. Nor did distance necessarily spell safety, the English penetrating far into Scotland and the Scots lifting cattle well into present-day Cumbria and Northumberland almost as far south as Newcastle.[12]

Riding season was generally from autumn to spring when nights were long, chance of detection less and escape easier, while summers were devoted to tending cattle on higher ground and growing crops for subsistence. Reivers gathered on the frontier on frosty nights, often with members of neighboring clans, and threaded their way on horseback through mazes of pathways toward their target of the evening. Upon completing their mission, they returned home through secret routes, their stolen booty rarely recovered. When followed by victims of an evening's raid on a "hot trod," they would lead their pursuers into marshes that locals knew well but which served to trap outsiders. Their light and fast-moving horses were trained to adjust their strides in order to avoid getting trapped into the bogs that dotted the area.[13]

---

[11] Fraser, *The Steel Bonnets*, 29–30.

[12] Watson, *The Border Reivers*, 22–23.

[13] James Lewis Armstrong, *Chronicles*, 61–63; Fraser, *The Steel Bonnets*, 50; Graham Robb, *The Debatable Land: The Lost World between Scotland and England* (New York: W. W. Norton & Company, 2018), 72. Reivers favored the Galloway nag, a small horse once found in the south of Scotland that became extinct the nineteenth century. It could travel long distances over difficult and treacherous terrain on winter nights, and its agility allowed it to round up cattle in the dark. Moffat writes that its skills and versatility were an important factor in the success of the reiving system. Moffat, *The Borders*, 321–323.

Borderers were a tough lot. In a land caught in the crossfire between political entities that invaded each other with frequentcy, they were hopelessy mired in a seemingly endless struggle between two nations. Challenges of survival in peacetime often mirrored those in war. The Borders had never known the rule of law; its inhabitants participated both as partisans in warfare between nations and as thieving perpetrators during periods of warlike peace that ensued in the interim. Somehow, they managed to achieve a status quo in those uncertain times. Sometimes victims and sometimes aggressors, they alternated between times of having their possessions raided and those when they plundered the goods of others. To keep an enemy from being able to pillage their livelihood and possessions, they unthatched and dismantled their stone cabins so that there was not much to burn and torched their homes and fields, fleeing to the safety of their lairds' towers. In times of dire crisis, they fled to the hills and the wilderness with their livestock and all they could move. During transborder conflicts, they conducted warfare by ambush, cutting supply lines and constantly harassing their invaders. Borderers learned to live on the move, to cut crop subsistence to a minimum, and to rely on the meat they could drive in front of them. They could build a house in a few hours and had no qualms about abandoning it; they could travel great distances at considerable speed and relied on their skill and cunning to restock their supplies by subsequent raiding.[14]

To Border inhabitants, times of war and peace were not very different. No side ever achieved decisive victory. Scots, usually at a disadvantage when combating the English both in the attack and defense of their strongholds, engaged in defensive warfare. They avoided pitched battles, preferring protracted war to exhaust the will and resources of their invaders. By destroying their own grain and any material that might afford relief to the enemy, they engaged in the devastation of their own countryside. Wars were never truly won or lost; in peacetime, rival clans never proclaimed victory. Warfare, full scale or communal, was always liable to break out again. There was no future for the Borderer in trying to lead a settled existence. "Might" was "right," and the weakest, unless supported by a strong surname, were out of the running. Godfrey Watson, in his book *The Border Reivers*, compared the process to a constant, ongoing version of "musical chairs." There were limited numbers of cattle and sheep on

---

[14] Fraser, *The Steel Bonnets*, 29.

the Borders and a fixed number of people to live off them. Livestock was regarded almost as a floating commodity, common to all, so that reiving became a game in which everyone reimbursed his losses with someone else's stock and only the weakest or least fortunate were the losers.[15]

The endemic violence of the raiding culture affected Borderers' attitudes toward work, time, land, wealth, rank, inheritance, marriage, gender, and personal relationships. Pastimes reflected a competitive physical culture. Borderers played "football," a precursor to present-day rugby, soccer, and American football, and held horse races, both of which were frowned upon by authorities because they were commonly used as covers by groups plotting raids or other suspect activities. They were horsemen who regarded pedestrians with contempt. Hunting, hawking, and fishing were popular, often providing an excuse for Anglo-Scottish fraternization. They gambled on cockfights and routinely wagered the spoils from a recent raid on a card game.[16]

Churches had once dotted the border but over time had been vandalized and laid to waste. The administration of religious rites became irregular, and a monk would visit villages once a year to solemnize marriages and baptisms. Robert Bruce Armstrong suggests that it is not surprising that inhabitants paid little attention to their religious duties. Efforts of the Catholic Church to restrain their excesses had so little effect that three years after his excommunication, an Armstrong laird, Sym of Whithaugh, boasted that he and his men had been instrumental in the destruction of no fewer than thirty parish churches. Fraser relates the tale of a visitor to particularly troublesome Liddesdale who, finding no churches there,

---

[15] Watson, *The Border Reivers*, 157.

[16] Fraser, *The Steel Bonnets*, 76–78. If daily activities lacked a sense of refinement, Border folk did excel in one area. They took great pride in their music and poetry, in which they described the exploits of their ancestors and themselves and had a gift for the spoken word. In reference to their illegal activities, Bishop Leslie wrote, "But if they are taken, their eloquence is so powerful, and the sweetness of their language so winning, that they even can move both judges and accusers, however severe before, if not to mercy, at least to admiration and compassion." For extensive descriptions of activities, traditions, and folkways carried from Northern Britain, including Borderland Scotland and Northern Ireland, to the American colonies, see Fisher, *Albion's Seed*, 654-747 and James Lewis Armstrong, *Chronicles*, 71, 73-74.

---

inquired, "Are there no Christians here?" receiving the reply, "Na, we's a' Elliots and Armstrangs."[17]

During nighttime raids, reivers in their thick leather jackets, or "jacks," and distinctive steel helmets, carrying their eight- to thirteen-foot spears, swords, and daggs, or large pistols, swooped down upon their targets on horseback. The size of the party depended upon the target. Smaller operations required six to eight riders. By contrast, a great laird might begin his "tryst" at a common muster point, gathering some two thousand men in the saddle. The sight of armed riders must certainly have been terrifying to weaker targets. It would probably be little comfort to them, however, that chroniclers of earlier times tended to paint the riders as "honorable thieves."

Bishop Leslie (Lesley), sixteenth-century bishop of Ross, described Borderers as being reluctant to cause blood to be shed except in the instance of a feud, "for they have a persuasion that all property is common by the law of nature, and is therefore liable to be appropriated by them in their necessity, but that murder and other injuries are prohibited by the Divine law."[18]

---

[17] Scott describes structures built by Christian missionaries to the area as early as 625 A.D. in *Border Antiquities*,

I: xxxiii–xxxiv. See also Robert Bruce Armstrong, *The History of Liddesdale*, 81; Fraser, *The Steel Bonnets*, 46. The irregular presence of clergy contributed to the curious custom of "handfasting" that allowed young men and women to live together by joining hands or "hand-fasting." The connection so formed was binding for only one year, at the expiration of which either party was at liberty to withdraw from the engagement or, in the event of both being satisfied, the relationship was renewed for life. Any children of this union were regarded as legitimate. This custom was apparently reserved for unions on one side of the border or the other. During the latter 1500s, the two countries increased their efforts to control cross-border alignment of the reiver clans. Couples living on opposite sides of the border who married without prior special permission could be punished by death. Watson, *The Border Reivers*, 180; Robb, *The Debatable Land*, 132.

[18] Sir Walter Scott, *Border Antiquities*, I: lxxvii–lxxx, II: lxv; Moffat, *The Borders*, 324. When alerted at night of an attack, Borderers signaled each other by burning fires atop their laird 's towers and by running full-speed relays of "fyre-crosses," burning straw, flax, or turf attached to a spear throughout the countryside. As a result of such warning systems, up to thousands of men could gather on horseback to meet the enemy in short periods of time. James Lewis Armstrong, *Chronicles*, 67.

George MacDonald Fraser notes that while there may be some basis of truth to this reference to a code of honor, written accounts from the era are rife with references to broken promises, unredeemed assurances, and downright treachery. There appear to have been times when Borderers used more prudence during raids because they did not want to start a blood feud. Borderers on both sides had more in common with each other than with fellow countrymen who lived outside the area. Intermarriage was common, and family clans often had branches on both sides of the border. A bond of professionalism existed between the reivers, and fugitives from the law on one side might find refuge on the other, much to the chagrin of the pursuing jurisdiction.

Fraser comments on the more romantic picture of the reiver as rough but generous, a product of his times who was no doubt a troublemaker but who was basically a decent person, having some peculiar patriotic aura about him as he set out upon his raids. He contends, however, that recorded incidents indicate that there would be little that would be considered attractive about this way of life. Treachery and intrigue, alliances and revenge, and a practice of blackmail for protection were all parts of the system. Blood feuds were rampant. Although not confined to the Borders, retribution of this form for a murdered kinsman was more common in this area than in any other part of Scotland. Raids were a fact of life and could be cruel. Fraser says that the Border reiver can be seen as he was—not at all heroic, but a nasty, cruel, mean-spirited ruffian who preferred a soft target provided by small farmers, widows, and lonely homesteads. He rode with overwhelming force, destroyed wantonly, beat up and even killed his victims if he was resisted, and literally stripped them of everything they had.[19]

Graham Robb, however, in his book *The Debatable Land: The Lost World between Scotland and England*, suggests that it would be a mistake to assume that all Borderers were engaged in endless reiving. Records of the era are comprehensive and list many culprits' names only once, and Robb notes that the majority of individuals named in records never took part in raids at all. He surmises that for many Borderers, the reiving expedition was a once-in-a-lifetime adventure and was perhaps a rite of passage. For every ballad recited by folklorists through the centuries commemorating

---

[19] Fraser, *The Steel Bonnets*, 44, 96–98; Fischer, *Albion's Seed*, 629; James Lewis Armstrong, *Chronicles*, 64. See also Scott, *Border Antiquities*, I: xlvi–xlviii.

famous raids or glorifying the feats of notorious reivers, there were likely a thousand well-worn tales regaling the of the day when Grandfather earned the right to adulthood by burning down a barn or making off with a farmer's sheep.

Robb notes that the object of reiving expeditions was not to kill others but to take their animals and whatever else came to hand, preferably with stealth and cunning, and finds some truth to earlier Romanticists' views that the reivers avoided physical harm to their victims. An entire season's reiving along the western sections of the border in 1589–90 during the heightened era of border disturbances, is recorded in a list of "bills" or official complaints in *Calendar of Border Papers*, prepared for English and Scottish wardens, or administrators. The largest raid was carried out by 204 riders, mostly Armstrongs and Elliots. A typical raiding party, however, was much smaller. The document lists a total of 53 raids, involving more than a thousand reivers, and in all those perilous high-speed excursions only three men were killed and two "maimed." Another document lists unresolved complaints relating to offenses committed by men of Liddesdale, possibly the worst of the raiders' roosts, between 1579 and 1587. A total of 123 houses were burned by more than 2,000 reivers in seven raids. Eleven men were killed, but all those perished in two raids led by the exceptionally violent and remorseless Armstrong, Kinmont Willie.[20]

★

---

[20] Robb, *The Debatable Land*, 69–70.

Kinmont Willie, perhaps the best known of the Border reivers, plundered on a large scale, striking not single houses but entire villages on both sides of the border. Documented in his infamous career that began around 1583 were large-scale, often daytime raids, where he engaged not only in stealing cattle and goods but also burning homes, taking prisoners, and wounding and murdering inhabitants. In 1585, he turned his efforts toward his own country, joining the Earl of Angus's campaign against the Earl of Arran and taking the opportunity to pillage Stirling. His biggest raid occurred eight years later when he again headed to the English Borders with one thousand men, carrying off more than two thousand animals and £300 in spoils. Fraser, *The Steel Bonnets*, 101–02.

Robb provides an example of the more "civilized" nature of reiving. He describes an exceptionally large raid in the winter of 1589–90 by some Elliots, Croziers, and associates directed against a wealthy servant's house

Firmly in the midst of the Border society were the Armstrongs, often described as the most troublesome and feared of the riding clans. They comprised a large force, often aligning with neighboring families, and probably were responsible for doing more damage than any two families

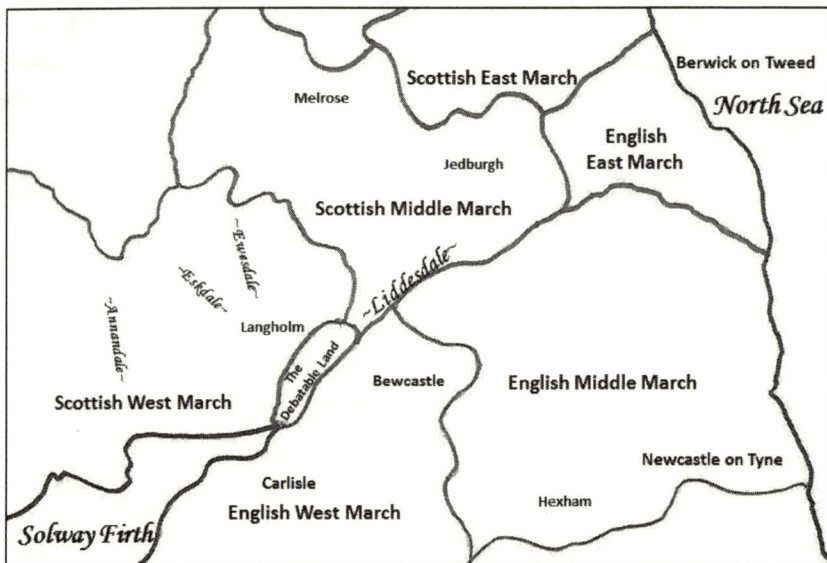

16ᵗʰ Century English and Scottish Border Marches

on the estate of Sir John Forster in Hethpool, two miles inside England along the northeastern stretch of the border. Upon their arrival, thirty riders proceeded to take eighteen animals and almost one hundred household items. Their heavily laden ponies returned bearing the weight of items that included weapons; breeches; doublets; shirts; a cloak and a jerkin (or jacket); a complete woman's wardrobe, including nightgowns and ribbons; some sheets and coverlets; a cauldron; a pan; a bolt of hemp; a pair of cards for carding wool; four children's coats; six shillings; a shroud; and as Robb adds, most impressively, a featherbed. This was a time-honored and, in some ways, orderly enterprise. While the reivers celebrated the haul and their wives and sisters tried on the garments, the "bereaved" made a careful note of every stolen item and its monetary value to be later submitted to the administrative wardens at their next meeting day. Robb, *The Debatable Land*, 71; Joseph Bain, ed., *The Border Papers: Calendar of Letters and Papers Relating to the Affairs of the Borders of England and Scotland*, vol. 1 (Edinburgh: H. M. General Register House, 1894), 348.

combined in Scotland or in England. At the height of its power around 1527, the clan, with its retainers and allies, could field around three thousand men. Although the family may have originated on the English side of the border, its power during the pivotal fifteenth and sixteenth centuries lay in Scotland. Its principal location was in that hot spot of the Scottish marches, Liddesdale, home to the clan's lairds at Mangerton, Whitlaugh, Raltoun, and Ailmore, their towers so close along the Liddel Water that their properties almost touched. The family's place of refuge was the Tarras Moss, described by Scott as a "desolate and horrible marsh" through which a small river flowed. Family offshoots, or "graynes," also resided in Annandale and Eskdale in the Scottish West March, as well as in the English West and Scottish East Marches. The family frequently rode with their neighbors, the Elliots, Nixons, and Croziers.[21]

Armstrongs were also present in what was known as the Debatable Land, that narrow tract of land running northeast from the Solway Firth that had served as a buffer between the two nations for several centuries. The whole area, only about ten miles long and six at its greatest breadth, assumed nuisance value out of all proportion to its geographical size. It was

---

[21] Fraser, *The Steel Bonnets*, 56–63. See also Scott, *Minstrelsy*, I: 49; Robert Bruce Armstrong lists some forty-five variations of the name "Armstrong" in his *History of Liddesdale*, 45. Legend surrounding the name "Arm Strong" acknowledges the clan's martial roots. When an ancient Scottish king's life was saved by Fairbairn, his armor bearer, the grateful monarch rewarded his squire with lands and title. Although variations of the tale differ in specificity, all attribute the name to one of great strength. The date at which this incident was to have occurred is elusive, but Armstrongs were documented to have been in present-day Cumbria in 1237. By the fourteenth century, Armstrongs had appeared on the Scottish side of the border. J. L. Armstrong notes that in 1528, the family was believed to have been three thousand strong. He cautions, however, that when the size of Border families was reported, the numbers often included their retainers and allied families. Despite their ability to muster large numbers of riders in their years of plundering the Borders, the number of actual Armstrongs was surprisingly small. The four main family branches numbered about seventy individuals in 1500; sixty years later, the graynes numbered about thirty men, and by 1597, only twenty-four. James Lewis Armstrong, *Chronicles*, 13, 115, 296. Current DNA research has pointed to the existence of a Pict progenitor. Bob Armstrong, "The Armstrongs: Pictish Warriors," last modified February 23, 2015, https://www.armstrongclan.info/pictish-warriors.html.

---

in that section of the Scottish West March that both England and Scotland claimed ownership and whose occupants were proverbial thorns in the sides of both countries. Since neither England nor Scotland acknowledged the other's claim of ownership, no side felt responsible for the activities of the people who lived there, and the area became a haven for the worst elements on the frontier. Here gathered a motley assortment of broken men who were English or Scottish as they pleased. The Armstrongs fit right in.[22]

Many tales of Armstrong exploits are recorded in ballads and folklore. One citing not only the clan's resourcefulness but also its gamesmanship toward flounting authority is especially revealing. Sir Robert Carey, the warden of England's West March, led a force into Liddesdale to avenge rampages by the Armstrongs on the English side of the border in 1598. Alerted to its coming, they collected their few belongings, horses, cattle and sheep, retired to Tarras Moss where there was sufficient dry ground for their herds and plenty of timber with which to build shelters, and settled in, prepared for an extended stay. At one point they sent a message to Carey saying that he was "like the first puffe of a hagasse, hottest at the first, and bade me stay there as long as the weather would give me leave."

Carey and his men had to bide their time while they quietly went to work to force the outlaws from their retreat. After some time he was able to position his men at strategic points around Tarras Moss in order to encircle the morass and block any exits. The operation was successful, and the miscreants were eventually arrested. Sir Walter Scott, in his *Minstrelsy of the Scottish Border*, wrote that years later the people of Liddesdale would retell the story of "Carey's Raid" but would add an additional detail. They related that although under siege, the Armstrongs were nevertheless able to send a raiding party into England and to plunder the warden's lands. On their return, they sent Carey one of his own cows, telling him that, fearing he might fall short of provisions during his visit to Scotland, they had taken the precaution of sending him some English beef. Scott noted that the tale was "too characteristic to be suppressed."[23]

★

---

[22] Robb, The *Debatable Land*, 3.

[23] Watson, *The Border Reivers*, 85; G. H. Powell, ed., *Memoirs of Robert Carey Earl of Monmouth* (London: Alexander Moring, 1905), 64. Scott, *Minstrelsy*, I: 56.

As early as 1249, England and Scotland attempted to bring some semblance of law to the area. Violence, even in times of so-called peace, had become endemic, and ordinary laws of the land were totally inadequate. The number and nature of the crimes committed were such that normal processes of law were not appropriate. Accordingly, the *Leges Marchiarum*, or Border Laws, were enacted, providing rules, at least in theory, for a complicated game that was played out on the border. This code, supplemented as time when on, was based partly on written law and partly on local custom and included rules that were binding to both countries as well as to the handling of local infractions. Thus, as Watson summarized, "A Borderer, therefore, was subject to three or four different collections of laws and regulations, which might well have been confusing if, in fact, he had paid attention to any of them."[24]

Infractions of laws concerning transborder issues dealt with such actions as alerting the opposing side to the advance of one's army or abetting it in the process, stealing goods from across the border, and harboring fugitives and liberating prisoners to more minor transgressions such as pasturing cattle or felling timber on the other's side. Regulations adapted to local custom on both sides dealt with a myriad of issues such as murder, acts resulting in wounding or maiming, robbery, destruction of property, receipt of stolen property, perjury, or fictitious complaints.[25]

Territory adjacent to the border on one side was divided into East, Middle, and West "Marches" with its counterpart on the other. Each had a governing officer known as a "warden." Additionally, troublesome Liddesdale had its own agent, known as a "keeper." The warden led the defense of his march against invasion during times of war and cooperated with his corresponding official in handling cases brought by opposing clans and individuals during times of peace. Though the rationale behind the system bears merit, the process had its shortfalls. Fraser notes that many of the wardens were themselves members of the worst raiding families or belonged to notorious feuding parties. Additionally, both governments used these positions to contain, embarrass, and spy on the other.[26]

---

[24] Watson, *The Border Reivers*, 41.

[25] Watson, *The Border Reivers*, 41–43; Robert Bruce Armstrong, *History of Liddesdale*, 12–13, 26–62. See also Scott, *Border Antiquities*, I: xcii–cxx for details concerning the extensive types of cases going before wardens.

[26] Fraser, *The Steel Bonnets*, 34, 132.

A warden oversaw the administration of a kind of martial law; he was all-powerful within his own area. If he thought fit to execute anyone who was caught red-handed, he did so and asked questions afterward. His office was a much sought-after appointment, not just for the power and prestige associated with the position but also for its perks that included provisions and forage for his personal guard of horsemen, payment to cover certain out-of-pocket expenses, and an official residence. He also stood to profit financially from the influence his position commanded.[27]

A warden's duties often involved assembling an armed force in times of war as well as in times of so-called "peace." When summoned, every able-bodied man was required to bear arms for the warden's forces to repel invasion or to keep order. Despite the holiday atmosphere of required muster days when the majority of the male population would gather, the duties involved in this system of conscription were not always to the liking of those drafted. An essential part of a warden "rode" was the burning of houses and of the crops of those singled out for retribution. Destruction of homes did not matter much to the Borderer since they could be quickly rebuilt, but burning crops upon which a neighbor was dependent for survival was a different matter. Watson notes that it was one thing to pursue someone who had just lifted your cattle or to help in carrying out an act of vengeance dictated by deadly feud, but it was another altogether to set out to punish people who might be related to you through marriage or with whom you might be allied and whose way of life, wherever they might happen to live, was much the same as your own.[28]

The great familiarity between reivers on both sides of the border was a constant concern for wardens. At any moment, war might break out or a punitive raid become necessary. Borderers then demonstrated that they might be led but could not be driven, wearing handkerchiefs on their arms and letters on their caps that were seemingly used by individuals seeking recognition by the enemy in order to be spared during conflict. The crosses of St. Andrew or St. George worn in battle to identify that combatant's nationality were so narrow "that a puff of wind might have blown them from their breasts."[29]

---

27 Watson, *The Border Reivers*, 38.
28 Watson, *The Border Reivers*, 38, 86, 88–89.
29 Ibid., 113.

Wardens from opposing marches typically met at a location near the border on a regular basis during a day of truce. From sunrise of the meeting day until daybreak of the next, an armistice was to be declared so that all attending could proceed safely to the conclave and home again. It was here that petitions for redress for property stolen or damage inflicted could be presented, and here that warden courts would provide judgment on cases before them. Individuals who had received injuries from parties from the opposite side had first to present their complaints to their own warden who in turn forwarded them to his counterpart. The accused were then exchanged, allowing the alleged perpetrators to be tried by their own wardens. Trials were subsequently held, money collected as payment for damages, and sentences pronounced.[30]

Central to the system was the idea of honor and respect for one's reputation for truthfulness and the keeping of a promise made. Perjury was taken seriously; its punishment was known as "bauchling." Proven liars and oath breakers were loudly and publicly vilified at warden meetings by bauchles who, among other tactics, carried gloves on the end of lances with which they pointed to men in question. A Borderer, having once pledged that he would make amends to an injured party, was expected to follow through on his promise. Chroniclers attest that a Borderer, when captured committing a felonious act, was customarily not confined nor arrested. He simply acknowledged that he was indeed a prisoner, and the time and place were set at which he was expected to meet to discuss his ransom.[31]

Punishments were severe. Guilt of treasonable offenses demanded decapitation while conviction of crimes involving other offenses might be addressed with less ceremony, giving rise to the term "Jedburgh justice," when men were said to be hanged first and tried afterward. Despite the serious outcomes of some trials, such occasions apparently provided an occasion for some frivolity. All did not conclude peacefully, however. B. Homer Dickson describes one day of truce when booths were erected, drink was sold, and an impromptu fair set up. Unfortunately, the mirth and good fellowship that began the meeting dissolved when the two wardens began to argue, and their respective sides "set to work with sword and spear and bended bow."[32]

---

[30] James Lewis Armstrong, *Chronicles*, 63–64; Robert Bruce Armstrong, *History of Liddesdale*, 17–26.

[31] Scott, *Border Antiquities*, I: lxxix–lxxx; Watson, *The Borders Reivers*, 153.

[32] B. Homer Dickson, *The Border or Riding Clans Followed by a History of the Clan Dickson* (Albany, New York: Joel Munsell's Sons, 1889), 8–9, 45.

Most cases were satisfactorily resolved, but some were not. The types of crimes heard by the wardens at their courts could be either relatively simple to discern or clouded by other factors. In his work *The Debatable Land*, Robb attempts to clarify decisions cited in court documents. Once-in-a-lifetime reivers usually returned the stolen goods or paid remuneration. The murderous reiver armies of a few petty warlords, hardened by military experience in the service of one nation or the other, fell into another category altogether, as did offenders engaged in long-running feuds, participants in wardens' punitive raids, some of whom were inspired by greed of revenge, and wandering gangs of professional thieves originating from outside the jurisdiction during the years of famine in the late sixteenth century.[33]

★

A pivotal event in the history of the Borders occurred in 1600 when, as one version of the story goes, the actions of gentlemen in attendance of Sir John Carmichael, warden of the Scottish West March, offended the family of an elderly member of the Armstrong clan. Vengeance for this perceived slight of honor ensued, and Carmichael was killed on June 16 near Langholm where he was to hold court. James VI, incensed by this last deed, ordered the succeeding warden to pursue the murderers relentlessly. Carmichael had been appointed warden of the area in preference to that of a Border chieftain, as had been the usual custom. Fraser notes that another reason for the assault may have been that Carmichael was regarded as an honest and efficient warden who served his post well and as a result had incurred the ill will of the locals. Murder plots were planned for him, but it was the Armstrongs and their associates who caught up with him. Although it took several years to do so, culprits were eventually captured, tried, and hanged.[34]

Three years later, James VI of Scotland became James I of England, assuming the thrones of two nations upon the death of his cousin, Elizabeth I. Determined to unite the two countries into one, to bury old quarrels and to keep the peace, his efforts to rid the Borders of their criminal elements increased. A final blow came the same week as he began his journey to England for his coronation when a group of two hundred Armstrongs with their retainers made a raid into present-day Cumbria, killing inhabitants and carrying off whatever booty they could. A furious James then sent an

---

[33] Robb, *The Debatable Land*, 71–72.
[34] James Lewis Armstrong, *Chronicles*, 296–98; Fraser, *The Steel Bonnets*, 141.

armed force after clan members with the instructions to wipe them out. Strongholds in Liddesdale were razed, and so many Armstrongs were put to death that they, as well as other clans James targeted, eventually accepted the fact that their old way of life was over.

James altered the time-honored way of life on the Borders. March law, which had ensured the region's peculiar unity and independence, was replaced by the law of the land. The old system of trods, trysts, bills, and bauchling was civilized and moderate by comparison with that he employed to pacify its population. Minor theft became punishable by death, and as the reivers were about to discover, state justice could operate with terrifying speed. Borderers who disturbed the pious dream of unity had been living for many years in a country in the middle of Britain, which was neither Scottish nor English. Those "mysguyded men" were now to be eradicated. "All theeves, murderers, oppressouris and vagabondis," declared James in 1604, must be rooted out; and severe and indifferent justice ministered upon all offenders. Technically, the purge was not a massacre since all those who were put to death received a trial. The trial, however, came after the execution. This efficient system was considered by the king an infinitely better means of furthering God's plan than the laws and customs of the Marches, which were now no longer in existence.

The other preferred solution to Border anarchy was James's order for the banishment from Scotland of "all idle persons," including "fairground charlatans, buffoons and strolling bards, and any call themselves Egyptians." All were to be expelled "to some other place, where the change of aire will make in them an exchange of their manners."[35]

The Armstrongs were not so easily gotten rid of. In 1607, a year after the execution of several of their number, they and the neighboring Irvins were still ensconced in every corner of the Debatable Land. Bent on self-destruction or unable to mend their ways, many had managed to break out of prison or to return from abroad. There they "impeded and stayed" the men who were sent to conduct a fresh survey of the area at the behest of Maxwell and Douglas, the new owners of the land granted them by the king. At that point, the men given the job of purifying and policing the Scottish Marches believed that deportation and trials were a waste of time and engaged in full-scale blitzkrieg.[36]

---

[35] Robb, *The Debatable Land*, 170–71.
[36] Robb, *The Debatable Land*, 175–76.

James didn't stop there. He appointed a board consisting of five Englishmen and five Scots to try Border criminals. No longer would an offender on one side be able to evade justice by fleeing to the other. Twenty-five mounted police were put on the border, and common folk were prohibited from carrying weapons.[37]

To weaken the Border clans further, a commission sat for twenty years to examine titles and property deeds. Since records more than likely had been destroyed by fire over the years, the inquiry also provided an opportunity for the adjudicators to increase their own holdings in cases where plaintiffs could not substantiate their claims. The halfheartedness with which some Border chiefs threw off their allegiance to the Catholic Church during the time when a Protestant king ruled both Scotland and England did not help their case, as others who had made more effort to do so received honors and lands. Much of the land encompassed within present-day Scottish Borders came into the possession of the Baccleuchs and remains in the family's ownership today.[38]

The king's efforts to bring the Borders into submission were as violent as the world he sought to destroy. Gallows were used extensively on the English side; thrifty Scots saved the expense of a rope by drowning their targets instead of hanging them, sometimes ten to twenty at a time. Entire families were outlawed en masse. Luckier individuals were conscripted by Walter Scott of Buccleuch to fight as mercenaries in Spain. Others moved by choice to newly formed Ulster plantations although some were banished there as a result of proceedings against them in the courts. Some permanently migrated to the English side of the border, and one branch of the Armstrongs relocated to the Netherlands. By 1610 to 1620, the Armstrongs, with few exceptions, had all but disappeared from their Liddesdale stronghold.[39]

Ulster

Under what circumstances John Armstrong's ancestors left Scotland for Ireland or, indeed, the identity of his immigrant forefather may never be known; but examination of individual histories presented in James Lewis Armstrong's *Chronicles of the Armstrongs* suggests a few possibilities.

---

[37] Leyburn, *The Scotch-Irish*, 12–13.

[38] James Lewis Armstrong, *Chronicles*, 300–01, 307.

[39] Fraser, *The Steel Bonnets*, 360–63.

Christie's Will, grandson of the notorious Johnnie of Gilnockie, emigrated to County Fermanagh sometime after 1630. Possibly one of his sons or accompanying Armstrong retainers left the plantation there and found his way to neighboring County Tyrone, recorded home of John's grandfather, and settled there at a later time. Departures from Ulster during times of crisis and the return of settlers from Scotland at their conclusions when leases on war-ravaged land were cheap make this scenario plausible. Another possibility lies with few surviving Armstrong soldiers who, after having been conscripted to serve in the European wars, found upon their return to the Borders that the family's land and property had been appropriated by others and may have ventured to Ireland at that time. Finally, and probably most likely, members of Armstrong graynes outside the hot spots of Liddesdale and the Debatable Land were drawn to the Plantation along with other Lowland families during its formative years. James Lewis Armstrong lists names of sons and grandsons of some known Liddesdale reivers who had established themselves outside the valley in lands farther to the west and into the English Borders. This population may have been ripe for the migration across the Irish Sea during the early to mid-1600s.[40]

---

[40] Johnnie Armstrong of Gilnockie was notorious even within the Armstrong clan and, as Fraser notes, a successful "scourge" of the Borders, levying blackmail throughout the English Marches and building up a private force of formidable reputation. By 1530, Scottish king James V had enough of rebellious Border clan activity and Gilnockie in particular. Although promising Gilnockie safe passage to meet with him, the king ordered the capture and execution of Armstrong and perhaps fifty of his men. Far from pacifying the region, the act inflamed it. Clan loyalty surfaced, and as a result, none of the Armstrongs or their allies came to assist James's forces twelve years later at the Battle of Solway Moss at which the Scots were soundly defeated by the English. Fraser, *The Steel Bonnets*, 225; James Lewis Armstrong, *Chronicles*, 316–20.

James Lewis Armstrong identifies four Armstrongs with descendants remaining on the Borders after James's purge of the family: Christie's Will, grandson of Johnnie of Gilnockie, left descendants in Canonbie. Archie the Jester, who found himself appointed to the king's court and granted lands in Ireland, left descendants near Bewcastle, on the English Borders. Armstrongs living on the Ewes Water could trace their ancestry to Andro in Kirktown, son of Ill Will's Sandy of Chengils in Liddesdale. Kinmont Willy, also the son of Ill Will's Sandy, left descendants at the Tower of Sark in Annandale.

These émigrés, the Armstrongs with their fellow Borderers and other Lowland Scots, were all part of a master plan to bring a civilized Ireland into Britain's realm. Ireland had long been England's wild stepchild. Ever since Norman King Henry II (1139–1189) invaded Ireland, the English had tried repeatedly to conquer or to pacify the island by one means or another. By the reign of Elizabeth I (1558–1603), England was able to maintain only a foothold in the countryside consisting of little more than an area around present-day Dublin. Any territory outside the "pale" was inhabited by those whom the English regarded as "Wild Irish," who lived in poverty under the control of powerful chieftains.

Elizabeth's greatest problems lay in Ulster. The northern section of Ireland was then controlled by Hugh O'Neill, Earl of Tyrone, and Red Hugh O'Donnell, Lord of Tyrconnell, who led an alliance of clans against the English in 1595. Elizabeth dispatched Charles Blount, Eighth Baron Mountjoy, who conducted a relentless campaign of destruction of food, houses, and cattle. Starvation and defeat induced the Irish to submit just as the queen lay dying. Mountjoy's "slash and burn" strategy nevertheless paved the way for eventual colonization in that newly depopulated area.[41]

James's original plan called for distribution of approximately one-half million acres to be assigned primarily to nobility and gentry from England and Scotland; but smaller allotments were also to be apportioned to veterans of the Irish wars, London companies, the Anglican Church, and Trinity College of Dublin. Additionally, land was set aside for the establishment of forts and towns, and finally, parcels were allotted to Irish of "good merit" who presumably would be able to take on native Irish as tenants. Among the grants made was that to James Hamilton, the First Earl of Abercorn who would colonize that part of the county of Tyrone in which John Armstrong's family eventually resided.[42]

From its inception, Ulster became the location of three peoples, each with different roles to play in the unfolding history of that part of Ireland. England was the absentee ruler; and at various times over the next 150 years, settlers of all country origins both profited and suffered under the politics and policies of its Parliament and Crown, its internal crises, and its church. The Scots, the eventual predominant population, brought with them the potentially unifying factor that later solidified their identity,

---

[41] Leyburn, *The Scotch-Irish*, 87; R. F. Foster, *Modern Ireland*, 34–35.

[42] Leyburn, *The Scotch-Irish*, 90-92. See also Foster, *Modern Ireland*, 63, 67.

the Presbyterian Kirk. Native Irish found themselves almost always on the wrong end of English policy. The interweaving of these three entities and the fallout from ecclesiastical, governmental, and economic policies directed from England were to play a major role in the gradual decision of approximately a quarter-million Ulster Scots to emigrate to America during the next century.

The Ulster Plantation eventually succeeded. There were, however, times of struggle for settlers arriving in the early years. Many absentee landlords appointed dishonest agents to oversee their holdings, and the general quality of settlers, particularly from Scotland, was regarded as poor. Firearms were few, and prospects for establishing an effective defense against a possible Irish uprising were slight. The condition of the land granted to tenants varied, and some areas included wastelands that had been ravaged by war.[43]

Threats, particularly to early settlers, were numerous. Many native Irish, removed from their lands, had been driven to the mountains or woods and lived by plunder. Large flocks of wolves roamed at night and often preyed upon settlers' cattle. The land was initially unfenced and undrained, much of it covered by woods, providing a safe haven for outlaws. On the other hand, rents were low and labor cheap. Initial laws banning the hiring of Irish labor were repealed, and settlers could get help for their farms. Renegade Irish were eventually caught, woods cleared, and swamps drained. With their lands leased at a nominal rent, their clothing and tools self-constructed, their planting of flax and abundant supply of wool providing materials for a fledgling textile industry, and livestock to sell, the colonists soon began to thrive.[44]

The arrangement seemed like a good deal for everyone concerned—everyone, of course, but the native Irish who were granted the poorer lands in less-accessible districts. Allotments to the English and Scots were kept together so that they might form communities and not mix with or marry the locals. The Irish were to be supplanted; they were to be regarded as little more than annoyances to be subdued and controlled. Summarily driven off the lands their ancestors had farmed for generations, they had no rights to

---

[43] Leyburn, *The Scotch-Irish*, 95; Charles A. Hanna, *The Scotch-Irish or The Scot in North Britain, North Ireland, and North America* (New York: G. P. Putnam's Sons, 1902), I: 501.

[44] Hanna, *The Scotch-Irish*, I: 501–02.

their own institutions nor voice in their government. The manifestation of this concept was to haunt Ulster repeatedly in years to come.[45]

★

The first pivotal crisis to threaten the welfare of the Ulster plantations coincided with the appointments of two Englishmen. In 1633, Thomas Wentworth was appointed Lord Deputy of Ireland, and William Laud became Bishop of Canterbury. Wentworth, upon coming to Ireland, was responsible for instituting two key policies, one economic and the other religious. While credited by James G. Leyburn in his work *The Scotch-Irish: A Social History* as an able man who was personally unselfish, honest, and intent upon giving Ireland stability and prosperity, he was also unwavering in his administrative policy. In order to protect the English woolen industry, Wentworth prohibited Ireland's own production of that commodity. Realizing the adverse impact the measure would have on Ireland's economy, however, he used his own money to foster a linen industry that later became a substantial source of revenue.[46]

Wentworth's second policy affected the very identity of Ulster Scots. James's son, Charles I, was then on the throne. As king, he was head of the Church of England and its counterpart, the Church of Ireland. Earlier, James had sought to bring the Scottish Kirk's liturgy in line with that of the Church of England. Charles continued his father's quest, resulting in rebellion over such policies in Scotland. Wentworth, acting on Charles's behalf, likewise pursued religious conformity in Ulster. In 1639, the directive was given that all Ulster Scots over sixteen years of age take the "Black Oath," swearing that they would obey the king's royal commands and declaring their disapproval of the recent rebellion in Scotland against his episcopal ordinances.

Archbishop Laud, to whom Churchill referred as "Charles' evil genius," mandated that Church of England liturgy be observed throughout England, Scotland, and Ireland. His work, the "Popish-English-Scottish-Mass-Service-Book," having already precipitated the rebellion by the "Covenanters" in Scotland 1637, became the focus of his attention in Ireland where he sought to require Presbyterian ministers to conform to the standards of the established church. Leyburn notes that the result was

---

[45] Leyburn, *The Scotch-Irish*, 95–96; See also Foster, *Modern Ireland*, 64.
[46] Leyburn, *The Scotch-Irish*, 121.

considered to be persecution, and those ministers who would not conform had no recourse but to leave the country. For five years after 1636, most Scottish congregations in Ulster were without ministers.[47]

Prior to Wentworth's actions to standardize the established church's liturgical practices, there had been only one official denomination in Ireland; formal Presbyterian Church government did not arrive until the creation of the Laggan Presbytery in 1649. The Church of Ireland at this time was strongly tinged with Scottish Presbyterian–inclined ministers and English Puritan elements. A number of clergy had come to Ulster who dissented from Anglican Church government, and early bishops had turned a blind eye to clerics who officiated in their parishes to congregants following a Presbyterian order of worship. Wentworth's actions altered the Confession of Faith, replaced bishops of questionable leanings with those of the High Church, and imposed penalties for nonconformity.[48]

The earlier rebellion of the Covenanters in Scotland set into motion a series of actions on the part of Charles that had disastrous consequences for Ulster's settlers of both Scottish and English origin. During that crisis, the king had considered invading Scotland to quell that discontented faction. In 1640, he directed Wentworth to raise an army of nine thousand men to participate in the invasion, most of whom were Irish Catholics. Before the army could embark for Scotland, however, Wentworth was recalled to England, and the army disbanded.[49]

Charles's directive to Wentworth was to yield unexpected results. The formation of Irish troops provided its leaders with the opportunity and organization to wage war against those who had taken over their country. Uprisings began in October 1641, leading to the rebellion that consumed the country for eleven years.

---

[47] Leyburn, *The Scotch-Irish*, 121–22; Winston S. Churchill, *The New World* (New York: Dorset Press, 1956), 198–206. See also Foster, *Modern Ireland*, 80–83.

[48] John Harrison, *The Scot in Ulster: Sketch of the History of the Scottish Population of Ulster* (Edinburgh: William Blackwood and Sons, 1888), 55–61; James Seaton Reid, *History of the Presbyterian Church in Ireland: Comprising the Civil History of the Province of Ulster from the Accession of James the First* (London: Whittaker and Co., 1853), I:154–67. See also *Londonderry 400: Plantation of the Walled City* (Belfast: Ulster-Scots Community Network, n.d.), 25–26. http://ulster-scots.com.

[49] Leyburn, *The Scotch-Irish*, 123. See also Churchill, *The New World*, 198–208.

In what began as a revolt under leadership of native Irish gentry, castles and towns over much of Ulster were seized by rebels. Initial bloodshed was limited, but soon the uprising's leaders lost control of the movement, and the fighting evolved into a vicious and cruel war. Churchill quotes historian Leopold von Ranke, "But no one can paint the rage and cruelty which was

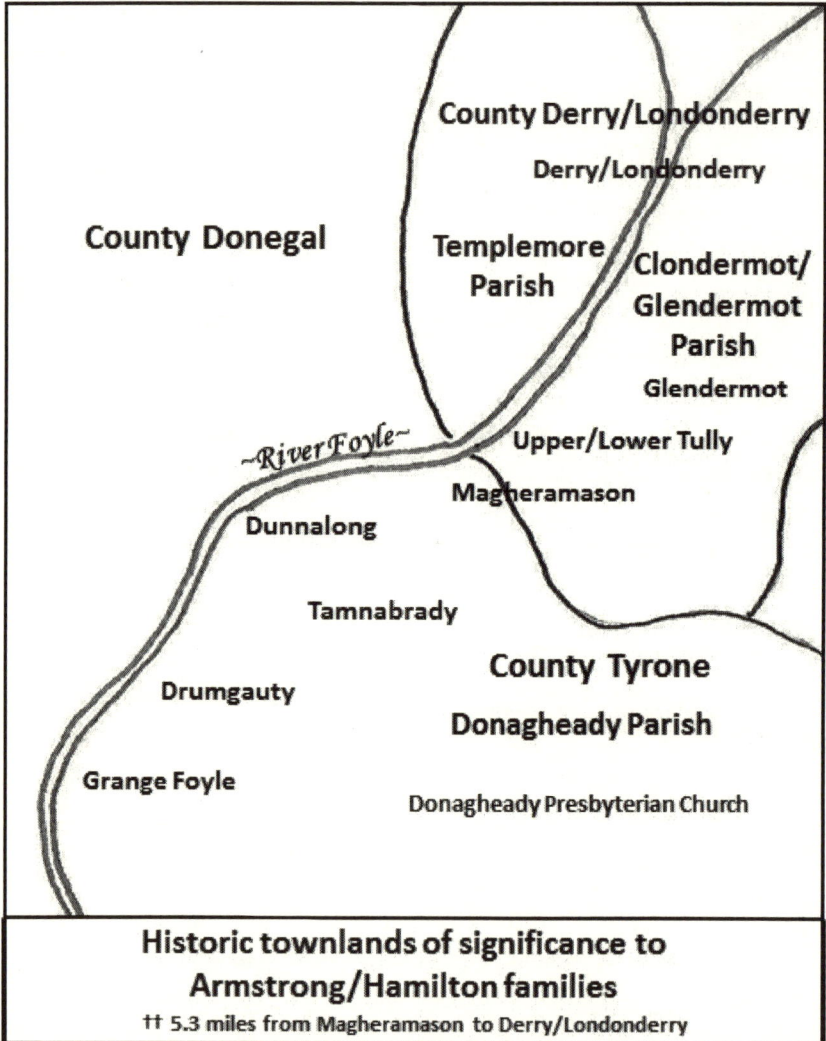

County Derry/Londonderry

Derry/Londonderry

County Donegal

Templemore Parish

Clondermot/ Glendermot Parish

Glendermot

~River Foyle~

Upper/Lower Tully

Magheramason

Dunnalong

Tamnabrady

County Tyrone

Donagheady Parish

Drumgauty

Grange Foyle

Donagheady Presbyterian Church

Historic townlands of significance to Armstrong/Hamilton families
†† 5.3 miles from Magheramason to Derry/Londonderry

vented, far and wide over the land, upon the unarmed and defenceless. Many thousands perished, their corpses filled the land and served as food for the kites."[50]

England was embroiled in its own dispute between the monarchy and Parliament at the time; and it was not until the close of the Civil War, the victory of Parliament, and the beheading of Charles I that it turned its full attention to Irish matters. In 1650, Cromwell himself went to Ireland and in one crushing campaign ended the rebellion. Leyburn states that the action was so thorough that it left scars that have never been forgotten or forgiven. Statistician Sir William Petty estimated that out of Ireland's population of 1,449,000, three-sevenths, or 616,000, perished by sword, famine, or plague. Of this number, 504,000 were Irish. Additionally, there were extensive deportations of native Irish to the West Indies, and another 30,000–40,000 left Ireland to enlist in European armies. Two-thirds of the good land in the country formerly held by the Irish now passed into the hands of the Protestants.[51]

Ireland was pacified by Cromwell, but at a price. Although the Presbyterian Scots were initially dealt with harshly because of their refusal to recognize the lawfulness of Cromwell's government and their vigorous denouncement of the beheading of Charles, he later granted allowances to the Presbyterian clergy. Under his strict rule, Ulster recovered steadily in the aftermath of the devastating blow of the rebellion. Scots settlements began to flourish. Leyburn notes that the "Lord Protector" tolerated no squabbles between Anglicans and Presbyterians.[52]

★

References to members of the Armstrong family in Donagheady Parish begin to appear around this time on tax lists and other documents. Little is known about the family, and what is certain was recorded by John Armstrong himself. His biographer, C. F. Cochran, states that he recorded the name of his paternal grandfather, John Armstrong, and those of his maternal grandfather and great-grandfather, Michael Hamilton and Edward Skipton, in a personal notebook when he was posted at the Falls of the Ohio in the late 1780s. References to the Hamiltons and the

---

[50]   Churchill, *The New World*, 225.
[51]   Leyburn, *The Scotch-Irish*, 124–25.
[52]   Leyburn, *The Scotch-Irish*, 126–27; Hanna, *The Scotch-Irish*, I: 579.

Skiptons can be found in recorded documents while those relating to the Armstrongs are more difficult to find. What is evident, however, is that the Armstrongs resided in the parish of Donagheady, part of the land tract in County Tyrone that had been granted to the Earl of Abercorn around 1610, whose manor at Dunnalong sat beside the River Foyle.[53]

Donagheady was also the home of John's mother, Jane Hamilton. Her father, Michael Hamilton, is recorded to have lived in the township of Drumgauty from 1717 to 1726 and in nearby Tullys in the adjoining parish of Glendermot in 1728 to 1748. Michael's death preceded that of his father, James Hamilton, who died about 1755. This James was the son of another James Hamilton of Magheramason, also in the parish of Donagheady, who died in 1734.[54]

The Hamilton lineage from which John Armstrong's mother was descended was not related to James Hamilton, the First Earl of Abercorn, nor to his successors to the title. Some of the Hamiltons in Jane Hamilton Armstrong's line used the family seal when signing documents, held lands under the earl, and passed the land on to their descendants by will for generations but were probably descended from a different branch of Hamiltons whose home was in Lanarkshire, Scotland, and whose estate, Priestfield, lay a few miles west of Hamilton Castle. The Scottish tradition of continuing the use of first names in family lines and the frequency of the name "James" truly cloud the matter, but it is safe to conjecture that Jane's immediate ancestors represent gentry rather than peerage.

Fortunately, Jane's mother's lineage is easier to trace. Her great-grandfather, Thomas Skipton, was born in England; educated at St. Paul's

53   Charles F. Cochran, letter to unknown recipient, September 28, 1915, and to Mrs. Spinning, September 11, 1915, in John Armstrong Papers, William. H. Smith Memorial Library, Indiana Historical Society, Indianapolis, Indiana. (PJA)

54   C. F. Cochran, *Seven Generations of the Ancestry of Captain Abram Piatt Andrew* (Washington, D.C.: National Publishing Company, 1924), PJA. Cochran referenced his findings based on wills that were recorded at the time of the deaths of the various Hamilton family members and was fortunate enough to have done so before such records were destroyed by fire at the Public Records office in Dublin in 1922. Cited townships of Magheramason, Drumgauty, and Grange Foyle are all in the extreme northwest corner of Donagheady Parish and are in close proximity to one another. What were once the Upper and Lower Tullies, although in the Glendermot Parish of County Londonderry, were almost adjacent to Magheramason.

School and Emmanuel College, Cambridge; became a lawyer and solicitor; and fled from London to Ireland in 1638 following his public outrage and subsequent warrant against him over the brutal treatment of his former law tutor in the London courts. Originally "opposing the Crown on account of encroachments on the rights of the people," he altered his views when he saw the excesses of the Parliament party and served as a volunteer against the Cromwellian forces in 1649. He married Charity Staples, daughter of Sir Thomas Staples of County Tyrone, and was later alderman and twice the mayor of Londonderry (Derry). Thomas's son, Alexander Skipton, followed in his father's footsteps and was mayor and sheriff of the city in 1704, marrying Jane Cary whose maternal grandfather was Sir Tristram Beresford, of Coleraine. Thomas's grandson and Jane Hamilton's maternal grandfather, Edward Skipton, was no mean figure himself. An officer in militia regiments, he inherited Tamneymore in County Londonderry and, continuing the family tradition of public office, was sheriff, alderman, and eventually mayor of the city in 1735.[55]

The plantation era ended in Ulster with the Rebellion of 1641. Settlers had been killed, fled to safer locations, or returned to Scotland. By the early 1650s, however, many had returned, occupying lands that had been devastated during the long years of warfare. The first references to the Armstrongs appear in a poll book for the Donagheady Parish in 1662, listing the names of those owing the tax. A John Armstrong living with his wife was classified as "yeoman" in the township of Taunaghbridy, or Tamnabrady, along with servant James Lockerby, and his name later appeared on hearth tax rolls in 1664 and 1666. Tamnabrady is now included in the Bready area, that vicinity in the northwest corner of the parish in which Jane Hamilton's family lived.[56]

★

---

[55] Cochran, *Ancestry of Captain Abram Piatt Andrew*, PJA. When describing events occurring within the city of Londonderry, or Derry, taking place in the 17th and 18th centuries, the author uses "Londonderry," its formal name at the time. Other references may include the latter term.

[56] The poll book also notes a William Armstrong and wife, classified as "servants" as living in the adjacent township of Tirunavghchor or Tamnaclare during this time period. Rev. J. Rutherford, *Donagheady Presbyterian Churches and Parish* (Belfast: McCaw, Stevenson, and Orr, Ltd., 1953), 106.

The year 1660 was pivotal in English history. Monarchy was restored with the arrival from exile of Charles II, son of the deposed king. Personally seeking religious tolerance, he was influenced by Parliament and the Church of England, political underdogs during the Cromwell years. Laws discriminating against non-Anglicans were passed that initially impacted Scotland but also found their way to Ulster. Sanctions on ministers of the Scottish Kirk forbade worship in groups with one person present who was outside the family unit. These were "killing times" when western Scottish lowland Covenanters fought a guerilla warfare against Charles' forces, precipitating increased emigration to Ulster from that group as well as from English members of Puritan sects who had supported Cromwell.

Meanwhile, the Church of Ireland's bishops began to exercise their newly returned power and their influence in Irish governmental affairs. Sixty-one Presbyterian ministers were ejected from their churches in 1661, forbidden to preach or perform sacraments and ordered out of parsonages provided them by their churches. Pastoral ordination was banned. An attempt was made to declare that all marriages that were not solemnized according to the ritual of the established church would be null and void. Four ministers from the Laggan Presbytery that included the Donagheady Parish were imprisoned, their release finally granted by Charles himself. In 1667, nineteen churchmen from Donagheady were excommunicated, left without guarantee of personal or property rights, among whom was John Armstrong. Scots gentry found their tenants oppressed, impoverished, rendered unable to pay their rents, and required to support a church they did not attend.[57]

However reluctantly the Armstrongs and members of other Border clans were to embrace Protestantism, much less to become engulfed in the tide of the Presbyterian Church that swept Scotland in the sixteenth century, they conceivably became followers of the Kirk, their national and religious identity maturing as subsequent groups of Presbyterian Scots continued to move to Ulster during times when the church was allowed to grow and prosper. Their resolve to support the Kirk was likely hardened in times of discrimination against it and its members. To be an Ulster Scot generally was to be Presbyterian. As new arrivals to Ulster, already known to be less than devout in practice of their professed Catholic faith, Armstrongs and

---

[57] Rutherford, *Donagheady Presbyterian Churches and Parish*, 19; Alexander G. Lecky, *In the Days of the Laggan Presbytery* (Belfast: Davidson and McCormack, 1908) 103–07.

other Borderers had to exercise the pragmatism that had long characterized their society. When settling in to an environment where their neighbors and landlords were Protestant and at the same time becoming aware of blatant discrimination against the Roman Catholic Irish, the path of least resistance was to adopt the religious practice of those around them, at least nominally. Few Catholics enjoyed equal status with their Protestant peers.[58]

Conditions during Charles II's reign eventually improved as discriminatory laws remained on the books but began to be ignored. Presbyterians slowly recovered a portion of their freedom, and gradually their ministers returned. Around 1670, permission was granted for Presbyterians to build new churches; and soon thereafter, Charles granted ministers a royal bounty, known as the "Regium Donum." On a list of ruling elders and commissioners to Presbytery from Donagheady was the name of John Armstrong who was instrumental in the hiring of that church's first minister.[59]

With growing prosperity in the latter years of the seventeenth century, coupled with poor economic climate in northern England, Ulster again became a gathering ground for Puritans, Quakers, and other European Protestants who blended well into the Ulster society. Economic setbacks did occur, however. Laws were enacted in 1665 and 1680 at the behest of English landowners who were alarmed at the success of Ireland's cattle ventures. Consequently, Parliament prohibited the importation of that commodity into England, thereby ruining Ireland's primary source of wealth. For a time, Ireland could send ships to the American colonies, but a Navigation Act of 1663 deprived her of this trade. Ireland's economy was saved by the manufacturing of wool, limitations on which had been rescinded by Cromwell; and at the time, the linen trade was thriving.[60]

★

---

[58] The Earl of Abercorn's brother who was Catholic, Sir George of Greenlaw, was a notable exception who occupied a position in a class far above the average settler to his lands. William Roulston, "Evolution of the Abercorn Estate in Northwest Ulster, 1610–1703," *Familia 1999: Ulster Genealogical Review*, no. 15 (1999): 56.

[59] Leyburn, *The Scotch-Irish*, 126; Rutherford, *Donagheady Presbyterian Churches and Parish*, 18–19.

[60] Leyburn, *The Scotch-Irish*, 127–28; Foster, *Modern Ireland*, 128–29.

The accession of James II (1685–88) brought another blow to the Ulster Scots. Charles's brother was an avowed Roman Catholic who sought to reinstate Catholicism as the national religion. Years of suppression of Catholics in Ireland were about to erupt in bloodshed. James's appointments of native Irish to key government and military positions promised dire changes. Englishmen were turned out of the army. Protestant regiments were disbanded. Hundreds of families fled Ulster in anticipation of what was to come. Meanwhile, James was driven into exile in France in 1688 by Protestant leaders in England; and William of Orange, grandson of Charles I, arrived in England from Holland to assume the monarchy. James, leaving exile from France and accompanied by French forces in an attempt to regain his throne, arrived in Ireland to join with the Irish army. A revolution that was accomplished almost without bloodshed in England turned long and bloody in Ireland.

In actions reminiscent of their grandfathers' Border experiences, frightened colonists feared another war and fled to safety, pulling down their homes and burning or destroying what they could not take with them. By March 1689, the countryside was devastated, and the northward-moving army had taken control of all Ireland with the exception of Enniskillen and Londonderry. Leyburn cites a French officer's description of County Londonderry. In a journey of forty miles, "only three miserable cabins" were left standing: "Everything else was rock, bog, or moor." Residents of Donagheady Parish, undoubtedly including the Armstrongs and their neighbors, hastened through this wasteland in their way to the gates of the walled city. Soon, its population of 2,000 had burgeoned to 7,000 soldiers and 30,000 refugees.[61]

Despite sickness, famine, and lack of supplies, the besieged city refused to surrender. Finally, after 105 days, the city was relieved by English supply ships. William's army later invaded Ireland, defeating James's forces. The years of the reign of the coregents William and his wife and cousin Mary brought relief to all parties. Freedom of worship was granted to the Irish Catholic population, Irish soldiers desiring to go to France were permitted to do so, and Presbyterians were reassured of their place in Ulster. With religious wars ending, families who had fled began to return.[62]

---

[61]   Hanna, *The Scotch-Irish*, I: 580–82; Leyburn, *The Scotch-Irish*, 130.

[62]   Leyburn, *The Scotch-Irish*, 129, 131; Hanna, *The Scotch-Irish*, I: 594.

What occurred during the siege and its aftermath changed the course of Irish history and the relationship of the Ulster Scots with their Anglican countrymen. During the worst of times, clergy and followers of both the Church of Ireland and the Scottish Kirk had shared a hellish existence as lack of water and food reduced the population to eating rats and mice, and sickness and the stench from the dead proved more fatal than wounds from enemy weapons. Both groups banded together within the besieged city throughout the worst of its days. Although figures vary widely, historians estimate that 9,800–15,000 soldiers and noncombatants died of fever, starvation, or wounds.

Not all went smoothly between the two groups after the war, however. Presbyterians saw what they considered grave injustices toward them by the occupying English forces and by local Anglican leaders. Commander of the relief forces, Major General Percy Kirke, refused to send soldiers into the countryside to protect the lives and property of settlers from marauding parties following the liberation of the city, officers from local Ulster Scots regiments were dismissed, and provisions were not available for the sick, many of whom died on the way to regain their homes. Feelings of resentment were already heightened against Kirke for his part in extending the length of the siege. In command of a large naval relief force that included soldiers and provisions, Kirke came within sight of the city, and fearing that his ships would be caught in the log booms and chains that had been laid across the mouth of the river, he ordered the fleet to turn around, sailed a few miles to the other side of the peninsula, and remained there for six weeks, not moving again until directly ordered to do so by William's military commander in Ireland. Adding to the resentment was the English House of Commons approval of £195,091 for Protestant regiments fighting the war, only a fraction of which was paid.

For many, however, the crowning blow lay in the glorification and monetary compensation of two additional English leaders whose actions during the siege threatened to unhinge a successful resistance. Church of Ireland Reverend George Walker was sent to London with an address to the king, received great acclaim, and published an account of the siege with himself as the hero of the operation. Far from being perceived as a hero by many within the walls during the siege, Reverend Walker at one point had tried to induce the city council to surrender. Adding further insult, he gave Presbyterians no credit for their defense of the city although they constituted 90 percent of the men in the ranks. Presbyterians also objected to the reward of £2,000 and an estate going to Captain Robert Corry, who had threatened to imprison anyone who took arms to defend the second besieged city of Enniskillen.[63]

The rift between the two groups deepened. For Ulster Scots, the insults at the hands of the principally English Anglicans burned for more than a century. For those who eventually left Northern Ireland to settle in America, the disregard for their contributions during the time of siege and its aftermath simply became one more bit of evidence that it was time to move on.[64]

The parish of Donagheady, with its proximity to Londonderry, had been hit especially hard. Large bodies of troops had been quartered along the River Foyle, and their foraging parties overran the whole area, commandeering cattle and corn. Homes and churches were burned to the ground and farmland laid waste. At the reinstitution of peace, however, survivors returned and began rebuilding their homes, their numbers increased by a final wave of Scots attracted by cheapness of farmland and new opportunities for trade.[65]

★

Once again, the fate of Ulster Scots that rose or fell according to the agendas of absentee rulers or actions of Parliament was about to take a dramatic turn for the worse. At the dawn of the eighteenth century, acts affecting them on religious and economic grounds were precipitated by directives of the English government that were the most harmful to date.

In March 1702, Presbyterians lost a friend and protector with the death of William. He was succeeded by Anne, daughter of James and sister of William's wife, Mary. Raised as a Protestant whose background was firmly Anglican, she approved the passage of a law from the High Church–controlled Parliament known as the "Test Act." Directed primarily toward Catholics, it contained a clause that was specifically aimed at subduing Ulster's predominantly Presbyterian population and also affected its other non-Anglican bodies, Quakers and Huguenots. Mandating that all holders

---

[63] Hanna, *The Scotch-Irish*, I: 600-02; William J. Roulston, *Researching Scots-Irish Ancestors* (Belfast: Ulster Historical Foundation, 2005), 9; Webb, *Born Fighting*, 107.

[64] Webb, *Born Fighting*, 109.

[65] Rutherford, *Donagheady Presbyterian Churches and Parish*, 22; Leyburn, *The Scotch-Irish*, 131.

of public office take sacraments according to the rites of the Anglican Church, it affected not only members of the Irish Parliament but also anyone holding civilian, military, or ecclesiastical office. Presbyterian ministers were turned out of their pulpits or threatened with legal proceedings. Because the sacramental test was made a condition of holding any military or civil office above the rank of constable, Presbyterians were forced to choose between their consciences and their offices. Twenty-four aldermen, burgesses, and sheriffs resigned their positions in Londonderry, among whom was John Armstrong's great-grandfather Alexander Skipton. Aldermen in Belfast withdrew en masse. When the Whig party came into power in 1709, attempts were made to persuade the Irish Parliament to repeal the act, but church bishops acted against such measures. Provisions were loosened in 1719 and later in 1737, but it was not until much later that the last of the Test Act articles was abolished. Not until more than fifty years later would Presbyterians again be allowed to serve in the military. By that time, many would already have vacated the country and would be eager to take up arms against the government that had subjected them to second-class citizenship.[66]

Ulster Scots had suffered religious restrictions before, but these were blatantly personal and discriminatory. This time, inheritance laws were affected. If on the death of a Protestant landowner, the natural heir was a Catholic, the latter was denied the stated property outright. If he were a Presbyterian, he was to be passed over in favor of a more remote family member who belonged to the established church. Nor were the dead themselves unaffected. In some parts of Ulster, burials could not be conducted unless a representative of the Church of Ireland officiated. Children of all Protestants not married in the Anglican Church were to be considered illegitimate, and Hanna notes that "many persons of undoubted reputation were prosecuted in bishops' courts as fornicators for cohabitating with their own wives." Children could no longer be taught by Presbyterian tutors. Presbyterians were compelled to pay tithes for support of rectors

---

[66] Alexander Skipton's name is among others inscribed upon a plaque in the First Derry Presbyterian Church commemorating its members who resigned their government seats at the passing of the Test Act of 1704. See also *The Story of the Presbyterians in Ulster: Pocket History and Heritage Trail* (Belfast: Presbyterian Historical Society of Ireland, n.d.), http://www.presbyterianhistoryireland.com; Hanna, *The Scotch-Irish*, II: 175–177; Leyburn, *The Scotch-Irish*, 167.

whose sermons they never heard and whose doctrines they did not accept while in addition, they had to support their own clergy.[67]

The aftermath of the siege of Londonderry and the later passage of the Test Acts were tipping points in the relationship between the Ulster Scots and their English overseers. Webb notes that the event became a wake-up call as to the former's collective status in what had become their homeland and a symbol for all the ills and betrayals that had hounded them throughout the preceding century. They were at odds with the native Irish, many of whom had been intent upon eradicating their presence. English rulers in London had urged them on but had then abandoned them during their critical times of need. Adding insult to injury, the Anglican elite in Ireland minimized their contribution once the siege had been lifted. Hardly a decade later, Parliament and the queen sought to exclude them from governmental, educational, military, and even religious authority in the very province in which their numbers and culture had become dominant and their labors had made a successful enterprise. Webb surmises that the siege reinforced the notion that the Ulster Scots were an isolated people who could depend only on each other, and its aftermath convinced many that they no longer belonged in Ireland's increasingly "toxic ethnic mix."[68]

Economic factors played perhaps an even larger part in creating the growing dissatisfaction among the Ulster Scots. The woolen industry had brought prosperity to Ulster, but apprehensive English competitors saw production in Ireland as threatening their own welfare and sought protection from the Crown for their product. Parliament passed the Woolens Act in 1699, prohibiting the exportation of Irish wool and woolen

---

[67] Leyburn, *The Scotch-Irish*, 164–68; Hanna, *The Scotch-Irish*, I: 618, II: 175; Webb, *Born Fighting*, 98. Since all burials traditionally took place in Church of Ireland churchyards, enterprising Presbyterians and others seemed to have found their way around having Church of Ireland officiants at their interments and subsequently having to pay the clergy to preside at the proceedings. In 1754, there were only five recorded burials in the Donagheady Parish. The Parish clergyman complained of the "indecent custom of interring without sending to the minister to attend—That the Papists should always, and the Presbyterians generally, omit it, is not to be wondered; but it is astonishing that those, who are of the Established Church, should choose to bury their deceased Friends like Dogs." Rev. E. T. Dundas, BA, *The History of Donagheady Parish* (Omagh: Tyrone Constitution, n.d.)

[68] Webb, *Born Fighting*, 100–01.

cloth. In two years following the law's passage, some 20,000 to 30,000 workers were out of jobs. Added to the economic despair caused by the curtailment of the woolen industry was the periodic depression of the price of Ulster's other successful export, linen, in foreign markets.[69]

It was, however, a practice known as "rack renting" that provided the final blow to the economy and one that precipitated the first large migration to America in 1717. The customary length of property lease in Ulster had been twenty-one or thirty-one years, the long leasing period having been an exceedingly motivating factor in drawing Scots to Ulster. Around this time, large numbers of lease renewals came due on property that had risen in value, and landlords saw fit to increase the rent substantially. Virtually all farmers, to include the Armstrongs on the Earl of Abercorn's estate, were affected since few in Ireland owned their own land until the late nineteenth century. Outraged leaseholders resisted. The highest bidders for new leases were often native Irish who joined with others to obtain a rental agreement.

Rack renting had dire results. For many, this was the last straw. Ulster Scotts considered their alternatives. They could return to Scotland or, particularly after the first wave of emigrants had shown the way, emigrate to America. Whole villages began to lose their Protestant element as ship after ship departed from Ulster ports. Nature collaborated in enhancing hard times. Insufficient rainfall between 1714 and 1719 resulted in ruined crops, curtailed the supply of flax for linen manufacture, and increased the price of food. Sheep died of foot rot. A smallpox epidemic hit Ulster in 1718, and the next three years brought fevers in the winter months.[70]

Wholesale migration from Ulster began and the tide of travelers to the American colonies could not be stopped. In five waves of movement lasting until the Revolution, around one-quarter million men, women, and children departed Belfast or Londonderry for American shores. America's gain was Ulster's loss. By one estimate, the Presbyterian population of Ireland declined by one-half between 1718 and 1775.[71]

---

[69] Leyburn, *The Scotch-Irish*, 158–60; Hanna, *The Scotch-Irish*, II: 174–175.

[70] Leyburn, *The Scotch-Irish*, 160–64; Roulston, *Three Centuries of Life in a Tyrone Parish*, 166.

[71] Leyburn, *The Scotch-Irish*, 180–81.
Emigration figures vary widely. Leyburn examines totals derived by various authors and studies. Conventional estimates of the number of Ulster Scots immigrating to America is around 200,000, but other estimates go as high as 300,000. The lower figure would mean that an average of 3,500 people

William Edward Hartpole Lecky sums up the situation this way:

> It would be difficult indeed to conceive a national
> condition less favourable than that of Ireland to a man
> of energy and ambition. If he were a Catholic, he found
> himself excluded from every position of trust and power,
> and from almost every means of acquiring wealth,
> degraded by a social stigma, deprived of every vestige of
> political weight. If he were a Presbyterian, he was subject
> to the disabilities of the Test Act. If he were a member
> of the Established Church, he was ever compelled to see
> all the highest posts of Church and State occupied by
> Englishmen. If he were a landlord, he found himself in
> a country where the law had produced such a social state
> that his position as a resident was nearly intolerable. If his
> ambition lay in the paths of manufacture or commerce,
> he was almost compelled to emigrate, for industrial and
> commercial enterprise had been deliberately crushed.[72]

★

Leyburn describes the Ulster Scot who now set his sights on American shores. He was a different person from his predecessors who had arrived in Ireland generations before. Social distinctions had changed his character. The disappearance of feudalism and absence of traditional family had released him from obligations to his laird and had given him the chance to live where he wanted and to work for whom he wished. No longer bound to farming, he could pursue manufacturing or trade. His performance as an individual and not his family's name determined his standing within his community; as his wealth increased, he was regarded as a substantial citizen.[73]

The Ulster Scot now thought of himself as Irish. His intermarriage with Puritans and Huguenots from England and the continent further defined his identity and broadened his horizons. His home was now

---

reached American shores from Northern Ireland in each of the fifty-eight years between 1717 and 1775 and the higher 5,175.

[72] William Lecky, *A History of Ireland in the Eighteenth Century*, I: 244–45.
[73] Leyburn, *The Scotch-Irish*, 140–42.

Ireland, having lived in its counties and townships for multiple generations. His forefathers had endured both the travails and the successes of the past 100-plus years. His family's blood had been shed there and his parents buried there. Scotland was a folk memory.[74]

To be an Ulster Scot was to be Presbyterian. Regardless of his religious convictions prior to departing Scotland, the Presbyterian Church became his identity, its conservative tenets determining his conduct and his relationships with his neighbors. His view of the king became shaped by the church and its tenet of religious freedom. It was superior to any order a king might make. If one church might revolt justly, so might another for the same reasons. His demand for liberty of worship as a religious minority in Ulster put him on the side of those who also demanded liberty of worship for all denominations when arriving in America. Presbyterians also had to claim their "rights of conscience" against the established church during times of discrimination in Ulster. When discriminatory laws were later passed in the American colonies, they and their Scots-Irish children demonstrated by their ready enlistment in revolutionary forces that they subscribed to the principle of armed resistance to a government they considered unjust.[75]

Men of Ulster fought native Irish during two major incursions. Once in America, they also lived on land that had been taken from the native populace. When such confiscation itself was declared legal by authorities, they fought to maintain the farms and property that they now considered theirs.[76]

James Webb notes that the Ulster Scots were descendants of the same men and women who had left embattled Border and Lowland areas. Conflict with the native Irish, especially after the insurrection of 1641, toughened and hardened a character that had never been soft. They had gleaned from the culture of one country and the land of another. They were a new people, strong and unfulfilled, ready for a new land. They took with them, however, a greater sense of injustice at the hands of the English governing class than anger toward their Irish neighbors.[77]

---

[74]   Ibid., 142–43.

[75]   Ibid., 146–47.

[76]   Ibid., 148.

[77]   Webb, *Born Fighting*, 116–17.

2

American Shores

It looks as if Ireland is to send all its inhabitants hither.
—James Logan, colonial secretary to William Penn[78]

Significant emigration from Ireland to the American colonies began around 1717 when an initial 4,000 to 5,000 Scots-Irish departed Ulster following years of drought and rack renting, the results of which saw farmers' rents raised exponentially on land they had tilled for as long as thirty years. A second larger wave from 1725–1729, attributed to poor economic conditions, crop failure, and rent increase, was so large that Parliament feared the loss of Ulster's entire Protestant element.[79]

Settlers during the earlier time period were drawn primarily to Pennsylvania although less-successful ventures were made toward settlement in New England. Calvinist-oriented Presbyterians should have fit right in to the Puritan society but found New Englanders disdainful of them, offended by their levels of illiteracy, slovenliness, and notable divergence from Puritan customs and habits. Presbyterians who expected religious freedom found it denied. The Congregational church was the established church in New England, and few from Ulster were willing to forsake the reformed tenets of Presbyterianism. By contrast, settlers

---

[78] James Logan (1729), The Logan Papers, III, quoted in Leyburn, *The Scotch-Irish*, 171.

[79] Leyburn, *The Scotch-Irish*, 169–70.

who entered the colonies through the Delaware River ports found their presence far more accepted, if not officially welcomed by James Logan, provincial secretary who felt that the Ulster Scots, who had prospered in times of direct conflict with opposing military forces and unfriendly neighbors, would provide islands of settlement in areas inhabited by the Native American population.[80]

A third period of emigration, largely attributed to conditions of famine, occurred in 1740–1741. By this time, the flow of Scots-Irish to the American colonies was so firmly established that their presence in Pennsylvania became an influential demographic in the Quaker commonwealth. Newer arrivals found properties in settled parts of the colony too expensive and began to push west and south into Virginia and the Carolinas.

Drought in Ulster and effective propaganda from America during 1754 and 1755 further increased the flow of emigrants. It was also during this time period that the colonies began to experience their first large-scale conflicts with specific Native American nations who began launching raids upon settlements in consequence of becoming displaced by ever-increasing numbers of frontiersmen flowing into their domains and invading their traditional hunting lands. Emigration ebbed during the time of the French and Indian War (1754–1763) but resumed from 1771–1775, largely due to rack-renting practices.[81]

Each wave of immigrants arriving on North American shores provided a stepping-stone for that which was to follow. The best advertisement for leaving Ireland came from those who had already ventured across the Atlantic. Family members remaining in Ulster realized that in leaving their Irish homes, they were not launching into a totally unknown land, but merely following in the footsteps of brothers, cousins, and friends who had

---

[80] Ibid., 91–92, 237–38. New England had seen the arrival of smaller numbers of emigrants from Ulster during the days of the Irish rebellion and later from Scotland when Cromwell ordered at least two boatloads of recalcitrant Presbyterians shipped to Massachusetts as indentured servants. James Logan was later forced to alter his opinion of the Ulster immigrants. Their behavior as pioneers, though demonstrating unquestioned bravery, yielded unexpected results. He noted, "A settlement of five families from the North of Ireland gives me more trouble than fifty of any other people." George Chambers, *A Tribute to the Principles, Virtues, Habits and Public Usefulness of the Irish and Scotch Early Settlers of Pennsylvania* (Chambersburg: M. A. Foltz, 1871), 10–11.

[81] Leyburn, *The Scotch-Irish*, 172–73.

already made the voyage. The prospect of being able to secure one's own land instead of holding a lease that might end in an enormous rent hike that could not be paid, freedom from religious and political restrictions, and for the ambitious, possible affluence and prominence within a new social framework were all enticing factors for the move across the ocean. For many, a system of indenture whereby one could have his way paid to the colonies in exchange for four to seven years of service was an attractive incentive.[82]

Thomas and Jane Armstrong departed for the American colonies relatively late within these waves of migration and are estimated to have embarked upon their transatlantic journey in 1754. In all probability, they were not making the journey alone. Well-organized groups consisting of several families or relatives traveled together or chartered their own ships. By the time of the family's departure from Ireland, the frequency with which ships sailed to the American colonies meant that immigrants generally had some degree of flexibility in making arrangements for their voyage and could benefit from information that was made available to them through advertising and by reports from previous emigres. The Armstrongs would have departed Londonderry, a port that afforded a direct route to Philadelphia rather than making secondary stops before embarking on Atlantic waters. They could shop comparatively and could consider ship size (a larger ship generally meant greater height between decks and increased overall comfort), the captain's reputation, and assurance that the ship's owner would also be traveling on board. In some cases, they attempted to discern whether the ship would carry only passengers who had prepaid for their passages or if the vessel would also carry those who crossed the Atlantic with the understanding that they would indenture themselves as labor to interested parties upon reaching Philadelphia. Generally, ships carried forty passengers who slept below deck in a cramped space, the height of which allowed only children to stand. Cost of the voyage was £4, including food and drink, which Marianne Wokeck in her article "Irish Immigration to the Delaware Valley Before the American Revolution" describes as plain but adequate. Generally, crowding was not an issue. This was not to say that the voyage was one of luxury. Miseries of seasickness, the belowdecks' stench of full chamber pots and illness that pervaded the close quarters were magnified when storms knocked the ship off course,

---

[82] Leyburn, 174-177.

---

adding weeks to the usual six- to eight-week travel time. During peak periods of immigration, particularly the late 1720s and late 1760s to early 1770s, vessels were more crowded, and sometimes ships ill-suited for an Atlantic crossing were used to accommodate the numbers who wanted to sail. Inexperienced captains might reduce provisions to gain more room for passengers, and occupants often became ill from insufficient food and confinement with large numbers in unheated spaces.[83]

After arriving in Philadelphia or other ports in the Delaware River basin, the vast majority of Scots-Irish disembarking at the time of the Armstrongs' crossing chose not to tarry in these areas because they were well settled and property was expensive. Most then began their trek westward along the Great Wagon Road that began in Philadelphia and continued through Lancaster County to the Susquehanna Valley and to points beyond. Thomas Armstrong's journey did not follow that pattern. Although eventually moving to Pennsylvania's Northumberland County, he did not do so until many years later. Instead, the Armstrongs headed up the Delaware River toward Hunterdon County, New Jersey.

★

[83] Marianne Wokeck, "Irish Immigration to the Delaware Valley before the American Revolution," *Proceedings of the Royal Academy*, Section C: Archaeology, Celtic Studies, History, Linguistics, and Literature 96C, no. 5 (1996): 103–19. Gottlieb Mittelberger, a traveler from Germany, describes in detail the hardship encountered by those leaving the Continent, the challenges endured onboard the ship and what awaited those who would become indentured servants upon arrival in Philadelphia. See *Gottlieb Mittelberger, Journey to Pennsylvania 1750 and Return to Germany in the Year 1754*, trans. Carl Theo. Eben (Philadelphia: John Jos. McVey, 1898), 13–45. Sources vary as to when registered ships departed Ulster in the early 1750s. R. J. Dickson writes that four ships departed Londonderry for Philadelphia between 1752 and 1754, one in 1752, two in 1753, and one in 1754. According to David Dobson, however, there were no ships departing Londonderry in 1753 and two ships, the *Ariana* and the *Buckskin*, arriving in Philadelphia in May and August 1754. The Armstrongs were likely passengers on one of these ships. Passenger manifests were not required until 1820. See Dickson, *Ulster Emigration to Colonial America, 1718-1775* (Belfast: Ulster Historical Foundation, 1966), 70, and Dobson, *Ships from Ireland to Early America 1623–1850* (Baltimore: Genealogical Publishing Company, Inc., 2004), I: 25; II: 10.

Why did the Armstrongs choose to settle in New Jersey? Scots-Irish émigrés tended to follow extended family members to various locales in the colonies, becoming part of instant communities. Thomas might have had relatives who preceded him to Hunterdon County, or he might have been traveling with others who had contacts there. Perhaps too the Armstrongs were looking for an environment that resembled the life that they were leaving rather than traveling to parts unknown. With enough capital gained from the sale of an unexpired lease in Ulster to purchase or lease land in New Jersey, they might not have felt the necessity to venture into the wilderness where land was practically free. The Armstrongs would have found an area where settlement had been begun by Quakers some seventy-five years before with a presence of Scots-Irish inhabitants, although not as dominant as in neighboring Pennsylvania. The county itself had become an established entity in 1713.[84]

The Armstrongs found their way to the township of Kingwood, which had separated from a larger township of Bethlehem in 1746, when its population totaled around 9,100. In an area whose western boundary was the Delaware River, its landscape in places presented a bold and picturesque view of perpendicular rocks and hanging ledges and in others gentle slopes and good farmland. Accounts tell of an abundance of timber, forests full of game, and the streams teeming with fish.[85]

The area soon became a beacon for settlers of several nationalities and religious leanings. By the time of the Armstrongs' arrival, Kingwood Township would have had Baptist, Methodist, and Presbyterian churches. By 1765, the whole county had nine Presbyterian, one Low Dutch (Reformed),

---

[84] Acreage in the New Jersey colony, originally divided into East and West Jersey tracts, had been granted to proprietors as early as 1663. Further subdivision had occurred in 1691 with the creation of the West Jersey Society's Great Tract, a joint stock company formed in London for the purchase of lands that included Hunterdon County.
Henry Race, "The West Jersey Society's Great Tract in Hunterdon County," *The Jerseyman* 3, no. 1 (1895), 1–5;
James P. Snell, *History of Hunterdon and Somerset Counties, New Jersey, with Illustrations and Biographical Sketches of Its Prominent Men and Pioneers* (Philadelphia: Everts & Peck, 1881), 162–89; Dermot Quinn, *The Irish in New Jersey: Four Centuries of American Life* (New Brunswick: Rutgers University Press, 2004), 32–33.
[85] Snell, *History of Hunterdon and Somerset Counties*, 155, 188, 391–92.

one German Reformed, three Anglican, two Quaker, and two Baptist congregations. A major road crossed the county that linked Philadelphia to Newark, and the county had smaller roads connecting settlements.[86]

George Mott, in his book *The First Century of Hunterdon County, State of New Jersey*, describes the political and social climate of the area thusly: "Political institutions were so liberal in their character that those who appreciated civil and religious liberty were attracted. And thus it came to pass that no county in the State had so mixed a population, composed, as it was, of Huguenots, Hollands, Germans, Scotch, Irish, English and Native Americans."[87]

The coming of a church into an area usually heralded the arrival of education, even if such efforts initially began as tutoring by the clergy. By the second half of the eighteenth century, schools began to appear in Hunterdon County as churches became more established. A Quaker meeting house was formed in Kingwood in 1730, and land for a school purchased in 1746. An Anglican church was already in the area. A school that the Armstrong children might have attended appears to have been begun as a joint venture in 1756 by Quakers, Anglicans, and Presbyterians living in the vicinity. As other churches were established, it is probable that more schooling opportunities arose.[88]

All these factors may have contributed to the Armstrongs' decision to settle in New Jersey rather than to venture into the Pennsylvania wilderness. In all probability, however, another more urgent factor might have influenced their decision. At approximately the time they arrived in America, reports were circulating that beyond the Alleghenies, the French were inciting Indians against English colonists. News of Indian movements in the Shenandoah Valley in 1753 raised suspicion that a storm of some sort was brewing; and the following year, open warfare broke out, heralding the beginning of the North American theater of the Seven Years' War between

---

[86] George S. Mott, *The First Century of Hunterdon County, State of New Jersey* (Flemington: E. Vosseller, 1878), 32; Snell, *History of Hunterdon and Somerset Counties, New Jersey*, 106.

[87] Mott, *The First Century of Hunterdon County*, 11.

[88] Frank E. Burd, "Education, 1964," *The First 300 Years of Hunterdon County, 1714-2014* (Flemington: Hunterdon County Cultural & Heritage Commission, 2014), 85–88. See also David Murry, *History of Education in New Jersey* (Washington: Government Printing Office, 1899), 13–18 for discussion of relevance of education to Presbyterian and Quaker settlers in West Jersey.

France and England, known in the colonies as the French and Indian War. At its formal conclusion in 1763, Pontiac's War ensued, continuing to make westward migration an unwise proposition.

★

At first glance, the marriage between Jane, daughter of Ulster gentry, and Thomas might appear to have been a mismatch. Leyburn notes, however, that throughout the Scots' residency in Ireland, lines between social classes became less defined. The poll book for the parish of Donagheady for 1662 lists a John Armstrong, quite possibly Thomas Armstrong's great-grandfather, as "yeoman" rather than "servant." Since virtually all who farmed in Ireland did not own their own land until the late nineteenth century, the nebulous distinction of "yeoman" in eighteenth-century Ulster might indicate that he held tenancy on land by an extended lease and was prosperous enough to employ his own servants and farm laborers, placing him somewhere below what might be considered gentry but above poorer tenant farmers. The wide variations in farming communities in terms of wealth, status, and social connections characterized a rural society that lacked clearly defined divisions between large well-established farmers and minor gentry. William J. Roulston notes that some of the yeoman class were as wealthy as minor county landed gentry. Similarly, there was often little difference between smaller farmers and their renters. The size of one's acreage mattered, as did the length of lease, customarily twenty-one or thirty-one years, or in many cases the length of "three lives," a virtual guarantee of holding property in perpetuity and affording freeholder rights. Lacking any specifics of the Armstrongs' holdings, it is logical to assume that they were firmly established tenants on the Earl of Abercorn's Dunnalong estate. In 1667, the aforementioned John Armstrong was a known member of the Donagheady community and church elder. Both possibilities put Thomas's family solidly in a respectable middle class of 18th century Ireland.[89]

---

[89] Leyburn, *The Scotch-Irish*, 141; Rutherford, *Donagheady Presbyterian Churches and Parish*, 56, 106; Stanley Stewart, *A History of Donagheady Presbyterian Church* (Strabane: Donagheady Presbyterian Church, 2005), 24. For information on leases for the Earl of Abercorn's estate, see Roulston, *Three Centuries of Life in a Tyrone Parish*, 166–67, 210–11, and Roulston, *Researching Scots-Irish Ancestors*, 14–15, 70–71.

Family lore suggests that Jane Hamilton was "disinherited" by her family with her marriage to Thomas Armstrong, which might be based on the appearance of her brothers' names in the will of her grandfather, James Hamilton. Jane's father Michael Hamilton predeceased her grandfather; and the names of her brothers James, Edward, and Michael are noted in their grandfather's will along with those of James's own sons and daughters. Jane is, however, mentioned in her father's will, proved April 26, 1749. Because only abstracts of these wills are now available, one is left to conjecture its contents. Monetary settlements might have been made to Jane and her sisters Betty and Frances at the time of their father's death, and property to be conveyed might have carried through to Michael's sons through her grandfather James's will.[90]

Roulston writes of the numerous Hamiltons in Donagheady Parish in the early eighteenth century in *Three Centuries of Life in a Tyrone Parish: A History of Donagheady, 1600–1900*. The Hamiltons of Magheramason and Lower Tully were cited as "gentleman" in registered documents and were counted among the freemen of Derry in 1746. Such status does not necessarily imply great wealth but indicates an economic status sufficient to hire undertenants to work one's lands. A freeholder held his lands under perpetual leases, usually dating from the early seventeenth century, and could also vote in Parliamentary elections. Jane Armstrong's immediate family may or may not have represented an overly affluent branch of the Hamilton family.[91]

What is clear, however, is that within the sparsely populated Dunnalong manor, the families of Thomas Armstrong and Michael Hamilton undoubtedly knew one another. Poll tax rolls of 1661–1662 for the entire 10,000-acre plantation indicated the presence of only seventy-seven yeomen and their wives, as well as eighty-two servants. Further analysis of the rolls indicates that in most of the townlands in the manor, there was only a single yeoman or farmer, John Armstrong being listed as such in Taunaghbridy (Tamnabready). That settlement, now included in present-day Bready, sits less than a mile along the main road from both Maghermason and Tully to the north and Drumgaudy to

---

90 Public Records of Northern Ireland (PRONI), Groves Manuscripts, T808/6134. www.proni.gov.uk/introduction_abercorn_d623.pdf. See also Cochran, *Seven Generations of the Ancestry of Captain Abram Piatt Andrew*, PJA.

91 Roulston, *Three Centuries of Life in a Tyrone Parish*, 89–90.

the south, settlements where the Hamiltons resided. The actual village of Donagheady is located two miles to the east of Drumgaudy and the site of the Donagheady Presbyterian Church. It is a safe assumption that the two families were probably neighbors for generations, worshipped together on Sundays, and shared drinks at the popular tavern at Drumgaudy. Jane Hamilton and Michael Armstrong might well have known each other their entire lives.[92]

What their motivations were for leaving Ulster at that time can only be surmised. Perhaps it was a matter of timing. Jane's father, Michael Hamilton, died in 1748 or 1749, and perhaps she was bequeathed money through his will. It is not known when Thomas's father died, or if his passing coincided with the couple's decision to emigrate. The timing of their departure is likely found in the sharp spike of both the expense and the length of continuing leases to land that was occurring throughout Ulster. Roulston notes that in 1749 James Hamilton, the Eighth Earl of Abercorn, sought to renegotiate the leases of his tenants in Dunnalong. Most had been for twenty-one years although others were for seven and fourteen years. Security of tenure was a major concern of the tenants, and many complained that their leases were not long enough. Abercorn then began granting new leases for twenty-one years but increased the yearly rent by about a third (i.e., from £15 to £20 per year) to compensate. Additionally, the earl continued to control the right of succession on a farm if the lessee died before the expiration of his lease. He appeared to be the final arbiter, particularly in cases of disputes between heirs, leaving one to speculate on the possibility of older Armstrong siblings.[93]

★

[92] Rutherford, *Donagheady Presbyterian Churches*, 106, 110. See also Bready Ancestry, "Poll Book for the Parish of Donagheady c. 1662" and "Hearth Money Rolls." http://www.breadyancestry.com.

[93] Depending upon his degree of ownership of the lease of Armstrong property, Thomas may also have gained necessary funds to emigrate through its sale. Cochran, Armstrong papers, PJA; William J. Roulston, *Parishes of Leckpatrick and Dunnalong: Their Place in History* (Letterkenny: Browne Printers, 2000), 52–53. Description of the Abercorn papers and property can be found on the PRONI website, http://www.proni.gov.uk/introduction_abercorn_d623.pdf.

Thomas and Jane arrived in New Jersey with daughter Ann ("Nancy") and son James, believed to have been born about 1750 and 1753 in County Londonderry. John was born shortly after arrival in New Jersey in 1755, and Hamilton soon followed.[94]

Jane Armstrong appears to have died some time prior to August 7, 1759, when her youngest child was probably still a toddler. At that time, Thomas's name appears on a calendar of wills listing his name as administrator of the estate of Leonard Kreutzer who was the father of his second wife, Anna Magdalena. The couple had two other children, Mary and Elizabeth, mentioned years later in Thomas's will.[95]

Thomas took up farming, his name listed among those in 1757 living in an area "Westward of Pierce's Road," a section of Kingwood Township in which he, at least initially, leased land. Leases were generally to last seven years. Given some financial assistance, tenants were expected to build log houses and barns with stables. They were to dig wells and plant orchards of up to two hundred apple trees with additional fruit trees placed about the house for shade. Tenants were also to clear one acre of

---

[94] C. F. Cochran to Dr. William Egle, July 7, 1901, in Armstrong Papers, PJA. Unfortunately, there appear to be no available church records of the marriage of Thomas and Jane Armstrong nor of their two older children's births or baptisms. One can only assume that they were a relatively young couple, probably marrying in the late 1740s with children born within a few years of their marriage.

[95] The name of Armstrong's father-in-law is recorded in various documents as Kreutzer, Kretzor, Critser, Cristor, and Critzer. Magdalena was later identified in Thomas's will as his wife, and additional documentation appears in Hunterdon County court papers as early as 1759 that were filed by Thomas and Anna Magdalena Armstrong against an individual who owed money to Anna Magdalena prior to her marriage. Kreutzer is listed as an early settler in the Alexandria Township, adjacent to Kingwood. "Thomas Armstrong & his wife vs. George Cotter," October 1759, and "Thomas Armstrong, Administrator for Leonard Kretzor vs. John Seger," November 10, 1760, are recorded in Hunterdon County court papers. Armstrong, named as Leonard Kreutzer/Critser's administrator on August 7, 1759, is recorded in A. Van Doren Honeyman, ed., *Documents Relating to the Colonial History of the State of New Jersey, First Series, vol. 32: Calendar of New Jersey Wills, Administrations, Etc., vol. 3, 1751–1760* (Somerville, New Jersey: The Unionist-Gazette Association, Printers, 1929), 81.

meadowland for each year of the lease and create fenced, plowed fields on the outside of the property in straight lines.[96]

Hunterdon County escaped the worst of the turmoil that plagued Pennsylvania during the French and Indian War. George S. Mott, in his book *First Century of Hunterdon County*, states that within that time period, emboldened Indians ventured into areas in close proximity to Philadelphia, causing residents to flee into New Jersey. Hunterdon County residents became alarmed and prepared for defense. The name of Thomas Armstrong appears with others on a petition dated February 27, 1756, to Governor Jonathan Belcher from the inhabitants of Kingwood Township expressing concern over the conflict with Native Americans in the neighborhood. Mott says, however, that those within the general area were uniformly peaceable and friendly in their intercourse with settlers although unrest was evident in Sussex and Warren Counties to the north.[97]

Thomas's farming ventures do not appear to have been entirely successful. He apparently suffered from cash flow woes typical of colonists at the time. Hard currency was scarce. In order to cover the value of goods to be bought and sold, individuals had to rely on credit and bartering to obtain needed essentials. His lack of success did not generate reluctance to exercise his use of the judiciary, however, as evidenced by numerous court documents.

An indication that Thomas Armstrong's financial fortunes appeared to have taken a turn for the worse appears in February 1765 when Samuel Purviance filed suit against him for the payment of £280. A short time later, on April 4, 1765, Armstrong appears to have signed a promissory note to pay Philadelphia merchants Andrew Reed and Charles Pettit £13.17s.7d by May 1 of that year or he would have to render more than twice that amount should he not be able to remunerate the original sum. Apparently unable to pay, his case was heard at the October 1765 term of the Inferior Court of Common Pleas, and he was held liable for the debt. In May of 1766, he was again summoned to court; and on the

---

[96]   Henry Race, "The West Jersey Society's Great Tract in Hunterdon County," 4; Henry Race, "Tenants of the West Jersey Society's Great Tract," *Hunterdon County Historical Society Newsletter*, Fall (1984), 423.

[97]   Mott, *The First Century of Hunterdon County*, 26; Snell, *History of Hunterdon and Somerset Counties, New Jersey*, 18; New Jersey State Archives Manuscript Collection, 1680s–1970s, New Jersey State Archives, Box 1-41, Folder 4-1, accessed through U.S. Census Reconstructed Records, 1660–1820, www. archives.com.

twenty-seventh of that month, the Hunterdon County sheriff was directed to confiscate Armstrong's property, the value of which was to be weighed against his financial obligation. Items seized represented the core of the family's possessions including bed and bedding, plow and harrow, wagon and gears, plates, basins, spoons, pots, cupboard, pails, lantern, chairs, churn, looking glass, and frying pan.[98]

Running concurrently with this suit was one that Armstrong himself had filed against James Brooks in October 1764 to be heard at the February 1765 session of court. In January 1765, he was deputized by the county sheriff to serve the "writt at his own Resque." The sum in question was £200 for trespassing damages. Apparently, some money was recovered, but the case was not resolved by the time Armstrong appeared in court to answer charges brought by Reed and Pettit in the October 1765 session because documents indicate that Armstrong again sued Brooks for £100 owed him as of June 29, 1765. This case was heard in October 1765 and decided in Armstrong's favor on the February 1766 session. Brooks's livestock and household goods were later seized to satisfy the debt to Armstrong.[99]

A final summons dated in August 1768 was for the October 1768 court session. Armstrong appears to have brought suit against Andrew and Mathias Parson in the Inferior Court of Common Pleas in reference to a debt of £20.13s.9d. A notation on the bottom of the summons states that "Andrew Parson is an old Man a Cooper" . . . "lives somewhere about Pittstown." Unfortunately, no information is available concerning the outcome of this procedure.[100]

How Thomas got in and out of his financial constraints is unknown. His fortunes must have improved at some point because he found the means to move his family to Pennsylvania and to purchase property in Northumberland County by 1770.[101]

---

[98] Hunterdon County Records, #31804, February 1765; #31907, August 1765; #12474, October 1765; #7609, May 1766; #20123, May 1766.

[99] Hunterdon County Records, #28521, January 1765; #22738, February 1766.

[100] Hunterdon County Records, #33518, August 1768.

[101] The names of Thomas Armstrong and son-in-law John McAdams appear on a list of men who were reimbursed for their services of removing Connecticut claimants from the Wyoming Valley, dated March 3, 1770. They could have rendered services as early as the fall of 1769. Julian P. Boyd, ed., *The Susquehanna Company Papers, Vol. 4, 1770–1772* (Wilkes-Barre: Wyoming Historical & Geological Society, 1933), 40.

One can only guess at the effect upon the Armstrong children of seeing family property confiscated and hauled away. To what extent that early humiliation affected John, then eleven years old, and led him to adopt future patterns of behavior that included a quest for financial independence, as well as regard for his personal reputation as a gentleman, officer, and businessman, can only be speculated upon. It is telling that years later, when Armstrong was an officer in the First Regiment, he carried a pocket notebook in which he had recorded the names of his grandfathers and great-grandfather who had apparently gained his respect by their actions or by their status in Ulster society. His heritage as a descendant of his mother's Ulster gentry was apparently well known to him although his memories of her must surely have been scant, having lost her by his fourth birthday. His writings as an adult reflect a demand for personal respect, spurred possibly by early memories of the family's financial humiliation and knowledge of his mother's lineage.[102]

In a letter written years later in reply to that of an unknown adversary, Armstrong indicated that he had entered the army "not having the advantage of an education," presumably that which might have been afforded to young men from wealthier families at the few colleges of the colonies at the time. He evidently received the schooling that was available in Hunterdon County, either at one of the church institutions or through tutors meeting with groups of children. It is likely that the Armstrong boys only attended school for a few years, as they were almost certainly needed to help on the family farm.[103]

---

[102] Charles F. Cochran, letter to unknown recipient, September 28, 1915, and to Mrs. Spinning, September 11, 1915; family record (Item #24) included in Armstrong Papers, PJA.

[103] Draft of letter, 1799, PJA; See Burd, "Education, 1964," 86–87, for specific information regarding the development of education in Hunterdon County. He describes the eighteenth-century school day as long, often continuing late in the afternoon to utilize existing daylight. Quality of teachers varied considerably. Many were itinerant, some of whom were well educated, but others with only a little more knowledge than their pupils. The scope of curriculum emphasizing rote learning was rudimentary at best, students mastering basic mathematics skills and learning to read using the New Testament or the New England hornbook, a tablet commonly used in early schools consisting of a piece of printed paper glued to a wooden board and protected by a flattened cow horn. Although the content varied over time, it typically displayed the alphabet and common syllable formations on its top half and the Lord's Prayer on the bottom.

Regardless of the quality or duration of instruction, Armstrong appears to have benefitted from his schooling. He wrote well. Although drafts of his correspondence often contain common misspellings of the time, they generally reflect correct grammar, with notable exceptions occurring during times when he made hurried notes. As an adult, he prided himself on his love of learning, evidently considering himself a gentleman with a gentleman's interest in refinement. Personal notebooks kept in both younger years and as he grew older reflect his familiarity with popular prose and poetry of the day.[104]

★

John's older sister Nancy married John McAdams in Kingwood in January 1766. Following the pattern of their Scots-Irish compatriots who tended to migrate westward whenever new lands became available for settlement, about three years later the extended Armstrong family packed what belongings they could transport and left Hunterdon County, traveling west to land newly opened for sale north of the convergence of the North and West forks of the Susquehanna River in what eventually was to become Northumberland County, Pennsylvania. Armstrong applied for the purchase of 300 acres of land located on the East Fork of Muncy Creek that flowed into the West Branch of the Susquehanna. Their site located over twenty-five miles upstream from the confluence of the two branches, the Armstrongs had moved to an area in stark contrast to that which they had left in Hunterdon County. In 1769, there were no churches, no schools, and with the exception of a few pockets of houses, only wilderness. By 1772, there were only four houses in the Sunbury-Northumberland area, and along the West Branch only about fifteen. The Armstrong family found themselves very much alone in their new surroundings, but the area soon began to attract Scots-Irish émigrés, and the population soon began to swell.[105]

---

104 A large proportion of Armstrong's papers located at the Indiana Historical Society consists of drafts rather than actual copies of his correspondence.

105 Kenneth D. McCrea, *Pennsylvania Land Applications, vol. 2, New Purchase Applications 1769–1773* (Philadelphia: Genealogical society of Pennsylvania, 2003); J. F. Meginness, *Otzinachson or a History of the West Branch Valley of the Susquehanna* (Philadelphia: Henry B. Ashmead, 1857), 124; Herbert C. Bell, *History of Northumberland County, Pennsylvania* (Chicago: Brown, Runk,

Thomas's sons James, John, and Hamilton were perhaps sixteen, fourteen, and twelve years old when they made the trek from Hunterdon County to their new home. Still a virtual wilderness, earlier European settlers lived with fresh memories of horror and bloodshed. Only five years had elapsed since the end of two periods of hostility that had gripped the area.

Prior to 1753, three entities intersected at Shamokin, home to the Lenape, or Delaware settlement at the confluence of the North and West Branches of the Susquehanna and site of present-day Sunbury. First came the early French and English traders who, in addition to creating a lucrative fur trade, obtained valuable geographic and political information for their governments and forged bonds with local tribes. They were joined in 1747 by members of the Moravian Church, who, having settled near Bethlehem, Pennsylvania, sought to bring Christianity to the Native American peoples by establishing a small mission at the village.[106]

The peaceful intercourse of the trader and the missionary with the tribes of Shamokin and the surrounding region was not destined to last. Pennsylvania's need for land to accommodate its burgeoning immigrant population, the struggle between France and England to attain dominance in the New World, and intertribal jealousies all were factors in raising the temperature in an area that eventually boiled over with a vengeance.

As initial settlements outgrew their boundaries, Pennsylvania realized the need to negotiate with Native American nations for land rights. Pivotal negotiations took place in conjunction with the Albany Congress of 1754, at which representatives from the northern British colonies met with Native American chiefs to discuss conditions and a defense against the growing threat of the French in Canada. Although not an official part of the conference, Pennsylvania authorities negotiated with representatives

---

and Company, 1891), 83. Thomas later purchased land in what was then designated as Point Township where the town of Northumberland now stands. Records show his tax obligations for 1781 for thirty acres of land and 1782 for fifty acres. He later purchased two lots in town, one of which he sold to John in 1781. William Henry Egle, MD, ed., *Pennsylvania Archives, Published Series, Series 3, Vol. 19* (Harrisburg: Wm. Stanley Ray, State Printer, 1897), *PA3*: XIX: 427–28, 461, 463, 508, 510, 561, 625, 707, 785; Northumberland County Deeds B:272, B:247; Armstrong and Cochran notebooks in Armstrong papers, PJA.

[106] Bell, *History of Northumberland County*, 26.

of the Iroquois confederation, better known as the Six Nations, to obtain rights for lands encompassing areas between the Delaware and Susquehanna Rivers, including land that would someday become part of Northumberland County. None of the confederation's members occupied any part of land sought by Pennsylvania, but its territory bordered that of the thirteen colonies, extending northward to southern Canada and westward into a part of the Mississippi Valley. The extent of its dominion, its absolute power, and intertribal organization rendered conquered tribes such as the Delaware and their neighbors, the Shawnee, of secondary importance. The resident Delaware, who were left out of the process entirely, were dissatisfied with the outcome of the agreement and either elected to stay in areas allotted them or to move west to the Ohio Country. Retaining a deep resentment toward the provincial authorities, they came under the influence of the French, whose presence west of the Alleghenies served to alienate them entirely from English interests. Ramifications of the Delaware disenchantment, and later that of the Shawnee, were to come full circle in the ensuing years.[107]

West of the Alleghenies only a few months earlier, the French, who considered the Susquehanna River to be the British colonies' western boundary, overpowered a small British contingent that had constructed a fort at the confluence of the Allegheny and Monongahela Rivers at present-day Pittsburg. Virginia had been granted lands that stretched to the Mississippi River through the colony's Royal Charter of 1609 and had begun to look toward the Ohio Country to lands occupied by the Delaware and Shawnee.

In response to the attack upon the fort that the French renamed "Fort Duquesne," the Crown dispatched General Edward Braddock, whose ill-fated mission to retake the fort was characterized by his tactless disregard of colonial advice and ignorance of Indian methods of warfare. France's Indian allies, stimulated by the utter defeat of Braddock at the hands of their combined forces, then broke loose upon frontier settlements from Canada to southern Virginia. Leyburn quotes a French captain who commented, "It is incredible what a quantity of scalps they bring us . . . These miserable English are in the extremity of distress."[108]

---

[107] Bell, *History of Northumberland County*, 25, 46. The Six Nations consisted of the Seneca, Onondaga, Oneida, Cayuga, Mohawk, and Tuscarora nations.

[108] Leyburn, *The Scotch-Irish*, 226–27.

Braddock's defeat was not lost on the Delaware who had remained neutral during his army's advance. Years of subjection to the dominant Iroquois and the final insult of agreements reached at the Albany Congress of 1754 through which the Six Nations had virtually sold Delaware and Shawnee lands out from under them, now brought their bitterness to the fore. Violence erupted in the Susquehanna Valley on October 16, 1755, when a party of fourteen Indians attacked the settlements at Penns Creek, followed by subsequent attacks in the sparsely populated area. Pennsylvania's Quaker government initially refused to lend support to the area's angered settlers, and the state assembly was eventually turned over to prowar members. Fort Augusta was erected at Shamokin in 1756 and became a fortress that provided a place for staging of troops for defense of the area and a refuge for friendly Indians and settlers. Its strategic location limited the effectiveness of enemy raids and allowed the Susquehanna Valley to remain under British control.[109]

The tide of the war turned in Britain's favor in 1758 when British regulars, aided by colonial militia, captured Fort Duquesne. Victory there was followed by capture of Quebec in 1759, and by 1760, the British controlled all of Canada. The Treaty of Paris in 1763 called for France to cede all of its possessions east of the Mississippi, including Canada.

Peace on the frontier was not to follow in the aftermath of a formal agreement between countries negotiated half a world away. Pontiac's War began in 1763 just as the French and Indian War ended. The Ottawa chief had convinced a loose confederation of warriors from various tribes of the Great Lakes and Ohio and Illinois Countries of the necessity of uniting in a massive attack on the English colonies in order to halt the relentless advance of European settlement into Native American territory. Virginia and Pennsylvania were particularly hard-hit, and in two years of terror, an estimated 2,000 settlers in Pennsylvania were killed with many more fleeing eastward. The war finally ended after two well-led British expeditions into the Ohio Country prompted a negotiated settlement.[110]

These periods of frontier warfare were pivotal in the evolution of the deteriorating relationship between settlers and their Native American neighbors. The Scots-Irish who headed westward during earlier waves of

---

[109] Bell, *History of Northumberland County*, 47, 50. Penns Creek flows into the Susquehanna about five miles opposite present-day Sunbury.

[110] Leyburn, *The Scotch-Irish*, 229–30. See also Richard White, *The Middle Ground: Indians, Empires, and Republics in the Great Lakes Region, 1650–1815* (New York: Cambridge University Press, 1991), 269–314.

emigration from Ireland typically settled on the frontier. Their growing presence and complete insensitivity to the Indian perspective regarding land rights were destroying the latter's way of life. From the settler's viewpoint, he had made a home in what, to him, had been wilderness and empty land; he had no intention of retiring meekly from what he had created by his own toil. Because his settlements were most subject to forays, he had personal reasons for bearing the brunt of years of guerrilla fighting. Old World concepts of the treatment of a captured enemy went out the window as he soon got over any notion of the "proper way to fight." If an Indian murdered a white man, the only way to fight back was to slay him, to scalp him, and to burn his village in a surprise attack. The brutal atmosphere of the frontier dulled whatever finer sensibilities otherwise compassionate people may have possessed.[111]

In 1764, following the long-awaited end of hostilities during the two wars, land that was to become Northumberland County was opened up for organized settlement. Further negotiations with the Six Nations at Fort Stanwix, in present-day Rome, New York, in November 1768 yielded increased territory to the north and west. Acreage was initially granted to soldiers serving in the recent conflicts, and on April 3, 1769, a land office opened for all applicants. Massive migration to the thinly populated area then commenced; and Germans, English, Welsh, and Scots-Irish began to flock to their own destinations within the territory. So rapid was the area's growth that the county of Northumberland was officially formed less than three years later.[112]

County settlement was largely by those without substantial means. Terms of purchase rendered it possible for men to buy and improve their own land, and to build a home without great financial outlay. A horse and cow and eight or ten acres of cultivated land constituted the taxable property of the great majority of farmers of that period. The man who brought with him several horses and cattle and means enough to employ others to assist him in clearing his land was evidently regarded as rich by his neighbors. Settlement was not easy. Acreage first had to be cleared

---

[111] Leyburn, *The Scotch-Irish*, 228, notes that Easterners could clearly distinguish between the characteristics of back-country settlers. In general, Germans, especially in Pennsylvania, avoided conflict with Indians. Many were pacifists, and others took pains to obtain Indian consent to their settlements. Scots-Irish, on the other hand, were known to be excitable and hotheaded.

[112] Bell, *History of Northumberland County*, 83, 85.

from the primeval forest, done commonly through the multiyear process of destroying trees by girdling them that resulted in more expedient use of surrounding land as it was exposed to sunlight, but later clearing remaining stumps with crude farming implements made for hard work. Thomas Armstrong must have been thankful for his three sons to help him start up his farm and to provide shelter for the family.[113]

★

Concurrent with the rapid settlement of Northumberland County, a hidden thorn lay in the flanks of its development, causing unrest among the locals that continued to fester for decades. The long-lasting dispute between the settlers from Connecticut within Pennsylvania borders, eventually known as the Pennamite-Yankee Wars, was centered upon ownership of a twenty-one-mile stretch of land along the North Branch of the Susquehanna known as the Wyoming Valley. Designated by Pennsylvania as part of Northumberland County and located about sixty-five miles upriver from Sunbury in the area that includes present-day

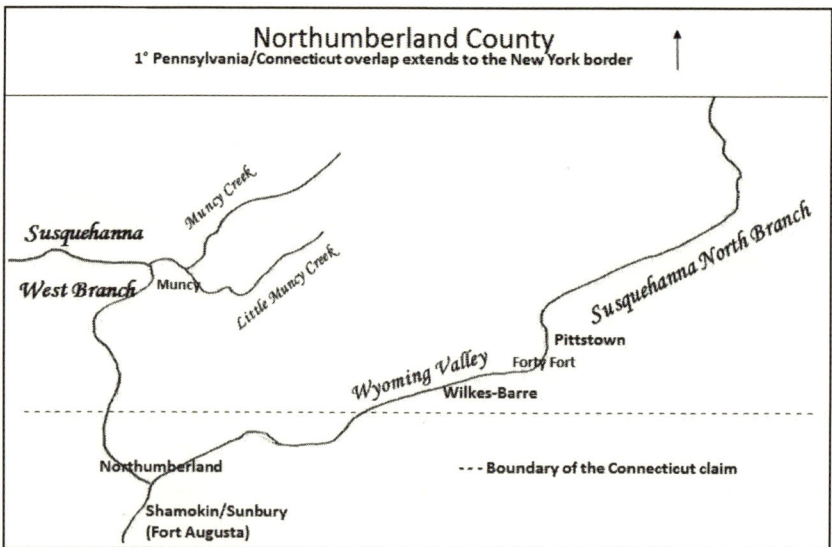

Northumberland County
1° Pennsylvania/Connecticut overlap extends to the New York border

Muncy Creek
Susquehanna
West Branch — Muncy
Little Muncy Creek
Susquehanna North Branch
Pittstown
Wyoming Valley — Fort / Fort
Wilkes-Barre
Northumberland
Shamokin/Sunbury (Fort Augusta)
- - - Boundary of the Connecticut claim

---

[113] Ibid., 87. Girdling is the complete removal of the bark from around the entire circumference of either a tree trunk or branch resulting in the eventual death of the area above the girdle.

Wilkes-Barre between Nanticoke Creek and the Lackawanna River, the dispute had its origins in the location of territory cited in the land grants of the two colonies. Imperial officials, who often possessed little knowledge of the American landscape they parceled out, issued vague or inaccurate patents that frequently interfered with earlier grants or encroached on competing claims. Charles II presented Connecticut a charter in 1662, granting its current territory plus "all lands west of it, to the extent of its breadth, from sea to sea." Nineteen years later, Charles granted William Penn his charter to include lands that extended to forty-three degrees north latitude and westward for five degrees. The two colonies overlapped by one degree and included lands in the Wyoming Valley, as well as that extending westward through the northern part of Northumberland County. Connecticut's interest in the western lands remained dormant for over a century until it experienced a land shortage in the 1750s, and its need for expansion resurrected its interest in the original seventeenth-century charter boundaries. Inhabitants of Connecticut set their sights on the rich Wyoming Valley.[114]

The Albany Congress of 1754 provided a venue for both Connecticut and Pennsylvania to negotiate with the Six Nations in order to claim land within the disputed territory. As noted previously, the Pennsylvania delegation's agreement with seventy representatives from the Six Nations opened up settlement in part of what was to become the sprawling Northumberland County. During this negotiation, Six Nations representatives pledged that they would not agree to any surrender of the Wyoming Valley, wanting to keep it in perpetuity. Regardless, only a few days later, agents of Connecticut's Susquehanna Company negotiated the purchase for valley lands in secret meetings with Mohawks who signed the agreement without consulting the council of the Six Nations. Under this agreement, Connecticut could claim not only the rich Wyoming Valley but other parts of Northumberland County under which Pennsylvania assumed it had proprietorship. Ironically, a conference that was to have resulted in improved Anglo-Indian relations and to foster intercolony cooperation served to increase tensions between Pennsylvania and Connecticut, Indians

---

[114] Alfred Mathews, *Ohio and Her Western Reserve* (New York: D. Appleton and Company, 1902), 58–61; Paul B. Moyer, *Wild Yankees: The Struggle for Independence along Pennsylvania's Revolutionary Frontier* (Ithaca: Cornell University, 2007), 16–17.

---

and whites, and the Iroquois who claimed jurisdiction over Wyoming Valley and other Native American tribes who made the valley their home.[115]

The Susquehanna Company made no move to settle the area for a period of eight years due to the unrest of the French and Indian War. In 1762, about two hundred Connecticut men arrived in the valley. Their timing was poor. Delaware warrors, unhappy with the situation, attacked the settlement in October 1764, killing twenty people and forcing the evacuation of others from the valley. The mysterious murder of Teedyuscung, an important Delaware chief, largely attributed to Connecticut settlers the year before, contributed to their unrest.

Settlers returned in 1769, this time with more men and the means to resist attack. In the intervening years, Pennsylvania had persuaded the Six Nations to negate their deal with Connecticut and founded a settlement within the valley themselves. There followed a succession of raids, sieges, and skirmishes between the two sides, all without lasting success for either. Later that year, Pennsylvania claimants, reinforced by a cannon and a two-hundred-man posse, overwhelmed and expelled Wyoming's Connecticut occupants. Though aggressive and heavy-handed, this act was accomplished without serious injury or loss of life. Thomas Armstrong and John McAdams apparently participated in this raid, the two receiving £4 for their efforts.

In 1771, Connecticut's claim was upheld by George III, precipitating the arrival of additional settlers who founded the town of Westmoreland in 1774. Connecticut pronounced the area, now with a population of 6,000 of its citizens, part of its Litchfield County. The region, however, had already been declared to be one of Northumberland County's seven townships at the time of its creation in 1772. By this time, Pennsylvanians living in the area were now allowed to purchase rather than lease property there and had strong personal motives for the expulsion of settlers under Connecticut's claim.[116]

---

[115] Moyer, *Wild Yankees*, 19–20. Reportedly, the deal was aided by the assistance of generous amounts of liquor available to the Mohawk representatives during negotiations. Roger R. Trask, "Pennsylvania and the Albany Congress, 1754," *Pennsylvania History: A Journal of Mid-Atlantic Studies* 27, no. 3 (1960):283.

[116] Moyer, *Wild Yankees*, 28; Boyd, The Susquehanna Company Papers, 1770–1772, 40. See also Mathews, *Ohio and Her Western Reserve*, 66–75; Anne M. Ousterhout, "Frontier Vengeance: Connecticut Yankees vs. the Pennamites in the Wyoming Valley," *Pennsylvania History* 62, no. 3 (1995), 339.

Antagonism grew as Wyoming divided into two groups: Yankees, as the settlers under Connecticut land grants were called, and the people the Yankees called Pennamites, or those claiming lands under Pennsylvania's jurisdiction. Connecticut settlers continued their advance into the area, building gristmills and forts, surveying land for new settlements, and setting up the five townships of Wilkes-Barre, Pittston, Kingston, Hanover, and Plymouth. The Continental Congress recommended that both sides peacefully settle the dispute, but the steadily increasing Connecticut presence in the valley and the rising number of ambushes and skirmishes between settlers in the disputed area led to escalation on both sides. Relations between the two groups became increasingly bitter, and rumors flourished. Pennamites worried that Yankees were going to fill up all the land as quickly as possible and win the controversy by sheer numbers. Yankees, on the other hand, warned each other repeatedly of Pennamite plans to attack and of the need to strengthen forts and to arm themselves.[117]

When Connecticut declared Wyoming to be part of Litchfield County in 1774, it determined that the western boundary of the town of Westmoreland extended to the Alleghenies, the line declared earlier by the Treaty of Fort Stanwix as a geographical division between land that could be occupied by European settlers and that reserved for the Indian nations. Subsequently, a significant part of Northumberland County in addition to the immediate Wyoming Valley came into dispute. Connecticut's claim now encompassed a swath of land stretching roughly from a point thirteen miles north of present-day Sunbury to the New York border. In reality, the Susquehanna Company sought not to stretch its claim all the way to the mountain range but to position settlements some fifty miles away to the West Branch of the Susquehanna on land that was already determined to be most of that part of Northumberland County that lay above the North Branch.

By June 1774, Connecticut settlers had arrived at the West Branch, taking up land on warrants granted them by the Province of Connecticut. Now the dispute over land and land rights became very close at hand. Northumberland County's growing population, centered at Sunbury and drifting northward up the West Branch, realized the threat by Connecticut settlers who could make claims to the very acreage they had already

---

[117] Ousterhout, "Frontier Vengeance," 342.

purchased. This was territory in which Thomas Armstrong and John McAdams had settled.[118]

It was time for action. Northumberland County Judge William Plunket called out the county militia to march against the intruders. On September 25, 1775, a group of fifty men left Sunbury, joined companies from other points, and proceeded northward to Warrior Run. The eventual clash between about five hundred Pennsylvania militia against eighty Yankees resulted in one fatality, several wounded, and all the Connecticut party being marched to Sunbury, the men taken to jail and the women and children sent back to the valley. Their moveable property was confiscated and their cabins burned. Not content with the expulsion of the Connecticut intruders from the West Branch, Plunket next undertook an invasion of the Wyoming settlement itself to rid the valley permanently of the Yankees. When the force of five hundred men reached its destination on December 23, however, it was met by three hundred Wyoming men and boys who had taken advantage of the valley's strong natural defensive terrain. A battle ensued on Christmas Day that resulted in bloodshed on both sides. Although Plunket's men suffered fewer casualties than the Yankees, the Pennsylvania advance was stymied. The Connecticut claimants occupied an impregnable position, and the Northumberland force subsequently retreated. The Yankees had little time to savor their victory, however, because greater issues were in the offing. After the Declaration of Independence was signed, both sides agreed to suspend hostilities in the area for the duration of the Revolution.[119]

No record remains of the men who comprised the Northumberland County militia force that participated in this campaign, but a force of five hundred men would almost certainly have required most of the available military-age manpower on the North and West Branches of the

---

[118] Both Thomas Armstrong and John McAdams are recorded to have settled near present-day Muncy Township, which encompassed land claimed by Connecticut claimants. *PA3*: XIX: 427-760. Kenneth D. McCrea, Pennsylvania Land Applications, vol. 2, 24.

[119] Ousterhout, "Frontier Vengeance," 345; Bell, *History of Northumberland County*, 96–98; Pennsylvania Historical Society, *The Fort Augusta Story* (Official Publication of the Fort Augusta Bicentennial Celebration, 1956), 36–37.

Susquehanna River. All three Armstrong brothers could well have been included in this number, if not their father and brother-in-law as well.

★

A description of the life and political atmosphere of Northumberland County in the summer of 1775 is recorded in the journal of Philip Fithian, a young Presbyterian minister visiting the area. Traveling to remote parts of the county but spending much of his time in Northumberland Township itself, he recorded both positive observations and potential concerns that could also have been voiced by young John Armstrong and his brothers at the time. Fithian viewed Northumberland and neighboring Sunbury as infant villages that were growing rapidly. He saw the richness of the countryside and its draw toward settlement, noting that there were already one hundred houses in Sunbury. The river was alive with boatmen. He spoke of preaching to congregations atop a wagon outside an unfinished meeting house one Sunday near Warrior Run and meeting with others in the settlement of Northumberland to build one there. He expressed foreboding, however, over reports of Indians taking eight horse loads of powder up country, fearing that "they have in view some infernal stratagem." Most notably, he heard locals in outlying areas speak with suspicion toward the Connecticut settlers living on unclaimed land and of the arrest of two men held in Sunbury on suspicion of selling rights to land under Connecticut's claim and the apprehension of townspeople that a mob might rise to release them.

Fithian's reporting noted a definite revolutionary spirit in the air. He witnessed the first company of thirty riflemen gathering at Northumberland that was raised in response to a resolution passed by Congress that would eventually join General Washington. Citizens were apparently kept informed, however belatedly, of what was happening on the war front by newspapers from Philadelphia and points east. Despite a two-week delay in learning of transpired events, the arrival of a newspaper apparently brought the opportunity for considerable debate among its readers. On one occasion, an article detailing a sermon was discussed. Said one gentleman. "Gunpowder and lead shall form text and sermon both."

Fithian was in Northumberland on Thursday, July 20, a day designated by the Continental Congress as one of fasting and prayer. Describing the town that morning as quiet with stores shut and all business laid aside, residents of the country which undoubtedly included the Armstrongs began coming into town midmorning for the eleven-thirty service. Held in what Fithian described as a new home, just covered, without partitions, he spoke in morning and afternoon services to a hefty crowd in a setting he described as "thronged"; people were inside, in the cellar, and many outside as well.[120]

Fithian's observations concerning the general tone of the populace of Northumberland County toward the upcoming conflict with Britain, particularly in the area on the county surrounding Sunbury and Northumberland, follow those of present-day historians concerning the attitudes of the Scots-Irish in frontier America. James G. Leyburn notes the mythology of the Scots-Irish that "to a man," they favored a break with Britain in 1775 and supported the War of Independence. Leyburn agrees that to a great extent, at least in some settlements, this was the case. Few Scots-Irish sold their property and departed for Canada or the West Indies rather than support rebellion against the Crown while this was true of many Englishmen and Scots. He quotes a New Englander who opposed the rupture with England as declaring the Scots-Irish to be, with few exceptions, "the most God-provoking democrats on this side of Hell." Leyburn asserts that if political opinion were founded upon logic, Scots-Irish should all have been ardent American patriots based on England's treatment of them, either from their earlier days in Scotland to their later days in Ulster. Now that she was again displaying her tyranny, Scots-Irish had a splendid chance not only to strike a blow for freedom but to pay off old scores. Their support of independence and of the war was ardent and practically unanimous in Pennsylvania, as well as in Scots-Irish populations in Virginia and the Carolinas. The Armstrong boys soon followed their neighbors into the fray. For them, it was a natural choice.[121]

---

[120] Fithian's diary June 27–July 24, 1775, in Bell, *History of Northumberland County*, 88–96.

[121] Leyburn, *The Scotch-Irish*, 305–06.

3

The Revolution, 1775–1778

These are the times that try men's souls.
—Thomas Paine[122]

On April 23, 1775, an express rider galloped into Philadelphia with the startling news of armed skirmishes between Massachusetts militiamen and British troops at Lexington and Concord. Within a few days, news of these events would have made their way westward to Sunbury and farther up into the Susquehanna River frontier. In response to the momentous event, the second Continental Congress hurriedly convened and passed a resolution on June 14, 1775, authorizing Pennsylvania to raise six companies of expert riflemen to join the New England militia in besieging British forces occupying Boston. John Lowden, one of the proprietors of Northumberland County, was commissioned as a captain of one of these companies and began recruiting men from the vicinities of Sunbury and Northumberland and settlements west of the Susquehanna River. His company of ninety-seven men was the first Northumberland County unit formed for military service in the Revolutionary War and was sworn into service on June 29, departing Northumberland on July 8.[123]

---

[122] Thomas Paine, *The American Crisis*, December 23, 1776.

[123] Heber G. Gearhart, "Northumberland County Troops in the Continental Line," in *Northumberland County in the Revolution*, ed. Charles F. Snyder (Northumberland County Historical Society, 1932), 31.

Although Thomas Armstrong's three sons, James, John, and Hamilton, were unmarried able-bodied men, none of them served in Lowden's company, the only unit raised in Northumberland County in 1775 to fight the British. Most historians of the period describe the prevailing attitude of a significant part of the colonial population following the incidents at Lexington and Concord as a *rage militaire*, referring to the spontaneous voluntary uprising in many colonies to take up arms against British rule. Since a large portion of the population of Northumberland County was Scots-Irish with a variety of reasons to resent British rule, it seems counterintuitive that the *rage militaire* did not extend to the North and West Branches of the Susquehanna. Although there appears no simple answer, plausible explanations may exist as to why the three Armstrong brothers did not go to war that summer.

To begin with, no one could simply enlist to fight in the Continental Army; it did not yet exist. The only way to answer the call to arms in Northumberland County that summer was to join the single rifle company raised by John Lowden, and the competition to be accepted by any of Pennsylvania's six authorized rifle companies was intense. A letter published in the *Virginia Gazette* described the difficulty in gaining a spot on the roster. One company had many more applicants than it could accept. In order to winnow the field, the commander drew a figure of a regularly sized nose on a board, placing it at a distance of 150 yards from a firing line, declaring that those who came nearest the mark would be enlisted. Sixty applicants hit the target.[124]

All three Armstrong brothers were relative latecomers to the frontier, having been raised in much more civilized New Jersey. Although all three would later prove to be successful military professionals, their skill with a long rifle simply might not have equaled that of their neighbors who had been raised on the frontier.

A second possible explanation is that because frontier life was far more difficult and dangerous than that in the more settled areas of Pennsylvania, some men of military age were reluctant to leave their families unprotected. Gregory T. Knouff notes that frontiersmen were reluctant to go to war not only because turning out for service would interfere with their agricultural pursuits, but they also feared that if war were to break out on the frontier in their absence, entire communities would be left unprotected. Men would

---

[124] Danske Dandridge, *American Prisoners of the Revolution* (Baltimore: Genealogical Publication Co., 1967), 14.

not join the main army only to leave their families and property vulnerable to despised Tory and allied Indian enemies.[125]

Certainly, one of the three Armstrong men could have been spared from the family's agricultural needs, but the danger from Indians on the Pennsylvania frontier was real. Samuel Hunter, colonel of the Northumberland County militia protested the calling out of his troops in September 1777 to face the British invasion of Pennsylvania, arguing that his men would not turn out, citing the threat of devastating hostility from Britain's Native American allies.[126]

Another more likely explanation is that one or more brothers were already performing service within the Northumberland County militia in its ongoing dispute with Connecticut settlers in the Wyoming Valley. The force of five hundred men who participated in the campaigns of 1775 would more than likely have included one if not all three of the Armstrong brothers.

According to Armstrong family lore, John Armstrong was driving a wagonload of wheat to Philadelphia when he encountered a recruiting party and decided on the spot to enlist in the Continental Army. Although it makes for a good story, the account is almost certainly false. By 1776, the Armstrong family lived nowhere near the capital. Any wheat going from the Sunbury vicinity to Philadelphia was probably sold to contractors who arranged to have consolidated shipments sent downriver to Harris's Landing (present-day Harrisburg) and then overland to the city. However, every family story contains some element of truth; and in this case, it was not John but his older brother James who was the first member of the family to answer the call to arms. With fighting halted in the Wyoming Valley in December 1775 and with no crops yet in the field, James must have learned that five new battalions of Pennsylvania soldiers were being raised and decided to go to Philadelphia to enlist. Whatever the circumstances, he entered the service as a private soldier in the Second Pennsylvania Battalion commanded by Col. Arthur St. Clair sometime between January 4 and February 20, 1776. The unit was soon ordered to depart for Canada to reinforce the American forces then besieging Quebec.[127]

---

[125] Gregory T. Knouff, "An Arduous Service: The Pennsylvania Backcountry Soldiers' Revolution," *Pennsylvania History* 61, no. 1 (1994), 50.

[126] Knouff, "An Arduous Service," 53.

[127] Francis B. Heitman, *Historical Register of the Officers of the Continental Army during the War of the Revolution* (Washington, DC: The Rare Book Shop Publishing Company, 1914), 74.

With James gone, there would have been increased pressure on John and Hamilton to remain on the farm to put in the next year's crop. John's enlistment was likely prompted by a Continental Congress vote on September 16 to increase the size of the Continental Army to eighty-eight regiments. Pennsylvania was to fill twelve regiments, and one of them, the Twelfth Pennsylvania, was directed to recruit its strength from Northumberland and Northampton Counties. William Cooke, the former sheriff of Northumberland County, was commissioned as its colonel. John may indeed have been delivering a load of wheat, but in Sunbury and not Philadelphia, where he encountered a recruiting party and decided to join up. Whatever the circumstances or his motivation, he enlisted in the Twelfth Pennsylvania Regiment in October 1776 and was appointed as a sergeant in the company of neighbor Capt. John Brady. John's appointment as a sergeant likely reflected confidence in his leadership potential and

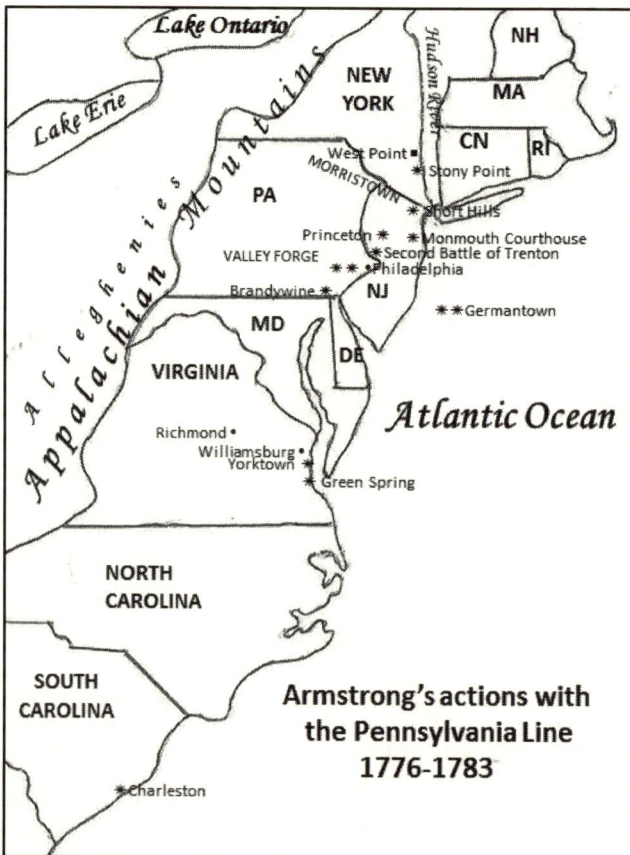

Armstrong's actions with the Pennsylvania Line 1776-1783

possibly his prior service in the county militia. Sergeants would have been responsible for instructing soldiers in the intricacies of eighteenth-century drill, teaching them to care for their weapons and equipment, maintaining cleanliness and good order in camp, and enforcing discipline in the ranks during battle. His appointment may also have been due to his ability to read, write, and to do simple arithmetic, skills required of both officers and noncommissioned officers.[128]

As the regiment formed in October and November, news of the crushing defeats suffered by Washington's forces on Long Island and New York City made its way to the frontier and no doubt imparted a new sense of urgency to its preparations. Although the Twelfth Pennsylvania was still far from meeting its authorized strength, Colonel Cooke reported to the local Council of Safety on December 2 that he had received an express from the Board of War to march his battalion immediately to Brunswick, New Jersey. Regrettably, the battalion was not yet supplied with provisions for their deployment, lacking such items as guns, clothing, and blankets. In compliance with these orders, the eight understrength companies departed Sunbury on December 18 in boats down the Susquehanna to Harris Landing and marched to Reading where they may have been issued some of the needed equipment and provisions from a military depot. They arrived in Philadelphia in late December to await further instructions. John Armstrong would not see home again for seven long years.[129]

★

The Twelfth probably reached Philadelphia on or after Christmas Day in 1776, contradicting another part of family lore that John participated in Washington's night crossing of the Delaware River and defeat of the Hessian garrison at Trenton on December 26. Upon reaching Philadelphia, the regiment was amalgamated with militia units from the frontier and other newly formed Continental regiments under the command of Brig. Gen. Thomas Mifflin. The new brigade crossed the Delaware on December

---

[128] Thomas Lynch Montgomery, ed., *Pennsylvania Archives, Published Series, Series 5, Volume 3* (Harrisburg Publishing Company, 1906) 671 (*PA5*: III: 671).

[129] Gearhart, "Northumberland County Troops in the Continental Line," 37; *PA5*: III: 671. Cooke's concern for clothing for his men probably referred to the lack of military uniforms. The men were likely dressed in their own clothing with rank denoted only by epaulets, sashes, or hat cockades.

29 and established its headquarters at Bordentown, a settlement south of Trenton on the Delaware. For the next three days, Mifflin attempted to mold this disparate force into a cohesive and disciplined unit capable of performing in combat. His order of the day for January 1, 1777, announced that Washington had alerted him to have his troops prepared to march that night or early the following morning "at a moment's notice."

However disorganized and poorly trained Mifflin's brigade, Washington urgently needed every man. The enlistments of all but a handful of his troops were set to expire on December 31. Unless he did something spectacular to restore the army's flagging morale and boost future enlistments, Washington knew that the Revolution would be lost. He realized that after crossing the Delaware on Christmas night and attacking the Hessian forces garrison at Trenton, he probably would not be able to hold the town when British reinforcements arrived. Consequently, he returned to the Pennsylvania side of the river the next day. With the expiring enlistments still on his mind, Washington abruptly reassessed the army's position and decided to move it back across the river into New Jersey and await an opportunity to strike another blow. By now convincing most of his soldiers to extend their enlistments, and expecting to be reinforced by Pennsylvania militia and two brigades under the commands of John Cadwalader and Mifflin, Washington placed the army along the south bank of Assunpink Creek and awaited the arrival of troops under the command of General Charles Cornwallis. The leading elements of Cornwallis's vanguard arrived at Trenton very late on the afternoon of January 2 and immediately attacked, trying desperately to overrun Washington's position before nightfall. The most vulnerable point was a stone bridge over the creek, which the British charged three times, only to be repulsed by artillery firing canister rounds at point-blank range. Night was falling when the main body of British units arrived on the field, and Cornwallis decided to wait until the next morning to continue the fight.[130]

Washington was now faced with a difficult decision. Large blocks of ice made the Delaware River impossible to cross back into Pennsylvania. If he remained along the creek the next day, Cornwallis would surely be able to cross the swamp on his right flank and pin his force against the

---

[130] William M. Dwyer, *The Day Is Ours! November 1776–January 1777: An Inside View of the Battles of Trenton and Princeton* (New York: The Viking Press, 1983), 328.

river. If he tried to retreat back to Philadelphia by going southward along the river to other crossing places, he might be overtaken on the march by British cavalry and his troops cut to pieces. To make the situation worse, neither Cadwalader's nor Mifflin's brigade had yet to join him. Rain-soaked muddy roads had greatly hindered their progress; troops marched most of the night and a good part of the next morning to cover the six miles separating Bordentown and Trenton. The two brigades totaling approximately 3,600 men finally arrived around eleven o'clock in the morning, a full five hours later than Washington had desired.

The historical image of George Washington is that of a wooden figure—humorless, tight-lipped, and taciturn, perhaps a little out of his depth as a military leader, doggedly pursuing a strategy designed to wear down the much larger British forces that opposed him. The actual Washington was a tall and imposing figure who almost always thirsted for battle. Whether he was on a horse or in a drawing room, he had a commanding presence that compelled the rapt attention of everyone around him. As a military leader, he was calm and composed, but often possessed of a volcanic temper that he struggled all his life to control, was unflinching in the face of battle, and had the courage of a lion coupled with the temperament and instincts of a riverboat gambler. He had already rolled the dice once and stolen a victory over the Hessian force garrisoning Trenton by making a dangerous night crossing of the Delaware River. Whatever his faults, he was the glue that held the Continental Army together in the darkest hours of the Revolution. Having at last managed to concentrate his scattered forces, and after a hastily called council of war to discuss the options with his commanders, he now elected to roll the dice again, boldly staking the outcome of the Revolution on a brilliant but exceptionally risky stratagem to move the entire army along the primitive back roads east and north of Trenton to attack the British rear guard at Princeton.[131]

The leading elements of the army started the twelve-mile march for Princeton just after midnight on the morning of January 3. Weather had not been Washington's friend. Unseasonable warmth and high volume of wagon traffic had churned the roads into a gluey morass that had impeded

[131] Alfred Hoyt Bill, *Campaign of Princeton, 1776–1777* (Princeton: Princeton University Press, 1948), 86; William Scudder Stryker, *The Battles of Trenton and Princeton* (Boston: Houghton, Mifflin, & Co., 1898), 254.

the movement of both troops and supplies for days. Now the weather became Washington's ally, falling to twenty-one degrees on the night of January 2 and not rising above freezing temperatures for the next ten days. As the army began its march, the mud on the road began to freeze and soon became as hard as pavement. The absence of the moon that night further helped to conceal the movement of the troops. Washington also deceived the British into thinking he was remaining in position by kindling huge bonfires all along the creek and ordering a few troops to remain behind to make digging and entrenching noises. Noise was to be kept to a minimum within the command itself. Wheels of gun carriages and wagons were wrapped in rags to mask the sound of movement, and unit by unit, the army slowly moved out of position.[132]

This was the second night road march in as many days for the men of the Twelfth Pennsylvania Regiment. An anonymous veteran described its difficulty. Many troops were "without shoes or other comfortable clothing, and as traces of our march towards Princeton, the ground was literally marked with the blood of the soldiers' feet." To make matters worse, the back road to Princeton had only recently been cut through a heavily wooded tract, and tree stumps in the roadway interfered with the movement of wagons and artillery.[133]

As dawn was breaking, the leading elements of the army came to a stone bridge two miles from Princeton. Here Washington divided his force, sending west a column comprised of Brig. Gen. Hugh Mercer's Virginia Continentals augmented with Maryland and Delaware troops, the Pennsylvania Rifle Regiment, and Cadwalader's militia brigade to cut off any British forces that might be moving along the main post road from Trenton. The second column was commanded by Maj. Gen. John Sullivan and consisted primarily of Maj. Gen. Arthur St. Clair's New England and Mifflin's brigades of which the Twelfth Pennsylvania was part. This force headed directly north and was expected to make the main attack at Princeton.

---

[132] David Hackett Fischer, *Washington's Crossing* (New York: Oxford University Press, 2002), 316.

[133] This statement probably applied more to the older veterans of the army. Newly arrived militiamen and the men like John Armstrong in the recently formed Continental regiment at least had warm clothing and the shoes they brought from home. Sergeant R——, "The Battle of Princeton," *Pennsylvania Magazine of History and Biography* 20, no. 4 (1896), 515. (*PMHB*)

While Washington's army was marching throughout the night, the commander of the British rear guard in Princeton, Lt. Col. Charles Mawhood, had been ordered to send a strong force to guard the wagons carrying food and ammunition to Cornwallis at Trenton. By dawn, two of the three British regiments were marching down the main post road to Trenton, leaving the last to remain in Princeton. Seeing an American force approaching the post road, Mawhood ordered his regiments to deploy in line and attack. Mercer's composite brigade of Virginia, Maryland, and Delaware troops was struck first. What appeared initially to be an effective defense was routed with the arrival of British reinforcements. Mercer was mortally wounded, and troops retreated to available shelter.[134]

As Mercer's force reeled and fell back, Cadwalader's militia units arrived to reinforce him, the first companies taking positions behind a fence where they could fire and reload rapidly at the advancing Redcoats. Despite their best efforts, some of the companies gave way and began to fall back. Washington, then with Sullivan's column, saw that Mercer and Cadwalader were in trouble and rode forward to take personal control of the battle. Riding to within thirty paces of the British line and mounted on a white horse, he was an easy target, yet emerged without a scratch.[135]

Other units from Sullivan's column began to arrive. Among them was Mifflin's brigade. John Armstrong and the Twelfth Pennsylvania Regiment went forward into the American line to the right of Cadwalader's position, as did Col. Edward Hand's Pennsylvania Rifle Regiment. Sergeant White was serving a cannon and later wrote of the charging Pennsylvanians, "I never saw men looked so furious as they did running by us with their bayonets charged." Washington halted the onrushing men, settled them down, and led them forward firing platoon volleys. The British line broke, Washington urged the men onward, and the backcountry Pennsylvania riflemen relentlessly pursued the British regulars.[136]

Sullivan's column easily pushed aside the British Fortieth Regiment and moved into Princeton. Two hundred British troops had sought asylum in Nassau Hall, the principal building of the College of New Jersey. According to legend, Capt. Alexander Hamilton, then commanding an artillery company, is credited with firing a cannonball into the building that

---

[134] Sergeant R——, "The Battle of Princeton," 517.
[135] Fisher, *Washington's Crossing*, 324.
[136] Ibid., 336.

decapitated a portrait of King George II. The British quickly surrendered. To Washington's chagrin, his victorious soldiers ransacked Nassau Hall, dragging out food, clothing, furniture, and even some paintings. In a letter to the president of Congress on January 5, Washington estimated he had inflicted five hundred British casualties with a loss of five officers and thirty soldiers. He also captured three hundred British soldiers, including fourteen officers.[137]

★

Washington had little time to savor the sweetness of victory. He knew that Cornwallis, stung by the humiliation of another defeat at the hands of the poorly armed and clothed Americans, would soon be in Princeton in pursuit. With the last of his troops departing Princeton barely an hour before the first British troops arrived from Trenton, the bone-tired men made a grueling fifteen-mile march northward to Somerset Courthouse where they arrived well after sundown, most collapsing on any convenient piece of ground to sleep fitfully through the freezing night. The next day, they moved farther north on to Pluckemin where they were allowed to camp for two nights to recover their strength before staggering onward to Morristown on January 6 where they finally halted, safely out of danger. Snow covered the ground, heralding the end of the military campaign season. Sgt. John Armstrong was thoroughly exhausted, but he could look back with satisfaction on what he and his regiment had accomplished. Three weeks earlier, they had departed Sunbury not knowing if Washington was defeated and the Revolution ended. They had been tested in battle and survived, as had the Continental Army. The crisis was averted for now; the Revolution would continue.[138]

Washington badly needed time to rest, regroup, and reorganize his rapidly dwindling army. He had begun the 1776 campaign with close to 20,000 men under arms; barely 3,000 made the march from Princeton into winter quarters, and this number soon dropped to less than 2,500 as

---

[137] Ron Chernow, *George Washington: A Life* (New York: The Penguin Press, 2010), 282; George Washington to John Hancock, 5 January 1777, Founders Online, National Historical Publications and Records Commission (NHPRC), http://founders.archives.gov.

[138] James McMichael, "Diary of Lieutenant James McMichael, of the Pennsylvania Line, 1776-1778," *PMHB* 16, no. 2 (1892), 141.

enlistments expired and the three Ds—death, disease, and desertion—took their toll. The number of men that arrived in Morristown on January 6, however, was fifteen times the size of the population of the town. With only fifty or sixty houses clustered around the village green, there was not nearly enough space to accommodate such a large force, so the men built fires and camped on the green and in nearby woods and fields. Soon, local civilian commissioners canvassed the area, assessing available space and designating how many soldiers were to be billeted in each house and barn. The Reverend Jacob Green in nearby Hanover invited fourteen officers and men to share his house with his wife and eight children. Mrs. Anna Kitchell housed sixteen soldiers and fed as many as forty each day. Some houses were designated entirely for troop billeting, and piles of straw were placed on the floor of each room to provide sleeping quarters for as many as twenty soldiers. Morristown was "devoid of beauty, both in its form and location," according to Lieutenant McMichael, but he found "the inhabitants very hospitable, all professors of the Presbyterian religion which renders them very agreeable to me." He also noted archly that "the young ladies here are very fond of the soldiers, but much more so of the officers."[139]

The most immediate problem faced by Washington at Morristown was the health of his men. Smallpox began to appear in camp, and Washington faced a difficult decision. Smallpox had long been a scourge of warfare and was a principal cause of the defeat of the American forces besieging Quebec in the 1775–1776 Canada campaign. Transmitted almost exclusively through person-to-person contact, the virus could also be spread through exposure to contaminated blankets or clothing. Unless the disease was quickly checked, the death rate might climb as high as 40 percent. Despite other primitive medical practices in the eighteenth century, a reliable preventative measure was found through inoculation. The process,

---

[139] John T. Cunningham, *The Uncertain Revolution: Washington and the Continental Army at Morristown* (West Creek, NJ: Cormorant Publishing, 2007), 26–27; McMichael, "Diary," 141. The geography of New Jersey dictated Washington's choice of Morristown to spend the winter. The two outer ridges of the Watchung Mountains form a gigantic fish hook, rising as high as 900 feet above the plains below, with few elevations lower than 500 feet. From these heights, Washington could keep a close eye on any movement the British might make toward him from New York City and Staten Island in the east or from New Brunswick in the south.

called variolation, involved lancing a pustule of someone suffering from smallpox and placing a small amount of the matter under the skin of the patient, usually on the arm. He would then contract a milder form of the disease than if he had been exposed through physical contact. He would, however, be contagious and had to remain under a strict quarantine to avoid contaminating others. From the onset of symptoms until the last scab fell off the body could take as long as thirty days. For at least two full weeks of this time, he would be too sick to perform any kind of work. Once recovered, however, he would be immune for life.[140]

Washington agonized over the dilemma. Although effective, the practice was not without the risk of 1 to 2 percent of soldiers dying from the process. Not only did variolation carry some risk for the troops involved, but if they were not properly quarantined, the disease might spread to the civilian population and to the rest of the army. The process had to be sequenced carefully; he could not afford for all the troops to be inoculated at one time and thus be unavailable for duty for weeks. The British might learn of the army's weakened condition and threaten combative action that his troops would not be able to answer. Washington finally decided in early February that the benefits of the procedure outweighed the risks. Sgt. John Armstrong, along with the other soldiers and officers of the Twelfth Pennsylvania, most certainly suffered through the variolation process sometime in February or March of 1777. Inoculating an entire regiment would have taken weeks since a portion of its strength had to be available to perform typical camp duties, guarding stores, maintaining arms and equipment, doing cooking and laundry, and conducting training. Although small detachments might have been assigned to scouting and patrolling parties, the Twelfth Pennsylvania would not have been involved in any major combat operations until all the soldiers had been inoculated and recovered from the ordeal.

The specific location and activity of the Twelfth Pennsylvania Regiment after the unit arrived at Morristown is unknown other than the location of its headquarters at the crossroads at Metuchin, between Quibbletown and Amboy. On May 22, 1777, it was assigned to the Third Pennsylvania

---

[140] According to the odds, the Twelfth Pennsylvania Regiment alone would suffer between three and five deaths following the procedure. Elizabeth A. Fenn, *Pox Americana: The Great Smallpox Epidemic of 1775–82* (New York: Hill and Wang, 2001), 19, 32–33, 92–94.

Brigade of the main Continental Army where it was combined with the Third, Sixth, and Ninth Pennsylvania Regiments. John was then reunited with his older brother James. The latter, having enrolled as a private in the Second Pennsylvania Battalion, had shortly been named as the regimental quartermaster before departing Philadelphia, possibly due to his organizational ability and level of literacy. He apparently demonstrated even more potential for leadership to his colonel, Arthur St. Clair, because by the time the Second Battalion reached Canada, he had been commissioned as an ensign, and six months later was a second lieutenant. John's ability had likewise been recognized by his regimental commander, William Cooke, because on March 13, 1777, he rose from the ranks and commissioned as an ensign. James's Second Pennsylvania Battalion had been deactivated and subsequently reactivated as the Third Pennsylvania Regiment. He and John were now brother officers in the Pennsylvania line. They would serve nearly side by side in some of the hardest fighting of the Revolution for the next year and a half.[141]

In the aftermath of the twin defeats at Trenton and Princeton, General William Howe, commander of British forces in North America, withdrew his army from all of New Jersey except for a small area along the Raritan River between New Brunswick and Perth Amboy, the effect of which yielded a positive outcome for colonial patriots. Americans who had lost faith in the independence movement and had rallied to the British in the fall of 1776 proved to be a minority in New Jersey. Many locals were invigorated by Washington's victories, and in the spring of 1777, resistance to the British presence in New Jersey grew into small-scale partisan warfare that eventually inflicted more casualties on the British and Hessian forces than they had lost in all their previous battles with the Continental Army. The British were reasonably well provisioned in New York City and remaining New Jersey outposts, but they lacked feed for their animals. Without adequate fodder for horses and oxen, they could not mount cavalry or haul artillery and wagons to support their outposts. Even while Washington's army was marching to Morristown, New Jersey, militia units spontaneously turned out in great numbers to attack British patrols and wagon trains whenever they left their cantonments to seize hay and oats from nearby farms.[142]

141 Heitman, Historical Register of Officers, 74–75; *PA5*: III: 671.
142 Andrew Jackson O'Shaughnessy, *The Men Who Lost America: British*

By March, as the men recovered from variolation and newly raised regiments began to swell the size of the army, Washington's troops again began to take the field. Because the Twelfth was composed of good riflemen and scouts, it was in high demand and seems to have operated in a wide area of New Jersey during the spring and early summer, participating in numerous skirmishes throughout the central part of the colony at Bound Brook, Piscataway, New Brunswick, Bonhamton, and other locales. In a letter to the Pennsylvania Council of Safety on March 10 while he was headquartered near Metuchen, Colonel Cooke wrote, "As my regiment is near the Enemy's lines, we are every week Scrimmageing with them."[143]

These engagements, large and small, came at a cost. According to Herbert Bell, editor of *The History of Northumberland County*, "The heaths of New Jersey, from Paramus to Freehold, by a line encircling Morristown and Bound Brook, were, in the summer 1777, dotted with the graves of the Eighth and Twelfth Pennsylvania."[144]

The Twelfth also participated in the major battle at Short Hills on June 26. Earlier in the month, Howe had attempted to lure Washington out of his Morristown location by marching large forces from Perth Amboy into central New Jersey and then returning them to their fortifications to the east. Washington took the bait and marched out of the hills. His forward division, led by Maj. Gen. William Alexander (known as Lord Stirling), included the Twelfth Pennsylvania Regiment and was ordered to shadow the British withdrawal. Two British columns quickly countermarched to bring Stirling to battle and cut off Washington's route of withdrawal. Outnumbered four to one, Stirling's men held firm to allow Washington enough time to maneuver back into the hills.[145]

★

Howe subsequently elected to withdraw completely from New Jersey and to consider other options for the rest of the year. He could move north up the Hudson River corridor in order to split the colonies in two and

---

Leadership, the American Revolution, and the Fate of the Empire (New Haven: Yale University Press, 2013), 101–103.

[143] Gearhardt, *Northumberland Troops in the Pennsylvania Line*, 43–44.

[144] Bell, History of Northumberland County, Pennsylvania, 111; *PA5*: III: 671.

[145] Alan Valentine, *Lord Stirling: Colonial Gentleman and General in Washington's Army* (New York: Oxford Press, 1969), 209.

deprive Washington of reinforcements and support from New England, he could capture Philadelphia by moving by sea up the Delaware River or Chesapeake Bay, or he could sail to Charleston to crush the rebellion in the south. Howe's army embarked on board British vessels on July 8, indicating that he would pursue one of these options.

Washington was forced to guess Howe's destination; an incorrect assumption would spell disaster. If Washington moved the army north to prevent a movement up the Hudson River, Howe could move unopposed on Philadelphia. If he remained in Morristown to protect Philadelphia, Howe could move either north or south unopposed. The day after Howe embarked from New Jersey, Washington learned that Major General St. Clair had abandoned Fort Ticonderoga at the southern end of Lake Champlain. With British forces in Canada already poised to move south, Washington felt he had no choice but to move the main army north to the Clove, a rugged defile on the western side of the Hudson River near West Point, to meet British aggressors descending from the north. When Howe sailed from Staten Island on July 23 and did not head for the Hudson, Washington figured that he had made the wrong assumption and moved his troops south near Trenton. When Howe failed to appear off the Delaware capes, Washington then moved the troops nearer to Philadelphia at Germantown.

By August 21, he thought he had again guessed incorrectly and concluded that Howe's target was Charleston. The very next day, however, Howe's armada was sighted in the Chesapeake Bay and three days later dropped anchor at the Head of Elk, the northernmost point of the Bay. Philadelphia was the target after all. The army was put into motion to march through Philadelphia and then south to confront the new threat to the capital. In evaluating Howe's decision to strike at Philadelphia through the Chesapeake, British historian George Trevelyan noted dryly that Howe was now ten miles further from Philadelphia than he had been the previous December when his forces were at Perth Amboy.[146]

Washington believed he had no option but to fight for Philadelphia. To reassure its citizens and overawe the Loyalist and Quaker elements, he decided to stage a massive parade through its streets on August 24. The parade, meticulously planned to impress the citizenry, was composed of

---

[146] Christopher Ward, *The War of the Revolution* (New York: The MacMillan Company, 1952), I: 332.

four of the five divisions of the army, all the artillery, and four dragoon regiments. Spacing between units was carefully arranged to create the impression of a larger force. Drummers and fifers massed in the center of each regiment so that the soldiers might keep in step. Nothing could be done about the men's torn and ragged clothing, but a sprig of evergreen was worn in every hat to give an illusion of uniformity. Anyone falling out was threatened with thirty-nine lashes. Troops began marching at dawn from Germantown in a light rain following violent thunderstorms the night before. By midmorning, the first troops began to march down Front Street. The main streets of Philadelphia were between fifty and one hundred feet wide, paved with cobblestones, and lined with brick or slate sidewalks upon which a large number of the city's 30–40,000 residents turned out to see the sight.

Washington and the Marquis de Lafayette, a newly arrived French aristocrat who at that time served on Washington's staff, led the massive procession on horseback. They were followed by the rest of the army staff, a troop of light horse, a pioneer company, and each infantry brigade followed by a battery of artillery, until all four divisions of the army passed by. The Third Pennsylvania Brigade was toward the end of the massive twelve-man-deep column, but no doubt both John and James held their heads erect and braced their shoulders as they passed the State House where they were reviewed by the Continental Congress. Finally, a troop of horse brought up the rear, and the army moved slowly out of the city. Observers estimated it had taken two full hours to pass any single point along the parade route. John Adams wrote to his wife Abigail, "They were extremely well armed, pretty well clothed, and tolerably disciplined . . . they don't step exactly in time. They don't hold their heads up quite erect, nor turn out their toes exactly as they ought. They don't all of them cock their hats, and such as do, don't wear them all the same way." Another observer, Alexander Graydon, was more charitable: "Though indifferently dressed held well-burnished arms and carried them like soldiers, and looked, in short, as if they might face an equal number with a reasonable prospect of success."[147]

★

---

[147] Ward, *The War of the Revolution*, 334–335; Thomas J. McGuire, *The Philadelphia Campaign*, vol. 1, *Brandywine and the Fall of Philadelphia* (Mechanicsburg, PA: Stackpole Books, 2006), 124–25; Alexander Graydon, *Memoirs of His Own*

Howe did not move immediately on Philadelphia. Neither his men nor the few horses that survived the voyage, short in distance but lengthy in duration, were fit for campaigning. Both had been confined on board ships in early July and by the end of August suffered from the effects of the stifling summer heat. Howe needed time to secure his lines of communication, to rest his men, and to find new horses for the coming fight. He spent the next two weeks skirmishing with small groups of light infantry and militia, plundering local farms for cattle and sheep, and weighing his options. The most direct path to the capital was across the narrow neck of the Delmarva Peninsula and up the west bank of the Delaware River, but taking such a route would allow Washington to secure one of his flanks on the river, reducing his own maneuvering options. He elected instead to divest his troops of their heavy baggage and move northward from the Head of Elk in two large columns commanded by Cornwallis and Hessian general Wilhelm von Knyphausen. Washington awaited him at Chadds Ford, a small village on the major road to Chester, arraying his troops along the eastern bank of the shallow but swift Brandywine Creek.

Washington had selected exceptionally good ground for defense. He positioned the Pennsylvania militia under Brig. Gen. John Armstrong Sr. on his left flank on the least likely avenue of approach. The center and right were covered by divisions commanded by Anthony Wayne and John Sullivan while smaller units covered other fording places to their right for several miles. On higher ground astride the main road heading uphill, he placed Nathanael Greene's division, keeping the two divisions of Adam Stephen and Lord Stirling in reserve nearby. A hastily organized light infantry brigade under Brig. Gen. William Maxwell was across the creek to provide early warning and to inflict casualties on Howe's vanguard as it approached. Altogether, he had approximately 15,000 troops in his command to face an equal number of British. If he made no tactical errors, Washington stood an excellent chance of winning the coming battle.[148]

Washington, however, had made a critical mistake. Although he had stationed forces to cover several of the fords on Brandywine Creek north of Chadds Ford, he failed to reconnoiter all of them. Howe made him pay

---

Time and Reminiscences of the Men and Events of the Revolution (New York: Lindsay and Blakiston, 1846), 290–91.

[148] John Armstrong Sr. was a Pennsylvanian who had earlier led British troops against French and Indian forces during the Seven Years' War.

dearly for the omission. At four o'clock on the morning of September 11, an hour before he put Knyphausen in motion toward Chadds Ford, Howe, with Cornwallis's division began a long road march toward crossings on the western and eastern branches of Brandywine Creek well to the north of Washington's right flank. Finding both crossing sites unguarded, Cornwallis moved uphill on a small narrow road that could easily have been defended by a handful of skilled riflemen. He reached the summit of Osborne's Hill at half past two where he was forced to rest his exhausted troops before they could march any further. About a mile ahead was a small Quaker meeting house. Resting in good spirits, they knew that they were well behind the rear of the American position and poised to cut off any chance that Washington might have to retreat.[149]

Soldiers of the Third Pennsylvania Brigade, part of Stirling's division under the command of Brig. Gen. Thomas Conway, watched all morning as the battle at Chadds Ford progressed. Its four regiments, James's Third, John's Twelfth, and the Sixth and Ninth, were badly understrength. When Washington belatedly realized the danger to his position, he ordered Sullivan, Stirling, and Stephen to move as quickly as possible to the vicinity of the meeting house, resulting in the crowd of troops moving briskly up a steep two-mile climb carrying muskets, forty rounds of ammunition, blankets, and knapsacks, a combat weight of approximately sixty pounds. At the top of the hill overlooking Brandywine Creek was the little village of Dilworth. To the left and about a mile beyond it was the meeting house. By three o'clock, covered in dust and gasping for breath in the searing heat, Stirling's and Stephen's divisions moved into position on a bald hilltop across the road. As the troops wiped the sweat from their faces and formed into two lines facing the enemy, they could see the British lines forming on Osborne Hill barely a mile away. Five light field pieces were positioned between the two American divisions to fire directly down the road. "They formed two lines in good order along their heights" observed a Hessian officer watching from Osborne's Hill. Even Cornwallis grudgingly agreed, noting curtly that "the damn rebels form well." Against Cornwallis's eight

---

[149] British troops had been marching for nearly eleven hours in excruciatingly hot summer weather. They had not eaten during that time, and Cornwallis recognized that they needed both food and water before going into battle.

thousand men, the American forces arrayed along the hill numbered barely four thousand. Sullivan's division, however, was nowhere to be seen.[150]

This would be the first real test in a major battle for the Armstrong brothers. Both had seen combat, but only in smaller engagements. Their only division-sized battle had been at the engagement at Short Hills. For the next one and a half hours, the brothers watched in fascination as the full panoply of the British Army formed for a major battle. Howe decided to attack directly down the road to Dilworth with British and Hessian grenadiers in the center, a Hessian jaeger battalion on his left, and a British Guards brigade on the right. The grenadiers in the center were already the tallest soldiers in the British Army. As they prepared for battle, they replaced their forage caps with bearskin hats that they carried flat in their knapsacks. Once unfolded, they added another foot to the grenadiers' height, rendering a fearsome sight. Leading the way were sixty-two fifers and drummers, equally resplendent in a sea of gold lace. At four-thirty, all stepped off with shouldered muskets, regimental colors in front, to the stirring tune of the Grenadiers' March. "Nothing could be more dreadfully pleasing than the line moving on to the attack," recalled Lt. William Hale of the Second Grenadier Battalion, "believe me, I would not exchange those three minutes of rapture to avoid the thousand times the danger."[151]

Sullivan's division finally showed up on the left flank as the British forces were closing the distance with the American line but did not have time to get in proper position before being scattered by the British guards. When artillery fire began, Jacob Ritter of the Bucks County militia who was with one of Conway's regiments recalled, "Bombshells and shot fell around me like hail, cutting down my comrades on every side, and tearing off the limbs of trees like a whirlwind; the very rocks quaked, and the hills that surrounded us seemed to tremble with the roar of cannon."[152]

When the grenadiers were one hundred yards from Conway's line, the drummers and fifers moved to the rear. At a distance of forty yards,

---

[150] Thomas Conway to Supreme Executive Council, August 15, 1777, *PA5*: I: 522–23. McGuire, *The Philadelphia Campaign*, vol. 1, 198.

[151] McGuire, *The Philadelphia Campaign*, vol. 1, 198; David G. Martin, *The Philadelphia Campaign, June 1777–July 1778* (Cambridge, MA: De Capo Books, 1993), 64.

[152] Gregory T. Knouff, *The Soldier's Revolution: Pennsylvania in Arms and the Forging of Early American Identity* (University Park, PA: Pennsylvania State University Press, 2003), 123.

Conway's regiments began firing by platoon volleys. The grenadiers fired one volley and charged with bayonet. As British forces began their principal drive up the hill, the fire became close and heavy. They forced temporary retreat five times, but each time the Continental forces regained their ground. After general fire that lasted an hour and forty minutes, during most of which Sullivan described as muzzle to muzzle, right and left flanks began to give way and the entire force had to abandon the hill; but not until, as Sullivan noted, "We had almost covered the ground between that and Birmingham meeting-house, with the dead bodies of the enemy." As the three shattered regiments retreated down the road to Dilworth, they were met by Greene's division that had moved up to reinforce them. He was barely in time to stem what might have been a complete rout of the entire army. As night fell, Cornwallis directed his exhausted troops to halt and reorganize during the night.[153]

Brandywine was a major defeat, but the troops had performed exceedingly well. American casualties, approximately 1,100 killed, wounded or captured, were double those of the British. The Twelfth Pennsylvania Regiment was in the area of the heaviest sustained fight, yet incredibly suffered only three recorded casualties. Maj. James Crawford and Capt. John Brady were wounded and 2nd Lt. William Boyd killed. Ens. John Armstrong distinguished himself by his performance in the battle. He was promoted on December 11, 1777, to the rank of second lieutenant with an adjusted date of rank of September 11.[154]

Howe was in no hurry to pursue Washington, spending four days after the battle resting his troops and collecting and burying the dead. On September 16, his force organized as usual in two columns commanded by Cornwallis and Knyphausen, he moved north, looking for a rematch. The two forces met near the White Horse Tavern, about ten miles south of Valley Forge. The weather then intervened in what has become known as "the Battle of the Clouds." A massive thunderstorm struck just as both armies prepared for battle. Sheets of rain pummeled both forces, soaking ammunition, drenching musket and cannons, and making the soft ground impassable for the units

---

[153] Thomas C. Amory, *The Military Services and Public Life of Major General John Sullivan* (Boston: Wiggin and Lunt, 1968), 48–50.

[154] *PA5*: III: 671; John B. B. Trussell, *The Pennsylvania Line: Regimental Organization and Operations, 1775–1783* (Harrisburg: Pennsylvania Historical and Museum Commission, 1993), 137. Casualty estimates for both American and British sides vary. See McGuire, *The Philadelphia Campaign*, vol. 1, 269.

to maneuver cohesively. Washington took the opportunity to move his army to safety, the footing so treacherous that the American troops required nine hours to move eleven miles to a bivouac area near Yellow Springs where they collapsed exhaustedly into the cold mud. Many had no blankets, having discarded them at Brandywine in the excessive heat.[155]

There could be no rematch with Howe without an immediate resupply of powder. Doing so precipitated a three-day ordeal of marching twenty-nine miles in the continuing rain to Reading Furnace and back, including a grueling all-night crossing of the Schuylkill River at Parker Ford in breast-deep water. Howe took this opportunity to move unopposed into Philadelphia on September 26, Congress having decamped to Lancaster eight days earlier. Washington was at least able to give his tired troops time to rest and to absorb the reinforcements now arriving in answer to the earlier call from Congress. His army was again approximately the same size as it was before Brandywine—eight thousand Continentals and three thousand militiamen. Howe sent relatively few troops into Philadelphia, preferring to station the bulk of his force at nearby Germantown where he could more easily maneuver against Washington if he desired. Washington saw an opportunity to strike with his now rested and reinforced army. He would slightly outnumber Howe's nine thousand troops and this time would have the advantage of surprise.

★

At seven o'clock on the evening of October 3, the lead elements of Washington's army departed for Germantown, sixteen miles away. The battle plan was Washington's most complicated to date. He apportioned his eleven thousand men into four columns that were expected to march at night on four separate routes over terrain that had not been reconnoitered and then to converge on Germantown at roughly the same time. Forces assigned the main attack proceeded in parallel columns commanded by Sullivan and Greene. In Sullivan's column, Conway's Third Pennsylvania Brigade with its four understrength Pennsylvania regiments that included the Armstrong brothers would lead the march, drive in the British pickets, and then move to the right to support the divisions of Sullivan, Stirling, and Wayne as they attacked the British left flank.

---

[155] Martin, *The Philadelphia Campaign, June 1777–July 1778*, 81–82.

Only Sullivan's column arrived on time. Conway's vanguard drove back the British picket line, but not before two fieldpieces were fired to signal an enemy attack. As the pickets were being driven in, they were reinforced by the British Second Light Company whose combined attack was so vigorous that Conway was forced to deploy his entire brigade on line to meet them. Sullivan deployed his own division and then Wayne's to make a bayonet charge. With the Armstrongs now in the thick of the fighting, the British retreated for more than a mile toward Germantown. By this time, Howe himself was on the scene berating the British light infantry for withdrawing from what he considered only a scouting party. At that very moment, grapeshot from an American artillery piece whistled through the leaves of the chestnut tree under which he was standing, revealing a much larger force than a mere scouting party. Howe realized he had been caught by surprise and rode back into Germantown to rally his army.[156]

Several complications that would bedevil the operation now became apparent. The first was fog, described by an American officer as being so thick that, combined with the smoke of battle, it brought on almost midnight darkness, making it impossible to distinguish friend from foe at a distance of five yards. The diminished visibility allowed 120 men of the Fortieth Regiment of Foot who were also retreating from the American onslaught to take shelter in a massive stone house along the main road that was owned by Chief Justice Benjamin Chew.[157]

A debate arose between Washington and senior officers about the Chew house as to whether it should either be bypassed or taken before the attack could continue. Most wanted to leave a regiment behind to surround the place while continuing the attack; but Henry Knox, the chief of artillery and a former bookseller who had widely read the military classics of the day, declared authoritatively that it was a major mistake while in enemy territory to leave an unconquered castle in the rear. Washington, always sensitive about his own lack of formal education, agreed that the "castle," that is, the Chew house, must be taken and the artillery prepared to do the job. Unfortunately, Knox's six-pound shots could only knock out the windows and doors; they merely bounced off the thick stone walls.

---

[156] Thomas J. McGuire, *The Philadelphia Campaign*, vol. 2, *Germantown and Roads to Valley Forge* (Mechanicsburg PA: Stackpole Books, 2007), 76.

[157] Tim Abbott, "Elias Dayton's Account of the Battle of Germantown," *Walking the Berkshires*, last modified October 4, 2012, http://greensleeves.typepad.com/berkshires.

The house was a major distraction from the overall operation, and it cost fifty-three American deaths, about one-third of those lost in the battle.

Meanwhile, Greene's column had arrived late, having four miles further to march at night than the other columns. Hearing the commotion at the Chew house, one of his division commanders, Stephen, moved without orders in that direction. Wayne and Sullivan had by this time moved beyond the house, but the noise of artillery firing in Wayne's rear convinced him that Sullivan and Stirling might be in trouble, and he wheeled about to their rescue. In the dense fog, his force collided with Stephen's division. Firing ensued, and both divisions quickly broke and fled from each other in panic and confusion. Sullivan was not in trouble from the enemy, but by now, his troops were nearly out of ammunition. The British pressed him back initially but soon concentrated their main effort on Greene, who also was compelled to withdraw. Washington tried to stem the retreat, but the soldiers merely waved their empty cartridge boxes at him, demonstrating why they were moving back. He had no choice but to save what he could of his army and to prevent a general rout from occurring.[158]

Howe seemed content to allow Washington to withdraw, having escaped near defeat by a hairsbreadth. The Battle of Germantown was a near success. Nearly every man had marched sixteen miles to Germantown, fought steadily for three hours, and then marched twenty-four miles in retreat, a total of forty miles in one day. In spite of the complicated plan, in spite of the disorienting sixteen-mile night march, in spite of the fog, and in spite of the Chew house, victory had been tantalizingly close at hand. As at Brandywine, the troops did not feel themselves defeated. They had fought well, and for the first time had driven a British army before them. Germantown eventually had wider consequences. The French foreign minister, the Count de Vergennes, had long been pondering an alliance with America. He was impressed that Washington had fought two consecutive battles against highly seasoned troops and had been close to victory in both.[159]

Howe wanted one final opportunity to best his foe before winter. On December 4, he sneaked out of Philadelphia at midnight with nearly his

---

[158] Ward, *The War of the Revolution, Vol. 1*, 368; John Lacey, "Memoirs of Brigadier-General John Lacey, of Philadelphia," *PMHB* 26, no. 1 (1902), 101–11.

[159] Chernow, *George Washington: A Life*, 311.

entire force, intending to strike Washington at Whitemarsh where the army was deployed and well protected by its cannon batteries covering all major approaches and its flanks surrounded by wooden abatis, obstacles formed by tree limbs arranged so that their sharpened points are faced toward the direction of the oncoming enemy. Washington chose not to maneuver away from such a strong position and waited for Howe to attack him. Howe was by now more cautious about dealing with Washington after his recent experiences at Brandywine and Germantown and elected not to attack. He returned to Philadelphia. For both sides, the 1777 campaign season was over.

★

On December 19, 1777, one year and a day after John Armstrong departed Sunbury, the leading elements of Washington's army entered winter quarters at Valley Forge. His miserable bedraggled soldiers had taken a full week to cover barely thirteen miles from Whitemarsh, having first camped without tents for four days in snow and sleet while waiting to be reunited with their baggage and then remaining another three days because the extreme cold had frozen the rutted roads into sharp, icy ridges that made travel nearly impossible for the mostly barefooted army. As they slowly made their way into Valley Forge, leaving bloody footprints in the road to mark their passage, Dr. Albigence Waldo, a surgeon in a Connecticut regiment, described their wretched, discouraged, and forsaken appearance, their bare feet seen through their worn-out shoes and clothing in tatters: "I am Sick, my feet lame, my legs are sore, my body covered with this tormenting itch—my Cloaths are worn out, my constitution is broken, my former Activity is exhausted by fatigue, hunger & Cold. I fail fast I shall soon be no more!"[160]

Unlike the previous winter encampment at Morristown, there were no houses or barns in which to find shelter from the icy north wind and no friendly villagers to offer a meal or a kind word. The tired soldiers found instead a large undulating plateau surrounded by low forested hills and protected by the Schuylkill River to the north, a wide creek to the west, and rolling terrain on the east and south. They slowly filed in to brigade bivouac sites marked out by regimental quartermasters and did little more

[160] Albigence Waldo, "Valley Forge, 1777-1778. Diary of Surgeon Albigence Waldo, of the Connecticut Line," *PMHB* 21, no. 3 (1897), 299–323.

the first day than huddle for warmth around fires. Conway's brigade was assigned a location near the base of a mountain overlooking the plateau, ironically named "Mount Joy."

Named for an old iron forge on a creek running into the Schuylkill River, Valley Forge was chosen for three reasons: its proximity to the British army now comfortably quartered in Philadelphia for the winter, its easily defendable terrain, and the agricultural abundance of the surrounding countryside. The region produced more wheat, grain, and livestock than any similarly sized area in the colonies and had to be protected from pillage by the British. As Joseph Ellis explained, "The central irony of the 'starving time' that would be experienced by the Continental Army at Valley Forge was that it occurred squarely in the middle of the richest and most productive agrarian community on the Atlantic coast." Nothing was readily available to the starving men, not food, not shelter, nor even water. Because there were no springs available on the plateau, all the freshwater needed for cooking, drinking, and bathing had to be drawn by hand from the Schuylkill or the few creeks that traversed the landscape. When a soldier from one of the Connecticut regiments, Joseph Plumb Martin, arrived at his billeting location, he paid his very last coin simply to obtain a single drink of water from another soldier's canteen. It was going to be a very long winter.[161]

Of the approximately 12,000 men that trooped into Valley Forge, at best, only a third were fit for duty. Of the rest, 2,000 were marked as unfit for lack of shoes and 3,500 were marked as "sick present," meaning confined to their huts or tents. The 2,000 men who were noted as "sick absent" were the most unlucky and in what passed for hospitals. Dr. Benjamin Rush stated, "There cannot be greater calamity for such men to come into our hospitals at this season of the year. I assert that the great majority of those who die under our hand perish with diseases caught in our hospitals."[162]

---

[161] Joseph Ellis, *American Creation* (New York: Vintage Books, 2007), 61. Joseph Plumb Martin is universally considered the authentic voice of the Continental private soldier, one of a few to write comprehensively of his Revolutionary War experiences after the war. Joseph Plumb Martin, George F. Scheer, ed., *Private Yankee Doodle* (Little, Brown and Company, 1962), 103.

[162] Ellis, *American Creation*, 63. The main problem was typhus, then known as the "putrid fever." It attacked not only the men, but their doctors and nurses as well. Many soldiers recuperating from battle wounds received at the battles of Brandywine and Germantown caught it and died.

For the men arriving at Valley Forge, the most immediate need was for food. Brig. Gen. James Varnum reported on December 20 that his division had been without any meat for two days and three without bread. For many soldiers, all that was available at the time was a thin paste made from water and flour that could be baked on hot stones placed around campfires and was universally known as fire cake.[163]

The lack of foodstuffs in camp quickly reached a crisis level. In a letter to Congress on December 23, Washington candidly laid out the dire situation confronting the army and his inability to remedy it, noting that there was not a single hoofed animal in camp and no more than twenty-five barrels of flour to feed 12,000 troops. Three or four more days of bad weather, he thought, might destroy the army.[164]

Despite the army's misery, Washington refused to allow the British to forage in the countryside without a fight. No sooner had Conway's brigade streamed into Valley Forge than it was ordered the next day to confront a large British foraging expedition that had crossed the Schuylkill River near Darby, Pennsylvania. In his December 23 anguished letter to Congress, Washington described what had ensued when he ordered troops into readiness to meet the expedition and was informed that the men were unable to stir due to lack of provisions and that an unsuccessful mutiny had broken out the night before.[165]

There is no evidence that the Twelfth Pennsylvania was involved in this mutiny, as the regiment did march out to confront the British although no fighting occurred. The episode, however, highlighted a steadily growing problem in the army. Colonel Cooke, the Twelfth's commander, unaccountably absented himself without leave for the entire period the regiment was involved in this operation. When he returned to Valley Forge ten days later, he departed for an additional period of two months, presumably returning home to Northumberland County while his men suffered in winter quarters. A general court-martial on March 10, 1778, found him guilty of two counts of absence without leave but innocent of an additional charge of granting furloughs to officers under his command and then reporting them absent without leave. Cooke resigned

---

163 Ward, *The War of the Revolution*, 545.

164 Hampton L. Carson, "Washington at Valley Forge," *PMHB* 43, no. 2 (1919), 107–108.

165 Carson, "Washington at Valley Forge," 105–06.

his commission and returned home, leaving Lt. Col. Neigal Gray in command, an unfortunate choice as Gray was later convicted by a general court-martial of the much more serious charge of defrauding soldiers of their rations for money. Because the regiment's major, James Crawford, had earlier been wounded at Brandywine and never returned for duty, the Twelfth was now without a single field grade officer and there is no indication one was ever appointed until the badly understrength regiment was dissolved on July 1, 1778.[166]

A larger problem within the Continental Army officer corps manifested itself not only within the Twelfth Pennsylvania but throughout other regiments at Valley Forge. Dr. Waldo's December 28 diary entry mentioned that fifty officers in General Greene's division had resigned the day before and that six or seven in his own regiment would do the same that day. Many officers had wives and families at home that were suffering through the winter, and the deteriorating value of the Continental currency was no longer sufficient to support them in their husbands' absence. Unlike enlisted men, officers were allowed to resign their commissions at any time without penalty, and many married men thought they had no choice but to go home.[167]

The misery associated with the army's wintering at Valley Forge was due in large part to the simultaneous collapse of the army's quartermaster and commissariat departments. Quartermaster General Thomas Mifflin had resigned in the fall of 1777 to take a position in a newly reorganized Board of War authorized by Congress. His successor had proven totally incompetent, and the army's entire logistical system had by December fallen into administrative chaos. Exacerbating the problem was the collapsing value of Continental currency. Farmers in Pennsylvania and New Jersey, given the choice of accepting the nearly worthless Continental dollar for their produce or the gold paid by the British army, naturally preferred the latter. Washington had little choice but to send out detachments of men to scour the countryside for food. This effort was barely sufficient to stave off starvation but not enough to alleviate the men's misery. Even the army's

---

[166] General Orders, Marcy 14, 1778, Papers of George Washington, Revolutionary War Series, Theodore J. Crackle, ed. (Charlottesville: University of Virginia Press, 2004), XIV: 171; *PGW/RWS*, XV: 295.

[167] Waldo, "Diary of Surgeon Albigence Waldo," 314.

horses eventually succumbed to starvation, and their rotting carcasses in the camp added to the unhealthy conditions.

Washington eventually had enough. On February 12, he issued a draconian order authorizing his troops simply to take what they needed from the local citizenry. All confiscated property was to be fully documented and paid for in certificates that he hoped would eventually be made good by Congress. Nathanael Greene was placed in command of this operation. A Quaker and a kindly man by nature, Greene nevertheless complied, writing later to Washington, "[The] Inhabitants cry out and beset me from all quarters, but like Pharaoh I harden my heart." Washington eventually made him the army's new quartermaster general, and within two months, the food situation stabilized.[168]

Washington also had to get his men out of tents and into more permanent shelter. The timbered hills overlooking the plateau provided a ready resource as the army's able-bodied men began to create a small city of wooden structures. Shelters were of a uniform design, roughly fourteen by sixteen feet, with six and a half feet of headroom. Inside, narrow bunks stacked in triple rows were built on either side of the door, and a fireplace provided enough warmth for a modicum of comfort. Many soldiers draped tents over their huts to keep the sharp wintry winds at bay. Officer's huts had wooden floors. Several problems with the design of the huts soon became apparent and would be corrected in future winter encampments. Many cabins were built on flat ground rather than on slopes, which meant that over time, they filled up with water and mud, and some were sunk a foot or two into the frozen soil, and they likewise soon became muddy. Additionally, the poor design of the fireplace created dense clouds of smoke inside the huts. By the onset of spring, Washington ordered many units out of the huts and into tents as a measure to improve the health of the troops. Whatever their flaws of design and construction, however, the huts probably saved the army that winter.[169]

The absence of proper clothing remained a persistent problem affecting all ranks. A Frenchman strolling through camp caught glimpses of soldiers using woolen blankets as cloaks and overcoats, realizing later that they were

[168] Terry Golway, *Washington's General: Nathanael Greene and the Triumph of the American Revolution* (New York: Henry Holt and Company, 2005) 161–62.

[169] Chernow, *Washington, A Life*, 325; James Thomas Flexner, *George Washington in the American Revolution, 1775–1783* (Boston: Little, Brown and Co., 1967), 226.

officers and generals. By mid-January, when the camp's huts were finally completed, some four thousand soldiers were so poorly clothed that they dared not venture outside. Some used pieces of their tents for shirts, coats, or footwear. All the while, fifty loads of clothing were in a warehouse in Lancaster, Pennsylvania, awaiting supply wagons that never arrived. The situation, at least for the officers, was eased by a stroke of luck. On the first of January, a British ship was seized on the Delaware River en route to supply the British garrison in Philadelphia. In it was found enough scarlet, blue, and buff cloth, hats, shirts, stockings, shoes, boots, and spurs to clothe, in Surgeon Waldo's opinion, all the officers of the army.[170]

In the mythology of the American Revolution, Valley Forge was the low point, a stern test of endurance and fortitude, a crucible that forged a force that eventually triumphed over Britain to win American independence. The cost was high. Close to 2,000 men died that winter, most from a combination of malnutrition, disease, and exposure. Others, weakened by the miserable conditions, died later, many needlessly due to congressional infighting, bureaucratic incompetence, and a dysfunctional logistics system. But no soldier marching out of Valley Forge that June would have imagined that war would go on for another five years, testing the endurance and fortitude of even the most ardent patriot. There would be worse winters ahead for the Continental Army and even more administrative mismanagement. Many officers and men would serve virtually without pay until the end of the war. Just how and why they were able to bear such hardship probably lies in the fact that a revolution of sorts had been wrought in the hearts and minds of those who survived the experience. According to Joseph Ellis, "The seeds of a truly national vision were planted at Valley Forge for the first time . . . At least the germ of this nationalistic perspective began to congeal within the officer corps at the time, alongside the belief that the Continental Army, not the state-centered Continental Congress, was the only surviving national institution that represented the American people as a whole." Along with the

---

[170] Chernow, *Washington, A Life*, 324; Flexner, *George Washington in the American Revolution*, 226. Golway, *Washington's General*, 160; Waldo, *Diary of Surgeon Albigence Waldo*, 322.

possibility of social mobility, this vision of allegiance and service to the new nation animated the ambitions of the Armstrongs for the rest of their lives.[171]

★

A more observable transformation within the officer corps and within the army itself took place during those winter months at Valley Forge. Fate stepped in to provide an unexpected solution to two problems endemic in the army, discipline and military proficiency, in the form of a foreign officer volunteering his services to the new nation. Lt. Gen. Baron Friedrich Wilhelm von Steuben arrived in camp at the end of February. Von Steuben's pedigree was vastly inflated, for although he had once been an aide-de-camp to Frederick the Great, king of Prussia, he had never advanced beyond the rank of captain. He was, though, a solid military professional who impressed all with whom he came into contact with his professionalism and devotion to their cause despite the fact that he spoke no English.

When Washington assigned him to inspect the army and give recommendations for how to improve its discipline and military professionalism, von Steuben was appalled by his findings. The army lacked any form of standard administration, or for that matter, organization. Some regiments were comprised of only three platoons of soldiers, and others had as many as twenty-one. Every state seemed to have a different drill system. Officers, following the English model, seemed to think their responsibilities for the men was to inspect the guard and stand in front of their formations during battle. All training was left to the noncommissioned officers whose standards varied considerably from unit to unit.[172]

Von Steuben determined that the key to the army's improvement was standardizing its drill and the responsibilities of leaders at every level of command. He also decided that the key to implementing the new standards was for him to demonstrate them personally. On March 19 with one hundred soldiers selected from all fourteen brigades of the army, and on the main parade field of the encampment, he began imparting proper drill procedure, first with twelve men forming a squad and gradually working up to the company level. Officers and enlisted men not on duty drifted over to the parade ground to watch the spectacle, occasionally

---

[171] Ellis, *American Creation*, 71.

[172] Thomas Fleming, *Washington's Secret War: The Hidden History of Valley Forge* (New York: Smithsonian Books, 2005), 213.

laughing at the baron's fractured English. Von Steuben laughed along with the bystanders at these lapses and soon won everyone over; observers quickly grasped the importance of his instruction. By March 24, he had impressed Washington as well, who ordered all brigades to perform the daily drill with their officers present and everyone to be under the personal supervision of von Steuben. Under the stern but patient gaze of the baron, the Armstrongs and their fellow officers received instruction that would become the early American army's standard for military procedure for decades to come.[173]

[173] Paul Lockhart, *The Drillmaster of Valley Forge: The Baron De Steuben and the Making of the American Army* (New York: HarperCollins, 2008), 87–116.

4

An Officer and Gentleman, 1778–1783

An officer is much more respected than any
other man who has a little money.
—Samuel Johnson[174]

Sometime in April 1778, John Armstrong was selected to be part of a "partisan corps" of cavalry and infantry under the command of legendary cavalry officer Capt. Allen McLane of Delaware. McLane had already made himself indispensable to Washington by providing reliable intelligence on British movements in and around Philadelphia and by keeping constant pressure on their foraging parties throughout the winter and spring. As the 1778 campaign season approached, Washington needed his talents more than ever. Although McLane had already recruited a troop of Delaware horse, he was now augmented with approximately one hundred infantry and cavalry troops, including a group of Oneida Indians. John Armstrong was one of these augmentees.[175]

McLane later wrote that Armstrong had been introduced to him by the Generals Lafayette and Maxwell. Recommended as a vigilant officer, Armstrong was included in the corps where the lieutenant served for

---

[174] Samuel Johnson to James Boswell, April 3, 1776, quoted in Robert Debs Heinl, *Dictionary of Military and Naval Quotations* (Annapolis: United States Naval Institute, 1966), 221.

[175] Ward, *The War of the Revolution*, II: 547.

almost two months, meriting McLane's acknowledgment of his "Assiduity and Bravery."[176]

One can only speculate why Lafayette recommended John Armstrong to McLane. The most reasonable explanation is that the two men met on the Brandywine battlefield when the marquis was near Conway's brigade during the hottest part of the fighting. Lafayette was wounded, and perhaps John helped him off the battlefield. John's relationship with Maxwell is easier to explain; Armstrong must have impressed the general by his conduct during a short period of attachment to his command while at Valley Forge. On one occasion, Armstrong, in command of thirty soldiers, encountered an enemy party of superior strength and effected their retreat with a loss of four to five of his men. The incident was noted in a letter later written to John by Col. Daniel Brodhead, former commander of the First Pennsylvania Regiment, and may corroborate anecdotes published in a local Cincinnati biography of Armstrong's service in the Revolution. More than likely, information for the article came from recollections of conversations provided by his son some years later, but they represent Armstrong's sole accounts of his experiences during the war and attest to the fact that he spent time in command of a mounted unit.

In one such story, John is described as having stationed his men inside a stone wall enclosing a cemetery while he rode forward to the camp of a group of British cavalry commanded by Major Banastre Tarleton. When a number of the cavalrymen gave chase, he deliberately slowed his pace, allowing them to come close behind him. Then nearing the graveyard, he spurred his horse, circling around to a back entrance and leaving his surprised pursuers open to the fire of his men. In another anecdote, he is quoted as saying that during his command, he only became alarmed one time during an incident that occurred when he and his men were resting in a meadow and were surprised by a troop of British horse. When spotted, they were within fifty yards of Armstrong and his men, and they were outnumbered four to one. The story goes that he laughed and told his anxious men to stand fast and to wait until the British were within twenty steps before firing. The first platoon's volley broke the enemy's advance and forced them to retreat and reform. He then ordered his second platoon to "face to the right about" and fire, scattering the horsemen again,

---

[176] Letter from Allen McLane to the President of a Court-Martial, Reading, Pennsylvania, June 21, 1783 (mistakenly dated, probably May 21, 1783), PJA.

continuing in this manner until his force was able to withdraw at a gallop. Although he was an infantry soldier, John would have been a dragoon, or mounted infantryman, while serving under McLane. In a draft of a letter presumably sent to a former officer in the Twelfth Pennsylvania Regiment several years after the war, he refers to a dispute between the two men over the payment for a horse in April 1778 that resulted in litigation in a civilian court. There would seem to have been no other reason for an infantry lieutenant to own a horse unless he needed it for mounted operations.[177]

As a part of McLane's partisan corps, John would have participated in the near debacle at Barren Hill on the eastern side of the Schuylkill River between Valley Forge and Philadelphia. Washington assigned about a third of the available troops at Valley Forge, approximately 2,200 men, to Lafayette, still a major general without a formal command, to provide security to the encampment and gain intelligence about British military activities. The arrangement proved to be a major tactical mistake: the force was too small to defend itself if the British came out of Philadelphia in strength and too large to move quickly away if they did. This is precisely what happened. Knowing immediately what Lafayette was up to and where his troops were located, the entire British force under the personal command of Howe moved out of Philadelphia to seize the two available fording sites and to trap Lafayette. Fortunately for the young marquis, McLane's men captured two British grenadiers that night who told them what was afoot. McLane ordered one of his companies to delay one of the British columns while he raced back to inform Lafayette of the danger to his command. He was barely in time. Lafayette was just able to march his force to the one ford still available to him and to get over the river before he could be trapped. Nevertheless, McLane and his men were officially recognized for their service that had enabled the marquis to make "a glorious retreat as well as a safe one."[178]

★

---

[177] Letter from Col. Daniel Brodhead to the President of a Court-Martial at Reading, Pennsylvania, June 1, 1783, PJA. Charles Cist, *Cincinnati Miscellany, or Antiquities of the West and Pioneer History and General and Local Statistics* (Cincinnati: Caleb Clark, 1845) I: 38. Draft of letter from Armstrong to unknown correspondent dated 1799, PJA.

[178] Ward, *The War of the Revolution* II: 564–67. An unexpected event occurred when British Dragoons suddenly came across McLane's Oneida Indians who

On June 19, a reinvigorated Continental Army marched out of Valley Forge, presumably all in step and in a proper formation due to von Steuben's reforms. In late April, the long-awaited alliance with France had been concluded, bringing with it the promise of better financial and logistical support. The British Army, now commanded by Sir Henry Clinton upon Howe's recall to England, had been ordered to abandon Philadelphia and was now moving back toward New York City. Congress had approved an extra month's pay for every soldier in camp, along with an extra ration of rum to celebrate the end of a very long and difficult winter. Their ranks had also been replenished by new recruits, and the size of the army was now virtually identical to the size that had marched in.

Washington was determined to strike a blow against Clinton's rear guard as it marched through New Jersey on the way to the safety of New York City and Staten Island. Washington called a council of war to discuss the prospects for a successful attack; the majority of his generals, most notably Maj. Gen. Charles Lee who had just been exchanged after being in British custody since December 1776, recommended against it. Only Greene, Wayne, and Lafayette argued for offensive action. Washington acceded to this cautious approach but dispatched a brigade forward to keep watch over the British movement. The next day, he changed his mind and decided to reinforce this advance guard, placing Lafayette in command with orders to look for an opportunity to engage the British rear guard. Lee, who had earlier acceded to the decision to put a more junior major general in charge of what was now a force of five thousand men, changed his mind and demanded to lead the guard himself. In honoring the principle of seniority, Washington entrusted the fate of the army to a man who had participated neither in the 1777 campaign nor the Valley Forge encampment and who did not believe American soldiers capable of standing up against British regulars. The stage was set for another debacle.

Washington directed Lee to meet with the senior officers of the units comprising the advance force and to develop a plan for the upcoming operation. When he met his subordinates, Lee simply told them he lacked sufficient information about the location of the British rear guard to develop a plan and that he would simply move forward until contact was made with the enemy and react accordingly. He made no further effort to

---

were picketing a main road. The Oneidas' war cries and screams frightened the British horses, and both groups immediately fled in opposite directions.

reconnoiter the field or gain the information needed. The next morning, as the separate units of the advance guard encountered British forces, the result was a series of uncoordinated movements by the several units while Lee provided no guidance and made little or no attempt to impose order. One by one, the disparate units began a withdrawal that quickly became a confused and chaotic rush to the rear. Washington was following behind Lee with the main army, intending to support his operations when he saw the first troops streaming to the rear. He immediately spurred his horse and galloped forward to demand an explanation from Lee. According to Joseph Plumb Martin, who was an eyewitness to the encounter with Lee, Washington was "in a great passion." With British artillery rounds impacting all around him, he demanded the officers of Martin's Connecticut regiment explain why they were retreating. Told they were following Lee's order, Washington swore, "Damn him," rounded on Lee, and took personal command of the battle. According to two of Washington's aides who were with him, Alexander Hamilton and James McHenry, what happened next at what would later be known as the Battle of Monmouth Courthouse was Washington's finest moment of the war.[179]

Continuing forward toward the oncoming British, Washington halted two withdrawing regiments and ordered them to hold off the British long enough for the rest of the army to occupy a defensive position on nearby Perrine Hill. Washington then positioned the army with Stirling's division on the left, Greene's division on the right, and Lafayette with the remnants of the advance guard forming a reserve in the rear. The Third and Twelfth Pennsylvania Regiments were positioned in the middle of the line roughly adjacent to Greene. Knox's artillery occupied a nearby hill where it could provide enfilading fire on the British as they moved forward along a long valley. As the units closed on the American position, the largest and most prolonged artillery duel of the entire war began. After an unsuccessful attack on Stirling's position by the British light infantry and the famed Black Watch regiment, Clinton realized that the American position was too strong to be taken and elected to withdraw. Wayne moved forward with three regiments, one of which was the Third Pennsylvania, to harass Clinton's troops.

---

[179] Alexander Hamilton to Elias Boudinot, July 5, 1778, Founders Online, https://founders.archive.gov. See also "The Battle of Monmouth, described by Dr. James McHenry, Secretary to General Washington," *Magazine of American History: With Notes and Queries* 3 (1897), 355–63; Martin, *Private Yankee Doodle*, 126–27.

After receiving several volleys, two retreating British regiments turned about and counterattacked, forcing Wayne to withdraw to a nearby parsonage. The hottest fighting of the day then ensued in an adjacent orchard occupied by the Third Pennsylvania Regiment. The British faltered, largely due to fire from American artillery. It was so heavy and accurate that a single American cannonball struck the muskets from the hands of an entire British platoon. The British infantry eventually withdrew down the valley as night began to fall. Washington organized a counterattack to drive the British completely from the field, but by the time it could be mounted, it was too dark. Washington ordered his troops to lie on their arms that night with the intention of renewing the battle early the next morning. But as dawn broke, it was clear that the British had resumed their movement back toward New York and were too far away to engage.[180]

John Armstrong's role at Monmouth was mostly that of an observer; the only casualties suffered by the Twelfth was from British artillery. What glory accrued to the Armstrong family that day rested on the shoulders of his brother, James, whose regiment heroically defended the parsonage against almost overwhelming odds. Technically, Monmouth was a draw, but the American side considered it a great victory. As Hamilton told his friend, Elias Boudinot, "The behavior of the officers and men was such as could not be easily surpassed. Our troops, after the first impulse from mismanagement, behaved with more spirit and moved with greater order than the British troops. You know my way of thinking about our army, and that I am not apt to flatter it. I assure you I never was pleased with them before this day."[181]

Von Steuben must also have been gratified to see the results of his training in discipline and maneuver fully vindicated. Not in any battle since Princeton had Washington performed so well. At Monmouth, he had by the power of his personality and tactical judgment literally snatched a brilliant tactical victory from the jaws of impending defeat. Three days later, the understrength Twelfth Pennsylvania Regiment was dissolved and its men assigned to the Third Pennsylvania Regiment. Astonishingly, John

[180] Ward, *The War of the Revolution*, I: 584.
[181] Alexander Hamilton to Elias Boudinot, 5 July 1778, Founders Online, https://founders.archives.gov /?q=%20Author%3A%22Hamilton%2C%20 Alexander%22&s=1111311111&r=198.

and James Armstrong now were serving side by side as brother officers in the same regiment. [182]

On July 4, the army camped at New Brunswick, where John and James Armstrong participated in celebrating the second anniversary of American independence with a parade and cannon salutes. Terry Golway notes, "The troops were given extra rations of rum, and there were shouts of laughter in the summer night. The gray, cold, and hollowed-out ghost of Valley Forge had been exorcised."

★

With the British Army once again concentrated in New York City, Washington became worried about the security of the Hudson River corridor and decided to march the army north. Joseph Plumb Martin described the movement as being made in "easy marches," meaning that the troops typically rose at three o'clock in the morning, marched no more than ten miles a day after breakfast, and halted by the early afternoon. Every third day the army was allowed to rest. In this leisurely fashion, the army crossed the Hudson River at Kings Ferry and established headquarters for the rest of the campaign season at White Plains. Little did Washington realize that he had fought his last major battle of the Revolution and that the only activities the army would undertake for the next three years would be a series of skirmishes and small unit operations.[183]

In August, Washington directed the establishment of a light infantry corps to be composed of three regiments of carefully selected men from several brigades to keep a close eye on the British in New York City and the

---

[182] This move created bad feelings among some officers as there were insufficient vacancies in the Third Pennsylvania to accommodate all the officers of the Twelfth. As a result, several officers of the Twelfth, including three company commanders, became supernumerary and were "deranged"—sent home to Northumberland County and were understandably bitter at the officers chosen to be retained in service. In a previously cited letter, one of them whose name is not known initiated civil court proceedings against John over the sale of a horse during Armstrong's assignment with McLane. He also cast aspersions on John's integrity apparently because John had been called to testify against Colonel Cooke at the latter's court-martial earlier that year. Two letter drafts, dated 1799, clearly indicate the hard feelings that endured some twenty-one years past the dissolution of the Twelfth Regiment. PJA.

[183] Martin, *Private Yankee Doodle*, 133.

surrounding environs. Its area of operation was roughly from Mamaroneck on Long Island to Dobbs Ferry on the Hudson River. Because the corps was only a temporary organization and no records of its precise composition are available, the question of whether John Armstrong was selected for it cannot be confirmed. Assignment was temporary; men were returned to their regiments during winter. In light of his good service with Maxwell and McLane and his selection for the Stony Point operation the next year, it is reasonable to think he served in the light infantry. Joseph Plumb Martin, who was selected for the corps, described it as consisting of about half New Englanders with the rest mostly from Pennsylvania. "The duty of the Light Infantry," he explained, "is the hardest, while in the field, of any troops in the army, if there is any *hardest* about it. During the time the army keeps the field they are always on the alert, constantly on the watch. . . . There is never any great danger of the Light Infantry men dying of the scurvy."[184]

Perhaps because the problems of the prior year's encampment at Valley Forge were a recent memory, Washington split the army into three widely scattered groups for the winter. One brigade remained on the west side of the Hudson River north of New York City; one brigade was sent to Elizabethtown, New Jersey, to keep a close watch on Staten Island; and the remainder, about 8,800 men including all the Pennsylvania regiments, moved back to the Watchung Mountains near the town of Middlebrook. Due to the mythology of Valley Forge the preceding year and the exceptionally harsh conditions experienced by soldiers the following year, the winter encampment of 1778–1779 gets short shrift in histories of the Revolution, but it was severe enough for Anthony Wayne. He wrote letters to Joseph Reed, the president of the Pennsylvania Supreme Executive Council, pointing out that many of his men were "quite destitute of blankets" and that the plight of his officers was "more intolerable than the soldiers." Wayne warned that many of them were asking for leaves and furloughs and that if these were granted, they were likely not to return. Despite Wayne's misgivings, however, most officers remained; and according to Dr. James Thatcher, a surgeon in a Massachusetts regiment, the bad weather and logistical problems did not inhibit their social life. He noted that "our officers have not permitted the Christmas day to pass

---

[184] Ibid., 136.

unnoticed" and that there was not a day "without invitations to dine, nor a night without amusement and dancing."[185]

Huts were again built, but unlike at Valley Forge, they were not dug into the frozen soil to prevent the floors from becoming soft and muddy. All had shingled roofs, and the fireplaces were better engineered. All the men got blankets and straw for bedding. The alliance with France had also produced, among other things, better uniforms for the troops. The weather was generally better than at Valley Forge, and the number of soldiers in hospitals was barely a quarter of the number hospitalized the previous year. And just as at Valley Forge, Martha Washington joined her husband as did the wives of several other senior officers, and their presence lent a touch of gentility to the lives of all the officers. The climax of the camp's social season was a huge gala on February 18, 1779, to celebrate the first anniversary of the alliance with France. A one hundred-foot-long pavilion was constructed for the occasion by the soldiers, and a band made up of enlisted men provided music for dancing. Guests from all over New Jersey came to celebrate the occasion, with as many as seventy ladies available for dancing with junior officers. Sixteen cannons roared salutes to the arriving dignitaries who enjoyed a multicourse dinner followed by fireworks and dancing until dawn.[186]

It was at about this time that the Armstrong brothers parted ways. The previous September, James was one of forty-one officers who signed a petition submitted to Washington protesting recently adopted promotion procedures following the amalgamation of regiments within the Third Pennsylvania. Apparently seeing little future in continuing in the Pennsylvania Line, by January 1779, he had joined Lee's corps of Partisan Light Dragoons, an elite force of combined cavalry and infantry under the leadership of Lt. Col. Henry "Light Horse Harry" Lee.[187]

★

---

[185] John T. Cunningham, *The Uncertain Revolution: Washington and the Continental Army at Morristown* (West Creek, NJ: Cormorant Publishing, 2007), 64, 67.

[186] Ibid., 71.

[187] Also referred to as "Lee's Legion." See William Thomas Sherman, "Lee's Legion Remembered: Profiles of the 2nd. Partisan Corps as taken from Alexander Garden's Anecdotes" (1822 & 1828 eds.), https://archive.org/stream/ LeesLegionRemembered (last update Nov 20, 2018).

Washington and Clinton both had only sparse resources available for the 1779 campaign season. Washington considered three available options—attack British forces in New York City and Newport, Rhode Island; mount a major expedition to subdue the troublesome Iroquois confederacy in the Niagara region; or remain strictly on the defensive. Since a major offensive action to push the British out of New York required more men than he could muster at the time, he recommended the last option to Congress. Already worried about the recent fall of Savannah to the British in January 1779, Congress agreed that the most prudent thing for him to do would be to conserve his strength and not risk further losses. Clinton likewise had too few troops to subdue the Americans in a pitched battle but decided to employ limited operations to lure Washington out of the Watchung Mountains, a feat that was ultimately accomplished in an indirect manner. He elected to leverage his naval superiority on the Hudson River, thereby threatening that vital corridor, a move he was confident Washington could not ignore.[188]

In late May, Clinton moved a significant part of his force north to seize Kings Ferry, a major crossing point on the Hudson south of West Point. The landing was protected on the eastern side of the river by Fort Lafayette at Verplanck's Point and on the western side of the river by Stony Point, a high promontory overlooking a ferry site on which a small fort had been built. He easily overwhelmed the fortifications' defenders and began to secure both positions in anticipation of an American counterattack. As predicted, Washington moved the bulk of his army north to West Point.

At about this time, John Armstrong, still in New Jersey, found himself under arrest and facing a court-martial for disobeying an order to send a prisoner in his charge to a court-martial proceeding. He apparently never received a legal order to do so, and he was found not guilty. The court

---

[188] Clinton also had fewer troops than he needed to subdue the Americans in the field. In order to protect their lucrative sugar trade in the West Indies from French attacks, he had been ordered to send eight thousand troops south to Florida and the Caribbean and to remain strictly on the defensive in North America. Both sides, therefore, had neither the manpower nor the political backing for a major campaign in 1779. See Michael Schellhammer, *George Washington and the Final British Campaign for the Hudson River, 1779* (Jefferson NC and London: McFarland and Company, 2012), chapters 1 and 4.

concluded that Armstrong had acted "as every good officer would or ought to have acted" and acquitted him with honor.[189]

In reviewing the army's daily general orders, the modern reader is struck not only by the frequency of officer courts-martial, but also by the triviality of many charges and why an incident so mundane as Armstrong's was not sorted out by the chain of command before resorting to formal judicial action. Joseph Ellis believes this was due to the growing sense among the officer corps that they were part of a new uniquely American aristocracy based on merit that promoted two overlapping patterns of behavior. The first was an obsessive concern with rank, including minute distinctions of seniority that often required courts-martial to resolve. While soldiers mostly suffered in silence, officers perpetually engaged in petty arguments about their relative status in the military hierarchy, at times resembling what John Adams observed, "apes scrambling for nuts." The second pattern of behavior was characterized by minor arguments that could escalate quickly to a matter of honor, often requiring formal adjudication before they led to personal challenges and duels. John's first court-martial perhaps evolved from the latter. It would not be his last brush with the army's judicial system.[190]

★

Clinton's move up the Hudson River defined the course of the 1779 campaign. Washington dispatched 4,000 men under the command of Maj. Gen. John Sullivan to upstate New York and Pennsylvania to quell problems with Britain's Native American allies. To deal with the new British fortifications, he elected not to use the main army but to assemble a new corps of light infantry troops to be commanded by Brig. Gen. Anthony Wayne. The corps was drawn from the three divisions under Washington's immediate command. The 1,200-man force was to be comprised of selected men organized into four regiments, each with two battalions of four companies. Each company was commanded by a captain and had one subaltern and three sergeants. All the officers were personally approved by

---

[189] Theodore J. Crackle, ed., General Orders, 27 May 1779, Papers of George Washington, Revolutionary War Series, XX: 642. (*PGW/RWS*).

[190] John Adams, The Letters of John and Abigail Adams (New York: Penguin Books, 2012), 212; Joseph Ellis, *American Creation* (New York: Vintage Books, 2007), 69-70.

Washington. Possibly because of his previous service with Allen McLane, John Armstrong was one of the junior officers selected for the corps. No company rosters have been located, so it is uncertain in which of the two battalions with Pennsylvanians John Armstrong served, but most likely he was assigned to the First Battalion of the Second Regiment, under the command of Lt. Col. Samuel Hay.[191]

Wayne arrived to take up his new command on July 2. Typically, Wayne was appalled at the appearance of his men and the support that had thus far been provided to what was supposed to be the elite of the Continental Army. Each man was dressed in his state's regimental uniform, and many were tattered and poorly repaired. Some men even lacked shoes. He complained to the commissary general that his corps had been greatly neglected in the receipt of needed goods, having only two days of fresh provisions since they had arrived at their appointed location, Sandy Beach, and not more than three days' allowance of rum in twelve days. He also wrote directly to Washington, requesting new uniforms for the men, provisions, rum, and von Steuben's blue book on drill. Washington replied he could not supply completely new uniforms but agreed to send each man one cap or hat, one blanket, one shirt, and one pair of shoes—and of course, the "blue books."[192]

Wayne had been directed by Washington to interpose his force between the British position at Stony Point and West Point, the protection of which was the army's top priority. He was also directed to look for an opportunity to strike the British if a favorable situation could be found. After reconnoitering and conferring with Lighthorse Harry Lee whose partisan corps was screening the area and gathering information (presumably with James Armstrong now attached to it), Wayne told Washington that it was likely impossible to storm the position directly, but it might be possible to take it by surprise. Lee then directed the redoubtable Allen McLane, whose troop of horse had now been placed under his command, to attempt to penetrate the British position under the guise of accompanying Mrs.

---

[191] Henry P. Johnston, *The Storming of Stony Point* (New York: James T. White and Co., 1900), 69, 71. Pennsylvanian Col. Richard Butler commanded the 2nd Regiment and Hay's 1st Battalion consisted entirely of Pennsylvanians. Two other companies of Pennsylvanians were in the 1st Regiment's 2nd Battalion under Major Thomas Posey.

[192] Schellhammer, *George Washington and the Final British Campaign for the Hudson River*, 126.

Smith, a local woman who lived there, back to her home. Dressed in a frontiersman's hunting shirt and carrying a long rifle, he appeared to be a simple woodsman. His disguise fooled the British officer who led him into the position where his practiced scout's eye noticed vulnerabilities in the defenses. When the British officer conducting him around asked if the fortification might be strong enough to keep Mr. Washington out, McLane replied coolly, "If I was a general, sure I am that I would not attempt to take it if I had fifty-thousand men." The officer seemed pleased as he departed.[193]

Wayne scheduled an inspection and parade for his men on July 15, the first time all had been assembled at one place at the same time. They were ordered to be freshly shaved, to have their hair powdered, and to parade with full field packs and one day's cooked rations. When the inspection was completed, Wayne ordered them to march out of the camp. Their route took them past the ruins of Fort Montgomery, around the base of Bear Mountain, passing near the Hudson River by Fort Clinton, near Doodletown, and over west Dunderberg Mountain, a total of thirteen miles on rough tracks with the men moving in single file. Since this was to be a night attack, all the men put pieces of white paper on the back of their hats so that they might be seen at close range by their comrades. The officers carried spontoons, also known as half pikes, a wooden staff with a sharpened point and edged crossbar while the soldiers carried unloaded muskets with bayonets attached. Orders were issued that any soldier who attempted to load a weapon, initiate action prematurely, "retreat one single foot," or "skulk" during the assault was to be put to death by the nearest officer. Lee's partisan force provided security for the movement and guided the troops through the swampy ground at the base of Stony Point to their planned line of departure. During this part of the operation, one man deserted, jeopardizing the entire operation. Lee ordered him hanged.[194]

Wayne then issued his attack orders. He divided his force into three parts. Butler's regiment would attack Stony Point on its northern flank while Wayne with two regiments would make the main attack on the southern flank. A third force of two companies of North Carolina troops was to make a demonstration in the center to distract the British guards.

---

[193] Alexander Garden, *Anecdotes of the American Revolution* (Charleston: A.E. Miller, 1828) II: 79.

[194] Johnston, *The Storming of Stony Point*, 71–77; Noel B. Gerson, *Light Horse Harry: A Biography of Washington's Great Cavalryman* (Garden City NJ: Doubleday and Company, 1966), 66.

The fort was protected at the bottom of the hill by a ring of wooden abatis. Small groups of men armed with axes and saws known as "forlorn hopes" because of the high casualties they were expected to take led each column. The men moved into position around midnight, and Wayne gave the order to attack at twenty minutes past the hour.

The sound of wood being chopped alerted the British that an attack was underway, and they fired cannons and muskets in the general vicinity of the noise. Because it was pitch-black, most shots were high of their intended marks. The forlorn hope of Wayne's column failed to break through the abatis, and the officers and men moving behind them grabbed axes and began chopping as well. Butler's advance party was more successful. His men poured through a gap and began to climb the steep hill in front of them, which was in places almost perpendicular. For John Armstrong, carrying an unwieldy spontoon and wearing flat-soled shoes, it was a difficult and treacherous climb amidst a hail of musketry. All the men stolidly moved forward in silence, heeding Wayne's admonition not to shout and give away their positions. A British musket ball grazed Wayne's scalp, knocking him down. Bleeding profusely from the head wound, he continued to direct his men forward. His column, now being led by Lt. Col. Christian Febiger, broke through its abatis and made its way up the steep hill to a more level piece of ground where they prepared to assault the inner defenses of the fort. In the darkness, the coordinated assault of the two columns soon degenerated into a series of separate actions by small groups of Americans and British defenders. The battle began to wind down as one by one, the British cannons were put out of action and isolated pockets of defenders surrendered and were disarmed. By two o'clock, Wayne wrote a brief but melodramatic note to Washington that said only, "The forts and garrison with Col. Johnson are ours. Our officers and men behaved like men who are determined to be free."[195]

The victory at Stony Point was purchased at the remarkably low cost of only thirteen dead and sixty-four wounded Americans. British casualties were much higher and included more than five hundred prisoners, among whom were six American deserters who were later court-martialed and hanged. The stores and equipment in the fort were "purchased" by Congress for around $158,000 and the money distributed to the officers and men making the assault. Typically, officers got more shares the higher

---

[195] Schellhammer, *George Washington and the Final British Campaign*, 152.

their rank, and the enlisted men got a single share although they had borne the brunt of the fighting. Nonetheless, a single share was worth about seventy-eight dollars, nearly a year's salary for a private soldier. Lieutenants got four shares, so John Armstrong would have received slightly more than three hundred dollars for his two hours of work that night. Congress also struck a gold medal for Wayne and silver medals for his key lieutenants. The victory was celebrated throughout the states, but curiously, Lee's men were omitted from the honors and rewards although they had played an important role in the operation. The men who made the assault were the "lions of the day" in camps and social circles and were cheered at dinners, fetes, and town meetings. A simultaneous planned attack on Verplanck's Point across the Hudson failed to materialize, but in the glow of victory, this detail was downplayed. The fort itself was abandoned a few days later after it had been completely stripped of its stores and armaments.[196]

★

After a similar raid on a British outpost at Paulus Hook, New Jersey, opposite Manhattan by Lee's partisan corps, the main army's active operations for 1779 ended. Washington continued to fortify West Point while Clinton, after receiving reinforcements, abandoned Newport and turned the focus of British attention south to the Carolinas and Georgia. With the threat to the Hudson River corridor abated, Washington decided to move the bulk of the army south into winter quarters at Morristown. While he established his headquarters in the town, most of the troops were a few miles south in an area known as Jockey Hollow where they chopped down nearly two thousand acres of timber and built a virtual city of a thousand log cabins. When Joseph Plumb Martin's Connecticut regiment arrived in the middle of December the snow was nearly foot deep. They were "naked, fatigued and starved, and forced to march many a weary mile, through cold and snow, to seek a situation in some (to us, unknown) wood to build us habitations to starve and suffer in."[197]

Trouble for the army was already looming on the horizon, however, since by early October, the quartermasters reported there was not a single pair of shoes in the army's depots and the situation was equally dire for shirts, overalls, and blankets. The problem this time was not with the

---

[196] Henry P. Johnston, *The Storming of Stony Point*, 100.
[197] Martin, *Private Yankee Doodle*, 66; 167–68.

army's administrative department, but with the value of the Continental currency, which now fetched only three cents to the dollar. As the value of its currency continued to plummet, Congress simply stopped printing new money and appealed to the states to pay their own troops in their state's currency. The states in turn increased the amount of their own paper currency in circulation, and the prices of commodities soared. By mid-December, Washington informed Congress that the army had gone for days without bread, making its prospects "infinitely worse than they have been at any period of the war and . . . unless some expedient can be instantly adopted, a dissolution of the army for want of subsistence is unavoidable."[198]

In this, the fifth winter of the war, the troops were now skilled at building their winter cabins. Each hut was approximately twelve feet wide and fifteen to sixteen feet long and seven feet high, with a gabled roof with wooden shingles and chimney on the back wall. Bunks for twelve men were built into the walls, and tables and chairs were fashioned from leftover wood. With an abundant supply of firewood, the men were generally warm inside although they remained hungry and shabbily dressed. Officers were under strict orders that their huts would not be built until all the enlisted men were housed. In a letter to his brother on December 22, Pennsylvania officer Lt. Erkuries Beatty wrote, "I think if you saw my Situation and way of living you would really Pity me, for colder weather I never saw in this time of year, and we are yet in our cold tents, we have just got the men in their Hutts, and it is so cold we cant get ours built, and what is worse than all we scarcely got anything to Eat." Beatty's plight was not quite as severe as that of the average soldier, however, because three days later, he also wrote of his Christmas Day activities: "I am just down from dinner about half Drunk, all dined together upon good roast & boiled, but in a Cold hut, however grog enough will keep out cold for which there is no Desiring, tomorrow we all dine at one with the Colonel, which will be another excellent dinner and I think you may call that fair living, but Ah! I am afraid it wont last many Days."[199]

[198] Chernow, *Washington, A Life*, 366.
[199] Joseph M. Beatty, Jr., "Letters of the Four Beatty Brothers of the Continental Army, 1774–1794," *Pennsylvania Magazine of History and Biography* 44, no. 3 (1920), 207–210 (*PMHB*).

Beatty was eerily prescient, for winter soon struck with a vengeance. Weather historian David Ludlow notes that in only one winter in recorded metrological history all statewide inlets, harbors, and sounds of the Atlantic coastal plain from North Carolina northeastward were frozen over and remained closed to navigation for a period of a full month and more. The snow began falling in Jockey Hollow on January 2 and continued for the better part of four days for a total of eighteen inches. The already meager supplies of food, clothing, and equipment that were being shipped to camp were stranded on the roads, unable to make it through the deepening snow drifts. "The Army is upon the eve of disbanding for want of Provisions," wrote Quartermaster General Greene.[200]

For most of the month of January, rations became increasingly scarce, and the bleak specter of starvation began to stare the men in the face. The situation was worse than at Valley Forge. Joseph Plumb Martin wrote that at one point, it snowed for four days successively with the accumulation of as many feet. The men were literally starving. Martin ate birch bark he had gnawed off a stick of wood. He saw several men roast their old shoes and eat them. One of the officers killed and ate his pet dog. Relief came at the end of the fourth day in the form of fresh beef and wheat, which the men devoured voraciously.[201]

As he had done earlier at Valley Forge, Washington was forced to forage in the surrounding countryside for food. He assigned quotas of provisions to be provided by every county around Morristown and directed his cavalry units to forage along the coast as far south as Cape May. Slowly, the crisis eased as food began to flow into the camp once the worst part of the winter passed.

As the food crisis abated, life in the encampment took on a more normal atmosphere. It was during this time that John Armstrong had his most serious encounter with Continental Army justice. This time, he was arrested and tried by general court-martial on the charge of "ungentlemanlike behavior in attempting to impose a falsehood" on his commander regarding his attendance at the regimental parade. Armstrong apparently was part of a court-martial panel at a time when the officers of the Third Regiment were all expected to be on parade. He must have

---

[200] David Ludlow quoted in Cunningham, *The Uncertain Revolution*, 101; Nathanael Greene quoted in Terry Golway's *Washington's General*, 213–14.

[201] Martin, *Private Yankee Doodle*, 172.

believed that serving on the panel was the more important duty, but his commander Thomas Craig obviously thought differently. Possibly wishing to head off future incidents by other officers, Craig wrote directly to both the president of the court and to the commander-in-chief in an effort to secure a conviction. "Should he come off clear," wrote Craig to Washington, "which I have some reason to judge from the color of the court, publishing the proceedings in my opinion may be attended with dangerous consequences as some of the officers will not think themselves obliged to look after the internal police of their companies while in duties of that nature." The court found him guilty and sentenced him to be cashiered. At this point, Washington intervened in John's favor, confirming the sentence of the court-martial, but setting aside the harsh punishment: "The Commander-in-Chief confirms the sentence; but from the general good character he has heard from Lieutenant Armstrong, he hopes what he was charged with proceeded rather from a want of recollection than from any ill design and is induced to restore him to his rank and command. He is released from arrest."[202]

★

No light infantry corps was formed in 1780. No major engagements occurred in the north during the 1780 campaign other than two large skirmishes with the British in the vicinity of the Springfield Gap in June. The only significant action involving John Armstrong that year was at the Bergen Blockhouse, a little-known action that nonetheless is listed among the regiment's battle honors. The "battle" occurred in July 1780 while Wayne, then in command of the First and Second Pennsylvania Brigades, about two thousand troops in all, was foraging for cattle in Bergen County, New Jersey, when they came across a blockhouse that had been constructed and manned by loyalists. Wayne was always looking for opportunities for offensive action and decided to capture it. Finding that the blockhouse was able to withstand the fire from his light artillery pieces, he decided to assault it with infantry. After the troops crossed the abatis and pickets that surrounded the blockhouse, they discovered that the only way into the structure was through a single subterranean passage wide enough for only one man to pass through at a time. With the men milling

---

[202] General Orders, 1 March 1780 and Col. Thomas Craig to George Washington, 1 March 1780, *PGW/RWS*, XXIV: 606–08.

about the blockhouse and casualties mounting without any prospect of success, Wayne prudently called off the attack, having sustained sixty-nine casualties including three officers and achieving no effect.[203]

The most significant event of the year in came in late September when the treason of Benedict Arnold, who was commanding the sensitive post at West Point, was uncovered. Washington rushed Wayne's two Pennsylvania brigades to West Point to prevent the British from exploiting the situation and soon moved his headquarters nearby to New Windsor a few miles north of West Point. He remained there for the winter but sent the bulk of the army back to Jockey Hollow. Wayne, in temporary command of the Pennsylvania troops in the absence of St. Clair, was uneasy about the condition and mood of the men. They were angry at three perceived transgressions by the Pennsylvania government: New recruits were being paid bounties in hard currency while veterans were scarcely paid at all and, if so, only in worthless paper currency; provisions and clothing promised when they enlisted were routinely being withheld; many men had enlisted for "three years or the duration of the war" and the state was failing to make any distinction for men who wanted to go home. For most men who had enlisted in the fall of 1777, the expectation that the war would last three years was so remote that many signed "for the duration" thinking this was the shorter period. In other cases, the men were not sure whether they had signed up for one or the other time period because the army's paperwork was a shambles. Most wanted to be mustered out after three years and then reenlist for the cash bounty currently being paid to new recruits.

Two weeks before the army's main body was due at Jockey Hollow, the Third Pennsylvania Regiment arrived to put the huts in order and make arrangements for their arrival. By December 7, the men were reasonably comfortable in the huts, but Wayne was concerned that they had received no alcohol for sixty days except for half a gill of rum two weeks earlier. Rum was considered to be an essential article of issue for soldiers in winter quarters to keep them warm on duty. Wayne grew more worried by the day, writing to Col. Francis Johnston of the Fifth Pennsylvania, "I sincerely

---

[203] Dr. H. H. Burleigh, "The Blockhouse at Bergen Wood," address given March 3, 1965. United Empire of Loyalists' Association of Canada, http://www.uelac.org/PDF/The-Block-House-in-Bergen-Wood.pdf.

wish the Ides of January was come and past. I am not superstitious, but can't help cherishing disagreeable ideas about that period."[204]

Late in the evening on January 1, 1781, most of the officers were in their huts hosting parties for colleagues about to depart for home. Congress had voted in October to reorder the Pennsylvania Line, consolidating eleven understrength regiments into six. Many officers would be "deranged," and they were understandably upset to be leaving. Lt. Enos Reeves of the Tenth Pennsylvania noted that the evening had begun as pleasantly as possible, beginning with an elegant regimental dinner and entertainment at which all the field and other officers from the regiment, plus a few from the German regiment, were present. The evening did not end as well.[205]

A disorder started in the huts of the Eleventh Pennsylvania around eight o'clock but quieted down until it broke out again an hour later, this time spreading to brigades on both sides of the Pennsylvania camp. Officers immediately turned out to quiet the men to no avail. During the action, two were shot and a third mortally wounded.[206]

Wayne was immediately on the scene and after hearing their grievances pleaded with the mutineers to return to their huts. The men patiently heard him out, but several platoons replied by firing their muskets over his head. Wayne then opened his coat and called out, "If you mean to kill me, shoot me at once. Here's my breast." They replied that it was not their intention to hurt or disturb any officer of the Line, "two or three individuals excepted." With that, the mutineers formed up and began marching out of the camp. About two-thirds of the Pennsylvania soldiers eventually joined the column. Wayne feared that the men might march north toward New York City and join the British. He gathered all the officers and took them ahead of the march out to the main road where they all pledged to sacrifice their lives if necessary to prevent the men from deserting. When the column reached the crossroads, it turned south instead of north. The men had no intention of joining the hated British, but they now planned

---

[204] Quoted in Carl Van Doren, *Mutiny in January*, 35. A gill is approximately one-quarter pint.

[205] John B. Reeves, "Extracts from the Letter-Books of Lieutenant Enos Reeves, of the Pennsylvania Line," *PMHB* 21, no. 1 (1897), 72.

[206] Lt. Francis White of the Tenth was shot through the thigh, Capt. Samuel Tolbert of the Second was shot in the belly, and Capt. Adam Bettin was mortally wounded by a mutineer after Bettin chased him with a spontoon. Cunningham, *The Uncertain Revolution*, 288.

to march to Philadelphia to air their grievances before the state's Supreme Executive Council. Wayne offered to lead the march but was told he could only follow if he wanted. Wayne took two senior officers, Cols. Richard Butler and Walter Stewart, with him and sent the rest of the Pennsylvania officers back to camp under the command of Col. Thomas Craig to take care of the soldiers who had not mutinied and to await further orders.[207]

The assembly marched to Princeton where, ironically, the mutineers arrived on January 3, the date of the battle four years earlier. Pennsylvania president Joseph Reed agreed to meet the mutineers and adjudicate their grievances but would do so in Trenton, not Philadelphia; and on January 9, they began their march westward. The attitude of the mutineers toward their officers during discussions came as a shock. Col. Francis Johnston of the Fifth was so badly treated by his men that he refused to participate in the deliberations of the state commission further unless expressly ordered to do so by Wayne. Other regimental commanders were similarly treated: Craig of the Third was threatened by men with firelocks; Proctor of the artillery was not allowed by his men to produce the men's signed papers before the commission because they knew they had been signed for the duration of the war; the men became so angry with the attitudes of their commanders that shots were fired one evening at Wayne's quarters. In the final settlement, about 1,250 men were discharged, representing over 50 percent of the Pennsylvania Line at the time.[208]

The mutiny was ended, but the contagion began to spread. When regiments of the New Jersey Line mutinied, Washington reached the limits of his tolerance. He refused to negotiate, demanded the unconditional surrender of the mutineers, and ordered Maj. Gen. Robert Howe to march with 600 troops from West Point to New Jersey, a risky strategy because there was no guarantee these troops wouldn't side with the mutineers. On January 27, Howe surrounded the recalcitrant troops, compelled them to surrender, and ordered a dozen mutineers to form a firing squad to execute the ringleaders. This brutal action ended the January mutinies.[209]

There is no record about the impact of the mutiny on junior officers like John Armstrong. Like his seniors, he must have been devastated on that New Year's Day when his men refused to obey his orders. It would have

---

[207] Van Doren, *Mutiny in January*, 46–48.

[208] Ibid., 150, 199.

[209] Ron Chernow, *Alexander Hamilton* (New York: Penguin Books, 2004), 390.

been equally mortifying and a further blow to his self-image as a man of honor and a selfless patriot to learn how many men secretly despised their officers. A final insult to all of them was that the forthcoming reorganization of the Line meant more derangements although John would be spared this indignity. With the mutiny over, but the bitterness of the experience lingering in everyone's mind, the remnants of the Pennsylvania Line were consolidated and reorganized for the forthcoming 1781 campaign. Wayne moved the remaining 1,150 troops back to Pennsylvania, gave the men a sixty-day furlough, and ordered the officers to begin recruiting new soldiers and reenlisting as many recently discharged soldiers as wanted to return to service. The Seventh, Eighth, Ninth, Tenth, and Eleventh Regiments were disbanded and the soldiers redistributed to the six remaining regiments. Craig's Third was sent to Reading, Pennsylvania, to be reconstituted while the other five regiments moved to other locations.[210]

★

The Pennsylvania Line was about to follow the thrust of the war southward. It was alerted in February to reinforce Lafayette who earlier had been sent to Virginia to protect that colony from a British invasion, but Wayne needed more time to recruit and prepare the new force. He expected to have approximately a thousand men under arms, but by May, only eight hundred were available to move south. The six regiments on paper were consolidated into two battalions of eight companies under the command of Colonels Stewart and Butler, the latter to whom John Armstrong was assigned. Before they began the move, however, another mutiny occurred. This time, the cause was dissatisfaction among the newly recruited troops about being paid in current banknotes without their depreciated value being offset. Neither Wayne nor his officers were in any mood for compromise or negotiations. Like Washington in January, he'd had enough and determined to suppress any further instance of mutiny, rebellion, or indiscipline in the ranks. Wayne convened a general court-martial, and of twenty men tried, seven were found guilty and sentenced to death. Wayne's disgruntled force finally departed York on May 26 and joined Lafayette at Fredericksburg, Virginia, twelve days later.[211]

---

[210] Van Doren, *Mutiny in January*, 202–03.
[211] Ibid., 234–236.

At last reinforced with good troops under a proven leader, Lafayette was now able to confront Cornwallis. The British general had been advancing westward toward Charlottesville to deprive the Americans of their food and supply magazines, but with Lafayette's more potent force in the field, he retreated back to Richmond, Lafayette following closely behind. The parties clashed on June 26, prior to which Lafayette, emulating Washington, had formed his own light infantry corps, augmented by cavalry. Reinforced by Butler's battalion, the force caught up with Cornwallis's rear guard near Williamsburg where a brief cavalry skirmish took place. Wayne, who had been following Butler with the rest of his brigade, pushed several companies forward to support the light infantry and cavalry. Cornwallis deployed his entire force to his rear guard, but no further fighting occurred. The engagement cost each side about thirty casualties. On the Fourth of July, the troops celebrated the fifth anniversary of American independence. The Pennsylvanians were in good spirits—they considered their operations to have saved Virginia from being overrun by Cornwallis.[212]

Meanwhile in New York City, Clinton felt threatened by Washington who had been reinforced by the French army under the command of General Rochambeau and ordered Cornwallis to send some units northward. Although he was irritated at this force reduction at the time when he was being pressed hard by Lafayette, Cornwallis dutifully complied and began to move his troops to Jamestown en route to Portsmouth where they would load on ships and return to New York. Lafayette saw an opportunity to strike while he was crossing the James River. Believing that the bulk of British troops had crossed over the river and that only a rear guard remained on the near side, Lafayette sent Wayne forward to attack it. Wayne sent Stewart's battalion and the light infantry corps forward to the Green Spring farm within half a mile of the British outposts on the river. Cornwallis realized what Lafayette was planning to do and had prepared a trap of his own. Having sent only part of his cavalry and the heavy baggage across the river, Cornwallis prepared to pounce on the advancing Wayne.

Wayne spent most of the afternoon of July 6 driving back British cavalry patrols and infantry pickets. Cornwallis resisted ordering a general attack that would almost certainly have crushed him while waiting to determine if it was an opportunity worth taking. Shortly before five o'clock, Butler's

---

[212] Henry P. Johnston, *The Yorktown Campaign and the Surrender of Cornwallis* (Freeport, NY: Books for Libraries Press, original 1881; reprinted 1971), 55–56.

battalion arrived to reinforce Wayne. Cornwallis now saw his opportunity and struck. As Cornwallis's men marched out of the woods where they had been concealed, Wayne realized he was outnumbered by more than five to one. Knowing that a retreat would likely be disastrous and that to wait simply for the shock of the enemy advance would likewise be a disaster, he chose the only remaining course of action that held a glimmer of hope.

In a move that was vintage Wayne, he attacked when almost any other man would have turned and fled. The Pennsylvania troops surged forward under a fire of musketry and grapeshot to within seventy yards of the enemy. Both combatants then came to a standstill, and for fifteen minutes, a sharp and well-contested action took place. As Lafayette moved forward to support Wayne, mounts began to be shot down from underneath the field officers, and all the artillery horses were killed in the fire. Six or seven Pennsylvania officers trying to save the American artillery pieces that were now without the means to be moved were wounded as well. Soon, Wayne's right flank was turned, and his men began slowly to withdraw through the swampy ground surrounding the battlefield. Only the lateness of the hour prevented the British from pursuing him to seal the victory. American casualties were considerable: four sergeants and twenty-five soldiers were killed and five captains, one captain lieutenant, four lieutenants, seven sergeants, and eighty-two soldiers wounded. Two cannons were also lost. The British suffered seventy-five casualties, including five officers. The Battle of Green Spring was John Armstrong's last major battlefield experience of the Revolution.[213]

By September, the news that Washington was marching south to Virginia with the main army electrified the command. Wayne's brigade moved to Williamsburg to await Washington's arrival, and on September 14, its entirety was paraded in the commander-in-chief's honor. Afterward, every officer in the command, including John Armstrong, had the opportunity to meet him personally. All the Pennsylvania officers went in a body to his house in Williamsburg where he stood in the door to receive them. According to Ensign Ebenezer Denny, "Officers all pay their respects to the Commander-in-Chief; those who are not personally known,

[213] Ibid., 61–67. In the Armstrong Papers at the Indiana Historical Society is a letter book dating from the revolutionary era. John copied Lafayette's division order published the day after the Battle of Green Spring that described the battle. There are no personal comments, but the entry indicates it was an event he wanted to remember.

their names given by General Hand and General Wayne. He stands in the door, takes every man by the hand—the officers all pass in, receiving his salute and shake."[214]

Wayne's brigade, part of von Steuben's division composed of 4,300 French and American soldiers, departed Williamsburg on its march to Yorktown on September 28. The 800 men that had left Pennsylvania in May had by this time dwindled to 550. Upon arrival at the heavily fortified British-controlled York River port, they began digging the first parallel trench opposite the British defense line, and the siege began. There would be no fighting for the Pennsylvanians at Yorktown, only hard work constructing trenches and bearing up under British counterbombardment. On the night of October 11, von Steuben's division was in the trenches when an artillery exchange ensued. A shell landed close to von Steuben who threw himself down into a trench. Wayne, who was nearby, stumbled over his body and fell on top of him. Von Steuben merely laughed and said, "Ah ha Wayne, you cover your general's retreat in the best manner possible."[215]

When the British surrendered on October 19, John Armstrong was among the spectators watching them march into an open field and deposit their muskets and regimental colors into a large pile. Denny noted that one of the tangible benefits of the surrender was the British store of clothing and equipment that now belonged to the Americans, a portion of which amounting to sixty dollars was furnished to each American officer.[216]

★

It had been nearly five years since John had left Sunbury. He could not possibly have imagined on that victorious day that the war would continue for two more years. The euphoria of Yorktown lasted barely two weeks before new orders were issued directing the Pennsylvania Line to march south to augment the army of Gen. Nathanael Greene, no longer the army's quartermaster, but the commander of all Continental Army

---

[214] Ebenezer Denny, *Military Journal of Major Ebenezer Denny: An Officer in the Revolutionary and Indian Wars* (Philadelphia: J. B. Lippincott & Co. for the Historical Society of Pennsylvania, 1859; republished by Forgotten Books, 2012), 39.

[215] Johnston, *The Yorktown Campaign*, 141.

[216] Denny, *Military Journal*, 45.

troops in the Carolinas. The force departed Williamsburg on the first of November under Maj. Gen. St. Clair with Wayne as second-in-command, a situation Wayne no doubt heartily detested. The march to South Carolina took nearly two months to complete, but according to Denny was "easy, regular marching; roads generally good, through sandy country." The force arrived at Greene's headquarters at the oddly named location "Round O," a distance of approximately 35–40 miles northwest of Charleston on January 4, 1782. Wayne was detached with a small force to conduct an independent campaign against the small British force in Georgia while the remainder of the troops under St. Clair, after a brief rest, continued on to reinforce the siege at Charleston. The rigors of the march and growing health problems evidently reduced the size of the Pennsylvania force more than their few desultory skirmishes with the British around Charleston. By the second week in March, the force was consolidated into two battalions.[217]

An officer in the Second Battalion, Lt. John Tilden, recorded many interactions between the Pennsylvania troops with the officers of Lee's Legion, who were also involved in operations around Charleston. Here, John Armstrong was once again reunited with his brother in the spring of 1782. James Armstrong by this time a captain, had served in the Carolinas for about a year, participating in numerous skirmishes with the British cavalry and fighting with Lee in major battles at Guildford Courthouse and Eutaw Springs as well as several minor ones at Quinby Bridge and Fort Cornwallis where he played a major role in arranging the surrender of American loyalist leader Col. Thomas Browne. He was captured by the British near Dorchester Courthouse in December 1781 when his horse stumbled and spent time on a prison ship in Charleston Harbor until he was exchanged, probably in March or April of 1782.

Rumors of negotiations with the British to surrender Charleston in return for a safe passage home largely put an end to active operations

---

[217] Ibid., 46. The march probably was not as easy as Denny stated. Typical of the journey was a stretch from November 19–23 when the men marched nineteen, fourteen, fifteen, and fourteen miles each day. When they got to South Carolina, the roads were rougher and the terrain wetter. On January 1, they crossed twenty swamps and creeks, "many deep." See also "Itinerary of the Pennsylvania Line from Pennsylvania to South Carolina, 1781–1782," *PMHB* 36, no. 3 (1912), 273–92 and John Bell Tilden, "Extracts from the Journal of Lieutenant John Bell Tilden, Second Pennsylvania Line, 1781–1782," *PMHB* 19, no. 2 (1895), 222.

in the fall of 1782. By November, with the surrender of Charleston looming and the death toll due to disease and poor diet climbing, Greene sent many Pennsylvanians home and consolidated the remainder into a single battalion. A group that departed Charleston by ship in November probably included John Armstrong. When Charleston finally surrendered in December, the remainder of the Pennsylvanians quickly followed them back to Philadelphia.

★

The final chapter of John Armstrong's Revolutionary War service began with his arrival at Lancaster, Pennsylvania, in late December. Almost immediately, he again found himself under arrest and facing a court-martial, this time charged with being absent without leave. While supervising repairs to a post in Lancaster, he was short of materials and applied for leave until more could be procured although his doing so is disputed in the charges. When he returned from this absence, he changed the duty roster, angering several junior officers who then lodged a complaint against him. A Lieutenant Martin stated that Armstrong failed to perform his duty as officer of the day because of an "engagement to drink tea with some of the ladies the following evening." Having just returned from a hard year in South Carolina, Armstrong must have been stung by the charges made by officers who had little or no combat service. In a letter addressed to them dated February 26, 1783, Armstrong wrote, "I did not suppose any gentlemen, in particular brother officers, capable of hurting the feelings of another in the manner you have wounded mine. . . . No, you have invented a method to impugn my character and wound my feelings." His accusers apparently used the language of this letter as the basis for an additional charge of "conduct unbecoming an officer and a gentleman." [218]

A general court-martial convened in Philadelphia on May 22 to hear the evidence against him. Col. Richard Butler testified that he had assigned Armstrong on December 23, 1782, to repair the barracks at Lancaster and that this was done satisfactorily. A Major Greene stated that

---

[218] Armstrong to his accusers, February 26, 1783, PJA. This is the best-documented of Armstrong's three courts-martial. The Armstrong Papers contain proceedings of the trial, dated May 22, 1783, Armstrong's statement to the court, dated June 10, 1683, and letters from William Henderson, Allan McLane, and Daniel Broadhead, May 21 and June 1, 1783, PJA.

Armstrong was also acting at times as adjutant at Carlisle, Pennsylvania. Armstrong, in a statement to the court, blamed the entire affair on one of the junior officers who instigated the signing of a complaint by ten others, pointing out that of that number, only two of the officers were in attendance at the court. He explained that his absence from Lancaster was because he had no materials to affect the repairs he was responsible for, that the duty roster problem was caused by his volunteering for duty on that day but remembered belatedly that he had another engagement, and that he had served honorably for seven years in combat while his accusers had no field service. He then entered into evidence three letters from Col. Daniel Brodhead of the First Pennsylvania Regiment, Maj. Allen McLane, and Capt. William Henderson of the Third and Twelfth Pennsylvania Regiments, attesting to his good character and exemplary service during the war. The verdict of the court was announced in the general orders for June 16, 1783; charges brought against Armstrong were unfounded. He was acquitted with honor.[219]

Of the more than one thousand courts-martial conducted by the Continental Army during the seven-year war, John Armstrong's name stands out as the only officer to have been tried three times. It was probably not a record of which he boasted in later years, but his familiarity with the court-martial system would prove beneficial a decade later.[220]

During the month of Armstrong's acquittal, most soldiers and officers in the army with the exception of the troops with Washington at Newburgh, New York, were given a six-month furlough with the expectation that their leaves of absence would become discharges upon the ratification of the ongoing peace treaty with Great Britain being held in France. Soldiers in the Pennsylvania Line had recently received three months of salary valued at twenty shillings in hard currency but worth only a tenth that amount in the inflated Pennsylvania currency. Several recruits at the depot in Lancaster became enraged at this "dishonest treatment" and traveled sixty miles to Philadelphia where they joined with more discontented soldiers at the local barracks. On June 20, approximately four hundred soldiers, many fortified with liquor from the local taverns, surrounded the state house in Philadelphia, home to both Congress and the Pennsylvania Supreme

---

[219] General Orders, 16 June 1783, *Writings of George Washington*, XXVII: 16 (*WGW*)

[220] James C. Neagles, *Summer Soldiers: A Survey and Index of Revolutionary War Courts-Martial* (Salt Lake City: Ancestry Inc., 1986), passim.

Executive Council, to demand redress. Alexander Hamilton was named to a committee of the Congress to deal with the matter, and he went across to the state house to deliver an ultimatum to John Dickenson, now the president of the Supreme Executive Council. It must guarantee the safety of Congress or else it would relocate to a safer location, which it did to Princeton the next day. The mutiny quickly collapsed.[221]

Unknowingly, John Armstrong, still in Lancaster, played a small role in this mutiny. One of the ringleaders was a junior officer named John Sullivan. On June 25, he wrote to Armstrong, who was acting in an administrative capacity at the barracks, "I shall esteem it a particular favour if you should take the trouble to send me to a place I shall appoint my port-manteau and some loose cloathes dispers'e thro' my room." Two days later, Armstrong received another note with instructions to release his belongings to his servant and to inform others concerning the settlement of his accounts and sale of his horses. In the future, he could be reached at the home of a publican in Cork. Unaware that Sullivan was being sought for his actions in the mutiny, he forwarded the items without hesitation. He might have wondered about one sentence in the letter, however, that read, "As a soldier and a man of honor I defy slander itself to assess my character and I most cordially wish my enemies and those of my brave little associates all the blessings they deserve. J. Sullivan." Given his luck with the military justice system, Armstrong was no doubt glad not to have been court-martialed again for aiding and abetting the escape of a wanted mutineer.[222]

Although he remained some weeks or months more at Lancaster, John Armstrong's Revolutionary War service was over. He was mustered out in December as a brevet captain when Congress formally dissolved the army. Many states had awarded certificates for bounty land on the western frontier. Not wanting to return home in rags, it was not unusual for the men to sell their certificates immediately to raise money for their homeward journeys. In what would become a precursor to a lifelong pursuit for property ownership, John was a ready buyer of these certificates. By the

---

[221] Charles J. Stillé, *Major General Anthony Wayne and the Pennsylvania Line in the Continental Army* (Philadelphia: J. B. Lippincott, 1893), 297–298 and Chernow, *Alexander Hamilton*, 181–82.

[222] Sullivan to Armstrong, June 25 and 27, 1783. PJA.

end of 1783, he had a list of thirty names of soldiers who had conveyed their land to him.[223]

In one of his last acts as commander-in-chief of the Continental Army, George Washington sent a list of the names of sixteen officers to Congress meeting in Annapolis. He had long urged that body to consider raising a small peacetime military establishment for the newly independent nation and wished before resigning his commission to recommend who should serve in it. "In addition to the testimony which accompanies them," he wrote, "I can only add mine, that most of the gentlemen, whose names are on the list, are personally known to me as some of the best officers who were in the Army." Included in the list of names were those of James and John Armstrong of Northumberland County, Pennsylvania.[224]

When John finally departed Lancaster, he could look back in wonder and pride at all he had seen and done in the Revolution. He had participated in major battles at Princeton, Short Hills, Brandywine, Germantown, Monmouth, Stony Point, and Green Spring; at the sieges of Yorktown and Charleston; and in countless skirmishes and minor engagements. He had endured the two terrible winters at Valley Forge and Morristown, the awful mutiny of the Pennsylvania Line in 1781, and seven arduous years of hard service, poor food and clothing, and little or no pay. But he had also distinguished himself in the eyes of men like Lafayette, Maxwell, Wayne, McLane, and of course, Washington. He had formed fast friendships with fellow officers who would serve with him again in years to come and would know key players in the future of the country's military establishment personally.

He was no longer the second son of a yeoman farmer scraping out a living on the far frontier of Pennsylvania. He was now in his own eyes an officer and a gentleman of the Continental Army, a founding member of the Society of the Cincinnati, and the first officer from Pennsylvania to affix his signature to the Society's roster for that state. He was above all else a soldier. In this profession, he would strive to make his mark in the world.[225]

---

[223] Document dated "1783," PJA.

[224] Letter to the President of Congress, 21 December 21, 1783, *WGW*, XXVII: 278–80.

[225] Genealogy Trails, "Members of the Pennsylvania Society of the Cincinnati, The Order in Which They subscribed, in December, 1783," http://genealogytrails.com/main/societyofthecincinnati.html#PENN.

5

Wyoming, 1783–1784

We have dispersed the Connecticut party,
but our own people we cannot.
—Justices Thomas Hewitt, David
Mead, and Robert Martin to
Pennsylvania's Supreme Executive Council,
August 7, 1784[226]

At war's end, John Armstrong was a mature twenty-eight-year-old officer who, like many of his colleagues, had known only the military during his adult life. The Continental Army formally ceased to exist in late 1783, and Armstrong wanted to continue military service through a proposed "peace establishment."[227]

Armstrong had considerable family in Northumberland County to keep him company as he contemplated his future. His brother Hamilton and sister and brother-in-law, Nancy and John McAdams, were there, along with his father, stepmother, and presumably his younger stepsisters Elizabeth and Mary. The elder Armstrong died within a short time of John's return. Thomas Armstrong's will dated September 25, 1783, stipulated

---

[226] *PA*1: X: 628–30.

[227] Armstrong's notebooks include two drafts of undated and unaddressed correspondence indicating his interest in continuing military service that were apparently written to mentors with influence in selecting officers should Congress authorize the formation of such a military force (PJA).

that his wife, Magdalena, have rights to his estate for the duration of her lifetime. John was named successor heir to his father's estate, through which he eventually inherited a lot in the town of Northumberland. Having previously purchased another lot from his father and stepmother in April 1781, he may have considered staying in Northumberland should other options not be available to him. In instructions to the executors of his father's estate the following winter, he directed them to rent out farmland he also apparently held, stipulating that another individual might have the upper fields, "but the lower one I will reserve for myself."[228]

John received an immediate inheritance of £30 in the form of forgiveness of debt he owed his father. In all likelihood, John's full siblings, Hamilton, Nancy, and James received the same amount, as did one stepsister, Mary, although the other, Elizabeth Wilson, was only to receive five shillings and was obviously not in her father's good graces. Why John was named as the successor heir rather than his older brother James is a matter of conjecture. James, having served in the South in Lee's Legion, eventually settled in Georgia. Perhaps at the time, John appeared to be the oldest sibling with strong ties to the area who could look after family interests. Perhaps too that perceived slight might have served as an incentive for James to join fellow Legion officers who made their way south after the war.[229]

The Northumberland County that Armstrong had left prior to going to war had changed dramatically in his absence. Settlers along the North and West Branches of the Susquehanna had lived in fear of attack by Native American warriors in alliance with British Tory units as whole townships were evacuated, homesteads and property destroyed, livestock plundered, and settlers attacked and killed. Active warfare threatened outlying areas for the better part of five years, which, as Herbert C. Bell notes, caused

---

[228] Northumberland County Book of Wills: 5: I: 25; Northumberland County Book of Deeds: B247, B272; John Armstrong to William Antes, January 16, 1784, PJA. Armstrong's estate inventory lists ownership of a lot in the town of Northumberland but also lists livestock and farming equipment. The Federal Supply tax roster for Mahoning Township, Northumberland County in 1782 notes his possession of 50 acres of land within that division. PA3: XIX: 508.

[229] The names of Hamilton, Nancy, and James were grouped together in Armstrong's will; but the amount due to them is missing in the document copied in Northumberland County probate records. They were likely bequeathed £30, a sum equal to the amount allotted to stepsister Mary and John's £30 debt forgiveness. Northumberland County Book of Wills: 5: I: 25.

more distress to inhabitants in that area than the large British Army of occupation caused in the East. Settlers north of the Susquehanna and along the West Branch were forced to seek refuge at Sunbury and points farther down the river during the "Great Runaway" of 1778 and "Little Runaway" the following year while their abandoned houses and farms were burned to the ground and violence continued. Not until after the war's end did settlement begin again and the county regain its pattern of growth.[230]

★

The Wyoming Valley was the scene of exceptional violence and destruction during the war. As settlers returned to the valley to reclaim their lands, the old conflict between Yankees and Pennamites again came to the fore. Disputes between the two factions erupted within the valley itself and evolved not only into armed conflict between the parties but also discord between factions of Pennsylvania's government. Ironically, it provided John Armstrong the opportunity to pursue his military career although in a very different manner from anything he had experienced during the Revolution.

During the initial war years, two Continental Army companies were raised to provide for the valley's defense; but they were later ordered to join Washington's forces following the disastrous New York City campaign, leaving the area's protection to the local militia. Lt. Col. Zebulon Butler returned home on furlough from his unit, the Third Connecticut Regiment, in early June 1778 to find the town in a state of alarm at the growing fear of attack by Tory and Indian forces in the isolated valley. Making his way to York where the Continental Congress was meeting, he appealed to that body for the return of two independent Wyoming companies that were then stationed at Lancaster. Their repositioning was approved, the units were amalgamated into one, and the men were reassigned to the valley to protect their families and property.[231]

The reorganization came none too soon. Affairs came to a head later that month when Maj. John Butler (no relation to Lt. Col. Zebulon Butler), veteran of the French and Indian War from upstate New York who had served in the British Indian Department, led his "Butler's Rangers," a

230 Bell, *History of Northumberland County*, 518.
231 Glenn F. Williams, *Year of the Hangman: George Washington's Campaign Against the Iroquois* (Yardley, Pennsylvania: Westholme Publishing, LLC, 2005), 107–08, 114; Ousterhout, "Frontier Vengeance," 330–63.

force of colonists allied with Britain with about seven hundred primarily Seneca warriors, downriver from Tioga Point into the valley. Along the way, they overwhelmed settlers in smaller fortifications before reaching a larger one at Forty Fort, the installation so named to note the original forty Connecticut settlers who had built it.

The Battle of Wyoming has been well recorded by historians but is nevertheless important to note here, if only because of its effect on the postwar condition of the valley and Connecticut settlers' claim to the land, paid for by the lives of its men. On July 3, 1778, the valley was the scene of one of the bloodiest battles of the war, the aftermath of which sparked the "Great Runaway" downriver to the rest of Northumberland County and greater Susquehanna. The battle is also known as the "Wyoming Massacre" for good reason. Offered terms of surrender by the Rangers, defenders Lt. Col. Zebulon Butler and Lt. Col. Nathan Dennison had no intention of surrendering the fort. Misreading signs of the numbers and actions of the approaching force, the 375–500 men at Forty Fort confidently advanced toward Ranger positions in battlefield formation with periodic firing to draw out enemy action. The bulk of Major Butler's warriors and Rangers, concealed in dense thickets and swampland, waited until the opportune time and then attacked with full fury, overwhelming the advancing Americans.[232]

Once the battle itself ended and the Wyoming men realized that their only option was retreat, the real horror began. As the men fled, warriors pursued them mercilessly. Most were hunted down, killed, and scalped, even as they attempted to surrender. Survivors later claimed that few actually fell in battle and that most were killed in its aftermath. Although casualty estimates vary widely, Glenn Williams sums up the discrepancy in figures thusly: "Regardless of how one counts the corpses, it was an overwhelming Indian and Tory victory."[233]

---

[232] Williams, *Year of the Hangman*, 127–29; Oscar Jewell Harvey, *A History of Wilkes-Barre, Luzerne County, Pennsylvania* (Wilkes-Barre: Raeder Press, 1909), II: 1005.

[233] Casualty estimates differ considerably. Differing sources list figures from 160 up to approximately 400 Wyoming soldiers lost and 3–80 Tory/Indian allies killed. See Williams, *Year of the Hangman*, 133, with detailed account of the circumstances surrounding the battle, 99–138. Figures are also noted in Ernest Cruikshank, *The Story of Butler's Rangers and the Settlement of Niagara* (Welland, Ontario: Tribune Printing House, 1893), 47–48 and Charles Miner, *History of Wyoming in a Series of Letters from Charles Miner to His Son, William*

When the Rangers' regular forces eventually departed the valley, the last vestige of control over their Native American allies disappeared. Survivors of the battle itself, their families, and valley neighbors fled to safety in the wake of homesteads burned to the ground and resulting carnage. Peace was eventually restored by a retaliatory expedition under the command of Gen. John Sullivan who proceeded up the North Branch of the Susquehanna the following year where he joined the army of Gen. James Clinton to attack the Iroquois in their own territory in New York. In spite of this and other punitive actions, the Pennsylvania frontier remained a dangerous place, and attacks upon isolated settlers continued. As late as the summer of 1782 when the war was generally over in the East, alienated Indian nations, for whom the real issue was one of survival rather than maintaining British colonialism, were still launching attacks in Northumberland County.[234]

★

Meanwhile, the question of state jurisdiction of the Wyoming Valley lay unanswered. In November 1781, the Continental Congress turned the matter over to the Court of Commissioners who met in Trenton the following year. In the decision rendered on December 30, 1782, that body ruled that Pennsylvania held legal claim to the territory but left unresolved the issue of individual land ownership. Pennsylvania regarded the Trenton Decree not only as a settlement of state jurisdiction but also of the titles to the land.[235]

Following the Sullivan campaign, a combined militia and Connecticut regulars manned the garrison in the valley. Given the dispute regarding state sovereignty, however, Congress decided to replace that unit with one aligned with neither Connecticut nor Pennsylvania, and in December, 1780, Washington ordered a unit from the New Jersey line to go into the

---

Penn Miner, Esq. (Philadelphia: J. Crissy, 1845), 228.

[234] See Harvey, *A History of Wilkes-Barre*, II: 984–1038 for detailed accounts of the event and its aftermath and Ousterhout, *Frontier Vengeance*, 350–51. From July 23 to August 8, 1782, twenty-one settlers were killed or captured. All those who lived above Northumberland on both branches of the Susquehanna were planning to move into the towns and had given up all thoughts of putting in fall crops.

[235] Frederick W. Gnichtel, *The Trenton Decree of 1782 and the Pennamite War* (Trenton: The Trenton Historical Society, 1920), 7–10.

valley to replace the existing force. Following the Court of Commissioners' decision, John Dickinson, president of the State of Pennsylvania, directed Capts. Philip Shrawder and Thomas Robinson of the Pennsylvania Rangers to assume command of the Wyoming garrison. When the Connecticut settlers learned that the two companies of Pennsylvania Rangers sent to replace Continental troops at war's end were there not only to guard against Indian incursions but also to protect Pennsylvania landholders' interests, the embers of unrest were again ignited. Thus began a series of events that eventually pitted not only Yankees against Pennamites but also Pennsylvania governmental agencies against one another.[236]

With the arrival of the Rangers, the military represented the only governmental presence in the valley, Connecticut jurisdiction having been abolished and Pennsylvania civil authority not yet in place. Captain Robinson wrote Dickenson in early May that peacemaking efforts between soldiers and inhabitants appeared to be working despite wrangling disputes and the litigious nature of the populace. He had concerns about crop planting that spring and what actions the military should take when those with opposing claims came to blows. Leaders of citizens' committees on both sides corresponded heavily with their benefactors in Connecticut and Pennsylvania legislatures.[237]

The atmosphere eventually turned sour, heralding the resumption of the struggle between Connecticut and Pennsylvania landholders that produced a level of bloodshed surpassing that of previous Pennamite-Yankee conflicts. Land and resources were already greatly reduced in the wake of the destruction wrought during the war years. Later, catastrophic

---

[236] Harvey, *A History of Wilkes-Barre*, II: 1201, 1224, 1227. See also Oscar Jewell Harvey and Ernest Gray Smith, *A History of Wilkes-Barre, Luzerne County, Pennsylvania* (Wilkes-Barre: Raeder Press, 1927), III: 1271, 1315. Provisions of the Constitution of the State of Pennsylvania provided the framework for a government of multiple branches that included the following: a legislative assembly of representatives from Pennsylvania's counties, a Supreme Executive Council consisting of twelve members that administered the business of the government, a president selected by both the assembly and council, a judiciary appointed by the assembly, and a council of censors that reviewed actions of the government and acted to "censure" activities not in accordance with the state constitution. All these institutions would eventually play a part in the saga of the Wyoming conflict.

[237] Samuel Hazard, ed., *Pennsylvania Archives, Published Series*, Series 1, Vol. 10 (Philadelphia: Joseph Severns and Company, 1854), 23, 48, 99–100.

flooding left much of the valley in ruin; and houses, cleared fields, crops, and livestock became items of contention over which settlers fought and died. Tensions that lay beneath the surface were compounded by the absence of a unified effective authority. Verbal sniping, physical altercations, armed conflict, injury, and death would haunt the valley for years to come.[238]

Affairs nevertheless remained manageable during the summer of 1783. A Pennsylvania commission had been sent to the valley that spring to take statements from the citizens' committees representing both Pennsylvania and Connecticut interests. Pennsylvania claimants proposed a plan that was understandably rejected by those from Connecticut that called for immediate relinquishment of half a Connecticut settler's land, with the forfeiture of the second half within eleven months, with slight concessions to widows of those who had fallen in the war. Adding fuel to the fire, in September, the Pennsylvania Assembly divided the valley into townships according to its own specifications and appointed local magistrates without the Connecticut claimants' consent.[239]

Meanwhile, Pennsylvania's Supreme Executive Council directed the creation of a special unit to replace the Rangers. This force was to consist of one major, two captains, four subalterns and men who had served in Pennsylvania forces during the war. Maj. James Moore was appointed to the command, and Captain Shrawder remained in the valley, reenlisting his company while Capt. John Christie recruited a company near Philadelphia. They would occupy the present garrison, now called Fort Dickinson.[240]

★

Armstrong's prospects for employment and for continuing his military career brightened at this development, and he received a commission as a first lieutenant in the Corps of Infantry on September 25, 1783, joining Captain Shrawder's company. For his services, he received £13 pay and subsistence per month.[241]

Captain Christie's company arrived in the valley on October 29, and controversy erupted over the forced billeting of parties of soldiers of both companies with inhabitants of the valley despite room available to them

---

[238] Moyer, *Wild Yankees*, 56–59.
[239] Miner, *History of Wyoming*, 318–28; Moyer, *Wild Yankees*, 43.
[240] *PA1*: X: 99–100; Miner, *History of Wyoming*, 330.
[241] *PA5*: IV: 822.

within the garrison, as well as reported rude and insolent behavior on the part of the troops toward the settlers. Tempers had already risen at the acts of an appointed magistrate to the area. The choice of Alexander Patterson was hardly without bias. He had previously headed the citizens committee representing Pennsylvania settlers, but his arrest of Lt. Col. Zebulon Butler on September 24 following Butler's expression of disgust at the treatment of some of his fellow Connecticut settlers further fueled Yankee resentment. Butler's arrest was pivotal in the relationship between Patterson, representative of the Pennamite faction, and those individuals responsible for law enforcement and judicial procedure of Northumberland County in Sunbury and foretold a pattern for events to come. Lacking an arrest warrant, Sherriff Henry Antes initially refused to hold Butler on charges brought by Patterson. Two newly appointed Wyoming justices then made out a warrant directing Antes to take Butler into custody; but the colonel, having secured bail, was soon set free by the sheriff.[242]

Other incidents followed. On October 31, Captain Christie assisted Patterson in the arrest of eleven citizens, holding some for over a week without arraignment or trial. Whether Armstrong participated in the arrest of the settlers is unknown nor is how he dealt with a situation that grew increasingly uncomfortable as time went on.

Connecticut settlers did not take Patterson's insults lying down, setting forth injustices and seeking redress through petitions to the Pennsylvania and Connecticut Assemblies as well as to Congress. Accordingly, the Pennsylvania Assembly sent a four-member commission from neighboring Northampton County to Wyoming to investigate the situation in late December. Although the subject of later disagreement in the assembly when depositions from claimants were reviewed, the petition of the Connecticut settlers was effectively denied through a committee report of the commission's findings on January 23, 1784, that it had found no evidence that irregularities had been authorized by Patterson the previous fall.[243]

At about this time, Lieutenant Armstrong's name began to be mentioned in correspondence between Major Moore and President Dickinson as a courier between Wyoming and Philadelphia. In addition to

---

[242] Miner, *History of Wyoming*, 331–33.
[243] Ibid., 337–38; 339–40.

his task of collecting pay for the troops, he undoubtedly filled the president in on details that could not be put into writing.[244]

Armstrong's trips to Philadelphia were significantly curtailed during the early spring of 1784 when floods ravaged the valley, adding to the misery of Yankee and Pennamite claimants alike. He described the scene in a letter of March 21 to his friend Dr. Reading Beatty:

> On the night of the 15th the river rose 10 feet in thirty-six Minutes, over flowed all this country, swept off greatest part of the Houses in the settlement with Horses Cattle & Grain. Several Houses with families in them were swept four Miles down the river, and landed safe on higher ground. Some saved themselves by climbing trees, where they continued for several hours. We were obliged to evacuate the Fort in which the water was four feet deep. The Ground at this time for several miles is covered with Ice four & five feet thick. What will become of the poor inhabitants God only knows . . . I sincerely Pitty the Inhabitants, the women & children in a particular manner.[245]

Compounding the misery inflicted by natural disaster that spring, garrison soldiers were tasked with the removal of fences, in essence destroying previously drawn boundaries in favor of those reformulated by Pennsylvania surveys. Connecticut settlers put up resistance, insisting on a legal trial of the issue but declaring that they would yield to a regular and fair judicial decision. Tensions mounted as Connecticut claimants struggled to survive. Yankee leader Col. John Franklin described the conditions:

> The greatest part of the settlers were in the most distressed situation—numbers having had their horses swept off by the uncommon overflowing of the river Susquehanna in the month of March preceding; numbers were without a shelter, and in a starving condition; but they were not suffered to cut a stick of timber, or make any shelter for their families. They were forbid to draw their nets for fish—their nets were taken from them by the officers of the garrison.

[244] Moore to Dickenson, February 1, 1784. *PA*1: X: 197–98, 207.
[245] Armstrong to Beatty, March 21, 1784, PJA.

The settlers were often dragged out of their beds in the night season by ruffians, and beat in a cruel manner. Complaints were made to the justices, as well as to the commanding officers of the garrison; but to no purpose—they were equally callous to every feeling of humanity.[246]

On May 11, Armstrong was ordered to proceed with fifteen men to Abraham's Plains and to disarm all the Connecticut settlers in that neighborhood. When his party entered the settlement, he found the men generally absent with reports that they were assembling in the hills, planning opposition.[247]

The following days presented a turning point in the relationship between Pennsylvania authorities in Wyoming, the Connecticut claimants, and the state of Pennsylvania itself. Not unexpectedly, accounts of the incident vary widely depending upon the perspectives of the persons reporting. What is certain is this: matters in the valley were tense. Connecticut settlers feared the seizure of their property, and a group was gathering with arms. Pennamite settlers took matters into their own hands and on May 13 and 14 drove 150 Connecticut families from their properties, essentially forcing them from the territory. In his letter to President Dickinson regarding the incident, Major Moore reported that the move was to expel those "conceived too dangerous to be permitted to remain." He noted that from information he had received, the conduct of the Pennsylvania settlers was "marked with the highest degree of Lenity."[248]

Others tell a different story. Miner notes that locals were routed at the point of bayonet "with the most high-handed arrogance" while homesteads burned. About 500 men, women, and children with scarce provisions made the sixty-mile trek eastward through the wilderness, and several died on route or after reaching settlements. When news of this removal reached civilization, Miner notes that popular opinion within the state turned firmly in favor of the displaced claimants and that the incident reinforced

---

[246] John Franklin's unpublished legal brief concerning the Susquehanna Company's case written circa 1794 is cited in Harvey and Smith, *A History of Wilkes-Barre*, III: 1325, 1376; Miner, *History of Wyoming*, 344; *PA*1: XI: 435–36.

[247] Moore to Armstrong, May 11, 1784, PJA; Moore to Dickinson, May 15, 1784, *PA*1: XI: 437–38.

[248] Moore to Dickinson, March 20, 1784, *PA*1: X: 222. Moore to Dickinson, May 15, 1784, *PA*1: XI: 437–38.

the Pennsylvania Assembly's prior decision to dismiss the two companies stationed at Fort Dickinson after the first of June.[249]

It is not clear what role garrison troops played in the May incident. Moore's report to Dickinson indicated that Pennsylvania claimants acted on their own. Yet Harvey and Smith cite a letter attributed to Moore that was written to a friend but also published in both Philadelphia and New Haven papers indicating not only his support but also his "complete approbation so heartily as to make me take a part in it." Clearly, they were more than innocent bystanders in the whole operation. Hearing word of the incident from Connecticut leaders who fled westward to Sunbury rather than eastward toward the Delaware River, Northumberland magistrates John Buyers, Frederick Antes, Christian Gettig, and Robert Martin wrote Dickinson on May 17 that they were at a loss to account for the outrageous conduct of the soldiery. Supreme Court circuit judges were due at Sunbury at the end of the month, and the matter went before the court at that time. Judges Thomas McKean and Jacob Rush issued indictments against Moore and forty-four others for riot and false imprisonment of the Connecticut claimants. They ordered bail for those indicted and appearance at the next session of court. John Armstrong's name appears in the list of the indicted.[250]

The conflict was clearly no longer merely a battle between two opposing groups of settlers; it became a three-way struggle between Connecticut claimants, Pennsylvania settlers and land speculators, and the state of Pennsylvania. Additionally, the affair represented a dangerous conflict of interest that the state allowed to take root among the men appointed to keep the peace. Four Wyoming justices appointed by the state in 1783—Alexander Patterson, John Seely, Henry Shoemaker, and David Mead—claimed land in the Wyoming Valley. Pennamites further undercut the state's ability to control events by gaining the cooperation of garrison officers who were desirous of claiming valley land themselves. Under such circumstances, officials could not serve as impartial umpires in the events that unfolded because they were themselves embroiled in the contest for property and power.[251]

---

[249] Miner, *History of Wyoming*, 344–46. The resolution for troop withdrawal from Wyoming as of June 1, 1784, was passed by the Pennsylvania Assembly on March 25. *PA*1: X: 224.

[250] Harvey and Smith, *A History of Wilkes-Barre*, III: 1383–84, 1389; *PA*1: X: 414.

[251] Moyer notes that Alexander Patterson issued sizable grants to Major Moore and other garrison officers. Moyer, *Wild Yankees*, 45–46; Harvey and Smith, *A History of Wilkes-Barre*, III: 1392. Armstrong apparently held land in

Immediately after the adjournment of the June 4 meeting of the court at Sunbury, Northumberland County sheriff Henry Antes started for Wilkes-Barre with warrants of arrest for all the men indicted the previous month. Upon his arrival he found the men at Fort Dickinson but was refused admittance. When he returned at a later date to execute the warrants, this time accompanied by the county coroner, he was again blocked from entry. When joined by some of the Connecticut men, one of their number was apprehended and beaten in front of the Sunbury officials. Antes realized that he could not fulfill his task without a posse and headed back again to Sunbury.[252]

Those indicted were eventually arrested, and to their total disgust, the act was accomplished by Connecticut claimants Franklin and Swift, who had been deputized by Sheriff Antes. Many charged with inciting riot were found guilty at trials held in November 1784. Issued particularly stiff fines were Major Moore and Henry Shoemaker, a justice of the peace, who were fined £100 and required to pay the costs of prosecution and to give security in the sum of £500 each guaranteeing their good behavior for twelve months. Others found guilty were held to less severe fines but required to post bonds as well. Armstrong, along with other subalterns of the garrison, was acquitted of charges of assault and battery, his only charge. It appears that the lieutenant managed to keep his name clear in this aspect of the morass that had become the Wyoming conflict.[253]

On June 13, Captains Shrawder and Christie were ordered to discharge their respective companies. A considerable number of the men, however, were immediately employed by Patterson who remained in possession of Fort Dickinson. Although fellow lieutenants Read, Ball, and Henderson opted to remain, Armstrong seems to have had enough of the situation even though Patterson himself had promised to pay those who continued with him.[254]

Wyoming, but the date of his acquisition is not known. See Frances Johnston to John Armstrong, October 12, 1791, and Armstrong to Johnston, April 23, 1792, PJA.

[252] Harvey and Smith, *A History of Wilkes-Barre*, III: 1391–92.

[253] The case became moot a short time later. On January 11, 1786, the fines of those found guilty were removed by act of the Pennsylvania Assembly. Miner, *History of Wyoming*, 348; *Minutes of the Supreme Executive Council of Pennsylvania* (Harrisburg: Theodore Fenn and Company, 1853), XIV: 622; Harvey and Smith, *A History of Wilkes-Barre*, III: 1452. Harvey and Smith note "Hamilton? Armstrong," but undoubtedly refer to John.

[254] Harvey and Smith, *A History of Wilkes-Barre*, III: 1389.

Connecticut forces now gathered in the hills at what they dubbed "Fort Lillopee" began to increase as more men returned. Now it was the Yankees' turn for revenge. Well-armed and increasingly impatient in their primitive surroundings, they began making forays into the valley during the latter days of June, and open warfare soon began. On July 20, a party encountered a group of Patterson's levies who opened fire on them, resulting in two deaths on the Yankee side and several wounded men on the other. This incident was quickly followed by another in which a party of about sixty Yankees marched down the west side of the river, dispossessing every settler not holding a Connecticut Claim, driving them to the relative safety of Fort Dickinson. The multiday operation concluded with the garrison resisting capture, the Connecticut claimants forced into retreat, and both sides suffering casualties. Messengers periodically arrived from Northumberland in an attempt to curb hostilities, but their efforts had little effect.[255]

John Armstrong unwittingly found himself in the middle of the conflict. Harvey and Smith speculate that Armstrong, no longer a part of the garrison's force, had traveled up the Susquehanna to Tioga Point to inspect lands in which he was interested. In a deposition given to Pennsylvania Chief Justice Thomas McKean on July 28, he stated that because he was not feeling well, he stopped in Wyoming upon his return to Sunbury on July 12 where he found newly arrived men from Connecticut near Forty Fort and learned that they had been engaged in various acts of harassment, beatings, and theft within the valley. Continuing downstream, he found thirty to forty more armed men waiting for reinforcements in order to launch an operation against Pennsylvania claimants. By the time he reached Fort Dickinson, settlers had already gathered there for protection and were joined days later by others who fled to the enclosure after the arrival of Yankees and subsequent firing on the fort. Armstrong himself was fired on when assisting widows and their children transfer to the safety of the garrison despite a two-hour cease-fire and reported that several family members had been wounded by gunfire in the process. Hostilities had not ceased by his departure on Sunday, July 25.[256]

★

---

[255] Miner, *History of Wyoming*, 347–48.

[256] *PA1*: X: 623–24; Harvey and Smith, *A History of Wilkes-Barre*, III: 1395.

Another John Armstrong now assumed a pivotal role in the history of Wyoming. Many chroniclers of the period do not look particularly kindly on this Armstrong's involvement in the events that followed. As secretary of the executive council, he directed officials at Sunbury on July 24 to "employ every legal means" to investigate the facts of the incident and "to proceed with utmost vigor & impartiality, so that every Person committing an outrage upon the peace of the County and the dignity of the State may be duly punished." Five days later, the council, having reviewed reports from Wyoming regarding the valley's state of affairs, resolved to send Secretary Armstrong and John Boyd, council member from Northumberland County, as commissioners to Wyoming to oversee matters. Sheriff Antes was directed to raise a posse from Northumberland to support militia from neighboring Northampton County consisting of three hundred infantry and twelve to fifteen light dragoons. When Armstrong reached Easton to rendezvous with the force, however, he discovered that only a third of the expected Northampton militia had turned out, and of that number, few were willing to proceed to Wyoming.[257]

When the Sunbury justices arrived in Wyoming, they found Pennamite and Yankee parties continuing their standoff and began negotiations requesting both sides to lay down their arms. Although the Connecticut party agreed to do so, the justices received only evasive answers from Patterson's men who were still occupying the garrison. Frustrated in their attempts to gain common ground with the Pennsylvania party, Justices Thomas Hewitt, David Mead, and Robert Martin wrote to the council "that had it not been through the cruel and irregular conduct of our own people the peace might have been established long since."[258]

Miner says that at this point, the justices permitted the Connecticut claimants to reclaim their arms for self-defense at which time they concentrated their forces at their former post on Abraham's Creek to await the arrival of commissioners Armstrong and Boyd. Arriving on August 8 with the message that they were there to restore peace and to stop the

---

[257] Minutes of the Supreme Executive Council of Pennsylvania, XIV: 167–68. Armstrong, son of Revolutionary War major general John Armstrong who had earlier gained fame of during the French and Indian War, later became a US senator and secretary of war and is generally referred to as John Armstrong Jr.; *PA*1: X: 295,303,304,631; *Minutes of the Supreme Executive Council of Pennsylvania*, XIV: 167–68.

[258] *PA*1: X: 628-30; see also Miner, *History of Wyoming*, 353.

immediate hostilities, the commissioners announced that there was to be a surrender of arms by both parties. Harvey cites Col. John Franklin's account of the circumstances surrounding the surrender of the Connecticut claimants resulting from Armstrong's adaptation of what might be better known as "bait and switch." They were informed that the Northampton militia had taken possession of the fort, that Patterson and others had been made prisoners, and that Yankees who had been forcibly dispossessed of their property were to be reinstated with their possessions. On the next day, Franklin was requested to order his force to assemble under arms. Since Patterson's party had already been disarmed, the commissioners wanted a physical demonstration that Connecticut forces had also submitted to the government's request to surrender their weapons, even though the commissioners stated that they were satisfied by the Connecticut party's earlier show of good conduct and peaceable disposition by laying down their firearms at the request of the Northumberland justices. Franklin continued that the commissioners had *"pledged their honor"* that no advantage would be taken of them. The party would be requested to surrender their arms, some who had warrants against them would be requested to post bail for appearing in court, and weapons would be restored to them within ten days' time.[259]

The event did not unfold as promised. No sooner had the Connecticut party laid down their weapons than Commissioner Armstrong gave the order for the militia to advance, to take up the grounded firearms, and to arrest the claimants. Not only had weapons not been surrendered by Patterson's men, but they also paraded under arms to assume custody of their Connecticut foes. The Connecticut party was eventually marched to confinement, thirty of whom were led southeast to Easton and forty-two westward to the Sunbury jail.[260]

The magistrates witnessing the events were stunned. They had been blindsided by the unexpected turn of events and the betrayal of the Connecticut settlers to whom they had given their pledge of equal justice, a

---

[259] Miner, *History of Wyoming*, 357; John Franklin's brief of 1794 cited in Harvey and Smith, *A History of Wilkes-Barre*, III: 1416–18.

[260] Miner, *History of Wyoming*, 357. Lt. John Armstrong and his brother Hamilton appear to have taken part in the operation launched at the justices' request, their names listed on the muster roll of Capt. John Loudon's Northumberland County volunteers who marched to Wyoming. Thomas Lynch Montgomery, ed., *Pennsylvania Archives Series 6, Vol. 3* (Harrisburg: Harrisburg Publishing Company, 1907), 935–36 and *PA1*: X: 322.

plan that they understood had the approval of the arriving commissioners. Justice Robert Martin appealed to the Council of Censors on August 14, describing in detail what had transpired, concluding, "It appears very clear to us, that the proceedings now at this place are carried on in so unfair, partial, and unlawful manner that we despair of establishing peace and good order in this part of the County."[261]

Once again, disagreements between Northumberland magistrates in Sunbury and Pennamite factions in the valley came to the fore. Prisoner releases began almost immediately upon their arrival at Sunbury as Yankees who posted bail began returning to the valley. In Easton, prisoners managed to escape captivity on September 17, and sixteen made their way back to Wyoming. Returnees managed to obtain ammunition and the weapons that had been taken from them earlier from a storehouse and mounted a brief siege of the garrison.

Lt. John Armstrong and his brother Hamilton were apparently part of the militia unit from Sunbury witnessing this turn of events on August 9, ending any official involvement the Sunbury brothers had in the whole affair. This was, however, not the case for the State of Pennsylvania nor for John Armstrong Jr.

★

On October 1, the Supreme Executive Council ordered a militia force of one hundred men to be drawn from Bucks, Berks, and Northampton Counties to proceed to Wyoming to put down the unrest arising from the return of the Yankee prisoners from Sunbury and Easton; but only forty Berks County militia reported for the operation. Armstrong's militia, augmented by Patterson's Pennamites, swung into motion, engaging in a skirmish at the Yankee stronghold of Fort Defence. They were unsuccessful in taking the fortification, however, and were forced to abandon their efforts. The following day, they dispossessed thirty families whose farms had been previously ordered restored to them.[262]

---

[261] Robert Martin to James Potter and William Montgomery, Members of Council of Censors, August 14, 1784, quoted in Miner, *History of Wyoming*, 357–58.

[262] Harvey and Smith, *A History of Wilkes-Barre*, III: 1423–24, 1433, 1440; *PA1*: X: 345.

By this time, the plight of the Connecticut settlers had gained national attention, and rifts in cooperation between state institutions and individuals within them became increasingly apparent. On September 10, prior to the Supreme Executive Council's order to send militia into Wyoming to put down unrest after the Yankees' release from imprisonment, the Council of Censors, having been alerted by Northumberland justices after the August incidents, requested documents from the general assembly concerning events that had transpired in the fall of 1783 and spring of 1784, but that body ignored the request. The following day, the Council of Censors published its findings in a stinging denunciation of the whole affair and the government's part in it, followed some days later by a further admonishment of the assembly for not turning over the requested documents. On September 15, the general assembly, composed of legislators from all counties in the state, passed an act calling for the restoration of property of settlers who had been dispossessed the previous May. Regardless, the Supreme Executive Council continued its harsh stance concerning events in the valley by calling for militia from Bucks, Berks, and Northampton Counties to keep order during the fall harvest and to assist in the arrest of troublemakers. When it met the first week in October, seven of its twelve members were absent, including an ailing President Dickinson whose written communication to the council voicing his disagreement to the proposed plan was ignored, and Armstrong returned to Wyoming. Lack of enthusiasm for any further action pervaded the rest of the state, reflected in the valley's neighboring counties' disinclination to call up their militias. Armstrong was eventually ordered out of the valley; and he, Patterson, and the militia departed Wilkes-Barre on November 27. Three days later, Yankee settlers burned the fort, ending that phase of the Pennamite-Yankee War. The act passed by the assembly restoring Connecticut claimants' lands as of September 14 was eventually honored, and settlers were left to organize their own governing councils.[263]

Wrangling over property rights continued for years. In September 1786, Luzerne County, which included the Wyoming Valley, was created from Northumberland County; and the following year Pennsylvania passed the Confirming Act reaffirming the rights of Connecticut settlers

---

[263] *PA*1: X: 347, 330, 361, 657; *PA*1: XIII: 640–641; *PA*2: XVIII: 640; Colonial Records: XIV, 218–24. See also Miner, *History of Wyoming*, 357–67 and Harvey and Smith, *A History of Wilkes-Barre*, III: 1432–1455.

whose claims predated the Trenton Decree. In 1799, an act for offering compensation to Pennsylvania claimants who held property in the valley's seventeen townships before March 28, 1787, provided for either direct payment from the state or the option of suing it, the value of the land to be adjudged by a jury. Commissioners resurveyed lots claimed by Connecticut settlers whose titles originated before the decree of Trenton and new certificates were issued.[264]

★

Lt. John Armstrong's interests were far removed from the Wyoming Valley by the time of John Armstrong Jr.'s September and October forays. Fortune had come his way in the form of an act of Congress on June 3, 1784, for the formation of a regiment of seven hundred men to be furnished by Pennsylvania, New Jersey, New York, and Connecticut to support the organization and settlement of the newly acquired Northwest Territory

---

[264] For details of this aspect of the complicated Wyoming saga, see Moyer, *Wild Yankees*, 68-195 and Miner, *History of Wyoming*, 371-460. Despite the creation of Luzerne County, tensions in the valley remained high, and at one point disaffected "Wild" Yankees loudly espoused independent statehood. Passage of the Confirming Act of 1787 granted Connecticut settlers holding lands prior to the Decree of Trenton the rights to their original lands but did not address titles on land claimed by settlers following the court's ruling, creating a division between Yankees willing to accept its provisions and those who did not. Additionally, property holders from both Pennsylvania and Connecticut living outside the valley and others eager to invest in parcels of land brought pressure on the Pennsylvania government that resulted in act's repeal in April 1, 1790. Pennsylvania slowly began to mediate the situation that became less intense as eager investors began to look westward toward purchasing cheaper lands in the Northwest Territory. In April, 1795, a statute was passed enacting penalties against anyone taking possession of lands within Northampton, Northumberland or Luzerne counties, with the exception of those claiming land under the original Confirming Act of 1787. The Compromise Act of April 1799 offered compensation to the Pennsylvania claimants of certain lands within the seventeen townships in the county of Luzerne and was followed by supplemental laws in 1802, 1805, and 1807. Paul B. Moyer notes that reconciliation between Yankee settlers and Pennsylvania moved forward with growing momentum after 1804 and was largely complete by 1810. The forty-year colonial land dispute had endured through a Revolution and its aftermath, the formation of a Constitutional government, and three presidential terms.

that had been ceded to the United States from Great Britain under the terms of the Treaty of Paris. Each state had the prerogative to appoint its own officers to the federal corps.

Pennsylvania was expected to supply the majority of men for the regiment, and Lt. Col. Josiah Harmar was accordingly selected as commander. He was directed to enlist a total force of three companies of infantry and one of artillery and three captains, three lieutenants, and three ensigns from the state. Harmar had served in the Third Pennsylvania Regiment from January 1781 to January 1783, and in that position, his career and that of Armstrong had overlapped for at least two years. Undoubtedly, Harmar knew the officer well.[265]

To Armstrong's disappointment, he received a commission as an ensign rather than a captain, his rank by brevet at the end of the war. Audaciously, he wrote President Dickinson on August 24 requesting an appointment at his former rank. In doing so, he was following a pattern characteristic of officers at the time in presenting arguments for their desired rank directly to higher authorities. Additionally, Armstrong had met and briefed Dickinson on several occasions throughout the past year regarding events in the Wyoming Valley and may have felt confident that his request would be approved.[266]

One can only assume that Armstrong was delighted at the prospect of again being part of a regular army unit and welcomed the opportunity to leave behind the scenes of endless wrangling and bloodshed between neighbors he had witnessed over the past year. Despite the disappointment in receiving a lower rank than he had wanted, he must have felt both pride and relief in receiving his commission, dated August 12, 1784.[267]

---

[265] *PA*1: 10: 309–10; 466; James Ripley Jacobs, *The Beginning of the U.S. Army 1783–1812* (Princeton: Princeton University Press, 1947), 16–18. Heitman, *Historical Register of Officers*, 209.

[266] *PA*1: 10: 315–16. Armstrong was not alone in receiving a rank lower than that in which he had previously served. Both of Armstrong's fellow Pennsylvania initial appointees as ensign, Andrew Henderson and Ebenezer Denny, served as lieutenants during the war. Heitman, *Historical Register of Officers of the Continental Army*, 151, 216.

[267] In an express from Wyoming to Dickinson on October 26, Commissioner Armstrong referred the president to Captain Armstrong who would relate facts concerning the arrival of Connecticut claimant and leader John Swift with reinforcements from up the river. Under what circumstances Armstrong now found himself in the Wyoming area is open to conjecture since he was

6

Birth of the Regiment, 1784–1785

*It will be judged necessary, I believe, to establish
for a time some troops, at suitable posts in the
Western territory, and to keep up a few men to
guard our public stores, but no standing army.*
—William Ellery[268]

By the close of the Revolution, Americans were tired of war and
everything that went with it. Gone was the spirit of cooperation between
colonies to rid the country of its British overseers. Most Americans lived
an insular life, their leaders thinking only in terms of their own state's
interests.

---

then actively engaged in Harmar's regiment. See Harvey and Smith, *A History
of Wilkes-Barre*, III: 1450 and *PA1*: X: 389. Also present in the minutes of the
Supreme Executive Council of November 10, 1784, was Armstrong's request
for reimbursement for past expenses. He sought fifteen pounds, ten shillings
for his services and expenses in riding as an express from Northumberland
County to Northampton County delivering dispatches to the Wyoming
Commissioners. Colonial Records, XIV: 254.

[268] William Ellery, Delegate to the Continental Congress from Rhode Island to
Jabez Brown, Deputy Governor of Rhode Island, April 10, 1784, in Paul H.
Smith and Ronald M. Gephart, eds., *Letters of Delegates to Congress, 1774–
1789, vol. 21, October 1, 1783–October 31, 1784* (Washington, D.C.: Library of
Congress, 1994), 508.

Congress was weak and ineffective. Its members came and went as they pleased and at the direction of their respective states; its sessions generally drew no more than a mere handful of men huddled together to legislate for some four million people scattered over 823,844 square miles. Under the Articles of Confederation, Congress had inadequate powers, no practical method of increasing them, and no effective means to enforce the few it actually possessed.

No armed body existed to support the rule of federal law. As of January 3, 1784, only seven hundred men remained in the army. Even this force was scheduled to be dismissed and replaced by skeleton units of twenty-five men at Fort Pitt and fifty-five at West Point to guard postrevolution equipment and stores. Lawmakers, remembering the grievances over pay expressed by soldiers during the short-lived Philadelphia Mutiny during the lingering days of the war, feared new disturbances and were inclined to abolish even this small remnant of the Continental Army. Representatives recalling years of effort to rid the nation of its occupation by the British army and its rule embraced the view that a standing military force in peacetime was inconsistent with the principles of a republican government, dangerous to the liberties of a free people, and a potential way of establishing despotism. Moreover, the cash-strapped nation could not afford it. Rather than a standing military, legislators tended to think in terms of militia forces, called up for short terms of duty and answerable only to the states that mustered them.[269]

Not all the nation's founding fathers shared this viewpoint. George Washington and a cadre of higher-ranking officers of the Continental Army recalled how hard they had worked during the early years of the Revolution to create a disciplined army capable of defeating the British in open battle and had concluded that regulars in long-term Continental units were superior to the ill-organized and untrained citizen militia regiments. When asked by Congress in 1783 to consider the nation's future defense needs, Washington and his associates unanimously recommended a small national military establishment and a complete overhaul of the militia

---

[269] Not only was the dispute between Pennsylvania and Connecticut roiling in the Wyoming Valley, but conflict over land also continued over New York's claim to territory within what would become the state of Vermont. Virginia and Pennsylvania also had yet to settle their final borders due to overlapping jurisdictions outlined in their royal charters. Jacobs, *The Beginning of the U.S. Army*, 13–14.

system. Their proposals became crucial to the Nationalist movement to strengthen the central government in the 1780s and later to Federalist policy in the 1790s. [270]

On May 2, 1783, George Washington presented a plan to Congress outlining a "Peace Establishment", proposing a regular force to garrison West Point and other posts on the frontiers as necessary "to awe the Indians, protect our Trade, prevent the encroachment of our Neighbors of Canada and the Floridas, and guard us at least from surprizes." Aware of the skeptical mood of Congress, he recommended only a modest total force of 1908 infantry and 723 artillery soldiers. His figures were increased in a plan later proposed by his former military aide and congressional delegate from New York Alexander Hamilton, but Congress took no action to implement either plan. Debates about the creation, size, and scope of a peacetime army continued between Federalist and anti-Federalist factions until the turn of the century, defining personal rivalries and laying the foundation for future political parties.[271]

Years of warfare resulted in a depression that the weak decentralized government could not resolve as long as each state jealously guarded its privilege to tax its inhabitants. No such authority existed at the federal level and, indebted internally and abroad for the cost of the war and still glutted with worthless paper currency from individual states, the United States government was unable even to settle payment accounts for war veterans.

The Treaty of Paris, signed September 3, 1783, formally ended hostilities between the United States and Britain and provided promise for the cash-strapped nation. Roughly one-quarter-million square miles of unsettled land ceded by Britain lay to the west. Well-connected individuals were eager to form land companies, to purchase large tracts from the government, and to resell acreage to an eager public. Men of more modest means savored the idea of buying and selling land in this new frontier as a way to build their wealth in an economy in which hard currency was difficult to come by. Settlers, having long since abandoned the quest to purchase expensive land in the East, had already migrated down the Shenandoah Valley into the backcountry of Virginia and the Carolinas

---

[270] Richard Kohn, *Eagle and Sword: The Beginnings of the Military Establishment in America* (New York: The Free Press, 1975), 9–10.

[271] Francis Paul Prucha, *The Sword of the Republic: The United States Army on the Frontier 1783–1846* (Lincoln: University of Nebraska Press, 1969), 5–6.

and had pushed into areas that would become Tennessee and Kentucky in search of cheap homesteads. Opening up the Northwest Territory for increased settlement appeared to be an answer toward solving the nation's many economic problems, and by the granting of bounty lands to Revolutionary War veterans, the government found a solution toward resolving its payment obligations to them.

Before Congress could appease speculators hungry for development, however, it first had to prepare the way for the territory's settlement. Despite having legal possession of the land in the eyes of European nations, the government had to negotiate agreements with resident Native American nations before any land could be surveyed for distribution or sale.[272]

Congress eventually conceded that the opening of the Northwest Territory required some sort of unified armed force. Troops were needed to accompany emissaries to treaties with Indian nations and impress the assembled tribes with American might. Squatters were already pouring into the Ohio Valley, threatening to deter future purchases of federal land, and the government needed a force to protect its citizens and to keep the peace. Additional manpower also was needed to accomplish the transfer of British forts along the Great Lakes ceded to the United States by the Treaty of Paris. Consequently, in June 1784, Congress authorized the creation of a new force to be drawn from four states organized as one regiment of infantry and two companies of artillery to serve for twelve months unless discharged sooner. Of the proposed 700-man force, Connecticut was to furnish 165 soldiers; New York, 165; New Jersey, 110; and Pennsylvania, 260. A total of 37 officers were to be commissioned and the whole operation was to be overseen by a secretary at war with a minuscule staff of three clerks and a messenger.[273]

Congress had established a small ineffective unit to do a job that, given even its most immediate tasks, called for several well-trained and equipped regiments. The tiny force was hampered from the start, but that it was created at all is remarkable. Despite the wrangling over the unwanted

---

[272] William H. Guthman, *March to Massacre: A History of the First Seven Years of the United States Army 1784–1791* (New York: McGraw-Hill, 1970), 1.

[273] Kohn, *Eagle and Sword*, 55; Guthman, *March to Massacre*, 5; Prucha, *The Sword of the Republic*, 8. See also John K. Mahon, "Pennsylvania and the Beginnings of the Regular Army," *Pennsylvania History* 21, no. 1 (1954), 39. The First American Regiment lives on today as the Third Infantry Regiment, "The Old Guard," posted outside Washington, D.C.

prospect of establishing a new military institution, the reluctance to pay for it, jealousy between the Southern and Middle Atlantic states bordering the frontier eager for government protection and the New England states that were not, and the lingering belief of many delegates that state militias could handle problems arising in peacetime, Congress grudgingly acceded to the force's creation.[274]

The tiny army faced formidable challenges from the start. None of the states mobilized militia units as a whole, instead opting to recruit enlistees soldier by soldier. New York, having sought and been denied Congress's approval to allow its own state military force, flatly refused to recruit its quota. In Connecticut, recruiting was delayed for months because the legislature adjourned before Congress passed the act authorizing the force. Pennsylvania expected Congress to underwrite the expenses of recruiting and supply but discovered the government would not do so until the men were recruited, assembled, and ready to operate under national authority. Pennsylvania's officers took oaths of loyalty to both Congress and to Pennsylvania's Supreme Executive Council, and the regiment's commander was to report to both.[275]

Chosen to command the regiment was thirty-one-year-old Philadelphia native Josiah Harmar. An orphan reared by Quaker relatives, Harmar joined the Continental Army in 1775 as a captain and emerged a brevet colonel, along the way forming a friendship with Thomas Mifflin, eventual governor of the state of Pennsylvania and president of the Continental Congress who pushed for his appointment as regimental commander. Distinguished more for organizational skill than personal bravery, Harmar's war service included the ill-fated Canada campaign in the winter of 1775, the winter at Valley Forge, and duty in 1782 as adjutant general with Greene in the South. He emerged from the war a young man with aristocratic pretensions and a passion for order. In 1784, Harmar was sent by Congress to carry the ratified peace treaty between Britain and the United States to the American commissioners at Paris where he met Benjamin Franklin and the Marquis de Lafayette who in turn facilitated

---

[274] Guthman, *March to Massacre*, 2. See Mahon, "Pennsylvania and the Beginnings of the Regular Army," 35–36 and Kohn, *Eagle and Sword*, 45–53 for a description of congressional debate concerning creation of a federal force.

[275] Kohn, *Eagle and Sword*, 63.

an audience for him with Louis XVI and Marie Antoinette. He wrote that he found London and Paris most enjoyable but highly expensive.

A man who enjoyed good food and wine, Harmar brought his wife, Sarah, with him to frontier posts where they made the best of rough-hewn garrison surroundings by furnishing them with furniture from the East and lavishly entertaining officers and guests. Considering himself firmly in the "gentleman" class, he was nevertheless an officer of the martinet variety who followed von Steuben's manual by rote and realized the necessity of economy while in the public service, a concept he continually stressed to those under his command.[276]

Overseeing the entire operation was Secretary at War Henry Knox. The former Boston bookseller and beneficiary of a good marriage was a figure not to be missed, towering over his contemporaries at a height of over six feet and weighing an estimated 280 pounds. Washington's former chief artillery officer was an ardent supporter of a strong national government and likely received his appointment because he possessed the confidence as well as the affection of his former commander.[277]

★

John Armstrong now found himself part of an officer corps in which he must have felt comfortable. During the first year of the regiment's existence, all officers were from the Pennsylvania Line, New Jersey's soldiers having been tasked to accompany commissioners to treat with the Six Nations at Fort Stanwix, New York. They undoubtedly knew one another, having served in the same regiments, participated in the same campaigns, and encamped side by side during long winters at Valley Forge and Morristown. Most were the veterans who had formed the hard nucleus of the Continental Army, the men who had supplied the backbone of the war effort for the long duration of the conflict whose median length of service was six years. Their wartime experiences provided a web of shared habits, loyalties, and memories as well as a common socialization into military life that served as a bond in the creation of a cohesive group.

---

[276] Alan Brown, "The Role of the Army in Western Settlement Josiah Harmar's Command, 1785–1790," *Pennsylvania Magazine of History and Biography* 93, no. 2 (1969), 161–63; Andrew R. L. Cayton, *Frontier Indiana* (Bloomington: Indiana University Press, 1996), 107.

[277] Cayton, *Frontier Indiana*, 108–09.

Armstrong's background was typical of other fellow officers. Most were relatively young men, the median age for entering military service being twenty-one, Armstrong's age when entering Pennsylvania's Twelfth Regiment. Most were too young to have accumulated much property or to have established stable civilian careers. Having spent nearly all of their adulthood in uniform, these men were soldiers in the sense that military service had been the central experience to that point in their lives. They were typical of perhaps two-thirds of the white population of the New England and Middle states, part of a broad middle class that included "respectable" small property holders, artisans, shopkeepers, professional men of local reputation, or like Armstrong, sons of fathers who were farmers. For many, Revolutionary War service had provided a channel of social mobility. Left rootless by the dissolution of the Continental Army, lacking the property or the social connections to merge easily into civilian life, and perhaps recalling with nostalgia the action and camaraderie of the war years, these men looked to service under Congress as a source of status and security.

William B. Skelton, in his study of the backgrounds of the men who comprised the regiment, notes that Armstrong's fellow officers were the result of a democratization process that accompanied the extended duration of the Revolution. At the beginning of the conflict, officers were traditionally drawn from the "better sort" of the populace, the families of merchants, lawyers, planters, and prosperous farmers who were most likely to be known to the governors and militia field officers who made appointments. In old-school British tradition, they were considered the natural leaders of the hierarchical society of the late colonial period. This pattern changed dramatically as the war progressed. Its length and subsequent vacancies in the officer ranks due to injury, death, resignation, and regimental reorganization provided the opportunity for many from humbler backgrounds to advance themselves. Leadership skill and valorous behavior enabled enlisted men such as the Armstrong brothers to advance into the officer class.[278]

★

---

[278] William B. Skelton, "Social Roots of the American Military Profession: The Officer Corps of America's First Peacetime Army, 1784–1789," *Journal of Military History* 54, no. 4 (1990), 435–43. For a description of the opportunities afforded to the officer class, see Holly A. Mayer, *Belonging to the Army: Camp Followers and Community during the American Revolution* (Columbia: University of South Carolina Press, 1996), 52–56.

Pennsylvania commissioned its officers on August 13, 1784. Their first duty was to recruit the men they were to command, a task far more challenging than they first expected. Congressional fears of creating too large an army proved groundless. Gone was the glamour and color of Revolutionary days, and new recruits were few and far between. Potential recruits recalled how discharged soldiers returned home from the war with partial or no pay, only to discover that their old jobs or businesses had vanished. They remembered that returning veterans were greeted not with a hero's welcome, but with scorn and disapproval. Neighbors suffering from the economic strain brought on by the war isolated themselves from the troubles of those who had served. An entire substrata of veterans sought refuge in the impersonal atmosphere of the cities along the Eastern Seaboard. In his detailed history of the First Regiment, William H. Guthman notes that they were a pathetic fraternity of forgotten souls, many of whom fell into lives of drinking and drifting.[279]

Unable to find enough suitable men willing to join the fledgling army, recruiters turned to those with few other options in life, many of whom enlisted for the promise of food, clothing, liquor ration, and, for some, the vision of settling on new land at the end of their time in service. They were successful in raising the assigned number of enlistees if not in filling the ranks with quality prospects. Harmar's return of troops to Pennsylvania's Executive Council dated September 25, 1784, noted a total close to its quota, reporting 256 noncommissioned officers and men in the regiment. As the officers led their recruited companies to a staging camp near the Schuylkill River, Harmar set about making soldiers out of the ragtag assembly by stressing proper military appearance and paying careful attention to the maintenance of equipment and weapons. By the end of September, he was seeing positive results, but his training time was cut short by receipt of orders to march the troops westward to Fort Pitt. The neophyte army was to accompany commissioners to old Fort McIntosh on the Ohio River where they would treat with representatives of the Wyandot, Delaware, Chippewa, and Ottawa nations.[280]

---

[279] Guthman, *March to Massacre*, 22.

[280] *PA*1: X: 338; Brown, "The Role of the Army in Western Settlement," 164–65. Harmar's correspondence with Pennsylvania's Executive Council during this period, as well as the regiment's monthly returns, appear through August 1785 in the *Pennsylvania Archives* and afford the opportunity to track the regiment's movements, as well as occasional notations concerning Ensign Armstrong and

The regiment marched to Fort Pitt in infantry companies under the direction of Capts. Walter Finney, David Zeigler, and William McCurdy and artillery company commander Capt. Thomas Douglass. Incidents on the journey provided a wake-up call to the problems presented by the quality and disposition of the new recruits. Guthman notes that during the long trip overland, the men, having trekked across the mountains in chilly autumn rain by day and sheltered at night in tents stretched on sodden ground, inadequately attired and unused to strenuous military travel, found sanctuary in the various towns at night with a crock of whiskey or flask of rum. Officers spent their time rounding up strays and stragglers. Many deserted, satisfied that they had received all the clothing they were going to be issued. Of the 256 noncommissioned officers and men listed in Harmar's return of September 25, 1784, 60 had deserted by December 1.[281]

In his autobiography, *A Narrative of the Life and Travels of John Robert Shaw, the Well-digger, Now a Resident of Lexington, Kentucky*, Shaw presents a picture of what the trek was like for the average enlisted soldier. The lengthy route began over the Wagon Road forged earlier by westbound settlers from Philadelphia through Lancaster, Carlisle, Shippensburg, and Chambersburg and across the Alleghenies to the northwest until it reached a small island opposite Fort Pitt. Shaw described several incidents caused by intoxicated recruits, attempted desertions, and harsh punishments doled out to those who engaged in drunk and disorderly conduct as officers attempted to keep the men together to maintain good order and discipline. He himself was not immune to mischief. One night, he got so drunk that he and a friend pulled down fences, letting cows, sheep, and horses into a farmer's garden. The evening ended with Shaw falling into a twenty-foot-deep well but emerging without permanent injury.[282]

Armstrong was assigned to Captain Finney's company. The unit set out from Philadelphia on September 22, 1784, arriving at Fort Pitt four weeks later. In light of the high percentage of recruits deserting from the company—Finney's numbers accounted for over one-third of the total

---

other officers.

[281] *PA*1: X: 338; Guthman, *March to Massacre*, 22–23; Jacobs, *The Beginning of the U.S. Army*, 19.

[282] John Robert Shaw, *A Narrative of the Life and Travels of John Robert Shaw, the Well-digger, Now a Resident of Lexington, Kentucky* (Lexington: Daniel Bradford, 1807), 86–90.

number of soldiers deserting from the entire regiment in the span of a little more than two months—his men obviously needed to be corralled.[283]

At Fort Pitt, Harmar continued his effort to mold his force through drill and performance of garrison duties. Adhering closely to the von Steuben doctrine, he stressed the need for discipline and order to create in his men "a just sense of their profession" and "honorable character of a soldier." Displeased with the quality of soldiers he found occupying the local fort, remnants of the force guarding postwar military stores, he noted that those left behind had adopted the same way of life as the residents of that frontier community, many of whom "lived in dirty log cabins and were prone to find joy in liquor and fighting."[284]

★

Fort Pitt eventually became a supply hub, its post–Revolutionary War skeleton staff replaced by Harmar's regimental soldiers when the bulk of the command moved thirty miles down the Ohio to Fort McIntosh. The latter fort, erected in 1778, had once been a well-built stockade occupied in the Revolution but had fallen into disrepair. When Harmar's troops arrived, they discovered that settlers bound for Kentucky had "destroyed the gates, drawn all the Nails from the roofs, taken off all the boards, and plundered it of every Article." In mid-January 1785, Harmar reported that his entire corps had been on constant fatigue since its arrival in order to restore the fort to a condition adequate for accommodating the treaty commissioners. The bulk of the heavy labor fell on the common soldiers whose chief solace was liquor, which invariably got them into trouble. Even officers sometimes fell prey to alcholic excess. John K. Mahon cites the account given by Arthur Lee, one of the federal commissioners to the treaty, who described an incident involving too much merriment on the part of some officers during a Christmas celebration. Artillery captain Thomas Douglas had his men haul a cannon onto the parade ground in the dead of night and fire repeated salutes. Harmar was not there, and Douglas would not stop when ordered to do so by the acting senior officer. When the troops were put under arms, drunken company commanders gave contradictory orders while swearing at and confounding the men.[285]

---

[283] *PA1*: X: 388.

[284] Jacobs, *The Beginning of the U.S. Army*, 15.

[285] *PA1*: X: 391, 395; Brown, "The Role of the Army in Western Settlement," 165.

The treaty to be signed at Fort McIntosh was the second between the United States and Native American nations, the first having been held at Fort Stanwix on the banks of the Mohawk River in present-day Rome, New York, the previous October. Although representatives from the Indian confederations, federal and state commissioners, and army escorts constituted the assembly, there was an unseen and uninvited guest. The British, from garrisons on the Great Lakes, continued not only to give material support to their native allies but also encouraged them to resist dealings with the new federal government.

Congress assumed that Britain would comply with the terms of the Treaty of Paris, believing that after the transfer of forts along the Great Lakes at Detroit, Mackinac, Oswego, and Niagara, the Indians would no longer have the support of their former patrons for hostile actions against American settlements. British agents, however, had other ideas; Britain was unwilling to give up its lucrative fur trade as well as proximity to the fledgling nation whose early years were marked with uncertainty and its future tenuous. In September 1783, the same month in which the Treaty of Paris was signed, British superintendent of Indian Affairs Sir John Johnson authorized a grand council at Lower Sandusky, present-day Fremont, Ohio. Britain, with support of key leaders, sought to unite the disparate nations into a confederacy to act as one voice against the Americans in order to accomplish the plan of having Indian nations and their territories serve as a buffer between the former colonies and Canada. At this vast gathering of representatives of thirty-five nations, British agent Alexander McKee carefully presented the situation in the following manner: although formal boundaries had been drawn to demarcate Canada from the United States, the land itself was still theirs. Britain would support the nations in any effort of the United States to deprive them of their homelands. [286]

See also Lewis E. Graham, "Fort McIntosh," *Western Pennsylvania Magazine* 25, no. 2 (1932), 93; Mahon, "Pennsylvania and the Beginnings of the Regular Army," 42–43; Daniel Agnew, *Fort McIntosh: Its Times and Men: With a Historical Sketch of the French and British Claims in the Northwest, and Their Meeting in Arms at the Head of the Ohio, and the Indian Incursions and Outrages in Western Pennsylvania and the Ohio Territory* (Pittsburgh: Myers, Shinkle and Company, 1893), 20.

[286] Downes notes that despite Indian nations' belief to the contrary, the British had no intention of actually providing troops to assist them in any armed conflict against the Americans. See Randolph C. Downes, *Council Fires on*

This new British policy had its first test at the initial treaty between the Iroquois nations and the American government at Fort Stanwix. Boding ill for the proceeding's outcome, tribal representatives from the western nations arrived before the commissioners were ready to begin and, frustrated by the delays, went home. Consequently, Cornplanter and Capt. Aaron Hill, chiefs of the Seneca and the Mohawk, assumed representation not only for the Six Nations but for all tribes east of the Mississippi River. Unified and confident following their meeting with the British at Sandusky a year earlier, the attitude of the American commissioners at Fort Stanwix left the chiefs stunned and the Six Nations splintered in its wake. Ready for talks of peace and affirmation that Congress's intention was to be friends with all Indian nations, the delegates settled back to listen to the "good counsel" of their new white fathers. Instead, Commissioners Richard Butler, Oliver Wolcott, and Arthur Lee issued a series of mandates that set the pattern for future dialogues and led only to dissatisfaction among the Indian nations that would be dispossessed of their lands and hunting grounds. All territory east of the Mississippi, they proclaimed, now belonged to the United States. Britain had lost the war, and the new government would control who lived where. Because they had backed the defeated British in their fight against the American colonies, the Indian nations had lost their lands as well. As a subdued people, they were not entitled to dictate terms. All Iroquois claims to lands west of New York and Pennsylvania were now relinquished and the tribes confined to certain areas of those states, subject to approval of state treaties. The treaty was reluctantly signed by the chiefs present but created friction between the leaders who had signed and those not in attendance.[287]

---

the *Upper Ohio until 1795* (Pittsburgh: University of Pittsburgh Press, 1940), 279-283, 288. See also Wiley Sword, *President Washington's Indian War: The Struggle for the Old Northwest, 1790–1795* (Norman: University of Oklahoma Press, 1985), 19–20; Richard White, *The Middle Ground: Indians, Empires, and Republics in the Great Lakes Region, 1650–1815* (Cambridge: Cambridge University Press, 1991), 434.

[287] Downes, "Council Fires," 290. Of the Six Nations, the Oneidas and Tuscaroras had been on good terms with the Americans during the war and remained so, their lands being secured for them by the Fort Stanwix treaty. The Mohawks turned more openly toward British support and sought lands in Canada. Senecas, Cayugas, and Onandagas remained on American soil and became increasingly compliant to the treaty directives, as their location made them

By late January 1785, newly rebuilt Fort McIntosh was ready to receive representatives of the Indian nations for a second treaty. Commissioners George Rogers Clark, Richard Butler, and Arthur Lee met at the Pennsylvania outpost with representatives from tribal groups that primarily inhabited present-day central and northern Ohio and Michigan. Although the chiefs present at Fort Stanwix had accepted terms of land forfeiture for the Iroquois nations that were predominant about Lake Erie and had also accepted terms on behalf of other nations inhabiting territory now claimed by the United States, other Indian leaders were not prepared to see their rights disposed of so cavalierly and accused the Six Nations of a breach of faith.

Treaty negotiations with Delaware, Chippewa, Ottawa, and Wyandot representatives opened in bitterly cold weather on January 8, 1785, and concluded on January 21. The commissioners outlined similar arguments presented to the Iroquois at Fort Stanwix: their territory now belonged to the United States and because of their alliance with Britain they might now be compelled to retire beyond the Great Lakes. The American people were of a generous nature, however, and were willing to overlook all that had passed, allowing the Indians to keep their lands west of the Great Miami River. In what would become present-day Ohio, nations would be allotted lands above an east-west line running through the state and were promised hunting rights onto ceded lands while game was plentiful and until white settlers arrived. At the same time, protection for American citizens attempting to settle on Indian lands would be withdrawn. All American prisoners taken over the years were to be released; and gifts of liquor, kettles, blankets, paint, lead, and gunpowder, albeit probably worthless due to a previously long period of storage, were presented. A specific request to receive tents was refused because they were too expensive. The hard-line approach of the commissioners was successful in the short term but indicated a naiveté toward the position of the Indian nations that eventually would be dispelled by the harsh reality of warfare.

most vulnerable to any directed hostilities. Sword, *President Washington's Indian War*, 23–26.

Land in the new territory was opened up for settlement, and the East waited impatiently to devour it.[288]

★

Ens. Ebenezer Denny described not only the scene of the treaty but also his expectation that the regiment would soon march to Detroit to occupy the British fort there, a mission that was never executed by Harmar's regiment and whose occurrence would not take place until the middle of the next decade. Rather, with the treaty signed and Congress enacting the Land Ordinance of 1785 allowing for land sales following an official survey of the ceded territory, the scope of the army's duties took a significant turn. The tiny corps was now tasked with two directives, the first of which was to guard survey parties in their monumental task of plotting the vast virgin territory. The designated zero point of the survey was located near Fort McIntosh, and the garrison was expected to furnish troops needed for the process in that quadrant. The second task involved keeping illegal American settlers out of Indian lands, thereby protecting the nation's future financial nest egg, lands destined to be granted to war veterans or sold to land speculators. The first was accomplished with great difficulty; the second would prove to be impossible.[289]

Believing that ownership went with occupancy, many newcomers, particularly the Scots-Irish, often did not trouble themselves with securing title to land they settled. As a result, Harmar's regiment had the unpleasant task of evicting many of them. The ugliness of the job of removing squatters within Pennsylvania itself, however, was partially relieved by the personal interest that many officers and public officials themselves had in the land; the government had earmarked all the ground between the Ohio River and the current state's western boundary for war veterans. Determined to keep that tract clear, and undoubtedly pressured by state officials to do so, Harmar evicted the settlers between Fort Pitt and Fort McIntosh,

---

[288] Prucha, *The Sword of the Republic*, 8; Sword, *President Washington's Indian War*, 28. Under terms of the treaty, the nations were forced to accept lands in the northern Ohio Territory bounded on the west by the Maumee River, the north by Lake Erie, the east by the Cuyahoga River, and on the south by the line drawn through the central part of what is now the state of Ohio. Downes, *Council Fires*, 294–95.

[289] Denny, *Military Journal*, 55.

although by his own statement, this was not one of his official duties as commander of the United States troops.[290]

Ensign Armstrong was likely present at the treaty at Fort McIntosh and involved in the exhausting effort to rebuild the fort prior to the conclave. Listed on the January 1, 1785, monthly return as "sick present," there is no notation on February's return, indicating that he was back on duty. His actions after the treaty are prominently recorded, however. On March 29, 1785, he was ordered to lead a party of twenty men about seventy miles down the Ohio River as far as Wheeling in order to evict squatters. As reported in letters to Harmar on April 12 and 13, Armstrong notified residents of their illegal presence, extracted promises to relocate, met with hostile occupants, destroyed buildings, and in one case arrested a settler. Torn between following his instructions and seeing the reality of the situation, he elected to grant reasonable time for the settlers to comply with directives in consideration of weather conditions and other mitigating circumstances. As a result, he returned to Fort McIntosh with a petition from occupants requesting additional time to clear their property. His findings confirmed informal observations that squatters were flooding into the territory, estimating that there were 300 families both at the falls of the Hocking River and on the Muskingum River while there appeared to be some 1,500 families farther downstream on the Miami and Scioto Rivers. He ventured the opinion that unless early action was taken by Congress to prevent trespassing on lands west of the Ohio, "that country will soon be inhabited by a banditti whose actions are a disgrace to human nature."[291]

---

[290] Brown, "The Role of the Army in Western Settlement," 167–68; Mahon, "Pennsylvania and the Beginnings of the Regular Army," 43–44. Land speculation was not limited to wealthy individuals. Embraced as an opportunity of investment when hard currency was rare, men of moderate means eyed the land soon to be opened, and John Armstrong and his fellow officers were no exception. Armstrong was already buying up tracts of donation land from his soldiers. PJA.

[291] Harmar to Armstrong, March 29, 1785, Armstrong to Harmar, April 12 and 13, 1785, Harmar to Henry Lee, May 1, 1785, cited in Alfred Thomas Goodman, ed., *Papers Relating to the First White Settlers in Ohio* (Cleveland: Western Reserve Historical Society, 1871), 3–6; William Henry Smith, ed., *The St. Clair Papers* (Cincinnati: Robert Clarke and Company, 1882), II: 3–5; Brown, "The Role of the Army in Western Settlement," 168; Mahon, "Pennsylvania and the Beginnings of the Regular Army," 43; *PA*1: X:448.

Subsequent missions by other regimental officers made it clear that although such expeditions to rid the area of squatters might yield short-term results, the efforts of a few soldiers were powerless to turn back the growing floodtide of settlement. At the first opportunity, large numbers of those ejected from their lands returned. Virginia's Kentucky territory offered no satisfactory refuge for uprooted settlers due in large part to confusion of land titles there. Because only an estimated one-tenth of Kentucky settlers held lands with clear deeds to their acreage, thousands originally headed for Kentucky to secure land on easy terms were disappointed and ended up settling on government lands to the north.[292]

Armstrong was tasked with at least one additional mission to evict squatters. Harmar informed Knox on June 15, 1785, that he had dispatched Armstrong's small force to Salt Springs, located in present-day Mahoning Valley of Trumbull County, Ohio, a few days after his return from Wheeling to dispossess a number of "adventurers" who had located there. The eviction was apparently accomplished without serious difficulty.[293]

By late April, Armstrong was temporarily assigned to Fort Pitt. His papers include instructions from Major Wyllys at Fort McIntosh on the April 29, 1785, to send three companies of men to that installation and a letter from Major Nicholas Fish on May 31 commending Armstrong on his favorable treatment of Indians who had come to Fort Pitt along with the major's request to take care of another party heading toward the fort that should be given six pounds of tobacco and a string of wampum, as well as eight days' worth of provisions to last them on their journey home.[294]

By April 1785, initial terms of enlistment were due to expire, and men who had signed up for one year's service were ready to go home. Harmar became alarmed. The regiment's tasks were increasing while its small force was diminishing daily due to death, desertion, and discharge. With few amusements, little clothing, indifferent rations, and scant pay, soldiers had

---

[292] Brown, "The Role of the Army in Western Settlement," 189.

[293] Goodman, "Papers Relating to the First White Settlers in Ohio," 3, 6.

[294] Wyllys to Armstrong, April 29, 1785, and Fish to Armstrong, May 31, 1785, in Cist, *CM* I: 6. The regiment began to be augmented by personnel from the remaining states tasked to supply soldiers for the force. Two majors, John P. Wyllys from Connecticut and John Francis Hamtramck from New York, joined the infantry command, and Major John Doughty, also from New York, came to the regiment as artillery company commander. Fish was commander of troops in New York and was also detailed duty at Fort McIntosh.

little reason to remain voluntarily in the service. Forbidding forests, tales of hostile Indians, continued physical hardships, and irritating control and military discipline increased their nostalgia for a different life. Many waited impatiently for the day of their discharge.[295]

Of the two hundred or more troops then in western Pennsylvania, most were to finish their enlistment by September 1785. Congress passed legislation on April 12, 1785, again authorizing an army totaling 700 men; but this time, those signing up would commit to three-year enlistments. The force would be comprised of eight companies of infantry and two of artillery, with one lieutenant colonel, two majors, eight captains, ten lieutenants to include an adjutant, quartermaster, and paymaster, ten ensigns, one surgeon, and one surgeon's mate. Only seventy men from Pennsylvania agreed to reenlist, and Harmar began recruiting to fill the balance of the state quota of 260 men. He also sent Pennsylvania governor Dickinson a list of the officers whom he believed should be retained in service. Ens. John Armstrong's name was on the list, as were all other serving officers.[296]

Recruiting parties were sent eastward, but efforts to fill the quotas met with results similar to those of the previous year. With the designated date for beginning surveying rapidly approaching and the army still under strength, the situation was eased by the arrival of a newly recruited company from New York in September that was immediately dispatched with the surveyors. Armstrong was among the officers sent to Philadelphia. As of August 1, he remained in the city with orders to recruit "30 stout, able-bodied men."[297]

On October 20, 1785, the list of Pennsylvania officers serving in the regiment was sent by that state to the secretary at war. John Armstrong's name had moved up the list and appeared with those of two other lieutenants. Stewart Herbert's name had been omitted, allowing for Armstrong's promotion to the higher rank.[298]

★

[295] Jacobs, *The Beginning of the U.S. Army*, 23.

[296] *PA1*: X: 466; Prucha, *The Sword of the Republic*, 9–13. See also William Addleman Ganoe, *The History of the United States Army* (Ashton, Maryland: Eric Lundberg, 1964), 92.

[297] Guthman, *March to Massacre*, 96; Brown, "The Role of the Army in Western Settlement," 168; PA1: X: 480, 490.

[298] *PA1*: X: 525. Promotions were based on date of rank and were dependent upon

In the meantime, Congress, in response to the demands of settlers and speculators, ordered Harmar to send troops with Indian commissioners Richard Butler, Samuel Parsons, and George Rogers Clark to the mouth of the Great Miami River for a third treaty. They were to meet again with representatives from the western nations but specifically with the Miami and Shawnee who did not attend the previous treaty at Fort McIntosh and whose warriors were already causing problems in Kentucky. Commissioners, fortified by their success in the two previous treaties, looked forward to arriving at a practical solution to these conflicts while Washington and other leaders realized that the outcome of this meeting would be a crucial test of the government's authority. As invitations went out to representative nations, Harmar sent Capt. Walter Finney and his company down the Ohio to the designated treaty site where in October and November 1785, they erected a stockade, blockhouses, and a council house that they appropriately named Fort Finney.[299]

Attracted by gifts of flour, rum, and tobacco, Wyandot and Delaware tribal chiefs, accompanied by their followers and families, were the first to arrive for the meeting. Having participated in previous discussions at Fort McIntosh, these representatives were invited to provide a moderating influence to the proceedings. Perceiving what lay ahead, however, Shawnee and Miami leaders disregarded messages to meet with commissioners, the results of the previous treaties at Fort Stanwix and Fort McIntosh having incurred their considerable indignation. As a result, commissioners were forced to bide their time until finally, on January 14, 1786, an advance delegation of Shawnee warriors appeared, accompanied by their women and children. Others soon

---

vacancies at the next higher grade. The process became one of contention between officers when those with previous Revolutionary War ranks were integrated into the regiment. Additional complications arose concerning Pennsylvania officers' service in the regiment during its first year and whether it should be considered militia or regular army duty.

[299] Armstrong may not have joined his company building Fort Finney. He had returned to Fort Pitt by mid-December, at which time he received orders from Major Hamtramck to assume command of the fort. He was to guard the public property with a contingent consisting of one sergeant and twelve men. Hamtramck to Armstrong, December 15, 1785, PJA. For description of the structure and site of Fort Finney, see Erkuries Beatty, "Diary of Major Erkuries Beatty, Paymaster of the Western Army, May 15, 1786 to June 5, 1787," *Magazine of American History* 1 (1877): 176.

followed although they represented only a fraction of the Shawnee Nation, most notably those from Mackachack in present-day Logan County, Ohio, who were in dire need of provisions, especially tobacco and corn. The Miamis and the majority of the Shawnees continued to shun the council. By late January, however, 318 Shawnees were present, a number large enough to justify convening the proceedings. During the ensuing three weeks, the commissioners endeavored to clarify the terms of the treaty, reiterating the surrender of the western territory by Great Britain to the United States and boundaries established at the Fort McIntosh conference. Reluctant to agree but faced with the bold resistance of the commissioners who threatened retaliation not only against them but also their women and children, the chiefs assented and the treaty concluded. In doing so, they acknowledged the sovereignty of the United States over all the territory ceded by Great Britain; the land between the Great Miami and the Wabash Rivers was to be reserved for them.[300]

To all appearances, the Shawnees had reconciled themselves to the terms of the treaty. The commissioners were confident that Congress could now instigate the surveying and selling of territorial lands without impediment. Scarcely had the Shawnees returned to their villages, however, before there were murmurings of discontent. A few weeks later, leaders declared that the treaty had been signed only to gain time in order to prevent the destruction of their villages by the Americans and that they had no intention of keeping the agreement.[301]

In his article "The Role of the Army in Western Settlement Josiah Harmar's Command, 1785–1790," Alan Brown notes that the Fort Finney treaty had particular significance because it was the last time the government presented the argument that the nations had no alternative other than to relinquish their lands since they, as British allies during the Revolution, had lost them when the latter accepted the peace terms of

---

[300] James Alton James, "Some Phases of the History of the Northwest, 1783–1786," in *Proceedings of the Mississippi Valley Historical Association for the Year, 1913–1914, Vol. 7*, ed. Benjamin F. Shambaugh (Cedar Rapids: The Torch Press, 1914), 191–93; Jacobs, *The Beginning of the U.S. Army*, 24; Brown, "The Role of the Army in Western Settlement," 166; Sword, *President Washington's Indian War*, 28–30. Denny provides a vivid description of the celebratory atmosphere accompanying the arrival of the Wyandot (Wyandotte) and Delaware leaders prior to the commencement of the treaty as well as the description of the trip down the Ohio, the fort, and the surroundings. Denny, *Military Journal*, 57–73.
[301] James, "Some Phases of the History of the Northwest," 191–93.

1783. This position might have been maintained had the United States government under the Articles of Confederation not been so weak and if the British could have been induced to leave their western posts and abandon their role as protectors of the Indians. Such was not the case.[302]

The United States had obtained agreements with the Iroquois at Fort Stanwix and the Delaware and Wyandots at Fort McIntosh without significant backlash. The situation changed after the treaty at Fort Finney. As they were to demonstrate on numerous occasions in the coming months and years, the Indian nations in the Northwest Territory did not regard themselves as a conquered people. Additionally, the federal government at the time had no appetite for a show of strength, choosing to avoid the expense and consequences of enforcing its position by raising and deploying more troops. There was little likelihood of peace in the newly opened territory until the United States demonstrated the power to enforce its demands, thereby convincing the western nations that they had no other option than to accede to its terms. Nevertheless, the government had every intention of pursuing its planned policy of opening the western lands for sale.[303]

During the first few months of its life, the tiny forerunner of the regular army was occupied with organizing itself, building fortifications, assisting Indian treaties, providing protection for surveyors, and attempting to keep the public land clear of squatters. As Mahon states, it was not, fortunately, called upon to fight. As the scope of the army's mission began to change from one of keeping settlers out of Indian territory and government lands to one of providing for their protection, that function would come soon enough.[304]

---

[302] Brown, "The Role of the Army in Western Settlement," 166–67. For an account of Indian reactions to the early treaties, see Richard White, *The Middle Ground*, 437–39.

[303] James, "Some Phases of the History of the Northwest, 1783–1786," 193; Brown, "The Role of the Army in Western Settlement," 166–67.

[304] Mahon, "Pennsylvania and the Beginnings of the Regular Army," 44.

7

Army Life

*Unfortunately, the Confederation did not always have
the money, and instead of borrowing it, Congress often
obliged the army to do without. The effect on the military
establishment was debilitating. . . . At various times the
soldiers lived on short rations because supplies were lacking
or went into the field with clothing in tatters, or without
essential apparel. The result was low morale, continual
desertion, habitual drunkenness, and mutinous behavior.*
—Richard H. Kohn[305]

The dawn of 1786 found Lt. John Armstrong at Fort Pitt atop the
expanding chain of garrisons along the Ohio River. He saw increasing
numbers of would-be settlers begin their passage down the river, ostensibly
bound for Kentucky but perhaps stopping instead on the river's north side
at locations he and his fellow officers had previously attempted to rid of
squatters. As supply officer, he received regimental news and gossip, as well
as requisitions from his colleagues downriver, and greeted fellow officers,
commissioners, surveyors, and contractors as they passed through the
garrison on their journeys westward, hearing tales of white settlements and
Indian unrest when they returned. He met with visiting Native American
delegations seeking supplies and food. As the fort's commander, Armstrong

---

[305] Kohn, *Eagle and Sword*, 69.

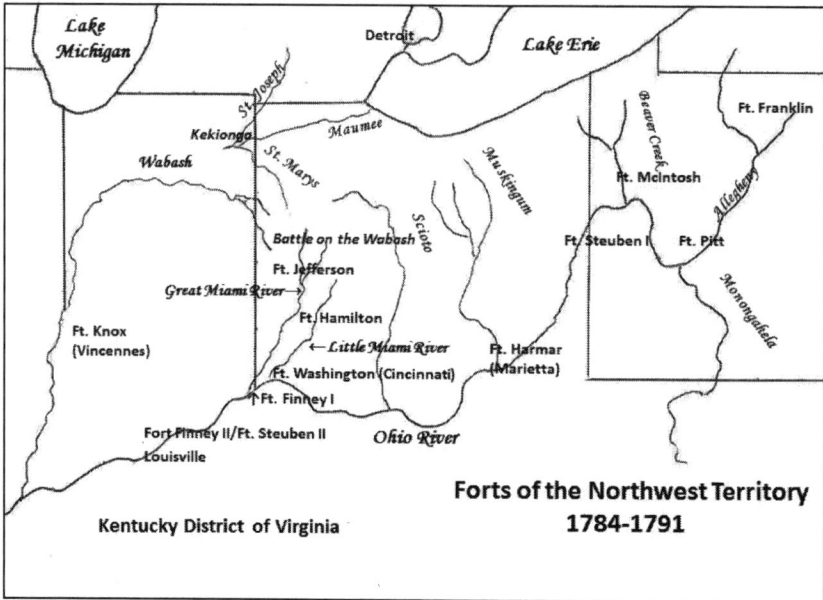

Forts of the Northwest Territory
1784-1791

managed the operation of the aging garrison and supervised its military and civilian inhabitants while interfacing with Pittsburgh's populace. He was in a prime position to witness the effects of the evolving missions of the already overstretched regiment.[306]

In the spring of 1786, the regiment's primary mission was preventing settlement north of the Ohio River by the increasing numbers of would-be squatters and a secondary mission of providing protection for surveying parties. These priorities were soon reversed. The army found itself too small to curb the burgeoning flow of settlers going downriver and better equipped to protect the surveyors. Accounts of river traffic passing the mouth of the Muskingum River in the seven months between October 10, 1786, and May 12, 1787, listed 177 boats; 2,689 passengers; 1,333 horses; 766 cattle; and 102 wagons bound for Limestone and Louisville. Because the travelers were allegedly bound for legal Kentucky settlements, the

---

[306] Correspondence between Armstrong and Harmar, Wyllys, and Ziegler from December 1785 to May 1786, PJA. Environs of early forts were crude, and the behavior of their inhabitants reflected life on the rough frontier. See description of Pittsburgh residents in Beatty, "Diary of Major Erkuries Beatty," 314.

army was powerless to interfere although some were later found crossing the Ohio into government territory.[307]

Accomplishing these missions required the army to be positioned both at points where surveying could begin and encroachment could be monitored. In October 1785, Capts. John Doughty and Jonathan Heart were directed to proceed to the mouth of the Muskingum River and to construct a fortification at what eventually became Marietta, Ohio. The location, excellent for preventing squatter settlements and executing their eviction from government lands, was also ideal for protecting the surveyors. The army's presence there would convey to the Indian nations that the government intended to protect legal settlers on the lands ceded to them by treaty. Named "Fort Harmar," the post became regimental headquarters the following summer when it was moved from Fort McIntosh.[308]

Garrison construction continued. In June 1786, within days of the completion of Fort Harmar, two companies under the direction of Capts. Walter Finney and David Ziegler were sent to construct a second fort at the Falls of the Ohio to protect the area's residents from Indian incursions. Since Fort Finney, which served as the treaty site earlier in the year, was now deemed nonessential, the officers were instructed to stop there to salvage useful building materials before heading further downriver.

The new fort was located on the north side of the Ohio River directly across from the settlement of Louisville in present-day Jeffersonville, Indiana. It was adjacent to Clarksville, home of Brig. Gen. George Rogers Clark, who, along with veterans of Virginia's Revolutionary War Illinois Regiment, had been granted tracts of land in the area. It was not surprisingly named "Fort Finney" after its builder, who by this time had gained considerable experience constructing or rebuilding facilities for the regiment. The fort eventually served as a base for communications and operations for points further down the Ohio.[309]

---

[307] John Parker Huber, *General Josiah Harmar's Command: Military Policy in the Old Northwest, 1784–1791* (PhD dissertation, Ann Arbor: University of Michigan, 1968), 58–59; Sword, *President Washington's Indian War*, 57.

[308] Guthman, *March to Massacre*, 38. For description of Fort Harmer, see Jacobs, *The Beginning of the U.S. Army*, 26–27 and Beatty, "Diary," 182.

[309] Guthman, *March to Massacre*, 39–40; "Falls of the Ohio" and "Rapids of the Ohio" commonly reference the fort's general location. For its description, see Lewis C. Baird, *Baird's History of Clark County, Indiana* (Indianapolis: B. F. Bowen, 1909), 138; Beatty, "Diary," 382.

Meanwhile, Harmar had directed Maj. John Hamtramck to Mingo Bottom. Now present-day Steubenville, Ohio, the area was located about forty-five miles downriver from Fort McIntosh. Once there, Hamtramck was to evict squatters and to erect a blockhouse for the protection of the surveyors and the recently appointed Geographer of the United States, Capt. Thomas Hutchins. Operating from the newly established Fort Steuben, Hamtramck commanded 200 men guarding multiple parties of surveyors, who, day and night, seven days a week, traversed the wilderness. The process was slow. By the end of December 1786, only four of the seven ranges had been surveyed, and work had to stop due to the severity of the winter and threat of Indian hostilities. The garrison was ordered abandoned in June 1787 in accordance with a directive from Congress for consolidating army forces downriver. Future surveying for the remaining ranges near Mingo Bottom was delegated to a small contingent of soldiers based at Wheeling. The name "Fort Steuben" was then transferred to the garrison at the Falls of the Ohio that had been previously known as Fort Finney.[310]

Rounding out the chain of forts to the north was Fort Franklin, erected at Venango by Capt. Jonathan Heart in 1787 at the confluence of the Allegheny River and French Creek to defend the frontiers of western Pennsylvania. By mid-1787, Harmar's army was stretched between seven forts along six hundred miles. Three were obsolete although not dismantled: Fort Pitt had a only small detachment of men, Fort Steuben at Mingo Bottom lay deserted, and the first Fort Finney at the Great Miami River was no longer necessary. Forts Franklin, McIntosh, and Harmar each

---

[310] Guthman, *March to Massacre*, 40; Richard H. Kohn, *Eagle and Sword*, 67; Harmar to Knox, June 7, 1787 in Smith, ed., *The St. Clair Papers*, II: 22–23. The surveyors' starting point was at present-day East Liverpool, Ohio, from which a forty-two-mile line was plotted to the west, establishing the northern boundary of the "Seven Ranges" survey. The expanse was then divided into seven townships, each six miles square. Range lines were subsequently plotted southward from that base line, each six miles apart until they intersected with the river. Surveyors started mapping within the first range that abutted the Ohio and worked toward the west, going further into the wilderness with completion of each ensuing six-mile-wide north-south column. For detailed information concerning the surveying process, see John E. Dailey, "Ohio Lands and Survey Systems," in *The American Surveyor*, December (2004), http://www.oldfortsteuben.com/admin/data/files/ TheAmericanSurveyor FabricOfSurveyingOhio December2004.pdf.

housed one regimental company, but the largest troop concentration of six captains and 329 men was now at Falls of the Ohio at the new Fort Steuben where Armstrong was soon to join his former company commander, Capt. Walter Finney.[311]

★

Life for enlisted soldiers on frontier outposts during the regiment's formative years varied considerably according to location and immediate circumstances. The men guarded vast stores of food, drink, and gifts for tribal chiefs when accompanying envoys to treaty sites. Soldiers paraded and fired salutes for visitors during military ceremonies. The bulk of their time, however, was spent at lonely outposts to which they stayed in close proximity as threats from Indians increased. Much of a soldier's time in service consisted of hard physical labor building or maintaining forts. Garrisons varied in size from large fortifications with wooden stockades, barracks, magazines, and other assorted buildings, to single blockhouses or camps consisting of a mere collection of huts. Regardless, the work to build and maintain them was exhausting. Commenting on the later construction of Fort Washington, Edward Coffman in his book, *The Old Army: A Portrait of the American Army in Peacetime, 1784–1898* writes of a sergeant's recollection that it took twenty to thirty men to pull one huge log into place. Troops lived in tents until the forts were completed. Major Hamtramck made the construction of Fort Steuben a contest, with six gallons of whiskey as the prize to the men who completed the first house. His ploy obviously worked because all the houses were done in eight days with only an additional twenty-five to complete the entire fort. Hamtramck told Harmar that he attributed this speed to the men's "great attachment to whiskey."[312]

Once garrisons were constructed, security was paramount. Surrounding perimeters were always kept clear; and work parties were continually formed to cut, pile, and burn brush, weeds, and fallen timber, as well as

---

[311] Guthman, *March to Massacre*, 41–43; Huber, *General Josiah Harmar's Command*, 82; For description of Fort Franklin, see Denny, *Military Journal*, 115–116.

[312] Excellent descriptions of garrison life can be found in Edward M. Coffman, *The Old Army: A Portrait of the American Army in Peacetime, 1784–1898* (New York: Oxford University Press, 1986), 15–26; Guthman, *March to Massacre*, 55–90; and Kohn, *Eagle and Sword*, 67.

to rid the area of any tall tree stumps. Sentries were ordered to be alert, especially at night, and the officer of the day was responsible for guards and patrols. Soldiers were not to wander from the garrison and continually kept in readiness in case of an alarm. Men left the fort in pairs, always carried their arms with them, and were ordered never to venture beyond hearing the signal of a beating drum. Gates of the fort were closed at sunset and not opened until sunrise. Countersigns, usually the names of people or places, were announced a day in advance of their use during the issuance of the daily garrison orders.

Times for morning and evening formations varied according to the season and the prevailing degree of danger. The two assemblies were essential to the routine of the regiment and served as the commandant's most direct means of communication with his men. Courts-martial were announced, their panel composition and verdicts read aloud, and punishment carried out before the assembled troops. Regimental and garrison orders were given and were often followed by the reading of the Articles of War.[313]

Since personnel, as well as food, clothing, ammunition, and almost every other essential had to be transported by water, soldiers built, repaired, caulked, and manned boats, mastering navigation of the rivers upon which their livelihoods depended. As hostilities increased in the late 1780s, marauding Indians discovered the army to be the most vulnerable when ascending the Ohio, Wabash, or other rivers in heavily laden boats moving slowly against the current. Despite the danger, the army still found water transport to be the most practical method of movement for men and supplies because of its speed, directness, and cost.[314]

For all his hard work, a private or noncommissioned officer could expect to receive annually a coat, two pairs of woolen overalls, one hat, four pairs of shoes and one pair of shoe buckles, one stock and stock clasp, one vest, two pairs of linen overalls, four shirts, four pairs of socks, and one blanket. The daily ration consisted of one pound of bread or flour, one pound of beef or three-fourth pound of pork, and one gill of common rum. Additionally, one quart of salt, two quarts of vinegar, two pounds of

[313] Guthman, *March to Massacre*, 10. Approved in 1775 by the Second Continental Congress, the Articles of War outlined sixty-nine regulations establishing the conduct of the Continental Army and provided the basis for revised codes until the Unified Code of Military Justice was adopted in 1951.

[314] Guthman, *March to Massacre*, 84–88.

soap, and one pound of candles were issued with every one hundred rations. Soldiers often augmented the rations by hunting or fishing.[315]

★

Officers' lives were similar to those of enlisted men in many respects. They lived and served in the same garrisons and companies, experienced the rigors of the frontier, and ultimately shared the dangers of combat. Despite these similarities, other differences markedly separated the two. Officers were superior by law; they ordered, and soldiers obeyed. In pay and social standing, the lowest-ranking officer occupied a position far above the most senior noncommissioned officer. For those who violated military laws, rank made a profound difference. Privates might be flogged and noncommissioned officers reduced in rank while officers usually got off with reprimands or suspension in rank. About the worst punishment an officer could expect was dismissal from the service.[316]

Officers maintained discipline, inspected men and quarters, sat on courts-martial, drilled the troops, supervised work parties, and traveled to secure pay and supplies. Record keeping was an integral part of the army's organization. Orders issued by regimental and garrison commanders were entered daily into a company orderly book by the adjutant and were read along with applicable congressional directives to the men on parade. Logistical accounts (number of men on duty, sick, on leave, deserting, detached, or captured) were kept in a company book, usually by the commanding officer. A weekly personnel return was submitted to Harmar at headquarters where a compilation of all companies commandwide was entered into a regimental book. Similar records were maintained for provisions, clothing, and weapons.[317]

Officers were at times tasked to explore wilderness territory, to lead surveying parties for routes overland, to conduct negotiations with foreign officers and representatives of Indian nations, and, eventually, to lead their men in battle. As the sole representatives of the United States government in remote areas, officers at times executed civil as well as military duties.[318]

---

[315] Congress of the United States, American State Papers 1789–1838, Military Affairs (Washington: Gales and Seaton, 1832), I: 6. (*ASP-MA*)

[316] Coffman, *The Old Army*, 28–29.

[317] Guthman, *March to Massacre*, 10.

[318] Coffman, *The Old Army*, 28–29.

Harmar firmly espoused von Steuben's methods of creating a well-disciplined corps, taking every opportunity to direct his officers' attention to the baron's Blue Book. Appropriate as von Steuben's doctrine might have been for unit organization and for teaching recruits the basics of military procedure, Guthman notes that the manual was created for combating British and Hessian troops who engaged in conventional military tactics and not for the backwoods guerrilla-style of fighting exemplified by highly skilled Native American warriors. This basic flaw, along with a myriad of other factors, contributed to the disasters that followed.[319]

The duty of recruiting new soldiers took officers back to their home states or to East Coast cities when the enlistments of most soldiers expired in 1785 and 1788, before the St. Clair campaign in 1791, and later in 1792 to enlist men for Maj. Gen. Anthony Wayne's legion. Leaving garrison life and returning to the amenities of the civilized world for several months was no doubt pleasant, but the recruiting challenge was just as great as it had been during the first days of the regiment. During good economic times, likely prospects dwindled, and officers were often in competition with one another to make their quotas.

Recruits were required to be in good physical condition, which in 1784 meant the absence of seizures, hernias, or incapacitating diseases and to be between the ages of sixteen and thirty. Recruiters' instructions were one thing; the inevitable pressure to fill quotas was another. When they had to compromise, recruiters often chose the latter. Most enlistees came from a part of society that had few other life options; more suitable candidates generally were not interested in military life.[320]

Officers had to maintain peace. Congress had made it clear that the nation could not afford a war, so positive relations with local Native Americans was of paramount importance. This aspect of frontier policy affected officers of all ranks, from the commander in his official dealings with tribal delegations to the lieutenant with his men in a lonely frontier blockhouse to whom Indians on the verge of starvation often came following ruined harvests or other misfortunes. Typical of such encounters was that of Capt. Jonathan Heart who was sent to Venango to construct Fort Franklin. He arrived in the area in May 1787, where he was confronted by nearby women and children who pleaded for food lest

---

[319] Guthman, *March to Massacre*, 11.
[320] Coffman, *The Old Army*, 14–15.

they starve before hunting season began. Heart told them that they were to receive fifty bushels of corn promised to them earlier by commissioner Richard Butler, but this failed to satisfy the delegation. When he received word that chiefs of the Seneca, Mohawk, and Wyandot tribes wished a council, he felt that transacting such business was not the duty of a junior officer, but since notification of his arrival had been made by Butler, and since the Indian presence would outnumber the men in his command, he deemed it unwise to deny them an audience.[321]

Depending upon the situation and the individual, an officer's attitude toward the local Indian population at such times was suspicion, fear, hatred, curiosity, sympathetic interest, or a combination of these views. As representatives of the national government and men originating from eastern states, they were less likely to share the extremes of local prejudices and might be expected to be more considerate toward the Native American populace than frontiersmen who were prone to retaliate indiscriminately against attacks on their settlements and isolated homesteads. As the number of incidents increased, however, and fatalities began to occur within the military community, officers had to come to terms with their attitudes toward a population that was rapidly becoming "the enemy."[322]

Officers enjoyed one sigificant amenity that was unavailable to the enlisted men. When the organized settlements that were to become Marietta, Louisville, and Cincinnati began to spring up along the Ohio, they associated with community leaders, often former Revolutionary War officers themselves, and their families. In his diary, Erkuries Beatty described his trip to the Falls of the Ohio in 1787 and noted that the officers appeared to be "exceedingly happy here, having the company frequently of a genteel circle of Ladies, who come over, dance of an evening and stay all night, as the officers have very neat rooms." Presumably, Armstrong was in a position by this time to enjoy the company of the local ladies as well.[323]

Some officers became interested in Indian antiquities, particularly the prehistoric mound complex outside Fort Harmar. Jonathan Heart's written descriptions were published and attracted attention in the East

[321] Guthman, *March to Massacre*, 58; Jacobs, *The Beginning of the U.S. Army*, 32–33.

[322] Coffman, *The Old Army*, 34–35.

[323] See Theodore Roosevelt, *The Winning of the West, Vol. 3: The Founding of the Trans-Alleghany Commonwealths, 1784–1790* (New York: G. P. Putnam's Sons, 1894), 22–24; Beatty, "Diary," 432; Denny, *Military Journal*, 237.

and abroad. Many officers shared enlightened Easterners' fascination with natural phenomena and were drawn to the rich fossil deposits found along the Ohio. A landmark frequently referred to by diarists was Kentucky's Big Bone Lick, downstream from present-day Cincinnati and site of a resting place of large prehistoric animals trapped in the surrounding marsh. Ebenezer Denny described the trip he made there in December 1785 with Captain Finney and a party of soldiers, recording in his diary that he had collected fossils of some astonishingly large bones; and in June 1788, Harmar tasked Armstrong to deliver those "of a huge, unknown animal" that the lieutenant had dug up to Philadelphia physician and anatomist Dr. Caspar Wistar.[324]

Letter writing also consumed large amounts of an officer's time. Armstrong's papers include not only drafts of his important letters but in some cases copies as well. Mail went up and down the river carried by fellow officers who had business at other posts, and many of Armstrong's letters to associates in the East were hand delivered by those on furlough. Understandably, delivery of correspondence was often delayed by months. Friends sent officers copies of newspapers, which were then passed from person to person.

Correspondence between officers and the secretary of war was commonplace in this small army, and subalterns and even their men did not hesitate to communicate to the highest authority. While most official correspondence included in his papers went to officers in his immediate chain of command, Armstrong frequently exercised this prerogative, and his papers contain several letters to Knox.[325]

---

[324] Guthman, *March to Massacre*, 62–63; Denny, *Military Journal*, 60, 227. Bones were likely those of a mastodon.

[325] Norman W. Caldwell, "The Frontier Army Officer 1790–1814," *Mid-America* 37, no. 2 (1955), 101–28. See Armstrong-Knox correspondence in the Armstrong's papers, October 30, 1789, July 17, 1791, March 5, 1793; Armstrong to Alexander Hamilton, September 17, 1791, Founders Online, http://founders.archives.gov/documents /Hamilton/01-26-02-0002-0306. Apparently, not all correspondence with those higher up in the command was necessarily appreciated by Armstrong's superiors. He had written to Knox in December 1788 concerning the lack of consideration of his brevet rank on occasions when he had to serve under militia officers, and Harmar later wrote, "Lieutenant Armstrong, I see, has been writing the War Office about brevet rank. He is a valuable officer, but instead of troubling you upon the occasion,

Regimental officers routinely engaged in land speculation. Revolutionary War veterans from Pennsylvania and New York serving in the regiment had already received land from their respective states. Additionally, having seen land that opened up for sale in 1787 and having taken part in survey operations themselves, many were in prime position to provide minute details of choice properties within the territory to their friends at home. Land investment was one of the few paths to wealth at the time. Most had no understanding of the concept of "conflict of interest." Armstrong was no exception and bought up his soldiers' claims whenever he could.[326]

Officers found it hard to live on their salaries even though their pay placed them in the country's middle class at a time when "hard money" was difficult to come by. The pay scale for officers and men, fixed in 1785–1787, was as follows:

Lieutenant colonel	$50 per month
Majors	$45 per month
Captains	$35 per month
Lieutenants	$26 per month
Ensigns	$20 per month
Surgeons	$45 per month
Surgeon's mates	$30 per month
Sergeants	$6 per month
Corporals, musicians	$5 per month
Privates	$4 per month

In lieu of rations, majors and lieutenant colonels got $20; captains, $12; lieutenants, ensigns, surgeon's mates, $8; and surgeons, $16 per month in subsistence pay. Forage allowances amounted to $12 per month for majors and $6 per month for company officers and surgeons.[327]

---

it is my opinion that he should have represented his grievances, if any there were, unto his commanding officer." Harmar to Knox, January 14, 1790, in Denny, *Military Journal*, 245.

326 Guthman, *March to Massacre*, 63.

327 Caldwell, "The Frontier Army Officer," 108; ASP-MA, I: 5–6.

Continuing a practice inherited from European armies and standard throughout American forces during the Revolution, officers were authorized personal servants. These "waiters" might have been enlisted soldiers, indentured servants, or slaves. Their use was not necessarily a mere status issue, although, as "gentlemen," officers they were expected to exhibit a way of life that distinguished them from the average man; such individuals were needed to cook for their officers, to tend their horses, to look after them when they were ill, and to run errands.[328]

★

Another tradition, and indeed a necessity, was the use of women to provide laundry services in support of the soldiers. They were authorized rations in Washington's army, some even fighting in battle; and after the war, they accompanied Harmar's troops to the frontier. Capt. Jonathan Heart noted in his orderly book that "provisions will be issued to the women in the garrison at the rate of four to a company."[329]

Women helped lighten the burden of life for soldiers in the grim, desolate places occupied by some of the frontier posts. Whatever else they did other than washing clothes was not specifically recorded unless they

---

[328] Mayer, *Belonging to the Army*, 170–77. Personal servants, contractors, family members, and women provided legitimate services to units during the Revolution, and their presence continued within the organization of the First Regiment. Armstrong's servants are not positively identified in his records, and he apparently had more than one throughout his career, receiving reimbursement for expenditures for himself and his servant on his trip to the Missouri River in 1790 and later having an orderly charged as a deserter during the St. Clair campaign. In April 1791, he assumed the indenture of John McIntosh from Col. Thomas Craig. Whether McIntosh became Armstrong's attendant or if he was part of Armstrong's efforts to enlist soldiers prior to the St. Clair expedition is unknown. Armstrong papers, March 8, 1780, and April 19, 1791, PJA; A. P. Nasatir, *Before Lewis and Clark: Documents Illustrating the History of the Missouri, 1785–1804* (Norman: University of Oklahoma Press, 1952), 141. Samuel Newman, "Captain Newman's Original Journal of St. Clair's Campaign," *Wisconsin Magazine of History* 2, no. 1 (1918), 71–72. Accessed March 20, 2021, http://www.jstor.org/stable/4630127.

[329] Coffman, *The Old Army*, 25.

---

got into trouble and attracted the attention of the command. Some were wives of soldiers; others were not.[330]

Women who worked for the army would not have been acceptable marriage partners for "officers and gentlemen." In her book *Belonging to the Army: Camp Followers and Community during the American Revolution*, Holly A. Mayer discusses the role of women in Washington's army. While her work reflects conditions during the Revolution, her observations regarding those in the postwar era also apply. The issue was ultimately one of class roles and expectations; one's place and behavior were defined by rank, civilian and military, and gender. Washington associated with women of his own social order, welcoming the presence of his wife and other senior officers' wives when they visited the camps, but he was uncomfortable with women from lower classes. He was used to dealing with ladies of high social status, courteous to women from the middling orders, but dismayed by white women in the lower ranks of society who seemed to adhere to a totally different social code. Most female camp followers lacked the polish and graces that defined the eighteenth-century lady.[331]

One of John Armstrong's notebooks contains his lengthy musings on "polite" society in Pittsburgh during his assignment to Fort Pitt in 1786. From his references, he seemed to have spent a great deal of time pondering the makeup of the female populace and measuring those ladies against a distant love interest for whose presence he was pining. The effect that distance, economic circumstances, social status of a junior officer, and well understood qualifications of a wife suitable for a "gentleman" had on Armstrong and his peers in finding a mate is difficult to gauge.[332]

Frontier life was harsh, and wives of officers are rarely mentioned in records until garrisons were more established and settlements were organized nearby. Real danger lay in the isolation and loneliness of frontier outposts. Coffman notes that living in such remote locations was hard enough on men but worse for women. Since an officer's wife was not supposed to associate with the laundresses or camp followers, her circle of society was extremely limited. Colonel Harmar's wife, however, accompanied him almost from the beginning of his command to Fort McIntosh, Fort Harmar, and Fort Washington and was later joined by a

---

[330] Ibid.

[331] Mayer, *Belonging to the Army*, 127.

[332] John Armstrong notebook, 1781–1813, PJA.

few other officer wives. Beatty noted in his diary that on one of his trips, he found Mrs. McCurdy at Fort McIntosh to be in a very bad state of health, and Ebenezer Denny recorded the marriage of Captain Zeigler to the daughter of a settler in Marietta in March 1789.[333]

★

Garrison life could be filled with endless days of monotony. To relieve boredom, many of the men and any children present trapped and domesticated baby animals so that each garrison had an assortment of "wild" pets. Gardening, hunting, and fishing helped pass the limited amount of free time both officers and men might have had and often supplied shortfalls in promised contractor-supplied provisions. Still, a bachelor officer's life was lonely. A few passed the hours reading or, as in Armstrong's case, laboriously drafting and copying letters and reports to superiors and associates.[334]

An occasional celebration relieved the harshness of frontier life. Holidays and important occasions provided the excuse for an extra allowance of whiskey, and the men looked forward to these events with enthusiasm. The Revolutionary War-inspired holiday St. Tammany's Day was observed on May 1 at the various garrisons, complete with decorated maypoles, dancing "with many curious antics," and drinking, carousing, and firing arms. Commemorations celebrating the anniversary of the nation's independence on July 4 were particularly noteworthy, with cannon firing and extra gills of whiskey being part of the day. Ebenezer Denny described this celebration by officers at Fort Finney in 1786:

> This day was celebrated with three rounds of small arms and three with the field-piece, after which the gentlemen all dined together. When dinner was over thirteen toasts were drunk, each accompanied with a round from the three-pounder, attended in the intervals by two drums, two fifes, and a couple of excellent violins.

[333] Guthman, *March to Massacre*, 61; Beatty, "Diary," 313; Denny, *Military Journal*, 131, 153; Coffman, *The Old Army*, 37. Capt. William McCurdy was significantly older than his fellow officers, having been born in 1730. Most junior officers were bachelors.
[334] Guthman, *March to Massacre*, 61; Coffman, *The Old Army*, 36.

The evening was spent as well as circumstances would allow it.[335]

Although that celebration appears to have been one not to have been missed, Denny described the commemoration of St. Patrick's Day that year that probably should have been:

> A majority of the men in the garrison are Irish. The soldiers requested to have the privilege of celebrating this day, as was customary. Accordingly the bung was opened and every man had permission to purchase and drink what quantity of liquor he pleased; and a pretty good portion did some of them take, for toward evening we had not six men in the garrison fit for duty, not even the guard excepted.

He noted that one man died the next day from the effect of too much alcohol.[336]

Celebrations at Fort Harmar, the Falls of the Ohio, or other large garrisons were the exception. Lonely outposts eventually dotted the territory from Fort Pitt to Louisville where life on a daily basis was less rosy. As settlements sprang up, detachments were delegated to provide for their defense in nearby blockhouses. Lonely tracts of dense woods full of bear, panther, and deer cut off the parties of from twenty-five to one hundred soldiers from civilization. So wild was the life in these places and, later, so certain the attack from Indians that officers or men dared not take their wives or families to such outposts.

Although the designs of individual forts varied, garrisons were usually built in stockade form. They were surrounded by rectangular fences of logs, pointed at the tops and loopholed for the flintlocks and iron and brass cannon and reinforced at the corners by blockhouses. The enclosure was usually divided into two parts by a high stockade fence similar to the outer one. In case a blockhouse or other wooden part was burned or a breach made in the outer fence, the occupants could retreat to one side or the other.

[335] Denny, *Military Journal*, 88–89; S. P. Hildreth, "Journal of Joseph Buell" in *Pioneer History: Being an Account of the First Examinations of the Ohio Valley, and the Early Settlement of the Northwest Territory* (New York: H. W. Derby & Co., 1848), 143.

[336] Denny, *Military Journal*, 79.

The two enclosures contained the guardhouse and parade area on one side while officer and enlisted quarters and the magazine were on the other. Supplies were usually placed inside the blockhouses.[337]

Sites for garrison construction were chosen with an eye for water supply within the walls. Outhouses were built outside the fortification, but there were also "necessary facilities" inside for use at night and when under attack. Violent prisoners were secured in a dungeon-like cellar called "the black hole," usually in heavy irons.[338]

Officers shared two-room quarters. Those of a commanding officer might have two rooms and a hall, but such an occurrence was a luxury. Enlisted men huddled together in cold barracks. Relying on open fireplaces for warmth while waiting for supplies delayed due to frozen rivers and enduring the monotony of long winters, many soldiers, not surprisingly, found solace in alcohol.[339]

★

Supply problems were never-ending. The Quartermaster Department that had supported troop operations during the Revolution had been abolished in 1785, and the army now relied on a system that depended on contractors. Sometimes far removed from the frontier, their sole purpose was to support the growing number of fortifications and the needs of soldiers who occupied them. Everything from basic supplies needed for survival in the wilderness, such as food, clothing, and munitions; those needed to tame it, such as axes, shovels, picks, and grindstones; and other necessities, such as candles and paper, came from the East. Since all goods were transported on the water, large periods of time occurred during the year when rivers were unnavigable due to ice, flooding, or low water levels; and the soldiers on the receiving end of the process suffered accordingly. Ideally, the regiment should have maintained a three-month supply of salt beef or pork. Hot weather and salt shortages, however, often made the curing process ineffective, and meat often spoiled. As open conflict with Indians increased, so did attacks on contractors' boats, and supplies and cattle were lost in the raids. By far, the larger problem, however, was with the system itself and the unwillingness of Congress to address not only the whole question of a peacetime force but also the money needed to support

---

[337] Ganoe, *The History of the United States Army*, 93.
[338] Guthman, *March to Massacre*, 61–62.
[339] Ganoe, *The History of the United States Army*, 93.

it. Repeatedly, Congress pursued a policy of awarding contracts to the lowest bidder, creating a system in which no one came out ahead, least of all the soldiers on the far end of the supply line.

Since contracts were let on an annual basis, the army saw a virtual seesaw of suppliers for its assigned rations. The government's initial contract in 1785 was with James O'Hara, a Pittsburgh-based veteran quartermaster officer who apparently accomplished his duties "tolerably well" despite complications arising from "the state of the frontiers and of public affairs." In 1786, the government awarded the contract to Turnbull, Marmie & Company, lowest bidders for the job. As Jacobs notes in *The Beginning of the U.S. Army, 1783–1812*, they were paid in depreciated Pennsylvania currency and retaliated by furnishing "depreciated" rations or none at all. During November of that year, troops at Fort Harmar often went hungry, getting only half their allowance of bread and meat. They might have starved the following January if Harmar had not advanced his personal funds to purchase provisions. For a time, conditions were so bad that he thought of abandoning the fort. Things began to improve in 1787, however, when the Board of the Treasury again let the contract to James O'Hara; but the next year, it again went to the lowest bidder, the firm of Elliott and Williams. Winning bids per ration for the four years in question began in 1785 at 13.5 ninetieths of a dollar and by 1788 had dropped dramatically, ranging from 7 to 16 ninetieths of a dollar, depending on distances to forts from Baltimore, Elliot and Williams's place of business.

Contractors were locked into the never-ending process of trying to collect payment from the cash-strapped government, either to purchase much-needed supplies or to receive payment for those already delivered. Keen competition every year forced prospective contractors to lower their bids and resulting profit margins to the point where it was impossible to break even on their investment, much less make money. To realize any sort of profit, they had to make up their losses by selling liquor and cheap merchandise to soldiers on payday. Either the contractors had to bid so low in order to be awarded the contract, forcing them to make up their losses with sales to individual soldiers, or they took the contract purposely at a low figure in order to do so. The end result was the same: the system allowed the contractor to take advantage of a soldier's needs, thereby making a constant debtor of him.[340]

---

[340] Guthman, *March to Massacre*, 63–69; Jacobs, *The Beginning of the U.S. Army*,

Not only did soldiers often go hungry, they also lacked adequate clothing and proper equipment. When Major Hamtramck's men accompanied surveyor Thomas Hutchins near Fort Steuben in 1787, soldiers lacked both provisions and equipment. Of the three companies of men assigned to Hamtramck, only thirty men were sufficiently equipped to permit their accompanying the surveyors. Nevertheless, the group carried on until November when freezing weather put a halt to the operation in spite of the fact that many of the men were "barefoot and miserably off for clothing."[341]

All too often, troops received inferior guns, bayonets, and cartridge boxes that had been turned in after the Revolution and stored in eastern depots. A contractor was supposed to supply such articles as were "indispensably necessary" when ordered to do so in writing by Harmar or post commanders, but the goods received frequently did not conform either to requisition or specification in respect to quality and quantity. During April 1786, Harmar reported that the shirts delivered were skimpy, of sleazy cloth, and would wear out in a week. Shoes were too small, designed for twelve- or fourteen-year-old boys, and of inferior leather. Coats provided in Philadelphia were so worthless that they would not have lasted through the march to Pittsburgh unless fatigue coats were worn part of the time. By October 1788, regimental soldiers on the frontier were short a year's supply of clothing, their allotment having been issued to new men recruited that year. Orders issued to ensure the longest possible wear for the short supply of uniforms read, "No soldier is to presume to wear his uniform coat on fatigue, on pain of being severely punished." Commanding officers were to inspect the clothing, arms, and ammunition of their respective companies every Monday and submit a written report to the commander that same day, specifying the condition of every article.[342]

These and similar problems plagued the system for years. Even after the new constitutional government was instituted in 1789 and later during the times of high-stakes expeditions, the army's problem of an adequate supply of food, munitions, and equipment went unresolved. Money was the primary reason—the government's lack of it, and the contractor's need for it.[343]

35–37.

[341] Alan S. Brown, "The Role of the Army in Western Settlement," 169.

[342] Jacobs, *The Beginning of the U.S. Army*, 37; Guthman, *March to Massacre*, 10.

[343] Jacobs, *The Beginning of the U.S. Army*, 35–37; Guthman, *March to Massacre*, 63–69.

The matter of pay presented even more problems. Paymaster Erkuries Beatty's odyssey to obtain funds in 1786 exemplifies the difficulty in getting pay to the troops during the formative years of the regiment. Soldiers were initially paid in Continental currency, but in 1786, Secretary at War Henry Knox made a strenuous effort to have payment made in "hard money" or specie. Beatty was directed to get an order from the Board of Treasury for that purpose. He succeeded in getting an order for $12,000 to be drawn from Pennsylvania's loan office, but the office had no money. When he was referred to the treasurer of Pennsylvania, there was no specie in that location. Beatty then called upon several county treasurers, collected what he could and ended up with enough specie to provide one month's pay to the troops.

Because of the scarcity of funds, troops seldom drew pay more than once or twice a year. By October 2, 1788, they had not been paid in twenty-one months although officers were able to draw subsistence and forage money they were due up to April that year. Armstrong received three years of back pay on January 26, 1790, covering his service from January 1787 to January 1790; he was not alone in experiencing the extended delay in receiving his accumulated salary. By the end of the decade, troops were owed nearly $150,000 in pay and subsistence.[344]

Lack of funds also limited army operations. In June 1786, Knox requested $1,000 to transport three tons of lead and powder to Fort Pitt for distribution to frontier posts but was refused despite the fact that Indian hostility was increasing and the need for ammunition was critical. The Board of Treasury claimed that its coffers were empty. Knox repeatedly reminded Harmar of the confederation's financial weaknesses and cautioned him to avoid any action that might lead to war. Near the end of 1786, Knox explicitly forbade offensive operations without specific orders from his office.[345]

★

Discipline, paramount to the regiment's foundation, defined daily life. Courts-martial were a regular part of garrison life and often consumed

---

[344] Beatty, "Diary," 380–81; Jacobs, *The Beginning of the U.S. Army*, 38; Kohn, *Eagle and Sword*, 69; Denny, *Military Journal*, 96; pay receipt, January 26, 1790, PJA.

[345] Kohn, *Eagle and Sword*, 69.

large portions of an officer's time. Men were brought up on charges for a myriad of reasons, including drunkenness, petty thievery, swearing at officers, or forging officers' names on permits for additional whiskey rations, as well as for more serious offenses, such as falling asleep while on guard duty or neglect of assignment. All were punishable by whippings, which consisted of twenty-five to one hundred lashes, administered during troop formation. Desertion, stealing government property, murder, aiding a prisoner to escape, major thefts, and assaulting Indians or civilians were punishable by execution, running the gauntlet, being drummed out of the service, or by multiple whippings carried out over a period of days. Soldiers were rarely executed during Harmar's time, however, and major punishments were restrained due to the necessity of retaining the offenders for military service. Severe sentences were not ordered unless the situation absolutely required it.

Based on the Articles of War formulated in 1775 by the Continental Congress, court-martial procedures originally required a panel of thirteen officers to adjudge the guilt or innocence of the accused soldier for trials where capital punishment might result. Regulations were altered in 1786 due to the lack of officers to serve on such courts. Original statutes regarding the size of the court were applicable to units of true regimental strength typical of those in the Revolutionary War rather than to smaller units spread hundreds of miles apart, which were more typical of the frontier army's structure. Revisions were made to allow as few as three commissioned officers to adjudicate trials of privates and noncommissioned officers whose offenses did not involve capital crimes. Such garrison trials could not impose sentences of imprisonment over one month or fines of more than one month's pay. Harmar reviewed the verdict of every court-martial, approving or disagreeing with the sentence imposed by the court, and he held the prerogative of altering the terms of punishment as he saw fit. Trials of enlisted soldiers accused of capital crimes or of officers accused officially of any illegality were to be tried by a general court-martial, requiring a panel of five to thirteen officers. Verdicts of general courts-martial were submitted to the Secretary at War for approval, and he in turn forwarded the proceedings and findings to Congress for final assent. Punishments were often altered by either the commander or Knox and were frequently reduced to a verbal reprimand. No fixed punishment existed for specific infractions, and often varying sentences were given to different offenders found guilty of the same crime.[346]

By today's standards, punishments were unusually cruel, but the world was a much less forgiving place in the late eighteenth century. In his work, *The Old Army: A Portrait of the American Army in Peacetime, 1784–1898*, Edward Coffman notes that brutality was inherent in the times. A fight could result in the loss of an eye or an ear or damage a vital organ, resulting in death, and the law showed little mercy to those convicted. Hanging, beating, and the slow torture of cruel prison conditions for those guilty of crimes and the equally barbarous treatment of the mentally ill in asylums were accepted by society. Later, reform movements ameliorated these practices; but in the late eighteenth and early nineteenth centuries, they flourished and often took the form of public spectacle. The army depended on discipline to maintain its character, and in keeping with the times, military punishments were often brutal. Harsh as the regiment's punishments were, though, they paled in comparison with the one thousand lashes the British Army administered to its soldiers at the time of the Revolution.[347]

Regardless, the severe punishments doled out for serious infractions paint a dim picture of eighteenth-century garrison life. Joseph Buell, a sergeant from Connecticut, noted in his journal the frequency of courts-martial at Fort McIntosh and, in particular, the January 1786 incident when Maj. John Wyllys ordered the immediate execution of three captured deserters without waiting for the formality of a court-martial. Buell described this incident as the most inhumane act he ever saw.[348]

★

---

[346] Jacobs, *The Beginning of the U.S. Army*, 35; Guthman, *March to Massacre*, 13–16. For a detailed explanation of the policies that determined court-martial procedures, see Bradley J. Nicholson, "Courts-martial in the Legion Army: American Military Law in the Early Republic, 1792–1796," *Military Law Review*, 144 (1994): 77–90 and Richard C. Knopf, "Crime and Punishment in the Legion, 1792–1793," *Bulletin of the Historical and Philosophical Society of Ohio* 14, no. 3 (1956), 232–238.

[347] Coffman, *The Old Army*, 23.

[348] Hildreth, "Journal of Joseph Buell," 141–42. Buell described the event that shocked the entire chain of command and led to a revision of court-martial procedures. Wyllys had conducted a trial employing only five rather than the

With pay in arrears; clothes in rags; crude, cold quarters; and food often dependent upon local hunting and fishing conditions because of inadequate supply procedures, a soldier did not have much to brighten his days of hard labor or monotonous garrison routine. For many, escape came in one of two ways—desertion or drunkenness. Desertion was the most obvious as well as the most extreme method, and many took this way out. Drunkenness, while still exposing the soldier to harsh punishment, was a more likely means of escape. Whiskey was already an integral part of a soldier's life. He received it as part of his daily ration, and if he was on a work detail, he might receive an additional amount. A garrison commander might also authorize extra rations on special occasions. If a soldier became ill, the only medicine he might get was more whiskey. Many, however, crossed the line between self-regulated consumption and drunkenness. Payday often meant a quick exchange of cash, a rare commodity on the frontier. Ebenezer Denny described the situation in which contractor O'Hara brought goods to encampments on payday and took in almost as much money from soldiers as was distributed, the men having permission to purchase and consume whiskey. He noted that for three days following soldiers' payday on March 1, 1786, there was scarcely one sober man in the garrison, excepting officers, and questioned how long the situation would have continued if the practice had not been stopped.[349]

Sickness and maladies of all sorts were another part of frontier life. Inadequately clothed soldiers exposed to the severe weather of the frontier

---

proscribed thirteen officers of two deserters who were found guilty, the results of their conviction and recommended sentencing forwarded to the War Office and congressional approval. In the interim, three additional soldiers took off. When they were apprehended, Wyllys had them shot. The major was later arrested and tried for the incident but was acquitted.

[349] Coffman, *The Old Army*, 21–23; Denny, *Military Journal*, 79. Rations authorized in 1787 and continued in 1789 included a daily allotment of one gill of rum per soldier. In 1790, the ration was changed to a half gill rum, brandy, or whiskey. As availability of molasses and sugar, obtained from the West Indies, became less likely following the Revolution, whiskey became America's drink. Brewed from local crops of corn, wheat or rye, settlers could brew it themselves, and commercial distillers established large operations on major waterways throughout the Ohio Valley. See ASP-MA I: 5–6; Nelson A. Miles, *Report of the Lieutenant-General Commanding the Army* (Washington: Government Printing Office, 1900), I: 212.

often suffered the consequences. Guthman cites Samuel Stearns's *North American Almanack* of 1776, which lists diseases common to the country at the time. Among the many cited were consumption or tuberculosis, rheumatism, smallpox, measles, malaria, conjunctivitis, tonsillitis, gout, diarrhea, dysentery, and pleurisy. He warned, "Those that wear dirty clothing and live an idle sedentary life and feed chiefly upon salt meat, old dry biscuit, farinaceous vegetables, Peas, Beans, and old cheese are subject to many dangerous diseases and especially the Scurvy." Guthman notes that Stearns did not include venereal disease, the "regiment reducer" common in the Revolution that had no cure. Diseases cited by Stearns had not changed by 1787. Wounds were slow to heal, and infections set in. The lack of "bark," or quinine, was particularly serious, as most of the men were afflicted with malaria at one time or another. Although an issued ration, another commodity in short supply was vinegar, a necessary dietary balance when large quantities of salted meat were consumed.[350]

By the time the French scientist Volney visited the Ohio River valley in 1796, little had changed. He found fewer than twenty homes free from fevers during a journey of some seven hundred miles, and, when stopping at Greenville, then headquarters of Anthony Wayne's Legion force, found some 300 of 370 soldiers ill with similar maladies. From the lowest-ranking enlisted man to the highest-ranking general, frequent illness was a part of frontier life.[351]

★

The frontier was a rough, wild place often populated by men and women incredibly hardened to their environment. Erkuries Beatty described the residents of Louisville during one of his trips to the garrison at the Falls of the Ohio. A group of officers had received a "polite" invitation to attend a barbecue from "the genteeler sort of people" to conclude with a dance in town in the evening. Beatty noted that only two officers intended to go, however, because "the people and they do not agree very well." He described another occasion at which he witnessed a fight between two locals who fought by biting each other, attempting to gouge out the other's eyes or grabbing the opponent's testicles. He was horrified by the spectacle and by the fact that no one tried to intervene, seemingly to consider that all was fair play. He

---

350 Guthman, *March to Massacre*, 55–56.
351 Caldwell, "The Frontier Army Officer," 120–21.

reported a third incident that occurred when one particularly notorious town bully grossly insulted an officer in a public house. The officer, who must have been of formidable size and strength, managed to overpower his aggressor and emerged only with a scar on his nose from an attempt of his opponent to bite it off. Beatty noted that several other such fracases had occurred between officers and locals and that the former subsequently did not cross the river without swords, pocket pistols, or daggers under their coats.[352]

Theodore Roosevelt described the situation in this way: although relations between officers and gentry were pleasant, those with frontiersmen were not. One group was rude, suspicious, lacked discipline, and looked with distrust and a mixture of sneering envy and hostility upon the other. Officers, products of rigid training and fixed ideals, felt little sympathy for the frontiersman's good points and were contemptuously aware of his numerous failings. As Indian hostilities increased and Kentucky militias began, first to act independently and later in conjunction with federal troops, basic disregard of one group for the other would not only plague operations but ultimately led to disaster when they eventually marched together to confront their mutual foes.[353]

Life for officers and enlisted soldiers in the early years of the First Regiment serving on the outposts of civilization was a challenge. Yet with resources stretched so thin, Harmar's regiment performed the duties Congress delegated to it as best as it could. It could not curtail the migration of illegal settlers or keep at bay the increasing assaults by isolated Native American parties, but by its very presence, it acted as the eyes and ears of the government in the west, relaying information about the British and their Indian allies, monitoring the pace and direction of settlement, and exploring the wilderness. The army built forts at strategic points along the Ohio that became stepping-stones not only for future settlement but also for use in the military campaigns that were to follow. No one will ever know for certain what incidents were prevented by the army's presence along the Ohio River. What is certain, however, is that the force was weak, woefully understrength, and at the mercy of a government that had yet to figure out how to support it while it wrestled with idea of its very existence.[354]

---

[352] Beatty, "Diary," 432–433.

[353] Roosevelt, *The Winning of the West, Vol. 3: The Founding of the Trans-Alleghany Commonwealths*, 22–24.

[354] Kohn, *Eagle and Sword*, 71–72.

8

The Temperature Rises, 1786–1789

So I don't know which is worse the Indians
or the people of this country.
—Erkuries Beatty, May 2, 1787[355]

In its first years of its existence, the army was preoccupied with building fortifications, guarding surveyors, accompanying commissioners on treaties, evicting squatters, interacting with friendly Indians, and dealing with internal supply, manpower, and morale problems. During this time, however, reports of incidents involving Indian raiding parties began to filter down through the command and provided an undercurrent of tension for both those going downriver to settle, legally or illegally, and for the soldiers protecting the country's interests. As early as April and May 1786, Armstrong, while commanding Fort Pitt, received word of small parties stealing horses and firing upon canoes to reports of larger groups crossing into Kentucky and attacking settlements there. By the summer, convoys were anchoring in the middle of the river for safety, and the garrisons were on alert. The situation would soon get worse.[356]

The army was initially forced to stand by as raids into Kentucky increased and retaliatory strikes by frontiersmen grew proportionately.

---

[355] Beatty, "Diary," 437
[356] Heart to Doughty April 27, 1786, and Doughty to Armstrong, May 8, 1786, PJA; Hildreth, "Journal of Joseph Buell," 143–44; Beatty, "Diary," 235.

In mid-1786, Secretary at War Henry Knox gave Lt. Col. Josiah Harmar authority to punish any assaults upon army posts, its troops, or legal settlers, but cautioned him to distinguish between isolated raiding parties and those acting under tribal orders lest any reprisal on the part of the army precipitate a costly war. The following year, a Wyandot party captured a soldier within sight of the Fort Harmar garrison. The unfortunate man was taken to their village and murdered, his scalp paraded through those nearby. It was the first regimental casualty, and the men were angry.[357]

Unrest had already taken on a new dimension further to the west. For over fifty years, residents of the village of Vincennes on the Wabash River had benefitted from proximity to Indian villages along nearby Maumee River tributaries and the access they afforded to the Great Lakes. Settled by French fur traders in 1732, it had fallen under the jurisdiction of the Crown under terms of France's agreement with Britain following the Seven Years' War. Now within United States territory, it was far removed from formal governmental authority and continued to rely upon the system of magistrates and a form of civic organization that had been implemented for the past half century. Locals, mostly traders, coexisted with tribes living along the Wabash tributaries, among which were the Kickapoo, Mascouten, Piankashaw, Wea, Delaware, Shawnee, and Miami. Described by traveler and land speculator John Filson in 1785, the town had some three hundred houses, "most of which makes a poor appearance but in general are convenient and clean," with numbers of its French residents having intermarried with local Indians. By 1786, however, residents had been joined by about seventy American families that had claimed lands in the area based on their participation in George Rogers Clark's occupation of the region during the Revolution while others had appropriated land by virtue of squatters' rights.[358]

The arrival of the Americans presented an unsettling dynamic to the existing cultural mix. The newcomers settled the land, whereas the French had merely occupied it. The European settlers generally had little interest in the land itself and were primarily engaged in trading their abundant crops, easily cultivated in the fertile valley, providing the basis of an economy directed toward New Orleans. Americans, on the other hand,

---

[357] Kohn, *Eagle and Sword*, 68.

[358] Richard White, *The Middle Ground*, 421–22. For additional description of Vincennes, see Jacobs, *The Beginning of the U.S. Army*, 26.

were obsessed with claiming the land as theirs and regarded the French as lazy, not utilizing the abundance they had before them.

The introduction of whiskey appears to have been a tipping point in the delicate social balance of European-American-Indian relations. Americans turned their corn into whiskey and supported themselves by selling it to the Indians. Alcohol had always been a prized commodity on the Wabash, but with the breakdown of traditional lines of authority following its transfer to American jurisdiction, it became even more valuable. Local magistrates tried to restrict its trade by levying fines on such sales, but their measures had little impact. More importantly, they were powerless to stop the disputes and behavior caused by its presence.

Besides the increased availability of whiskey and the rising number of incidents of violence between Europeans and Indians attributed to it, the introduction of alcohol as a means of local revenue disrupted the well-established system that had previously allowed townspeople to prosper in a world of long-distance commerce. Now there was money to be made locally, the effect of which drastically altered the once self-regulated society.[359]

With the arrival of alcohol, older chiefs accustomed to acting as mediating agents within their tribal units were rendered powerless to control their younger warriors whose impulsivity was matched by that of the American settlers. Local magistrates managed to remain officially uninvolved in much of the chaos until mid-1786 when a particularly heinous incident forced their hand.

On June 20, Indians ambushed Daniel Sullivan and a party of Americans who were working in their cornfields, wounding two men, one of whom was critically injured. Sullivan was the de facto leader of the American community and was described by Vincennes magistrate Jean Marie Philippe LeGras as "very dangerous . . . and pernicious to the public peace." Following the attack, Sullivan and his men stalked into Vincennes, seizing and killing the first Indian they found who happened to be a sick man under the care of the French, later scalping him and dragging his body "like a pig on the tail of a horse." This incident differed from those previously arising from disputes between local Indians and American settlers; it had taken place in the town, thus implicating the French and threatening to turn the area into a bloodbath. LeGras ordered all Americans out of the area, but they refused to go. An estimated 450

---

[359] Cayton, *Frontier Indiana*, 55–56, 91–93.

to 700 warriors soon arrived from the Wabash villages and threatened to exterminate "the Big Knives." Fortunately, LeGras and other magistrates were able to defuse the situation and to persuade the warriors to depart.[360]

News of these events created a stir in the Kentucky territory and the state of Virginia itself. Kentucky settlements had long been the targets of horse thefts, property attacks, and murder at the hands of raiders crossing the Ohio; and settlers saw Wabash tribes as the source of many of these incursions. Punitive forays by a handful of local frontiersmen only intensified the situation. As one county lieutenant put it, "Scarcely a week has passed without some person being murdered."[361]

The federal government's inaction concerning the issue and intense pressure from its citizens living in the territory prompted Virginia governor Patrick Henry to authorize the Kentucky militia to take action to defend the region. Territoral officials chose to interpret the governor's ruling as the go-ahead to conduct offensive operations against offending tribes. In September 1786, a large force was assembled in Jefferson County, Kentucky, and Revolutionary War hero George Rogers Clark was ready to lead the charge.[362]

Clark, known for his successes in campaigns against the British and their Native American allies in the West, had originally been appointed brigadier general of the Virginia militia by Gov. Thomas Jefferson. Bold and unapologetic in his animosity toward Indians, his attitude was typical of the frontier philosophy of Indian management— intimidation, or as he put it, "to keep them in awe."[363]

Conditions did not bode well for the campaign from its start. Clark had planned to execute the operation against the Vincennes-area tribes with a force of about 2,000 men but was forced to proceed with a militia of about 1,200. Faced with a variety of logistical problems, the frustrated Clark eventually advanced without an expected shipment of lead, instead casting ammunition from pewter dishes, cups, and other metallic articles.

Signs of the mission's impending failure became evident even before Clark reached Vincennes. His men marched overland, but supplies were sent by water and were delayed, perishable goods spoiling along the way.

---

[360] White, *The Middle Ground*, 424–25; Cayton, *Frontier Indiana*, 94.

[361] Sword, *President Washington's Indian War*, 31–33.

[362] Cayton, *Frontier Indiana*, 95.

[363] Sword, *President Washington's Indian War*, 33; White, *The Middle Ground*, 368–71.

Clark nevertheless pushed on toward the Wabash villages, but by this time, volunteers began to talk about going home. Without provisions, deep in enemy territory, and realizing that Indians had been alerted to their coming, his men lost their incentive to be there. Additionally, reports of Clark's frequent drunkenness did not inspire confidence, and his troops finally refused to obey orders, marching home in a disorderly mob. With only remnants of his original force, Clark returned to Vincennes and garrisoned the town.[364]

★

Word of Clark's dismal campaign was not well received by Congress. Eager to extend its authority into previously unreached territory now under jurisdiction of the United States, on April 24, 1787, it directed Knox and subsequently Harmar to dispossess "a body of men who have in a lawless and unauthorized manner taken possession of Post St. Vincents in defiance of the proclamation and authority of the United States." By mid-June 1787, Harmar, his staff, five infantry, and one artillery company had gathered at the Falls of the Ohio. Harmar sent word ahead to inform the residents of Vincennes that the arriving troops were not villains but regulars sent by the government in order to preserve good faith and to protect its legal inhabitants.[365]

The operation was the first major endeavor for the regiment as a whole, companies having been transferred from Fort Harmar and the now downsized Fort Steuben built to support the surveying process, to the garrison at the Falls, now known as the new "Fort Steuben." Leaving Lieutenant Kingsbury, two noncommissioned officers, and thirty men to man the fort, Captain Zeigler and company started down the river in eight Kentucky boats and two keelboats loaded with cattle, horses, and flour on July 6 and were followed two days later by Major Hamtramck with a party of one hundred men. The parties rendezvoused at Pigeon Creek, 180 miles below the Falls where cattle, horses, necessary baggage, and fifteen days of provisions were removed from the boats and loaded in an overland convoy headed by Lieutenant Colonel Harmar. Artillery pieces and other heavy baggage were entrusted to Major Hamtramck who was to

---

[364] Sword, *President Washington's Indian War*, 35–37; Roosevelt, *The Winning of the West, Vol. 3*, 83–84.

[365] Cayton, *Frontier Indiana*, 110–111; Brown, "The Role of the Army in Western Settlement," 170; Denny, *Military Journal*, 98–99.

proceed down the Ohio and up the Wabash to Vincennes. Harmar started overland on July 11 with the rest of the troops and cattle, accomplishing the trek of seventy miles in seven days. The journey was tough on the men. Each soldier carried sixteen pounds of flour in addition to his arms. The weather was extremely hot, and the men were thirsty. Armstrong, in Captain Finney's company, accompanied Harmar overland and described the conditions as disagreeable with the weather warm, water lacking, and the terrain "a desert."[366]

The regiment was greeted by relieved townspeople and friendly Cherokees who had sought refuge with the French from rival Chickasaws and unfriendly frontiersmen in Kentucky. After their experiences with the Kentucky militia, locals viewed the soldiers as belonging to another nation, calling them "real Americans."

Hamtramck arrived with boats and baggage on July 25 but had left a portion of the cargo with Ensign Ryker Sedam and a small contingent of soldiers at the mouth of the Wabash because shallow water prevented a clear passage up the river. The following day, Armstrong and fifty soldiers were dispatched to assist Sedam in bringing up the remainder of the stores.[367]

The trip presented unexpected challenges. On the second day of the journey downriver, the company came upon a canoe that had fallen behind Hamtramck's convoy and discovered the badly mutilated bodies of a soldier from Captain Zeigler's company and a Frenchman who was with him. A third man had been taken prisoner.

After burying the two men, Armstrong's detachment encountered a party of Spaniards who reported that they had come across a group of forty Piankashaws who told them they were on their way downriver to attack Ensign Sedam's company. With that information, Armstrong's men wasted no time, rowing downstream ninety miles in one day. They arrived at the mouth of the Wabash fortunately to find Sedam's party unharmed and embarked upriver, accompanying the convoy carrying five boxes of clothing, ninety barrels and thirty-two kegs of flour, nineteen barrels and twenty-three kegs of whiskey, four boxes of military stores, one barrel of butter,

---

[366] Harmar to Knox, August 7, 1787, in Gayle Thornbrough, ed., *Outpost on the Wabash, 1787–1791* (Indianapolis: Indiana Historical Society, 1957), 34 (*OOTW*); John Armstrong to Richard C. Anderson, August 8, 1787, PJA; Denny, *Military Journal*, 99–101; Hildreth, "Journal of Joseph Buell," 154–58.

[367] Denny, *Military Journal*, 101–02.

one of beer, and one box of soap. Proceeding up the Wabash cautiously, Armstrong reconnoitered potentially dangerous areas and positioned troops on the shore to stand guard until the boats passed by safely.

Meanwhile, Harmar had dispatched soldiers under Hamtramck's command to rendezvous with Armstrong's party after reports reached Vincennes that the Piankashaws were lying in wait to attack the convoy. The parties met eighteen miles below Vincennes and continued upriver safely, arriving on August 5. Obviously pleased with the efforts of his exhausted men, Armstrong reported to Harmar that he had allowed each man an extra gill of whiskey per day and two extra gills during their race downstream to the Ohio.[368]

Harmar's visit had multiple objectives; mission priorities included preventing illegal encroachments on public lands now belonging to the United States, protecting private property from arbitrary invasion by illegal militias, and making peaceful overtures toward the area's Native American tribes. Additionally, he had to placate locals still reeling from Clark's ill-fated retaliatory campaign. Accordingly, Harmar posted copies in both French and English of the 1783 congressional proclamation against intruders in the Northwest Territory, which, he reported, "amazed the inhabitants exceedingly, particularly those who stile [sic] themselves Americans." He thought his actions would have the proper effect on Kentuckians, especially veterans of Clark's campaign who eyed the lands of the Wabash that by law were the property of the United States.

Immediately after his arrival, Harmar met with eight Piankashaws who had traveled from Terre Haute to speak with him. They exchanged small gifts, and Harmar assured the delegation of the friendly intentions of the United States. When he learned of the murdered men on the Wabash and of the planned attack on his men at the mouth of the river, however, Harmar changed his message, warning the chiefs of the dangers inherent in bringing down the "vengeance of the United States." Assuming his diplomatic role, he then asked them to send messages to the chiefs of all the Wabash tribes to assemble at Vincennes for a future meeting with him the following month.

---

[368] Armstrong to Harmar, August 8, 1787, and Harmar to Knox, August 7, 1787, *OOTW*, 34–44; Armstrong to Richard Clough Anderson, August 8, 1787, PJA; Denny, *Military Journal*, 103–04.

Most of Harmar's time at Vincennes was spent trying to sort out land records. During the general's visit, locals drew up a petition to Congress requesting that titles granted prior to the cession of the territory from France to Britain at the close of the Seven Years' War be honored and that those settlers be allowed to retain their deeded lands. While he considered all property in the area as belonging to the government, Harmar admitted that many of the Kentucky militia who had participated in unsuccessful raids on the Indian villages had taken up "tomahawk rights" on choice tracts.[369]

While waiting for his meeting with the Wabash chiefs, Harmar traveled west to Kaskaskia and Cahokia, outposts on the Mississippi River that had seen no American authority since the end of the Revolution. Returning to Vincennes in September, he hosted a meeting with 120 Piankashaw and Wea tribesmen. Although the chiefs professed "nothing but peace and friendship for the United States," Harmar ignored the time-honored practice of gift giving. Americans, he said, were warriors who did not come to purchase their friendship with trinkets, but "barely to take them by the hand if they chose to give it; if they did not, it was a matter of indifference." Richard White attributes Harmar's heavy-handed attitude as contributing to future unrest in the region.[370]

Official diplomatic and administrative duties completed, Harmar and the core of the regiment began departing Vincennes at the end of September. Maj. John Hamtramck and ninety-five men remained behind to construct a permanent garrison in the settlement. Completed in mid-1788, Fort Knox became regiment's westernmost fort.[371]

Armstrong remained at Vincennes until October 1787 when his company, now commanded by Capt. Joseph Asheton, returned to the Falls via the Wabash River. In late August, many soldiers at Vincennes became ill, several of whom eventually died. In September, a party of soldiers traveling overland to the Falls were attacked by a party of Indians, and only two of the fifteen men survived.[372]

★

[369] Cayton, *Frontier Indiana*, 112–13; Guthman, *March to Massacre*, 45–46.

[370] White, *The Middle Ground*, 429.

[371] Guthman, *March to Massacre*, 47.

[372] Captain Finney's resignation from the regiment was noted on Harmar's August 7, 1787, Return of Troops. *PA*1: 11:173–74; Hildreth, *Journal of Joseph Buell*, 156; Denny, *Military Journal*, 107.

Clark's campaign in the fall of 1786 was not the only Kentucky offensive against Indian marauders. The second, led by Clark's associate, Benjamin Logan, also proved to be a disaster, but for entirely different reasons. Launched at approximately the same time as Clark's foray against the Wabash Indians, Logan raided the Shawnee villages located up the Mad River in present-day Logan County, Ohio. Clark's larger operation was planned to attract the attention of watchful Indians in what is now central Ohio and to draw warriors away from the Shawnee villages. Ostensibly, Logan's mission was justified retaliation, based on the premise that the tribe had violated terms of the treaty signed earlier in the year at Fort Finney. Randolph Downes notes, however, that the Shawnees had mistakenly been held responsible for incursions made by Mingo and Cherokee tribesmen.[373]

Logan's mostly mounted force of 790 men departed Limestone on October 1, 1786, and proceeded north to the well-known Mackachack towns of the Shawnee. During the operation, they burned seven villages, killed ten chiefs, damaged crops, and slaughtered cattle. They did their greatest long-term damage, however, in exactly the wrong place and to the wrong person. Residing in one of the towns was an aging chief, Moluntha (Malunthy), signer of the treaty at Fort Finney and a known moderating voice among the Shawnee. His warriors absent on a hunting expedition, Moluntha made no effort to defend his village. As recently as May, he had received assurances from American commissioners that his tribe was included among those who were friends of the United States. On the force's arrival, he hoisted "the thirteen stripes" on his sixty-foot flagpole to receive the approaching Americans.

Amid the confusion of the riders' assault, Moluntha first attempted to flee but finally surrendered himself and his wives and children. Carrying a peace pipe, the bewildered chief awaited the opportunity to shake hands with the Americans. In the group was a man named Hugh McGary who had been largely responsible for a defeat of Kentuckians by the British and their Indian allies along the Licking River at Blue Licks in August 1782. Still thirsty for revenge, he approached Moluntha and asked him if he had been at Blue Licks. The old chief either did not understand the question or merely agreed benevolently, saying yes to appease an obviously angry man. McGary immediately swung an ax upon Moluntha's head, splitting

---

[373] Downes, *Council Fires*, 298.

it open, and proceeded to scalp him. In the chaos that ensued, the force plundered empty huts and captured a few prisoners.[374]

Logan's men returned to Kentucky, exultant in their success. There had been, however, no important objectives achieved, and to many who had been required to go as part of the inexpertly led militia, the experience had been particularly odious. McGary was brought to trial and found guilty of murder, behaving in a disorderly manner, and "in part" guilty of insubordination; but tried by a court of thirteen Kentucky militia officers, he received a sentence of suspension from rank for one year—a proverbial slap on the wrist. Of greater impact was the reaction to the affair by the Shawnee, incensed at the death of the aging chief and the raids on their villages. Instead of being intimidated, they responded with retribution. As early as December 1786, a frontier army officer noted an upswing in raids, saying, "There are more Shawnees now on the south side of the Ohio River than have been discovered at one time for two years past."[375]

★

Despite these incidents, settlers continued to make their way down the Ohio to Kentucky while Congress finalized its plans for sale of the nation's Northwest Territory. The Land Ordinance of 1787 laid the groundwork for the eventual creation of the states of Ohio, Illinois, Indiana, Michigan, and Wisconsin. This landmark document created a framework for administering the territory with a federally appointed governor, secretary, and three judges. It also included guarantees of personal rights and addressed social parameters such as the creation of schools, abolition of slavery, and a halt to the practice of involuntary servitude. The policies were all the more remarkable considering it was written by a Congress very much in disagreement amongst itself on a variety of issues during the precise time period when a constitutional convention was convening to settle the underlying principles for a stronger national government.

Large tracts of land began to be sold immediately following the ordinance's July 13 adoption. The promise held by the territory's status as a "cash cow" would eventually be realized, but not without hiccups along the way while the government dealt with both payments and defaults from various land schemes. Its first sale went to the Ohio Company of

---

[374] Downes, *Council Fires*, 298; Sword, *President Washington's Indian War*, 37–39, 44.
[375] Sword, *President Washington's Indian War*, 41.

Associates, a joint-stock company of former Continental Army officers and soldiers. The deal was a bargain for both sides; the stockholders got lots of land inexpensively while the government got men committed to its success. Its New England organizers were fervent exponents of national authority who would prove to be strongly supportive of both federal and territorial governments. A second sale proved emblematic of the absence of the concept of "conflict of interest" that characterized the times. Congress sold a huge tract of land between the Little Miami and Great Miami Rivers to John Cleves Symmes, a congressman from New Jersey prior to passage of the ordinance. Cleves's organization proved less devoted to national interests than the Ohio Company and emerged later as a sizeable factor in the eventual distribution of regimental forces.[376]

With the adoption of the land ordinance, the army once again saw a mission change. Fort Harmar, built to protect the Ohio lands from the intrusions of white settlers, was selected by the Ohio Company as the location of the territory's first large-scale settlement, and settlers began to arrive in April 1788 to establish the town of Marietta across the Muskingum River from the garrison. The army's role now became one of protection for legal settlers rather than the expulsion of illegal ones, not just in the vicinity of Fort Harmar but also along the Ohio as land opened up for settlement.

Not surprisingly, these developments heightened the tension between Native Americans and white settlers. Even prior to the issuance of the Land Ordinance of 1787 and the noticeable upswing in traffic of settlers heading downriver, matters began to deteriorate. Clark's and Logan's expeditions had been incendiary, fueling raids by Indians into the territory that were in turn met with settler retaliations of increasing cruelty.

By the late 1780s, the flood of newcomers to the western lands had so populated Kentucky that incursions south of the Ohio River by large raiding parties were no longer practical; most forays into the interior were now of a limited nature, usually involving stealing horses and killing an occasional isolated settler. After such attacks, warriors generally scurried back across

---

[376] Cayton, *Frontier Indiana*, 118–19. Cayton notes the serious overlap between individuals engaged in land speculation and those appointed to government positions in the Northwest Territory. Two of the first three territorial judges, Samuel Parsons and James Varnum, were directors of the Ohio Company; and the third was John Cleves Symmes. The territorial secretary, Winthrop Sargent, was also the secretary of the Ohio Company.

the Ohio River, often just ahead of an angry posse of frontiersmen that was certain to follow. As an alternative to the Kentucky raids, tribesmen began to concentrate on the hundreds of travelers passing down the Ohio River who were vulnerable targets with none of the risks associated with raids in the settled areas. The use of decoys, Indians speaking English who dressed as white travelers in distress or unfortunate captives themselves, wild-game calls, and seemingly abandoned or disabled rivercraft were among the various ploys utilized to lure unsuspecting occupants of boats heading downstream to the riverbank. Warriors would suddenly appear to kill and scalp passengers outright or select prisoners to be marched to distant villages. Many of these were either killed along the way or marked for death by torture, slavery, or ransom once they reached their final destination. Conversely, children and youths were commonly adopted by their captors. Who lived and who died unspeakably painful deaths was often seen by survivors as a capricious choice made by their captors.[377]

In this atmosphere of mutual hatred, unavenged murders, and long-suffered injustices, bitterness and rancor spilled over into atrocities that further intensified the conflict. Each new barbarity seemed to beget a more brutal and unreasoned response by both sides. Increasing ferocity, particularly on the part of younger warriors, evidenced by dismemberment and gross mutilation of fallen victims, began to characterize frontier Indian attacks in the late 1780s and early 1790s. Responding in kind, the American frontiersmen demonstrated a cruel viciousness of their own. Settlers in one Kentucky county were so embittered that they decided to poison the food stuffs, particularly potatoes, corn, and wheat that were typically stolen during raids. Men like Hugh McGary were all too common along the frontier. In addition to his murder of Chief Moluntha, he had a long history of blind animosity toward Native Americans. On one occasion, he pretended to befriend a lone Indian encountered on the trail, savagely bludgeoning him with a large club once his fellow traveler's back was turned.[378]

Kentucky frontiersmen were often indiscriminate in their retribution. In July 1789, Maj. John Hardin conducted a raid with 220 Kentuckians directed toward Wea towns in the Wabash valley. They encountered a hunting party of 22 Shawnee men, women, and children peacefully

---

[377] Sword, *President Washington's Indian War*, 72.

[378] Ibid., 69–78.

encamped with fires burning and horses grazing. Without waiting for orders from Hardin, the vanguard attacked, killing three men, three women, a boy, and an infant before the rest managed to escape. Hardin's raiders were soon strutting about Vincennes displaying the grisly scalps of their victims, while Fort Knox's commandant, Major Hamtramck, seethed with rage.[379]

In his travels up and down the river as the regimental paymaster, Erkuries Beatty heard tales of kidnappings, murder, and torture of settlers at the hands of Indians and witnessed cruelties instigated by frontiersmen on unfortunate, often innocent Indians. On one occasion he described the cruel torture of two boys who had been taken prisoner and used as victims when teaching dogs to hunt Indians. At the same location, he saw the surviving women and children of Logan's raid, "the men all killed they could catch." Although locals faulted the raiding party for killing Moluntha, Beatty reported that Logan got credit for the murder of his men.[380]

Warfare, still isolated and sporadic, slowly grew more intense. Increasingly, the government in the East and inhabitants of the West argued over which nations were involved and whether settlers or Indians were responsible for the fighting. Westerners continually pressed Congress for help, but they sensed reluctance, even hostility to their pleas. Easterners blamed much of the conflict on greedy frontiersmen who encroached on Indian land, who murdered and tortured as savagely as their foe, and who in spite of treaties assaulted Indian villages, often indiscriminately. Westerners viewed government authorities as "eastern," uninterested and biased against frontier needs. The federal army seemed too weak and too scattered to afford any real protection. Western settlers boiled with resentment, denied the protection they believed they were owed as American citizens.

★

Out of these differing perceptions emerged two schools of thought on how to deal with the deteriorating situation. One was military, the other diplomatic. George Washington and others unhesitatingly endorsed the latter path. Viewing white aggressors and Native American agitators

---

[379] Ibid., 77.
[380] Beatty, "Diary," 435–37.

equally guilty in creating and maintaining hostilities, they felt the solution lay in agreeing to mutually accepted boundary lines. The government should negotiate with the Indian nations generously, fairly, and in good faith while taking care not to yield nor to grasp too much. War was too expensive and should be avoided at all costs. On August 9, 1787, a congressional committee presented its report to that body. It conceded that past treaty measures had not been effective in achieving positive objectives and outlined several suggestions: making general treaties with multiple nations that addressed common interests rather than with individual nations or regional alliances, eliminating the use of language that connoted superiority, conducting proceedings on a more equal footing, and convincing the nations of the justice and humanity, as well as the power of the United States. Pessimism about the outcome of talks and pressure from land speculators, however, pushed government negotiators to adopt unyielding positions on key issues: any new treaty should result in no change to either the terms of previous agreements or to existing boundary lines.[381]

The government's new approach, however, was to be far more conciliatory. Instead of insisting that the nations had lost their land as a result of "the principle of conquest," the theme of previous negotiations and a line of reasoning that infuriated the Indians, Knox and others felt that the only method to which tribal representatives would agree to relinquish their lands was by the formal sale of "right of soil," a tradition employed earlier by the British in colonial America. By this time, Congress was willing to expend money on the peace process, having begun to realize some revenue from the sale of its lands. It assumed that the nations would accept monetary compensation, which, in reality, had little relevance to their way of life. In essence, the whole process was to be an enormous charade.[382]

The call for another treaty actually originated from Indian factions. The collective nations, generally discontented with the entire chain of events since the end of the Revolution, believed that a new deal was now in order. Representatives from the Six Nations, the Wyandot, Delaware, Shawnee, Ottawa, Chippewa, Potawatomi, Miami, and Cherokee tribes,

---

[381] Kohn, *Eagle and Sword*, 93–94; Reginald Horsman, *Expansion and American Indian Policy, 1783–1812* (Norman: University of Oklahoma Press, 1992), 41–42.

[382] Horsman, *Expansion and American Indian Policy*, 44–45.

as well those of the Wabash confederacy met in council at Brownstown at the mouth of the Detroit River in December 1786 to reconfirm their resolve to act as a confederation as originally agreed upon at their meeting at Sandusky in 1783.

The confederacy decided to reject all former treaties and to request a reopening of the issue of land boundaries. Besides voicing its displeasure that Indian nations were not represented at the peace treaty between Great Britain and the United States at the close of the war, the confederation expressed its dismay at the unwillingness of the government to deal with the nations as one body. The petition to Congress requesting a new treaty also included the demand that until a new agreement could be negotiated, surveying of the Seven Ranges should cease since the land was ceded through the accord signed at Fort McIntosh, which the nations considered invalid. Unfortunately, the petition took a surprisingly long time to reach Congress and even more time for that body to act on it. The decision to treat with the assembled nations was not made until almost a year later in October 1787. Although the meeting was to be held three months later at Fort Harmar, it did not take place until over a year later in January 1789. Within that time span, the settling of lands north of the Ohio had proceeded so rapidly that renegotiating boundaries was clearly a moot point.[383]

Joseph Brant was one of the leading figures at the preliminary conclave in Brownstown. This remarkable man, a Mohawk chief of proven leadership and recognized talent, had been mentored as a youth by Sir William Johnson, British superintendent of Indian Affairs. His sister Molly was the influential administrator's consort, and Brant was educated in white schools, became a convert to the Anglican Church, and had once assisted in the translation of the gospel of Mark into the Mohawk language. He traveled to England in 1775–76 and later became the official translator for the Six Nations. Forever a British loyalist, he held the rank of captain in the Indian department throughout the Revolution but preferred to fight as a war chief because that status gave him command of more men in battle than was customary for a captain. Active primarily in campaigns in the Mohawk Valley, but also dispatched to Ohio Indian villages to encourage inhabitants to take arms against invasion by forces led by George Rogers Clark during

---

[383] Downes, *Council Fires*, 299; Prucha, *The Sword of the Republic*, 18; White, *The Middle Ground*, 433, 443; Sword, *President Washington's Indian War*, 41.

the war, he emerged as the perfect soldier and inspiring leader, possessed of remarkable physical stamina, courage under fire, dedication to the cause, and known to his British counterparts as a complete gentleman. Continuing his advocacy for his people, he returned to England in late 1785 to plead for more generous treatment for the Six Nations than they had received after the terms of peace and had also asked for assurances of the continuation of their alliance. Brant was to work tirelessly in his efforts to maintain the Indian confederacy in its negotiations at the forthcoming treaty.[384]

Unfortunately for Brant and others espousing a united front in dealing with the government, within the nearly two-year span between the conclave on the Detroit River and the treaty held at Fort Harmar, schisms among nations had begun to destroy the confederation's solidarity on three crucial fronts. Wyandots and Delawares found themselves unable to accede to the confederacy's insistence of an Ohio River boundary and cessation of the surveying of the Seven Ranges. In the event these provisions were not honored by the government, the confederation would be obligated to attempt to stop the surveying process by force as well as to move upon settlements on land already ceded. The Wyandot and Delaware would then be forced to participate in a war in which their people, who were closest to the American settlements, would be the first to be struck and possibly destroyed in retaliation.[385]

A second rift developed within the Iroquois confederation itself. The Seneca, the most western of the Six Nations were, like the Wyandot and the Delaware, in a precarious position in the case of war with the United States. They had long been inclined to abide by the decision of the treaty of Fort McIntosh in regard to their lands. Furthermore, their chief spokesman, Cornplanter, had worked hard to achieve Congress's guarantee of trade and protection for his people and had succeeded in getting that body to state that Seneca hunting grounds would remain inviolate. The establishment of Fort Franklin along the Allegheny River in Pennsylvania in April 1787 represented the United States' commitment to the Seneca nation.[386]

---

[384] Barbara Graymont, "Joseph Brant," *Dictionary of Canadian Biography*, vol. 5, 1801–1820, http://www. biographi.ca/en/bio/thayendanegea_5E.html; Sword, *President Washington's Indian War*, 53.

[385] Downes, *Council Fires*, 301.

[386] Ibid., 302.

A third threat to Indian unity occurred between Brant and the tribes of the Wabash and Maumee River valleys. Brant sought to bring something new to the table by presenting a compromise to the previously insisted-upon Ohio River boundary. Aware of the burgeoning American settlements north of the Ohio River at Marietta, Brant had persuaded eastern tribes to yield a portion of their lands, provided that the Americans would show some evidence they would negotiate fairly. Brant's attempts to enlist the support of the Seneca, Delaware, and Wyandot Indians, who represented the right wing of the confederacy in favor of conciliation with the United States, infuriated the Wabash-Maumee nations. The Wabash, primarily the Wea and Piankashaw, and Maumee Valley tribes, composed chiefly of the Shawnee, Miami, and Kickapoo, represented the extreme left wing of the confederacy and had consistently refused to make any concessions regarding the boundary. Their defiance had only been reinforced by Clark's raid.[387]

Complicating the process were the British whose interests were intertwined with those of the Indian nations. Following the council's meeting at Brownstown, it reconvened at the Miami towns in October 1788 to plan for the upcoming treaty. At what turned out to be a chaotic meeting attended by 1,000 to 3,000 tribesmen, bitter divisions between the factions became apparent as the British took a far more active role in deliberations. Reports from Major Hamtramck in August 1788 confirmed that British agent Alexander McKee had warned the Indians not to attend the upcoming treaty because it would serve no purpose; whatever would be promised to the Indians in the way of peace would be broken immediately by the "Kentuck people." Hamtramck also reported that the British had directed the Indians to agree to nothing short of a permanent boundary line of the Ohio River and should that request be refused, to attack the American garrisons and settlements immediately.[388]

For the disheartened Brant, the October summit was clearly a disaster. The Wyandot, Chippewa, Ottawa, Pottawattamie, and Delaware, rather than plunge headlong into a destructive war, agreed only to negotiate for a revised boundary and in the process would yield small parts of their territory. The Shawnee, Miami, and Kickapoo, whom Brant regarded as

---

[387] Ibid., 303–04.

[388] Guthman, *March to Massacre*, 160; Hamtramck to Harmar, August 31, 1788, in *OOTW*, 114–120; White, *The Middle Ground*, 444.

"so much addicted to horse-stealing that it will be a difficult task to break them of it," declared for war rather than give up any of their country and would not attend a treaty with the government. He saw no solution to unite the two factions.[389]

---

[389] Downes, *Council Fires*, 301–04; Sword, *President Washington's Indian War*, 60–61, 65.

9

Another Treaty, Another Misstep, 1787–1789

This was the last act of the farce. The articles were signed.
—Ebenezer Denny at Fort Harmar, January 11, 1989[390]

The arrival of the governor of the Northest Territory of the United States, Maj. Gen. Arthur St. Clair, was announced on July 9, 1788, at Fort Harmar by formal presentation of arms and discharge of thirteen rounds from a six-pounder. Appointed in December 1787, he had already been advised by Congress regarding the acceptable parameters for any forthcoming treaties.[391]

Scots-born St. Clair had arrived in the colonies as an ensign in the British Army. He served with Maj. Gen. James Wolfe during the siege of Quebec, following which he married the daughter of prosperous Bostonians. Acquiring a large estate with funds derived from the dowry of his wife and the amount saved from his own fortune, he resigned his commission and joined an enclave of Scottish families in western Pennsylvania where he became prominent in politics, military affairs, and local society. In his prime in 1775 when he accepted a commission in the Continental Army as colonel, he was described as a man of "imposing appearance, graceful, cultivated, whose agreeable and intelligent conversation,

---

[390] Denny, *Military Journal*, 130.
[391] Denny, *Military Journal*, 121; Guthman, *March to Massacre*, 62.

captivating manners, and honorable principles won all hearts." He served with Washington at Trenton and Princeton and was well known to John Armstrong whose Pennsylvania unit he commanded during the southern campaign. Although rising to the rank of major general, St. Clair was never an outstanding leader. Court-martialed but exonerated for the loss of Fort Ticonderoga in 1778, he returned to his Ligonier estate to find that his fortune had been lost due to property mismanagement in his absence, whereupon he returned to Pennsylvania politics and entered Congress. Wiley Sword notes that St. Clair, now fifty-two years old, corpulent and severely affected with gout, had resigned his position in Congress to manage the destiny of the western lands without the slightest knowledge of Native American perspectives on the situation.[392]

Preparations for the treaty were hampered from the start. Originally to be held at the Falls of the Muskingum in present-day Zanesville, Ohio, in May 1788, it was delayed due to St. Clair's insistence upon Fort Harmar as an alternate site following an incident whose magnitude the governor greatly misjudged. Ensign Nathan McDowell's detachment of twenty men had been tasked to construct buildings to house the treaty proceedings and had almost completed its assignment when it was attacked by a party of ten to twelve Chippewas. Soldiers were able to get to cover but suffered casualties. Once the men were able to answer the Indians' fire, the warriors left. When a friendly Delaware came onto the scene, McDowell sent him to Fort Harmar to relay news of the incident. St. Clair, who had been in the territory less than a week, was infuriated by what he termed an insult and an indignity to the United States and sent a message to Indians meeting at Brownstown, chastising them for disrespect and "unprovoked hostility," demanding an explanation, and declaring that any future conference would be held on an American site. Ironically, three days after his dispatch, he received notice of appropriation of additional monies for the treaty and a letter from Knox detailing Congress's anxiety in the matter of quieting all disturbances among the Indians.[393]

St. Clair's handling of the isolated attack by a handful of Indian banditti put the new treaty in jeopardy. He was now under pressure from the administration for a rapid peace and soon began to worry about

---

[392] Smith, ed., *The St. Clair Papers*, I: 5–14 (*SCP*); Kohn, *Eagle and Sword*, 92; Sword, *President Washington's Indian War*, 53.

[393] Sword, *President Washington's Indian War*, 62–63.

receiving a timely answer from the Indian nations to his ultimatum of July 13. Moreover, reports confirmed that a party of Chippewas from Canada and not part of the confederation seeking a new treaty had carried out the attack.

More disquieting reports arrived in late October when word that the western nations at the grand council on the Maumee River had resolved to insist on the Ohio River boundary and would not travel farther than the Falls of the Muskingum for a treaty. This news generally paralleled a series of reports of recent violence in other frontier areas that included attacks on parties of soldiers. In late July, a party of Kickapoos had attacked Lt. William Peters and thirty soldiers near the mouth of the Wabash River. Eight of his men had been killed and ten wounded, and a boat laden with provisions had been lost to the attackers. Late in September, a party headed by John Armstrong had been fired on while heading down the Ohio near the mouth of the Scioto River, resulting in one man wounded. In October, an army lieutenant at Fort Harmar reported that a soldier recently captured by Indians near the Falls of the Ohio had been killed and mutilated in a ghastly manner. "Not content with scalping him," the officer complained, "[they] cut him in four quarters and hung them up on the bushes." Clearly, the time when Indians distinguished between "real American" soldiers and the frontier banditti "Big Knives" was over.[394]

Meanwhile, Josiah Harmar was tasked to ensure the safety of confederation members arriving for the conclave. Troops were instructed to treat the Indians with respect and had previously been ordered not to make hunting expeditions up the Muskingum or near encampments where friendly tribesmen might be staying lest any untoward incident take place. In the same vein, Harmar's orders to David Zeigler whose assignment it was to escort members of the Six Nations down the Ohio cautioned him of rumors that several "vagabonds" around Wheeling were intent upon firing on the party.[395]

Events continued to bode ill for the treaty. Tribal representatives requested that St. Clair reconsider his decision to hold the conference at Fort Harmar as an indication by the government that it was prepared to bargain in good faith. Some confederation members evidently feared the repetition of hostage taking employed previously when tribal members were

---

[394] Sword, *President Washington's Indian War*, 64–65; Denny, *Military Journal*, 127.
[395] Denny, *Military Journal*, 155–56.

detained for the return of American captives. Others feared an attempt to poison the whiskey intended for their consumption or that they might be presented with blankets infected with smallpox.[396]

Reportedly in a surly mood and ill with gout, St. Clair missed this opportunity for reconciliation. He flatly denied the confederacy's request. The decision to hold the treaty at Fort Harmar had been enacted due to the "insult" of the federal troops at the original meeting site, and assembling there would be an affront to the dignity of the United States.

Representatives of the Six Nations and Western confederacy responded angrily.

> From the misconduct of a few individuals who live at a great distance . . . and are little concerned with a union with you, you have extinguished the council fire . . . We look upon [this] extremely hard, particularly as we have been exerting ourselves for several years past to bring the whole of the Indian nations of this country to agree to come to some terms of peace with the United States.[397]

Since the nations had mutually agreed that they would go no further than the original treaty site, they notified St. Clair that they would not participate. A messenger from the chiefs, however, then revealed the full extent of the compromise over the Ohio River boundary that the moderates had been able to obtain at the Miami conference. Couched in words expressing the desire for peace but asserting a firm position that their proposition was a boundary line that they were not willing to exceed, they asked for a prompt reply due to the lateness of the season.

St. Clair again missed the opportunity for reconciliation, labeling Brant's hard-won compromise as "altogether inadmissible." When they received St. Clair's reply in late November, most of the chiefs, particularly Brant, were outraged. His final communication to St. Clair was to the effect that nothing more could be done than what had been offered, warning him against establishing treaties with individual representatives and that little attention would be paid to any agreements such parties might make. Although he and his fellow leaders of the Six Nations were within

---

[396] Sword, *President Washington's Indian War*, 65; Denny, *Military Journal*, 127.

[397] Sword, *President Washington's Indian War*, 65.

sixty miles of Fort Harmar at the time, they departed in order to meet up with a delegation from tribes who were two days away to dissuade them from attending the treaty.[398]

Hopes of accomplishing any meaningful agreement had vanished. Although St. Clair immediately intensified preparations to hold a face-saving treaty with the Senecas and other American-aligned Indian factions, he had effectively alienated vital moderate leaders. While St. Clair prepared for the expected arrival of chiefs disposed toward productive relationships with the government, Joseph Brant and the Mohawks, Shawnees, Miamis, and Delawares returned to their homelands, determined to resist the American "backwardness."[399]

Brant's refusal to attend the proceedings and the apparent division of the Indian confederacy played right into St. Clair's hands. As he had hoped, the chiefs who began to arrive at Fort Harmar were hesitant and divided. Many expressed anger at Brant, which worked in St. Clair's favor as he set about dictating the terms of the meeting.

Two treaties were consequently concluded, one with the Iroquois in attendance and one with the rest of the tribal representatives. Both were nearly identical to those negotiated previously. The same boundaries were delineated and the same lands were set aside for the Indian nations. They would be allowed to hunt within the ceded territory as long as they "demeaned themselves peaceably" and molested no Americans. Horse stealing by both Indians and frontiersmen was to be met by strict punishment. Traders to the Indian country would be required to get official licenses from the governor of the Northwest Territory. Chiefs would pledge to warn the United States of all hostile movements of other tribes and endeavor to stop their invasion, and a reciprocal pledge would be given by the government. Land granted to the nations would be theirs, but they in turn would pledge not to cede it to any country other than the United States.[400]

Monetary compensation was written into the agreement. The Six Nations, with the exception of the Mohawks who did not attend, were to receive $3,000, the amount of which was equal to the cost of gifts they then received, as well as consideration of an additional quantity of goods.

---

[398] Sword, *President Washington's Indian War*, 64–67.

[399] Ibid., 67.

[400] Downes, *Council Fires*, 306.

Remuneration to the Wyandot, Delaware, Ottawa, and Chippewa tribes in attendance was to total $6,000, to be allotted in the same manner. The government could consider itself to have "purchased" the rights to the lands.[401]

The chiefs withdrew to consider the terms they were about to sign. They recognized immediately that it was substantially the same treaty that they had seen before. On subsequent days, they decided to propose Brant's boundary compromise, but their eloquent oratory had no effect. St. Clair flatly rejected the proposal, and there was nothing for them to do except cede to the terms dictated by the Americans.[402]

St. Clair's intransigence had effectively removed the vital "middle ground" in Indian-US government relations. Leadership of the Indian confederacy now passed into the hands of the more war-inclined western nations. Brant's moderate faction had been alienated, and the confederacy had been gleaned of its more pacific elements. The tribes that gathered at Fort Harmar were now so removed from the mainstream that they could no longer serve as a calming influence. America was being inextricably drawn into war at a time its leaders most hoped to avoid one.[403]

★

Government under the Articles of Confederation was ending. With the vote of New Hampshire's assembly on June 21, 1788, nine of thirteen states had approved the Constitution, and it became the law of the land. Congress sat in session for the first time on March 4, 1789. Out of sheer necessity, it passed an act on September 29, 1789, the last day of its first

---

[401] Congress of the United States, American State Papers, Indian Affairs, I: 5-8 (*ASP-Indian Affairs*).

[402] Downes, *Council Fires*, 305–09; Randolph Chandler Downes and Harlow Lindley, *Frontier Ohio, 1788–1803* (Columbus: The Ohio State Archaeological and Historical Society, 1935), 9–16. See also Denny, *Military Journal*, 127–130. White notes two interesting postscripts to the whole affair. At the conclusion of the proceedings, St. Clair found he had no white wampum, the color of peace, to make treaty belts. He had only black wampum, the color signifying war or death. Thus, he could not present belts to confirm or validate the treaty, as was the time-honored custom. Additionally, with few exceptions, the Indians signing the treaty were neither war leaders nor established chiefs, whose signatures meant little. White, *The Middle Ground*, 446.

[403] Sword, *President Washington's Indian War*, 67–68.

session, approving the army's size of 840 men previously authorized in October 1787 although only about 672 soldiers were actually in the service at the time of the law's passing. Designed to be a makeshift measure until the needs of the country could be more thoroughly assessed, the troops were granted the same pay and allowances they had held previously. The regiment was already stretched thin, and Harmar continually juggled men and stores to meet the ever-growing needs of the expanding frontier. Pennsylvania garrisons began at Fort Franklin. Fort Pitt had only one officer and a few men to receive and forward supplies. Fort McIntosh was expected to be replaced by a blockhouse a few miles up Big Beaver Creek to "cover the country." Army headquarters were at Fort Harmar, which had four companies intended to reinforce posts either up or down the river. At Fort Steuben were two companies to protect that region and to provide a link to the garrison on the Wabash. The latter, Fort Knox, had two companies and four small brass cannons.

With the passage of the defense bill, Henry Knox, now the Secretary of War in that newly created department, continued to make the case for a larger force, but it was not until the following year that Congress was receptive to increasing its size. In the meantime, the problems faced by the nation's woefully undersized "Sword of the Republic" continued to multiply.[404]

★

Settlers continued to arrive at way stations along the Ohio in ever-increasing numbers. From December 1787 to June 14, 1788, Harmar, now commissioned brevet brigadier general, reported from his headquarters on the Muskingum that more than 6,000 individuals had passed down the river during that time. Not surprisingly, the number of hostile Indian actions and subsequent retaliatory forays continued to rise. Knox commented that "it would be a point of critical investigation to know on which side they have been the greatest."[405]

---

[404] Prucha, *The Sword of the Republic*, 14–15; Jacobs, *The Beginning of the U.S. Army*, 43–44.

[405] Harmar received the promotion ostensibly to avoid disputes over rank on occasions when regulars were to be used in conjunction with the militia. In a true reflection of the times, he received an increase in rank but not in pay. Brown, "The Role of the Army in Western Settlement," 173 (*PMHB*).

Following the exit of the moderate faction, the center of gravity of the Indian confederation shifted westward to the villages at the headwaters of the Maumee River, home of Miami tribes. Fort Knox, closest to the area but farthest from support of the regiment, became the proverbial hot spot. By the spring of 1789, conditions were dire. Maj. John Wyllys, commandant of Fort Steuben, declared that Indian attacks into Kentucky from "that nest of villainy the Miami Village" were so frequent that communications with Fort Knox could not be maintained without fifty or sixty troops accompanying every convoy. Between May and September 1788, four federal detachments passing between those posts were attacked. Kentuckians resumed their raids, and in August 1788, Patrick Brown led a band of sixty frontiersmen to Vincennes and insolently defied Major Hamtramck's order to withdraw. When the major requested Brown to produce his official orders, the Kentuckian was unable to do so. Because he had only nine men fit for duty that day, Hamtramck was powerless to stop Brown and his men from stealing horses that belonged to friendly Indians actually employed by the government or from attacking and killing friendly Piankashaws. If Brown had attacked Wea or Miami tribesmen, he would have had more justification, but his choice of the Piankashaw only increased Indian hostility.[406]

The year 1789 saw a rise in Kentucky freebooting expeditions, as well as the beginning of the government's endorsement of such tactics. Kentuckians had high expectations about the ability of a new stronger federal government to arrest the mounting Indian attacks upon their settlements but soon perceived that their situation was not fully understood. The disillusionment that accompanied the Indian attacks in the spring of 1789 precipitated even more action on their part. The mortifying behavior of Major Hardin's men that summer along with reports that there were to be three more such expeditions baffled Harmar. He suggested that there might have been federal endorsement of the Kentucky policy, writing to Knox on October 19, 1789, "Will you be pleased to give me particular and especial directions how to act with the inhabitants of Kentucky? Perhaps they may be secretly authorized to form these expeditions."[407]

---

[406] Hamtramck to Harmar, August 31, 1788, in Thornbrough, ed., *Outpost on the Wabash*, 114–20 (*OOTW*).

[407] Downes, *Council Fires*, 311–12; Downes and Lindley, *Frontier Ohio*, 1788–1803, 19.

If Harmar was in doubt, Hamtramck must have been thoroughly confused. He and his men witnessed the retaliatory raids between Indians and Kentuckians and, with his small force, was powerless to prevent it. His letter to Harmar on May 21, 1788, reflected his frustration on multiple issues, among which was the fact that scalps were being brought into town daily, supposedly from Kentucky, and he decided to ban the Weas from Vincennes if the practice continued. He reported that none of his soldiers had reenlisted, and that it was unlikely any would.

Hamtramck's letter to Harmar on August 12, 1788, recounted an attack on Lieutenant Peters's supply convoy, the arrival of which he believed was well known to the Indians. He reported that the garrison had been without flour or pork for two months and that he was afraid all communication with the garrison at the Falls would be shut down due to the attacks on the convoys. He also related the sobering news concerning the fact that the village and soldiers were sick and without medicines to induce vomiting or bark to treat malaria, adding that he thought that the artillery company stationed there would have better luck reenlisting its men if it were stationed elsewhere. Artillery captain William Ferguson wrote Harmar that in addition to the garrison being ill, there was no whiskey, soap, nor candles and that vinegar was seldom if ever issued.[408]

Yet another example of the ineffective position of the regiment at Fort Knox occurred a few months later. A large party of Shawnee passed through Vincennes with three white prisoners whom Hamtramck managed to rescue by providing the group with provisions from his stores. The army's position was so weak that Hamtramck had to rely on bribery rather than force to accomplish whatever needed to be done.[409]

★

As reenlistments began to come due in 1788 and 1789, officers were sent east to fill their quotas and to replace their depleted ranks. The process was more successful at the Falls than at Vincennes. Captain Asheton's company in which Armstrong served reenlisted almost its entirety. Armstrong did

---

[408] Hamtramck to Harmar, May 21 and August 12, 1788, and Ferguson to Harmar, August 11, 1788, *OOTW*, 76–79, 104–09.

[409] Guthman, *March to Massacre*, 160–61; Hamtramck to Harmar, October 13, 1788, *OOTW*, 120–26.

his part to fill Pennsylvania's quota, reenlisting three men and signing up five others in December 1787.[410]

It took a strong individual to remain a soldier. Aside from the obvious challenges of Indian attacks, hard physical labor, sickness, and malnutrition, the men were plagued with slow communication not only from friends and family in the East but also within the regiment itself. This lack of communication contributed to uncertainty about the status of Indian affairs, making an officer's duties of diplomat and protector that much more difficult to execute.

Officers were concerned about their evolving role in keeping the peace. Hamtramck's lengthy letters to Harmar reflect his frustration at not being able to respond to incidents involving Wabash area Indians raiding into Kentucky or the retribution by Kentucky "banditti." Soldiers along the Ohio were caught between containing the actions of hostile Indians on one side and belligerent whites on the other. Since most officers were from northern states, they were quick to blame southerners, particularly Virginians living in Kentucky, for all the subsequent Indian trouble.[411]

★

The arrival of settlers purchasing the land legally put additional demands on the regiment's limited manpower although their enclaves differed greatly in their need for protection by federal forces. The Ohio Company benefitted from proximity to Fort Harmar, located a stone's throw across the Muskingum River. The well-organized village grew rapidly, populated by New Englanders who built their own blockhouse at their settlement "Campus Martius."

Less self-sufficient were the settlements arising from sales by John Cleves Symmes, who had signed a contract in 1788 for one million acres lying between the Little Miami and the Great Miami Rivers that were divided into three tracts. The first, Columbia, was established on the banks of the Little Miami River by Benjamin Stites and a large number of settlers

---

[410] Certificate by Wyllys, December 21, 1787, PJA. Harmar to Knox, June 15, 1788, *OOTW*, 87. Armstrong might have recruited in the East in 1787. His papers include a receipt dated October 18, 1787, for a bill £2 8sh 6p from Dr. Matthew Maus of Northumberland, indicating that he could have returned to the area at that time.

[411] Guthman, *March to Massacre*, 142–43, 158.

from New York and New Jersey and was the future home of Armstrong when he left the army in 1793. Losantiville, laid out across the Ohio from the mouth of the Licking River, later became the town of Cincinnati, attracting investors and settlers from Kentucky. Symmes himself chose to develop the third, which he dubbed "North Bend" at the mouth of the Great Miami. Of the organizers of the three settlements, Symmes was in the most need financially, and the necessity of attracting potential purchasers for his land was vital to his personal solvency. Consequently, the former congressman lobbied influential friends in the government to protect his investment. His demands and the government's agreement to provide him with federal forces to protect his holdings compelled Harmar to continue the juggling act of covering the territory at a time when the army's resources were already stretched to the breaking point.[412]

On February 2, 1789, Symmes arrived at North Bend with a company of infantry commanded by Lt. William Kersey. Enduring intense cold, the soldiers quickly constructed crude shelters from boards ripped from their boats. Arriving almost empty-handed into the wilderness, the soldiers had to depend on Symmes's bounty for survival. When inhabitants of neighboring Columbia became fearful of an Indian raid, a sergeant and eighteen men were dispatched to protect them. They managed to keep the Indians away, but the area flooded, and water rose to the loft of their blockhouse. On another occasion, Kersey detailed a sergeant and twelve men to accompany settlers proceeding downriver to the Falls. The trip was short-lived because ice soon wrecked their boats, and the hope of continuing onward was abandoned. With no assurance that his men wouldn't starve in that present location, Kersey elected to move the detachment downriver to Fort Steuben, resulting in North Bend's lack of any army protection. Major Wyllys, then in command of the garrison at the Falls of the Ohio, subsequently dispatched Ensign Francis Luce and regulars to go back upriver to North Bend.

Symmes was incensed. He wrote Jonathan Dayton, a business associate and New Jersey politician, asking him to contact Knox and have Kersey punished. Once Harmar learned what had happened, he ordered not only a company commanded by Capt. John Mercer to the Great Miami but Lieutenant Kersey to return as well.

---

[412] Downes and Lindley, *Frontier Ohio*, 61–63.

Meanwhile, Ensign Luce and his seventeen men carried on at, as Kentuckians dubbed it, the "North Bend Slaughter House." Except for guns and ammunition, the soldiers had almost nothing. They had no tools to perform the work that was expected of them, lacking even axes and saws. Symmes supplied what he could, and after working a week, Luce's men built a blockhouse of sorts. When it proved only large enough to shelter the troops in case of attack, however, the settlers were unhappy.[413]

Between June and September 1789, the administration was subjected to a continual stream of pleas to protect the Ohio Valley frontier, most coming from Kentucky and from Symmes. Both groups, as well as the Ohio Company, had politically powerful conduits directly into Congress. Their cries for help, complaints, and accusations of insensitivity to the lives and property of frontier citizens came through loud and clear. The administration listened sympathetically, promising protection but at the same time pointing to the lack of money and the problems of transition in the government. To placate Symmes and the Kentuckians, Harmar was ordered to shift the bulk of the army and his headquarters westward and to build a new fortification in Symmes's territory. Accordingly, Fort Washington was constructed in present-day Cincinnati. Knox, aware of a possible backlash from the settlers at Marietta, ordered troops to be moved "silently and without any great notoriety" one company at a time so that residents of the Ohio Company would not be alarmed nor the Indians provoked. The new arrangement further stretched the army, and the consequent reconfiguration of troops left the Ohio Company settlements largely unprotected. After a summer of sporadic Indian attacks, requests for aid were still coming in, and appeals found their way directly to the president. Simply put, the army was too small.[414]

★

Richard H. Kohn cited the administration's next move as one which at the time seemed prudent, but which in retrospect became another step down the inevitable path to war. In a letter to Washington, Governor St. Clair outlined the deteriorating situation in the territory, decrying the lack of regulars and predicting war if the Kentuckians could not be

---

[413] Jacobs, *The Beginning of the U.S. Army*, 31–32; Huber, *General Josiah Harmar's Command*, 170–73.

[414] Kohn, *Eagle and Sword*, 96–97.

restrained. In 1787, Kentucky had been authorized to hold a militia in readiness to unite with federal troops should the situation be necessary, and the following year, Congress passed a similar resolution requesting backup militia from Virginia and Pennsylvania. St. Clair now asked for new authorization to call out the frontier militia as a way to conciliate settlers and to deal with the Indians from a position of strength.

When the president submitted St. Clair's request to Congress on September 16, 1789 and it was subsequently approved, most of the regular troops were offended. Regulars and militia forces were from two different worlds. The federal corps had been recruited mainly from eastern states; the militia were Kentucky and Pennsylvania frontiersmen, and there were enough differences between the two groups to create antagonism if not outright scorn. Harmar had previously told Knox that the earlier 1788 resolve would defeat all the plans of the regular army if militia colonels should "take command of the Majors of the regiment." He continued that it was "lamentable that instead of calling the militia, the government is so feeble as not to afford three or four regiments of national troops properly organized who would soon settle the business with these perfidious Villains upon the Wabash."[415]

By 1789, the army already had plenty of experience with militias and wanted no more. Officers had seen the results of the infamous Logan operation in 1786 and had noted the disastrous performance of the Kentuckians during Clark's expedition when large portions of his force had deserted en masse. From 1786 through 1789, retaliation by Kentucky frontiersmen continued to antagonize federal troops and Indians alike.[416]

Armstrong had firsthand knowledge of the Kentucky militia. In November 1788, he was tasked to march to Vincennes as part of a supply convoy under the command of a Kentucky militia officer. Not shy about reporting his dissatisfaction to Harmar and sensitive to the issue of rank, he wrote of the "injury done me by being ordered to march to Post Vincennes under the command of a militia officer on state affairs." Even allowing for bias on Armstrong's part, his criticisms seem well founded. The militia was mounted, and it drew far ahead of the regulars who were on foot, leaving Armstrong and his party far behind and virtually unprotected with the packhorses and cattle. His men exhausted from having to keep a

[415] Guthman, *March to Massacre*, 150–51; Kohn, *Eagle and Sword*, 97–98.
[416] Guthman, *March to Massacre*, 151.

steady pace without breaks in order to maintain contact with their escort, Armstrong eventually insisted that the procession halt for fifteen minutes in the middle of the day so that his men could rest. On one instance, the mounted troops were so far ahead that Armstrong did not even hear gunfire the party had directed toward buffalo. The supply train seldom got going before nine o'clock in the morning, and lack of scouting caused Armstrong's men to ford through the middle of a creek in the cold weather. Armstrong learned later that by crossing some distance farther down the trace, they would not even have gotten their feet wet. He estimated that a trip that took twenty-nine days could have been accomplished in nineteen, not a small factor with men carrying several days' provisions on their backs and marching in cold weather.[417]

★

Armstrong was stationed at Fort Steuben at the Falls of the Ohio from mid-1786 until 1790 during which time he witnessed the flood of migrants into the area, heard of attacks on settlements by groups of hostile Indians, and felt growing resentment for the militia expeditions that made the army's mission even more challenging. He was detailed to command supply convoys up and down the river and had duty at a blockhouse his detachment had built overlooking the Ohio at the appropriately named "Armstrong's Station." Correspondence also indicates that he had the company of his brother Hamilton while stationed at Fort Steuben whom he described as a "sober, active young man." The younger Armstrong served as an unofficial officer designated as a "cadet" who, along with other duties, acted in the capacity of transmitting messages and supplies between stations until being commissioned as ensign following the Harmar campaign in 1790. In recommending his appointment to Knox, St. Clair noted that Hamilton had served as a volunteer for two years and was

---

[417] Armstrong to Harmar, November 6, 1788, PJA; Armstrong to Harmar, December 29, 1788, *OOTW*, 143–44. Following the expedition, Armstrong, rankled by his experience with having to serve under the militia captain, wrote Knox in December 1788 regarding the validity of his brevet rank of captaincy following the Revolution in relation to that of militia officers. The secretary of war responded that he had no immediate answer to his question and that he would have to ask the president for guidance on the policy. Knox to Armstrong, October 30, 1789, PJA.

known to him as a deserving young man and a good woodsman who had on several occasions been in command of detachments, always acquitting himself well.[418]

Armstrong undoubtedly had numerous encounters with hostile Indians during his assignment at Fort Steuben. His papers indicate that one mission apparently found him more apprehensive than most. On May 25, 1787, he reported an expedition in which he led a party composed of his own men plus eight others. They set out from Clarksville to find a group of Indians that had recently killed neighboring settlers. Armstrong reported that they tracked the group for ten miles before sighting and pursuing the party, subsequently capturing five horses and collecting articles left behind. The day before engaging in this mission, Armstrong recorded these instructions in his notebook: "In case I get killed by any axident doctor Allison will please to act as my executor in conjunction with my Brother Hamilton Armstrong. The Doctor will please to attend to the papers he will find in my trunk."[419]

One supply mission to Vincennes in May 1789 was particularly significant. Major Hamtramck had previously informed Capt. Joseph Asheton, then Fort Steuben's commander, of his dire need of provisions for his 140 men. Asheton dispatched Armstrong with one ensign, one cadet, and forty-three noncommissioned officers and privates along with seven months of supplies in boats guarded by fifty armed men. Once entering the Wabash, he dispatched small parties onshore to scout for signs of Indians

---

[418] Armstrong to William Alexander, September 5, 1788, PJA; St. Clair to Knox, October 29, 1790 *SCP* II: 188–189. Family lore attributes Armstrong with command of Fort Finney/Steuben. This was not the case. Upon Capt. Walter Finney's departure in June 1787 and the consequent name change of the garrison to Fort Steuben, Maj. John Hamtramck, followed by Maj. John Wyllys, was designated commander of the installation. Wyllys remained in command until the spring of 1789. Replaced by Joseph Asheton, records indicate that the captain continued his command at least through May 1791. Armstrong was a junior officer while serving at the Falls and was not promoted to his captaincy until October 1790. Numerous references to Wyllys's and Asheton's commands appear in Harmar's letters found in Thornbrough's *Outpost on the Wabash, 1787–1791* and in his letters included in Denny's *Military Journal*.

[419] Armstrong to Wyllys, May 25, 1787; Armstrong to Johnston, June 28, 1787, in Cochran notebook; Armstrong's notation in his notebook, 1785–1790, PJA.

who might be lying in wait to ambush the convoy. He reported skirmishes with two parties of Indians but attempted to avoid larger numbers of warriors in the area. At one point, his party stopped to bury the mutilated body of a soldier sent to meet the detachment. In his report to Harmar, Hamtramck credited Armstrong for the party's hard work and his safe arrival due to the captain's "great attention."

Armstrong characteristically reviewed the mission's standard procedures, noting that soldiers should operate the boats rather than men supplied by contractors who had no knowledge of the river and were unacquainted with the use of the oar or a setting pole. The trip up the Wabash, he said, would have taken half the time had soldiers manned the boats. Also criticizing the amount of rations issued to his soldiers, he noted that an allotment of one per day was too small for men performing such hard work and that he had distributed extra whiskey for their efforts. Armstrong's party returned to the Falls on June 25, 1789, after a journey of twenty-six days.[420]

By this time, donation lands for Revolutionary War soldiers had been designated, and Armstrong began his quest to acquire land in earnest. His papers include numerous records of purchasing soldiers' land rights and other sales he witnessed for fellow officers. He had started his first venture in large-scale land speculation, writing to Col. Francis Johnston, Major McConnell, and Maj. William Alexander concerning a tract of 17,000 acres at the mouth of Captina Creek between Wheeling and Marietta and the need to purchase warrants for that amount, requesting 500 acres for his trouble. He had personally toured the acreage on his way from Fort Pitt to Fort Harmar upon his return from the East in September 1788.[421]

Copies of Armstrong's successive army commissions are included in his papers at the Indiana Historical Society, beginning with his September 1783 appointment by the Supreme Executive Council of Pennsylvania

---

[420] A setting pole was used to push off of the river bottom in order to guide the boat in the desired direction. In his letter to Hamtramck on February 20, 1790, Harmar noted that Armstrong had "been so constantly employed upon, in going backwards & forwards to the Post," *OOTW*, 221. Asheton to Hamtramck, May 31, 1789; Armstrong to Hamtramck, June 11, 1789; Hamtramck to Harmar, June 15, 1789; Armstrong to Asheton, June 25, 1789, *OOTW*, 172–78.

[421] Armstrong letters to Johnston, McConnell, and Alexander, September 5, 1788, PJA.

as first lieutenant in Maj. James Moore's infantry company at Wyoming and followed by appointments to the ranks of ensign and lieutenant from August 1784 through April 1788 by that body. On September 29, 1789, John Armstrong again received a commission as a lieutenant in the Regiment of Infantry, this time signed by George Washington under the new constitutional government. Having served six years on the frontier as a junior officer and having watched his fellow officers slowly rise in rank as vacancies occurred, he had yet to achieve the brevet rank awarded him at the close of the Revolution. The following year, he finally received his long-coveted promotion, but 1790 would prove to be a pivotal one which he was fortunate to survive.

10

The Missouri County, 1790

It is a business much easier planned than executed.
—John Armstrong, June 2, 1790[422]

In the far reaches of the United States lay the long-neglected settlements of Cahokia and Kaskaskia. In early 1790, Washington dispatched St. Clair to address the myriad of problems in that part of the territory once held by the French, British, and later the United States that had been forced to rely on its own resources since Virginia, whose charter included lands stretching to the Mississippi, had six years before relinquished its claim to areas north of the Ohio to the federal government. Seeing not only the need to send the governor to the Illinois country to address neglected administrative problems, military men Washington and Knox also realized that they needed knowledge of the terrain and resources not only of the land lying in present-day Indiana and Illinois but also of Spain's enormous territory west of the Mississippi. Vast sections of land west of the Wabash lay uncharted, and the administration wanted maps with which to negotiate its unknown landscape and to develop potential routes to the Great Lakes. Determined to improve not only their knowledge of the land and rivers lying within the territorial United States, they also flirted with

---

[422] Armstrong to Harmar, June 2, 1790, in Colton Storm, "Lieutenant Armstrong's Expedition to the Missouri River, 1790," *Mid-America: An Historical Review* 4, no. 3 (1943): 185.

the idea of secretly exploring tributaries to the Mississippi lying within Spanish territory. Accordingly, in the waning days of 1789, Knox directed Josiah Harmar to take the following action:

> Devise some practicable plan for exploring the branch of the Mississippi called the Messouri, up to its source and all its southern branches, and tracing particularly the distances between the said branches and any of the navigable streams that run into the Gulf of Mexico.

Unaware of the magnitude of the proposed task, Knox continued his directive:

> You will easily see that this object cannot be undertaken with the sanction of public authority. An enterprising officer with a non-commissioned officer well acquainted with living in the woods, & perhaps capable of describing rivers and countries, accompanied by four or five hardy Indians perfectly attached to the United States, would, in my opinion be the best mode of obtaining the information requested.[423]

Since any exploration of the Missouri River and its tributaries involved entering Spanish territory, Knox emphasized the operation's covert nature. The individual involved in the expedition should be "habited" like an Indian and reveal no sign of any connection with the nation's army; he would carry no written orders.[424]

Harmar was skeptical of the plan but chose to honor the directive he was given, tapping John Armstrong for the task. The lieutenant received his

---

[423] A. P. Nasatir, *Before Lewis and Clark: Documents Illustrating the History of the Missouri, 1785–1804* (Norman: University of Oklahoma Press, 1952), 135–37.

[424] Storm, "Lieutenant Armstrong's Expedition," 181, 187–88; Reuben Gold Thwaites, ed., *Original Journals of the Lewis and Clark Expedition, 1804-1806* (New York: Dodd, Mead, and Company, 1904), VII: 199; Nasatir, *Before Lewis and Clark*, 135–42. Few maps of the territory existed at the time, and Storm notes that the reference most commonly used was probably that of Jacques Nicholas Bellin done in 1750 that was based on La Salle's observations along the Mississippi watershed in the previous century.

verbal orders at Fort Washington in late February. His written instructions reflect Harmar's misgivings about the feasibility of conducting such an exploration and also his determination to pass on the responsibility for making the ultimate decision to proceed to Governor St. Clair.

> I have already made you acquainted with the business which you have to undertake, provided the Governor of the Western Territory should Judge it advisable—If not, You are to return from the Illinois Country to Post Vincennes, & explore the Wabash river, & give me a particular report of its communication with Lake Erie, the depth of the Water, the distances &c—if it can be done with safety, proceed to the Miami Village, in which case it will be necessary to have an Escort of Friendly Indians to accompany you—you will endeavor to return to Head Quarters by Land, after this business is effected.[425]

Departing Fort Washington on February 22, stopping at Fort Steuben to get his affairs in order, and delivering supplies to Vincennes en route, Armstrong reached the Mississippi on March 23 and the garrison at Kaskaskia a few days later. He was to deliver a letter from Harmar to the governor who was then at the Illinois garrison and to transmit information verbally that could not be put into writing.[426]

When St. Clair arrived at Kaskaskia in early March, he found its inhabitants in a sorry state. Local government was practically nonexistent and the community in shambles. The river had flooded multiple times, sweeping away crops or preventing them from being planted. Indian trade had disappeared, and former friends were now hostile. Adding to the misery, an untimely frost had decimated the previous year's corn crop. Busy with attempting to sort out governmental affairs, St. Clair undoubtedly welcomed the appearance of an unexpected officer on the scene of so much misery. In his article, "Lieutenant Armstrong's Expedition to the Missouri River, 1790," Colton Storm noted that immediately upon Armstrong's

---

[425] Harmar to Armstrong, February 20, 1790, PJA. See also Storm, "Lieutenant Armstrong's Expedition," 181–82.

[426] Armstrong Notebook, February-October 1790, PJA.

arrival at the garrison, he was put to work trying to remedy a serious lack of supplies.[427]

By all appearances, St. Clair nixed the whole operation, citing its impracticability due to the fact that "it is a point on which some people are feelingly alive all over, and all their jealousy awake. Indians to be confided in, there are none." He apparently ventured further concerns to Knox and Harmar through Armstrong, apparently not willing to risk transmitting them on paper.[428]

Armstrong's comments regarding future ventures into the Missouri country were more positive. In his report made upon his return to Fort Washington on June 2, the lieutenant stated that he believed that provided with the proper equipment, he could have made the passage. By giving generous gifts to some of the nations on the Missouri during a tour of eighteen months to two years, needed information might be obtained. Should he again be called upon to go on such a mission, he would need oilcloth for securing papers as well as a half-faced camp or tent of the same material. He also wrote, "If it is a matter of consequence to the United States I am of opinion there would be less difficulty in the execution at present than at an afterday." He submitted an invoice of goods necessary

---

[427] Storm, "Lieutenant Armstrong's Expedition," 183. Armstrong undoubtedly pursued personal business during his time on the Mississippi. He had taken an interest in the estate and property of Richard McCarty, Revolutionary War officer in Virginia's Illinois Regiment under George Rogers Clark who had posthumously been awarded land in what would become Clark County, Indiana, and the location of Armstrong's current duty station at Fort Steuben. Prior to serving in the Illinois Regiment, McCarty, a French-Canadian trader, had owned land and a mill in Cahokia. Armstrong had been in contact with McCarty's lawyer in Canada and had offered to serve as agent in the sale of McCarty's lands. He needed documents from Kaskaskia and Cahokia to support McCarty's ownership of lands on the Mississippi and conveniently found himself in the region to search for them. Michael J. O'Brien, *The McCarthys in Early American History* (New York: Dodd, Mead, and Company, 1921), 142–44. Armstrong's papers include correspondence regarding McCarty's lands that begins in 1788 and continues well past his death in 1816.

[428] *SCP* I: 164–65; St. Clair to Knox, May 1, 1790, in Storm, "Lieutenant Armstrong's Expedition, 183–84; Thwaites, *Original Journals of the Lewis and Clark Expedition*, VII: 200.

for trade in the country and believed that a connection with local traders might take place, resulting in little expense to the government.[429]

Other facts lead to the conclusion that Armstrong did not complete the mission originally detailed by Knox. St. Clair's official response was definitive in his "no go" decision for the Missouri expedition, citing specific reasons for not doing so in letters to Knox and Harmar on May 1 and 2. Armstrong in his official report to Harmar, written after his return to Fort Washington, further delineated reasons for not undertaking the journey. St. Clair had thought that perhaps the only way to make the trip would be to go in the guise of a trader, and Armstrong noted that the Spanish commandant was well aware of the quantity of furs and goods that went up and down the river, a fact that presumably would point to his presence as an outsider in the territory. Additionally, Armstrong did not know of Indians "well attached to the United States."[430]

Armstrong apparently gained official permission from St. Clair to conduct limited information-gathering ventures. A short distance upriver from Kaskaskia was Ste. Genevieve, and further north, the Illinois settlement of Cahokia looked across the river at the village of St. Louis. He recorded that he met the commandants of the two garrisons in Ste. Genevieve and St. Louis through the introduction of a priest and apparently established positive relationships with them.

> While at St. Genavieve & St. Louis being on an
> intimate footing with the Commandants of each place . . .
> I endeavord to learn when conversing of the Mississippi &
> Missouri whether either of those Gentlemen had Maps or
> descriptions of these Rivers taken by private adventurers,
> not explained by Maps several of which they showed me,
> but such only as we have in the United States.[431]

---

[429] Huber, *General Josiah Harmar's Command*, 183–84.

[430] Armstrong to Harmar, June 2, 1790 in Storm, "Lieutenant Armstrong's Expedition," 184–85; *SCP*, II: 136, 144.

[431] Armstrong's memorandum, May 1790, PJA. He was possibly introduced to Spanish administrators in Ste. Genevieve and St. Louis by one of two priests associated with churches on both sides of the river, Father Paul de St. Pierre and Father Pierre Gibault. See John Rothensteiner, "Paul de Saint Pierre: The First German-American Priest of the West," *The Catholic Historical Review* 5, nos. 2 and 3 (1919), 201, 203–205, 214.

The Illinois Country

Mississippi River

Illinois River

River Bluffs

Les Petites Cotes

Missouri River

St. Louis

Cahokia

Kaskaskia River

← Kaskaskia-Cahokia Road

Kaskaskia
Ste. Genevieve
†

Mississippi River

Spanish Louisiana

† Remains of the village of Kaskaskia
devastated by flooding in 1861 and
subsequent channel shift of the Mississippi
to the east

Ohio River

Apparently managing to speak with prominent locals on both sides of
the river, Armstrong also gained information from fur traders instrumental
in the founding of Ste. Genevieve and St. Louis, among them Auguste
Chouteau, Jean Gabriel Cerré, Sylvester Labadie, and Charles Gratiot. He
was able to copy a map of the Missouri territory, recorded geographic notes

from Chouteau, and also obtained a sketch of the Illinois River and notes of its connections with Lake Michigan.[432]

Contrary to information included in St. Clair's and Armstrong's official reports, family tradition holds that Armstrong did, indeed, venture up the Missouri on this mission, citing the biography written by his son, William G. Armstrong, in Charles Cist's *Cincinnati Miscellany or Antiquities of the West* in 1845. In it, the younger Armstrong stated,

> He immediately started on this tour, and proceeded up the Missouri some distance above St. Louis, *not with an army to deter the savages, nor yet an escort, but entirely alone!* It was his intention to examine the country of the upper Missouri, and cross the Rocky Mountains—but meeting with some French traders, was persuaded to return in consequence of the hostility of some of the Missouri bands to each other, as they were then at war, that he could not safely pass from one nation to another.[433]

Certainly the son's account is strong testimony that Armstrong ventured well past St. Louis, as there would hardly be a better informant than Armstrong himself. Later reasoning by C. F. Cochran, his biographer who maintained the collection of Armstrong papers now housed at the William H. Smith Memorial Library at the Indiana Historical Society, was that such an expedition could have taken place, a theory supported by the absence of entries in Armstrong's journal and the lack of existing correspondence in Armstrong's papers between the time of his arrival at Kaskaskia on March 28 and May 1 when St. Clair wrote to Knox that Armstrong had "been here for quite some time," as well as the secret nature of the mission that precluded neither Armstrong nor St. Clair from maintaining any information relating to the expedition in writing.[434]

---

[432] Memorandum, May 1790, PJA; For information concerning Illinois River documentation, see Colton Storm, "Lieutenant John Armstrong's Map of the Illinois River, 1790," *Journal of the Illinois State Historical Society* (1908–1984), 37, no. 1 (1944): 48–55.

[433] Cist, *CM* I: 40.

[434] Cochran lamented the fact that although he was the main custodian of Armstrong's correspondence and other records, some papers had been retained by other family members and speculated that pertinent documents might

A third possibility lends truth to the theory that Armstrong indeed ventured into Spanish territory although not on the grand scale noted by his son. St. Clair knew Armstrong's talents well, having served as division commander of the Pennsylvania Line during the last years of the Revolution, participating in the Siege of Yorktown, the journey south into the Carolinas, and the operations surrounding Charleston. He had ample opportunity to have learned further of the lieutenant's resourcefulness during the almost two years he had been governor of the Ohio territory and would have recognized him as an officer well suited to operate alone in the wilderness. He may have officially declined authorization for Armstrong's mission with the understanding that he would turn a blind eye toward the lieutenant's wandering into Spanish territory on a limited basis. St. Clair, then conducting business in Cahokia, did not correspond with Knox and Harmar regarding Armstrong's mission until days before Armstrong departed upon his homeward journey. In all likelihood, Armstrong carried the letter to Kaskaskia to be sent eastward or conveyed St. Clair's message to Harmar himself.

Armstrong could have made headway into an area where few lived without traveling great distances from the settlement at St. Louis. Despite his son's assertion that the lieutenant was "entirely alone," Armstrong had the company of his "servant" who could have provided needed power for manning a canoe against river current. Additionally, as a soldier accustomed to traveling long distances on foot, he could have reached the Missouri River easily by land. He could also have traversed trails on horseback.[435]

---

have been lost or deliberately carried away prior to his attaining them, a factor further clouding the question of Armstrong's venture into Spanish territory. C. F. Cochran to Reuben Gold Thwaites, September 18, 1905, PJA. Interestingly, Armstrong's papers presently include a memorandum to paymaster Erkuries Beatty dated April 16, 1790, directing him to pay Armstrong's accounts, indicating that on this date, falling midway during his time in the area, Armstrong was at the garrison at Kaskaskia or in Cahokia where parties returning eastward would have transmitted the memorandum to Beatty.

[435] The governor's approval of the lieutenant's character and abilities was later demonstrated by St. Clair's appointment of Armstrong as a Hamilton County judge within months of his army resignation in 1793 and that of Armstrong's position as treasurer of the Ohio territory three years later. SCP, II: 175–76. Armstrong's fastidious nature is reflected in his per diem request for reimbursement for expenses for both himself and his servant for "Seventy Dollars and thirty-nine nineties of a Dollar." He also requested reimbursement for his horse that he had purchased for $40 and subsequently

One scenario for a venture into the Missouri country centers upon the location of a natural ford across the Mississippi approximately twenty-five miles north of Cahokia. The ancient "Trail to the Village of the Missouris" originated above the confluence of the Missouri with the Mississippi and paralleled the river's north bank as it meandered westward into central Missouri. Following the trail approximately twenty-five miles, he could easily have reached the tiny hamlet of Les Petites Cotes (present-day St. Charles, Missouri), a settlement of approximately twelve houses that served as a jumping-off point to the west for a small number of trappers, traders, and river men. There he could have gained valuable information regarding conditions on the upper Missouri. By traveling alone or with one companion, he would not have called undue attention to himself for the brief period of time he spent either in the area or shortly beyond it.[436]

Armstrong may also have been the source of information for St. Clair's later description of a site along the Mississippi River bluffs near the mouth of the Illinois River about thirty-five miles upriver from Cahokia as the ideal location for a future military post. On his way northward to gather rudimentary information concerning the Illinois waterway and its possible connection to the Great Lakes, Armstrong might have considered possibilities for entering the Missouri country upon his return. If traveling by land, he would have passed the river's natural fording point and noted it for later use. If traveling by water, upon his return from the Illinois River, he could have entered the Missouri country by crossing the long, narrow

---

delivered to Major Hamtramck. Armstrong to Harmar, June 2, 1790, in Storm, "Lieutenant Armstrong's Expedition," 185–86.

[436] Daniel T. Brown, *Westering River, Westering Trail: A History of St. Charles County, Missouri to 1849* (St. Charles, Missouri: St. Charles Historical Society, 2006), 81. The course of the Mississippi River has altered considerably since Armstrong's journey westward. Natural phenomena, such as the New Madrid earthquakes of 1811–1812 and periodic flooding and channel shifting of the Mississippi have changed the landscape, as have dams along the waterway from Minnesota to its confluence with the Ohio River at Cairo, Illinois, and levies and dykes throughout its entirety. For information concerning the history of river alteration, see U.S. Army Corps of Engineers, "Geomorphology Study of the Middle Mississippi River," last modified December 2005, http://www.mvsc.usace.army.mil/arec/Documents/Geomorphology/Geomorphology_Study_of_The_Middle_Mississippi_River.pdf, accessed May 24, 2021.

peninsula separating the two rivers over an ancient Indian portage or entered the Missouri downstream at the confluence of the two rivers.[437]

Regardless of whether Armstrong actually ventured into the Missouri territory or how he got there, John Parker Huber notes that the lieutenant's trip was not in vain. He established useful contacts, prepared an invoice of necessary supplies, and secured valuable maps with descriptions of terrain, the first of the country west of the Mississippi secured by a government-ordered expedition. Harmar, in a letter to Knox following Armstrong's return, noted that the lieutenant had shared information with him that he had obtained from men who had explored the country extensively. All his reports were eventually transmitted to Knox and to the president.[438]

---

[437] *SCP*, II: 175–76. Armstrong could also have reached the Missouri River by land by following a more direct route although one with the possibility of being noticed in its initial stages, by following an old Indian trace leading roughly twenty-five miles from the St. Louis riverfront west to the Missouri's south shore across from Les Petites Cotes. Daniel T. Brown, *Westering River*, 81, 95.

[438] Huber, *General Josiah Harmar's Command*, 181–84; Storm, "Lieutenant Armstrong's Expedition," 186–88 and Storm, Harmar to Knox, February 20, 1790, 182. Armstrong made other explorations westward. In a letter to his brother James in 1810, he wrote that he had traveled to the Missouri Country in 1807. He added that "in this country we think nothing of a journey of 2 or 3000 miles . . . in the years 97 & 98 I spent two summers in the woods without seeing any white man but these of our party's." John Armstrong to James Armstrong, June 22, 1810, PJA.

Armstrong again ventured westward in 1808. In a memorandum indicating that he was about to take a journey to the Mississippi and his "life being uncertain," he listed property within his ownership, one piece of which was "on the Mississippi the number of acres not ascertained" Memorandum, September 24, PJA. Upon his return to the Mississippi in 1808, he would have encountered both Merriweather Lewis and his friend and occasional Columbia business associate William Clark in St. Louis serving as Governor of the Territory and Superintendent of Indian affairs, respectively. References to Armstrong's connection with Clark can be found in James J. Holmberg, ed., *Dear Brother: Letters of William to Jonathan Clark* (New Haven: Yale University Press, 2002), 44, 48-49, as well as multiple copies of correspondence or mention of Clark in the Armstrong papers; Stephen E. Ambrose, *Undaunted Courage, Meriwether Lewis, Thomas Jefferson, and the Opening of the American West* (New York: Simon and Schuster, 1996), 416, 437- 38.

Armstrong departed Kaskaskia around May 8, traveling overland through present-day southern Illinois. Upon his arrival at Fort Knox, he assessed the feasibility of accomplishing Harmar's second assignment, exploring the Wabash and its links to waterways to Lake Erie, as well as proceeding to the Miami villages. He apparently chose to exercise discretion over valor. Armstrong's report of June 2, 1790, to Harmar clearly indicates that he attempted no such exploration: "I found from the hostile disposition of Indians on the Wabash that it was unsafe to attempt exploring that & the Moami Rivers &c."[439]

Although Armstrong determined that the conditions for making a detailed survey of the Wabash and its connections to waterways leading to Lake Erie were unfavorable at the time, he did attempt to follow Harmar's directive to proceed to Fort Washington by an overland route. Although credited by William G. Armstrong as traversing and exploring "the then wilderness of Illinois and Indiana," his trip overland from Vincennes to Fort Washington on the final leg of his journey appears to have been more "traversing" and less "exploring." Armstrong reported that he set out eastward in the company of two Indians but wrote that after proceeding for two days, one of his companions became sick and the other "lame," and they refused to continue on that route. He was successful in convincing them to accompany him to the alternate destination of Fort Steuben,

---

[439] Armstrong reached Fort Knox prior to May 16. His papers include detailed mileage landmarks between southern Illinois creek and river crossings from Kaskaskia to Vincennes.

Armstrong's papers suggest a small mystery concerning the last leg of his journey homeward and his earlier directive from Harmar to chart the course of the Wabash and connections to Lake Erie. This information was apparently forwarded to Harmar prior to Armstrong's descent down the Ohio. An entry in Armstrong's handwriting appears to be a copy of the document submitted by Hamtramck to Harmar on March 17, 1790. Armstrong was in Vincennes when Hamtramck's letter to Harmar was written. Armstrong may have penned the document based on information from local traders and neighboring Indians familiar with the upper Wabash prior to his departure downriver. Hamtramck to Harmar, May 16, 1790, *OOTW*, 216, 225–27, 233; Armstrong papers, PJA; Storm, "Lieutenant Armstrong's Expedition," 185.

however, and eventually made his way to headquarters at Fort Washington where he presented his findings to Harmar.[440]

★

Armstrong had missed out on a lot during his time in the west. While he was away, isolated Indian attacks had continued not only upon settlers but also on army detachments. Maj. John Doughty and a party of fifteen men had been on what was designated as a mission of peace to the Cherokee Nation along the Tennessee River in late March 1790. His party was attacked, and a four-hour battle ensued, during which six men were killed and five injured. Doughty and the survivors managed to make their way back to the Ohio River, but with their reduced manpower, they were unable to fight the current, so they went downstream. Upon reaching the Mississippi, they found refuge at L'Anse à la Graisse south of the confluence of the two rivers and were eventually rescued by a detachment of soldiers from Kaskaskia. Armstrong undoubtedly got all the details firsthand from the bedraggled officer when his depleted party arrived at the Illinois outpost in early April.[441]

Attacks also continued along the Ohio. Major Hamtramck wrote St. Clair in mid-April, citing reported incidents that had taken place in the territory, particularly upon settlers and merchandise-laden boats going downriver near the mouth of the Scioto River the previous month. An attack had also occurred on the river south of Fort Steuben and one north of it upon a small Kentucky settlement.[442]

Kentucky district judge Harry Innes summed up the situation a few months later. Since he had arrived in Kentucky in November 1783, more than 1,500 people had been killed or taken prisoner; and upward of 20,000 horses had been stolen along with other property of value consisting of money, merchandise, household goods, and clothing. He complained that

---

[440] Sources vary regarding Armstrong's departure from Vincennes for Fort Washington. Armstrong's letter included in Storm's article states that he departed Vincennes on May 13; Hamtramck's letter to Harmar that was to be carried by Armstrong was dated May 16. See Storm, "Lieutenant Armstrong's Expedition," 185 and *OOTW*, 233–34.

[441] Doughty to Wyllys, March 25, 1790, and St. Clair to Knox, May 1, 1790, *SCP* II: 134, 137. L'Anse à la Graisse would become New Madrid, Missouri.

[442] Hamtramck to St. Clair, April 19, 1790, *SCP*, II: 135.

although the federal government had been repeatedly informed of the incidents that occurred almost daily, the Kentuckians had received no satisfactory information regarding the government's intention to afford them relief.[443]

Armstrong probably did not hear of a sizeable operation involving several of his fellow officers and regimental troops until he reached Vincennes in May. Harmar had clearly chafed under the constant depredation of settlers and his men along the Ohio River. On April 15, he progressed upriver from Fort Washington with 120 regulars and was joined by about 200 Kentucky militia under the command of Brig. Gen. Charles Scott to rout a nest of "vagabond Indians" that had been raiding boats on the Ohio near the Scioto River. The operation was a failure. Once soldiers reached the Scioto, no fresh signs of Indian presence were found, and the militia began clamoring to go home.

Incidents continued. On May 12, tribesmen attacked a federal convoy of six boats under the command of Ensign Asa Hartshorne nine miles above Limestone, Kentucky at which five men were killed and eight were taken prisoner. Harmar bristled at this latest incident. "The Indians have been and still are damned troublesome," he told one friend in June. "I am in full hopes that the new government will give me the materials to work with, and the next year be prepared for a general war with them."[444]

★

William Guthman notes that like Harmar, officers on the frontier as well as the administration knew that an eventual showdown was

---

[443] Innes to Knox, July 7, 1790, quoted in Charles Elihu Slocum, *The Ohio Country Between the Years 1783 and 1815* (New York: G. P. Putnam's Sons, 1910), 53; American State Papers (ASP)-Indian Affairs, I: 88.

[444] Sword, *President Washington's Indian War*, 85–86; Wilkinson to Harmar, April 7, 1790, and Harmar to Knox, June 9, 1790, in Papers of the War Department: 1784–1800, Roy Rosenzweig Center for History and New Media, accessed March 28, 2021, https://wardepartmentpapers.org/s/home/item/40743; http://wardepartmentpapers.org/s/home/item/42175. Original Source: Post-Revolutionary War Papers, RG94, National Archives and Records Administration, https://wardepartmentpapers.org/s/home/item/40531; official Hartshorne report, May 30, 1790, Harmar to Knox, June 9, 1790, *ASP-Indian Affairs*, I: 91–92.

inevitable. Their hopes were placed in the new government's ability to build a more substantial military, but there was still strong resentment in Congress against a large standing army. The legislative body had little feel for the hostilities occurring along the country's western borders; the territory was too remote to make any impression on many members from the eastern states.

The Secretary of War submitted a plan for an enlarged army to Washington who in turn passed it to Congress on January 21, 1790. It called for a small corps of artillery and engineers and a legion consisting of 2,033 officers and men for the protection of the frontiers and the manning of magazines and arsenals under the provision that soldiers be enlisted for a certain period of time, after which they would return to civilian life. He also called for the establishment of a well-constituted militia to supplement this new force in which men from 18–60 would be required to perform military duties. Such a citizen army would not only defend the country against its enemies, but would also create "a glorious national spirit." Knox ventured that use of the militia would be politically acceptable and cheap compared to long-service regulars. In view of an upcoming expedition against the Indian nations, it was the only force available. Congress did not accept even this modest plan.[445]

Congress was finally forced to address the question of national defense it had too long deferred and acknowledged its responsibility to protect settlers on land they had legitimately purchased from the federal government. An act on April 30, 1790, increased the size of Harmar's 700-man force to 1,216 to be organized into a regiment of infantry and a battalion of artillery. Men were to be enlisted and officers commissioned for only three years, a limit that temporarily skirted the issue of creating a permanent standing army. The law came with a price tag for the soldier, however. Although it raised the pay of the commanding officer and provided pensions for soldiers wounded in the line of duty, the legislation lowered the pay of all the other ranks just at the time when the army faced its most significant challenge. Army historian William Adelman Ganoe summed up the legislation thusly: "It then tore down the whole structure by

---

[445] Guthman, *March to Massacre*, 174; Jacobs, *The Beginning of the U.S. Army*, 44; Kohn, *Eagle and Sword*, 108.

cutting the pay of the private to $3 per month, and deducting besides $1 for hospital stores and clothing, so that he really received only $2 in cash."[446]

★

Washington, Knox, Harmar, and St. Clair continued to wrestle with the question whose answer became increasingly obvious. Particularly in the case of the Indians along the Wabash who continued to raid into Kentucky and along the Ohio, full-scale war looked more and more likely, but attempts to avoid it nevertheless had to be conducted. Knox had genuine qualms about the extent of any operation. He summed up his feelings in a report to Washington in June 1789, citing two ways to deal with the situation. The first was to raise an army with the purpose of crushing the refractory nations entirely, and the second was to treat with them, outlining explicitly their rights and limits while at the same time exercising equal justice to any offenders on the American side who violated the terms of an agreement. Assuming that in the event of war, the army could rout the enemy forces, Knox questioned the morality of such an operation. A strong believer in Native American rights as prior occupants of the soil, he felt that land should not be taken from them unless done with their free consent or by right of conquest in the event of a justifiable war. Dispossessing them in any other manner would be a gross violation of the fundamental laws of nature. Even in the case of a justified war, there was another major factor to consider: the cash-strapped government simply could not afford it.

---

[446] Congress approved the following pay scale:

Lieutenant colonel commandant	$60 per month
Major commandant of artillery	$45 per month
Majors	$40 per month
Captains	$30 per month
Lieutenants	$22 per month
Ensigns	$18 per month
Surgeons	$30 per month
Surgeons' mates	$24 per month
Sergeants, senior musicians	$5 per month
Corporals	$4 per month
Privates, musicians	$3 per month

Jacobs, *The Beginning of the U.S. Army*, 50; Guthman, *March to Massacre*, 6, 145; Ganoe, *The History of the United States Army*, 96. Under the previous act of Congress of October 1787, privates had received $4 per month.

Knox favored the second option. He called for treaties and agreements whereby the nations would be paid for their land, reasoning that the situation would ultimately resolve itself. Future settlement of lands bordering Indian territory was inevitable, and the game upon which the Native American inhabitants relied would surely diminish. Lands valuable to the nations solely as hunting grounds would lose their productivity, and they would eventually be willing to sell tracts they had been granted through treaty. Knox predicted that within fifty years, the Indian population would be significantly reduced. He was emphatic on one point, however. The United States had to gain possession of the posts on the Great Lakes still occupied by the British. Possession of these strategic garrisons would serve to awe neighboring nations or, in the event of their continuing resistance, enable the government to operate against them with a much greater prospect of success.[447]

Washington also leaned toward a policy based on treaties and strategic placement of army garrisons, as well as trade in order to "establish peace upon the foundation of Interest and friendly intercourse." Congress, however, continued to delay enacting legislation to support such a policy, to appropriate money for negotiations, and to increase regimental size to support additional garrisons. The president clearly wanted to avoid war if at all possible but was realistic enough to hedge his pronouncements with caveats. The previous October, he had requested St. Clair's assistance in determining the mood of the Wabash Indians, directing him to ascertain the likelihood of either a positive response toward peace initiatives or an inclination toward war. Washington sought to discover the following:

> Whether the Wabash and Illinois Indians are most inclined for war or peace. If for the former, it is proper that I should be informed of the means which will most probably induce them to peace. If a peace can be established with the said Indians on reasonable terms, the interests of the United States dictate that it should be effected as soon as possible. You will, therefore, inform the said Indians of the disposition of the General Government on this

---

[447] Guthman, *March to Massacre*, 162–65; *ASP-Indian Affairs*, I: 12–14.

subject, and of their reasonable desire that there should be
a cessation of hostilities as a prelude to a treaty.[448]

The wording of Washington's letter of October 6, 1789, proved to
be pivotal in the history of the territory. Historian Wiley Sword notes
that Washington stressed that the governor's conduct should reflect the
government's desire to avoid a war. If, however, hostilities should continue
and *if the President could not be advised in time*, Washington authorized St.
Clair to call on the lieutenants of Virginia (i.e., Kentucky) and Pennsylvania
counties for detachments of militia to augment federal troops in "offensive
or defensive" operations. Furthermore, St. Clair and Harmar must agree
"conjointly" on such action.[449]

In January, St. Clair forwarded the task of determining the disposition
of the Wabash and Miami area tribes toward peace to Major Hamtramck
at Vincennes. Sword contends that the governor's written query was little
more than an ultimatum consistent with his intention to obtain a peace by
using strong language that threatened military action. At one point, St.
Clair asserted, "I do now make you the offer of peace; accept it or reject it
as you please." By reaffirming the mandate-style diplomacy used in past
negotiations and treaties that had so alienated moderate and hostile factions
alike, St. Clair derailed what Washington intended as an earnest attempt
to initiate a substantive dialogue with the Wabash nations. St. Clair chose
to rely on indirect correspondence rather than personal negotiation and
consented to meet with chiefs only when they had assembled at Vincennes
in compliance with his instructions.[450]

Andrew R. L. Cayton in his work *Frontier Indiana* notes that
Hamtramck could predict the response of the Wabash Indians. Piankashaws
and others along the lower Wabash were inclined toward peace, but their
neighbors to the northeast in the Miami villages were not. Nevertheless,
he dispatched Pierre Gamelin, a well-regarded French magistrate, to

---

[448] Washington to St. Clair, October 6, 1789, *SCP*, II: 125–26; Kohn, *Eagle and Sword*, 100–01; Knox to Harmar, December 19, 1789, *OOTW*, 210–12.

[449] Washington to St. Clair, October 6, 1789, *SCP*, II: 125–126; Sword, *President Washington's Indian War*, 84; Downes, *Council Fires on the Upper Ohio*, 314. See also Knox to Harmar regarding the president's response to Kentuckian Samuel McDowell, December 19, 1789, *OOTW*, 211–13.

[450] Sword, *President Washington's Indian War*, 84; St. Clair to Hamtramck, January 23, 1790, *SCP*, II: 130–32.

ascertain the intentions of the local tribes. When Gamelin ran into an old enemy and decided to return to Vincennes, Hamtramck commissioned his brother, Antoine, the local clerk of court, to assume the duty. He departed Vincennes on April 5, traveled as far as the village at Kekionga, known as "Miami Town," at the confluence of the St. Marys, St. Joseph, and Maumee Rivers in present-day Fort Wayne, Indiana, and returned the next month, making his formal report to Hamtramck on May 17.

Gamelin's mission had been difficult. Tribes along the Wabash, skeptical of their history with the government in general and with Kentucky filibusters in particular, deferred their answers until Gamelin had met with tribal chiefs at Miami Town. Once there, he spoke to an assemblage of Miami, Shawnee, and Delaware, as well as French and English traders. They listened respectfully, but they indicated their displeasure until Gamelin assured them that he was there to offer peace and not to coerce them to accept it. They gave Gamelin no formal answer, claiming the need to consult with the British at Detroit before responding. By all appearances, however, they were skeptical of the message. Blue Jacket, leader of the Shawnee, made it emphatically clear that he did not trust the Americans. "From all quarters," he complained, "we receive speeches from the Americans, and not one is alike."[451]

Gamelin had to return to Vincennes without a definitive answer. He found that Indians on his way back to Vincennes expressed approval of the fact that there had been a lack of resolution on the part of the Miami tribes. What was interpreted as a positive sign by the Wabash Indians that the chiefs at Kekionga were not at that time committed toward direct confrontation was interpreted quite differently by Washington, Knox, St. Clair, and Harmar, who saw the results as indicating a disinclination toward a peaceful solution.[452]

★

The die had been cast. Backwoods merchants, prominent landowners, and civil and militia officials had long badgered Congress and the administration for federal action to quell the bloodshed. As protests

---

[451] Cayton, *Frontier Indiana*, 139–43.

[452] Cayton, *Frontier Indiana*, 141–43; St. Clair to Hamtramck, January 23, 1790, *SCP*, II: 130–31. See also Hamtramck to Harmar, March 17, 1790, and May 16, 1790, *OOTW*, 223–24, 233. Gamelin's deposition appears in *ASP-Indian Affairs*, I: 93.

---

continued to pour in during the spring and early summer of 1790, Knox approached the president and obtained Washington's permission to undertake an offensive expedition. In his instructions to Harmar, dated June 7, 1790, Knox ordered his senior military commander "to extirpate, utterly, if possible, the said [Indian] banditti." This, he said, was to be "a standing order" until accomplished.[453]

In a summary statement dated May 27, Knox outlined recommendations for an expedition to address the source of incursions that were the most troublesome—the continuing attacks on boats going down the Ohio and the raiding of Kentucky settlements. Optimistically, he considered that the hostilities represented the actions by not more than 200 "banditti Shawanese and Cherokees, and some of the Wabash Indians on the north-west of the Ohio" and estimated that a force of some 100 regulars and 300 mounted militia engaged for a period of thirty days would be sufficient to quell the "bad people." Following the president's approval, Knox wrote to Harmar and to St. Clair with orders to that effect, asking them to discuss the best method for eradicating the hostile groups while not interfering with the plans for a general accommodation "with the regular tribes." Reginald Horsman notes that it was typical of Knox's optimism and blindness to the situation that he believed hostilities were merely the work of a small group and did not represent general resentment on the part of the greater Indian nations.[454]

Richard H. Kohn notes that the decision to punish the Indians by mounting a federal offensive, even on a limited scale, was the administration's Rubicon: Washington and Knox had committed themselves to the use of force, an undertaking that led directly to war. In their minds, the action was only a punitive expedition designed to eliminate bandits and restore peace. Only the troublemakers should be targeted; there should be a distinction between renegades and Indians acting under tribal authority.

---

[453] Sword, *President Washington's Indian War*, 87. Earlier discussions included the establishment of garrisons at the Miami villages. This idea was tabled when Harmar estimated that it would take a force of 300 to 400 soldiers to man a fortification and a well-established pipeline for provisions and supplies to support it. Harmar to Knox, June 16, 1789, referenced in Downes and Lindley, *Frontier Ohio*, 19.

[454] Horsman, *Expansion and American Indian Policy*, 85; Summary Statement of the Situation of the Frontiers by the Secretary of War, May 27, 1790, and Knox to St. Clair, June 7, 1790, *SCP*, II: 146–148; Knox to Harmar, June 7, 1790, ASP- Indian Affairs, I: 97.

Knox ordered St. Clair to offer the Wabash tribes peace when the troops arrived at their villages. To Knox and the president, the expedition was a compromise, a contingency measure. Unknown to them, St. Clair was already capitalizing on instructions issued him the previous October that permitted him to call up a militia force of 1,500 men from Kentucky and Pennsylvania. Hence, the governor was committing the nation to using force in a manner not previously conceived by the administration.[455]

Believing that war was finally at hand, St. Clair, returning from his duties in the Illinois Country in early June and having been apprised by Hamtramck that the results of the peace overture to the Wabash and Miami had been unsatisfactory, had hastened to Fort Washington to confer with Harmar, collecting army contractor Robert Elliott along the way.

Harmar and St. Clair did not share Knox's optimism concerning the degree of resistance they might encounter; they felt his estimate of 200 "banditti" responsible for recurring incidents was unrealistic. The problem was not solely with the Shawnee. The entire Miami nation, plus others on the Maumee and upper Wabash Rivers, in addition to the Shawnee, had rejected past peace overtures. St. Clair and Harmar estimated that the affiliated tribes could field at least 1,100 warriors, a number that led them to opt for a larger two-pronged operation. Marching northward from Fort Washington to the Miami villages under Harmar would be a force composed of 300 regulars and 1,200 Kentucky and Pennsylvania militia. A smaller body of 400 Kentucky and Vincennes militia and 100 regulars from Fort Knox commanded by Major Hamtramck would proceed up the Wabash to either the Wea or Vermillion villages in order to divert attention away from activity surrounding Kekionga, the primary target of the operation. Harmar's force would march on September 25 and would be preceded by Hamtramck's departure from Vincennes the week before. St. Clair wasted no time in relaying instructions he had received from the president the previous fall, sending letters to nine Virginia and four Pennsylvania counties, calling each to supply their portion of the 1,500 man quota.[456]

How did Harmar reconcile himself to a plan involving such heavy reliance on the militia? He and his officers had repeatedly recoiled at the poor results of authorized and unauthorized raids into the territory by Kentucky frontiersmen. His men, John Armstrong among them, had

---

[455] Kohn, *Eagle and Sword*, 102.

[456] Kohn, *Eagle and Sword*, 102–03; Downes and Lindley, *Frontier Ohio*, 23.

voiced personal displeasure and disappointment in serving with militia forces. The regimental commander must have had a foreboding of things to come when he wrote his friend Thomas Mifflin in Philadelphia to the effect that "our regular force is to be small; there is a prospect of being joined by a considerable body of militia, who I hope will stick to the text, and not leave me in the lurch."[457]

Still, says Wiley Sword, Harmar was a reasonable man who understood the practical limitations of his regular force. Effective militia performance was so essential to his mission that he adopted an almost conciliatory tone toward the military amateurs. Harmar adopted the motto "One Mind" that he professed to regulars and militia alike to appeal for unity and cooperation.[458]

Following his meetings with Harmar and Elliott, St. Clair set out for New York to lobby for his plan. On August 23, 1790, Knox, on behalf of the president, approved the modified operation, yielding to the governor's firsthand knowledge of his estimate of Indian strength and putting trust in Harmar's approval of the plan. They may also have realized that several of their original assumptions had been incorrect. They had wrongly identified the factions at the source of the problem, and they now recognized a major flaw in their proposed use of fast-moving cavalry. The militia provided the mounted cavalry; the army had none. Unless regulars were used in the operation, the government could neither command nor control the expedition. Additionally, a cavalry of four hundred horsemen would be hard-pressed to carry thirty days' worth of rations. Furthermore, it would be an impossible task to distinguish "good" from "bad" Indians while rapidly advancing in order to avoid attacking the wrong parties. At any rate, St. Clair had already mobilized the militia. So, reports Wiley Sword, in spite of recognized bad feelings between the army and the militia, the secretary of war and the president unhappily approved the St. Clair–Harmar plan. He adds that although the administration accepted the revised plan, it neither approved nor accepted the assumptions behind it. Knox still wanted the army's movements to be rapid and decisive, even though the mission was largely to be carried out by soldiers on foot.[459]

---

[457] Harmar to Mifflin, September 4, 1790, in Denny, *Military Journal*, 257.

[458] Sword, *President Washington's Indian War*, 92.

[459] Sword, *President Washington's Indian War*, 86; Kohn, *Eagle and Sword*, 103.

What began in the spring of 1790 as a pacific overture to the Wabash and Miami tribes had become by midsummer an armed crusade. That a general large-scale offensive into Indian territory in quest of "banditti" might be regarded by the region's native peoples as aggression of the first magnitude involving desecration of its lands and rights was totally ignored by the planners.[460]

How could did this have happened? Richard H. Kohn suggests that what no one realized at the time was that the proposed military strategy now controlled the government's Indian policy; in effect, the tail was wagging the dog. A 2,000-man two-pronged expedition fully committed the nation's military, political, and moral prestige when no such commitment had been intended or desired. Just why Washington and Knox blundered in such a fashion is a matter of conjecture. Indian unrest, not only in the Ohio territory but also to the south in treaty disputes with the Creek Nation, was only one of a myriad of issues facing the new government. At the time, the administration feared that war was imminent between England and Spain and could envision a scenario in which the United States could literally be caught in the middle of fighting between the two nations' colonies of Canada and Louisiana. Consequently, Washington and his advisers may have decided to demonstrate the nation's own military potential as a deterrent.

Kohn also says that the administration kept Indian policy separate from foreign policy; diplomatic efforts to negotiate the transfer of the Great Lakes forts to American hands were ongoing despite evidence that British occupation of these garrisons was linked to the deteriorating Native American-United States relations. He further asserts that whatever the secondary goals of the campaign were, the administration's assumptions about the use of force were fallacious and its knowledge of the western situation imprecise. The president and his secretary of war, under intense pressure from Westerners, from politicians, and from its own understanding of governmental responsibility, made this decision during a year when they were preoccupied with other critical issues, among which were acceptance of Hamilton's financial program, fierce bargaining over the location of the nation's capital, and the threatened war between England and Spain. St. Clair presented his plan for the administration's approval during a week when the government was in chaos, offices dismantled, and records

---

[460] Sword, *President Washington's Indian War*, 87.

packed up for the transfer of the capital from New York to Philadelphia, the president personally supervising the transportation of his household goods. The administration wanted peace with the Indians, so it decided to force them into it. Kohn notes that both Knox and Washington clearly saw the dangers and disadvantages of inaction but not the risks of going forward. That Harmar's force could be defeated never occurred to either of them.[461]

Harmar and St. Clair, with the approval of Knox and Washington, all seasoned military men, should have seen the warning signs. They had opted for an offensive military campaign with limited preparation and resources, one that required the timely coordination of two widely scattered forces composed largely of inexperienced soldiers. Wiley Sword notes that the army was now being asked to save a situation created by mistakes in Indian diplomacy and interior affairs on the part of the federal government, even though it was ill prepared to do so. Despite the circumstances, Josiah Harmar and his men were ready to go. The chance to retaliate against the tribes had long been sought by army leaders; their growing bitterness, exacerbated by a long-standing defensive posture, was responsible for the eagerness that now pervaded frontier posts.[462]

The stage was now set for the drama about to unfold. Attacks along the Ohio River continued. Casualties incurred in the July attack on Ensign Jacob Melcher's party returning from Tennessee to Vincennes, further intensified the smoldering anger of the soldiers. On the eve of the offensive, the army high command seethed with resentment.

Wiley Sword adds an ironic postscript. Around the time St. Clair and Harmar were concluding their plans for the autumn offensive, a delegation of Potawatomi and Miami Indians arrived at Vincennes to discuss peace in accordance with the directives included in St. Clair's message to the Wabash and Miami nations earlier that year. At the time of Gamelin's visit, several tribes had agreed to respond to St. Clair's invitation at a later date. Hamtramck turned them away, basically telling them that they should have come when invited in the spring and that the governor had left the region. He reported that "they went a way much disatisfyd."[463]

---

[461] Kohn, *Eagle and Sword*, 104.

[462] Sword, *President Washington's Indian War*, 87.

[463] Melcher to Hamtramck, July 28, 1790, and Hamtramck to Harmar, August 20, 1790, *OOTW*, 238, 247; St. Clair to Knox, September 19, 1790, in *ASP-Indian Affairs*, I: 95–96; Sword, *President Washington's Indian War*, 88.

11

Kekionga, 1790

They fought and died hard.
—John Armstrong, October 18, 1790[464]

Full-scale war was coming. The operation would render the enemy helpless in a smooth, sudden stroke, its towns and crops destroyed and its leaders made to yield to the might of the government of the United States.

Whatever preconceived notions the administration had of achieving a quick, decisive victory, reality set in as Harmar and his men greeted the September arrival of what was to be the bulk of their fighting force. Instead of experienced Kentucky frontiersmen, the majority of newcomers appeared to be levies and substitutes totally unfamiliar with military life. "They appear to be raw and unused to the gun or woods; indeed many are without guns, and many of those they have want repairing," wrote the regiment's adjutant, Ebenezer Denny.[465]

If Harmar and his officers were dismayed by what they saw upon the arrival of the Kentucky militia, they must have been beside themselves when the Pennsylvania militia showed up later that month. The proposed force of 500 well-armed men was 200 short. Many were scarcely able to

[464] Armstrong's notebook, February–October 1790, PJA. See also Cist, *CM* I: 195–97.

[465] Denny, *Military Journal*, 140; Sword, *President Washington's Indian War*, 92. The Kentucky militia had apparently been told that weapons would be repaired upon arrival at Fort Washington.

bear arms, being too old, too young, or infirm. Not only did some carry weapons that were in bad shape, many brought none at all. Some had never fired a gun. Army historian James Ripley Jacobs notes that added to the general condition of "stupidity and awkwardness" was indifference; their primary reason for enlisting had been free government transportation to the West. Harmar had no choice but to use them as they were; there was no time for training. Frost would soon make the grass unfit for grazing and the projected system of utilizing packhorses for transporting equipment and supplies would be in jeopardy.[466]

If the quality of the militia units was not bad enough, Harmar had to resolve issues of command within their leadership. Lt. Col. James Trotter disputed the Kentucky militia command of Col. John Hardin who was his senior in rank. So many Kentuckians threatened to go home if Trotter were not given command that Harmar had to find a compromise. Trotter would command the three Kentucky battalions, and Lt. Col. Christopher Truby would head the Pennsylvania battalion. All four units would then be under Hardin's direction. Although the immediate structural problem was solved, personal animosity continued between the two Kentucky officers.[467]

To add to these challenges, the operation was micromanaged by Knox who had already proven himself too far away to appreciate the scope of Indian resistance, much less the battlefield conditions. Knox directed Harmar to execute rapid movements to "astonish" the enemy, yet to be cautious and guard against surprise. Knox also advised Harmar that as many of the rifle-armed militia as possible were to be resupplied with smooth-bore muskets because rifles were not good arms in a close fight.[468]

To add to the pressure under which Harmar found himself, Knox warned him he had received credible reports that he was "too apt to indulge" in excess "in a convivial glass"; there was considerable doubt about Harmar's "self-possession." Accordingly, Knox wanted the commander to understand that the outcome of the expedition was extremely important not only to the government but to his own career. If the campaign failed because of Harmar's drinking, the officer's reputation "would be blasted forever."[469]

---

[466] Sword, *President Washington's Indian War*, 94; Jacobs, *The Beginning of the U.S. Army*, 53.

[467] Sword, *President Washington's Indian War*, 94.

[468] Ibid.

[469] Sword, *President Washington's Indian War*, 95; Knox to Harmar, September 3, 1790, cited in Founders Online, http://founders.archives.gov/documents/

St. Clair also issued directives. The governor, who had retreated to territorial headquarters at Marietta, instructed Harmar not to restrain the militia and to take advantage of their "savage ferocity." In essence, Harmar was to chastise the Indians as well as their French and English trader allies for their treachery. Vengeance was to be a primary objective. Corn, expected to be hidden in the traders' houses, was to be destroyed; and plunder of their merchandise was preferred over general confiscation. Peace overtures were not to disrupt these punitive measures unless they were backed by the security of hostages.[470]

At this point, the secretary of war made an astonishing decision. Knox directed St. Clair to alert the British commandant at Detroit of the government's planned expedition against the Wabash and Miami confederacy in order to prevent any misinterpretation of the mission.

St. Clair duly obliged, sending notice by private messenger on September 19, informing Maj. Patrick Murray of the expedition whose sole design was of "humbling and chastising" those factions whose "depredations are become intolerable" and assuring him of the "pacific disposition" of the nation toward Britain and all her possessions. He added that the United States did not expect Britain to aid its Indian allies and requested the commandant to restrain British traders in the area who appeared responsible for instigating much of the "injurious" action. The idea of notifying the British of the forthcoming operation appeared to come from Knox himself. When he learned of it, Washington described himself as "apprehensive," convinced that the action was premature and rife with possible unfavorable consequences.

By notifying the British, St. Clair compromised any possibility of surprise. Both Knox and St. Clair, as well as many of their contemporaries familiar with the unsettled situation in the Northwest, firmly believed that the British were at the core of the behavior demonstrated by warring groups and that until key posts in the region were relinquished by Britain,

---

Washington/05-06-02-0323. James M. Perry notes that heavy drinking was probably no more of a problem for Harmar than it was for many officers at the time who regularly consumed vast quantities of wine and spirits at the table. Food was Harmar's real passion, and his letters are full of references to fish, game, fruit, and vegetables of the region. See Perry, *Arrogant Armies: Great Military Disasters and the Generals behind Them* (New York: John Wiley and Sons, 1996), 40.

[470] Sword, *President Washington's Indian War*, 96.

the situation could never be resolved peacefully. How Knox could have been so naive as to expect the commandant at Detroit not to share this intelligence with his native allies is difficult to understand. Washington's apprehension was well founded given the fact that the British were not only encouraging refractory Indian nations to stand firmly against the United States but were also supplying them with provisions and ammunition.[471]

Perhaps the most significant problem, however, lay in the basic assumptions concerning what would occur when Harmar's force faced the Indian nations prepared for war. William Guthman in his work, *March to Massacre: A History of the First Seven Years of the United States Army*, notes that Knox did not count on a major battle taking place. In the secretary of war's mind, the forthcoming expedition was meant only to burn towns and crops and to show the Indians that the nation's force could reach their far-flung villages. He believed the war chiefs might select a location affording ideal cover and concealment from which to ambush oncoming units, but he also believed experienced Kentucky woodsmen and swift-riding mounted militia would discover the trap and be able to prevent a surprise attack.

What Knox completely overlooked was the Native American genius for tactics and ability to outsmart opponents in combat. The mere fact that a large well-equipped force was about to lumber through the forest and brush, the cacophony of which would resonate for miles, was in Knox's mind all that was necessary to frighten the inhabitants; when their homes and crops were burned, their punishment would be complete. Knox did not consider that while the caravan was loudly making its way through the countryside, Indian scouts would be carefully scrutinizing its every movement, assessing how the men marched and camped, and how well trained and accustomed to the woods they appeared to be. All this information would then be given to the war chiefs who would select the most advantageous place and time to strike.[472]

Josiah Harmar too was either unaware of his enemy's talent for assessing an adversary's weaknesses or chose to disregard it. In his journal

---

[471] St. Clair to Major Murray, September 19, 1790, and Washington to Knox, November 4, 1790, in Smith, *SCP*, II: 186–87; Perry, *Arrogant Armies*, 39; Guthman, *March to Massacre*, 178–79. Messages were also sent to the more peaceful Wyandots, Ottawas, and Senecas. Michigan Pioneer and Historical Society, *Historical Collections*, XXIV: 97–103.

[472] Knox to St. Clair, September 14, 1790, *SCP*, II: 181–182; Guthman, *March to Massacre*, 183–184.

entry of May 15, 1788, Col. John May, a former Massachusetts militia officer on his way to Marietta, described meeting Harmar at Pittsburgh and accompanying him and a small party up the Monongahela River to the scene of Braddock's defeat by French and Indian forces over thirty years earlier. Bones still littered the ground. May observed that Braddock had engaged the enemy with traditional platoon firing, sometimes advancing in a solid column. Meanwhile, the Indians fought an entirely different kind of battle, shooting from hidden positions, and little by little, eventually tore Braddock's force to pieces. The field trip vividly demonstrating the inappropriateness of the British tactics in the face of unconventional Indian warfare was clearly lost on Harmar as he led his force northward to the Miami villages two years later.[473]

The regimental commander, ever the devotee of Baron von Steuben, failed to see how a system designed to defeat European armies was inappropriate for frontier warfare. No apparent effort was made to prepare the force for meeting an enemy that employed tactics far removed from those presented by British and Hessian troops during the Revolution. Indian tactics were no secret. From Braddock's monumental defeat to frontier fighting against the Indian allies of the British during the Revolution, colonials had gained firsthand knowledge of Native American warfare. Guthman notes that no preparatory training in Indian guerilla warfare was ever imposed on Harmar's army or that of his successor, Arthur St. Clair.[474]

Harmar's expeditionary force faced a formidable array of leaders. Foremost was Little Turtle, a Miami war chief who had fought in Kentucky during the Revolution, later adding to his reputation by leading

---

[473] John May, *Notes on Journals and Letters of Colonel John May of Boston Relative to Two Trips to the Ohio Company in 1788 and '89* (Cincinnati: Robert Clarke Company, 1873), 48–49.

[474] Guthman, *March to Massacre*, 11. If Harmar and St. Clair hadn't absorbed lessons learned from fighting on the frontier during the Revolution, Indian leaders had learned quite a lot. Perry cites Sullivan's victory over the Iroquois in northern Pennsylvania and New York during the Revolution. Warriors of the Six Nations made a fatal mistake of fighting to save one of their main villages in present-day Elmira, New York, and subsequently paid the price for doing so. Warring chiefs concluded that towns and villages were no place to make a stand against traditional armies, a strategy that would be repeated by the Miami confederation. Perry, *Arrogant Armies*, 37, 40.

successful raids against settlements there and along the Ohio River. War chief Blue Jacket, a white man captured and adopted by the Shawnee, and Miami chief Le Gris were also part of the leadership living nearby. These men were principals in a confederation that, ever since the Indian center of gravity had shifted westward, included not only the Miami and Shawnee but also factions of the Ottawa, Chippewa, Sauk (Sac) and Fox, Potawatomi, Winnebago, Wyandot, Kickapoo, Piankashaw, Wea, and Delaware nations, plus a few Senecas, Mohawks, and Mingos.[475]

Nor were Harmar's forces planning to invade some remote Indian village in the woods. They were headed to the Miami towns located at the confluence of the St. Marys and St. Joseph Rivers from which flowed the Maumee River eastward to Lake Erie. To the northwest was the Eel River, flowing in the opposite direction to the Wabash, itself a short portage away. The area between the watersheds had become home to several communities of Native Americans, most of whom were ill disposed toward the United States and staunch defenders of the Ohio River boundary for Indian lands who had refused to sign any treaties with the government. The village of Kekionga, or Miami Town, seat of that nation's power, was located on the north bank of the Maumee opposite the mouth of the St. Marys. A sister settlement was situated on the opposite shore of the St. Joseph. Additional Shawnee, Delaware, and Potawatomi enclaves dotted the area. At least 1,000 people lived in the area in some 300 bark cabins surrounded by vegetable gardens, cattle and horses, and acres of corn growing along the banks of the rivers. Miami chief Le Gris's village was also home to a few dozen French and British traders.[476]

Trade played a large role in the culture of the Miami towns. As white settlement increased in the south, a large volume and variety of items were transported northward. Articles in the villages became more diverse as the sources and outlets for goods increased and as the British attempted to maintain alliances through such trade. Cloth in various textures and colors

---

[475] Cayton, *Frontier Indiana*, 147–48; Perry, *Arrogant Armies*, 32. St. Clair had estimated that 1,100 warriors would possibly be brought into action from the Miami-Wabash vicinity alone, and Knox surmised that an even greater number should be counted on if these were joined by the Wyandot and Delaware and those of the St. Joseph and Illinois tribes. Knox to St. Clair, September 14, 1790, *SCP*, II: 182.

[476] Cayton, *Frontier Indiana*, 144; Huber, *General Josiah Harmar's Command*, 227–28.

became widely available, as did bridles and saddles, farm implements, housing materials, and a great variety of domestic items.[477]

The area was part of a long-standing multiracial, multiethnic world. Author Richard White in his book, *The Middle Ground: Indians, Empires, and Republics in the Great Lakes Region, 1650-1815*, says that despite the tendency of speakers within the confederation councils to stress color and the need to resist the "whites," the confederation "middle ground" at the Miami villages was not necessarily racist. Indians continued to adopt whites and to marry them. Tribesmen drank with them, ate with them, fought alongside them, had sexual relations with them, and exchanged goods with them. The British were a major presence in their lives.

A description of this world has been provided by trader Henry Hay who spent the winter of 1789–1790 in Kekionga. Hay, son of a British deputy Indian commissioner, had known many of the community's residents since childhood; and his writings described the interwoven worlds of Indian, English, and French societies that existed in the villages where cultures intermingled but remained intact. He described teas, afternoon parties with hostesses serving French liquor, and even balls. Native Americans participated in this common society but only at certain points and in certain ways. Little Turtle and his brother-in-law Le Gris commonly ate with Hay and his host but did not take dinner. They came in the evening when they "drank tea, also madeira," or more commonly, they breakfasted with them.[478]

Cayton notes, however, that it would be wrong to romanticize life in the towns. In addition to the normal cycles of illnesses, deaths, and difficulties of surviving hard winters, concern over the ever-approaching Americans was omnipresent. Then there was the plight of the captives. Of the prisoners abducted during raids on the Ohio and white settlements, some were adopted and others held for the purpose of information,

---

[477] Stewart Rafert, *The Miami Indians of Indiana: A Persistent People, 1656–1994* (Indiana Historical Society, 1996), 38. Kekionga had streets and sidewalks, a council hall and a ballroom, and even a brothel. Little Turtle's house had glass panes in the windows, framed paintings on the walls, and near the back door, a five-seat privy. Noted in Perry, *Arrogant Armies*, 32.

[478] White, *The Middle Ground*, 448–53; Henry Hay's journal can be found in M. M. Quaife, ed., *A Narrative of Life on the Old Frontier; Henry Hay's Journal from Detroit to the Mississippi River* (Madison: State Historical Society of Wisconsin, 1915), 208–61.

given relative freedom of the place, and eventually ransomed to British authorities. The less fortunate were made slaves while others were tortured and murdered. Cayton says that even the merry Hay, who spent much of his time drinking and flirting with European and Indian females of full or mixed-blood descent, paused for a moment when he saw a dead man's heart, "...a small stick run from one end of it to the other & fastened behind the fellows bundle that killed him, with also his Scalp."[479]

Hence, Harmar's force set out from Fort Washington with the cards stacked firmly against it. Its enemy knew its destination, was led by astute war chiefs commanding disciplined warriors with superior fighting skills, and had received material support from the British. Its mission was to be accomplished by a slow-moving train of men, horses, cattle, and cannon noisily plodding through woods, bogs, and streams, the militia largely untrained and untested, and senior leaders fixated on a mode of warfare only suited for conflict in a world far distant from the Ohio frontier. What could possibly go wrong?

★

The combined militia of 1,133 men commanded by Colonel Hardin left Fort Washington on September 26. On September 30, Harmar and the federal troops marched in two small battalions under the commands of Majors Wyllys and Doughty accompanied by Captain Ferguson's company of artillery with three light brass pieces. The addition of 320 federal troops made a total of 1,453 men under Harmar's command. Meanwhile to the west, Major Hamtramck's force departed for villages on the upper Wabash on the same day, having been delayed by the late arrival of the militia only the day before.

Harmar's regulars caught up with Hardin's militia on October 3, and the commander spent the remainder of the day organizing the line of march, issuing orders of battle and encampment, and elaborately explaining the details of the operation to the militia officers. The army resumed its advance on October 4 and the following day was reinforced by mounted infantry from Kentucky.[480]

---

[479] Cayton, *Frontier Indiana*, 145–46.

[480] Guthman, *March to Massacre*, 187; Sword, *President Washington's Indian War*, 98; Denny, *Military Journal*, 142.

The columns were led by spies and guides, followed by an advance company of 30 men who were in turn followed by 24 trailblazers flanked on either side by small bodies of cavalry. Behind them plodded a militia battalion from Kentucky. The federal regiment followed, proceeding in two columns with artillery, the general staff, musicians, and colors in the center. Behind were two columns of Pennsylvania and Kentucky militia flanking ammunition, baggage, and provisions of flour and salt carried by 578 packhorses followed by 175 cattle. To the rear were a third Kentucky militia batallion and the rear guard. While trailblazers hacked through woods, fields, and brush to clear the way for man, beasts, and cannon, the force lumbered slowly forward, averaging about ten miles per day. When moving through open country, the unit moved faster; at other times, progress slowed while soldiers, horses, and livestock maneuvered through roots and brush.[481]

The enormity and composition of the march that stretched for two miles made it almost impossible to keep the various units in their proper positions or to keep the packhorses together. Wiley Sword observes that the march could be better compared to a herd of elephants trampling through the underbrush than to a stealthy approach of a raiding column intent on surprising their enemy. Yet as the army approached the Great Miami River near present-day Piqua, Ohio, on October 9, having traveled about ninety miles from Fort Washington, there had been no sign of surveillance by the Indians or any recent presence.[482]

At the end of the day, the men formed a large hollow square. Baggage, horses, cattle, and stores were herded into the center, around which a line

---

[481] Guthman, *March to Massacre*, 187–88; Jacobs, *The Beginning of the U.S. Army*, 54. For details of the order of march, encampment, and battle formation, see *ASP-Military Affairs*, I: 20–36. Firsthand accounts of the operation are included in several sources. See Denny, *Military Journal*, 141–49; Frazer Wilson, ed., "Harmar's Campaign," *Ohio Archaeological and Historical Quarterly* 19, no. 4 (1910): 393–96 (*OAHQ*); Basil Meek, "General Harmar's Expedition," *OAHQ* 20, no.1 (1911): 74–108. John Armstrong's daily journal is found in James McBride, *Pioneer Biography: Sketches of Some of the Early Settlers of Butler County, Ohio* (Cincinnati, Robert Clarke & Company, 1869), I: 107–145 and *CM* 1: 195–197. Original documentation can be found in Armstrong's notebook of February–October 1790 at PJA.

[482] Guthman, *March to Massacre*, 187; Sword, *President Washington's Indian War*, 96; Huber, *General Josiah's Command*, 226.

of sentries was stationed. At night, horses were hobbled and tied, and grass was cut and brought to them. Security for the cattle was just as rigid. Yet many horses disappeared over the course of the expedition, either due to carelessness on the part of the militia who neglected to restrain them or by theft from Indians. Patrols were sent out at daylight each morning to round up as many strays as could be found before the army resumed its movement.[483]

Meanwhile, Little Turtle and the war chiefs closely watched the progress of the column. There was no concealing the noisy, undisciplined army moving slowly northward. Scouts reported observing men who were apparently unaccustomed to the country and officers who found it difficult to control them. The operation's objective was well known. When St. Clair's message reached its destination at the British garrison at Detroit, messengers and observers were quickly dispatched to the Miami towns and tasked to report on the progress of the American expedition as well as to aid and advise the war chiefs in their resistance to the greatest extent possible. Not only had the British supplied the tribes with arms, ammunition, and provisions, they were also physically present to render moral support to their allies.[484]

---

[483] Sword, *President Washington's Indian War*, 6. Michael S. Warner offers another theory for the disappearance of roughly one-third of the six hundred packhorses, suggesting that the high loss rate was due to the fact that the army had to reimburse contractors and owners for horses lost on the march, thus making it a profitable incentive for the civilian packhorse drivers to have their charges "lost" or "stolen" by invisible Indians. In contrast to its problems with packhorses, Harmar's expedition lost virtually none of its beef cattle, nor did the mounted riflemen complain of losing their animals. See Warner, "General Josiah Harmar's Campaign Reconsidered: How the Americans Lost the Battle of Kekionga," *Indiana Magazine of History* 83, no. 1 (1987): 60.

[484] Sword, *President Washington's Indian War*, 98–99. Return J. Meigs Jr., the young attorney who had been selected to deliver St. Clair's message of September 19 to the British, arrived in Detroit the second week in October and was coolly received at the garrison. Major John Smith, Major Murry's successor at Fort Detroit, issued his reply on October 14, writing that the military preparations by the Americans had caused no "uneasiness" and that the Indians had not received any encouragement or assistance in committing depredations along the Ohio River. See Michigan Pioneer and Historical Society, *Historical Collections*, XXIV: 102–03.

Residents were not idle as the army slowly advanced toward them. Alarmed by reports from various sources of an exaggerated number of troops heading their way, perhaps from six to eight thousand in number, leaders called for help from other villages. Although many tribesmen came, by mid-October, the chiefs could muster only about 600 warriors. Reluctantly but firmly, they began to evacuate their towns. The Delaware went south toward the White River; the Shawnee, with most of the European traders, went down the Maumee River toward Lake Erie and Detroit; and the Miami headed to the northwest in the direction of the Eel River. With women, children, and infirm now dispersed, warriors quickly slaughtered cattle and hid as much of their corn harvest as they could. Shortly after dawn on October 15, they set fire to their villages in order to keep them out of the hands of the Americans and then went into hiding.[485]

On October 10, Harmar's advance party came to the Great Miami where they found an abandoned canoe drawn up on the opposite shore of the river. Scouts discovered the skin of a freshly killed bear cub cut up into small pieces adhering to nearby tree stumps. Sword says that veteran Indian fighters immediately realized the chilling significance of their discovery. Not only had the column's progress been closely monitored by unseen eyes as it ventured northward, this was a warning that many white scalps would soon be taken. Consequently, one half-pound of powder and one pound of lead was issued to each rifleman, and twenty-four buck-and-ball cartridges were allotted to each musket-armed infantryman. Commanding officers were ordered to check each man's arms to ensure that they were in good order and loaded.[486]

Harmar's army was now marching through flat terrain with lakes, meandering streams, and dense undergrowth. It had proceeded some 125 miles above Fort Washington by October 12 and the following morning captured one of two Shawnees, evidently sent to spy on the army, who told interrogators that the Indians were preparing to abandon their villages. Harmar decided to strike while they were still in the process of razing their homes and crops, hoping for a successful fight and the capture of their supplies. He compensated for the army's slow pace by sending a mounted detachment forward under the command of Colonel Hardin to reconnoiter the area. The troops were eager to go; officers cast lots to take

---

[485] Cayton, *Frontier Indiana*, 150–51.
[486] Sword, *President Washington's Indian War*, 97; Denny, *Military Journal*, 143.

their places on the expedition. Of the six hundred men selected, only fifty were regulars under the command of Capt. David Zeigler.

October 14 dawned rainy and cold. Hardin's troops got a late start but were able to make up for the delay, arriving at the deserted villages the following afternoon. The men pitched camp and waited for the main body to arrive. Temptation was too great for the idle soldiers, however, and despite repeated orders to maintain vigilance, parties of thirty to forty men began to disperse in all directions, taking what they could find and not returning until they grew tired of pillaging the remains. Harmar arrived on October 17. The expedition had now reached its destination, some 170 miles above Fort Washington, and formal destruction of the settlements began the next day. The apparent walkover victory emboldened even the officers, and they began to talk about a movement westward toward the Wea villages and a possible rendezvous with Hamtramck, whom they assumed was moving up the Wabash. To their disgust, however, they could barely maintain control of the militia as the undisciplined troops foraged about the area looking for what one called "hidden treasure."[487]

★

Indian foreknowledge of his mission was only one piece of information Harmar was missing. The second lay 150 miles to the southwest. The master plan of launching a two-pronged offensive was no longer viable. Hamtramck's mission to divert the Indians' attention from Harmar's march on the Miami towns by proceeding up the Wabash toward the Wea villages had been delayed. Getting a late start due to the belated arrival of the militia, the major had set out with 330 men, only 50 of whom were regulars. Short of his projected strength of 500 men, he had to leave "the sick and lame of Kentucky and ours in the garrison which amounted to about ninety men." Estimating that his enemies in the vicinity of the Wabash numbered about 750, Hamtramck had reason to be intimidated. His instructions were to raid Vermillion, L'Anguille, or the Wea Towns; but the choice was left to his discretion. Hamtramck chose the Vermillion village at the mouth of the river of that name on the Wabash as his initial objective. Arriving there on October 10, however, he found it had been completely abandoned.

---

[487] Jacobs, *The Beginning of the U.S. Army*, 56–57; Cayton, *Frontier Indiana*, 151; Denny, *Military Journal*, 145.

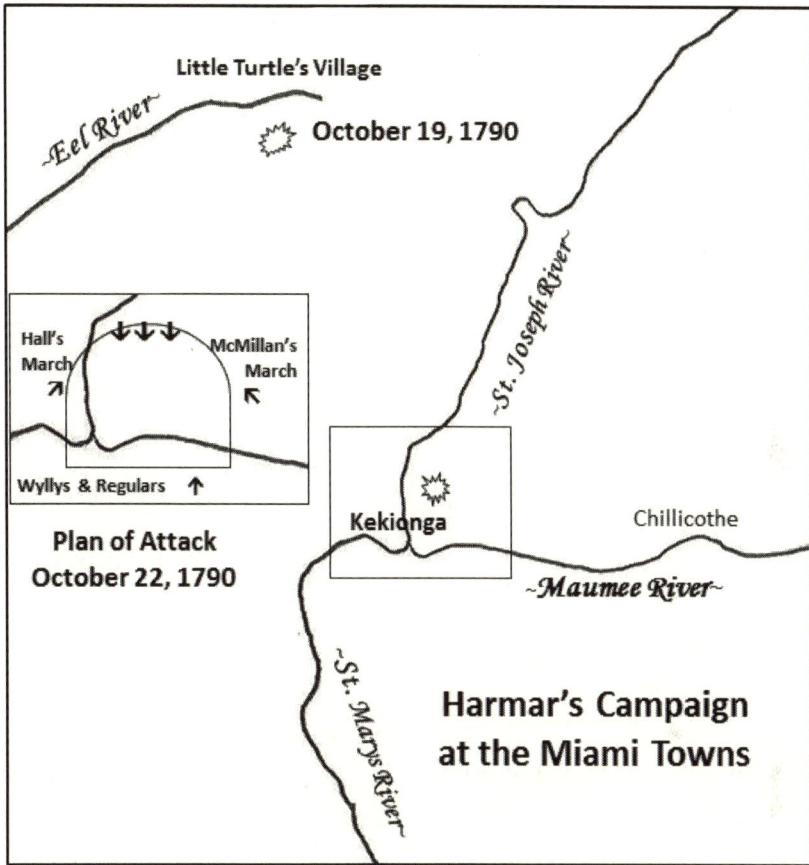

Harmar's Campaign
at the Miami Towns

Hamtramck next anticipated moving on to the Wea towns, but his command soon dissolved. Although no hostile Indians had been seen on the march, the militia threatened mutiny. Some had already deserted, and when news spread through the camp of the proposed Wea raid, more departed. Those remaining wanted to go home, using the shortage of rations as an excuse. Hamtramck doubted he could keep any of the unruly militia with him much longer; stern measures might indeed provoke outright mutiny. Fearing an encounter with the Wea with a reduced force, he broke camp on October 14, disappointed that he had failed to deliver on his part of the bargain. He started the journey homeward only to have several horses stolen along the way.[488]

---

[488] Sword, *President Washington's Indian War*, 97–98; Hamtramck to Harmar, November 2, 1790, in Thornbrough, *OOTW*, 259–64.

Meanwhile, Little Turtle and his allied warriors waited patiently for the Americans wandering about their villages to make a tactical mistake. During the night of October 17, they drove away an estimated 50 to 100 packhorses and a few cavalry mounts. The loss of so many packhorses was severe, and all thoughts of advancing to the Wabash were promptly forgotten. Harmar had already decided to send out a reconnaissance detachment, having learned from an old Frenchman who was found near the towns that warriors were scattered in the woods due to the inability to fight because of insufficient assistance from other tribes. He dispatched Lieutenant Colonel Trotter with a 300-man force that included Armstrong's 30-man company, part of the cavalry, mounted infantry, and militia. They were to be gone three days and travel northwest of the abandoned villages to look for the absent warriors. The unit proceeded only about one mile when a lone mounted Indian was discovered along the path. He was pursued, shot, and killed. As the horsemen made their way back to the column, they saw another mounted warrior and chased him. In a scene reminiscent of an English fox hunt gone awry, the Kentucky cavalry and mounted militia tried to run the second man down, leaving their waiting infantry without orders and in confusion for nearly a half hour. Armstrong then asked permission to separate from the main body to prepare an ambuscade. After his men were in position for some time, a Kentucky cavalryman who had become separated from the group during the previous chase approached in a gallop, terrified because he had encountered some 50 warriors from whom he had barely escaped. Trotter decided to abandon the idea of mounting an ambush and instead began searching for the war party, marching in several different directions until nightfall looking for more signs of Indians. When Trotter heard the six-pounder discharged at the main encampment at sundown, he thought it was a signal for the detachment to return to camp. What was to have been a three-day expedition ended that night. Evidently satisfied that he had killed two Indians, Trotter returned two days earlier than ordered.[489]

Incensed at the shameless, cowardly conduct of the militia, Harmar ordered the same detachment to go out again the following morning. Hardin demanded that he lead the contingent in order to restore the honor of the militia, a request to which Harmar agreed. After Harmar heard

---

[489] Guthman, *March to Massacre*, 189–90; Sword, *President Washington's Indian War*, 104–06; *ASP-Military Affairs*, I: 26–27.

Armstrong's version of the day's activities, he subsequently reinforced the lieutenant's command with his subaltern, Lt. Asa Hartshorne, and twenty militia, detailing him to proceed with Hardin the next day.

Hardin's force of 180 men, including Armstrong's company of thirty regulars, set out from their camp on the St. Joseph River at midmorning on Tuesday, October 19, marching sixteen miles northwest of Kekionga toward the Eel River. Ironically, they were heading directly toward the village of Little Turtle, the most capable Indian leader in the Northwest Territory. Although he lacked any support from other villages that day, Little Turtle could not ignore the threat to his village and quietly massed his approximately 150 warriors.

Ebanezer Denny watched the reluctant militia's departure that morning. He later reported that by the time Hardin's men had traveled three miles, fully a third of his force had dropped out of the ranks and returned to camp.[490]

Following the trail that Trotter was to have taken the preceding day, Hardin's party came to an area showing signs of recent encampment. Hardin halted his force for about a half an hour to reconnoiter the area. When the troops were finally called back into formation, Hardin in his haste to resume the march forgot about one company that had been sent some distance away. After marching two or three miles, he realized his error and sent Major Fontaine back with part of the cavalry to bring the party forward.

Continuing onward, Hardin's column was strung out in single file for nearly a half mile along the trial when Armstrong heard what he thought to be an alarm fired some distance ahead. He also discovered the tracks of a horse that had come down the trail and apparently had turned around, heading back in the direction from which it had come. Armstrong told Hardin of his findings, warning him that Indians were possibly waiting in ambush nearby. His advice was not taken, and no additional precautions were put into place. Confident that even if warriors were awaiting the advancing troops there would be no attack, Hardin moved forward at the head of the column. Although he may have been attempting to redeem the

---

[490] Cayton, *Frontier Indiana*, 151; Denny, *Military Journal*, 145–46; Guthman, *March to Massacre*, 190; Sword, *President Washington's Indian War*, 106. *ASP-Military Affairs*, I: 27.

militia's honor in the wake of its performance the previous day, Hardin's bravado proved fatal.

The trail led toward a small meadow surrounded by heavy timber and a swamp on one side. At the far end of the opening were scattered what appeared to be discarded Indian goods and a spreading fire. The possibility of booty broke the militia's discipline entirely as several men rushed to get a share of the treasure. Little Turtle had set the trap. Hardin's men had taken the bait and now he and his warriors waited to spring it. They were carefully hidden in the woods beyond the fire with muskets leveled.[491]

Suddenly from about 150 yards away, warriors began firing into the front of Hardin's column and advancing toward it. Their first fire, a rolling fusillade, came from the right side of the meadow, striking several militiamen. In shock, both the militia and regulars reflexively recoiled to the left, only to take a point-blank volley from other warriors hidden in that direction. Sword describes the scene of confusion that quickly disintegrated into chaos. The rear of the column had not yet come up when the militiamen in front bolted in retreat. Armstrong and Hartshorne attempted to form a line of regulars in the meadow, but so many militia broke through their ranks that the formation was continually thrown into disorder. Behind them, the single-file column of infantry refused to advance and support Armstrong's wavering line. Instead, they ran wildly from the field. Most of the militia fled without firing a shot, throwing down fully loaded muskets and fleeing rearward as fast as they could, pushing Colonel Hardin back with them. Despite the panicked flight of the militia, Armstong's men, together with a small number of militia who had joined them, stood their ground and fired at targets in the underbrush that surrounded them.

Little Turtle, seeing the disorder, signaled an immediate charge. From out of the underbrush on both sides of the meadow poured the Miamis with a few Shawnees and Potawatomis. Some were mounted, others carried rifles, and the advance warriors brandished only tomahawks and scalping knives. Once the regulars had expended a single round from their ponderous Revolutionary War muskets, there was no time to reload, and they withstood the charge only with fixed bayonets. Seeing warriors coming at them from all sides, Armstrong and Hartshorne almost

---

[491] Jacobs, *The Beginning of the U.S. Army 1783–1812*, 57; Guthman, *March to Massacre*, 190; Cayton, *Frontier Indiana*, 152.

certainly would have tried to form their men into a circle facing outward for better survivability, but it cannot be known if they succeeded. They were surrounded immediately with each man desperately fighting for his life. What is certain is that one by one, the men began to succumb to the overwhelming odds. The victorious war cries of Little Turtle's men could be heard nearly a mile away.

Amidst the screams of the wounded and dying men and swirling gunsmoke Armstrong knew that his command was about to be annihilated and shouted the order to those still standing to disperse and to try to make their way back to Harmar's camp. Individual retreat from the scene of bloodshed was now the only option, and the scattered remains of Armstrong's men were mostly chased down and slaughtered. All thirty regulars but only nine Pennsylvania militia stood their ground that day. Armstrong lost all but six of his men, and none of the militia that had remained with him survived.[492]

The account of Thomas Irvin completes the story. An ensign in Captain Faulkner's forgotten Pennsylvania militia company that had been remembered belatedly by Colonel Hardin and retrieved by Major Fontaine, he related that when the major finally located the company, he, having heard the gunfire, assumed that the Indians were retreating and informed Captain Faulkner of that fact. The officers had never believed that the Indians would launch a surprise attack and were shocked when they encountered two fleeing mounted militiamen who called out, "For God's sake retreat you will Be all Killed there is Indians enough to Eat you all up."[493]

Now moving cautiously ahead, the detachment of about seventy-five men passed a small creek. Once on the other side, they met a horde of badly frightened militia who gasped that they were just ahead of the Indians. Faulkner's troops "took to the trees," forming an irregular line across the trail. The militia quickly streamed past. Only four mounted officers led by Hardin remained with the new line. A few Indians then appeared, halting about ninety yards away. With Faulkner's troops growing more anxious by

---

[492] Jacobs, *The Beginning of the U.S. Army 1783–1812*, 57; Guthman, *March to Massacre*, 191; Sword, *President Washington's Indian War*, 107–08; Huber, *General Josiah Harmar's Command*, 229–30. See also Armstrong's testimony, *ASP-Military Affairs*, I: 27.

[493] Guthman, *March to Massacre*, 191; Wilson, "Harmar's Campaign," 394–96.

the minute, Hardin and the others delayed until they were convinced there would be no further stragglers. Then they resumed their retreat.

It was after dark when the bedraggled remnants of Hardin's patrol reached camp. Hardin was said to have broken down in tears when he related to Harmar how the "cowardly behavior" of his militia had led to a complete defeat. Immediately, the general ordered a six-pounder fired at hourly intervals throughout the night to guide the stragglers in. Then he began to count the casualties. Rumors of a massacre began to spread through the camp, creating panic among the militia. Sword noted that Harmar was so dumbfounded by the affair that he could not answer Hardin when he pleaded to return to the battlefield with another detachment the following day.[494]

Varying accounts of Armstrong's activities following his company's annihilation exist, but there are substantiated facts that underscore his resourcefulness during the episode. He was extremely lucky to have escaped with his life; both Armstrong and Hartshorne survived through unexpected twists of fate. It is likely that Little Turtle's warriors did not pursue the two men and any others who managed to distance themselves from the immediate scene of hand-to-hand combat because they were busy scalping the dead and wounded and stripping their bodies looking for valuables. Hartshorne ran into the nearby timber and fell over a log behind which he managed to hide. According to the biography written by his son years later, Armstrong was also saved by a tree, throwing himself down in the grass between an immense oak stump and a log where he stayed during the three remaining hours of daylight. From his vantage point, he watched warriors pass and repass, gaining an idea of the size of the force that had decimated his unit and witnessed their ritual desecration of the remains of fallen soldiers.[495]

Armstrong's son continued his father's tale. At nightfall, although he was within proximity of the warriors' noisy celebration, he decided it was dark enough to make an escape. On his third step away from his hiding place, he was heard by nearby Indians, a yell was given, and the assembly went silent. He took off running, jumped into the nearby swamp, and hid there throughout the night. It was immediately surrounded by Indians

---

[494] Sword, *President Washington's Indian War*, 108–09.

[495] Jacobs, *The Beginning of the U.S. Army*, 57–58; *CM*, I: 39; ASP- Military Affairs, I: 27.

looking for him, their search not ending until the moon went down and they retired to their fires. The younger Armstrong quotes his father as saying,

> The ice was frozen to my clothes, and very much benumbed, I extricated myself from the pond, broke some sticks and rubbed my thighs and legs to circulate the blood, and with some difficulty at first, slowly made my way thro' the brush. Believing the Indians would be traveling between their own and the American camp, I went at right angles from the trace about two miles to a piece of rising ground, thinking to myself it is a cold night, if there are a Indians here, they will have fire, if I can't see theirs they can't see mine, and fire is necessary for me. I went into a ravine where a large tree was blown up by the roots, kindled a fire, dried myself, and laid down and took a nap of sleep. In the morning, threw my fire in a puddle of water, and started for camp.[496]

Armstrong then took a circuitous route back to the location in which the army had encamped prior to his departure, being careful to avoid leaving tracks, but when he approached the site, he realized that the army had moved, the ground now occupied by parties of Indians. He was eventually guided by the homing signal of cannon fire and finally made it into camp that evening, now located two miles away in the deserted Shawnee village of Chillicothe.[497]

---

[496] *CM*, I: 40. Family lore surrounds a powder horn around which an animal skin was at one time secured. According to his son's account Armstrong spent several hours with much of his body submerged in the dark, cold swamp water while successfully hiding from Indians searching for him and also managing to keep his musket dry by supporting it on his shoulders during the ordeal. Although protecting his musket in this way, gun powder and cartridges became waterlogged. Armstrong later lit a fire to warm himself during which his powder horn cracked by exposure to its heat. When he reached camp, he shot a squirrel and stretched its skin around the horn to seal its crack.

[497] Armstrong's description of his escape is included in *CM*, I: 37–41, as well as in the Armstrong papers. Other accounts varying slightly in detail can be found in C. W. Williamson, *History of Western Ohio and Auglaize County* (Columbus,

Harmar's bewilderment at the situation caused by the utter cowardice shown by the militia turned to outright rage when Armstrong stumbled into camp and gave his account of the incident. An irate Armstrong announced that he would never again willingly fight alongside or under the command of any militia officer. Without delay, Harmar published general orders announcing that, should there be a repetition of the prior day's "shameful cowardly conduct" by the militia, he would "order the artillery to fire on them."[498]

Twenty-four regulars sacrificed their lives that day. Six years after its formation, the First Regiment of the United States Army had seen genuine combat with an enemy. The fact that all thirty of Armstrong's men held fast under fire provides an ironic twist to the event, setting a tradition of discipline and pride passed down through successive generations of the Army throughout the nation's history. Sword noted that the event was perhaps a humble beginning for the modern United States Army but one in which a proud combat tradition was established. Armstrong recorded this entry in his journal:

> On the 19th Col. Hardin commanded in lieu of Colonel Trotter; attacked about one hundred Indians, fifteen miles west of the Miami village, and from the dastardly conduct of the militia, the troops were obliged to retreat—I lost one sergeant, and twenty-one out of thirty men of my command. The Indians on this occasion gained a complete victory, having killed in the whole, near one hundred men, which was about their own number. Many of the militia threw away their arms without firing a shot, ran through the federal troops & threw them in disorder.

W. M. Linn & Sons, 1905), 34, and McBride, *Pioneer Biography*, I: 132–136.

[498] Sword, *President Washington's Indian War*, 109; Brian Krieger, "Power Struggle in the Old Northwest: Why the United States Won and the Indians Lost the Indian War, 1786–1795" (master's thesis, North Carolina State University, 2008), 77, http://www.repository.lib.ncsu.edu. Krieger states that when Armstrong and Hartshorne returned to camp, they were determined to kill the militia who had abandoned them and their comrades during the fight. Maj. John Wyllys and his men restrained the bedraggled officers before they could make good on their threats.

Many of the Indians must have been killed, as I saw my men bayonet many of them. They fought and died hard.[499]

Overnight, the tenor of Harmar's expedition was altered. Where there had been an eager quest for vengeance and a reckless disdain for the enemy, now only a cold, uncertain fear prevailed. Harmar now had little confidence in his predominantly militia army. His mission had been to destroy all the Indian villages, and he chose to accomplish that goal before something happened to prevent it. On Wednesday, October 20, the army burned all the towns near the forks of the Maumee. Stacks of corn, beans, vegetables, hay, and fences went up in smoke. Harmar reported that his men destroyed some three hundred houses and around twenty thousand bushels of corn. He was convinced that the total destruction of the Miami towns would break up the Indians' base of operations. Meanwhile, he made preparations for a return to Fort Washington. Provisions were running low, and the loss of so many packhorses crippled the army's transportation. The following day, Harmar led his army eight miles away from Kekionga, declaring his mission accomplished.[500]

Throughout the day, Hardin lobbied Harmar to allow him to go back to the villages to punish any returning Indians. Although skeptical of the plan at first, Harmar had heard from scouts that about 120 warriors had come back to Kekionga several hours after the army's departure. Harmar admittedly was looking for some means to embarrass his enemy and worried about a possible ambush on the way back to Fort Washington. Sword notes that inwardly, the general must also have been anxious to retaliate for the drubbing that his troops had taken on October 19. Hardin found his opening. The general relented, but this time, he determined that regulars should lead the operation. Harmar was initially determined to rely on his regulars to conduct the mission because he felt that they would

---

[499] Sword, *President Washington's Indian War*, 108. The exact number casualties from Armstrong's unit varies slightly, depending on the publication. He testified at Harmar's board of inquiry that he lost twenty-four federal troops while his journal records twenty-one dead. His entry on October 20 completes his journal, and it is possible that he later realized that additional men had been killed. PJA; *CM*, I: 196–97 and *ASP-Military Affairs*, I: 27. Regardless of the precise number of casualties, the courage of the unit to stand as a whole is significant.

[500] Cayton, *Frontier Indiana*, 152–53; Sword, *President Washington's Indian War*, 109.

remain steadfast under orders, but since only 60 could be spared for the operation, he realized that the bulk of the force still required heavy use of the militia. Accordingly, he appointed Major John Wyllys to command a force of regulars augmented by 300 militia under Hardin's command and 40 horsemen under Major Fontaine.

The 400-man force departed the army's main body at 2:00 a.m. on October 22. Upon approaching the rivers, Wyllys divided his men into three columns. Major Horatio Hall was to lead 150 Kentucky militiamen in a circuitous route to the northwest, crossing the St. Marys River and doubling back toward Kekionga, entrapping warriors there. At the same time, Maj. James McMillan with the remainder of the Kentucky force would encircle the village from the east, cutting off possible escape in that direction. Once all were in place, Wyllys' regulars accompanied by Major Fontaine's 40 cavalrymen would lead a frontal assault, hoping to drive the Indians north where they would be confronted by the waiting militia units.[501]

The return of Harmar's troops came as no surprise to the war chiefs. Shawnee, Miami, Ottawa, Sauk, and Delaware tribesmen began to file out of Kekionga during the night, passing noiselessly into the underbrush. Despite the destruction of their homes and shortage of provisions and ammunition, they were in high spirits. By dawn, the warriors lay in wait along the banks of the Maumee.[502]

Denny recorded the events of October 21 in his journal:

> The wings commanded by Majors Hall and McMillan came upon a few Indians immediately after crossing the Omee, put them to flight, and contrary to orders, pursued up the St. Joseph for several miles. The centre division, composed chiefly of the regular troops, were left unsupported. It would seem as if the enemy designed to draw the principal part of the force after a few of their people, while their main body attacked Major Wyllys.[503]

---

[501] Cayton, *Frontier Indiana*, 153; Sword, *President Washington's Indian War*, 110–11.

[502] Sword, *President Washington's Indian War*, 110–11.

[503] Denny, *Military Journal*, 147–48. Accounts in current publications vary in detail and perspective. See Sword, *President Washington's Indian War*, 110–16; Jonathan Heart's description in Guthman's *March to Massacre*, 192–94;

Due to the confusion caused by the militia's premature advance and subsequent counterattack by Little Turtle's forces, Major Wyllys had been unable to organize his men who were still coming into the area. During the impasse, Major McMillan arrived on the scene, swinging back with his column immediately upon hearing the firing. Crossing the Maumee, his infantry easily made it to the opposite shore and temporarily gained control of the fight, the Shawnees and Miamis promptly running for cover and taking a heavy volley from the Kentuckians as they dispersed. McMillan's men launched their pursuit, followed by Wyllys's regulars who, crossing the Maumee, began to file past the ruins of deserted Kekionga through the large desolate cornfield earlier razed by the American army. Suddenly, a war cry filled the air. From out of the underbrush poured the largest body of warriors yet seen in the vicinity of the Miami towns.

Although accounts give varying details of the fighting that took place that day, one thing is clear. Little Turtle had duped the army into chasing his decoys and had caught an isolated detachment in the open plain where there was little cover to mask their vulnerability. His warriors exercised extreme discipline not to reveal the extent of their strength until the Americans were fully exposed. Indians were suddenly among Wyllys's men in the cornfield. The regulars fought with their bayonets, having no time to reload their single-shot flintlock muskets; their enemy used tomahawks and spears. What had minutes before been a quiet river was suddenly a cauldron of yelling, cursing men and braying mounts. Capt. Joseph Asheton reported catching a glimpse of Wyllys sitting on the ground with his hand grasping his breast, surrounded by Indians. When Wyllys's large cocked hat was seen being flaunted and worn by a warrior, the men realized the major's fate.[504]

Battered and bloodied soldiers now retreated into the deserted Kekionga ruins, leaving their dead where they fell. There they discharged, cleaned, and reloaded their muskets and rifles before beginning a retreat toward Harmar's distant encampment. The last thing many of them saw was the figure of Lt. Ebenezer Frothingham, sitting pale and bleeding by the Maumee, too exhausted to go on and escape the fate that he must have

---

John Parker Huber, *General Josiah Harmar's Command*, 232–35; and Warner, "General Josiah Harmar's Campaign Reconsidered," 43–64.

[504] Sword, *President Washington's Indian War*, 112–14; Denny, *Military Journal*, 147–48; *ASP-Military Affairs*: I:28.

known awaited him. That day, Frothingham, Wyllys, and the 49 regulars who had remained by their officers' sides were killed. The dead, wounded, and missing amounted to 180.[505]

One of the great mysteries of the day was the conflicted reporting given to Harmar concerning the engagement's outcome. When a bloodied and badly frightened Kentucky cavalryman reached Harmar's encampment and reported the entrapment of Wyllys's forces and the fighting that ensued, the commander sent Kentucky militiaman Major Ray with a detachment to meet the survivors. When Hardin, who had led the westward column, approached Ray, Hardin told him that his Kentucky troops had managed to drive many approaching Indians into the St. Joseph River, and asked the major merely to wait until the remainder of the militia arrived and then to withdraw to camp. Making his way to the army's encampment, Hardin found Harmar and immediately related an exaggerated account of the fighting. Harmar recorded in his journal that night that the detachment under Wyllys and Hardin had "performed wonders, although they were terribly cut up" and that "the militia behaved themselves charmingly." He closed his entry by observing, "The savages never received such a stroke before in any battle that they have had."[506]

It wasn't long before the returning militia reached the camp in complete disorder, so panicked that they appeared to be in near revolt. Rumors of the slaughter of federal regulars circulated through the encampment. Coming to terms with the reality of the situation but still believing his army's mission completed, Harmar decided to depart Indian country before his army disintegrated, not waiting for stragglers and leaving the dead untended on two battlefields. His neglect of this duty of honor was a certain admission of defeat, a fact remembered by veterans over a half century later. Officers later explained Harmar's decision to do so was based on his belief that the packhorses would not be able to stand the strain.[507]

Harmar embarked on a return journey that Denny described as slow and difficult. One-third of the packhorses had died or been lost, and supplies had to be carried by soldiers. Litters had to be made for the

---

[505] Cayton, *Frontier Indiana*, 153–54; Sword, *President Washington's Indian War*, 114–15; Jacobs, *The Beginning of the United States Army*, 59.

[506] Sword, *President Washington's Indian War*, 115–16; Warner, "General Josiah Harmar's Campaign Reconsidered, 54; Meek, "General Harmar's Expedition," 93.

[507] Warner, "General Josiah Harmar's Campaign Reconsidered," 55–64.

wounded. On October 23, Harmar abandoned the encampment, leading a strung-out procession that continued for twelve days. The weather had turned cold, and one night, a driving rain turned into snow. Men trudged along in the often bleak and rainy weather. Frost came early that year, and good grazing was no longer available; the animals were fed with flour to keep them going. The militia soldiers were generally out of control, paying little or no attention to orders, and the regulars in the ranks behaved little better. In brazen disobedience, they left the column and fired their weapons when and where they chose. At one point, Harmar had to order the federal troops to parade with fixed bayonets to quell a threatened mutiny by the militia. Finally on November 3, 1790, Harmar reached Fort Washington where he immediately began the process of discharging the militia.

Harmar had earlier considered taking action against insubordinate militia officers but reconsidered this move, fearing it might break up the army and inhibit future operations. Ultimately, Hardin persuaded him to issue orders discharging the militia with "honor and reputation." In typical Harmar fashion, he hosted an elaborate dinner for all his field officers and a number of his friends.[508]

What was horror for the Americans was triumph for the Miami, the Shawnee, and their allies. They had exacted a terrible price upon the Americans for the loss of their property and crops. The burning of their towns meant little to them. Little Turtle and the war chiefs had outfoxed and outfought the Americans at every turn. They had humiliated the United States, and as Harmar gathered the remnants of his forces for their trek southward, they took ritual revenge on the bodies of their dead and wounded enemies and three unfortunate soldiers they had captured.[509]

Harmar's expedition had narrowly avoided total annihilation by a gift of sheer fate. Blue Jacket and other principals urged an attack on the retreating column by 700 warriors. A plan was formulated and agreed upon; all they had to do was merely to await the departure of the Americans from their encampment, the time when the army's remnants would be most vulnerable. The evening was clear, and the full moon bright. But as the evening progressed, the face of the moon began to be covered by shadow. A lunar eclipse, the first in several months, an ominous, foreboding sign

---

[508] Jacobs, *The Beginning of the U.S. Army*, 59–60; Sword, *President Washington's Indian War*, 119; Denny, *Military Journal*, 149.

[509] Cayton, *Frontier Indiana*, 154; Downes, *Council Fires on the Upper Ohio*, 315.

of possible ill fortune, gave the allied tribes second thoughts. The Ottowas were the first to withdraw from the planned operation and were soon followed by others. A bitter Blue Jacket commented that they were obliged to let the Americans retreat, adding that if the warriors had been able to attack in concert, a total and decisive victory would have resulted.[510]

★

Harmar's initial communiques to the secretary of war claimed victory but admitted severe losses. The general himself considered the mission's objectives reached; houses and crops were razed and upward of an estimated 100 warriors had been slain. Others, however, immediately recognized the expedition's failure and couched their comments in those terms. Resentful Kentucky militiamen accused Harmar of cowardice and general incompetence, and rumors spread eastward like wildfire. Congress reacted to reports of the campaign's failure with outrage. Although untrue, accusations that Harmar had been drunk the whole time gained wide acceptance in the absence of any other logical explanation of defeat and in the end saved the administration from an embarrassing public debate over policy. Knox and Washington kept their official reactions to a minimum, preferring to let Harmar bear the torrent of criticism alone.[511]

Lt. Ebenezer Denny was dispatched from Fort Washington to deliver Harmar's official report and arrived in Philadelphia on December 14, 1790 bringing with him official dispatches and his own observation of militia shortcomings, an explanation that reinforced long-standing prejudices already held by Knox and the president. Dave R. Palmer notes in *1794: America, Its Army, and the Birth of a Nation*, that for nearly a month past Denny's arrival the capital was still abuzz with talk condemning Harmar because many found it hard to credit the official accounts and preferred to believe that Harmar was a drunkard rather than to admit that the militia system had failed. Public opinion remained unchanged until John Armstrong arrived on January 5, 1791, to tell his harrowing first-person account of the battles, including damning stories of the militia failures. Washington and Knox had been set to believe the worst about the regimental commander; but with firsthand information from Denny

---

[510] Sword, *President Washington's Indian War*, 117–19.

[511] Warner, "General Josiah Harmar's Campaign Reconsidered," 55; Harmar to Knox, November 6, 1790, *ASP-Indian Affairs*, I: 104.

and Armstrong, a very different picture emerged. Both attributed the defeat entirely to the militia. Composed of substitutes, poorly armed, badly equipped, and officered by inexperienced men instead of prominent Indian fighters, it had been uncontrollable, disobedient, and at crucial times openly mutinous. Battles had been lost because the militia had run or had acted impulsively, exposing the regulars to attack and decimation.[512]

Realizing that Knox and Washington were disappointed in the campaign's outcome and reeling from disparaging charges to his character, Harmar initially considered resignation but later decided to clear his name through a court of inquiry. Officers whose testimony would be crucial to the process, however, were not immediately available, and Harmar had to wait almost a year for his day in court.

Not until September 15, 1791, did the inquiry begin at Fort Washington. Its presiding officer was Maj. Gen. Richard Butler, and Lt. Cols. George Gibson and William Darke completed the three-person board. All were well known on the frontier and understood its problems, and Butler had been instrumental in negotiating the treaties of Fort McIntosh and Fort Finney a few years earlier. The tribunal deliberated for nine days, examining witnesses ranging in rank from ensign to major. The principal officers of the militia were informed of the investigation, but none came to testify. In the year since the campaign, they had become widely scattered and had their own businesses demanding their attention. Jacobs notes that they may also have felt that the evidence they would present might be as harmful to them as to Harmar. Consequently, not only were all the witnesses regulars, but many were also officers who had served under Harmar's command since the formation of the regiment.

The board's decision fell firmly in Harmar's favor; his performance and integrity were restored. It found his personal conduct "irreproachable" and his plans of march, encampment, and battle "judicious and well calculated." Decisions to send detachments from the main body on October 14 and 19 were well justified, and the mission of returning to Kekionga led by Wyllys and Hardin on October 21 was based on logical assumptions; its failure was only due to the fact that orders were not properly executed. Harmar was completely exonerated, and his conduct merited high approbation.[513]

---

[512] Kohn, *Eagle and Sword*, 107; Dave R. Palmer, *1794: America, Its Army, and the Birth of the Nation* (Novato, California: Presidio Press, 1994), 181.

[513] Jacobs, *The Beginning of the U.S. Army*, 63–64; Guthman, *March to Massacre*,

In their testimonies, Harmar's loyal officers were quick to come to his defense, blaming the militia's shameful performance for disasters that occurred on the expedition. Guthman, however, notes one consistent omission in the depositions that were taken during the official inquiry. There was no recognition of the superior tactics of Little Turtle and his warriors in the description of the army's defeat. Even Armstrong, a trained officer with fourteen years of military experience, could not allow himself to acknowledge the masterful tactics of the Indians against the overconfident American force. His reports do not even hint that the enemy had anything to do with its victory; he merely criticized the cowardice and inability of the militia as compared to the regular army.[514]

Jacobs notes that despite the court's decisions, it was impossible to hide the fact that the expedition had failed. In the quest to render the Miami tribes so fearful that they would abandon their raids along the frontier, the government had sent over 1,400 men northward to show the nation's armed strength. Instead of impressing them with the army's might, Harmar's troops had advertised their own incapacity, and the mission's outcome induced their adversaries into greater acts of destruction. They had inflicted only trifling losses to the assembled warriors at a very heavy cost to themselves. About one-seventh of the expedition's number became casualties. Of the 320 regulars, 75 were killed and 3 wounded; of the militia, 108 were killed and 28 wounded. Equipment had been lost or destroyed, large quantities of rations had been wasted, and significant numbers of horses had been killed, stolen, or had otherwise disappeared.[515]

★

The benefit of over 200 years of hindsight provides a clearer view of the failed campaign, and several historians have critiqued the episode. The expedition was flawed from its inception. Culpability for any military failure starts at the top, and Washington cannot be exempted from his share of responsibility. Harmar, argues James M. Perry, may not have been the best choice to lead a campaign whose outcome was at that moment

---

191, 195; *ASP-Military Affairs*, 1: 20–36.

[514] Guthman, *March to Massacre*, 191.

[515] Jacobs, *The Beginning of the U.S. Army*, 60. Information sent to Fort Detroit presented from the British and Indian perspective appears in the Michigan Pioneer and Historical Society's *Historical Collections*, XXIV: 102–109.

so important to the prestige of the new government. Given the high stakes, Washington could have replaced Harmar, who as a lieutenant colonel in the Revolution, had neither previously planned nor executed a large military campaign. Whether or not having a seasoned former Revolutionary War general in charge of the operation, if indeed a suitable one could have been found on short notice, might have altered its outcome given other circumstances surrounding the campaign remains a moot issue. Washington, though, clearly had his doubts that Harmar was the right man for the job. He was unpopular with influential Kentucky politicians; and reports of his drinking, whether or not true, had reached both him and Knox. The president's words when he first heard about the campaign were damning:

> I expected little from the moment I heard he was *a drunkard*. I expected less as soon as I heard that on *this account* no confidence was reported in him by the people of the Western Country—And I gave up *all hope* of Success, as soon as I heard that there were disputes with *him* about command.[516]

Washington could also have demanded the troops be trained in frontier fighting. Given his own history with General Braddock thirty-five years earlier and his knowledge of the bloody experiences of militia and regular army forces fighting Indians on the frontier during the long years of the Revolution, he should have grasped that necessity.[517]

Michael S. Warner cites other factors in the mission's failure that could be attributed to miscalculation by individuals in the higher ranks. Goals for the mission were obscure, if not completely based on faulty assumptions. Knox and St. Clair agreed that the expedition should "chastise" the hostile tribes by striking at their towns and destroying their homes and crops,

---

[516] Perry, *Arrogant Armies*, 46–47; Washington to Knox, November 19, 1790, and Knox to Harmar, September 3, 1790, cited on Founders Online, http://founders.archives.gov/documents/Washington/05-06-02-0323. In Harmar's favor and a fact most likely considered by Washington and Knox was that he had commanded the regiment commendably for six long years and was indisputably knowledgeable of the myriad of issues surrounding the territory's settlement and its defense.

[517] Perry, *Arrogant Armies*, 46–47.

although Knox later seemed to have had second thoughts, writing St. Clair in September that its outcome would either force the Indians to terms or become the basis of even wider warfare.[518]

Warner agrees with historian Richard H. Kohn that the entire chain of command must share responsibility for committing the prestige of the United States to a venture uncertain of purpose and constructed of half measures. Harmar's eagerness to injure the foe that had given him six years of frustration is understandable but cannot excuse his undertaking such a dangerous and yet tentative campaign.[519]

The configuration of the expedition itself suffered from several weaknesses. Harmar's force was too large and too slow to surprise anyone. His men walked at least 150 miles in order to get to the Miami towns, having to cut a paths through the wilderness as they went. Travel by river might have been a better option. Warner suggests that going up the Great Miami River as far as present-day Piqua, Ohio, about eighty-nine miles from Kekionga, would have saved time and left horses and men in better shape for the campaign. Although originally contemplated by the campaign's architects, the plans were abandoned due to the expense.[520]

In executing the operation itself, the militia forces were with few exceptions a complete disaster. Knox expected seasoned frontiersmen; instead, he got substitutes, old men, boys, and otherwise unacceptable candidates. Warner suggests that Harmar's unpopularity in Kentucky might have made more qualified men reluctant to join the expedition. Kentuckians also disliked army officers, and some apparently believed the campaign was doomed from the start. The dismissive attitudes of federal officers toward the militia didn't help the situation.[521]

Many militia members had indeed showed little or no willingness to work as a team or to carry out orders at critical times during the campaign. Jacobs suggests their skills lay in other areas. When used in Wayne's later campaign as messengers, scouts, or on patrols, they performed with distinction; when faced with possible annihilation in battle at Kekionga,

---

[518] Knox to St. Clair, September 14, 1790, *SCP*, 2: 181–83; Warner, "General Josiah Harmar's Campaign Reconsidered," 56.

[519] Warner, "General Josiah Harmar's Campaign Reconsidered," 62; Kohn, *Eagle and Sword*, 104.

[520] Warner, "General Josiah Harmar's Campaign Reconsidered," 60–61.

[521] Denny, *Military Journal*, 140; Warner, "General Josiah Harmar's Campaign Reconsidered," 57–58.

they sometimes fought as bravely and as fiercely as the regulars. They had their own methods, however, that could not be altered except by considerable training. Warner suggests that given the opportunity and more time, Harmar might have molded most of the militia troops into passable soldiers, but time was not on his side. The Kentucky militia began arriving at Fort Washington a scant two weeks before the army was to march, and the Pennsylvanians arrived with only a few days to spare.[522]

Low pay was certainly not an incentive to serve. Militia privates received three dollars a month. A man who left his family and farm at harvest season to serve for sixty days could thus count on hardship, danger, and only six dollars for his trouble.[523]

Harmar's expedition cannot be considered a total failure, although its immediate aftermath only aroused Indian hostility rather to compel errant tribes into submission. Guthman maintains that the campaign demonstrated that a large force could penetrate the uncharted forest, cutting its own roads as it marched. Without the benefit of accurate maps or supply posts along the way, it could reach a destination as far away as the Miami villages. Harmar's army returned well fed and did not endure severe hardship on the march itself. The country was no longer uncharted, and accurate maps were now available for future expeditions. Merely to have made the expedition was something of an accomplishment.[524]

Despite the disastrous outcome, officers and men had now experienced warfare against the hostile tribes, and many problems in transportation and supply had been partially solved for a larger number of men than had ever previously maneuvered in that section of the country. Harmar led mixed troops of cavalry, infantry, and artillery; had been gone thirty-four days; ran three separate operations against the enemy; and covered approximately 340 miles, all the more remarkable considering that the total force had been hurriedly assembled and formed into organizations that had never before operated together. However ingloriously, Harmar managed to return his army as a tactical unit; those who participated had learned a great deal.[525]

---

[522] Harmar to Hamtramck, November 29, 1790, *OOTW*, 268; Jacobs, *The Beginning of the U.S. Army*, 63–65. Warner, "General Josiah Harmar's Campaign Reconsidered," 58.

[523] Warner, "General Josiah Harmar's Campaign Reconsidered," 58.

[524] Guthman, *March to Massacre*, 195.

[525] Jacobs, *The Beginning of the U.S. Army*, 60–61.

Warner also credits Harmar with developing a sound plan of executing a two-pronged operation. Sending Hamtramck with a diversionary force against the Wabash tribes provided a move that distracted potentially hostile tribes and kept them from joining the main body at the Miami villages. Although this secondary mission accomplished nothing of positive value, perhaps six hundred warriors remained on the Wabash in the hope of ambushing his force.

Although faulted by contemporaries and some historians, Harmar's decision to return to Kekionga on October 22 to attack returning warriors appears shrewd in retrospect. Warner notes that the overall plan was solid; had it worked, the expedition might be remembered quite differently. The scheme failed because it asked too much of its militia components, but the troops under Hardin and Wyllys still inflicted heavy casualties.

Harmar's caution also merits praise. Waiting warriors never found an opportunity to assault his camp or his marching columns. Christopher W. Wingate in his study of the early United States Army notes that the commander's insistence on all around security while marching, the use of breastworks, the formation of a square encampment to prevent infiltration or surprise, and the daily use of scouts to reconnoiter well ahead of the main body had merit. Warner suggests that Harmar recognized the weakness of his force and the perils it faced. When the general erred, it was usually on the side of caution.[526]

Warner is not without criticism of Harmar's decisions, however. Having reached the Miami towns and set his army to their destruction, and having accomplished the campaign's stated mission of destroying the villages and crops, he still sought battle. He put his militia troops at considerable risk on October 18 and 19 by sending them far from camp in the hope that they would find and defeat the fleeing tribesmen. Yet despite his disappointment with the militia's performance, he kept at least 80 percent of the regulars with him at all times. Warner suggests that Harmar apparently placed little trust in the abilities of his regular officers and soldiers, an unusual observation given Harmar's intimate knowledge of his own troops over the preceding six years.

---

[526] Christopher W. Wingate, *Military Professionalism and the Early American Officer Corps, 1789–1796* (Fort Leavenworth: Combat Studies Institute Press, 2013), 56; Warner, "General Josiah Harmar's Campaign Reconsidered," 61–62.

Although emboldened by their rout of the Americans, the warring tribesmen suffered damage not apparent by their obvious victory. They had indeed forced their opponents to engage in the kind of warfare in which they excelled: they conducted successful ambushes from well-concealed locations, enticed militia officers into splitting their forces, and ran decoys to distract and lead the army into attacking positions favorable to their massed warriors. All of these brilliant tactics were executed on their home ground, however. Previously, they had chosen sites from which to attack settlers and soldiers far to the south, knowing that they could always retreat to the safety of the Miami towns where they enjoyed the protection of the British and were too far away to suffer any meaningful retribution from the United States Army. That era had now ended.[527]

So too had the initial chapter of the United States' first peacetime army come to an end. No longer a series of detached units manning strung-out forts charged with protecting settlements that dotted the western territory, it had now experienced its first defeat as a unified fighting force. Following the court of inquiry decision, Josiah Harmar resigned his commission and returned to Philadelphia. Historian Alan Brown gives him appropriate credit in hindsight as a man who served his nation well but whose services later generations have overlooked or remembered only for his army's defeat. Harmar and his small force performed substantial services for the nation, aiding settlement and helping to establish the authority of the United States on its western frontier. Harmar must be credited for hastening the settlement of the Ohio Country. Personally honest, he refused many opportunities to further his own fortunes or those of less scrupulous friends. Had someone less honest and effective held his command, the establishment of American authority in the West could have been immeasurably delayed.[528]

Mistakes made during the army's first large-scale campaign under Harmar's leadership should have been instructive in planning future operations. Guthman notes that a late start in the year meant that frost soon eliminated grazing for horses, and that untrained militia only hurt, not helped, the regular army. These lessons were soon forgotten as preparations for an inevitable follow-on campaign got underway. Once again, planners considered the number of troops necessary for such an

---

[527] Guthman, *March to Massacre*, 195–96.
[528] Brown, "The Role of the Army in Western Settlement," *PMHB*: 177–78.

operation but were ultimately forced to compromise on both the quantity and quality of recruits. Clever Indian tactics were quickly forgotten in the haste to build another army to achieve what Harmar's force could not.[529]

It was a foregone conclusion that Harmar had to surrender his command, but the president's selection of Arthur St. Clair as his successor proved to be a most grievous error. To quote James M. Perry, "Harmar was a calamity; St. Clair would be a catastrophe."[530]

---

[529] Guthman, *March to Massacre*, 195–97.
[530] Perry, *Arrogant Armies*, 47.

12

St. Clair's Campaign, 1791

*I figure to myself that this campaign will be more
fatiguing and hazardous than any I have served in.
We have to march thro an Enemy country and in it
to establish the posts, and that in the winter season
too—would it not be as pleasant to spend the winter
in Philadelphia—a fine peace establishment this.*

—John Armstrong[531]

A furlough for the newly promoted Capt. John Armstrong was long
overdue. Making the "Waggon Inn" on Market Street his home after
his arrival in Philadelphia in early January, he settled in to await the
administration's plan for the inevitable campaign that was to follow.[532]

Armstrong and his fellow officers remained intensely loyal to their
commander. Having already met with the secretary of war and confirming
Ebenezer Denny's account of the October expedition, the captain wrote
two letters to Harmar reporting disparaging remarks he had heard about
the general but assured him that he had not been deserted by his friends.
Harmar's papers include additional letters from other officers, and all

---

[531] Armstrong to Francis Johnston, August 30, 1791, PJA

[532] Armstrong's official date of promotion was September 26, 1790. Francis
B. Heitman, *Historical Register and Dictionary of the United States Army*
(Washington: Government Printing Office, 1902), I: 170.

signed a statement expressing their support and their hope that he would continue in his service to the regiment.[533]

Armstrong found Philadelphia's political climate charged not only with anger over the late military disaster but also with reports of raids by emboldened warriors on two key settlements. On January 2, the Big Bottom blockhouse thirty miles above Marietta on the Muskingum River was attacked by Wyandot and Delaware tribesmen. Thirteen occupants were killed, and five Ohio Company associates were taken prisoner.[534]

A few days later, a party under the direction of Shawnee war chief Blue Jacket and adviser Simon Girty arrived at Dunlap's Station, a blockhouse housing a thirteen-man federal detachment protecting thirty-five settlers about seventeen miles north of Cincinnati, and ambushed a four-man surveying party. One man was instantly killed, and another, Abner Hunt, was thrown from his horse and captured. The remaining two men managed their escape back to the station.

The garrison awoke the next morning to the sight of two hundred warriors surrounding the stockade. When the installation's commander, Lt. Jacob Kingsbury, declined their demand to surrender, gunfire ensued, and the station found itself under siege. As the incident unfolded, the unfortunate Hunt was first forced to act as an intermediary between the Indians and the garrison and later tortured to death in full view of the stockade's defenders. By the time the blockhouse was relieved, the

---

[533] Armstrong apparently briefed Knox on several issues related to the overall campaign. His papers include the draft of a letter to clarify a statement that he had made concerning the army's contractors, citing specific instances in which his troops had not only been ill served in the procurement of provisions but had been taken advantage of when having to purchase overpriced goods. Armstrong to Knox, February 21, 1791, PJA. See also George Morgan to John Armstrong, February 25, 1791, PJA and Meek, "General Harmar's Expedition," *OAHQ*, 95; Officers' correspondence with Harmar can be found in Richard C. Knopf, ed., The Harmar Papers from the Clements Library Ann Arbor, Michigan (Columbus: Anthony Wayne Parkway Board, 1954), 169, 172, 181, 200, 202.

[534] Fortunately, upon reaching Detroit, prisoners were greeted sympathetically by the British and traders, a few ransomed for their release and another adopted by the Indians. See Theodore Roosevelt, *The Winning of the West*, Part 5, "St. Clair and Wayne" (New York: Current Literature Publishing Company, 1905), 139–40. Sword, *President Washington's Indian War*, 128–29.

Shawnees had disappeared, leaving in their wake burned homesteads, dead cattle, and ruined crops and possessions.[535]

The assaults upon Big Bottom and Dunlap's Station were not isolated occurrences. Among other attacks were those on an entire family taken captive in Allegheny County, Pennsylvania, and another at the home of a settler living twenty-three miles from Pittsburg. Initially received as friends, the party murdered the family of eleven, pitching their bodies into the flames of their burning cabin. Terrified inhabitants of Pittsburgh sought arms from Fort Pitt and were issued one hundred muskets while settlers living in remote areas fled to nearby stations.[536]

★

William H. Guthman notes that despite the rise in incidents, the question of supplying additional troops for a second expedition against the Indians was the subject of considerable controversy in Congress and citizens along the Eastern Seaboard. Once again, the administration had to balance the thorny issues of creating a permanent military institution and funding its operations to solve the ever-increasing Indian problem against the indifference of average citizens far removed from the frontier.[537]

In late January, Knox, on behalf of the president, proposed another full-scale operation to Congress. His plan called for an enlarged force of 3,000 men that would be so powerful it could defeat any combination of warring tribes, even if aided by the British. Maintaining peace afterward would be ensured by establishing a permanent garrison at the Miami villages and other subsidiary posts necessary for supply and communication with Fort Washington. The administration next requested money to create a second regiment of regulars of about 1,000 soldiers to man additional garrisons planned to stretch from the Ohio country southward into Georgia to monitor the activities of southern tribes. With a force of regulars totaling 2,000 men, approximately 1,200 would be available for a campaign against the defiant nations of the Western confederacy. The remainder of the

[535] Sword, *President Washington's Indian War*, 126–28; McBride, *Pioneer Biography*, I: 14–21; 87–89; 146–47.
[536] Jacobs, *The Beginning of the U.S. Army*, 67–68.
[537] Guthman, *March to Massacre*, 200.

expeditionary force would be levies, volunteers enlisted by the government only for the duration of the campaign.[538]

To forestall the anticipated opposition, Washington arranged for Congress to receive a letter from Rufus Putnam, organizer of the Ohio Company at Marietta, concerning the incident at Big Bottom. Entered into the Congressional Record on January 27, 1792, Putnam had described his situation as critical, concluding that "our present situation is truly distressing; and I do, therefore, most earnestly implore the protection of Government, for myself and friends inhabiting these wilds of America."[539]

The strategy worked. Representatives from New England, the most vocal opponents of the administration's policy, knew Putnam, a Continental Army officer from Massachusetts who ended the war as a brigadier general, and recognized not only that the Ohio Company was backed financially by New Englanders but also that some 70,000 of them had migrated to the frontier since 1786. The bill was approved.[540]

Passage of the revised military authorization of March 3, 1791, set the administration's wheels spinning. The operation's starting date was set at July 10, slightly more than four months' time from the bill's passage, so haste was imperative. The campaign was to be preceded by at least one preliminary raid on the Wabash tribes by Gen. Charles Scott and his Kentucky militia. Meanwhile, men had to be recruited by officers yet to be commissioned, the enlarged army reorganized, uniforms and equipment manufactured and distributed, transportation of troops to Fort Washington arranged, and campaign logistics settled. These monumental tasks were to be accomplished at a time when both a government bureaucracy and permanent military establishment experienced in such undertakings were practically nonexistent. Knox had already submitted a thirty-five-page document to the president outlining precisely what steps needed to be taken, right down to the details of strategy and orders to be issued to the

---

[538] Kohn, *Eagle and Sword*, 109. In addition to establishing a permanent garrison at the Miami villages, the administration hoped to settle the question of a territorial boundary. Knox assumed that the army's disciplined valor would triumph over the "undisciplined" Indians and that they would sue for peace in their defeat. They would then have to concede to new boundary lines redrawn to the west. Knox to St. Clair, March 21, 1791, *ASP-Indian Affairs*, I: 172.

[539] Kohn, *Eagle and Sword*, 110; Rufus Putnam to Washington, January 8, 1792, *ASP-Indian Affairs*, I: 121–22.

[540] Kohn, *Eagle and Sword*, 110.

various commanders of militia and regular army units. Maj. Gen. Arthur St. Clair had already been selected to command the force, and Armstrong's former regimental commander Maj. Gen. Richard Butler designated as second-in-command. By March 21, Knox issued detailed orders to both St. Clair and Butler. With weekly reports to be submitted to keep the administration regularly informed, the government was finally assuming control over its army and its military operations. In this case at least, Washington and Knox had learned from prior mistakes.[541]

Appointments to key positions had to be made. The quartermaster department had been abolished in 1785, and reinstatement was essential to provide the myriad of goods necessary to support the 3,000-man force. Clothing, blankets, medicines, instruments, tents, ordnance, boats, horses, and equipment of all sorts fell into the purview of newly appointed Quartermaster General Samuel Hodgdon, formerly commissary general during the Revolution.

An estimated 4,000 rations per day were deemed necessary to supply the force following its departure from Fort Washington. Responsibility for this daunting task fell upon the army's contractor, William Duer, who had served for a short time as assistant secretary of the Treasury and was a close friend of Hamilton, Knox, and Washington.[542]

Armstrong and some of his fellow officers can be pictured on March 3, 1791, as lingering about Congress Hall while voting took place and buttonholing Knox as soon as possible to receive their recruiting assignments. Since officers were to get a bonus of two dollars for each man recruited and mustered, they jumped at the chance to begin their assignments. Armstrong was apparently near the head of the line; in his letter to Harmar on March 9, 1791, Ebenezer Denny wrote that Armstrong had already gotten his instructions and was beginning recruitment activities that day while he and Erkuries Beatty still waited to learn their fates.[543]

Armstrong wasted no time. This notice appeared in Philadelphia's *American Daily Advertiser* on March 22, 1791.

---

[541] Kohn, *Eagle and Sword*, 111; Knox to St. Clair, March 21, 1791, *ASP-Indian Affairs*, I: 171–74.

[542] Guthman, *March to Massacre*, 207–08.

[543] Guthman, *March to Massacre*, 201–02; Denny, *Military Journal*, 257; Richard M. Lytle, *The Soldiers of America's First Army, 1791* (Lanham, Maryland: Scarecrow Press, Inc., 2004), 34 notes that recruiting to fill vacancies in the First Regiment was to take place in Maryland and New York.

Captain Armstrong informs his fellow Soldiers and others, who may wish to inlist, that he has commenced Recruiting in the city of Philadelphia, where a generous Bounty and other Encouragement will be given. Young Men who wish to become Adventurers in a New Country, by joining this Command, may acquire a Knowledge of the Western World, subject to no expence; and after serving a short period, set down on their own Farms, and enjoy all the blessings of Peace and Plenty.

John Armstrong, Captain
1st Regt. United States
Philadelphia, March 14, 1791[544]

Recruiting for the Second Regiment took place primarily in the New England states and in South Carolina and Delaware. Two regiments of levies to serve for a period of six months were to be raised in New Jersey, Pennsylvania, Maryland, and Virginia and from territory south of the Ohio River. The administration, having learned its lesson about relying on militia units, planned to call them up only in the event of a serious manpower shortage.[545]

When filling leadership roles in the new regiment, Knox had the unique opportunity both to play politics and to fulfill the need for competent military leadership. A New Englander, Maj. Jonathan Heart, formerly of the First Regiment, was selected to be the new regiment's commander. Most of the company officers selected were men who had seen combat service in state Continental lines during the Revolutionary War and had a history of proven ability and untarnished reputation.[546]

The president took a direct hand in selecting leadership positions for the levy units. His friend, Lt. Col. William Darke, was selected to

---

[544] Guthman, *March to Massacre*, 30. Regimental officers had learned from experience; the actual work of recruiting was done for existing regular army units by trusted sergeants and corporals who accompanied their recruiting officers eastward. Lytle, *The Soldiers of America's First Army*, 35.

[545] Knox to Washington, December 26, 1790, and Knox to St. Clair, March 21, 1971, *ASP-Indian Affairs*, I: 139, 171; Guthman, *March to Massacre*, 208.

[546] Lytle, *The Soldiers of America's First Army*, 27.

command the First Regiment of Levies and in turn nominated young officers capable of recruiting infantry companies in Virginia.

Maj. Gen. Butler selected battalion commanders for the Second Regiment of Levies who would recruit their company officers. He ensured, however, that two of his younger brothers, both highly competent combat leaders, were offered commissions.[547]

Newly formed companies were to make their way to Fort Pitt either by land or by marching to present-day Brownsville, Pennsylvania, where they could travel up the Monongahela River to Pittsburgh. The contractor was to arrange for provisions along the way and for arms, accoutrements, and ammunition to be issued from storage at Fort Pitt. Quartermaster Hodgdon was to proceed to the fort to purchase 110 horses for the cavalry and boats for the conveyance of the troops and supplies down the Ohio and arrange for roughly 300 packhorses to be purchased in Kentucky. Hodgdon was given $20,000, an amount that could be increased with St. Clair's authorization. By the end of May, all principals had been given their orders, and essential details worked out so that the operation could proceed smoothly. Armstrong completed enlisting his company of seventy-six men, gathered his recruits in Philadelphia, and departed for Fort Pitt by way of Reading and Lancaster on April 27. The captain and the army were ready to proceed.[548]

★

Randolph Downes and Harlow Lindley in their work, *Frontier Ohio, 1788-1803*, note that the ill-fated Harmar campaign had a peculiar effect on both parties involved. Its outcome had provided enough of an Indian victory to hearten tribesmen but did not discourage the Americans from making a further attempt to negotiate for peace. The administration still hedged in the decision to commit the army to another military campaign. It believed that the majority of United States citizens wished to avoid war because the cost in lives and dollars might far exceed any advantage that could be gained by such an action. If negotiations succeeded, the government would save money and win public approval; if not, there would be no doubt about the government's pacific intentions. So at the same time it readied the army for combat, the administration implemented a

---

[547] Ibid., 30–31.
[548] Guthman, *March to Massacre*, 209, 212.

new two-stage diplomatic offensive. The first stage, an invitation to the western tribes, was pure politics, a transparent attempt to avert accusations of aggression or genocide. Col. Thomas Proctor, a former artillery officer and close friend of Knox, was dispatched to persuade friendly Senecas to accompany him to Miami and Wabash lands in order to negotiate a peace treaty.[549]

The initial signs seemed positive. Seneca chief Cornplanter had been in Philadelphia in December. When he was advised not to allow his young warriors to join in any hostile actions against the United States, he assured the administration that tribesmen under his influence would not only remain on friendly terms with the government but would also attempt to prevent further violence on the part of the western nations. Arrangements were then made for him to travel to the Ohio territory. Proctor was to rendezvous with Cornplanter at his village in western New York following the chief's trip homeward.[550]

Matters went downhill from there. As Cornplanter's party was making its way westward, a small group of Virginia militia patrolling the woods southeast of Pittsburgh encountered a raiding party. The militia gave chase, and their scouts followed one group to the mouth of Big Beaver Creek, a known Native American gathering place. When they later attacked and killed peaceful Delawares, Indians in the Pittsburgh area retaliated immediately. Suddenly, western Pennsylvania was embroiled in war. In the confusion that ensued, Cornplanter's entourage was apprehended by a Pennsylvania militia detachment as it made its way up the Allegheny; he and his tribesmen were forced to put to shore, eventually fleeing into the underbrush. Although a federal noncommissioned officer was aboard their large garrison boat, which was loaded with provisions for Fort Franklin and with gifts presented to the chief in Philadelphia, the cargo along with several canoes in which the Senecas were traveling was seized, taken to Pittsburgh, and sold as captured property.[551]

When Knox heard of the unrest in western Pennsylvania as well as the diplomatic disaster that had befallen Cornplanter's party, he tried to

---

[549] Downes and Lindley, *Frontier Ohio*, 26; Kohn, *Eagle and Sword*, 112; *ASP-Indian Affairs*, I: 171.

[550] Guthman, *March to Massacre*, 201; Knox to Proctor, March 11, 1791, *ASP-Indian Affairs*, I: 145–46.

[551] Sword, *President Washington's Indian War*, 133–34; St. Clair to Knox, April 19, 1791, in Smith, *SCP*, II: 205.

contain the spreading regional hostilities by ordering an investigation and by assuring Cornplanter that the Big Beaver massacre was a tragic mistake. To ensure the compliance of the other Iroquois nations, the decision was then made to seek a second peace initiative, and Pennsylvanian Timothy Pickering was sent to assemble representatives of the Six Nations to cement their friendship with the United States and prevent an alliance with the hostile tribes farther west.[552]

When Proctor met up with Cornplanter at Fort Franklin on April 8, the rattled chief and his men had second thoughts about continuing their western mission. They insisted that he travel to Buffalo Creek, present-day Buffalo, New York, where a full council of the Six Nations might consider the proposal. Upon arriving at the meeting site two weeks later, Proctor found the assemby politically divided and many chiefs infuriated by his requests. After nearly a month's delay, the council finally agreed to send a small six-chief delegation with Proctor to the western country, but the entire plan was soon aborted. Because so much time had elapsed, the parties could no longer proceed by land and had to travel by water to reach their destination. The Senecas refused to cross the lake in small boats and the British, who controlled navigation on the Great Lakes, denied Proctor's request to charter a vessel adequate for the lake's waters.[553]

Even before a lack of transportation precluded Proctor's effort to gain the Senecas' help in establishing a peace mission with the western nations, things had already begun to fall apart. During the month Proctor was biding his time at Lake Erie, Pickering's invitation arrived asking the Iroquois to discuss a separate peace treaty with the United States at Painted Post, now Newton, New York. Downes and Lindley note that the Six Nations at Buffalo Creek interpreted this as an attempt to keep the nations from speaking in unity and therefore a blow aimed at the confederacy. To add to the confusion, another message came from St. Clair, urging the Iroquois to take up arms against their brother nations to the west. Befuddled by the confusing mix of diplomatic initiatives, they resolved to take the path of least resistance and remain neutral. A disappointed Proctor

[552] Kohn, *Eagle and Sword*, 113.
[553] Sword, *President Washington's Indian War*, 134–135.

finally departed Buffalo for Fort Franklin on May 21, two weeks past the predetermined May 10 deadline for his return.[554]

★

Meanwhile to the south, the clock was ticking down the precious days before the planned expedition, and the Ohio River was becoming a bloodbath. On March 27, Capt. David Strong's large party was attacked near the mouth of the Scioto, resulting in the deaths of twenty-three men. In the same week, a raiding party captured a fifty-foot pirogue, subsequently attacking a keelboat and killing its dozen passengers. The frontier was aflame with bitterness when St. Clair wrote to Knox in May of a late-blooming plan to counter raids along the Ohio frontier. Several offers of monetary rewards for Indian scalps were being circulated. One Ohio country resident boasted, "We . . . have by subscription raised £50 per scalp for the first Indian [brought in], £30 for the second, and £20 for the third." Fear permeated the settlements.[555]

According to Knox's instructions, the initial raid to "soften" resistance of the Wabash tribes that was to be led by General Scott could not begin until news of Proctor's peace efforts was known. If word of his mission's outcome had not been received by May 10, preparations for the raid could proceed. Such a campaign would merely be a prelude to the larger effort and would include the taking of prisoners, particularly women and children. By treating them humanely, the Americans would be able to demonstrate their capacity for compassion and possibly incline other nations toward peace. On May 23, Brig. Gen. Charles Scott, accompanied by Col. John Hardin and fellow Kentuckian James Wilkinson, crossed the Ohio River with a force of 800 men, many of whom were veterans of the Harmar campaign with a score to settle. Initially headed north, as if advancing toward the Miami villages, they later swerved westward toward the Wabash.

Scott and his men found few warriors in the area. Contrary to the fears of Kentuckians and the administration, Little Turtle and other leaders were not then contemplating an organized attack on the Americans. An unusually cold and snowy winter had decimated the buffalo population in the Illinois country. That natural disaster in their hunting grounds, along with the impact of the destruction of the harvest at the Miami villages

---

[554] Downes and Lindley, *Frontier Ohio*, 28; Guthman, *March to Massacre*, 203.
[555] Sword, *President Washington's Indian War*, 136–138.

during the Harmar campaign, meant that leaders were more concerned with survival than conquest. Some headed to Detroit to ascertain continued support from the British while others rebuilt the Miami villages. Still others moved up the Maumee and settled at the mouth of the Auglaize River, about halfway to Lake Erie. When word of Scott's raid reached the Auglaize settlements, an estimated 2,000 warriors hurried to the Miami towns, thinking that the location was the expedition's main objective. Another 500 left the Wabash to join their brethren, leaving the actual target of the raid largely unprotected.[556]

Upon reaching the Wabash, Scott split his force, sending Hardin and 200 men to two small Kickapoo villages, Wilkinson with 360 men to Kethtippecanuck, eighteen miles northeast on the Tippecanoe River, and himself to Ouiatanon, site of Wea villages near present-day Lafayette, Indiana. Meeting minimal resistance, they destroyed towns, burned cornfields and gardens, and took 41 prisoners, mostly women and children, holding them initially at Fort Steuben but eventually delivering them to Fort Washington as ransom for peace.[557]

The war machine was indeed ramping up, but delays had already pushed the July start of the campaign into the fall. St. Clair decided on a second raid and authorized Wilkinson, accompanied by 500 mounted Kentucky militia, to conduct another operation, this time on Miami villages at Kenapakomoko, situated near the junction of the Eel and Wabash Rivers near present-day Logansport, Indiana. The expedition had questionable success. Horsemen had to negotiate bogs and marshes of the upper Wabash country, and the mission had to be discontinued when provisions ran short and 279 horses became lame. Wilkinson's men managed to burn a few towns, destroy 430 acres of corn, and take 34 prisoners. The militia encountered few warriors not only because tribesmen were widely dispersed on scouting and procurement missions, but also because illness had incapacitated a large percentage of the region's inhabitants. Wilkinson, ever the self-promoter, presented inflated accounts of his success, asserting that he had destroyed the chief town of the Wea Nation. Washington was so pleased by his glowing report, a copy of which Wilkinson intentionally

---

[556] Cayton, *Frontier Indiana*, 155–56; Guthman, *March to Massacre*, 202; Knox to St. Clair, March 21, 1791, *ASP-Indian Affairs*, I: 171.

[557] Sword, *President Washington's Indian War*, 141; Cayton, *Frontier Indiana*, 156–57.

forwarded to the government in Philadelphia, that a special congratulatory message was issued thanking him for his "zeal, perseverance, and good conduct." [558]

★

These expeditions added to the misery of the upper Wabash Indians but had little strategic impact. By August, most of the warriors had gathered in the Maumee Valley where an estimated 1,400 Native Americans from the entire Great Lakes region arrived to discuss the next step in their dealings with the United States under the watchful eye of British agents who were at the time caught in the middle of the evolving policy of their own government.

Sir Guy Carleton, the governor of Quebec and now known as Lord Dorchester, was in a tight spot. He had sought renewed guidance from England following the Harmar campaign and the commencement of open hostilities between the Indian confederacy and the United States. Delay in receiving a reply, however, left him and his subordinates with no authoritative word regarding Britain's commitments to its Indian allies, and they had to interpret generalized instructions to resolve specific situations. Britain had no interest in war with the United States, but her authorities also needed to appease their Native American neighbors. Until he heard otherwise, Dorchester attempted to sustain normal relations with both sides, leaving it to his superiors in England to initiate a change in policy.

Without specific guidelines, British agents further down the chain of command adapted policy as they saw fit. Most significant among this group were the operational officers directly charged with managing Indian contracts, particularly three American defectors to the British cause during the Revolution who were strongly anti-American in their sentiments, Alexander McKee, Matthew Elliott, and Simon Girty. McKee, in particular, was active in arranging for provisions and supplies for the western nations. With his assistance, additional quantities of corn were requisitioned under the guise of providing for the assembled nations who would debate peace terms.[559]

---

[558] Guthman, *March to Massacre*, 203; Sword, *President Washington's Indian War*, 156–58.

[559] The three agents had strong Shawnee ties. All were married or had been married to Shawnee women, and all had Shawnee children. Girty, a white

Stung by the loss of so many women and children during the Wilkinson raid, the immediate reaction of the assembly was outrage. The Wabash villages had been attacked at the time when, to the east, a body was gathering to deliberate renewed measures to determine new boundary lines and the assurance of British support. A delegation headed by Joseph Brant had traveled to Quebec to confer with Lord Dorchester regarding a possible compromise on the confederation's firm demands of an Ohio River boundary. Resurrecting his attempts to find a way out of conflict with the United States following his unsuccessful efforts prior to the Treaty of Fort Harmar, Brant proposed that if the United States agreed to a boundary on the Ohio River that excluded land east of the Muskingum and sent no army into Indian country, the confederation would make peace with the Americans. Although the Miami and Shawnee predictably would oppose to such a measure, a massive gathering of confederated nations was planned on September 1 at the Maumee rapids to hear from the returning delegates. Wilkinson's raid, followed by intelligence of St. Clair's planned advance up the Great Miami, drew an even greater number of participants than had been expected.[560]

Unfortunately, the delegation's peace proposal went for naught as the opportunity to present it to the waiting tribes never occurred. When Brant and his party reached the Maumee rapids in October to present their compromise plan, they were too late. The entire council had gone forward to defend the Miami villages against St. Clair's oncoming army.[561]

Earlier that spring, Knox had instructed St. Clair to remain open to the possibility of negotiating a peace with the Wabash and Miami nations. His letters to St. Clair of May 12 and May 19 prior to the time of Proctor's return indicate that a quantity of Indian goods suitable for gifts would be shipped to him in the event of a treaty. His correspondence also reveals his knowledge of Brant's mission to the western Indians seeking agreement on a boundary compromise. Knox's hopes to avoid conflict, however faint or ill conceived, were for nothing. Despite Brant's efforts to garner a compromise within the confederation, Britain's policy ambiguities, and

---

man with a pronounced hatred toward Americans, was particularly vilified as a front-line adviser to raiding parties. Matthew Elliott's name arose a few years later in connection with that of Wilkinson during the Wayne campaign. Sword, *President Washington's Indian War*, 43, 122–26, 141.

[560] Sword, *President Washington's Indian War*, 158.

[561] Ibid., 159.

the administration's overtures to avoid another confrontation, the United States was going to war. Wiley Sword notes that at the very time Indians were debating terms for a negotiated settlement, Wea tribesmen ventured to Fort Washington where they had been invited to reclaim their wives and children. They could only look with despair at the helpless, miserable prisoners while the federal government refused to consider their release and were even informed that since they had acted more like children than men, peace would be denied to them. Representatives of all Wabash nations would have to come in before amnesty could be granted.[562]

The Wea tribesmen seeking to free their wives and children were not the only Native Americans visiting Fort Washington. In an effort to gain knowledge about the force that was inevitably to invade its territory, the confederation had dispatched Tecumseh, an English-speaking Shawnee, to gain information. Dressed in white man's clothing and a wide-brimmed hat, Tecumseh visited Cincinnati six times and Fort Washington, four. Assuming the demeanor of an Indian on a mission with the army, he purposely went about reading posted general orders and eavesdropping on conversations, becoming such a familiar figure that no one questioned his presence. Tecumseh later trailed the army as it progressed northward, relating information on a daily basis to a relay of runners who reported to Little Turtle and the war chiefs.[563]

★

Troops began reaching Fort Pitt in May with John Armstrong's company arriving on the twenty-fifth. Upon his departure from Philadelphia, he had received explicit instructions from Knox concerning expectations for his soldiers' demeanor and the officer's responsibility in

---

[562] Sword, *President Washington's Indian War*, 142; Knox to St. Clair, May 12 and May 19, 1791, *ASP-Indian Affairs*, I: 176.

[563] Allan W. Eckert, *A Sorrow in Our Heart: The Life of Tecumseh* (New York: Bantam Books, 1993), 419–20. Tecumseh and his brother Tenskwatawa, known as the Shawnee Prophet, later established Prophetstown near present-day Lafayette, Indiana. Tenskwatawa became a powerful spiritual leader influencing Delaware, Shawnee, and Miami followers to renounce their evil habits and undergo a spiritual and cultural rebirth in order to resist ever-increasing American influence. In 1811 Governor William Henry Harrison destroyed Prophetstown near the confluence of the Tippecanoe and the Wabash Rivers. Cayton, *Frontier Indiana*, 205-222.

assuring good behavior. Knox had no wish for the repeat of the drunken behavior that had characterized past marches and had left in its wake the destruction of private property and ill will among local residents. Armstrong corresponded with Knox along the way concerning the issuance of haversacks, and the secretary arranged for their delivery at Fort Pitt. His company headed downriver about June 1, apparently the first unit to depart.[564]

It was around this time that things began to go wrong and Knox's detailed plan for the expedition began to unravel. The available federal troops on-site were simply too few. When St. Clair assumed active command at Fort Washington in mid-May, he counted only 75 soldiers fit for duty. When he consolidated soldiers from supporting garrisons, the First Regiment numbered only 299 men. Of the 420 men whose enlistments expired during 1790, only 60 had reenlisted. There was little incentive to stay on the part of privates whose already meager pay had been reduced by the act of April 30, 1790. Additionally, the regulars had received no pay for 1790 and would receive nothing until the following April.

Additions to the First Regiment came slowly. Maryland lagged in recruiting its quota, and Massachusetts and Pennsylvania failed to reach theirs. Knox reported a deficit of 300 men, approximately one-third of the First Regiment's full strength. Recruiting for the Second Regiment was worse; enlistments totaled about 550 soldiers, or 60 percent of that unit's complement. Enrollment for the six-month levies was anticipated to be 2,000 men, but only 1,674 soldiers were enlisted. With an overall deficit of approximately 1,000 men, the projected design of the campaign force was in jeopardy.[565]

The shortfall in enlistments went hand in hand with the quality of troops that had been recruited. Sword notes that it should have been

---

[564] *ASP-Military Affairs*, I: 37; Knox to Armstrong, April 26, 1791, Armstrong to Knox, May 10, 1791, PJA; Charles Cist, *CM* I: 174. His company having been decimated during the Harmar campaign, Armstrong may have assumed command of Jonathan's Heart's company who in turn became commander of the Second Regiment and recruited enlistees for that unit. Included in the Armstrong papers is a payroll dated June 22, 1791, for the "late" Captain Heart's company.

[565] Jacobs, *The Beginning of the U.S. Army*, 76–77; *ASP-Military Affairs*, I: 36; Sword, *President Washington's Indian War*, 146–47.

self-evident almost from the beginning that the quality of the army as a whole would be contingent upon the caliber of the recruits and their discipline and training. The administration had grossly misjudged the amount of popular support for the campaign. It was apparent from their appearance upon arrival at Fort Washington that the newly recruited regulars were largely men whose lives held few options; they had been hastily thrown together and sent west totally unfamiliar with army methods and frontier life. Sadly, the recruiting results for the levies mirrored that of the regulars.[566]

The reasons behind this lack of success in achieving the desired quantity and quality of recruits are not difficult to discern. Jacobs cites the labor shortage that existed in even the most populous sections of the country. All those willing to work found ready employment. In spite of the $6 enlistment bounty, good men were wary. If they wanted to go west, marching as enlisted men offered the least congenial way. A private's pay of $3 a month was not much of a lure, especially when one-third of it was inevitably deducted for clothing and medical care in addition to that forfeited for lost or damaged equipment. If these drawbacks failed to keep a prospective recruit from signing up, fear of the Indians might. At best, the life of a recruit was hard, made worse by the government's failure to keep implied or direct promises, and pay was always late.[567]

As recruiters had found in previous years, enlistment appealed only to the few or those without hope—aimless drifters, sailors who had missed their ships, prisoners, farm boys or apprentices already worn out by their labors in their present locations. Recruiting parties knew their haunts; they sounded the fife and drum on the village common where the poor and homeless gathered and marched through the main streets and darkened alleys of towns and cities, beating more loudly and blowing more shrilly as they passed noisy inns and whorehouses.

Jacob adds an insightful note that ignorant and indifferent men have in the past been turned into skillful and heroic soldiers through three staples of regular service—able leadership, training, and adequate supplies. Unfortunately, the army of St. Clair lacked all three essentials.[568]

---

[566] Sword, *President Washington's Indian War*, 147.

[567] Jacobs, *The Beginning of the U.S. Army*, 77.

[568] Ibid., 79. Not all recruiters had to rely upon enlisting unsuitable candidates. Lytle notes that officers well known for their Revolutionary War service, including Lt. John Platt recruiting for Capt. Robert Kirkwood of Delaware

In mid-June, Knox advised St. Clair of the projected manpower shortfall and alerted him to the necessity of recruiting militia from the frontier, rendering the entire argument for using levies in preference to the militia moot. Knox suggested calling up mounted militia in the belief that they would be more effective than the usual drafts of infantry, but St. Clair rejected the idea, reasoning that a mounted force was inappropriate on an extended slow-moving expedition. It would also be more expensive. By choosing to ignore the more elite mounted Kentucky volunteers who had proven successful under Scott and Wilkinson in favor of the militia, the same unruly and inept elements were conscripted that had failed in Harmar's campaign. By this decision, St. Clair fatally weakened an army already characterized by inexperience and diminished numbers. Of the eventual 2,418 men participating in the campaign, less than 300, old enlistees from the First Regiment, had military experience.[569]

Jacobs suggests that St. Clair himself was a significant factor in the failure to recruit satisfactory local militia. Kentucky settlers' initial enthusiasm surrounding another military campaign against the marauding tribes quickly waned when they learned that St. Clair was to be in charge. They felt he lacked insight into their problems and was wholly unfit to conduct a war against the Indians. His appointment of Winthrop Sargent, a confirmed Federalist and dour New Englander whom they thought sour and rigid, as secretary of the territory and as the army's adjutant general did nothing to lessen their misgivings. Preferring to follow men like Scott and Wilkinson, they were induced to serve in the campaign only because of their desperate need for protection, hard money, and a keen sense of adventure.[570]

---

and Jonathan Snowdon recruiting in New Jersey, had reputations for successful leadership and achieved rapid results for recruiting for the Second Regiment in their states. See Lytle, *Soldiers of America's First Army*, 45.

[569] Sword, *President Washington's Indian War*, 147–48; Knox to St. Clair, June 23, 1791, *ASP-Indian Affairs*, I: 178; Guthman, *March to Massacre*, 219.

[570] Jacobs, *The Beginning of the U.S. Army*, 75–76. The appointment of Sargent, a civilian, as the army's adjutant general, ruffled even the regular military's feathers. Once regarded as the best-dressed man in the Continental Army— his field kit included pewter plates made by Paul Revere—Sargent had been handpicked by his friend, St. Clair. The governor had to obtain special permission from Knox for Sargent's appointment, as there had been no previous provision for the position. All this was unsettling to the regular

Then there were the delays. As the operation's projected summer starting date drifted into early fall, newly recruited units belatedly filtered into Fort Pitt. Because of the brief training period available before setting out, St. Clair told Butler, who had been delegated to coordinate affairs at that way station, to send the recruits to Fort Washington as soon as they arrived, detaining them just long enough to assemble entire companies. His order provoked a major source of contention, Butler having received conflicting directives from Knox telling him to deploy part of the levies for temporary protection of settlements along the upper Ohio River. This would enable him to dismiss militia from parts of Pennsylvania and Kentucky as well as to assure relief of the settlements of Marietta and Gallipolis downriver.[571]

Butler's mission was additionally hampered by the inability to outfit the troops with basic essentials for the campaign. Contractor William Duer had mismanaged advance funds that had been appropriated for provisions, utilizing them for personal investments, and had sent little or no money to agents at the recruiting rendezvous points and at Fort Pitt. Butler could not, therefore, furnish the new men with their traveling rations, nor did he have any boats available for their transport. Meanwhile, the levies were ripe for dissension. Many officers did not get along with Butler and threatened to resign. The general also saw the strength of the battalions drain away through discharge, smallpox, accidents, and desertions.

Butler's problems did not stop there. Quartermaster Samuel Hodgdon proved incompetent. His almost criminal mismanagement resulted in a shortage of tents, knapsacks, camp kettles, cartridge boxes, and pack saddles. Items forwarded from Philadelphia by the penny-pinching Hodgdon were of poor quality. Pack saddles were unfit for use because they were so large that Butler dubbed them "elephant sized" and could have been procured in Pittsburgh for half the price. Arms that had been forwarded to Fort Pitt had not been properly inspected prior to shipping, and many were unfit for use and required repair before being issued. The

officers, many of whom resented such a politically inspired intrusion. See Sword, *President Washington's Indian War*, 162.

[571] Guthman, *March to Massacre*, 213; Knox to Butler, May 5, 1791, *ASP-Indian Affairs*, I: 186. In 1790, the Scioto Company enlisted French settlers to immigrate to the Ohio Valley. Once there, they discovered that they had been misled and their settlement, Gallipolis, was actually part of the Ohio Company's holdings.

supply of shoes for the levies was so minimal that 2,000 pairs had to be ordered from Philadelphia late in June. The immediate crisis was solved by the purchase of shoes William Duer had on-site, but they proved to be of such poor quality that many did not last more than four days. Amid the confusion, new recruits were held up at all the various rendezvous points, some getting drunk and many deserting.[572]

By July 10, only a few units had made their way to Fort Washington. Armstrong's and Montfort's companies of the First Regiment and Kirkwood's company from the Second Regiment had arrived in mid-June, as well as three small companies of levies; but shortly thereafter, river navigation ceased for a month due to low water levels. By late August, St. Clair's force at headquarters still numbered less than 600 at which time he had to reconcile himself to the use of the militia. Further delay was not an option. Unless the army could begin its march before cold weather set in, operations would have to be canceled until the following year. Such a scenario would be ruinous to an administration counting on a quick victory to retrieve its prestige and to curtail criticism of its Indian policy. Besides, too much money had already been spent on the recruitment, outfitting, and transportation of the levies. Knox began pressuring St. Clair to hurry his preparations.[573]

Accommodations necessary to get the campaign going seemed never ending. When regulars from the First Regiment's other garrisons assembled at Fort Washington and prisoners taken during Scott's raid of the Wea villages were transported from Fort Steuben, new buildings had to be constructed to house them. Gun carriages that had been used in the Harmar expedition were unfit for service, those that came from Philadelphia were worthless, and new ones had to be built. Major Ferguson had arrived with materials with which to make ammunition, but none of it had been prepared ahead of time. A laboratory had to be prepared for

---

[572] Guthman, *March to Massacre*, 213–14; Sword, *President Washington's Indian War*, 48, 150–51; Kohn, *Eagle and Sword*, 114.

[573] Arthur St. Clair, *A Narrative of the Manner in which the Campaign Against the Indians, in the Year One Thousand Seven Hundred and Ninety-one, Was Conducted, Under the Command of Major General St. Clair* (Philadelphia: Jane Aitken, 1812), 10–11; Lytle, *Soldiers of America's First Army*, 48–50; Winthrop Sargent, "Winthrop Sargent's Diary While with General Arthur St. Clair's Expedition Against the Indians," *OAHQ* 33, no. 2, (1924): 239; Kohn, *Eagle and Sword*, 114; *ASP-Military Affairs*, I: 37.

making musket and artillery cartridges as well as howitzer shells. Arms were in bad repair; and axes, camp kettles, canteens, knapsacks, kegs for the musket cartridges, spare cannonballs, and ammunition boxes had to be made. Ropes and cartridge boxes needed repair. Splints for the wounded procured from Philadelphia were useless and new ones had to be devised. All this took a great deal of time and labor since shops had to be built and tools had to be fashioned. The process required men who knew how to do these things—smiths, carpenters, harness makers, wheelwrights—who were not readily available. Fortunately on July 28, a detachment of Maryland levies arrived, among whom were a number of artificers. Men who thought they had enlisted to fight Indians had to be taken away from training in order to build and repair the equipment for the campaign, an occurrence neither to their liking nor to their officers. St. Clair commented that Fort Washington looked as much like a large factory on the inside as it did a military post on the outside.[574]

Horses were too few, and their handling was incompetent. When one hundred arrived from Fort Pitt, they were put ashore on the Kentucky side of the Ohio where pasturage was excellent and raids by Indians unlikely. Within twenty-four hours, seventy went temporarily missing. The forage master, W. Dunn, who was short of both bells and hobbles, knew nothing about his job. At feeding time, the grain was scattered on the ground instead of being placed in troughs. While attempting to ingest the grain, horses injured each other by kicking and biting. Some swallowed dirt and rubbish with their feed and died as a consequence. St. Clair noted that Dunn should have carried a bell himself; otherwise, he'd be unable to find his way out of the woods.[575]

Contractor William Duer and his agent, Israel Ludlow were responsible for accumulating sufficient stores for the frontier garrisons and at the same time feed an army of 2,500 men, a monumental task calling for organization of the first order. Jacobs notes that Duer further complicated the problem by his eagerness for personal profit and a canny unwillingness to take financial risks. Although Knox had assured Butler in June that rations for six months would be available for posts to be established along the line of communication to the Miami towns, by early August, Ludlow complained that he still lacked authority to buy animals to transport

---

[574] Guthman, *March to Massacre*, 214–15; St. Clair, A Narrative, 10–12.

[575] Jacobs, *The Beginning of the U.S. Army*, 82.

provisions. In desperation and by his own authority, St. Clair directed the purchase of 656 horses.[576]

★

On August 7, St. Clair, with approximately two-thirds of the men promised to him, led his untrained and undersupplied army six miles north of the settlement to Ludlow's Station. It was time to move. Five weeks had already passed since the date originally set for the opening of the campaign, and some troops had been on-site for over a month. Fields surrounding Fort Washington had been entirely depleted by foraging livestock. Drunkenness among the recruits had been a significant problem, and troops needed to be further away from the temptations of readily available whiskey and the come-on of passing boatmen needing hands and enticing would-be deserters. Additionally, the army's relationship with the locals had deteriorated after Harmar's campaign. The militia had taken the heat for the expedition's defeat, and interactions between regulars and townspeople were often strained. When discord erupted in July, St. Clair placed Cincinnati under martial law, throwing Judge John Cleves Symmes into a rage. His later correspondence hinted of the town smarting under military control, and he cited eight regimental officers who, in his estimation, had exceeded their authority in the past while under Harmar's command, "beating and imprisoning citizens at their pleasure," among whom was John Armstrong. Moving the army out of Cincinnati seemed the best solution for all concerned.[577]

St. Clair had been the recipient of all these logistical problems with no help from the people he needed most. Butler did not arrive at Fort Washington until September 7, and immediately thereafter, his time and attention as well as that of Lieutenant Colonels William Darke and George Gibson, commanders of the two levy regiments, was consumed by Harmar's court of inquiry, which lasted until September 23. Hodgdon, whose responsibility it was to supply the very equipment that St. Clair

---

[576] Jacobs, *The Beginning of the U.S. Army*, 83–84; Sword, *President Washington's Indian War*, 162.

[577] Jacobs, *The Beginning of the U.S. Army*, 85; John C. Symmes to Jonathan Dayton, August 15, 1791, in Williamson, *History of Western Ohio and Auglaize County*, 42–45. Symmes apparently held no grudges against newly arrived levy officers, whom he felt were looked down upon by the regulars.

needed, finally departed Philadelphia in June but remained at Pitt until he left with Butler and the remainder of the forces. St. Clair's biographer, William Henry Smith, notes,

> There was neither quartermaster nor commissary; the commanding general was both. He was also chief artisan, and superintended the construction and repair of every thing . . . the thousand details incident to the creation and preparation of an armed force, without the means which may be commanded in an old country.[578]

As time ticked away and the commanding general viewed the condition of equipment and quality of his recruits, St. Clair continued to tend to his duties as governor of the territory. His already precarious health and energy suffered as a result. Smith adds,

> But though genius were never more fruitful and energy more tireless, yet even St. Clair found it impossible to improve the quality of the powder; to make an elephantine pack-saddle fit the back of an Indian pony; to transform raw lines into veteran soldiers in a week; make honest men out of rogues; nor by command, similar to that of Joshua of old, stop the sun in its course and delay the revolutions of the seasons.[579]

The problems of the campaign to come were not lost on its officers. John Armstrong wrote his friend Francis Johnston from Ludlow's Station, noting that the start of the expedition was already a month late, that Butler and the rest of that army had not arrived, and that he presumed that St. Clair would have to rely on the Kentucky militia as the strongest part of the army. He added that the cavalry horses sent from Pittsburgh were already worn out and blamed the army's quartermaster Samuel Hodgdon for the campaign's delays. "He is not yet arrived & you know the movements of an Army depend much on his exertions, whether he wants abilities or inclination I cant determine but there is a deficiency some where."[580]

---

[578] Smith, The St. Clair Papers, I: 172.

[579] Ibid.

[580] Armstrong to Johnston, August 30, 1791, PJA.

Before St. Clair departed for Kentucky to collect additional militia on September 1, he instructed Major Hamtramck, now commander of the First Regiment, to move his troops to the site of the first intermediary fort to be built as soon as surveyors marked an appropriate route to follow. Bad weather delayed the regiment's departure from Ludlow's Station until September 8, and it took three days for it to march eighteen miles to the appointed spot on the Great Miami River. In a foreshadowing of problems to come, the men had to cut their way through swamp and heavy timber with few good axes. To keep them serviceable, soldiers continuously operated forge and grindstone. After enormous labor on the part of the men, a way was finally opened through the forest for carts, wagons, packhorses, and artillery.[581]

By September 19, the First Regiment, probably including Armstrong's men, had begun construction of the garrison that St. Clair would name Fort Hamilton and completed it by September 30. With only 100 axes available when at least 1,000 were needed, soldiers had to take turns using the equipment, causing a delay in the fort's estimated construction time.[582]

Upon his return from Kentucky, St. Clair was relieved to learn of the arrival of not only the remainder of troops from Fort Pitt but also that of Butler, Hodgdon, and Gibson. The campaign could now get underway. The newly arrived troops departed Ludlow's Station a mere seven days later as the army began its journey northward. Led by a fifty-seven year old general afflicted with gout and harassed by a host of worries and apprehensions, it was largely an untrained patchwork of the urban unfortunate, would-be adventurers, and dirt-poor settlers with a smattering of military professionals thrown into the mix. Few realized what they were up against. They would soon face an enemy possessing a minute knowledge of the woods, streams, and trails that lay ahead of them and who were experts in the type of fighting in such terrain. Confident in

---

[581] St. Clair to Hamtramck, August 30, 1791, *SCP*, II: 239–40; Sargent, "Winthrop Sargent's Diary," 240. Considerable coming and going of regimental officers between the construction site and Fort Washington must have taken place since most were called upon to testify at General Harmar's court of inquiry at some time from September 15–23. Jacobs, *The Beginning of the U.S. Army*, 87, describes the construction of Fort Hamilton.

[582] Guthman, *March to Massacre*, 218.

the wisdom of their chiefs and hungry for revenge, the army's foes bided their time waiting for just the right conditions to strike.[583]

Josiah Harmar, seeking to make a quiet departure from Fort Washington, delayed his journey eastward until the conclusion of his court of inquiry and the exodus of troops. Before leaving, he shared his thoughts with his aide, Lt. Ebenezer Denny who recorded:

> He saw with what material the bulk of the army was composed; men collected from the streets and prisons of the cities, hurried out into the enemy's country, and with officers commanding them, totally unacquainted with the business in which they were engaged, it was utterly impossible they could be otherwise. Besides, not any one department was sufficiently prepared; both quartermaster and contractors extremely deficient. It was a matter of astonishment to him that the commanding general, who was acknowledged to be perfectly competent, should think of hazarding, with such people, and under such circumstances, his reputation and life, and the lives of so many others, knowing too, as both did, the enemy with whom he was going to contend.[584]

[583] Jacobs, *The Beginning of the U.S. Army*, 84.
[584] Denny, *Military Journal*, 170.

13

Massacre on the Wabash, 1791

A knowledge of the collected force and situation of
the enemy; of this we were perfectly ignorant.
—Ebenezer Denny[585]

St. Clair remained at Fort Hamilton only long enough to see it completed before returning to Fort Washington on October 2 to greet Lt. Col. William Oldham, commander of the Kentucky militia. Recruitment had been disappointing; Oldham arrived with fewer than half of the expected 750 men whom St. Clair immediately sent northward to join the army. Their arrival was heralded by the usual sarcasm, particularly among the regulars for whom the memory of Harmar's ill-fated expedition was deep-seated. An undercurrent of skepticism ran through the army, especially when it became evident that many of the conscripts were old and "by no means woodsmen." Because of their unreliability they were not assigned regular duties, and their presence added to the deteriorating climate of St. Clair's army. Dissension arose between regular and levied officers and schisms festered within the army's command. No basis for seniority had been established between levy colonels William Darke and George Gibson, causing a heated dispute between the two. Darke was ultimately given seniority based on his previous army service, but the roughhewn Virginian had already earned the enmity of many regulars

---

585 Denny, *Military Journal*, 171.

305

for his lack of professionalism. They likewise objected to the presence of civilian Adjutant General Winthrop Sargent, chafing at his austere disposition, haughty demeanor, and stern demands. Even St. Clair admitted Sargent was "very obnoxious" to them.[586]

In St. Clair's absence, Maj. Gen. Richard Butler marched the army northward from Fort Hamilton to the site of the next projected fortification. Troops departed Fort Hamilton on October 4 leaving behind a garrison mostly of "convalescents or men improper for actual service." Before returning to Fort Washington, St. Clair issued explicit instructions regarding the cutting of two parallel roads through the forest, adhering to his belief that the arrangement afforded greater flexibility for defense in the case of attack, but Butler soon discovered that the task was impossible. The poorly equipped army was moving through a virgin forest of white ash and white oak trees two to six feet in diameter standing 50 to 80 feet high. After fording the waist-high and rapidly flowing waters of the Great Miami and enduring cold and intermittent rain, the army managed only to advance a mile and a half through the wilderness on the first day. Axes were so improperly tempered that they dulled rapidly. Only ten men were assigned to each work detail with relief granted every two hours. Even the promise of an extra ration of liquor failed to speed the road-cutting process. After one day's march, Butler modified St. Clair's order, deciding to cut one rather than two roads. Butler's modification yielded a slight improvement, but after four days the army had covered only about 22 miles.[587]

James Ripley Jacobs describes the scene of the ponderously moving force. Fall had by now set in, the forest leaves had begun to turn yellow, goldenrod was turning brown, and the ill-clad soldiers occasionally shivered in the chill autumn air. Because the campaign had not been able to attract competent frontiersmen or Indians as guides, the surveyors and riflemen set out first, traveling far ahead on a compass bearing to mark out the road. Next came the woodcutters with an armed detachment for protection. The advance party and the main body of troops followed, divided into two columns with ten pieces of artillery spaced throughout. A small detail of troops followed to protect drovers herding rawboned

---

[586] Guthman, *March to Massacre*, 222–23; Sword, *President Washington's Indian War*, 160, 162.

[587] Sword, *President Washington's Indian War*, 161; Wilson, Journal of Capt. Daniel Bradley, 21, http://oldnorthwestindianwar.blogspot.com/p/daniel-bradley-was-not-militiaman-he.html; St. Clair, *A Narrative*, 16.

cattle, 656 heavily laden contractor-supplied packhorses transporting provisions, and 300 army-owned horses carrying supplies. The main body of cavalry reconnoitered the flanks. Farther out, a detachment of riflemen filtered through the woods, preceded by selected scouts moving swiftly but cautiously. A rear guard protected the tail of the long column. As the enormous caravan lumbered through the otherwise quiet wilderness, the noisy, cumbersome army plodded along accompanied by the sounds of trees being cut ahead, drums rolling behind, hungry horses neighing, and cattle bellowing. Profanity dotted the air as herders swore at livestock and soldiers swore at their officers who swore back at them.[588]

For the next ten days, the army slogged through woods, swamps, and open stretches of plain, seldom covering more than six miles a day. As time went on, fatigue increased, signs of Indians became more frequent, and desertions became epidemic. Patrols and messengers had to be selected with care; men assigned to such details too often failed to return. Detachments of recruits arrived periodically, but their quality and appearance afforded little encouragement to their officers. All that kept these and many others with the army was their terror of the Indians, their dread of one hundred lashes as punishment for attempted desertion, and the hardships they would undergo in trying to navigate homeward through the forbidding, all-encircling wilderness.[589]

Added to the scene were the camp followers, estimated at some stages of the march to be upward of 200 men, women, and children. St. Clair was accompanied by a Wea youth whom he called Billy to serve as a messenger. Major Heart and Captains Shaylor and Newman had their sons with them. Included in the number were civilian employees managing livestock and conveyance of supplies. Four women were usually allowed per company to wash, cook, clean, or mend for its soldiers. That estimate of 136 to 152 women was further increased by those who worked the same jobs for contractor and quartermaster employees. Many others were doubtlessly present, including wives of officers, noncommissioned officers, and men. Jacobs notes that militia units were prone to take with them whomever they pleased. Some women carried babies, others were pregnant. Regardless of the part they played in the operation, all imposed an added burden on the

---

[588] Jacobs, *The Beginning of the U.S. Army*, 88; Sword, *President Washington's Indian War*, 162–63.

[589] Jacobs, *The Beginning of the U.S. Army*, 89.

contractor in providing rations as the line of communications continually lengthened.[590]

When St. Clair and his staff rendezvoused with the army on the evening of October 8, the general fumed at its lack of progress. Wiley Sword notes that the relationship between Butler and St. Clair, decidedly cool following the delay of troops on the upper Ohio, now assumed a new acerbity. When Butler attempted to explain his reasons for altering St. Clair's directive to cut two parallel roads, the latter was abrupt and icy. Deeply offended by St. Clair's attitude, Butler withdrew from any contact with headquarters other than that of a perfunctory nature and purposely avoided his commander's presence.[591]

Force strength prior to the beginning of the expedition in late September was 2,300 men with the expectation of additional militia, but its numbers had already begun to decline. Men were already deserting, an observation easily made by Tecumseh's spies quietly observing the army's progress from behind cover. Worrying more about where he was going and how he was going to get there, St. Clair apparently did not give his enemy's plans a second thought.[592]

St. Clair was chagrined to find the climate of his command increasingly rancorous and was even more alarmed to discover the supply system in such a dire condition. When passing through Fort Hamilton, he found that the expected quantity of rations to be stored at the garrison had not been delivered. Although he fired off a blistering letter to the contractor's agent, the situation did not materially improve. By October 12, the army's supply of flour, issued as rations to every soldier for making bread, was down to only three days. Additionally, despite the procurement of 656 packhorses in September, the situation barely a month later was a cause for alarm. The

---

[590] Jacobs, *The Beginning of the U.S. Army*, 89–90; Richard M. Lytle, *Soldiers of the First American Army*, 71. Some wives were believed to have accompanied their husbands' units only to Fort Hamilton. It appears likely, however, that most did not. Thomas Irvin, waggoneer for an artillery carriage, noted that St. Clair had issued an order prohibiting nonessential women from proceeding with the army, but that many disregarded the order. When the men began crossing the river, the women did as well and later rode on the artillery carriages, some astride the cannons. See McBride, *Pioneer Biography*, I: 154.

[591] Sword, *President Washington's Indian War*, 161.

[592] Guthman, *March to Massacre*, 227–28; Knox to Washington, September 24, 1791, in Smith, *SCP* II: 232; St. Clair, *A Narrative*, 63.

dwindling number of horses was directly traceable to the horsemaster's negligence and incompetence. The situation got worse with the arrival of cold weather and diminished forage. Already weak and emaciated, they died so rapidly, said one soldier, that nearly every prairie and swamp was littered with their carcasses.[593]

★

The army arrived at the site chosen for the second fort forty-four miles above Fort Hamilton on October 12. Work began two days later in cold rain and hail. Because good axes were still scarce, only 200 men were assigned to the work detail while the rest of the army generally languished in the small leaky tents, mistakenly procured on Knox's advice that heavy tents would be improper for rapid marching. Soaked to the skin, so many men were sick from exposure and insufficient rations that St. Clair began to doubt if the campaign could continue. The clothing issued to the levies was in tatters, shirts shrank to the point they were almost useless, and shoes purchased from Duer's stock continued to fall apart. Moreover, there was uncertainty about ammunition since musket cartridges were soaked by rain in the leaky storage tents.[594]

The army was unable to move until the completion of the new Fort Jefferson on October 24. During its construction, the problems inherent in venturing increased distances from Fort Washington became evident. Leaders were faced with the grim reality that the distance the army could advance depended on remaining within reach of a supply convoy, a problem that eventually defined the entire campaign. By October 19, the supply of flour was critically low. As a result, troops were put on half rations. Lt. Ebenezer Denny also noted that all the army's horses, quartermaster's as well as contractor's, had been sent back to transport provisions.

St. Clair had assigned nearly all the 300 army-owned baggage horses to the contractor, and when the army moved again, the troops had to leave behind anything, including clothing and personal items, that could not be carried in a knapsack.[595]

---

[593] Sword, *President Washington's Indian War*, 162; *ASP-Military Affairs*, I: 37; *SCP*: II, 246–47.

[594] Sword, *President Washington's Indian War*, 163.

[595] Denny, *Military Journal* of Ebenezer Denny, 157; Sword, *President Washington's Indian War*, 163.

———

The men had long since tired of receiving irregular rations and the bad weather. When the levies' six-month enlistments began to expire, necessitating the dismissal of entire companies, large numbers of militia began deserting. St. Clair, nagged with fear that his army would break up with the departure of the levy regiments, vowed to push on. Sword notes that not only did St. Clair want to get them into action by November 3 when they would all begin leaving, he was also determined to progress further into hostile territory, making their departure less appealing.[596]

Although light frost had dotted the landscape since October 4, severe frost was now discernable in the morning sun. Denny wrote that the night of October 20 had gotten so cold that ice nearly one-half-inch thick had formed on the water. Livestock handlers were forced to search for uncompromised pastureland on which the horses and cattle could graze during the day, and the men gathered grass for them to consume at night.[597]

A shipment of flour and cattle arrived on October 22, finally allowing the army to resume its advance. Butler, concerned that the entire slow-moving force was taking too long to reach its ultimate destination, requested permission to lead one thousand men ahead to the Miami villages to start constructing a post there. St. Clair refused.[598]

On the following day, the nearly completed Fort Jefferson, stocked with two cannons, was turned over to Captain Shaylor of the Second Regiment in command of ninety men, most of whom were too ill to continue the march, a number that would soon be augmented by another thirty sick men, women, and children who would remain at the garrison when the army advanced. Instead of conducting a ceremonial dedication of the fort, St. Clair ordered all soldiers to assemble to witness an execution. The general had imposed the death penalty on three men to restore a measure of discipline and apparently felt at this point that examples had to be made to discourage further desertions. Two condemned men were artillerymen from the First Regiment who, having stolen their officers' horses and some of their clothing, were caught trying to desert to the British; and the third was a levy who had murdered a fellow soldier and threatened the life of an officer. Initially, there had been three men from the First Regiment charged with desertion, one of whom Private William

[596] Denny, *Military Journal*, 157; Sword, *President Washington's Indian War*, 165.

[597] Denny, *Military Journal*, 157–58.

[598] Sword, *President Washington's Indian War*, 165.

May was in Armstrong's company and may have been his orderly. May escaped with his life, being sentenced to receive one hundred lashes at five different times. Ironically, May, whom many regarded as the instigator of the plot and whose character Sargent described as "infamous," was tasked with a specific mission the following year that provided vital information to the government.[599]

The army, through discharge, desertion, disease, and detachment, was now composed of 1,770 noncommissioned officers and privates as it filed out of Fort Jefferson on October 24. Signs of recent Indian encampments dotted the area, which Sargent attributed to hunting parties. Denny recorded that St. Clair had been ill for some time and on that day was scarcely able to accompany the army.[600]

Soldiers remained encamped in the rainy, damp weather for the next five days to allow a detachment of fifty militiamen to march with the surveying party to explore the country ahead and to await a shipment of flour. Indians began to be sighted, decreasing the possibility of a surprise attack upon the Miami villages. Sargent recorded that he considered the mission now impossible to continue due to the impending dismissal of the levies and the likely departure of the militia to follow but that St. Clair continued to insist upon moving on in order to keep the army intact.[601]

Relief came to the stalled army on October 28. Seventy-four horses arrived, carrying twelve thousand pounds of flour and providing four days of rations as well as clothing for the First Regiment. Regimental officers were directed to fill vacancies in their ranks with levies, and the promise of new clothing enticed forty to enlist. Increased sightings of Indians prompted commanders to direct troops to be under arms from the morning's first drumbeat.[602]

At this point, seventy-four miles from Fort Washington, John Armstrong estimated that the force was still some forty miles from the

---

[599] Sargent, "Winthrop Sargent's Diary," *OAHQ*, 247–48; Newman, "Captain Newman's Original Journal of St. Clair's Campaign," 71–72; Lytle, *The Soldiers of America's First Army*, 80; Sword, *President Washington's Indian War*, 165.

[600] St. Clair, *A Narrative*, 63; Denny, *Military Journal*, 159; *ASP-Military Affairs*, I: 37; Sargent, "Winthrop Sargent's Diary," 248.

[601] Sargent, "Winthrop Sargent's Diary," 248–50; Denny, *Military Journal*, 159–60.

[602] Denny, *Military Journal*, 160.

Miami villages. Like Denny and Sargent, he expressed doubt that they could reach their destination in the current season but that St. Clair was determined to do so. In his letter to his friend Richard C. Anderson, he noted that prospects for provisions were poor and the horses worn down from fatigue and want of forage. Levies sued daily for their discharges, and he expected that three or four companies would leave in a few days, followed by others. He continued,

> I pray God that should the General proceed the Ennemy may not be disposed to give us battle. Our force does not exceed sixteen hundred and they the worst and most dissatisfied troops I ever served with. The Federal troops altho under some discipline are chiefly recruits unaccustomed with the use of fire arms, or the yells of Savages. Figure therefore to yourself what will be the consequence of a serious attack.[603]

The army advanced again on Sunday, October 30, and marched six miles, the men carrying rations for three days so that remaining horses could transport baggage. In the meantime, a party of Chickasaws, newly arrived from Fort Washington and longtime enemies of the western tribes, had been sent out on an extended reconnaissance patrol. St. Clair had been so ill that he had to be carried on a litter. Denny doubted that the general would be able to proceed.[604]

After one day's march, the army stopped again for two days to await provisions. The horses that were to carry the army's baggage were unable to do so, and a portion of it had to be left on the road, causing part of the corps to endure the night's violent storm and wind without their tents. The militia was by now totally out of control; between sixty to seventy men marched off, threatening to stop an expected supply train. Then on October 31, St. Clair made what turned out to be the most pivotal decision of the campaign; he dispatched the entire First Regiment to pursue the deserters to protect the oncoming convoys. By this action, the army lost at one stroke three hundred of its best troops and the only ones who had

---

[603] Armstrong to Anderson, October 28, 1791, PJA.

[604] Denny, *Military Journal*, 160–61; Sargent, "Winthrop Sargent's Diary," 250.

prior experience in Indian warfare. Ironically, the first convoy arrived that evening, and a second was expected within a few days.[605]

The army again set off on November 2 and covered seventeen miles in two days despite rain and light snow. Increased numbers of Indians were sighted, but riflemen pursued them with little success. The command now felt that they were observing scouting parties rather than experiencing chance encounters with Indians hunting for game.

★

Events the following evening set the stage for impending disaster. Disagreement over an appropriate campsite caused the army to march almost until dark. The only high ground available was not large enough to accommodate the entire army, so the militia camped across a nearby creek, the upper reaches of the Wabash River. Due to the lateness of the hour, defensive works were not built. The Kentucky militia, now openly defiant and unresponsive to their officers' orders, complained they were too fatigued and refused to leave the camp to join the main body. The army, already reduced in size, had separated its units. The men were hungry, exhausted, and cold. Having collapsed in a location surrounded by good cover, they were completely exposed because no defensive measures had been taken. The tactical mistake the Indians had patiently waited for had now been made, and the waiting warriors silently began moving into attack positions throughout the dark night.[606]

That evening, Capt. Jacob Slough of the Pennsylvania levies was directed to lead twenty-three men to apprehend Indians believed to have been stealing horses. About a mile from the army's encampment, Slough and his men, concealed in the bush, observed multiple parties of Indians. Slough decided to return to camp and, once back within the lines, reported to Colonel Oldham, the Kentucky militia commander, who agreed with him that an Indian attack was imminent. Oldham told the captain to report his findings immediately to St. Clair. Slough, however, went first to Butler's tent. Awakening the general, Slough asked if he should relay

---

[605] Denny, *Military Journal*, 162–63; Sargent, "Winthrop Sargent's Diary," 251.

[606] Denny, *Military Journal*, 163–65; Sargent, "Winthrop Sargent's Diary," 252–53; Guthman, *March to Massacre*, 234.

his findings to St. Clair. Butler dismissed the captain, telling him to go to bed. St. Clair never received the report.[607]

It was a cold, restless night. Sargent heard about fifty shots fired by sentinels, surmising that some were perhaps directed at an enemy but the rest fired for no particular reason. Meanwhile, Little Turtle and his war chiefs were making their final plan for an early morning attack. While the soldiers slept fitfully, Little Turtle massed his warriors, Wyandots on the right; Ottawas, Chippewas, and Potawatomis on the left; and the Indians most directly threatened by St. Clair, the Shawnees, Delawares, and Miamis, in the center.[608]

The attack came after parade the next morning. Still one-half hour before sunrise, the men had been dismissed, many going back to their tents or huddling around fires preparing breakfast. First came the yells, described by Sargent as an "infinitude of horse-bells" lasting for about five minutes. An ominous quiet followed. Then a burst of musket fire and the whistling drone of bullets broke the silence as hundreds of screaming warriors rushed out of the woods and quickly overran the army pickets, reaching the militia units first. Sargent recorded that they barely had time to get off one shot and ran "helter-skelter" into the main camp, followed closely by their assailants.[609]

Advancing in irregular lines, the warriors demonstrated clearly defined tactics. Filing to the right and to the left, they completely surrounded the camp, killing and cutting off nearly all the guards. Moving quickly from one tree, log, or stump to the next, they approached under cover of the smoke-filled musket fire. Artillery and returning gunfire from the soldiers made a tremendous noise but produced little positive effect. The left flank gave way first, but a reformed line managed to push the aggressors back. St. Clair, adrenaline pumping through his gout-ravaged body, led the charge himself. Lieutenant Colonel Darke mounted a charge with part of the second line to drive the warriors westward across the stream but was unable to sustain this temporary advantage. In the end, troops fell back, and the advancing Delaware and Shawnee closed in again.[610]

---

[607] Guthman, *March to Massacre*, 236–37.

[608] Cayton, *Frontier Indiana*, 159; Sargent, "Winthrop Sargent's Diary," 257.

[609] Jacobs, *The Beginning of the U.S. Army*, 105; Sargent, "Winthrop Sargent's Diary," 258. See also Lytle, *The Soldiers of America's First Army*, 91–108 and Sword, *President Washington's Indian War*, 176–88.

[610] Jacobs, *The Beginning of the U.S. Army*, 107.

Three separate charges were made in rapid succession by troops from the Second Regiment and available levy and militia companies. Many men followed their officers without flinching, using bayonets and gun butts to drive the Indians from cover; but valor alone could not suffice as the casualties began to mount steadily. After each rush forward, they had to fall back once more; and each time, the ring of hostile fire that encircled the camp grew smaller.[611]

In some parts of the perimeter, the Indians played a game of "cat and mouse" with the defenders. Forced back into cover by musket fire, they returned again and again, often skipping out of bayonet reach and then advancing again. The wounded were taken to a central location within the camp where the men who had panicked at the onset of the attack had crowded together.[612]

Already reduced in number by Darke's earlier charge, the Second Regiment, many of whose members had never before fired so much as a blank cartridge, remained the only sizeable body available to face the crisis that was unfolding along the line facing the Wabash. Here, the mounting pressure on the thin blue line near the artillery produced a near massacre. Little Turtle had appointed his son-in-law, William Wells, and a handpicked group of Miamis to kill the gunners manning St. Clair's eight cannons. It was now apparent they would soon be overrun, and in desperation, another bayonet charge led by Second Regiment commander Maj. Jonathan Heart was launched to save the artillery. Maj. Thomas Butler, brother of the major general, had already been wounded in the leg. Propped up on horseback so he could continue to fight, he joined his battalion of Pennsylvania levies. Charging directly into the center of the Indians' crescent formation, Heart's and Butler's men were devastated by tremendous fire. Heart was killed almost immediately; Butler, on horseback, was such an easy target that he was hit soon after the charge began. Only three officers of the Second Regiment escaped death that day, one of whom was badly wounded.[613]

The artillery pieces so laboriously transported nearly one hundred miles overland produced a great volume of noise but did little to frighten

---

[611] Ibid.

[612] Denny, *Military Journal*, 165–66.

[613] Sword, *President Washington's Indian War*, 184; Jacobs, *The Beginning of the U.S. Army*, 107; Lytle, *The Soldiers of America's First Army*, 94.

the Indians or to provide tactical advantage. The gun crews were quickly obliterated, and their replacements fared no better; at one location, the bodies of men working the guns were piled to the height of the cannon muzzles.[614]

Officers were singled out in an effort to destroy discipline and coordination. Richard Butler fell while moving down the lines directing his men. When the attack began, St. Clair was not yet in his uniform. He wore a rough blanket coat and a three-cornered hat; and by the end of the day, eight balls had passed through his clothes, and one had grazed the side of his face. Two horses he attempted to ride were shot down, along with his orderly.[615]

As the enemy fire continued with unabated fury, men were falling in every part of the camp. In his work *Pioneer Biography: Sketches of the Lives of Some of the Early Settlers of Butler County, Ohio*, James McBride relates Thomas Irvin's description of the battlefield. Stationed near the cannons, Irvin witnessed the ground covered with the bodies of the dead and dying, freshly scalped heads steaming in the cold morning air. The ravine ran with blood.[616]

Men became disoriented and bewildered. While the battle raged in one place, bizarre scenes unfolded in others. Soldiers could be seen grouped together around the fires, doing nothing but presenting convenient targets for the enemy. At one point, dazed men broke into officer marquees and ate the breakfasts abandoned by the men who had been called into battle. Officers attempted to rouse the wandering soldiers with little success. St. Clair drew his pistol, swearing to shoot anyone who refused to fight. Women who had taken shelter in the center of the encampment tried to goad the men with their angry taunts. In the course of a few hours, nearly

---

[614] Jacobs, *The Beginning of the U.S. Army*, 106; Lytle, *The Soldiers of America's First Army*, 96.

[615] Sword, *President Washington's Indian War*, 180; Jacobs, *The Beginning of the U.S. Army*, 108–09.

Jacobs notes that the Indians admired Butler for his dauntless courage. After gaining possession of the camp, they secured his body, cut out his heart, and devoured it in the hope of acquiring some of his valorous qualities. Sargent details other instances of bravery among the men, both the fallen and survivors. "Winthrop Sargent's Diary," 266-69.

[616] McBride, *Pioneer Biography*, I: 167–68.

all of them would be butchered, their bodies mutilated. Only three of the known thirty-three present are believed to have escaped.[617]

★

Denny noted that the battle lasted between two to three hours, and it was after 9:00 a.m. when the order for retreat was given. By gathering the remnants from several battalions and forming them into one body, a few officers led the effort to escape by executing a charge with themselves in front and the men following. A surprised enemy gave way, and for a few minutes, the retreating mass was left undisturbed. Soon recovering, warriors pursued the fleeing soldiers for about four to five miles before returning to plunder the field of battle. He recorded later, "Delay was death; no preparation could be made; numbers of brave men must be left a sacrifice, there was no alternative."[618]

"The conduct of the army after quitting the ground was in a most supreme degree disgraceful," wrote Sargent. "Arms, ammunition and accoutrements were almost all thrown away, and even the officers in some instances divested themselves of the fusees and cartridge boxes." Men were literally running for their lives. Sword describes a case of one harried fugitive who found that because so many arms with fixed bayonets had been discarded by the men ahead of him, he had difficulty avoiding being stabbed as he ran through the brush. It took Denny and other officers on horseback two hours to reach the front of the body where they attempted to bring it to a halt. Not entirely successful, they at least formed a semblance of a moving blockade to slow it down and bring the retreat under control.[619]

Accounts of the twenty-nine-mile retreat to Fort Jefferson are fraught with tales of sheer misery. Benjamin Van Cleve, who ran provisions with the packhorse train, described running and pulling an injured boy for two miles until he was finally able to put him on a horse that already had two men on it. He fell behind because of a leg cramp and was within one hundred yards of the rear where pursuers were tomahawking wounded men

---

[617] Sargent, "Winthrop Sargent's Diary," 268; Jacobs, *The Beginning of the U.S. Army*, 109.

[618] Denny, *Military Journal*, 167; McBride, *Pioneer Biography* I: 169; Sargent, "Winthrop Sargent's Diary," 261.

[619] Denny, *Military Journal*, 167; Sargent, "Winthrop Sargent's Diary," 262; Sword, *President Washington's Indian War*, 189.

trying to keep up with the retreating army. He stopped to tie a handkerchief around a man's knee and saw the Indians coming closer. He threw off his shoes, found that the cold ground renewed his energy, and began to run again. After passing about a half-dozen men, he figured that it was safe to slow down and fell in with Ensign Shambaugh, a First Regiment officer who had manned and then spiked artillery before retreating, and with Corporal Mott and a woman known as "Red-Headed Nance." Both were crying, Mott lamenting the loss of his wife and Nance her infant child. Shambaugh was nearly exhausted and held on to Mott's arm. Van Cleve carried the officer's fusee and accoutrements and led Nance. The foursome hung together for the rest of the journey, arriving at Fort Jefferson a little after sunset.[620]

For St. Clair's shattered army, with nearly two-thirds of its personnel and all of its equipment lost, the trek back to Fort Jefferson was an excruciating ordeal. Ice "as thick as a knife blade" filled the ruts, and slushy snow lingered in the shaded areas. Many men were shoeless. Others, having limped from the battlefield following the earlier action, were found crawling and staggering along the road with the blood oozing from their scalped heads. William Darke, his wounded thigh so sore and stiff that he could scarcely move, found the agony of the retreat beyond description. Maj. Thomas Butler, with one leg broken and the other mangled by a gunshot wound, was saved when his brother Edward ripped up his own shirt to staunch the flow of blood. Carried by three alternating stragglers and Edward, Thomas found each step such torment that he cried out to be left on the ground and allowed to die. At last, a lone mounted dragoon was persuaded to take the wounded major behind him, but the lack of medicine and provisions at Fort Jefferson necessitated a continuation of the painful march. Butler had to wait to receive adequate treatment until he reached Fort Washington six days later.[621]

Abandoning their pursuit of the fleeing army after a few miles, Little Turtle and Blue Jacket's victorious warriors returned to the battlefield to

---

[620] Lytle, *The Soldiers of America's First Army*, 173; Beverley W. Bond Jr, ed., "Memoirs of Benjamin Van Cleve," *Quarterly Publication of the Historical and Philosophical Society of Ohio* 27, nos. 1 and 2 (1922), 27 (*QPHPSO*); Catherine Miller was known as "Red-Headed Nance" because of her long flowing auburn hair. Her abandoned baby was reportedly recovered by the Indians and raised in a Sandusky village. Sword, *President Washington's Indian War*, 190.

[621] Sword, *President Washington's Indian War*, 190–91.

inspect their captured booty, including 1,200 muskets and bayonets, 8 cannons, and the personal possessions and uniforms of the officers. In their triumph, they tortured and burned wounded men and prisoners and mutilated and dismembered the dead. Propped up against a tree, Maj. Gen. Butler, who as a commissioner in the 1780s had repeatedly explained to Indian nations how Americans owned the land of the Northwest by right of conquest, found death in the form of a tomahawk to his skull. His scalp would be carefully dried and preserved, so that it might be sent to Joseph Brant to chide him for his absence. Nearby lay the remains of St. Clair's army, cold and unmoving. In mock tribute to the greed of the white man, the victorious warriors crammed earth into the mouths of the slain Americans, occupying only in death the land they had sought to conquer.[622]

When they discovered that the convoy they were to intercept had not yet been sent forward, Major Hamtramck and the First Regiment returned northward. Having encamped during the night near Fort Jefferson, they had passed that garrison the next morning when they heard distant cannon fire. Hamtramck ordered the regiment to proceed with muskets loaded and bayonets fixed. They marched several miles before encountering retreating militiamen who told of the army's disaster. Shaken and uncertain of what to do, the major decided to retreat to Fort Jefferson, sending Lieutenant Kersey forward with a small detachment to meet the body of the retreating army and to learn what had happened. Hamtramck reasoned that if the army was indeed defeated, Fort Jefferson would be the nearest point of refuge, and it must be secured.[623]

As the bedraggled remnants of the army staggered into the crowded garrison, St. Clair called a meeting of officers and took stock of what had happened that day. It was evident that more than half of the army had been killed or wounded. It was also clear that conditions at the fort were dreadful. One officer wrote that as soldiers straggled through the gates in broken clusters throughout the late afternoon and into the evening of November 4, the chaotic scene was horrid beyond description. The compound offered little respite for the forlorn, defeated men. There was nothing to eat; the fort was reduced to a single day's flour ration and was

---

[622] Cayton, *Frontier Indiana*, 160–61; Sword, *President Washington's Indian War*, 191.

[623] Denny, *Military Journal*, 168. Hamtramck's decision was not without controversy. Darke later unsuccessfully charged Hamtramck with abandoning the retreating men, many of whom were wounded and might easily have been saved. Sword, *President Washington's Indian War*, 190.

entirely without meat. With the expectation that pursuing warriors would soon attack the post and possibly cut off the convoy that was now on its way from Fort Hamilton, St. Clair decided that the army had to retreat southward, leaving only the badly wounded and a small detachment at Fort Jefferson.[624]

Heading out into the frigid darkness at 10:00 p.m., the ragtag exhausted force kept moving throughout the night. Staggering soldiers in the drawn-out procession had not eaten for twenty-four hours, had engaged in a three-hour battle while seeing their comrades meet their deaths, had fled for their own lives covering twenty-nine miles to Fort Jefferson, and now had begun an all-night march. Snow that fell two days earlier had since melted, and the ground was covered with ice about an eighth of an inch thick. Men splashing through water and ice in the darkness and stumbling over tree roots could hardly keep up. Some fell out on the side of the trail to rest even though they had neither blankets nor shelter from the cold. Finally, at around dawn on November 5, St. Clair agreed to stop until the expected convoy arrived.[625]

Fortunately, the information concerning the pack train was correct. The convoy reached the famished troops at about nine that morning, and rations were issued to the men to sustain them until they reached Fort Hamilton. A fire was soon kindled and ash cakes prepared. Remaining provisions were sent on to Fort Jefferson under a full company escort. Then in the early afternoon, the weary troops resumed their retreat southward.

Armstrong was with the First Regiment when it was sent south on October 31 to meet the supply train and would have supported the wounded and worn-out men on their trek from Fort Jefferson to Fort Hamilton. Accounts of the evacuation lend credence to family lore concerning Armstrong's part in the operation. His company was covering the rear. Armstrong, having dismounted so his horse could carry two men, spotted Capt. John S. Gano seated on a log. The two men dismounted the horse and placed the exhausted Gano astride. By alternating opportunities between the three men to ride along the route, the party made its way to safety. If he hadn't known Gano before aiding him on the journey south, the encounter was indeed fortuitous, as the territorial army officer who had surveyed the campaign's route, a future Hamilton County official

---

[624] Sword, *President Washington's Indian War*, 192; Denny, *Military Journal* 169.

[625] Lytle, *Soldiers of America's First Army*, 112; McBride, *Pioneer Biography*: I: 170.

and an Ohio militia major general, was surely instrumental a short time later in introducing Armstrong to his future wife. He became Armstrong's brother-in-law a little more than a year later.

St. Clair reached Fort Hamilton the morning of the November 7 and immediately dispatched Capt. Joseph Montfort and a sizable part of that garrison to Fort Jefferson with as many medical supplies as were on hand. By noon, the fort was ready to receive the remainder of the survivors, and arrivals found soldiers at Fort Hamilton waiting to distribute food and available supplies. Sargent reported that most of the First Regiment accompanying the wounded had straggled in by evening. In only two days, the massacre's survivors traveled a distance that had previously taken them an entire month to negotiate.[626]

Arriving levies and militia soon discovered that Fort Hamilton was not the last stop. Both were generally out of control, and Fort Washington was a better choice for their immediate relocation. Remnants of St. Clair's army set out for headquarters, leaving the garrison under the command of Captain Armstrong with fifty men of the First Regiment. Armstrong would hold that command for the greater portion of the following year.[627]

★

A motley caravan of militia and levies eventually made it to the banks of the Ohio the next afternoon. There, the full extent of the disaster became obvious. A staggering 55 percent of the American combatants had become casualties; the dead and missing numbered 630 by Denny's count. Three-fourths of the entire Second Regiment had been lost. Of approximately 1,400 persons present at the battle, fewer than 500 remained uninjured, and many of the survivors were noncombatants. The officer corps was reduced by half; 69 of the 124 commissioned officers present were reported killed, wounded, or missing. More than 280 wounded lay at outpost Forts Hamilton and Jefferson. An estimated 30–50 women with the army died as well. Although unknown to the army leadership at the time, Indian fatalities numbered just 21 killed and 40 wounded, and the expedition's defeat was produced by a force of only 700 men, roughly one-half of the American soldiers at the Wabash that day. The campaign

---

[626] Lytle, *Soldiers of America's First Army*, 112; Downes, *Council Fires on the Upper Ohio*, 318; Cist, *CM* 1: 41.

[627] Sargent, "Winthrop Sargent's Diary," 254.

had resulted in the worst defeat that would ever be suffered by American forces against the Indian nations.[628]

In addition to the enormous human toll were the massive losses of equipment and supplies, valued at nearly $33,000. All the artillery had been abandoned, as well as baggage wagons, tents, and traveling forges. About 400 riding and packhorses were left behind, and this number did not include many belonging to the contractors. Few men carried with them on their one-hundred-mile flight anything but the clothes that they wore and the food that they hoped would keep them from starving. A money chest containing $1,938, as well as a great number of axes, spades, mattocks, and tools of the blacksmiths, carpenters, armorers, and tinsmiths, fell into Indian hands.

An ironic postscript to the battle was supplied by the party of Chickasaw Indians sent on a reconnaissance mission a few days before the attack. Sargent noted that on their return, they reported encountering a lone warrior near the Miami towns who, thinking he was with friendly Indians, boasted to them that he'd been in a fight with the Americans in which there were only 700 warriors and that his arm was quite weary with tomahawking. They shot him.[629]

★

The battered fragments of what was once an army gathered forlornly at Fort Washington where little awaited them. There was no room in the garrison, so with winter approaching, troops camped outside while officers found houses for themselves. With all their equipment lost, there was little

---

[628] Denny, *Military Journal*, 171–174; Kohn, *Eagle and Sword*, 116; Sword, *President Washington's Indian War*, 195; Downes and Lindley, *Frontier Ohio*, 29. Casualty figures vary. A few officers cited by Denny as injured later died as a result of their wounds. Jacobs cites 657 officers, enlisted personnel, and civilian employees killed and 271 wounded. The exact number of women fatalities is not known. Kohn bases his information on estimates of 50 women killed by statements of an officer with the campaign. Sargent, with a report of 30 fatalities, may only have reported "official" women accompanying the task force. Estimates appear to represent minimum numbers rather than maximum figures. See Jacobs, *The Beginning of the U.S. Army*, 115. The estimate of Indian casualties varies more widely. Sword reports 61 casualties in contrast to those reported by Downes and Lindley, who list losses of 150 men.

[629] Sargent, "Winthrop Sargent's Diary," 255.

with which to set up camp. No blankets nor extra clothing were to be had, and long untended wounds became infected. With the exception of regular units, military discipline no longer existed. The only positive aspect of the situation was that the militia quickly headed for home. Levies who, aware that they had only a short time to serve, paid no attention to their officers and spent most of their time annoying townspeople. St. Clair neither issued payments nor recorded formal discharges; enlistment records had been lost on the battlefield, and he chose not to examine payrolls. Clouding the matter was the fact that many of the men had thrown away their arms, for which St. Clair felt they should be charged. By now, the levies were so ragged and devoid of equipment that they were half naked. Finally, they were promised clothing from the Fort Washington stores, but only if they consented to have the cost deducted from their pay. Most got very little of what they had been promised in compensation for their six months' service. Jacobs notes that they generally received ambiguous certificates of indebtedness, exchanging them for varying quantities of frontier whiskey, thus amounting to the soldier's final compensation for all his months of hardship and suffering.[630]

Meanwhile, the wounded remained at Fort Jefferson in the wake of the departure of everyone fit enough to make the trek southward. There was uncertainty about the fate of the troops abandoned there, and it was assumed that the garrison was now under siege. St. Clair belatedly sent a fifty-man escort with a packhorse convoy on November 10 that was followed the next day by one hundred men from the First Regiment. Reaching the fort was a challenge due to the deeply mired roads and nearly unfordable rivers. They found the fort secure but in dire straits. The 116-man garrison had been reduced to eating "horse flesh and green hides."[631]

Ironically, Fort Jefferson was saved partly by the weather. With winter cold rapidly approaching, the Shawnees, Miamis, and Delawares were forced to depart from the scene of their victory in order to hunt game. Summer crop yields had been insufficient to sustain the tribes of the Maumee and Wabash regions, and rains had flooded the vast cornfields adjacent of the towns on the upper Maumee River. Additionally, existing

---

[630] Jacobs, *The Beginning of the U.S. Army*, 116; Sargent, "Winthrop Sargent's Diary," 254; Sword, *President Washington's Indian War*, 194.

[631] Sword, *President Washington's Indian War*, 199; Sargent, "Winthrop Sargent's Diary," 256.

stores had been nearly exhausted as warriors gathered to await the arrival of the American army. Thus, at the optimal time for attacking Americans when they were weakest, much of their force had scattered.[632]

★

On November 9, St. Clair began penning his official report to Knox and the president, sending his initial dispatch through Kentucky. Lt. Ebenezer Denny was again selected to travel to Philadelphia to relay the bad news in person. So disheartened by the disaster and sick of military life that he soon refused a promotion to captain and resigned his commission, Denny nonetheless departed for Philadelphia on November 19. St. Clair followed as soon as he regained his health some three weeks later.

Denny arrived in Philadelphia on December 19, immediately calling on Knox and meeting with the president the next morning. Washington had by that time cooled down after receiving the initial news of the defeat. In a tale that is now legendary, the president was entertaining guests at dinner when a dispatch arrived from the War Department. Although he wished not to be disturbed, his private secretary, Tobias Lear, entered to whisper news of the courier's presence. Leaving the dinner table briefly to read the document, Washington returned and graciously continued the evening's festivities. After the guests had departed and only in Lear's presence, Washington fairly exploded. In that same room the preceding spring, Washington declared that he had given St. Clair one final warning—to beware of surprise. Bellowing invectives and gesturing wildly, Washington damned Arthur St. Clair with a fury that completely intimidated and awed Lear. Finally drained of emotion and collapsing on a sofa, the president sat in silence. When he finally spoke after regaining his composure, he vowed that St. Clair would have justice and that he would receive him without displeasure and hear him without prejudice.[633]

★

St. Clair soon had the opportunity to have his case heard. Because there were no active-duty officers of equal rank to form a legal military

---

[632] Sword, *President Washington's Indian War*, 196.

[633] Sword, *President Washington's Indian War*, 201; Denny, *Military Journal*, 175–176.

court, the House of Representatives formed a special committee to review the campaign, conducting that body's first congressional investigation. This was potentially a source of embarrassment to the administration. One governmental body threatening to pass judgment on another was not only unprecedented, it might also be dangerous. Washington held one of the first full meetings of his cabinet where the issue was debated extensively. Ultimately resolving to turn over all appropriate documents to the committee, it retained the authority to withhold papers that might "injure the public."

A hearing before the House of Representatives could not have worked to better advantage for St. Clair who had served as president of that body in 1787. His close friend Thomas Fitzsimons chaired the committee, and several of its members were former cronies. Committee sessions in the following weeks included heated testimony. Its decision of May 8, 1792, exonerated the major general. In its opinion, the campaign's failure could in no way be ascribed to his conduct at any time before or during the action. The primary causes of the operation's failure were gross mismanagement of the quartermaster and contractor departments as well as the lack of discipline and experience of the troops. It also referenced Congress's delay in authorizing the offensive, thus limiting the time required to mount the campaign that summer. The committee also interpreted the administration's orders regarding its execution as "express and unequivocal," precluding St. Clair from exercising discretion relative to proceeding with the campaign.[634]

Alarmed by the committee's preliminary report, members of the administration lobbied doggedly to change its substance since some, particularly those associated with contractor William Duer, might be named in a potential scandal. As Congress resumed later that year, Knox requested reopening the investigation. The committee was subsequently restructured, and a second revised report was submitted in February 1793, acknowledging that certain mistakes had been made in the original. The

---

[634] Sword, *President Washington's Indian War*, 292; Jacobs, *The Beginning of the U.S. Army*, 118; ASP, Military Affairs, 37–39.

issue was allowed to die when the revised report was tabled by the House and the committee discharged.[635]

★

Historians cite the multiple causes of the campaign's failure identified by the committee and provide several more. Blame for the resounding debacle begins with Congress itself by its procrastination and evasion of responsibility. The administration presented its request for an augmented force as early as December 8, 1790, but it was not until March 3 that legislation was passed providing for additional troops. By then, there was no longer sufficient time to recruit, outfit, transport, and train a force capable of successfully completing an expedition during the summer months.[636]

Christopher W. Wingate also notes the administration's pressure on St. Clair to persevere with the campaign after its many delays. Correspondence between Washington, Knox, and St. Clair reveals a level of inflexibility and one-way communication. The administration provided firm guidance but ignored St. Clair's warnings that the army suffered from a lack of training, organization, and logistical readiness for offensive operations. St. Clair was repeatedly pressed to commence the campaign even as late as September 1, at which time Knox wrote that by "every principle that is sacred, to stimulate your operations in the highest degree, and to move as rapidly as the lateness of the season and the nature of the case will possibly admit."

Washington and Knox were kept apprised of the delays that occurred that were out of St. Clair's ability to control. With Harmar's disaster a fresh memory, and as military men who oversaw logistical operations through the long years of the Revolution, they should have known the risks inherent in conducting a campaign so late in the year. Unquestionably, enormous funds had already been expended, and levy regiments recruited for only a limited term; but the commander in the field should have been allowed to use his discretion about whether to continue an expedition in light of the many negative factors that threatened success. The nation paid

---

[635] *ASP-Military Affairs*, 36–39; Sword, *President Washington's Indian Wars*, 202–03.

[636] Jacobs, *The Beginning of the U.S. Army*, 118.

a very high cost for Knox and Washington's impatience and the mission's ultimate failure.[637]

The president, together with his secretaries of war and treasury, were ultimately responsible for poor choices in selecting the army's contractor and quartermaster. The price allowed for troop rations was set so low that it realized only a minimal profit margin for contractors who, as might have been expected, resorted to chicanery. William Duer was no exception. As the recipient of $75,000 in advances for the purchase of army supplies, he instead used the money for his own land-speculation activities. Already under severe monetary pressure for liabilities incurred in stock speculation, Duer, on April 28, 1791, with $15,000 in his pocket from a treasury advance on the army contract, proceeded to loan $10,000 to his good friend. Henry Knox. Together they formed a secret partnership to speculate on New England lands. Knox and Duer were so heavily involved in arranging the details of their land scheme that from April to July 1791, Duer grossly neglected the army contract. Sword notes that not only did he give insufficient time and attention to organizing and maintaining a viable supply system, he siphoned off the funds advanced for procuring flour, beef, and other provisions. Duer's agents at Fort Pitt and other locations received few funds to purchase needed supplies. Hence, an abrupt stoppage in provisions occurred when merchants refused to grant further extension of credit. Guthman notes, "This misjudgment of the contractor's ability on the part of the War Department, along with its ignorance of the enemy's capabilities, were probably the greatest contributions to the defeat of the army."[638]

Quartermaster Samuel Hodgdon, another friend of Knox, had served in the Revolution as commissary general of military stores but, despite his experience, lacked ability for the job and was often careless in his business transactions. Although he received his appointment in March, he remained in Philadelphia until June 4, more than a month past the date that Knox had planned for him to be with the army. Ostensibly, he was in Philadelphia to order supplies and to arrange transport but demonstrated repeatedly that he lacked the judgment to purchase goods of the right

---

[637] Wingate, *Military Professionalism and the Early American Officer Corps*, 27–28; St. Clair, *A Narrative*, 5.

[638] Sword, *President Washington's Indian War*, 149–50; Guthman, *March to Massacre*, 208.

quantity and quality. His incompetence and Duer's mismanagement of funds caused needless delays as the troops transitioned through Fort Pitt, setting back the start of the campaign and cutting short the time officers might have used to mold and train their companies. Knox should have seen to the speedy delivery of those supplies.[639]

Then there was the choice of St. Clair to lead the campaign. Jacobs notes that the general was loyal to the administration but evoked neither enthusiasm nor confidence in anyone. His decision to include Winthrop Sargent as adjutant general, a position that had to be created for him, was questionable. Loyal, energetic, and in many ways able, Sargent's habitual austerity and chilly aloofness, as well as his ill-concealed contempt for the frontiersmen, repelled and alienated the very people with whom he was compelled to work. He was ill fitted to defuse the animosity between regulars and militia and unable to win the wholehearted support of higher-ranking officers.[640]

Neverthelss, the onus of responsibility still falls on St. Clair. He was, indeed, the recipient of insufficient and unacceptable quantities of munitions, equipment, packhorses, and other campaign requirements and by all accounts did his best to correct the situation; but during the staging phase of the operation, he made several trips to Kentucky to plan raids, secure supplies, or collect militia while leaving no second-in-command to deal with the logistical nightmare at Fort Washington. As precious time elapsed while troops filtered down the Ohio, the First Regiment was idle at Ludlow's Station and could have begun constructing Fort Hamilton and saving two weeks of good weather. He refused Butler's technical advice and opinions, and their estranged relationship possibly led to Butler's fatal hesitation in alerting St. Clair to the likelihood of attack on November 4. Pressed by superiors to start the campaign, confronted with an inadequate logistical system, and forced to manage a patchwork army of regulars, militia, and levies, he became testy, unreasonable, and exhausted. His insistence on regular army discipline also alienated the militia and levies. Kohn notes that the general held courts-martial for officers who violated minor administrative rules, including one for bad

---

[639] Sword, *President Washington's Indian War*, 150–51. Knox's private correspondence reveals that he tried to get Duer to adhere to his responsibilities but covered up for him as much as possible. He also belatedly admonished his friend Hodgdon, telling him that he should have been at headquarters "long ago."

[640] Jacobs, *The Beginning of the U.S. Army*, 79–80.

language to a superior. St. Clair later reported that so many punishments had been inflicted that his orderly journal read mostly as a "book of pains and penalties."[641]

All these factors resulted in a command climate so poor that his second-in-command withheld vital information about the enemy situation. Jacobs acknowledges that St. Clair was ill and that the adjutant general was captious and irascible, but his key subordinates should have shown sufficient professionalism to ensure that their commanding general was informed of the presence of nearby warriors following Slough's discovery the night before the attack. Butler, Gibson, and Oldham were all aware of Captain Slough's discovery. The fact that Butler and Oldham fell in battle and Gibson later succumbed to wounds does not free them from the fact that they failed miserably to perform a simple act that might have saved not only their own lives but also those of many of their men.[642]

St. Clair must also take responsibility for violating two key precepts of military practice, intelligence, and security. During the long march, St. Clair had no idea of the enemy he was facing, in contrast to that of the Indians who knew where he was every moment of its march, not to mention how many men were in the ranks and how many had deserted. Even days before the battle, he wrote that he thought his "force sufficient, though I have no manner of information as to the force collected to oppose us." St. Clair seems to have paid little attention to the urgent need to locate his enemy. He rarely dispatched scouting parties, and when he did, no reports were made to him in person. His use of the Chickasaw for long-range reconnaissance, knowing that they might be gone as long as ten days, was a huge mistake. He consistently chose to misinterpret increasing signs of Indian presence, attributing those seen as hunters, as well as considering men missing from guard duty as having deserted. Sword notes that the general persisted in his belief that his numerical superiority and better-disciplined army could best any force that the Indians might present even though he had no idea of their strength.[643]

---

[641] Kohn, *Eagle and Sword*, 115; Sword, *President Washington's Indian War*, 165.

[642] Jacobs, *The Beginning of the U.S. Army*, 104.

[643] Downes, *Council Fires on the Upper Ohio*, 319; Sword, *President Washington's Indian War*, 168; Roosevelt, "St. Clair and Wayne," 155–156; Wingate, *Military Professionalism and the Early American Officer Corps*, 56.

St. Clair made other poor decisions that affected force security as the prospect of battle drew closer. He decided to send the First Regiment, the army's strongest unit and the only one with combat experience, away from the main body at the time when the signs of Indian presence had increased. Wingate notes that he inexplicably allowed low levels of security deep in the heart of hostile territory. He placed the militia troops, arguably the poorest and least trustworthy, in the most exposed location the evening of November 3. He should have insisted that despite the late hour, breastworks be constructed. If he had ordered scouts to search the area that night, he could hardly have escaped the conclusion that the enemy was close at hand and that he should immediately take special precautions for the safety of his command. He should have ensured that Lieutenant Colonel Oldham, commander of the Kentucky militia, perform his rounds early the next morning in compliance of orders issued the night before to preclude the possibility of surprise. Roosevelt notes that given the army's circumstances, victory would hardly have been possible, but the overwhelming nature of the defeat might have been precluded by attention to these factors.[644]

St. Clair possessed other weaknesses fatal to the successful exercise of high command. He had no adequate appreciation of the fundamentals of Indian fighting. Jacobs notes that he could have learned from Scott, Wilkinson, and Harmar what personnel, supplies, and transportation were necessary for the operation; but even after consulting with them and others, he did not focus his efforts on these three fundamental requirements.[645]

In fairness, Jacobs highlights other facts about Arthur St. Clair that are easy to forget in the aftermath of such a disaster. He was both brave and loyal. He obeyed the wishes of his superiors, even when doing so ran counter to his better judgment and resulted in injury to his own reputation. When he failed, he accepted his share of blame. Jacobs says that there was something essentially patrician in his dignity, much that was praiseworthy in his sense of justice, and a good deal that was splendid in his acceptance of responsibility. Though a failure as a general, many still considered him a man of unquestionable worth.[646]

---

[644] Roosevelt, "St. Clair and Wayne," 174; Jacobs, *The Beginning of the U.S. Army*, 104; Wingate, *Military Professionalism and the Early American Officer Corps*, 57.
[645] Jacobs, *The Beginning of the U.S. Army*, 121–22.
[646] Ibid., 122.

St. Clair's biggest sin was his failure to halt the campaign at the time of the expiration of the levies. Good judgment dictated its postponement until the following spring, a measure followed by his successor Anthony Wayne, thus allowing for the construction of a fort for communications before winter and thereby speeding the campaign the following year. Given the pressure he apparently felt as an officer loyal to the specific directives of Knox and the president, this was an action he either did not or could not consider.[647]

Guthman presents one final glaring omission in the records concerning failure of the campaign. Multiple factors leading to its defeat are noted in the accounts of all those involved, but no references were made to the tactics of the Indian fighters or to their superior fighting skills. Occasionally, the style of "Indian warfare" was mentioned, but the capabilities of the Indian warrior compared to the American soldier were not discussed. Although Sargent noted that the Indians were difficult to see because they were "concealed" and that they charged "with a very daring spirit," and St. Clair noted the army rose to fight a "superior enemy" that attacked unexpectedly, neither commented on whether their strength emanated from numbers, fighting skills, or use of superior tactics. As in the aftermath of the Harmar expedition, military officers simply could not or would not give their enemy credit for the decisive victory. Little Turtle had organized his warriors into a self-sustaining combat unit and placed it in a perfect location to annihilate St. Clair's forces. Mission priorities, to remove leadership by targeting uniformed or mounted officers at every opportunity and to eliminate the artillery, were clear and entrusted primarily to a dedicated group of about three hundred sharpshooters under the command of William Wells.[648]

★

"BLOODY INDIAN BATTLE," screamed a Boston broadside, printed with two rows of twenty black coffins over the headline. News of the disaster did not require such dramatic publication on the frontier. Demands from alarmed citizens of Marietta caused St. Clair to reapportion his meager troops there. Pittsburgh residents looked upon the recent developments as a prelude to disaster and demanded an adequate garrison, more arms, and

---

[647] Guthman, *March to Massacre*, 221; Kohn, *Eagle and Sword*, 115.

[648] Guthman, *March to Massacre*, 230; Sargent, "Winthrop Sargent's Diary," 260; St. Clair, *A Narrative*, 54, 70; Lytle, *Soldiers of America's First Army*, 94.

additional ammunition for their common defense. Settlers abandoned their farms on the Allegheny, Muskingum, and Great Miami Rivers and found shelter in larger and safer places.[649]

The settlers' outrage was not lost on their influential contacts in the East. On December 26, the administration presented a plan to Congress calling for a complete revision of the army's structure. With a proposed strength of 5,168 men whose pay was to be liberally increased and who would serve for a minimum of three years, the force would include an entire regiment of riflemen, expanded use of cavalry and mounted militia, and the utilization of friendly Indians to serve as scouts and spies. After intense debate, the bill passed without revision. The mood of the public had been truly reflected in Congress, and Washington won a major victory. The administration ironically had at last gotten the army it had always sought because of two military disasters. The United States was now totally commited to victory in the Northwest Territory and to mobilize sufficient resources to achieve this objective. As to the question regarding who would assume the reins of command, one thing was certain. It would not be Arthur St. Clair.[650]

In the frigid January days that followed, James Wilkinson, now appointed lieutenant colonel commandant of the army's Second Regiment, led three companies of volunteers from Columbia, North Bend, and Cincinnati to the scene of the army's camp on the Wabash to bury the dead and to retrieve any property that could be salvaged. One hundred fifty mounted horsemen plowed through two-foot-deep snow drifts to arrive at the eerily silent, colorless scene where they discovered bodies covered so deeply that their presence was discernable only by rounded rises in the terrain where they lay. Many had been dragged from beneath the snow and eaten by wild animals. Seventy-eight bodies were found along the trail between the the battlefield and the point where the Indian pursuit terminated. McBride surmises that there were probably many more to be found as the injured and exhausted men crawled out of sight and perished alone. Scalped and stripped of clothing that was of any value, their bodies blackened by frost and exposure, few could be identified.

---

[649] Sword, *President Washington's Indian War*, 199; Downes, *Council Fires on the Upper Ohio*, 320.

[650] Sword, *President Washington's Indian War*, 204; *ASP-Indian Affairs*, I: 197–99.

The volunteers attempted to dig a large pit to collect and bury the frozen bodies, but due to the rock-hard ground and the enormity of the task, probably only half were interred. Securing one remaining six-pounder, two intact gun carriages, and a few muskets, Wilkinson's men departed the scene. There, in the silent gloom at the headwaters of the icy Wabash, the heart and soul of St. Clair's army remained until Gen. Anthony Wayne returned with men on Christmas Day 1793 to establish a permanent camp at the site and render a proper burial to the fallen.[651]

---

[651] McBride, Pioneer Biography, I: 30–35; Sargent, "Winthrop Sargent's Diary," 270–72.

14

Wilkinson, 1792

To Draw his portrait needs no pencil nice
For all his composition is vice on vice.
—Anthony Wayne, January 29, 1795[652]

With the departure of the remnants of St. Clair's army on November 7, Fort Hamilton became the primary operations center for the evacuation and relief of the wounded who had been left stranded in the wretched conditions at Fort Jefferson. Armstrong now found himself in the center of an administrative storm. Literally everything needed to be taken care of, not only for the men in his command, but also for the wounded who continued to stagger into the overcrowded fort. Receipts for issuance of rations fill Armstrong's files from the assumption of his command well into the new year. Correspondence with St. Clair and Quartermaster Samuel Hodgdon reflects the dire needs of the men. Soldiers were threadbare, the horses needed corn, and the men even needed kettles to cook their rations. More housing had to be found to accommodate not only the expanded number of men at the garrison but also the wounded and convoys passing through on their way to and from Fort Jefferson. Armstrong needed more

---

[652] Wayne to Capt. Henry De Butts, January 29, 1795, from Wayne Papers, Historical Society of Pennsylvania, quoted in Richard H. Kohn, "General Wilkinson's Vendetta with General Wayne: Politics and Command in the American Army, 1791-1796," *Filson Club History Quarterly* 45 (1971), 369.

able-bodied men to enlarge the fort and to provide for its defense, and his soldiers needed tools to accomplish these tasks.[653]

The wounded continued to file into the garrison. In his report to St. Clair on November 10, Armstrong reported that thirty-six men coming from Jefferson were ambulatory and another twenty-four, some of whom were on litters, had to be transported by wagons or horseback. They were accompanied by an additional number of troops who were ill. Some then continued onward to Fort Washington on the river, and Armstrong was kept busy directing the construction of flatboats for that purpose.[654]

St. Clair remained at Fort Washington until early December, leaving Maj. David Zeigler in charge of the garrison. Prior to his departure to Philadelphia, he wrote Armstrong an encouraging letter, expressing his confidence in the captain's ability to attend both to the fort and to its men and his trust that the post would be defended against attack. He advised Armstrong to send out reconnaissance parties and to establish modes of communication with Forts Jefferson and Washington. His parting words were, "I wish you, sir, a happy command."[655]

Armstrong ended the year with a company of 106 men that included five sergeants, five corporals, and two musicians. Also with him was Lt. Asa Hartshorne, with whom he had shared his near-death experience at the Miami villages the previous year. His company also supported activities in surrounding areas including Dunlap's Station, and in January, he sought the eviction of some of its settlers within John Cleves Symmes's purchase. Symmes, not uncharacteristically, railed against such heavy-handedness on the part of the military and Armstrong in the affair.[656]

★

[653] Armstrong to St. Clair, November 29, PJA; Armstrong to Hodgdon, November 13 and 23, 1792, and December 4, 11, and 24," Papers of the War Department, http://wardepartmentpapers.org/s/home/item/42175. (See also .../42212, 42214, 42246, 42282, and 42317).

[654] Armstrong to St. Clair, November 10, 23, 29, 1791, PJA.

[655] St. Clair to Armstrong, December 7, 1791, in Smith, SCP, II: 273–274.

[656] Returns of December 25 and December 31, 1791, PJA; John Cleves Symmes to Elias Boudinot and Jonathan Dayton, January 25, 1792, in Beverly W. Bond Jr., ed., The Correspondence of John Cleves Symmes: Founder of the Miami Purchase (New York: Macmillan Company, 1926), 161.

On October 22, 1791, George Washington appointed Kentuckian James Wilkinson as the lieutenant colonel commandant of the Second United States Infantry Regiment. Although leading previous desultory raids against the Wabash Indians, Wilkinson, former Revolutionary War brigadier general turned politician, had not taken part in St. Clair's expedition. The one-time "boy general," having falling on financial hard times, eagerly accepted his appointment but did not report to Fort Washington until early 1792. For the time being, he accepted a diminished rank without complaint, but that changed after the formation of the Legion of the United States in the next few months.[657]

With the exception of Benedict Arnold, Wilkinson has the justly deserved reputation as the most devious and treacherous officer ever to achieve high rank in the United States Army. Unlike Arnold, his duplicity, although widely rumored, was not discovered in his lifetime. He has since been the subject of numerous works attempting to unravel the motivation behind his schizophrenic army life in which he served simultaneously as the army's commanding general and that of a paid spy for Spain which distributed at least $32,000 for his services over the six-year period from 1790–1796. To provide a detailed analysis of his actions prior to his assumption of command of the army in Ohio in early 1792 is well outside the bounds of this work. Nevertheless, in order to understand the difficult situation in which Armstrong found himself ten months later and the poisonous command climate that existed in the reorganized army Legion during the time Wilkinson was in charge of troops awaiting the arrival of the forthcoming campaign's commander Gen. Anthony Wayne, it is necessary to review the background of the man who eventually assumed command of the country's army after Wayne's death, the man Theodore Roosevelt described as

> a good-looking, plausible, energetic man, gifted with a
> taste for adventure, with much proficiency in low intrigue,
> and with a certain address in influencing and managing
> bodies of men. He also spoke and wrote well, according

---

[657] Jacobs suggests that Wilkinson had no desire to be included in an operation led by St. Clair whom influential Kentuckians considered ill-suited for command. He was reluctant to participate in a failed exercise where his reputation might be injured through the fault of others. See Jacobs, *Tarnished Warrior: Major-General James Wilkinson* (New York: The MacMillan Company, 1938), 114.

to the rather florid canons of the day. In character he can only be compared to Benedict Arnold, though he entirely lacked Arnold's ability and brilliant courage. He had no conscience and no scruples; he had not the slightest idea of the meaning of the word honor; he betrayed his trust from the basest motives, and he was too inefficient to make his betrayal effective. He was treacherous to the Union while it was being formed and after it had been formed; and his crime was aggravated by the sordid meanness of his motives, for he eagerly sought opportunities to barter his own infamy for money. In all our history there is no more despicable character.[658]

One can only imagine what Roosevelt might have written had he known the full extent of Wilkinson's treachery. In the last years of the nineteenth century, a cache of papers relating to his activities was found in Baton Rouge, Louisiana. Not until the first quarter of the twentieth century, however, when historians began to dig through the estimated 200,000 documents sent back from Havana to Madrid in 1888, was the smoking gun of treason finally uncovered. Hundreds of letters, reports, comments, and assessments exchanged between Wilkinson, a.k.a. "Agent 13," his handlers, and the Spanish officials to whom they reported testify to the scale and importance of his activities.[659]

[658] Theodore Roosevelt, *The Winning of the West, Vol. 3: The Founding of the Trans-Alleghany Commonwealths*, 123–24; Of the $32,000, Jacobs notes that Wilkinson personally received $26,000. Jacobs, *Tarnished Warrior*, 152.

[659] Andro Linklater, *An Artist in Treason: The Extraordinary Double Life of General James Wilkinson* (New York: Walker Publishing Company, Inc., 2009), 5. Credit for initial uncovering of this information is attributed to Charles Gayarré who discovered Wilkinson's correspondence with the Spanish government in Madrid in the 1830s. Some seven decades later, Sr. Gonzalez Verger and William R. Shepherd found and organized approximately 4,800 documents in the Spanish archives. Shepherd published *Guide to the Materials for the History of the United States in Spanish Archives* (Washington, D.C.: Carnegie Institution of Washington, 1907), and his papers are included in the Library of Congress manuscript collection. See also Roscoe R. Hill, *Descriptive Catalogue of the Documents of the United States in the Papeles Procedentes de Cuba Deposited in the Archivo General de Indias at Seville* (Washington, D. C.: Carnegie Institution of Washington, Issue 234, 1916), xxvi.

How Wilkinson managed his affairs as senior general of the United States army while engaged in clandestine partnership with the Spanish government continues to be a subject of conjecture. Wilkinson's friendship with government officials in New Orleans and his early trading practices on the Mississippi when the river was officially closed to traffic from the United States raised eyebrows. Andro Linklater, author of Wilkinson's biography, *An Artist in Treason: The Extraordinary Double Life of General James Wilkinson*, notes that although his activities were certainly suspect, they time and again escaped positive detection. He was repeatedly referred to as a "Spanish pensioner"; numerous publications accused him of being a traitor; an entire Kentucky newspaper, the *Western World*, was devoted to exposing him; and accusations of collusion were made by congressmen of every political persuasion. Nor were these charges overlooked. Presidents George Washington, John Adams, Thomas Jefferson, and James Madison, together with half a dozen secretaries of war, not to mention a score of their cabinet colleagues, were all aware of his close contacts with the Spanish authorities in New Orleans and Madrid.[660]

Yet for any number of reasons best understood in the context of the state of the union during its precarious infancy, authorities chose either to cast a blind eye toward Wilkinson's reported activities or to use him for their own purposes. He was also incredibly lucky; ample opportunities existed for his lucrative career as a Spanish operative to be up, but good fortune always intervened. Frequently suspected, he was never caught.

For John Armstrong and the rest of the army, Wilkinson's appointment had serious consequences far removed from the latter's clandestine activities. With the passage of legislation for the formation of a five-battalion "legion" in March 1792, Wilkinson once again achieved brigadier general status and became second-in-command under Anthony Wayne. Wilkinson, convinced the job should have been his, set out to discredit Wayne at every opportunity. His duplicity was such that historians credit him with attempts to sabotage his own army's campaign leading up to the 1794 battle at Fallen Timbers by colluding with army contractors to delay shipment of provisions in order to discredit Wayne's leadership. One fact is certain, however: through Wilkinson's cunning manipulation, a once cohesive officer corps split irrevocably into two factions, one loyal to Wayne and the other loyal to Wilkinson, leaving long-lasting scars in the

---

[660] Linklater, *An Artist in Treason*, 3.

corps. Armstrong found himself caught squarely in the middle. Historian Richard Kohn described the situation:

> In all of the disputes over the various conspiracies in the West between the Revolution and the War of 1812, historians have agreed on one thing: James Wilkinson was involved. Frederick Jackson Turner set the tone in 1856 when he called Wilkinson "the most consummate artist in treason that the nation ever possessed." But plots with foreign governments and with such adventurers as Aaron Burr were only part of Wilkinson's career. At heart the man was driven by a relentless personal ambition. All his life he schemed for wealth and preferment, and nowhere was it more evident than in his five-year struggle to oust General Anthony Wayne and take over the command of the fledgling American army.[661]

★

Joseph Wilkinson was a small Maryland plantation owner who died when his son James was six years old. Linklater theorizes that in his father's absence, Wilkinson projected the picture of the ideal gentleman. He wrote that his father's last words to him were "My son, if you ever put up with an insult, I will disinherit you." Whether or not these were indeed his words, the idea expressed was deeply embedded into the son's personality. As an adult, the merest suggestion that his actions had been inappropriate were met with explosive anger and, occasionally, challenges to settle the matter by a duel.[662]

---

[661] Kohn, "General Wilkinson's Vendetta," 361–62; Richard H. Kohn, *Eagle and Sword*, 178–80; Wayne to Knox, December 23, 1794, and January 29, 1795, in Richard C. Knopf, *Anthony Wayne: A Name in Arms* (Pittsburgh: University of Pittsburgh Press, 1960), 373, 377, 383, (*AWNIA*); Timothy M. Rusche, "Treachery within the United States Army," *Pennsylvania History: A Journal of Mid-Atlantic Studies* 65, no. 4 (1998), 478–91; Jacobs, *Tarnished Warrior*, 155–56.

[662] Linklater, *An Artist in Treason*, 10; James Wilkinson, *Memoirs of My Own Times* (Philadelphia: Abraham Small, 1816), I: 8.

At seventeen, Wilkinson was sent to Philadelphia to become a physician. This opened his eyes to the prospect of a better life. It was exciting to be in a bustling city of 40,000 residents, paved streets, a university, a hospital, theaters, and the ambiance of polite society whereby a young man short on money but long on charm could hope to flourish. Linklater surmises that his formal education took second place to Wilkinson's interest in the city's social scene.

The newly minted teenage doctor soon found himself practicing medicine in Monocacy, Maryland, with his heart apparently not in his new profession. When news of the shots fired at Lexington reached the town, his immediate response was to join the fight against the British, prompted perhaps more for the excitement of battle rather than the love of liberty. Riding off every week to drill with an independent rifle company in Pennsylvania, he soon left Monocacy for more exciting venues. An eager young officer who would "bend or blend," tactfully courting the friendship of senior officers who might promote his advancement, he soon found himself an aide to Gen. Nathanael Greene. In April 1775, he was transferred to a New Hampshire regiment; and toward the end of the month, he was among reinforcements that were marching northward to join the army in the ill-fated Canada campaign.[663]

Once in Canada, he crossed paths with the celebrated general Benedict Arnold who had a history of mentoring promising young officers and joined his staff as an aide-de-camp. Although still in his teens, Wilkinson assumed command of nearly one hundred men, guiding them safely up the Hudson, through Lakes George and Champlain, and across tangled wilderness before crossing the St. Lawrence River, demonstrating initiative, physical hardiness, and the frequent exercise of good judgment along the way. Given his supreme confidence and insatiable ambition, he was destined for rapid advancement. Jacobs notes that his value to the service consisted of his adaptability, eagerness to please, diplomatic smoothness, and unusual strength of mind and body, the characteristics of a perfect staff officer.[664]

By July 1776, following the disastrous retreat of the American army from Canada, Wilkinson was a brigade major assigned to the staff of Brig.

---

[663] Jacobs, *Tarnished Warrior*, 2–8; Linklater, *An Artist in Treason*, 12–13; Wilkinson, *Memoirs* I: 12–13.

[664] Jacobs, *Tarnished Warrior*, 9, 12.

Gen. Arthur St. Clair at Mount Independence, opposite Ticonderoga, New York. That summer he contracted typhoid fever, part of the epidemic that swept through the ranks, and was evacuated to the south end of Lake George and then to Albany. Following two to three months of illness and recuperation, he found his old brigade disbanded and attached himself to the recently appointed commander of the troops returned from Canada, Maj. Gen. Horatio Gates, who was on his way to join Washington in New Jersey with reinforcements. Following Gates's decline of Washington's offer of command at Bristol in preparation for the army's raid on Trenton, the general traveled to Philadelphia. Wilkinson accompanied him, the lure of the city strong and the opportunity to see friends even stronger. Nominally assigned as a staff officer under St. Clair who had been assigned another brigade, he wisely decided to join him, arriving on Christmas Day in time for the army's night crossing of the Delaware and particpated in the battles of Trenton and Princeton.[665]

Wilkinson did not remain with Washington at Morristown that winter, but instead was assigned to one of the new battalions authorized by Congress in December 1776. He received a promotion to lieutenant colonel and was selected for recruiting duty in Maryland and Pennsylvania. He maintained contact with Gates who was lobbying Congress in Philadelphia for command of the Northern Department of the Continental Army and quickly assented when the general asked him to serve on his staff.

As aide to Gates during the pivotal battle for Saratoga, Wilkinson ran reconnaissance missions for the general and played a significant part in negotiating Burgoyne's surrender. It was at this point, however, that Wilkinson ran afoul of his former benefactor, Benedict Arnold. Arnold, subordinate to Gates during the exercise, bristled at restrictions placed on him during the protracted, deadlocked campaign. Relations between Gates and Arnold were cool from the start, and Gates at one point dispatched Wilkinson to stop Arnold from heading into battle. Later, in the course of his staff duties, Wilkinson reassigned designated units to the headquarters rather than to Arnold, heightening the latter's animosity toward his former aide. Weary of Arnold's belligerence, Gates eventually relieved him of command.[666]

---

[665] Ibid., 18–26.

[666] Ibid., 26, 35–38.

It was while working under Gates that a pivotal point in his career occurred, revealing an aspect of his character that emerged periodically throughout his life. Harkening back to his dying father's words regarding personal honor, Wilkinson turned on Gates, his current father figure and mentor. He would later demonstrate similar traits in his dealings with John Armstrong.

The incident unfolded in the following manner. After Gates's victory at Saratoga in October 1777, Wilkinson was given the honor of delivering the news of victory to Congress, temporarily meeting in York. Wilkinson took his time getting there, covering the distance of 285 miles in eleven days. He was not well, and the weather was bad. During a stopover in Reading, the local commander, Maj. Gen. William Alexander, Lord Stirling, invited him to dinner. As the evening progressed, Stirling fell asleep, leaving his young guest to be entertained by his aides, James Monroe and William McWilliams. Late at night with abundant drink and an attentive audience at hand, the twenty-year-old, by his own admission, indulged in "conversation too copious and diffuse for me to have charged my memory with particulars." However, his audience, particularly Major McWilliams, recalled that Wilkinson betrayed a confidence Gates had shared with him and duly reported Wilkinson's conversation to Stirling, specifically his claim that Gates received a letter from Brig. Gen. Thomas Conway that had included this comment disparaging Washington: "Heaven has been determined to save your Country; or a weak General and bad Counsellers would have ruined it." Conway's purported attempt to remove Washington as the army's commander became known later as the "Conway Cabal."[667]

When Wilkinson eventually arrived in York with the news of victory at Saratoga, a relieved Congress called for a day of Thanksgiving. Gates

---

[667] Linklater, *Artist in Treason*, 48; JWM, I: 330–31. When Conway, an Irish-born volunteer from the French army, sought to enter the service of the Colonies, he was granted the rank of brigadier general. He commanded the brigade at the Battle of Brandywine in September 1777 in which the Armstrong brothers fought and afterward was critical of Washington's performance there while boastful of his own. Congress later promoted him to the rank of major general despite Washington's opposition based on his conviction that other valuable longer-serving senior officers were more deserving of the leadership position. Heartened by the support that politicians had apparently given him, he tried to get Washington relieved and Gates placed in supreme command of the army. Jacobs, *Tarnished Warrior*, 43–44, 47.

was now the man of the hour, but his request for Wilkinson's promotion to brigadier general stuck in the congressional craw. Some members were loath to honor Wilkinson who was already high ranking for his years and were irritated by his delay in delivering a dispatch of such high importance to the waiting body. His rapid advancement belied the time-honored tradition of promotion by seniority and prompted several complaints from colonels of regiments that the elevation of an untried and unblooded officer, a staff officer who had never actually led troops in battle, would be a travesty. Much to their resentment, Wilkinson was awarded the brevet rank of brigadier general on November 6, 1777.[668]

It didn't take long for Gates to learn that some of his private correspondence had become common knowledge. When Wilkinson returned to Albany on December 8, 1777, Gates spoke of his suspicion that Col. Alexander Hamilton was the source of the leak. Hamilton visited Gates in early November and had been left alone in a room where he could have found Conway's letter and copied it. Wilkinson tried to dissuade his general from this belief, suggesting instead that Colonel Troup, another of Gates's aides-de-camp, might inadvertently have alerted Hamilton to its contents.

The matter was temporarily laid to rest when Wilkinson embarked on an inspection tour of northern forts, and Gates headed south to York to assume new duties as president of the Board of War. Wilkinson later wrote that he felt no personal concern regarding the matter because Gates had read the letter publicly in his presence and he, Wilkinson, had not spoken of it with evil intent. Nevertheless, when the issue was raised by Gates, Wilkinson kept silent. Worse yet, he tried to pin the blame on a fellow officer.[669]

Shortly after Wilkinson's return to Albany in early February, he received a letter from Lord Stirling demanding to know the precise wording of Conway's correspondence with Gates. When questioned by officers while at Whitemarsh, Wilkinson had apparently refuted his original words regarding the letter's content, and now Stirling wanted both the truth and a copy of the communication. Wilkinson replied that he couldn't remember what he had said when he was Stirling's guest and expressed his indignation at being requested to produce an extract of Conway's letter.

---

[668] Jacobs, *Tarnished Warrior*, 45–46; Linklater, *Artist in Treason*, 50.
[669] Wilkinson, *Memoirs* I: 373–76; Linklater, *Artist in Treason*, 52–53.

Regardless of his new rank, Wilkinson was clearly junior to a respected senior officer and was fully responsible for the predicament in which he found himself.[670]

Gates learned of Wilkinson's indiscretions directly from Washington, and when he confronted his former aide, Wilkinson refused to acknowledge any wrongdoing. Instead, he challenged Gates to a duel, writing, "In spite of every consideration, you have wounded my honor, and must make acknowledgment of satisfaction for the injury."

In response, Gates quoted extracts from a letter he had received from Washington, clearly showing the path Wilkinson's remarks had taken to reach his attention. In what might once have been forgiven by Gates as an act of youthful indiscretion, Wilkinson aggravated the situation by continued denial and efforts to cast blame upon a wholly innocent friend. James Ripley Jacobs notes that in the hope of escaping blame for his poor judgment, Wilkinson attempted a deception and now found himself held up to public scrutiny as an unfaithful subordinate. His judgment now proven to be immature, he seemed to think that a display of physical prowess might exonerate him from his previous errors and lack of moral courage.[671]

Gates agreed to meet Wilkinson behind the "English" church in York on the morning of February 24, 1778; but before Wilkinson left his quarters, he learned that Gates was nearby and wanted to see him. Although Wilkinson's later story was that Gates broke into tears and declared that he had no desire to injure him, "my child," over the affair, Jacobs contends it was more likely that Gates apparently had no appetite for answering the challenge of a subordinate. All was apparently forgiven, and Wilkinson again joined Gates working at the Board of War.[672]

Wilkinson was content until he journeyed to Valley Forge in March to settle matters with Lord Stirling. Gates and Washington had by this time reconciled their differences, and Wilkinson was allowed to read correspondence that had passed between the two generals. Learning what Gates had thought of him prior to their own rapprochement, Wilkinson disparaged both Gates and Conway in a conversation with the commander-in-chief. He later regretted this act of impertinence and knew that sooner

---

[670] Wilkinson, *Memoirs* I: 383–85.

[671] Jacobs, *Tarnished Warrior*, 51–52; Wilkinson, *Memoirs* I: 385–88.

[672] Jacobs, *Tarnished Warrior*, 52–53.

or later his remarks would make their way to Gates. His mentor might then become his enemy. To preempt the situation, on March 29, he fired off a letter of resignation to Henry Laurens, president of Congress, resigning from the Board of War and accusing Gates with acts of treachery and falsehood. Congress accepted his resignation but directed that the letter be returned as "improper to remain" within its files.[673]

The matter did not rest there. During the summer of 1778, Wilkinson was called to testify on behalf of St. Clair, then on trial for charges connected with his abandonment of Fort Ticonderoga the previous year. Gates was also called to testify, and the two showed up at about the same time. Their mutual animosity rising to the surface, Gates apparently made remarks about Wilkinson's conduct at their encounter in York. Incensed, Wilkinson again challenged Gates, and this time the latter accepted. Parties agreed to meet near Harrison, Westchester County, New York, on September 4, 1778. Each was to fire three times, but when Gates' pistol twice flashed in the pan and misfired, Wilkinson shot in the air, an action that should have satisfied honor on both sides. Gates refused to fire a third time. The appointed seconds interceded, and the principals shook hands. Gates declared that Wilkinson had "behaved as a gentleman" at York. A paper to that effect was signed by Gates's second and given to Wilkinson's second, but Wilkinson refused to provide a similar certificate for Gates. Meeting the next day to work out the issue, Wilkinson again refused to provide the certificate and further inflamed the situation by calling Gates a rascal and a coward and challenging him to yet another duel. The general ignored him and ended the affair by walking away from a man so clearly out of control.[674]

★

[673] Jacobs, *Tarnished Warrior*, 55–56; Wilkinson, *Memoirs* I: 394–441; Linklater, *Artist in Treason*, 57–59.

[674] Linklater, *Artist in Treason*, 59; Jacobs, *Tarnished Warrior*, 57–58. Following the abortive meeting in St. Clair's headquarters, Gates's and Wilkinson's seconds, Tadeusz Kosciuszko and John Barker Church, continued the disagreement. Both were supposed to appear for St. Clair's defense but pushed each other aside trying to enter the courtroom at the same time. They subsequently drew their swords and began to fight until driven off by guards.

Wilkinson then returned to Philadelphia and married his beloved Ann "Nancy" Biddle. If anything good can be said of Wilkinson, it was his choice of a marriage partner and devotion to her. Whether a conscious calculation or not, Ann was the daughter of John Biddle, a respected Quaker businessman, and Wilkinson married into a family with connections that served him well in the future. Regardless, Ann herself is described by contemporaries as remarkable for her strength of mind and character, and Wilkinson was apparently smitten by her.[675]

Wilkinson left the army following his resignation from the Board of War in March 1778 and received a congressional appointment as the army's clothier general the following year. Money was tight, Continental currency daily diminishing in value, and when the offer came for the position, Wilkinson gladly accepted it. The annual salary of $5,000 had been turned down previously by two others because it was inadequate, but Wilkinson eagerly embraced the money and the opportunity to be back in army circles. He inherited, however, an inefficient system in which administrative defects, a scarcity of material, and lack of adequate transportation created a thankless situation.[676]

Wilkinson resigned from his position in March 1781. When the novelty of it wore off, he found his duties irksome and neglected them. Additionally, his salary was reduced to $2,500 and not promptly paid. He had purchased a 444-acre estate outside Philadelphia at a bargain price, relishing the idea of supervising its pasture and farming land, cattle, fine horses, and distillery. After Washington approved Wilkinson's appointment, the commander-in-chief was chagrined to discover that his clothier general was more interested in spending his time in Philadelphia with his growing circle of friends than at army headquarters where the duties of his office could be most effectively discharged. Washington repeatedly enjoined him to attend to the duties his position entailed and even wrote to Congress requesting its authority be brought to bear to motivate the negligent official. On this occasion, Wilkinson evinced better judgment when faced with criticism than he had shown during his wrangle with Gates. Jacobs surmises that giving up uncongenial work did not seem to disturb him; he merely regretted that he had been unable to use his

---

[675] Jacobs, *Tarnished Warrior*, 60.

[676] Ibid., 62–64.

position as a means for acquiring another for which he was more adequately suited.[677]

Wilkinson soon tried his hand in politics, was elected representative to the Pennsylvania Assembly from Bucks County, and became a general in the Pennsylvania militia. His personal debts were accumulating, however, and he began to think that the West, Kentucky in particular, held the promise of better things. By the end of 1783, he was at the Falls of the Ohio, joining others who had already grabbed choice parcels of land with which they would make their fortunes.[678]

James Wilkinson stood out within this wave of pioneers. His exceptional war record, political contacts, medical knowledge, and outgoing personality all counted in Kentucky's turbulent frontier society. Despite having limited funds at his disposal, within three months, he had purchased considerable acreage on the Kentucky River and filed claims for more on the Licking River and at the Falls of the Ohio. Backed by wealthy friends in Philadelphia, he set up a store in Lexington with two partners from his days on Gates's staff, Isaac Dunn and James Armstrong (no relation to John Armstrong), and in 1786 built a tobacco warehouse, which in Virginia's tobacco economy was equivalent to setting up a bank. Within three years, he became a leading figure in Kentucky's emerging social, business, and political communities and had become embroiled in the rising conflict between the eastern establishment and western frontier regarding the country's relationship with Spain.[679]

A party with a keen interest in the relationship between alienated Westerners and the US government, Spain continued to hold possession of East Florida, what is now the present state's peninsula, and West Florida, which extended from the panhandle west to the Mississippi River. Territory north of the thirty-first parallel and east of the Mississippi had been ceded to the United States by Great Britain at the Treaty of Paris and included land that eventually became parts of Alabama and Mississippi. Concerned about American expansion westward, Spain, like its British counterpart to

---

[677] Ibid., 61–62, 64–66. Following the British evacuation from Philadelphia, influential residents determined to rid it of those held to be Tory sympathizers. In May 1779 Wilkinson was given the opportunity to purchase a choice, confiscated property at a fraction of its cost through his connection with his father-in-law.

[678] Ibid., 68–69.

[679] Linklater, *Artist in Treason*, 72, 74.

the north, sought alliances with Indian nations to use as buffers between its domain and the United States. The Creeks in Georgia were unhappy with treaties struck in the early days of the republic, and the Cherokee, Choctaw, and Chickasaw nations in North Carolina, as well as in present-day Kentucky and Tennessee, likewise saw their lands threatened as federal and state authorities haggled over treaty boundaries and land rights.[680]

Spain found the new land-hungry republic at its back door and, apprehensive of the country's expansion, attempted to throw both enticements and roadblocks into its neighbor's way. Following American independence, Spanish officials in New Orleans encouraged American settlers not only to migrate to Florida but also to cross the Mississippi into Spanish territory. By enticing disaffected westerners, it hoped to gain a population with loyalties to Spain rather than to the United States. The Kentucky territory was central to the discord, dismayed by the government's lack of protection against marauding Indians and frustrated by the extended delays in attaining statehood. French citizens in Vincennes and the Illinois country were discouraged at the breakdown in their local governments and the failure of the United States to organize civil affairs in the remote parts of the new nation's territory. Additionally, many objected to the provision in the Land Ordinance of 1787 prohibiting slavery and found relocating to Spanish territory an attractive proposition.[681]

Spain closed the lower Mississippi River and the port of New Orleans to American goods in 1784. The measure proved a significant blow to the developing Northwest Territory economy and in particular to Vincennes and Illinois residents, having always depended on two-way river trade to ship agricultural products down the Ohio and Mississippi and to receive goods from New Orleans in return. Many felt that they had been sold out by a Congress that had allowed Spain to close the Mississippi to the benefit of Eastern fishing and agricultural interests. The United States attempted to regain its use through a treaty in 1786, but the question was unresolved, and Congress, without funds and in need of Spain's trade to its eastern ports, failed to pursue the issue. The debate lingered for several years, sharpening the divide between regional interests. Rumors

---

[680] Prucha, *The Sword of the Republic*, 43–53; Horsman, *Expansion and American Indian Policy*, 24–31.

[681] Hamtramck to Harmar, March 28, 1789, *OOTW*, 158–159; St. Clair to John Jay, December 13, 1788, *SCP*, II: 103–04.

and threats abounded to the point where the preservation of the Union was in play. Plots by westerners to seize Natchez and New Orleans from Spain and thus open the river were circulated, and for a time, war with Spain was a possibility.[682]

★

John Armstrong found himself a minor player in this unfolding crisis. In March 1787, a Charleston, South Carolina, newspaper published a letter by Capt. John Sullivan concerning the closing of the Mississippi to American trade, announcing that Westerners were ready to defend their "commercial rights" with a force of "50,000 veterans in arms." Ironically, this was the same John Sullivan who four years previously had been an instigator of the Philadelphia Mutiny whom Armstrong had known when he was stationed at Lancaster at the war's end.

When Secretary of State John Jay notified Knox of the letter, the latter directed Harmar to interfere, by force if necessary, with the execution of any such plan. Armstrong was directed to discover the truth of the matter and arrived in the Holston River country on April 8, 1788. This autonomous region, now part of eastern Tennessee, then known as "Franklin," had been ceded to Congress by the state of North Carolina in 1784 and at the time, political factions had designs of its being admitted to the Union as an independent state. The region's waterways converge downstream with the Tennessee River and eventually flow into to the Ohio.

Armstrong visited the counties of Sullivan, Washington, and Greene to interview residents. He concluded "there is not, and has not been, any design formed or forming of the nature mentioned in the letter signed John Sullivan, nor has he ever been in that settlement." Locals were at the time embroiled in a dispute between two opposing politicians.[683]

---

[682] Guthman, *March to Massacre*, 45; Harmar to Knox, May 14, 1787, in Denny, *Military Journal*, 217; White, *The Middle Ground*, 419.

[683] Samuel Cole Williams, *History of the Lost State of Franklin* (New York: The Press of the Pioneers, 1933), 236–37; Theodore Roosevelt, *The Winning of the West, part 4: Franklin, Kentucky, Ohio, and Tennessee* (New York: The Current Literature Publishing Company, 1905), 227–28; Harmar to Knox, January 10, 1788, *OOTW*, 65–66; Harmar to Wyllys, July 16, 1788, in Denny, *Military Journal*, 222–23, 231. Sullivan was refused payment and "commutation" in 1786 by Congress, having "withdrawn himself from the United States without

Theodore Roosevelt summarized the issue. The government need not have been alarmed by a potential large-scale movement by backwoodsmen against Spain. What was becoming evident, however, was a growing conspiracy between Spanish authorities in New Orleans and selected men of influence within the western territories. Spain feared invasion and tried to insulate itself from US-control by attempting to induce westerners to influence their states and territories to align themselves with Spain. Spanish authorities knew they held two trump cards—the ability either to let loose or to restrain the Creeks and other nations within the southern territories and the enticement of free navigation on the Mississippi. Administrators in New Orleans located prominent men whom they judged eager for such personal concessions, and James Wilkinson emerged at the top of their list.[684]

Wilkinson had quickly immersed himself in Kentucky politics, becoming part of the anti-Virginia movement. Besides that state's inability to protect Kentuckians from Indian attacks, the confusion over land titles reigned supreme, complicated by the long-distance processing of claims and Virginia's decision to mortgage much of Kentucky to fund its wartime expenditures by issuing paper money backed by land in the West. The end result saw wealthy Eastern speculators owning huge quantities of treasury bills and certificates entitling them to ownership of up to one-third of all Kentucky land. Poorer settlers who came west might discover that they were barred from the best ground or that farms they worked really belonged to someone else. Additionally, Kentucky settlers and tradesmen had no particular loyalty to the government of the United States but relied on it to bring diplomatic pressure upon Spain to open the Mississippi River. Having access to the river was not only the key to Kentucky's eventual prosperity but to a calculating Wilkinson as well. Already experiencing financial difficulty, he had run up lines of credit with friends in order to make large purchases of land. His tendency toward extravagance meant that most of his partnerships unfortunately ended in quarrels and litigation.[685]

In late 1783, Wilkinson began to assume an active role in Kentucky assemblies discussing separation from Virginia and eventual statehood.

---

leave obtained before the conclusion of the war." John C. Fitzpatrick, ed., *Journals of the Continental Congress 1774–1789* (Washington: U.S. Government Printing Office, 1934), XXX: 355.

[684] Theodore Roosevelt, *The Winning of the West, part 4: Franklin, Kentucky, Ohio, and Tennessee*, 228; Williams, History of the Lost State of Franklin, 235.

[685] Linklater, *Artist in Treason*, 75–76.

When the Virginia legislature enacted terms for separation in what was known as the first enabling act in 1786, some Kentucky leaders were satisfied with its measures that called for a convention to vote formally on statehood, the creation of a suitable constitution, and a congressional vote approving the state's admission into the Union. Others were unhappy because under the proposed terms, another Kentucky convention was necessary before further action could be taken. Wilkinson was in the latter camp. Discord increased the following year when Virginia passed a second act postponing separation until January 1789 to follow the establishment of the new government. Unrest had also increased in 1787 with unfounded rumors of the approval of the Jay-Gardoqui Treaty with Spain that continued closure of the Mississippi in return for increased trade that favored East Coast interests. Wilkinson and his allies realized that they could expect little help from the federal government. Kentucky should become independent and deal on her own terms with other countries as she pleased.[686]

Wilkinson decided take matters into his own hands. After being denied permission through official channels to travel to New Orleans, he wrote directly to Francisco Cruzat, commandant of the Spanish fort at St. Louis, whom he addressed in the most benevolent of terms. Not only did he apologize for the behavior of freebooters under George Rogers Clark who had seized Spanish goods at Vincennes, but he also warned of a possible attack on the post at Natchez by a group led by a Colonel Green and promised to do everything in his power to foil the attempt. Confident of the outcome of his plan to gain entry into New Orleans, he advertised for consignments of ham, tobacco, and butter to be carried down the Mississippi for sale there. When his fifty-foot-long flatboat departed Louisville in April 1787, Wilkinson left behind crowds of approving Kentucky settlers.[687]

His ploy worked. Using his polished charm and the gifts of two Virginia thoroughbred horses to wheedle entrance into the Spanish territory, he worked his way down the Mississippi to New Orleans, gathering letters of recommendation from post commandants en route.[688]

---

[686] Linklater, *Artist in Treason*, 77-79; Jacobs, *Tarnished Warrior*, 74–76.

[687] Linklater, *Artist in Treason*, 79–80.

[688] Linklater, *Artist in Treason*, 82; Arthur Preston Whitaker, "James Wilkinson's First Descent to New Orleans in 1787," *Hispanic American Historical Review* 8, no. 1 (1928), 82–97.

He hit it off well with the two men he needed to impress most for his master plan to succeed. Gov. Don Esteban Miró and his chief financial officer Don Martin Navarro were both competent and respected administrators serving the Spanish government in New Orleans. The trio met several times, ostensibly discussing Wilkinson's wish to sell the goods he had brought with him, but both parties' motives soon became clear. On August 8, 1787, Wilkinson was granted a permit to bring in or sponsor shipments of Kentucky goods. In return, Wilkinson delivered a 7,500-word report that became known as his "first memorial," a document outlining the political future of the western settlements. Wilkinson indicated that he had made the voyage to New Orleans at the request of Kentucky notables to determine Spain's interest in opening negotiations to admit it under Spain's protection as its vassal. Thus began Wilkinson's official interactions with Spain in which he bent the truth for his own personal gain, trading personal integrity to satisfy financial greed and the craving for self-importance.[689]

Key to Wilkinson's proposal was the denial of access to the Mississippi for American goods. River access was essential in gaining the loyalty of Kentuckians. Wilkinson recommended that Spain should absolutely refuse the right of navigation of the lower Mississippi to the American government in order to force the settlers to look to Spain for that privilege. This was the heart of what became known as the Spanish Conspiracy, to induce Kentuckians to leave the Union and become part of the Spanish Empire by offering the reward of free trade on the Mississippi. Wilkinson promised to act as Spain's agent to make this come about.[690]

Although his recommendation to shut the Mississippi River to American traffic was in complete contradiction to the policy he espoused in Kentucky, Wilkinson insisted that a man of great popularity and political talent would be able to alienate western Americans from the United States, destroy any insidious designs of territorial rival Great Britain, and throw the Kentuckians into the arms of Spain. Such a person would need to be rewarded for his efforts and be allowed to ship goods to New Orleans free of charge. He, of course, was that man.[691]

---

[689] Linklater, *Artist in Treason*, 83–85; William R. Shepherd, "Wilkinson and the Beginnings of the Spanish Conspiracy," *American Historical Review* 9, no. 3 (1904), 498–503.

[690] Linklater, *Artist in Treason*, 85.

[691] Ibid., 86.

In his memoirs, Wilkinson denied that he had done anything more than offer empty promises in return for the commercial advantage of importing tobacco and other products to New Orleans. Regardless, on August 22, 1787, Wilkinson signed a formal document "transferring my allegiance from the United States to his Catholic Majesty." For others who would later make similar declarations in order to attain trading privileges, this act amounted to no more than a step toward closing a deal, but Wilkinson added this statement expressed in words clearly intended to carry weight with the two men he most wanted to impress:

> Born and educated in America, I embraced its cause in the last revolution, and remained throughout faithful to its interest, until its triumph over its enemies. . . . This occurrence has now . . . left me at liberty, having fought for her happiness, to seek my own. [But] circumstances and the policies of the United States having made it impossible for me to obtain this desired end under its Government, I am resolved to seek it in Spain.

Linklater notes that despite the declaration that he could not be accused of having broken any law or of tarnishing his honor by changing his allegiance, Wilkinson's instructions to Miró and Navarro were clear. Should their plans not work out, he relied on them to "bury these communications in eternal oblivion."[692]

Before departing New Orleans, Wilkinson set up a system of complex ciphers to communicate with his handlers. The use of ciphers was commonplace in an era in which there was no assurance a letter might be opened by anyone along the way to its recipient, but Wilkinson's use of it was exceptional, coding documents up to thirty pages in length.[693]

Wilkinson was welcomed as a hero upon his return to Kentucky. Within weeks, he assembled a fleet of twenty-five large flatboats to transport unprecedented quantities of tobacco, flour, and ham down the Mississippi. Sent under the direction of Wilkinson's partner in the Lexington store, Isaac Dunn and assistant Philip Nolan, the fleet made it successfully to

---

[692] Linklater, *Artist in Treason*, 86–87. See also Shephard, *Wilkinson and the Beginnings of the Spanish Conspiracy*, 496–97 for complete transcript of oath and Wilkinson, *Memoirs of My Own Times*, II: 108–15.

[693] Linklater, *Artist in Treason*, 88, 333–34.

the port city and realized a $9,830.50 profit. Intoxicated by this return, Wilkinson, in conjunction with Daniel Clark, an Irish-born merchant in New Orleans, and Dunn, spent almost $20,000 on return cargo bound for Kentucky consisting of luxury goods, including sugar, linen, wine, and brass candlesticks with the hidden agenda of impressing its residents with the advantages of the New Orleans trading route.[694]

Meanwhile, another Kentucky assembly had convened. Deciding unanimously on separation from Virginia, it had drafted a petition for admission to the Union to be delivered to Congress, but Kentucky's request was rejected on the ground that no additional state should be admitted before the organization of the new federal government. The assembly then called for a subsequent meeting to be held in November 1788 to discuss achieving entrance into the Union, obtaining unrestricted navigation of the Mississippi, and forming a constitutional district government. Congress's refusal to address Kentucky's status that summer and essentially placing the issue on hold for two years had played directly into Wilkinson's hands. Relying on Miró's ignorance of existing politics, Wilkinson assured him that with only two notable exceptions, all important delegates were decidedly in favor of separation from the United States and ultimate alliance with Spain. Miró was duped and expected November's assembly to decide on an independent Kentucky's alliance with Spain. In New Orleans, Miró wrote Spanish minister Don Antonio Valdes of the coming assembly, noting that the affair had progressed more rapidly than he had anticipated.[695]

Wilkinson and his associates suffered a setback at the November convention. Word of their plan for secession from the Union had surfaced and crystallized opposition among the party of large plantation owners whose property titles might be questioned should Kentucky become a sovereign power. Delegates were not ready to make the double leap of both defiance of the state of Virginia and rejection of the United States authority. The assembly agreed to meet yet again following the election of the new federal government.[696]

---

[694] Ibid., 91.

[695] Jacobs, *Tarnished Warrior*, 88–89. See Charles Gayarré, *History of Louisiana, vol. 3: The Spanish Domination* (New Orleans: Armand Hawkins, 1883), 194–98, 221–22 for Miró's optimistic views concerning the progression of events, copies of his letters from Wilkinson, and his correspondence with Spanish ministers.

[696] Linklater, *Artist in Treason*, 94–95. Gayarré, *History of Louisiana, Vol. 3: The Spanish Domination*, 228.

Wilkinson's correspondence with Miró following the November convention typified what became his pattern of reporting incomplete truths and blatant deception to his patrons while highlighting his own endeavors to manipulate events. Linklater notes that in February 1789, relying on lack of timely communications between Kentucky and New Orleans, Wilkinson sent Miró a long account of his performance at the convention that was almost entirely deceptive. Although the event had ended in failure, Wilkinson claimed that support for their cause had grown.[697]

Jacobs observed, "As a political chameleon Wilkinson was peerless. When circumstances demanded, he changed the color of his faith; in Kentucky he was one person; in New Orleans, another. Whether here or there he appeared to be in entire accord with those whom he would influence, employing their weaknesses to serve his ends." He adds that it was in this mindset that Wilkinson wrote Miró in 1789 that he had become "a good Spaniard."[698]

Wilkinson now found additional reasons to enhance his web of deceit, the most immediate being his precarious financial status due to a life of

---

Wilkinson was not alone in support of a separatist movement. Kentucky notables John Brown and Harry Innes, who later became Kentucky's delegate to Congress and the state's attorney general were initially identified both with the movement and with the legitimate agitation for statehood into which direction the issue inevitably merged. Roosevelt notes that many undoubtedly honorable men shared Wilkinson's views, but he was nonetheless critical of them because by proposing to enter into a separatist scheme, they were disloyal to their country and coerced by motives of private gain. He concedes, however, that given the weakness of the Union and the problems it faced at the time, only the most far-seeing and patriotic men could render unswerving loyalty toward it. Wilkinson, though, conspired for its breakup by working to persuade Spain to adopt measures that would damage both eastern and western sections of the country and increase the friction between them. Not only did he want to see the Spanish plans come to fruition, he sought to retain monopoly of the trade with New Orleans as long as possible. By receiving payment for his services to Spain, Wilkinson entered into a corrupt conspiracy with Spanish authorities to dismember the Union. See Roosevelt, *The Winning of the West, Vol. 3: The Founding of the Transatlantic Commonwealths, 1784-1790*, 141–44, 151.

[697] Linklater, *Artist in Treason*, 95, 98.
[698] Jacobs, *Tarnished Warrior*, 92.

extravagance and failed business ventures. The shipment of luxury goods to Kentucky conceived by Wilkinson, Clark, and Dunn that departed New Orleans in September 1788 made slow headway up the Mississippi and was crushed in Ohio River ice before reaching its destination. Dunn, distraught over his wife's infidelity and the loss of his personal investment in the disastrous shipment of goods, committed suicide the following June. His death, Wilkinson told Miró, entailed a burden on him of $10,000. To recoup his losses, Wilkinson sent another larger fleet transporting tobacco down the Mississippi in the spring of 1789 and was forced to borrow from wealthy speculators to support the venture. This trip was successful, the purchase of 235,000 pounds of tobacco assured. Wilkinson accompanied his next shipment in June 1789. These successful transactions were not enough to pay his expenses, however. When at the end of the 1789 season, a courier from New Orleans arrived in Kentucky with two barrels of silver to pay the farmers for the tobacco they had entrusted to Wilkinson, there was not enough to cover what was owed them. Their anger and abuse began the erosion of Wilkinson's popularity in Kentucky.[699]

Wilkinson's one hope of economic rescue lay in his relationship with Miró, but he was also alarmed that others might share his favored status. Spanish policy toward the United States was about to change. In May 1788, Spain's minister to the United States, Diego de Gardoqui, received notice of his country's intent to boost the population of its North American colonies by attracting settlers to its side of the Mississippi by offering free land, access to the river, and religious tolerance. All at once, Wilkinson's privileged position was threatened by others who might take advantage of Gardoqui's offers, including George Rogers Clark, Friedrich von Steuben, Daniel Boone, and John Sevier, founder of the short-lived Franklin colony who assured the minister that the settlers in eastern Tennessee were unanimous in their desire to form an alliance with Spain and to put themselves under its protection. Additionally, by December 1788, Col. George Morgan had already received permission to create a settlement on the Mississippi that was appropriately dubbed "New Madrid." Wilkinson attempted to counter such colonization by requesting 60,000 acres on the Yazoo River, allegedly to serve as a buffer state between the United States and Spanish territory, but in actuality to draw immigrants away from the New Madrid enterprise. He then unsuccessfully endeavored to discredit Morgan with

---

[699] Linklater, *Artist in Treason*, 99.

Miró, but the governor, impressed with Morgan, felt that he would be a great asset to Spanish policy in Louisiana. Although New Madrid was eventually colonized, Morgan ultimately abandoned his involvement in the project, but not before making known to Ambassador Gardoqui his uncomplimentary views about Wilkinson's Yazoo River scheme and the latter's partnership with Miró. By the end of the controversy surrounding the New Madrid project, both Morgan and Wilkinson had exchanged verbal shots through their respective benefactors. Given Wilkinson's penchant for holding grudges, it is conceivable that John Armstrong's association with Morgan at the time regarding an unrelated land purchase might have prejudiced his future commander against him. Whether at this point Wilkinson was aware of Morgan's other business transactions or was privy to Armstrong's partnerships and land purchases is not known.[700]

It took nearly eighteen months for the official response by the Spanish Council to Miró and Wilkinson's "First Memorial" to reach New Orleans. Received in early 1789, it outlined policies contrary to those they had proposed. Not only was the Mississippi to be opened for trade, but tariff would also be a mere 15 percent duty on goods sold. Migration to Louisiana was to be encouraged, and a ban was placed on any help given to Kentucky's secessionist movement. Such positions spelled financial disaster for Wilkinson. He subsequently formulated a second memorial to the Spanish government with Miró and Navarro on the assumption that Spain was out of touch with the swiftly changing events in the Mississippi Basin and that its leaders failed to understand that their plan was the key to political influence in the region. This time, Wilkinson had to couch his proposals in an entirely different manner while continuing to present his argument for personal advantage. Since easy immigration to Louisiana had been decreed, Wilkinson now changed course, declaring himself an ardent advocate for its prosecution. In place of stirring up revolution in Kentucky, he urged that "secret and indirect" agencies should be set into motion for

---

[700] Linklater, *Artist in Treason*, 97; Max Savelle, "The Founding of New Madrid, Missouri," *Mississippi Valley Historical Review* 19, no. 1 (1932), 30–56. See also Wilkinson to Miró, February 14, 1789, in Gayarré, *History of Louisiana*, 241–46, 264–68. Armstrong's correspondence includes an agreement made January 30, 1789, between Morgan, George McCully, and Armstrong for the purchase of thirty thousand acres of land twelve miles below the Wabash River, a follow-on survey dated May 1, 1789, and correspondence of February 25, 1791, PJA.

its separation and independence from the United States. He would make Kentucky a barrier state and bind her to Spain by ties of mutual advantage. New Orleans should be made a free port to sea trade, made prosperous by the West's ability to dispose of its products. The Mississippi had to be closed, but influential men given commercial advantages to advertise the advantage of Spanish protection. Whatever the program, Wilkinson still needed money to sustain the propagation of Spanish interests. Additionally, Wilkinson urged paying off Kentucky notables who might influence their state's political leanings. He provided a list of twenty-two people who should be offered bribes, some of whom at one time might have supported Wilkinson's plan but who had since fallen silent after the formation of the new federal government. Nearly all were friends or enemies he wished to buy off. Wilkinson stressed his zeal and loyalty to Spain's interest, at one point asking Madrid to grant him a military commission.[701]

The Spanish Council was not fooled. Linklater surmises that it must have been clear that the memorial was designed for Wilkinson's own benefit, an inference reinforced by the request for a loan of $7,000. But the significance in Wilkinson's request for a Spanish commission was not lost on Miró. Armies required oaths of loyalty. Wilkinson had crossed the line and was prepared for treachery.[702]

---

[701] Linklater, *Artist in Treason*, 98, 100–01 and Jacobs, *Tarnished Warrior*, 95–96. Wilkinson's friends included his lawyer Harry Innes, at that time a federal judge, and his enemies included Humphrey Marshall, once his partner but now suing him over a failed land deal. Wilkinson's second memorial appears in full in William R. Shepherd, ed., "Papers Bearing on James Wilkinson's Relations with Spain, 1787-1816," *American Historical Review* 9, no. 4 (1904), 748–66. Accessed through JSTOR, March 21, 2021. https://doi.org/10.2307/1834098 Wilkinson had earlier been approached by John Connally, a British spy from Canada investigating loyalties of Kentucky settlers with the hidden objective of inducing them "to throw themselves into the Arms of Great Britain" by promising money, ammunition, and ships to help them open Mississippi navigation. In his correspondence to Miró, Wilkinson took full credit for cleverly dispatching him from the territory.

[702] Linklater, *Artist in Treason*, 101. Miró's communication with Valdes of May 22, 1790, reiterates a prior recommendation that Wilkinson be given a $2,000 pension from the Spanish government. He additionally recommended that payment also go to Benjamin Sebastian, whom Wilkinson had identified as a true and trusted friend of Spain, with the thought of Sebastian keeping an eye on Wilkinson. Gayarré, *History of Louisiana*, 286.

When Wilkinson returned to Kentucky in October 1789, he moved his family to Louisville. Most of his real estate had to be sold. He had stayed so long in New Orleans in 1787 that his expenses ate up all but $377 of the $10,185 his cargo earned. The following year, tobacco sales brought in $16,372; but expenses left only $6,251 in Mexican silver dollars for Abner Dunn, brother of his deceased partner, to bring north for payment to his suppliers. In 1789, Wilkinson sent down 342 hogsheads of tobacco; and although almost one-third was found to be so rotten it could not be brought to market, the remainder sold for $18,131. Once investor Daniel Clark received his share, Miró took his $3,000 cut, and other expenses were paid, Wilkinson was left with just $49 and nothing to invest in next season's trade. Whatever credit Wilkinson still had in Kentucky now depended on the goodwill of New Orleans. Without Miró, he could not survive.[703]

However indebted he felt toward Miró in his ever-deepening spiral of dependence, how he might have justified to himself the following act that clearly crossed the line into treason is a question that only he could have answered. In the spring of 1790, Wilkinson learned of the government's plan to establish an overland route from Kentucky to New Orleans and wrote Miró to set the Creeks upon the army unit led by Maj. John Doughty that was initiating this new line of communication. Nearly annihilated by Cherokee, Shawnee, and Creek warriors, the mission's survivors had to be rescued from their final destination on the Mississippi River during Armstrong's stay at Kaskaskia. Wilkinson would likely have been in Louisville when Doughty's party departed Fort Steuben. When the mission's fate became known, Wilkinson must surely have had to come to terms with his own part in an act of betrayal of an American officer whom he undoubtedly knew and the subsequent death of his men in order to further a relationship with Spain. Knowing Wilkinson's involvement in this incident makes accounts of his later attempts to undermine Wayne easier to fathom.[704]

Miró gave Wilkinson $7,000 with the understanding that should the Spanish court fail to allow it as pension money, the amount would be repaid. Jacobs, *Tarnished Warrior*, 97.

[703] Linklater, *Artist in Treason*, 103.

[704] Washington to the Chiefs of the Choctaw, 17 December 1789, Founders Online, http://founders.archives.gov/documents/Washington/05-04-02-0293. See also Jacobs, *Tarnished Warrior*, 102.

In December 1789, Virginia passed legislation paving the way for Kentucky's statehood. June 1, 1792, was selected as the date when the separation from Virginia would occur, at which time it would become the nation's fifteenth state. Wilkinson knew that he could no longer continue to interest Miró in their original scheme of winning Kentucky and exerted every effort to get what he could from the perquisites he already enjoyed. He tried constantly to show that benefits for him would best promote the interests of Spain. He harped on the prospect of dangerous emigrants coming into Spanish territory and obstructing expeditions from upriver. Above all, he advised the Spanish government to adhere to the initial provisions noted in the pending Jay-Gardoqui treaty and make conditions as oppressive to westerners as they would be beneficial in the East, This would create more disunion and encourage more immigration, thereby supporting their common aims.[705]

Meanwhile, Wilkinson's business ventures, characterized by carelessness and bad luck, were floundering. In 1790, his associate Philip Nolan lost two-thirds of the cargo he took down the swollen Kentucky River. Having appealed to his creditors in January 1791 for an extension on his loans, Wilkinson made one last attempt to realize a profit and sent roughly 200,000 pounds of tobacco to New Orleans; the sale failed because much of it was in poor condition and Madrid had arbitrarily capped sales of the product at 40,000 pounds. Wilkinson's days as a trader were over. He was equipped for only one other profession and began looking for ways to reenter the military.[706]

★

Following the defeat of Harmar's expedition in October 1790 and the increase in raids into Kentucky, settlers clamored for retribution. When Wilkinson offered to lead a column of volunteers in a retaliatory raid, he wrote Miró, "The voice of all ranks called me." However, he overestimated his popularity. Not until the spring of 1791 did the Kentucky committee authorize a punitive raid, and command was given to Gen. Charles Scott with Wilkinson in a subordinate role. After leading a second raid which he commanded, Wilkinson took credit for his marginal achievement, trumpeting his success to Knox and indicating his desire to reenter military

---

[705] Jacobs, *Tarnished Warrior*, 101.
[706] Linklater, *Artist in Treason*, 105–106.

service, presenting himself as a patriotic frontiersman anxious to serve his country. Underlying his rhetoric was another plan. He now set his sights on commanding the new army Congress had authorized in response to Harmar's defeat.[707]

The obvious question is how Wilkinson could possibly have been considered for a command given his lackluster performance as clothier general ten years before, his apparent disregard for Washington's opinion of him at that time, and the numerous warnings the administration had received concerning questionable dealings with the Spanish government. Wilkinson's friend John Brown, a member of Congress, alerted him to an embarrassing story circulating in the East concerning "an influential American . . . engaged in trade to New Orleans and [who] now acts the part of secret Agent for Spain in Kentucky and employed by that Court through Miró for the purpose of effecting a separation of Kentucky from the Union." The strong innuendo against Wilkinson originated in a thirty-page paper sent to Washington on September 30, 1790, by James O'Fallon, land speculator and brother-in-law of George Rogers Clark. This followed a letter sent by Thomas Marshall, father of future Supreme Court Justice John Marshall, in October 1789 in which he sketched the outline of the Spanish conspiracy to effect a violent separation from the United States. Marshall insisted that he had seen a letter from Miró promising to place Wilkinson's ideas before the king of Spain. In his response to Marshall, Washington indicated that he had heard previous information in this vein and that he was alarmed by the news Marshall had shared.[708]

---

[707] Linklater, *Artist in Treason*, 107–08. See Wilkinson to Knox, August 26, 1791 and Knox to Washington, September 22, 1791, Founders Online, https://founders.archives.gov. Another member of the Marshall family, Henry, Wilkinson's political nemesis and nephew of Thomas, was ironically instrumental in Wilkinson's appointment. When criticized for recommending him, he defended his course thusly: "I consider Wilkinson well qualified for a commission . . . I considered him dangerous to the quiet of Kentucky, perhaps to her safety. If the commission does not secure his fidelity, it will at least place him under control, in the midst of faithful officers, whose vigilance will render him harmless if not honest." Royal Ornan Shreve, *The Finished Scoundrel: General James Wilkinson, Sometime Commander-in-chief of the Army of the United States, Who Made Intrigue a Trade and Treason a Profession* (Indianapolis: Bobs-Merrill Company, 1933), 86.

[708] Jacobs, *Tarnished Warrior*, 104–05; Linklater, *Artist in Treason*, 108.

The answer to the question of Wilkinson's appointment was rooted in his popularity in Kentucky. Richard Kohn notes that the administration's policy had been to suppress talk of secession by attaching leading Kentuckians to the national government. Wilkinson had a considerable following in the future state and powerful friends whose support it coveted. His raid into Indian territory had been touted as successful, so he was a natural choice for a leadership position in an army smarting from defeat and unpopular in Kentucky. He had only to await the outcome of St. Clair's campaign that more savvy Kentuckians felt was doomed for defeat. When the president appointed him lieutenant colonel commandant of the Second Regiment on October 22, 1791, Wilkinson sat out the ongoing campaign and awaited news of its failure. And fail it did.[709]

---

[709] Kohn, "General Wilkinson's Vendetta," 362; Jacobs, *Tarnished Warrior*, 114–15.

15

Fort Hamilton, 1792

There are very few nights that we are not under arms,
being alarmed by our sentinels firing on the enemy,
who, we know, have two or three spies constantly
about us. We dare not go beyond the gates.
—Unidentified frontier officer[710]

In March 1792, Washington and his advisers began the difficult task of selecting the right man this time to lead the reorganized army. It was a decision not to be taken lightly. The federal government could not risk yet another disastrous defeat. Responsibility rested ultimately upon Washington's shoulders; the success of his administration might well depend on the person who would now command the country's military forces. Failure was not an option.

Washington and his close confidants considered sixteen former generals. All were flawed in some way. Some were unknown, others too old, and some "never discovered much enterprise." His own choice was the current governor of the state of Virginia, Henry Lee, Revolutionary War "Light Horse Harry" of Lee's Legion, but because Lee had been only

---

[710] Quote from *Carlisle (PA) Gazette and the Western Repository of Knowledge*, November 28, 1792, cited in Alan D. Gaff, *Bayonets in the Wilderness: Anthony Wayne's Legion in the Old Northwest* (Norman: University of Oklahoma Press, 2004), 83.

a colonel at the end of the war he knew that more senior officers would refuse to serve under his command.

Political considerations also clouded the issue, and candidates had their own influential backers. Army historian James Ripley Jacobs notes that the president wanted the appointment to dampen political opposition and build public confidence in the war effort. As Washington lamented to his friend Lee, "to attempt to please everybody is the sure way to please nobody."[711]

Finally, in mid-April, the president reluctantly picked the least bad choice, forty-seven-year-old Maj. Gen. Anthony Wayne. Regarded initially by Washington as "open to flattery; vain; easily imposed on; liable to be drawn into scrapes" and likely "addicted to the bottle," whatever misgivings he might have had, Jacobs theorizes that the president recognized that Wayne possessed the potential for greatness. Wayne served with Washington during eight trying years of the Revolution, leading his men through the misery and death of the Canada campaign, fighting bravely at Brandywine and Germantown, and emerging with his patriotism unshaken and his will unbroken. His bayonet assault upon Stony Point was legendary, and he had saved West Point from the treachery of Benedict Arnold. In later war years, he had won the deep admiration and friendship of the commander of the Southern Department Maj. Gen. Nathanael Greene as he evicted the British from Georgia. Washington was convinced that Wayne possessed one eminent quality—a dominating desire to meet and annihilate the enemy.[712]

When Wayne accepted the command on April 13, he quickly discovered that he was to head an organization that existed only on paper. The War Department prematurely released the names of four men who had been appointed to the rank of brigadier general, but only James Wilkinson had accepted and the other three positions remained vacant. Staffing the First and Second Regiments was also a problem because so many officers in the latter had been killed in the St. Clair campaign.

Leadership positions needed to be filled, and wrangling over the merits and shortcomings of officers considered for promotion once again occupied the minds of Knox and the president. Of the three majors in the

---

[711] Kohn, *Eagle and Sword*, 125; Sword, *President Washington's Indian War*, 205; Jacobs, *The Beginning of the U.S. Army*, 126–27.

[712] Jacobs, *The Beginning of the U.S. Army*, 127.

First Regiment, only John Hamtramck was considered, David Zeigler having resigned in March 1792 and the other, Richard Call, not considered promotable due to unspecified "imputations" against him. There were no available majors in the Second Regiment—Jonathan Heart, killed in battle, and others, Lemuel Trescott and John Burnham resigning after Wilkinson, a civilian, had been promoted lieutenant colonel over them. David Strong, John Smith, and Joseph Asheton, senior captains from the First Regiment, were assigned to fill these vacant majorities in the Second Regiment, and Erkuries Beatty was designated as major in the First Regiment.[713]

Although Congress had approved three new regiments, the War Department decided to organize only two. Knox called on men with experience in Indian campaigning to fill the positions of major. Thomas Butler, Henry Gaither, John Clark, Henry Bedinger, and Alexander Trueman had been part of St. Clair's campaign, and William McMahon was a noted and experienced Indian scout. Once these assignments had been secured, the War Department decided to bide its time in order to determine which officers would prove worthy of promotion to lieutenant colonel. Vacancies at the company level in the First and Second Regiments were filled by advancing officers based on date of rank.[714]

In addition to considering the merits of individuals to occupy leadership positions in the restructured army, now renamed the Legion of the United States, Washington and Knox moved to correct problems that had plagued past campaigns. They instituted major changes to the accounting and contracting system by authorizing the Treasury Department to approve requests for salary, subsistence, recruiting, and contingent expenses; and to let all contracts; to handle all purchases of supplies and provisions; and to oversee the disbursement of pay and subsistence to regimental and company paymasters. Intent on not repeating past mistakes, they appointed James O'Hara quartermaster general with two deputies, Maj. Isaac Craig

---

[713] Gaff, *Bayonets in the Wilderness*, 35.

[714] Gaff, *Bayonets in the Wilderness*, 35–36. Armstrong, with promotion date of September 26, 1790, was not sufficiently senior to be considered for the rank of major at the time initial staffing decisions were made. See "Roster of the Officers of the 'Legion of the United States' Commanded by Major General Anthony Wayne," *PMBH* 16, no. 4, 423–29 for a listing of officers' dates of rank.

and Maj. John Belli, who would operate on both ends of the supply line to facilitate movement of goods between Pittsburgh and Cincinnati.[715]

The War Department outlined stringent policies regarding enlistment. Recruiters were directed to conduct themselves "with candor, integrity, and industry" and were cautioned not to abuse the system in an effort to fill their companies. Unless discharged sooner, soldiers were to be enlisted for a term of three years, and each was to receive a bounty of eight dollars to be paid only after taking an oath of allegiance.

Recruiting officers were to receive two dollars per enlistee although payment was withheld if the recruit deserted before leaving the rendezvous point. Quality over quantity was stressed, but Alan Gaff notes that officers were nevertheless encouraged to fill their companies because any marked deficiency in numbers would be reported to the president who could revoke their commissions. While the War Department assumed that quality soldiers would be forthcoming, captains and lieutenants, as usual, took anyone who could be had.[716]

★

Companies of enlistees began to arrive in Pittsburgh in early summer. Wayne soon found conditions there unsuitable for the growing number of men clustered within Fort Fayette, a small compound that had replaced Fort Pitt as a supply depot in the center of town. Wayne realized immediately that the garrison, built to accommodate only a company-sized unit, could not begin to satisfy his needs, not only because of its size but also due to its location. Liquor and women were too easily available, and the new men

---

[715] Kohn, *Eagle and Sword*, 124.

[716] Gaff, *Bayonets in the Wilderness*, 37–38. Recruits were to have been between eighteen and forty-five years of age, at least five feet five inches tall "without shoes," and "healthy, robust, and sound in his limbs and body." They should not be intoxicated at enlistment, nor could they swear to the oath until after a waiting period of at least twenty-four hours. No persons of African descent nor Indians were to be recruited. Officers were not to enlist vagrants, and if possible, recruits were to be "natives of fair conduct or foreigners of good characters for sobriety and fidelity, who have been some years in the country." Recruiting instructions, Henry Knox to Benjamin Briggs, March 31, 1792, PWD, accessed March 29, 2021, http://wardepartmentpapers.org/s/home/item/42661. Original source: Isaac Craig Papers.

were easily deprived of their pay, enlistment bonuses, and money realized from selling their clothing or equipment. Wayne could control liquor within his encampment but not outside its walls, and his dealings with civil authorities were unsatisfactory. He subsequently seized the opportunity to move his army twenty-two miles down the Ohio, created an encampment high above the river with plenty of timber for huts, and appropriately named his new station "Legionville." There, in what was a major difference between this and prior campaigns, Wayne set about preparing his men for what was to come and assiduously began the process of molding his collection of misfits into soldiers.

Not unlike the recruits of previous campaigns, the new enlistees were mostly "waifs of misfortune." During the Revolution, Wayne was noted for being a bit of a martinet. At Legionville he instituted strict policies for both men and officers that defined the army as he thought it should be. Many men were not accustomed to such high standards of cleanliness and neatness, and he insisted that officers set an example. Clothing was to be kept presentable; needles, thread, and patches were issued to all units. Those not turned out properly at reveille were deprived of their half gills of whiskey. Men detailed for guard duty were to be freshly shaven and powdered and to have their arms in perfect order. Sloppiness was rewarded with a penalty of twenty lashes.

He instituted changes in health care and emphasized proper hygiene among the troops. Legionville was kept thoroughly policed. Adequate numbers of latrines were dug and maintained by fatigue details. Kitchens were kept in order, and rubbish was prohibited from being dropped on the parade ground. When ill, soldiers were required to report to the hospital where the patients' daily rations of whiskey were bartered away for vegetables. Men were detailed from companies to provide help in the hospital, and two women were hired to cook for and nurse the sick. Soldiers were inoculated against smallpox.[717]

Wayne's primary objective was to maximize his army's preparedness. To achieve this end, discipline was key. Although measures punishing military infractions and criminal behavior had been an integral part of army routine and practice, neither Harmar nor St. Clair had imposed such a draconian disciplinary routine as that instituted by Wayne, and

---

[717] Jacobs, *The Beginning of the U.S. Army*, 129–34; Wayne to Knox, September 14, 1792, Knopf, *AWNIA*, 98–99.

both officers and enlisted men chafed under his iron rule. Army historian Wiley Sword notes that Wayne's orderly book for 1792–1793 reads largely a treatise on harsh punishments. Punishment was immediate and seemingly of an inconsistent nature depending on circumstances. Penalties ran the gamut from the mere issuance of reprimands to hanging or death by the firing squad. The most frequent form of discipline was flogging, often reserved for soldiers found sleeping on duty or evidencing an intention to desert. Capital punishment was generally reserved only for repeat offenders. Branding and running the gauntlet were commonplace. Lighter sentences, such as drumming a convicted soldier out of camp, forcing him to wear his coat inside out, or shaving his head were designed to shame those found guilty of lesser crimes. Above all else, punishment was meant to provide examples of what would happen to others should they digress from the expected norm of behavior. Confinement was not used; men were needed too badly to be wasted through its practice.

Knopf notes that although disciplinary measures imposed by Legion courts-martial were often severe, practices were in line with civil legal procedures at the time. He further notes that a study of court records suggests that Wayne, who approved or disapproved all sentences, valued men as individuals and that each convicted soldier received his thoughtful consideration before a sentence was confirmed.[718]

Just as Wayne made certain that his men understood his standards of discipline, he ensured that they would attain competency in the field. Recruits regularly practiced offensive and defensive drills. Wayne recognized the value of an accurate and rapid rate of fire and had his infantrymen repeatedly practice loading and firing with wooden snappers rather than expending precious powder and flints. Riflemen retrieved bullets from trees serving as practice targets and reclaimed the lead. He modified musket design in order to speed up the loading process. Sham battles were conducted to instill a sense of realism. He wrote to Knox in late July that he would soon provide his infantrymen with powder, although of an inferior grade, suitable only for such practice, to "inure the Cavalry to noise & fireing in their front, as well as to practice the Musketry to load & fire in full troot [sic, trot]". He later commented upon his success: "The

---

[718] Sword, *President Washington's Indian War*, 232; Knopf, "Crime and Punishment in the Legion," 237–38. See also Nicholson, "Courts-Martial in the Legion Army," 77–109.

very men who four or five weeks since, scarcely knew how to load, or draw a trigger, begin now to place a ball in a deadly direction."[719]

Wayne realized the value of esprit de corps. Battalion-sized flags and distinctly colored uniform trim and cap bindings and plumes in white, red, yellow, and green were ordered to correspond to the colors of each of the four sublegions. Wayne and others soon began to perceive a pronounced change in the character of his army.[720]

★

Wayne was eager to deploy the Legion down the Ohio well before winter set in. His force once in place, he envisioned a desultory expedition composed of mounted volunteers and regulars conducting road-cutting operations. Washington and Knox, however, held other ideas as to how the campaign should unfold. The prospect of war continued to be unpopular in the East, and political considerations drove the administration once again to negotiate with the Indian nations, initially to demonstrate to the country and allies that in spite of its military buildup, the government still preferred a peace settlement. A more important consideration, as usual, was money. Funding was difficult enough during times of peace and even greater in the event of war. European nations were unwilling to make loans until the new government of the United States had proven its stability. Taxes were deeply resented, and the one on whiskey was so hateful that rebellion was stirring in western Pennsylvania. The United States' status as a nation continued to be discounted by the British, and the Spanish were equally contemptuous, while France pressed the United States to continue the countries' alliance forged during the Revolution. With public doubt and criticism of the war following St. Clair's defeat reaching a crescendo, and with the need to keep the enemy off balance while its military forces were rebuilt, the administration had decided as early as January 1792 to dispatch emissaries to the Indian nations to determine any possibility of negotiation leading to peace.[721]

For the first of such missions, Knox sent Capts. Peter Pond and William Steedman to Forts Niagara and Detroit to "mix with the Miami

---

[719] Sword, *President Washington's Indian War*, 234; Wayne to Knox, July 27, 1792, *AWNIA*, 50.

[720] Sword, *President Washington's Indian War*, 235.

[721] Jacobs, *The Beginning of the U.S. Army*, 149–50.

and Wabash Indians" to ascertain their intentions regarding a possible peace and to persuade some of the most influential chiefs to travel to Philadelphia for talks with the administration. Their message, however, was perceived as arrogance. Conceding that United States forces had been defeated only a few months before, they threatened to send larger numbers in the next encounter and called on the Indians to "ask a peace of us." The purely cosmetic gesture ended in failure when the emissaries were unable to persuade the British to let them travel on Lake Erie to arrive at a negotiating site, and they had to turn back.[722]

The government also sought assistance from moderate Native American factions to influence a peace process. Representatives of the Six Nations who had been in Philadelphia in mid-March to discuss their own settlements with the government agreed to travel to a grand council that was to meet on the Maumee later in the year. Not only did the United States want to keep the Iroquois neutral, but they also hoped that they might assure the assembled chiefs that the United States wanted no lands but those obtained in a fair treaty. Mohawk chief Joseph Brant was persuaded to agree, and Knox dispatched Capt. Hendrick Aupaumut of the Stockbridge Indians to attend the council as well.[723]

Setbacks to Knox's plans occurred in early April 1792 when he instructed Maj. Alexander Trueman and Kentucky militia colonel John Hardin to act as emissaries, the former to the Maumee villages and the latter to the Wyandot towns on the Sandusky River. Neither made it to his destination. Their deaths were later confirmed by William May whom James Wilkinson had sent out independently to determine the fates of two other unfortunate emissaries, Freeman and Gerrard, whom he had dispatched earlier to carry messages of peace to Kekionga.

Rufus Putnam, the leader of the Ohio Company settlements at Marietta, was dispatched by Knox in May to contact hostile tribes on the Maumee. He was to meet them at Fort Jefferson to convince them that the government genuinely sought peace and to persuade them to journey to Philadelphia for formal negotiations. Delayed at Marietta until June 26, Putnam arrived at Fort Washington only to learn that a party of Indians

[722] Kohn, *Eagle and Sword*, 143; Horsman, *Expansion and the American Indian Policy*, 90; Knox to Captains Peter Pond and William Steedman, January 9, 1792, *ASP-Indian Affairs*, I: 227.

[723] Horsman, *Expansion and American Indian Policy*, 92; *ASP-Indian Affairs*, I: 233.

had attacked hay cutters on June 25 near Fort Jefferson. He believed the attack was directed toward him and abandoned his original plans, traveling instead to Vincennes to meet with the Wabash tribes in an effort to detach them from alliance with those of the Maumee.[724]

The administration clung to a thin thread of hope that a peace treaty might be possible. Putnam's meeting with the Wabash nations was somewhat productive; a treaty signed with them reinforced their intention to abstain from joining their brothers in war against the government. The administration now put its hope on the Six Nations persuading members of the council of its peaceful intentions and saw Brant's cooperation as encouraging, although he himself realized the fallacy in the government's continued proposal to occupy lands ceded earlier under the provisions of the Fort Harmar treaty. To maintain a resemblance of peaceful intent, Knox ordered Wayne to block any Kentucky forays into the territory until the effects of the peace overtures were known. He was to make no provocative

---

[724] Kohn, *Eagle and Sword*, 144, 146; Sword, *President Washington's Indian War*, 210–12. William May, the soldier whose life had been spared six months earlier during the St. Clair campaign while his two companions were executed on charges of desertion, was a man with cunning survival instincts and described by Wilkinson as "one of the most sublime scoundrels in the army." He set out from Fort Hamilton on April 13 and discovered the bodies of Trueman and two others seven days later. Apprehended by a party of Chippewas and Mingos, he was taken to a trading town on the Ottawa River, beaten and condemned to death but saved by Simon Girty and sent with a party of twenty-two Indians to attack Fort St. Clair around May 1. Returning northward, the party stopped at the site of St. Clair's battle where he learned the location of cannon hidden in the area. Taken to Detroit, he was purchased by British agent Matthew Elliot to work on a cargo schooner. He later identified distinctive scalps and heard the stories behind the deaths of both Trueman and Hardin from Indians he had transported. May eventually made his way to Pittsburgh and reported his findings to Wayne. Later, as part of the recovery mission to the scene of St. Clair's defeat on Christmas Day 1793, he directed the general's men to the buried cannon that were subsequently salvaged. Gaff, *Bayonets in the Wilderness*, 81; Sword, *President Washington's Indian War*, 211, 256; ASP- Indian Affairs, I: 243. Wilkinson to Armstrong, April 10, 1792, in John B. Dillon, *Oddities of Colonial Legislation in America* (Indianapolis: Robert Douglass Publisher, 1879), 506. May's instructions can be found in Armstrong's October 1990 papers at the Indiana Historical Society and were probably read to May before his departure.

military movements. Wayne and Wilkinson were both enraged because some of those murdered while on diplomatic missions had been military officers. They felt the men had been sacrificed to a useless policy of peace and appeasement. Nevertheless, Knox refused to give up hope.[725]

★

While Wayne was consumed with training in Legionville and the administration with peace overtures to various tribal entities, the army's new second-in-command, James Wilkinson, was overseeing his part of the operation farther down the Ohio. According to instructions from Knox, the new brigadier general's mission in the Northwest was three-fold: assure Native Americans of the federal government's desire for peace while attempting to learn all that he could about their intentions, numbers, and allies; establish one or more posts along the line of communication between Forts Hamilton and Jefferson; and lay in "abundant" provisions at advanced posts, particularly flour and salted meat, in addition to the amounts needed to last both garrisons for three to four months. This arrangement allowed Wilkinson to operate independently despite being subordinate to Wayne since the transmission of orders over long distances was slow and often interrupted and because most problems could be solved locally to better advantage. As John Armstrong discovered, however, while making sense on an organizational and logistical level, the system afforded the opportunity for Wilkinson to operate virtually unchecked.[726]

Wilkinson, in charge of what remained of St. Clair's woefully depleted army, set about the business of running his sphere of operation with unbounded energy. By mid-March, he had led a party of two hundred men to complete a post between Fort Hamilton and Fort Jefferson, which he christened "Fort St. Clair." Armstrong, commanding Fort Hamilton, was directed to expand that fort and to begin concerted efforts to plant hay to lay in store for the coming operation. Soldiers at Fort St. Clair

---

[725] Kohn, *Eagle and Sword*, 145–46; Sword, *President Washington's Indian War*, 219.

[726] Jacobs, *The Beginning of the U.S. Army*, 142; Knox to Wilkinson, February 11, 1792, Papers of the War Department, 1784–1800, Roy Rosenzweig Center for History and New Media, accessed March 29, 2021, http://wardepartmentpapers.org/s/home/item/42482. Original Source: James Wilkinson Manuscript Collection, Dawes Memorial Library, Marietta College.

and Fort Jefferson were to do the same since all three posts were to be way stations for troops and supplies. Commanders were given detailed instructions concerning the safety of their installations and that of convoys passing between them. Wilkinson issued a series of orders to promote pride, health, and cleanliness among troops that mirrored those of Wayne. Soldiers assigned to guard duty were to appear with their arms "in prime order," dressed in their best uniforms, and were to be shaved with their hair powdered. Latrines were dug two hundred yards from posts with a "necessary for the night" prepared closer to quarters. Sentinels were posted to prevent "wood, water, or any kind of filth" from being thrown on the parade ground. When work parties put in long hours during inclement weather, their rations were increased by one-half. Extra whiskey was issued on Christmas, but its sale to soldiers was strictly forbidden. Card gambling was also prohibited.[727]

★

Armstrong appears to have developed a positive relationship with his commander. His writings indicate that his duties at Fort Hamilton were challenging but that his accomplishments were gratifying and recognized approvingly by Wilkinson. Impressed with the beauty of his surroundings, he shared his thoughts regarding its future value in land development with Francis Johnston. Situated twenty-five miles north of Wilkinson's headquarters at Fort Washington on the banks of the Great Miami River, the scene was one of exceptional abundance. Jacobs describes the land as rich and the woods full of game. Ducks and wild turkeys were plentiful, and an abundance of fish could be netted in improvised seins. Multitudes of carrier pigeons sometimes huddled closely together in nearby trees after nightfall. Vegetables were assiduously cultivated because they were not included in the army rations, often with seeds provided by General and Mrs. Wilkinson. By the summer of 1792, Armstrong was raising beans, peas, corn, and even strawberries in spite of cutworms, yellow bugs, caterpillars, and grasshoppers.

Clearing the land surrounding the garrison provided a considerable challenge. Timber was thick and heavy, and marauding Indians were always a threat. Once the necessary clearance was achieved, the great effort

---

[727] Gaff, *Bayonets in the Wilderness*, 92.

resulted in only small areas of cultivation. If the ensuing crop escaped drought or destruction by Indians, soldiers were turned out to help with the harvest. At day's end, oxen carts pulling huge wagonloads of hay accompanied by a guard and workers with pitchforks and scythes returned to the garrison. Not far from the stockade, they tossed off the loads, piling them high in rounded stacks where they remained until the construction of a storage area within the walls of the fort could be completed. For their work, the men received a daily extra half gill of whiskey or had a dime added to their pay.[728]

Armstrong's other major project was to enlarge the fort that had been hastily constructed less than a year before. Not only was it to be redesigned to accommodate the ever-increasing numbers of men stationed there in its capacity as a way station for supply trains going back and forth to Forts St. Clair and Jefferson, but it also had to be expanded to accommodate the valuable stores of hay harvested from its fields. Wilkinson intended to make Fort Hamilton his headquarters upon Wayne's arrival at Fort Washington. Armstrong issued frequent updates to Wilkinson regarding not only his progress in cultivating the hay but also improvements to the fort that included making space for one thousand barrels of provisions and constructing a well, cistern, cellar, fish pond, a two-story soldiers' barracks, and officers' quarters, as well as improving its fortifications.[729]

Armstrong managed and monitored the wagon convoys proceeding between Fort Washington and Fort Jefferson. His men also constructed and manned flatboats to carry men and goods down the river as well as to convey parties across it. Packhorse teams were designated for bulk transport of goods, but river travel was generally easier and safer.

Additional men and teams of work animals were always in demand to accomplish the multitude of assignments laid upon Armstrong and his counterparts at the forts to the north. Specialized tools and implements were habitually in short supply, their availability dependent upon shipments from Pittsburg. Despite the reorganization of quartermaster operations, supply problems remained. Gaff notes that goods often arrived downriver in jumbled confusion. Packages were directed to officers no longer present,

---

[728] Armstrong to Francis Johnston, February 11, 1792, PJA; Jacobs, *The Beginning of the U.S. Army*, 147–48.

[729] Armstrong to Wilkinson, May 15 and June 1, 1792; Wilkinson to Armstrong, May 24, 1792, PJA.

uniforms might be dispatched in numbers to outfit full companies that were below strength, and musket balls might be labeled as horseshoes.[730]

Armstrong's correspondence with Wilkinson during April 1792 continually reflected shortages in items necessary for completing his assigned tasks and for provisioning his men. Carpenters arrived without tools and without the means of hauling timber. Reiterating to Wilkinson that without the necessary implements, he would not be able to carry out the general's orders, he added, "You must be tired of the repeated applications made for them." His letter of September 13 typifies his concerns regarding clothing for his men:

> I must, my dear general, in justice to my own feelings and to the men I command, repeat my complaint on the subject of clothing. It is known to you, sir, that my command has been a continued scene of fatigue and it is a reflection upon the nation that the men should serve six months without clothing. They are now performing the duties of soldiers without shirts or shoes, and seven months' pay due them. What can the public expect from men thus treated?—called upon, naked as they are, to perform the hardest service—destitute of money to purchase for themselves even a chew of tobacco.[731]

Overriding the entire operation of Fort Hamilton was the safety of the fort itself, its men who served as messengers, and those who transported supplies along the approximately seventy miles between Fort Washington and Fort Jefferson. Armstrong's men were continually tasked to guard

---

[730] Gaff, *Bayonets in the Wilderness*, 90–91.

[731] Armstrong to Wilkinson, April 27, 1792, in Cist, *CM* I: 168; Dillon, *Oddities of Colonial Legislation*, 506. In this sense, the term "nakedness" might have been literal. When soldiers were rotated out of Fort St. Clair in December 1792, editor of the *Kentucky Gazette* John Bradford noted, "He observes that these troops cut a shocking figure, and look more like a band of beggars than Federal soldiers posted for the defence of our frontiers . . . For they were not only bare of shirts, and bare headed, but were without a single pair of shoes, and a majority of them were obliged to conceal their posteriors with ragged blankets." Quoted in Gaff, *Bayonets in the Wilderness*, 91.

timber-cutting parties, construction crews, hay cultivators, pack trains, and those engaged in other assorted duties. The threat of attack was real.

Armstrong reported frequent Indian sightings to Wilkinson, assuring his general that he continued to take positive measures to heighten security around the fort and to prevent incidents from occurring under his command. On April 5, he reported sightings at both Fort Hamilton and at Dunlap's Station, during which all the cattle at the latter location had been driven off. Armstrong was convinced that warriors remained in the woods nearby his garrison and were "waiting for a scalp, in which I trust they will be disappointed." On May 9, he wrote that the horse of James McDonald, sent on an express run to Fort Washington two weeks earlier, had returned without his rider and he feared the messenger was dead.[732]

Earlier in the year, Capt. Joseph Shaylor, commander of Fort Jefferson, left that post with a small hunting party that included his son. The group was ambushed, and the younger Shaylor was killed. The captain was relieved of command and tried by a court-martial for leaving the garrison. His replacement, Capt. Joseph Montford, was himself slain on April 27 when he was lured outside the fort by turkey calls. Wilkinson issued a directive prohibiting all commanding officers from leaving the walls of their respective garrisons beyond musket range.[733]

Armstrong outlined his own security measures in his letter to Wilkinson on April 5, 1792. Convinced that small parties of Indians were continually in the neighborhood, he ordered that no soldier was to go 250 yards from the fort without permission from the commanding officer. When wood for fuel was needed, the men of each room were to go as a group conducted by a noncommissioned officer, and half the party were to carry arms.

Tensions reached a climax in mid-July during the height of hay cutting. Armstrong assured Wilkinson that at the time that both the crop and bullocks were safe and that the men would be able to camp on the enclosed parade ground the following day. He was conscious of his exposed situation, however, aware of Indian presence, and feared that a force of three hundred tribesmen might attack the operation. He estimated that only two more

---

[732] Armstrong to Wilkinson, April 5 and May 9, 1792, PJA.

[733] Gaff, *Bayonets in the Wilderness*, 12; Command orders, February 13, 1792, PJA.

days would be necessary to complete the task of bringing in approximately 150 tons of wheat.[734]

★

Wilkinson was firmly in command of the western forces, but wounds to his ego at not being chosen to command the army continued to fester. As the sole general officer from the Revolution on active duty at the time the selection was made, Wilkinson was consumed with the belief that the job should have been his. As long as Wayne was in Legionville, Wilkinson managed to live with the situation. Given the state of his financial affairs, he had little choice. Correspondence between the two was civil, but almost immediately, Wilkinson attempted to erode Wayne's authority. Wilkinson corresponded independently with the War Department, ostensibly to give Knox a direct and speedy channel of communication, but found use of this method as a means to bombard the secretary with complaints, proposals, and questions about supplies, strategy, and a myriad of details related to the army's organization. Wilkinson's letters to Wayne, while polite, were arrogant and overbearing. In November 1792, he elaborated in finest prose his desire for mounting desultory actions along the Maumee River:

> I must be candid to say that I earnestly wish for it, that I may be able to present to you a few Brilliants to lay at the feet of our President . . . cannot you suffer me to make a winter excursion, destroy the villages at the confluence of the Tawa and Glace River, and Erect Fort Wayne on the St. Mary's?" [735]

On several occasions, Wilkinson used Wayne's distance to question or modify specific orders. In November 1792, Wilkinson sent the general a twenty-seven-page letter describing the forts near Cincinnati as a separate district and requested additional prerogatives for himself. Wayne went directly to Knox to confirm Wilkinson's subordinate position.[736]

---

[734] Armstrong to Wilkinson, April 5, 1792, PJA; Armstrong to Wilkinson, July 14, 1792, *CM*, II: 27–28.

[735] References to the Ottawa and the Auglaize Rivers. Wilkinson to Wayne, November 28, 1792, Wayne Papers 23: 53 in Cochran notebooks, PJA.

[736] Richard H. Kohn, "General Wilkinson's Vendetta," 363.

Besides attempting to carve out an independent command, Wilkinson used other ploys to undermine Wayne. Jacobs notes that Wilkinson carefully maintained cordial relations with important politicians, particularly his old Kentucky friends, feeding them confidential information about the government's plans and openly criticizing military strategy. He entertained lavishly and cultivated his ties to the militia, giving them tasks that were seldom too onerous, such as participating in the winter expedition to the site of St. Clair's defeat. Despite the fact that construction of Fort St. Clair began as early as December 1791 by Maj. John S. Gano of the territorial militia whose men worked to complete the outpost and clear the surrounding grounds under extreme winter conditions, he claimed the credit for himself, noting to his friend Harry Innes that he had completed the task using fewer men and in less time than that which had been required for the building of either Fort Hamilton or Fort Jefferson.[737]

Wilkinson hosted prominent members of the territory and Hamilton County on May 1, 1792, to celebrate the frontier holiday of St. Tammany's Day. The party drank toasts accompanied by cannon salutes to the nation, President Washington, Congress, the Atlantic states, the western settlements, and others. Jacobs notes that among the sixteen toasts, one saluting the Indian nations most certainly would have been forgotten. Peace had to be maintained until negotiations were settled in spite of the fact that attacks had become more brazen as time went on. He suggests that Wilkinson would have preferred to launch 750 mounted men and 9 companies of infantry against them, a plan larger in scale but similar to the short aggressive campaign he had led in August the preceding year. Such an expedition would not have achieved any lasting results, but it might have enhanced his reputation among regulars and volunteers before Wayne's arrival. It might also have made people forget Charles Scott, the Kentucky militia general whom Wilkinson considered a rival.[738]

Wilkinson's most serious attempt to undermine Wayne involved splitting the loyalties of the officer corps. From the beginning, Wilkinson spoke disparagingly of Wayne to other officers. With grace and charm, he soon cultivated a small coterie of close friends and confidants within

---

[737] Jacobs, *The Beginning of the U.S. Army*, 144–45.

[738] James Ripley Jacobs, *Tarnished Warrior* (New York: The McMillan Company, 1938), 125–26.

Wilkinson's party was noted in John Bradford, ed., *Kentucky Gazette*, May 26, 1792.

the ranks. His posturing set the stage for conflicts to come. Wayne's delayed arrival in May 1793 eventually brought the two leaders together, and factions loyal to one general or the other developed rapidly. Wayne was not blameless, the ironclad discipline he imposed as he endeavored to transform the army made him unpopular in some circles. As Erkuries Beatty wrote to his friend Armstrong, "When he speaks, Heaven shrieks, and all stands in Awe."[739]

The exponential growth of the army created a fertile field for discord among the junior officers. The small officer corps that had composed the First Regiment only a few years before had been a tightly-knit group of Revolutionary War veterans who had shared hardship, death, deprivation, regimentation, and sometimes unmitigated boredom, not only during the long war years, but also on the isolated and sometimes brutal frontier. Christopher W. Wingate, in his comparison of the early U.S. army with the modern-day force, notes that available records and correspondence indicate few instances of dissension or conflict within the old officer corps and substantial evidence of a shared commitment to group values and loyalty. Almost ten years after the close of the war, many commissioned officers were from a new generation without knowledge of army customs and without those shared experiences that promoted an esprit de corps similar to that found in Harmar's army.[740]

Disputes in rank had always been an issue but soon became even more pronounced as bored officers became suspicious of one another. Young men with little knowledge of army etiquette took their cues from more senior officers. Both Wayne and Wilkinson oscillated from friendliness to angry hostility. Though each cloaked his feelings under a surface coating of formality, subalterns could sense the two general's animosity toward each other. Officers of longer service, mostly in the First and Second Regiments, tended to align with Wilkinson, particularly since they had been under his command prior to Wayne's arrival and because they disliked Wayne's demeanor, calling him "Ole Tony," "Old Horse," or "Mars" whenever they dared. Junior officers, including those of the newly formed Third and Fourth Sublegions, dependent on Wayne's favor for promotion more often favored the major general. The division was not ironclad, however, for like

---

[739] Kohn, "General Wilkinson's Vendetta," 363; Beatty to Armstrong, January 5, 1793, PJA.

[740] Wingate, *Military Professionalism and the Early American Officer Corps*, 84, 86.

the nation itself, the new army was riven by political factions, the Federalists supporting Wayne and the "democrats" backing Wilkinson. Some officers who might normally have opposed Wayne doubted Wilkinson's integrity, given the frequent rumors of Spanish intrigue that circulated about him. Men disciplined by either general joined the clique of his rival. As personal animosities arose between the two groups, arguments resulted in duels, an occurrence not generally reported in early regimental days.[741]

Wilkinson's disparaging comments were not limited to denigrating Wayne alone. Army historian James Ripley Jacobs notes that Wilkinson's egotism was so pronounced that he had little patience for the ideas of others. He had a low opinion of his associates, characterizing his officers as a group of incompetents who had a "painful deficiency of service and talents." Some in the First Regiment were "peddlers, others drunkards, and nearly all of them fools" and declared that a few had gone only a "little past the hornbook" while others could scarcely sign their names. In a letter of March 13, 1792, to his brother-in-law Clement Biddle that apparently by design found its way to Secretary Knox and to President Washington, Wilkinson tore into Maj. David Zeigler, the officer left in charge of Fort Washington in the absence of St. Clair prior to his own appointment. He described Zeigler's feud with then quartermaster Hodgdon, noting among other things, "He is a most insensible Blockhead, as seditious as any old Sargent, & destitute of every Ray of duty beyond the police of a company & the Minutiae of the parade."

Not content to stop there, Wilkinson continued, "Our friend Harmar since his unfortunate propensity to drink, has introduced & established the most disgraceful & pernicious habits in the 1st Regt, acting without check,

---

[741] Harry Emerson Wildes, *Anthony Wayne: Troubleshooter of the American Revolution* (Westport: Greenwood Press, 1941), 386–87; Kohn, "General Wilkinson's Vendetta," 364; Jacobs, *The Beginning of the U.S. Army*, 154; William Henry Harrison observed that "there were more duels in the Northwestern Army between 1791 and 1795 than ever took place in the same length of time and among so small a body of men," cited in Freeman Cleves, *Old Tippecanoe: William Henry Harrison and His Time* (New York: Charles Scribner's Sons, 1939), 15.

restraint, or control, he has sacrificed every thing to the capricious will of his officers, and I found them pettish & impatient as indulged Children."[742]

★

Wilkinson's command responsibilities did not prevent him from continuing his association with Spain. On December 21, 1791, shortly after accepting his commission, he wrote his benefactor Don Estaban Miró, asking for ideas on the "principal subject," the alignment of Kentucky with Spain. Shortly thereafter, Francisco Louis Hector, Baron de Carondelet, replaced Miró as governor of Louisiana; and it was now up to him to provide an answer. Not as savvy to Wilkinson's requests for money as his predecessor, Carondelet soon granted Wilkinson an annual pension of $2,000 retroactive to the first of the year 1789. Seven thousand dollars was to be deducted from that amount, however, representing the sum that Miró had previously advanced as a loan. Sometime during 1792, $4,000 was secured from New Orleans by Louisvillian Michael La Cassagne who in turn delivered it to Wilkinson on August 4. The amount was $3,000 more than was actually due at the end of the year, but opportunities for remitting so large an amount were infrequent. Wilkinson later declared that he ultimately received only $2,600, the balance of the sum possibly appropriated by La Cassagne, one of his creditors.[743]

Jacobs notes that Wilkinson could not abstain from the prospect of such money. On the contrary, the general tried to evince such zeal for the service of Spain that Carondelet would be deeply impressed and the pension money continued, if not increased. Again professing his allegiance and offering advice in a letter to the governor in December 1792, he

---

[742] Jacobs, *The Beginning of the U.S. Army*, 142; Wilkinson to Clement Biddle, March 13, 1792, included in a letter of April 16, 1792, from Henry Knox to George Washington. http://founders.archives.gov/documents/Washington/05-1--02-0167. Zeigler had served with the regiment since its inception and had been a respected officer throughout the Harmar and St. Clair years. Weary of coping with Wilkinson's schemes and machinations, Ziegler not only gave up his command but also resigned from the army on March 5, 1792, later becoming mayor of Cincinnati. See George A. Katzenberger, "Major David Ziegler: Biography of the First Mayor of Cincinnati," *OAHQ* 21, no. 2 and 3 (1912), 156.
[743] Jacobs, *Tarnished Warrior*, 133–34.

declared, "I have not abandoned those views, principles and attachments which I professed to Miró."

Wilkinson's biographer Andro Linklater notes that the report was imaginative, lively, and permeated with untruth. The general claimed to be in command of "2000 select troops composed of Musketeers, Chasseurs, Light, and Artillery" and to be paid "independent of prerogatives and facilities 3000 dollars a year." Despite these emoluments, he professed to be so disillusioned by having to soldier under "an incompetent Secretary of War and an ignorant Commander-in-Chief" that he wished to be given a commission in the Spanish army where his passion for "military fame" could be gratified. His rhetoric, which included the inflation of his powers and pay scale, as well as the feigned indifference to his career, was designed to make Carondelet realize how much he was worth. Linklater notes that the clear implication behind his words was that Spain should consider paying the general more to keep him from resigning. Militarily, Wilkinson noted that Spain had little to fear from its North American neighbor due to the "intestinal discord" between New England and the South and between the Atlantic states and the West. He continued that the conflict "renders the whole [nation] weak and contemptible, the occasion is favorable to Spain and you know how to improve it." [744]

Linklater notes that the letter was pivotal in Wilkinson's intrigue with Spain. Wilkinson had crossed the line. He was no longer a private citizen; he held the rank of brigadier general in the service of the United States. His actions had moved well beyond political grandstanding. A soldier who aided a foreign power violated his military oath and could be court-martialed; if charged with attempting to suborn others from their loyalty to the United States and found guilty, Wilkinson might face the death penalty for treason. [745]

Wilkinson was hooked. He had entered the army burdened with debt, and his condition had not improved substantially despite his payment from Carondelet and his army salary. By January 1792, Wilkinson had sold his properties in Frankfort, the proceeds of which went to former partner Peyton Short, who in turn assumed a number of Wilkinson's debts. The arrangement did not pay Wilkinson's most pressing obligations, however, and he had to send Henry Innes money from his army pay to satisfy his

---

[744] Jacobs, *Tarnished Warrior*, 134; Linklater, *An Artist in Treason*, 122–23.

[745] Jacobs, *Tarnished Warrior*, 134; Linklater, *An Artist in Treason*, 123.

creditors. Eager to maintain the judge's friendship, he offered to give him "uncontrolled power over my whole property in your own language." In November 1792, he sold the Louisville property to La Cassagne; and the following January, he turned over his interest in about 150,000 acres to Benjamin Sebastian, who in turn assumed responsibility for more of his debts.[746]

While determining how to solve his financial woes and contemplating how best to present himself to his Spanish benefactors, Wilkinson continued his double life as commander of the western army at Fort Washington in the company of his wife and children. There he oversaw the preparations for the campaign to come, putting out fires, large and small.

★

From all appearances, Armstrong had every reason to believe that he held Wilkinson's trust and approval. Their correspondence was frequent and generally congenial. The tone of letters exchanged between the two indicated that Wilkinson was pleased with Armstrong's attention to fulfilling the general's numerous directives and respected the captain's qualities as an officer. Wilkinson at times appeared unusually candid with his subordinate, although his motive behind doing so might have been to guage the degree of loyalty Armstrong held for his old commander. Referring to Wayne his May 24, 1792 letter, he wrote, "The almighty Big General has, I believe, conceived some jealousy of me; he may make the attempt, but shall not violate my rights with impunity." In a letter the previous month, Wilkinson cited Knox as the "God of War" in his opinion about the reorganization of the army: "If the God of War were not unfriendly to you, you should soon be a major." Armstrong apparently inferred that he was not on the secretary's good side, replying on May 16, "I am sorry that the God of war has formed any unjust prejudices against me. I will not suffer him to do me injustice & ask no favour."[747]

---

[746] Jacobs, *Tarnished Warrior*, 128–29, 133–35. Ironically, less than twelve months following the sale of the Lexington property, Kentucky's legislature chose it as the site of the newly independent state's capital. Land values quickly rose, and the fortune that Wilkinson always dreamed of passed instead to his creditors. Linklater, *Artist in Treason*, 120, 21.

[747] Wilkinson to Armstrong, April 29, 1792 and May 24, 1792; Armstrong to Wilkinson, May 16, 1792, PJA. Some sixty letters between Armstrong and

A further indication of Armstrong's approval by his commander appears in the general's letter of May 11, 1792, thanking the captain for his security precautions involving a convoy to Fort St. Clair: "I love a man who thinks, too few do so, and none else should command." Wilkinson went on to reassure him, "You may rest satisfied that the command of Fort Hamilton, shall not be changed whilst I have influence in any instance, until some general movement takes place—'Let him who wins wear, He who woos enjoy,' will I believe be the motto of my colors." Later that month, he wrote that he was pleased with both the plan and the progress being made toward the fort, which he would occupy later in the year.[748]

Armstrong appeared comfortable with his commander. His letter of March 29 expressed thanks for the general's confidence in him and his pleasure at the prospect of Wilkinson having command of the army. In another letter, apparently written to justify his actions concerning a recent incident concerning a contractor's convoy, he began with the salutation, "My Dear Friend." Wilkinson had apparently received a heated complaint from a contractor whose men had been delayed in crossing the river at Fort Hamilton. Armstrong defended his actions by noting the danger of the operation at the time, citing the high water level, the availability of only a small flatboat for transport, and the approaching darkness. He suggested that the person making the report must have been "young in service" and "possessed of more passion than judgement" to have considered transporting the men across the river while leaving nearly one hundred horses unguarded. He was sure that the affair must have been unfairly represented to Wilkinson and cited the section and article of the Articles of War to justify his actions. Regardless, Armstrong thanked the general for his advice regarding formal reprimands against civilian contractors.

Armstrong was forthright in rendering his opinions to Wilkinson. When he received new forms on which to report ration returns, Armstrong indicated that their use was not sufficient to note issuance to artificers, wagoners, and packhorse men or to indicate allotment of extra rations. He concurred with Wilkinson's earlier comments regarding the current status of local forces. "Our Regt. Is broken indeed, and not benefitted much by

---

Wilkinson written between February 5 and September 23, 1792, can be found in the Armstrong manuscripts and in easily retrieved sources, such as those included in Cist's *Cincinnati Miscellany*.

[748] Wilkinson to Armstrong, May 11, 1792, *CM*, I: 223; Wilkinson to Armstrong, May 24, 1792, PJA.

---

the commanding Officer being at so great a distance. Who I presume would reduce some companys to fill others and send the supernumerary officers on the recruiting service." He shared his beliefs regarding the wait that the army was forced to undergo prior to commencing the forthcoming campaign, writing Wilkinson in July that destroying Indian cornfields would make them more inclined toward peace than would treaties. Additionally, Armstrong felt sufficiently comfortable in his relationship with Wilkinson to seek his help in intervening on his behalf with the secretary of war from whom he needed a copy of his commission to support his claim of rank against officers of the Second Regiment, having addressed Knox earlier but not having received an answer.[749]

He adapted his usual forthright writing style on at least one recorded occasion to emulate that of his commander. Either apparently pleased with his own progress in early June or in an attempt to impress his general, he wrote,

> I am pleased with the idea of having much of your company this summer. I have happily anticipated your wishes. I have a cellar adjoining the well, and in part of it a cistern that contains about four hundred gallons, which I will fill with water once every day, which serves to keep the cellar cool, and answers the purpose of a fish pond.

He continued by wishing Mrs. Wilkinson a pleasant and safe journey to Philadelphia and wrote, "Will you come and eat strawberries with us? If we had a cow you should have cream also. Green peas we have in abundance. If you should spare some radish seeds, their produce would hereafter serve to ornament your table." [750]

As the summer progressed, the relationship between Wilkinson and Armstrong began to show minor rifts. In the same letter in which Armstrong invited Wilkinson to dine with him at Fort Hamilton, he described an incident involving Lt. Bernard Gaines. The lieutenant had

---

[749] Armstrong to Wilkinson, March 29, May 16, July 17, June 21, 1792, and Wilkinson to Armstrong, April 29, 1972, PJA. Note: At the time of Armstrong's letter posted in March, Wilkinson was the commanding officer of the remaining First and Second Regiments. Selection of Wayne as commanding general of the Legion was not made until mid-April.

[750] Armstrong to Wilkinson, June 1, 1792, PJA.

needlessly drained the garrison's cistern, incurring the considerable task of refilling it with 300–400 gallons of water. As a consequence, Armstrong had ordered him to "attend the filling and emptying it" for a month. Gaines replied that he would disobey such an order, and Armstrong had referred him to the eighteenth chapter of the "Baron's instructions." Gaines wrote a letter to be included with that of Armstrong to his commander. Wilkinson's reply of June 6 rebuked Armstrong, counseling him that the better way of handling the situation would have been to admonish the lieutenant in private and ordering him to relieve Gaines from the menial duty imposed upon him. He did, however, sign himself as "Your Friend" rather than the customary "Your Obedient Servant."[751]

In mid-August, Armstrong had a row with Ensign Hastings Marks. The officer with business at Fort Hamilton considered himself not subject to Armstrong's orders and returned to Fort Washington rather than continuing his obligations there. Armstrong noted bluntly that if he had forfeited his commander's confidence, "for God sake relieve me."[752]

By mid-September, construction of Fort Hamilton was nearing completion, but the clock was ticking down prior to Wilkinson's assumption of command later in the month. Armstrong's correspondence belies a sense of frustration in his attempts to complete the garrison to the specifications of his commander. He wrote that every exertion was being employed to complete the building process as soon as possible, but days had been lost due to wet weather and illnesses of the mason and one of the sawyers. Wilkinson's rooms were at that point habitable but not quite done. The magazine and storage buildings were nearly complete but not the stables.[753]

Armstrong's letter to Wilkinson on September 17 indicates that he had a strong disagreement with deputy quartermaster John Belli who in turn complained to Wilkinson about Armstrong's interference with his department, possibly concerning packhorse teams sent to Fort Hamilton. In his correspondence with Wilkinson, Armstrong allowed that Mr. Belli must have been unacquainted with army policy to assume that his department was an independent one and answerable not only to the commanding officer but also to discretionary powers of garrison

---

[751] Wilkinson to Armstrong, June 6, 1792, PJA.

[752] Armstrong to Wilkinson, August 21 and 22, PJA.

[753] Armstrong to Wilkinson, September 15, 1792, CM, I: 67. The incident with Belli may have the basis for one of the charges issued against Armstrong in February 1793.

commanders on-site. Armstrong continued that he considered his conduct while in command as being accountable to his commanding officer but not to one in any of the army's adjunct services. He continued by venturing his opinion that the quartermaster department was as "lame" under Mr. Belli as it had been under his predecessor.[754]

Armstrong's command of Fort Hamilton ended the following week. The following orders were issued on September 23:

> The interest of the service making it necessary to increase the garrison, the Brig. Genl. will take the command to-morrow, and he would be deficient in Justice did he let slip the occasion, to Acknowledge the Merits of Capt. Armstrong, the Present Commandant, for his Officer Like Caution and Vigilance, and his great industry and attention during the very arduous duties to which he has been Exposed, by which he has rendered much advantage to the Nation and acquired great Credit to himself.[755]

Armstrong wrote Wilkinson on the same day that while in command, he had endeavored to act on military principles and if he had erred, he had done so through a mistaken zeal for the good of service. He trusted that his tenure had been marked with due attention to the public interest and had met with Wilkinson's approbation.[756]

★

One hundred thirty miles to the north, over one thousand chieftains, warriors, and their families were congregating at the confluence of the Maumee and Auglaize Rivers. Representatives from thirty nations with varying degrees of investment in the outcome of the proceedings awaited the long-delayed opening of boundary talks. The assembly began gathering in mid-July and drifted into the area well into September. Sauks and Foxes arrived from the northern regions as did the British-allied Seven Nations of Canada, the more neutral Six Nations from the Buffalo Creek

---

[754] Armstrong to Wilkinson, September 17, 1792, PJA.
[755] Orders of September 23, 1792, PJA.
[756] Armstrong to Wilkinson, September 23, 1792, PJA.

region, and Senecas of Cornplanter's division, now aligned with the United States. Creeks and Cherokees came from the South; and a large contingent gathered from the Great Lakes, including Ottawas, Wyandots, and Potawatomis. The inveterately hostile Shawnees and Miamis were in their home territory. A few Wea and Wabash chiefs attended who were dissatisfied with the results of the Putnam negotiations. Also arriving in time for the proceedings were British agent Alexander McKee and several British observers.[757]

All was not well at the gathering. Reports of activity surrounding construction of the army's advanced forts were particularly disruptive, creating considerable ferment among the more moderate factions. Famine in the region led to the late arrival of many participants because they had to spend the summer hunting, and by late September, some of the Ottawas had already departed for home, tired of waiting for the council to begin. Frequent outbursts between rival contingents contributed to the deterioration of morale; incessant backbiting and preliminary sparring dominated meetings between individual nations. Additionally, political realities were such that control of the general confederacy rested with the resident Shawnees and that nation, long regarded as the most warlike of the Northwest tribes, jealously guarded its leverage.[758]

The administration's hopes for conveying its peaceful intentions had rested heavily on Joseph Brant. Although agreeing with the government in June to meet with the conclave, he fell ill and was delayed in undertaking his journey westward. The council convened on September 30, but Brant did not arrive until October 8 after the council closed. In his absence and after much discussion and posturing, the council determined that its prior position that the Ohio River remain the fixed boundary between the United States and the Indian Nations be upheld. Additionally, it demanded restitution of lands already ceded under past treaties and the destruction of the advanced posts within Native American territory. If the United States was sincere in its desire for peace, emissaries were invited to attend a future council to be held the following spring at Lower Sandusky. Forays into the Ohio settlements were already in the works and a raiding party led by Little Turtle was already preparing for a sortie after receiving its annual supplies from McKee's storehouse. For his part, Brant, greatly displeased with the

---

[757] Sword, *President Washington's Indian War*, 223.
[758] Ibid., 225.

result of the late council, returned homeward. His actions thereafter were characterized by a growing intolerance of what he regarded as radical elements, particularly the British Indian agents who aided and encouraged the "hot-headed" hostiles.[759]

The Six Nations representatives were tasked to report the council's decisions to the administration. Before meeting with Knox, however, the Iroquois leaders met, planning their presentation carefully to reflect their own influence in the proceedings. Deleting the council's demands of land restitution and the dismantling of advanced installations, presumably Forts Hamilton, Jefferson, and St. Clair, they conveyed the council's long-held stance on the Ohio River border, as well as the notice of a future conclave to which United States representatives were invited. Even though he was apprised that the Shawnees would only agree to terms of peace that stipulated an Ohio River boundary, Knox nevertheless seized the opportunity to meet with the assembled nations the following spring. Responding to the Shawnees, the Miamis, and their allies on December 12, 1792, Knox reported that the president embraced the proposal and would send commissioners to meet at the appointed time and place. Promising to furnish a full supply of provisions for the treaty, Knox then related the essential aspect of the bargain: "We shall prevent any of our parties going into Indian country, so that you may with your women and children rest in full security. We desire and shall expect that you call in all your warriors and prevent their going out again. It will be in vain to expect peace while they continue their depredations on the frontier."[760]

Knox wrote Wayne on December 7 of the forthcoming arrangements. No offensive operations were to be undertaken, but the troops should observe the highest degree of military vigilance in all respects.[761]

Wayne was virtually livid about these restraints. Asserting that it was humiliating beyond comprehension "to remain with our hands tied" while the enemy could act with impunity on the offensive, Wayne expressed his disgust at the prospect of protracted negotiations. The November 6 attack

---

[759] Ibid., 213, 225–29; The other government emissary Hendrick Aupaumut, "Captain Hendricks," was equally unsuccessful in efforts to sway discussion. Sword notes that he was soon discredited by Alexander McKee who asserted that Aupaumut was a spy sent by the "Big Knives" to estimate the numbers of the hostile Indians.

[760] Sword, *President Washington's Indian War*, 227–228.

[761] Knox to Wayne, December 7, 1792, *AWNIA*, 148.

on a packhorse convoy outside Fort St. Clair only increased his indignation. His impatience was matched, however, by the resolve of the president of the United States to proceed with caution.[762]

As Washington and his administration pinned their hopes on a future council with the Indians either to gain an improbable peace or to satisfy public opinion, Wayne and Wilkinson impatiently readied their commands for the operation to come, hampered and frustrated by their inability to control the events around them. John Armstrong remained at Fort Hamilton, no longer titular commander of the post, but head of his company and awaiting the time when Legion units could at last unite and the long-awaited operation could begin. The delay, however, might benefit him as he considered taking a long-awaited furlough. Armstrong had little idea at the time that his military career was about to take a sharp, unexpected downward turn.

---

[762] Sword, *President Washington's Indian War*, 228.

16

A Court-Martial at Fort Hamilton, 1793

*In short every measure has been persued to immolate
my reputation upon the Alter of Malice.*
—John Armstrong[763]

As the warm days of September drifted into fall, John Armstrong could have reflected on his army career with much to be proud of. He had overseen the transformation of Fort Hamilton, readied the garrison for the forthcoming operation, and surrendered his command with honor. As he considered a timeline for his eventual promotion, he wondered about his role in the next campaign. He shared frustration concerning its delays with his commander; the entire operation seemed in limbo with the greater part of the army mired in Legionville for at least the upcoming winter. He had spent a long year on the frontier, however, and now might be a good time to take a long-needed break. Possibly to prevent denial of his application for leave of absence based purely on personal reasons, he cited medical concerns on his request of October 16, 1792, enclosing certificates from the Legion's surgeon general, longtime regimental comrade Richard Allison, and surgeon's mate Joseph Phillips. Both attested to Armstrong's physical discomfort in the right hypochondria that likely originated from "severe duty on General Harmar's expedition" that increased in cold weather;

---

[763] Undated document, captioned "Hartshorn and Ewing" (1792), PJA.

they recommended a visit to the West Indies for relief or eradication of the condition.[764]

The lingering fall weather, however, yielded a sudden chill in the air between Armstrong and Wilkinson that turned to frost within a short period of time. Possibly attributed to the former's request for furlough, the cause was more likely based on other factors. Taking action against Armstrong at this time may have been Wilkinson's opening gambit to rid his command of Harmar's old officers now in line for promotion to ensure the advancement of others favorable to him. Unfortunately, Armstrong unwittingly provided the opportunity for Wilkinson to make his move. In mid-October, the captain apparently made indiscreet comments in the presence of Lt. John Wade who reported the conversation to Wilkinson. Perceiving an immediate change in his relationship with his commander, Armstrong subsequently addressed Wilkinson in writing, attempting to explain the thrust of the discussion he feared had been misrepresented to the general.

Although the contents of the alleged conversation were not indicated in Armstrong's letter, his words in explanation of the event proved damning. He committed the bold but unpardonable sin of suggesting that Wilkinson showed favoritism toward Wade whom Armstrong regarded as a young man of merit who, if he checked some "improper habits," would make a valuable officer and whose "usefulness has naturally attached to him [sic]." He continued, "But those attachments my Dr. Genl. might be wrong when the exercise of your rank is used to support improper measures taken by a

---

[764] Armstrong to Wilkinson, October 16, 1792, and statements by Joseph Phillips, October 3, 1792, and Richard Allison, October 12, 1792, PJA. The right hypochondria is the area of the upper abdomen in which the liver and gallbladder are located. Armstrong's physicians suspected an "obstruction or induration of the liver." In his efforts to bring what he conceived a lax officer corps into compliance, Wayne was generally intolerant toward those who requested leaves of absence, suspecting that many sought them only to escape labor. Although he could hardly be accused of such, Armstrong may have decided it prudent to present his case by citing documented medical concerns arising from his well-known experience in the Harmar campaign. See Wildes, *Anthony Wayne, Trouble Shooter of the American Revolution*, 376. Ironically, Wayne never applied this standard to himself. He often took lengthy furloughs during the Revolution.

favorite." He further asserted that if Wade were to be considered a spy on officer conversations, "it will end in his ruin."[765]

The conversation reported by Wade apparently pertained to the following of certain directives; Armstrong was unapologetic. He would adopt and support any policy made by Wilkinson, but until directed to do so, he would follow previously outlined procedures. He continued that he wished Wilkinson consider his letter of a private nature and would welcome his response, adding, "If I have introduced any improper idea assure you it has not proceeded from a wish to hurt your feelings. I should be sorry to incur your displeasure on the occasion."[766]

How could Armstrong have had the audacity or poor judgment to infer that his commanding officer was guilty of favoritism? Given his frequent written and in-person contacts with Wilkinson, Armstrong must have been familiar with the general's low tolerance for criticism or heard of it from others. A veteran officer on the cusp of promotion to major should have anticipated the potentially adverse consequences of such an allegation. In the captain's defense, however, he must have felt compelled to relate his side of the story. He might also have been comfortable conveying his thoughts frankly in what he assumed was a private letter given the relationship he assumed to have maintained previously with the general. Whatever his motivation, the die was now cast and his fate was sealed.

Seemingly oblivious to any indication of events that were to follow, Armstrong wrote Wilkinson again two days later, but this letter was of a completely different tenor. His leave apparently granted, he wrote,

> Impressed with the feelings of gratitude I beg leave to acknowledge the polite attentions and Sivilities you have paid me since I had the honour of serving under your Command, and wish you Sir to rest assured they will not be easily erased from my mind. The confidence you have been pleased to place in me on some occasions imboldens me to request that if a reduction of the Army should take place or a promotion happens during my intended tour, I may not be injured in either instance in consequence of my

---

[765] Armstrong to Wilkinson, October 21, 1792, PJA.

[766] Armstrong to Wilkinson, October 21, 1792, PJA. See Wayne Papers XXII: 79 from Pennsylvania Historical Society, in Charles F. Cochran's notebooks, PJA.

absence from the Army. Your simpathetic breast for the sufferings of an old soldier insures to me this attention."[767]

He continued by expressing his reluctance to leave the army, his friends, and his company whose command was apparently to go to his longtime subordinate, Asa Hartshorne. He hoped that Wilkinson would "give them some attention," and in the event of Hartshorne's promotion (and implied subsequent reassignment), Armstrong requested that leadership fall to an officer who would treat the men with justice and humanity. Armstrong also requested permission to write to the general during his absence.[768]

Armstrong later related to Wayne what happened next.

> I left Fort Hamilton on the 26 of October with an intention of going to Philadelphia & the day previous asked the Gel. if there was not some complaint Lodged against me by the QM. He said there was but he took no previous notice of it. I then byed [sic] he would previous to my departure give me an opertunity of acquiting myself by producing the Officers who had served with me. He said it was unnecessary that his Gel. Order was justification of my conduct. He then bought from me my bedding, slats, etc. to the amount of Sixty Dollars lent me his horse to ride to Washington [and] said the next day he would be there & give me a furlough. On the 27th he arrived and immediately after ordered me under arrest.[769]

Armstrong was to discover the full import of his mistaken assumption that his past relationship with Wilkinson held any sway in his present situation. Upon his arrest, he immediately wrote his commander, regretting that there could be anything personal in his detention and confident that the testimonials he had received from Wilkinson attesting to his behavior during his command would protect him from such an examination of his conduct. Being assured that no just grounds for prosecution existed, he requested a court of inquiry in order to clear his name rather than a

---

[767] Armstrong to Wilkinson, October 23, 1792, Wayne papers, XXV: 88 in Cochran notebooks, PJA.

[768] Ibid.

[769] Armstrong to Wayne, March 23, 1793, PJA.

court-martial proceeding. He also requested to know the charges against him. In closing, he continued, "From the Proofs I have had of your candour, sevilities, and friendship I trust this will not be denied me."[770]

The captain received a terse reply the following day. Armstrong was not to consider Wilkinson his friend, for "it is improbable that I should hold any man to be my Friend, or that I should continue His, who could tell me a falsehood to embroil me with my officers, and without cause, or without provocation could outrage my feelings in the manner done by your Letter of the 21st Inst." The general continued, however, that the captain should not consider him his enemy and that he would continue to offer him every consistent civility in his power which he would do "for the Credit of your profession, & of humanity." He hoped that Armstrong would be able to acquit himself of the very heavy charges against him that would be specified as soon as he finished his pending public dispatches. The request for a court of inquiry was denied.

Reiterating his belief that the general must have misunderstood the intent of the conversation that took place at Fort Hamilton and assuring him that his letter of October 21 was not meant to offend, Armstrong replied that a personal conference would clear up the matter to his commander's satisfaction. Wilkinson responded the next day that he would "cheerfully" grant the captain a meeting at the first moment of his leisure, which "shall be duly announced to him." Whether Armstrong eventually got to plead his case in person is unknown.[771]

Armstrong now knew that he was in serious trouble. On November 1, he sat down to write the one person who might help him out of the situation in which he now found himself but also probably the one individual for whom his accuser held the most contempt—Maj. Gen. Anthony Wayne, commander of the Legion of the United States. He was a comrade in the Pennsylvania chapter of the Society of the Cincinnati and the man under whose direction Armstrong had fought at Stony Point,

---

[770] Armstrong to Wilkinson, October 26, 1792, PJA. Courts of inquiry differed significantly from general courts-martial. In the Legion, use of this process provided an aggrieved officer the means for clearing his name of camp rumors. The court consisted of only three officers who interviewed witnesses concerning the allegations against the accused. See Nicholson, "Courts-Martial in the Legion Army: American Military Law in the Early Republic, 1792–1796," 106.

[771] Wilkinson to Armstrong, October 27, 1792, and October 28, 1792, PJA.

Green Spring, and the siege of Yorktown in the Revolution. He was also with Wayne during the Southern campaign and the long winters at Valley Forge and Morristown years earlier. Beginning his letter by apologizing for writing, Armstrong explained the details of his arrest, telling Wayne of his rendering an opinion on a "point of duty" in a conversation a few days prior to his departure from Fort Hamilton and consequently incurring the displeasure of his commanding officer. He had been on his way to Philadelphia when he received his arrest notice. Had it taken place at Fort Hamilton, he would have viewed the matter differently, but now he believed his arrest was determined some days before he had set out. Confident that no criminal charges against him could be supported, he assumed that the cause for arrest must have originated in "personallity, ill nature or malice." He hoped that his trial might be delayed until the arrival of the Legion commander and, fearing undue command influence by Wilkinson, could be adjudicated by a court selected from its entire line.[772]

Armstrong's letter was not the sole piece of correspondence dispatched from Fort Washington that day. Wayne soon received a letter from his second-in-command who assailed Armstrong's character in blazing terms. He explained to Wayne that his arrest was not for any personal insolence shown to him, but for a catalogue of charges "substantiated by testimony which would blacken the Character of a Clive, or a Hastings." Wilkinson had not yet framed the formal charges due to other pressing duties, but he assured Wayne that "speculation, peculation, and fraud and felonious Acts make a part of the list." He acknowledged regret for arresting any officer on such charges, much less a man of Armstrong's long service and real utility, "for to do Him Justice, he is one of the best officers under my Command, in point of Industry, caution, and resource, but he is a Man of unbounded rapacity, one of the first born Sons of Sedition, a despot to his Inferiors, a Master Speculator, a Man of duplicity & falsehood, and in short a proper Subject for an Example." He added that he had approved Armstrong's request for a furlough based on statements made from sublegion medical officers concerning the captain's health and had given him leave to go to Philadelphia.

> When in fact he exhibits every mark of vigorous high
> Health, & is able to kill any officer under my Command

---

[772] Armstrong to Wayne, November 1, 1792, PJA.

on Fatigue; and at the same time, I have strong reasons
to believe that his real intention was to carry into Effect
some Land Jobing Scheme during the ensuing Session
of the Congress, that he had predetermined never to
join the Army more, but to hang on and draw his Pay
as a Convalescent, so long as the imposition could be
supported.[773]

When Armstrong received the charges for his prosecution eight days
after his arrest, Wilkinson cited attention to his public dispatches as cause
for the delay. Given their ambiguous nature, he could well have spared
himself the unnecessary postponement.

1st Speculation, Peculation & Fraud
2nd Usurpation of Power
3rd Inattention to, & dissipation of the public property
4th Holding forth doctrines & opinions, subversive of the
    just principles of Subordination, & Discipline, and
5th For Conduct unbecoming a Gentleman & an officer[774]

Armstrong had been ordered to confine himself to the garrison and to
the village of Cincinnati, but asserting that his health required exercise on
horseback, he requested and received permission to ride occasionally as far
as Columbia. The captain also requested that when his company's clothing
arrived, he might be allowed to outfit his men at Fort Hamilton.[775]

On November 8, 1792, Armstrong received four long-delayed letters
from Francis Johnston. In a lengthy response, he addressed Johnston's
questions about purchasing a large tract of land, the receipt of seeds that
Johnston had sent, and the latter's purchase of three shares of Delaware
and Schuylkill Canal stock for Armstrong. Nowhere did he refer to his
present circumstances to his friend, but in a tone either romantically naive
or unbelievably practical, he noted,

[773] Wilkinson to Wayne, November 1, 1792, Wayne Papers, XXII: 95 in Cochran
notebooks, PJA.
[774] Wilkinson to Armstrong, November 3, 1792, PJA.
[775] Armstrong to Wilkinson, and Wilkinson to Armstrong, November 4, 1792, PJA.

I sent you five hundred dollars which you will please to lay out as you think proper. Perhaps it would purchase a good *wife* if I become a farmer. You know I shall want one—and will take the liberty of asking my good Friend Mr. G to think of one for me. Pray is Miss S—D—g married. I have been in love with her these three years, but have not been in a situation that would justify my telling her so.

So fared the love life of a career officer on the far western frontier.

Finally, in words that obliquely hinted of his present situation, he wrote that since he had left his command, three men had been captured at Fort Hamilton. Additionally, six soldiers had been killed, six men wounded, and one hundred horses lost in an incident near Fort St. Clair, adding in a note of self-advocacy that he had "lost no scalps" during his own ten-month command. Forwarding a copy of Wilkinson's published statement of September 23, he added, "The inclosed copy of a gel. order will ivence to you with what honour I resigned my command."[776]

Armstrong was apparently not the only old Harmar officer in Wilkinson's headlights. In a private letter to Wayne on November 28, the general's second-in-command included a copy of Erkuries Beatty's resignation. The previous day, the First Sublegion major had requested a leave of absence that Wilkinson had denied, inviting him to "dine with me this day" so that the general could relay the reasons for his refusal. After what must have been a head-spinning meeting for the long-serving Beatty, the major submitted his resignation that evening, also requesting time to settle his accounts once he arrived in Philadelphia. Wilkinson issued a formal letter of acceptance noting his approval of Beatty's request, "altho

---

[776] Armstrong to Johnston, November 8, 1793, PJA. Armstrong referenced the attack on November 6, 1792, of a detachment of Maj. John Adair near Fort St. Clair resulting in fifteen casualties and most of the horses lost. The fort's commander, Capt. Daniel Bradley, gave little aid to the hard-pressed pack train, pleading that by virtue of the order given previously to garrison commanders by Wilkinson, he had to limit himself and his men to defensive measures only. Jacobs, *Tarnished Warrior*, 126–27. A reflection of the difficulty of receiving correspondence from the east that was dependent upon delivery by friends or associates, Johnston's letters were dated November 26, 1791, and May 16, July 2, and August 27, 1792.

I cannot approve of the practice of continuing the pay and Emoluments of an officer, after He ceases to earn them." In forwarding Beatty's application to Knox, he wrote, "My Motives for accepting his Commission so abruptly, are a satisfactory knowledge that he is abandoned to the wretched habits of drunkenness—He was once a clever Fellow but is lost."[777]

The brigadier general also set his sights on Richard Allison, another Harmar officer who, like Armstrong and Beatty, was a veteran of the Pennsylvania Line. Presently the Legion's surgeon general, Allison had attested to the captain's medical condition: "I can only say that I consider Him every way unworthy of the appointment & that so long as he continues here, the Leaves of Sedition will continue to ferment." Wilkinson believed that Allison was considering resignation, and the general's plan was that the doctor should be ordered to Legionville, at which time he would resign. "I wish you to make the Experiment, in order to get rid of Him if possible—for he possesses neither Education, Industry or humanity . . . I will cheerfully attend the sick in his place, & will do them more justice."[778]

The departure of other officers in the past year was not lost on Armstrong. Some may simply have had enough of the service following St. Clair's defeat, but the captain had reason to suspect Wilkinson of trying to rid the Legion of its "old" officers, particularly veterans of the former Pennsylvania Line. Of the thirteen Pennsylvania officers and two surgeon's mates who composed Harmar's officer corps in 1784, seven remained on active duty as of January 1, 1792. Since Wilkinson's arrival, Armstrong had witnessed the controversial resignations of David Zeigler in March and Erkuries Beatty in November 1792. Ebenezer Denny and Joseph Asheton had also resigned their commissions that year although neither is known to have had a direct conflict with Wilkinson. Surgeon's mate Richard Allison remained in the Legion although Armstrong would no doubt have been aware of Wilkinson's displeasure with his longtime friend. The last officer in the initial regiment, Thomas Doyle remained in the army until 1796, but not before becoming a victim of Wilkinson's wrath when he attempted to thwart the general's attempt to escape exposure of his intrigue with

---

[777] Wilkinson to Beatty, November 27, 1792, and Wilkinson to Wayne, November 28, 1792, Wayne papers, XXIII: 53–55, Cochran notebooks; Beatty to Wilkinson November 27, 1792, Gratz Papers, Pennsylvania Historical Society Miscellaneous Collection included in Cochran notebooks, PJA.

[778] Wilkinson to Wayne, November 28, 1792, Wayne papers, XXIII: 53–55, Cochran notebooks, PJA.

the Spanish government. The purging of officers from the Pennsylvania Line who had served under Wayne's leadership seems to have been part of Wilkinson's effort to rid the Legion of those who might be more loyal to Wayne than to him. All except Allison were majors or senior captains soon eligible for promotion to that rank. Removing them from the command opened the way for advancing men loyal to Wilkinson.[779]

Wilkinson's obvious effort to purge his immediate command of Pennsylvania officers is doubly interesting due to the rationales he offered to Wayne when describing their shortcomings. His indignation at the prospect of Beatty drawing allowances in Philadelphia while attending to his personal affairs and Armstrong receiving pay while on leave prior to a possible decision to leave the army pales in comparison to his own ongoing dealings with the Spanish government, his failed business efforts, and his

---

[779] Both Allison and Doyle served with the Legion until it was abolished in 1796. The War Department discharged thirty-four officers, and among them were the last officers from Harmar's original force. See Coffman, *The Old Army*, 7. In late 1794, Thomas Doyle, a Wayne loyalist, commanded Fort Massac, a fort on the Ohio River in present-day southern Illinois where he found himself caught up in Wilkinson's attempt to whisk away the murderers of a courier carrying money from New Orleans that was destined for the general. Wilkinson, afraid their presence in Kentucky too risky, had them rounded up and sent downriver to New Madrid, accompanied by an army lieutenant and a Kentucky lawyer. Their boat was spotted trying to slip past the fort at night, and Doyle, suspicious of the movement, apprehended its occupants and refused to honor a written order from Wilkinson granting the party free passage downriver. Doyle delayed the group's departure until an interpreter could be found to question the assailants, but luckily for Wilkinson, one arrived from New Madrid who knew of the general's involvement in the matter and subsequently translated the accounts of the accused to hide any reference to Wilkinson. Doyle eventually released the party but later felt his commander's wrath for not honoring orders to let the party proceed. Linklater, *An Artist in Treason*, 143, 145–46; Ebenezer Denny, following his resignation from the federal force, accepted a commission in the Pennsylvania militia in March 1794 and served on the northwest Pennsylvania frontier. Denny, *Military Journal*, 179. Joseph Asheton had commanded the western movement of several hundred new recruits for the upcoming campaign and held command of the Legion's Sikes Run training camp until September 1792, when he was transferred to the Fourth Sublegion. Entering into an extended leave of absence, his resignation was accepted on November 27, 1792. He died the following year. Lytle, *Soldiers of the First American Army*, 190–91.

---

current state of near insolvency. His admission that he feared Armstrong's mission in Philadelphia might be to carry out "some Land Jobing" scheme may harken back to his animosity toward George Morgan with whom Armstrong had previously conducted business. He might also have been envious of Armstrong's success in accumulating choice parcels of land while his own investments had floundered.[780]

It took over a month for correspondence from Armstrong and Wilkinson to reach Legionville. The tone of Wayne's response to his second-in-command on December 10 was unsympathetic. Noting the lateness of the season and the need for Dr. Carmichael, the surgeon presently at Legionville, to remain on-site, Wayne wrote that Wilkinson should endeavor to make Dr. Allison more attentive to his duty. Nor did he express an overly sympathetic view of Wilkinson's staffing difficulties. He noted that Wilkinson's picture of the character of his majors and senior captains was far from pleasing, "but we must get over those difficulties; purgation's the idea strongly impressed, in which you may rest assured of every Legal support."[781]

Wayne responded to Armstrong on the same day. Since he was unaware of the circumstances of the captain's case, he regretted being unable to intervene. He could not interfere with Wilkinson's authority given the

---

[780] Armstrong did in fact have a land scheme that he was pursuing with Francis Johnston and possibly others with George Morgan. He had identified 95,000 acres "on the west side of Miami" for potential purchase, and Johnston had sought individuals who, although interested, were not willing to risk investment at the time due to unrest in the region. Armstrong's correspondence with his confidant Johnston is not, however, indicative of any immediate plans to leave the army. Armstrong to Johnston, March 29, April 23, November 8, 1792; Johnston to Armstrong, July 24 and August 2, 1792; Morgan to Armstrong, February 25, 1791, and May 1, 1789; purchase agreement, January 30, 1789, PJA. Armstrong also had at least one financial encounter with Wilkinson while stationed at Fort Steuben. A curious entry noted in his papers indicates that Wilkinson was indebted to Armstrong for £10/18/9. Wilkinson's associate Philip Nolan submitted payment, requesting Armstrong forward the sum to William Crogham for Wilkinson's credit. Armstrong later received that sum from Crogham. The amount in Pennsylvania currency equated to approximately $30, a sum in excess of a lieutenant's monthly pay of $26 at the time. Receipt June 2, 1789, PJA.

[781] Wayne to Wilkinson, December 10, 1792, Wayne papers, XXIII: 81 in Cochran notebooks, PJA.

fact that the brigadier general, commanding in a "distant" quarter, was authorized to order and to hold courts-martial. Nevertheless, Wayne's tone was sympathetic, the general wishing "as an old brother Officer" that there had been no cause of arrest and, if groundless, sincerely wishing him an honorable acquittal.[782]

Extracting himself at least temporarily from the gloom of Fort Washington during the Christmas season, Armstrong apparently spent considerable time visiting nearby Columbia. His friend "Mr. G.," to whom he referred in his letter to Johnston, could well have been Maj. John Stites Gano who would have introduced him to Tabitha Goforth, younger sister of his wife Mary. Gano and Mary had traveled down the Ohio in 1788 with Benjamin Stites to the mouth of the Little Miami River, establishing Columbia as the first of the Cincinnati settlements. Mary's father William Goforth, mother Catharine, and younger siblings arrived the next year. Goforth, by the time of Armstrong's first interaction with the family, was serving as one of three Hamilton County judges of the Court of Common Pleas and a justice of the Court of General Quarter Sessions of the Peace. However rushed their courtship, Capt. John Armstrong and Tabitha Goforth were married on January 27, 1793, at Gano's Columbia home. A reflection of the times, Tabitha was at eighteen years, eleven months, half of John's mature age of thirty-seven.[783]

One wonders just how enthusiastically Judge Goforth greeted the prospect of having Armstrong, then under the cloud of military justice, as a husband for his young daughter. Armstrong clearly had Gano's approval. It is possible that Goforth, by that time intricately involved in Cincinnati and territorial affairs, had his own doubts about Armstrong's primary accuser and more than likely had heard the rumors concerning Wilkinson's

[782] Wayne to Armstrong, December 10, 1792, Wayne papers, XXIII: 80 in Cochran notebooks, PJA. In contrast to the position he held concerning noninterference with judicial matters administered by Wilkinson during the time when the main body of the army was in Legionville, Wayne was never reluctant to intervene in the military justice system when his favorites were involved during the Revolution. He often protected Cols. Thomas Craig and Richard Butler when they were charged with serious offenses.

[783] Tabitha Goforth Armstrong Lockhart's pension application, W10202, 696, 698, http://searchancestry.com. Charles Theodore Greve, *Centennial History of Cincinnati and Representative Citizens* (Chicago: Biographical Publishing Company, 1904) I: 177, 336, https://archive.org.

involvement with Spain and the general's trail of financial insolvency. As Hamilton County judge, Goforth had experienced at least one direct run-in with Wilkinson in an incident that occurred the previous June. Drunken soldiers on pass caused a myriad of problems for the civilian populace surrounding Fort Washington, as well as the military establishment that had to corral them. Hoping to improve the situation, Wilkinson ordered that any soldier found drunk outside the garrison would immediately be dealt fifty lashes. When Ensign William Henry Harrison found an inebriated artificer and gave him the stipulated number of lashes as well as administering ten more to his companion for objectionable interference, the pair, asserting that they were civilians not under military control, filed assault charges against the ensign, resulting in the issuance of a warrant for the officer's arrest. Wilkinson exempted the artificers from any punishment in the future and forbade the service of the arrest warrant on the military reservation. Judge Goforth subsequently ordered Harrison's arrest wherever found. When the deputy sheriff attempted to take him into custody, the ensign sent the law officer sprawling. Wilkinson decided that the best course of action was to get Harrison out of the neighborhood and ordered him to accompany Mrs. Wilkinson and their three boys to Philadelphia.[784]

When he returned to Fort Washington after his wedding, Armstrong found a letter from Erkuries Beatty that filled him in on the news from Pittsburgh. The talk among the officers there had not been in Armstrong's favor, but his friend related the circumstances of the charges to some and reported he had been able to bring a few to more favorable points of view. His opinion of the group and of the command climate, however, was not encouraging. "This only between you & me Jack—If I get away from

---

[784] Harrison eventually gave himself up, received a severe judicial scolding, and was locked up in McHenry's tavern for twenty-four hours where he put in the time "in jollification with some boon companions." Jacobs, *The Beginning of the U.S. Army*), 146; *Cincinnati, "the Queen City": Newspaper Reference Book* (Cincinnati: Cuvier Press Club, 1914), 9, https://babel.hathitrust.org. Goforth, as a county official, was also acquainted with Wilkinson socially. He is listed as among the thirty-five guests attending the general's lavish St. Tammany's Day dinner on May 1, 1792, who paid fifteen shillings for the honor. "List of Dinner Attendees, May 25, 1792," Papers of the War Department, https://wardepartmentpapers.org.

Legion-ville with whole bones I shall be mighty glad, for I understand there is nothing but snubbing going on there on all quarters."[785]

He later heard from the army's paymaster, Caleb Swan, who also wrote from Legionville, giving Armstrong the conciliatory news that Wayne had expressed some unhappiness at hearing of Armstrong's arrest, thinking him "an old, and as he had always thought, a meritorious officer." Alluding to the camp's climate, Swan continued by saying that he didn't converse freely with anyone there due to a "want of harmony and a boasted ignorance." He ended by writing, "Don't show my letter to any body."[786]

By mid-January, Armstrong had begun planning his defense but had not yet received any further specification of charges following the general ones issued in November. He wrote Wilkinson on January 18 that he needed evidence from Samuel Alexander, late superintendent of artificers at Fort Hamilton, asking that he be summoned to attend the trial since questions might arise during the proceedings that Alexander could address. Wilkinson replied that he had no power to detain the superintendent since the latter was not under military orders, but later granted the captain permission to take Alexander's deposition.[787]

Orders for Armstrong's trial were published on Thursday, February 7 and listed the names of thirteen members of the panel consisting of three majors, five captains, and five lieutenants to begin deliberations on the following Wednesday at Fort Hamilton. On the same day Capt. Thomas Cushing, Wilkinson's adjutant and designated judge advocate for the proceedings, informed Armstrong that the court would begin hearing testimony from seven witnesses on February 8. When Armstrong again requested the specific charges against him so that he could prepare questions for the witnesses, Cushing replied that he could not inform Armstrong which parts of their testimonies would apply to his case because the court itself had not yet received notice of the charges. Testimony of the witnesses on February 8 would be used to determine them.[788]

---

785 Beatty to Armstrong, January 5, 1793, PJA.

786 Swan to Armstrong, February 5, 1793, PJA.

787 Armstrong to Wilkinson, January 18, 1792, and Wilkinson to Armstrong, January 18 and 19, 1793, PJA.

788 Armstrong to Cushing, February 7, 1793, PJA; Sub-legionary Orders and Cushing to Armstrong, February 7, 1793, Wayne papers, XXV: 23, 88 in Cochran notebooks, PJA. Witnesses on February 8 were to be Lt. Asa Hartshorne, Quartermaster John Belli, and Mr. Ewing of that department;

Records of Armstrong's trial were destroyed by the fire that swept through the War Department office in November 1800, and no official account of proceedings now exists. From Armstrong's correspondence with Wayne, Wilkinson, and others, however, a picture emerges of a legal process against the captain marked by irregularities in the military judicial system that were unusual even by the permissive standards of the day. Armstrong was no novice to the military court system. During his seventeen years of army service, he had participated in untold numbers of courts-martial as witness, serving or presiding on panels, and as defendant himself in three trials during the Revolution. It was abundantly clear that the deck was firmly stacked against him. Wilkinson, commander of forces in the West, had been given a free hand by Wayne to handle affairs in his area; and he was using undue command influence to leverage charges against the captain. Armstrong, struck by procedures which seemed unusual to him, recognized its danger early in the process. In a statement to the court he noted,

> Witnesses Gentlemen against me have repaired to this place by the General's order I believe before that for forming the Court was given. So tenatious [*sic*] have been the supreme authority of vesting too much power in the

---

Robert Benham, representative of contractors Elliot and Williams in charge of packhorse deliveries; Sergeant Wilson, apparently one of Armstrong's company's noncommissioned officers; Mr. Shaw; and Mr. Smith. Bradley Nicholson notes in his article "Courts-martial in the Legion Army: American Military Law in the Early Republic, 1792–1796" that the Articles of War provided an outline for military justice by mandating what was to be done but lacking direction on how to do it, having little to say about matters such as challenges to the panel, evidence, forms of punishment, or other important details associated with the judicial process. In the absence of statutory detail, courts relied on both military tradition and civilian practices that were both written and unwritten. Although some procedures noted in the progression of Armstrong's trial may seem unusual to current standards, they may have been within accepted bounds of tradition at the time. As Armstrong later pointed out, however, several practices used against him were clearly in violation of the Code of Military Justice. See Nicholson, "Courts-Martial in the Legion Army: American Military Law in the Early Republic, 1792–1796," 84.

breast of the commanding officer that in their appendix to
the Articles of War they have carefully guarded against it.[789]

Armstrong had been put under arrest four months earlier on generic
charges made by Wilkinson that lacked any specification, and no further
clarification had subsequently been provided. With Armstrong's trial
scheduled to commence on February 13, the court-martial panel had no
idea whether the charges against him had any foundation. The session on
February 8 was apparently designed by Wilkinson and Cushing to have
members hear testimony that would determine the specific charges under
which Armstrong would subsequently be tried. In essence, the court was
directed to witness a fishing expedition by the prosecution to find some
basis for the charges Wilkinson had made. Their very presence in the
room at what amounted to a pretrial investigation by the prosecution
undoubtedly would influence their perception of Armstrong's innocence
or guilt, as well as to expose them to the tenor of the command climate
surrounding Armstrong's case. Armstrong was unable to present organized
rebuttal questions to witness testimony since he had no prior knowledge
of what he would hear. Wilkinson could get away with such blatant
interference because Wayne was far away and refused to intervene. As the
trial progressed, other inequities soon emerged.

On February 9, Cushing informed Armstrong of the eight charges
against him and added a ninth on the following day.

-   The erasing or causing to be defaced the brand of a horse Creature
    not your own property, and causing the said Creature to be branded
    with your own Brand made for the purpose by a public Artificer
    for claiming the said Creature as your own property, and as such,
    offering her for sale, and for offering to purchase from Lieutenant
    Hartshorn, another Creature, to which neither he, nor you, had
    an equitable Claim, for a few pounds of Powder
-   For receiving from Sergeant Sheets a considerable sum of money,
    and afterwards for conduct in that transaction bearing Strong
    marks of a fraudulent design

---

[789] Armstrong to the president and members of the court, February 1793, PJA.
Efforts to reconstruct War Department records have resulted in *Papers of the War
Department 1784-1800*, an online repository of over 42,000 documents drawn
from institutions and private collections. https://wardepartmentpapers.org.

- For speculating on your own soldiers in the sale of shirting
- For receiving from different Contractors property for the labor of the men of your Company contrary to military usage, and not accounting for the same
- For engaging to advance for the DQM [Gen_] to the artificers, a considerable sum of money, and afterwards refusing to fulfill this engagement, because you could not become the Pay-master and thereby retain this money in your own [word missing]
- For contumaciously and insolently resisting the orders of the Sub-Legionary General, delivered by his aid de camp
- For uttering opinions of your Superior Officer, tending to subvert subordination and destroy all Confidence in him, and for declaring that you would resist, any orders which were not delivered to the Sergeants Call, and avowing your Right and your determination to crit [word missing] on and to fault, such arrangements of your superiors you did not like
- For trampling upon the Rights of your fellow Citizens & Tyrannizing over your inferior officers And, for telling the Sub-Legionary General a falsehood calculated to imbroil him with a brother [word missing]
- For ordering the assistant-Quarter-Master to deliver forrage for any horses emploied as [exp_] or otherwise, promising to give him the necessary vouchers when called on for this purpose, and neglecting and refusing to do the same; whereby a waste and dissipation of the public property has taken place, and the Quarter-Master is disenabled to account for such as has been properly applied[790]

Armstrong's correspondence clearly revealed his plan of defense, as well as providing insight into his strong will and determination not to fold under increasing pressure to do so. Well versed in the Articles of War and military justice procedures, he was not going to give up without a fight. He wrote to Wilkinson immediately after receiving the specific charges that his defense required three things. First, because some of the charges referred to incidents that had occurred prior to Wilkinson's assuming command, Armstrong's defense would require the testimony of the army's

---

[790] Cushing to Armstrong, February 9 and 10, 1793, PJA.

late commander, Maj. Gen. St. Clair, and two other witnesses who were then in Pennsylvania. Accordingly, he requested postponement of his trial until the spring when those individuals along with the rest of the army would arrive within the immediate command. Secondly, in order to receive a fair and impartial trial, he requested that proceedings be moved from Fort Hamilton to Fort Washington, away from possible influence upon the jury that might be generated by its commandant, Brig. Gen. Wilkinson, and coincidentally the instigator of the charges against him. Finally, he confronted Wilkinson with the fact that given the charges, the general would have to present testimony himself although Wilkinson had previously assured him that he would not come forward in his prosecution. Armstrong understood the obvious. The general's appearance and testimony for the prosecution could have no other effect than to influence the jury further against Armstrong, all members of which served directly under his command.[791]

Wilkinson's response was quick and indignant. Armstrong's request was an insult to the honor of the officers who would hear his case. His appeal was "irreconcilable to your own principles, to common Justice, & to common Sense, and therefore cannot be admitted." Stating that he would not appear for Armstrong's prosecution further than he would "be bound by Honor, by Duty, and by conscience to prove that you told me a falsehood," he noted that the court would determine what evidence would be necessary for Armstrong's defense and would render impartial justice.[792]

Armstrong continued to rely upon his past court-martial experiences. Trial proceedings began as scheduled on February 13 but were adjourned until the next day so that he could apply to Wilkinson to seek reduction of the number of officers on the court. Wilkinson had impaneled thirteen officers for the trial, some of whom were new to the army. Armstrong requested that the number be reduced to either seven or nine, but Wilkinson refused, stating that he had no intention of using his power to dissolve the court and "to wound the feelings of the ablest and most respectable officers of the Army." In correspondence with Wayne, he cited the captain's tactics as being calculated merely to delay justice.[793]

---

[791] Armstrong to Wilkinson, February 10, 1793, PJA.

[792] Wilkinson to Armstrong, February 10, 1793, PJA.

[793] Armstrong to Wilkinson, February 13, 1793, and Wilkinson to Armstrong, February 14, 1791; Wilkinson to Wayne, February 11, 1792, Wayne papers, XXV: 20 in Cochran notebooks, PJA. Armstrong had the right to request a

In his second letter to Wayne dated February 18, Armstrong wrote that he had been refused the privilege of objecting to any one of the members of the court although he had offered to accept any number above that of four provided the jury was composed of "old officers." Armstrong's panel was to be composed of the following members: Maj. David Strong, president; Majors Rudolph and Bedinger; Captains Doyle, Kingsbury, T. Lewis, Gibson, and Lee; Lieutenants Ingersoll, Shambaugh, Demlar, Van Rensselaer, and Covington. Of those assigned, all but Van Rensselaer, Covington, Gibson, and Lee were known to have participated in the St. Clair campaign, whether on the military operation itself or in garrison. They were most likely the officers to whom Armstrong objected and were in all probability the men most inclined to be swayed by their obligations toward Wilkinson. Article 11 of the 1786 appendix to the Articles of War states that "no officer shall be tried but by a general court-martial, nor by officers of an inferior rank if it can be avoided." Wilkinson apparently chose to ignore this provision.[794]

Armstrong related the positive news to Wayne that the court had agreed to allow reasonable time for him to collect witnesses and prepare for trial, but he acknowledged that his chances for success were "doubly

---

smaller panel and to object to specific members of the jury. Articles of War adopted at the onset of the Revolution mandated that general courts-martial be adjudicated by a jury of thirteen officers. This document was amended in 1786, then citing the minimum number of panelists to five for general and three at special courts-martial. As an officer, Armstrong would be tried by a general court-martial that would be heard by anywhere from five to thirteen officers, but should not consist of less than thirteen "where that number can be convened without manifest injury to the service." Bradley J. Nicholson writes that in light of cliques and rivalries, it was an intelligent practice to allow the accused and the judge advocate to challenge the selection of individual officers but also notes that doing so was a tricky proposition. Objecting to an officer as a member of the court without assigning any cause would be a reflection upon his character as a man of honor. See Nicholson, "Courts-Martial in the Legion Army: American Military Law in the Early Republic, 1792–1796," 83, 103. The May 31, 1786, appendix to the Articles of War can be found in William Winthrop, *Military Law and Precedents, Second Edition* (Washington: Government Printing Office, 1920), 972, https://www.loc.gov/rr/frd/Military_Law/pdf/ML_precedents.pdf.

[794] Armstrong to Wayne, February 18, 1793, Wayne papers, XXV: 23, 90 in Cochran notebooks, PJA; Winthrop, Military Law and Precedents, 973.

hard." His frustration evident, he was candid in his opinion of Wilkinson and the court. The general was clearly his avowed enemy as was the judge advocate, Thomas Cushing. He perceived that members of the court to whom he objected had subsequently become biased against his case.[795]

Capt. Thomas Cushing deserves special mention. His position was far from impartial, and he was clearly Wilkinson's man. An officer in the Revolutionary War from Massachusetts and son of Supreme Court Justice William Cushing, he had been commissary agent at Fort Washington prior to rejoining the army. He was again commissioned captain in the Second Regiment in 1791 and spent an extended period of time recruiting a company in his home state. Arriving at Fort Washington after the completion of the St. Clair campaign, his company accompanied Wilkinson's resupply and recovery effort to Fort Jefferson and to the site of St. Clair's battlefield in January 1792. He was with Wilkinson during the construction of Fort St. Clair and remained there as the commanding officer upon its completion.[796]

Cushing had been captured by the British during the Revolution and, having spent time in a British military jail, lost his chance for promotion. Upon reentering the service as a captain, he considered himself entitled to a majority as soon as a vacancy occurred. When the opportunity arose, however, Wayne pushed for the promotion of two other officers. The captain protested to Wayne, but to no avail. In a typical Wilkinson move, the brigadier general promised to pull strings on Cushing's behalf. Cushing became his right-hand man and an avowed Wayne enemy. One party helped the other. So engaged was Cushing with Wilkinson's welfare that he apparently loaned him a substantial sum of money. James Ripley Jacobs cites Cushing as one of the individuals to whom Wilkinson was struggling to repay $900 in the spring of 1792.[797]

The most crushing argument against Cushing's impartiality, however, was that he was one of six captains of the Second Regiment who had submitted a memorial to Knox disputing John Armstrong's date of rank and contesting his seniority in the line for promotion to major. Response to their memorial was still pending during Armstrong's trial. With

---

[795] Armstrong to Wayne, February 18, 1793, Wayne papers, XXV: 88 in Cochran notebooks, PJA.

[796] Lytle, *Soldiers of the First American Army*, 207–08.

[797] Wildes, *Anthony Wayne, Trouble Shooter of the American Revolution*, 390, 405–06.

Armstrong possibly out of the picture, Cushing would be next in line. In light of Wilkinson's relationship with Cushing and his penchant for rewarding those he considered faithful, Cushing's status for promotion immediately behind Armstrong may well be considered the decisive factor in Wilkinson's interest in seeing the demise of Armstrong's army career.[798]

Armstrong's papers include an undated letter to be read to the court, which judging from its tenor might have been presented as an opening statement on February 13. Referring to the Articles of War, Armstrong reminded members of the court that they had the right to determine the time frame necessary for the gathering of evidence. He was confident that on the basis of his performance of the past seventeen years and past approval by his superior officers, he could not have committed any crime that "demands immediate example" or that the service would be injured by a delay of his trial. Acknowledging that the charges against him were heavy, he stated that he would be embarrassed in appearing before the court were he not convinced of his own innocence as well as the justice that would be exercised by the panel.

Armstrong was unrelenting in his criticism of both Wilkinson and Cushing, the latter of whom was undoubtedly in the courtroom in his capacity as judge advocate. "Witnesses Gentlemen against me have repaired to this place by the General's order I believe before that for forming the court were given," directing the court to consider provisions in the appendix to the Articles of War guarding against vesting too much power with the commanding officer. He further reminded the court that the charges against him had sprung from alleged incidents that had occurred prior to Armstrong's relinquishing command. Correspondence between Armstrong and his commander concerning these incidents would substantiate the fact that the latter had been apprised of their occurrence. He saved his best shot for Cushing. "And Gentlemen give me leave further to observe, in all cases and on all courts where I have had the Honour to sit as a member, I always considered the Judge advocate interested for the

---

[798] Armstrong's biographer, Charles Cochran, suggests that Wilkinson's promotion of Cushing to major was well planned and that Wilkinson had earlier misled Armstrong as to his approval of the captain in order to blindside him. Once the general had located his headquarters at Fort Hamilton, he could delve into any rumors, founded or unfounded, regarding the captain and manufacture charges against him. Cochran to Gayle Thornbrough, March 1959, PJA.

Prisoner as well as for [the] United States. But sorry I am to observe that the present advocate has not pushed any one point that might operate in favour of me but on the contrary has acted the part of Prosecutor in council against me." Armstrong clearly felt Cushing's bias toward doing Wilkinson's bidding.

At the beginning of his trial, Armstrong submitted a list of twenty-six witnesses that he deemed essential for providing evidence for his defense, adding that more might be required as the trial progressed. Along with the name of the absent St. Clair were those of fellow officers, enlisted men, contractors, and artificers. Armstrong wrote to the court's president and its members on February 16, thanking them for their decision two days earlier to grant him a reasonable time to prepare for his trial "which I trust no principles will induce you to depart from." He also requested that prosecution witnesses not be questioned until he was able to assemble those for his defense. Doing so would be unfair. "Such an examination gentlemen might tend to <u>Stab my character</u>." Not mincing words, he suggested that the commanding officer or "any other person" could circulate proofs that might prejudice present or future courts or act against his favor should a reduction of the size of the Army take place before the conclusion of his trial and result in his derangement. Appealing to the court's sense of justice, he reiterated his request for sufficient time to gather defense witnesses in order to present his evidence to the court and felt that no inconvenience to the army would occur from such an arrangement.[799]

Sunday, February 24, 1793, was a pivotal day in the unfolding sequence of events. Wilkinson had heard enough of Armstrong's requests and rhetoric and had clearly lost his patience. The following early morning order was issued to the president of the court, David Strong:

> Having reported to the Sub Legionary Gel. that the Prisoner has refused to plead to the charges exhibited against him—the Sublegionary General thinks proper to order that the Court resume this trial ten O'Clock this day and should the Prisoner Still refuse to plead, the Court will proceed agreeable to the principles and practices of all Judiciary criminals civil and Millitary and

---

[799] Armstrong to Major Strong, February 13 and 16, 1793, and February (undated), 1793, PJA.

in his presence are to take all the testimony which may be offerd after which the prisoner is to be called upon to make his defence and should he still stand mute or refuse to offer any defence, then and in that case the Court are to make up their Judgment upon the Testimony before them and are to pass Sentence accordingly.

When he later sent a copy of the notice to Wayne, Armstrong noted, "By this order I was dragged to trial unprepared & after the Court had agreed I should have until the 20th May to collect my witnesses." What accounted for Wilkinson's overturning the court's decision is a matter of conjecture. Wilkinson cited administrative concerns to Wayne. He had to schedule additional court-martial proceedings for Maj. John Smith, whose case was unrelated to that of Armstrong, for which he also had to impanel thirteen officers, possibly those also adjudicating Armstrong's trial. Perhaps Wilkinson simply tired not only of Armstrong's demands to follow accepted customs of military justice in the governance of his trial and the perceived insolence on the part of the captain in reminding him and the court of these practices. More than likely, however, was the court's decision to grant the trial's continuance until mid-May, at which time the remainder of the Legion and its commander would have arrived at Fort Washington. At that time, Wilkinson would no longer be the ranking officer to review court-martial proceedings. His unscrupulous practices could be discovered by more experienced officers, and Armstrong might be cleared of charges against him if his trial were adjudicated by another panel or its decisions reviewed by Wayne.[800]

Although proceedings of the court on February 24 are unknown, from the volume of correspondence of that date in his papers, Armstrong apparently objected to the sudden overruling of the court's decision to allow

---

[800] Sublegion orders Fort Hamilton February 24, 1793; Wilkinson to Wayne, March 9 and March 27, 1793, Wayne papers, XXV: 69, 107 in Cochran notebooks, PJA. Major Smith, as commander of Fort St. Clair, abandoned his post by fleeing the garrison in the belief that his subordinate officers were planning to poison him. His trial was held on March 7, four days following Armstrong's resignation. Found guilty by the court and sentenced to dismissal from the service, Smith later appealed to Wayne, who reinstated the major. See "General Wayne's Orderly Book," *Michigan Pioneer and Historical Collections* (Lansing: Wynkoop Hallenbeck Crawford Company 1905), XXXIV: 422-23.

him sufficient time to procure testimony from witnesses necessary for his defense by either allowing him to gather depositions from key witnesses upon their arrival with the Legion later in the spring or granting him the privilege of traveling to their present locations in the East. He received a terse notice from Cushing stating that it would be "utterly improper irreconcilable to the public service, that either you or the Judge advocate acting for the United States, should be permitted to traverse the Country from this place to Philadelphia to collect testimony in the case in which you are interested."

Not deterred and perhaps figuring he had nothing to lose at this point, Armstrong replied that he did not agree with the general's opinion and that the ruling appeared calculated to deprive him of vital testimony of St. Clair and other material witnesses. Again citing the Articles of War, he continued,

> The Judge advocate or some person appointed by him or the General may attend at taking such depositions—any Officer therefore in the City Philadelphia or at Pittsburgh may be appointed on behalf of the United States and my attendance can be no injury to service as I am not in command. I shall therefore demand this as my just privilege, and when the General gives me permission— which I demand as a right [—] you shall be notified of the time aggreable to the plan given me and according to the rules and Articles of War. This I trust will not be denied me.

Armstrong's audacity infuriated Wilkinson who directed Cushing to respond, "I have exhibited to the General your letter of the last evening, and he desires me to inform you, that if you offer such another instance of Insolence to him thro any channel, he will exert the Law Martial upon you in its utmost strength."[801]

The exchange of letters of February 24 continued. Cushing informed Armstrong that he had arranged to take the deposition of Abner Dunn in

---

[801] Cushing to Armstrong, February 24, 1793; Armstrong to Cushing, February 24, 1793 and Cushing to Armstrong, February 25, 1793, Wayne papers, XXV: 88 in Cochran notebooks, PJA.

Cincinnati on February 26 and also sought information on Armstrong's plans to depose Israel Ludlow and Abijah Ward in order to direct an official representing the United States government to attend. Armstrong replied that depositions might be taken by a justice of the peace, but suggested that it would not be out of order to wait to depose the men until after the prosecution's case against him had closed. He added that it would be necessary for him to be present for such events, but his request was denied.[802]

Little is known about the week following the last documented court meeting on Sunday, February 24. Since Cushing had indicated that he would be attending Abner Dunn's deposition in Cincinnati during the first part of the week, the court would logically not have met until his return. That Friday, Armstrong wrote his third letter to Wayne, advising him that he was now on trial despite having been given until May 20 by the court to gather witnesses and Wilkinson's intervention to begin immediate proceedings. The court was to proceed to examine prosecution witnesses and to pass sentence. Because many requests to which he was entitled had been rejected, he felt that justice had been denied and wrote that his intention was not to present his defense. Instead, he appealed to Wayne to form a court selected from the entire line of the army, which presumably would meet following the Third and Fourth Sublegions' arrival downriver.[803]

Despite Armstrong's "no-defense" strategy, his papers indicate preparation for a rebuttal of charges against him. Detailed notes address each of the nine formal charges, outlining not only rationales behind his actions in each case but also references of physical proof to support his innocence. He was prepared to cross-examine witnesses for the prosecution, among whom appear to have been Brigadier General Wilkinson, Quartermaster Ewing, and his clerk Sergeant Wilson. Many questions appear to have been designated for Lieutenant Hartshorne referencing Armstrong's disagreements with Wilkinson, particularly the incident regarding

---

[802] Cushing to Armstrong and Armstrong to Cushing, February 24, 1793, PJA. Israel Ludlow was a surveyor and early settler of Cincinnati and founder of "Ludlow's Station." Armstrong described Abijah Ward as "late artificer." Article 10 of the 1786 appendix to the Articles of War mandated the presence of both the prosecutor and the accused when depositions would be taken by an appointed justice of the peace. See Winthrop, *Military Law and Precedents*, 973.

[803] Armstrong to Wayne, February 28, 1793, PJA.

Lieutenant Gaines, concerns over quartermaster supplies, and dealings with contractors. Most interesting was this question to be addressed to Hartshorne regarding Wilkinson: "Did he not request you to inquire of my men if they had not been wronged and to collect for him every matter of complaint you could against me [?]" Whether Armstrong was able to address any of these questions to called witnesses is unknown, but his scribbled notes indicating that he was prepared to do so.[804]

Something damning to Armstrong's chances of acquittal apparently occurred within the next two days. Wilkinson might simply have further intervened in the judicial process, or Armstrong might have come to the realization that he could not win his fight. It is, however, more likely that an event of a more sinister nature took place. In a later letter to Wayne, Armstrong wrote that at this point, his resignation from the army seemed the only alternative. Although he despaired in doing so, the captain penned this draft:

> I do certify that at the commencement of the prosecution against me, from information I received, that the General had tampered with my Noncommissioned officers and soldiers. I conceived it provided from Private resentment. I am now convinced this information was ill founded—and my arrest and [illegible] should be withdrawn, and I shall declare in writing that no expression of mine hereafter shall tend to convey such an Idea or cast any reflection on him.[805]

Wilkinson, not satisfied, had Cushing issue an alternative statement for Armstrong's signature.

> I hereby certify and acknowledge that I am satisfied General James Wilkinson in the Arrest served upon me in November last in the charges contained in said Arrest and the prosecution which ensued, has been influenced

---

[804] Armstrong papers, February 1793, PJA.

[805] Armstrong to Wayne, March 1, 1793, PJA; draft of statement, dated February 1793, PJA.

by motives and considerations of Public duty and not by any impulsions of private pique or personal resentment.[806]

Apparently realizing he had little choice, on March 3, Armstrong agreed to sign the certificate while also attempting to shield himself from future action. He later wrote Wayne that he thought his signature unfortunate and would have suffered anything rather than to have signed it.

> I have a short time since formed a connecion in this country and having spent the morning of my life in the army wish to injoy the afternoon in private Society. My character as an officer and a man has heretofore been marked with propriety. The certificate presented me by Captain Cushing I will sign & at the same time would thank you if you can [illegible] give me a discharge from the Army that may prevent the ill-natured from casting inflictions on me hereafter.[807]

Armstrong's formal resignation of March 3 bore no relationship to his court-martial nor to his present army status, which, as stated, was seemingly untrue: "Having lost my commission on the deficit of the Army commanded by Major Gen St. Clair I beg leave to offer this as my resignation to any command in the Army hereafter in consequence of such Commission or appointment."[808]

---

[806] Armstrong statement, March 3, 1793; Wayne papers, XXV: 88, Cochran notebooks, PJA.

[807] Armstrong to Wilkinson, March 3, 1793, PJA. Leaving the army as an officer in any other way besides honorably carried a heavy price. Article 22 of the 1786 appendix to the Articles of War states, "In all cases where a commissioned officer is cashiered for cowardice or fraud, it shall be added in the sentence that the crime, name, place of abode, and punishment of the delinquent be published in the newspapers in and about camp, and of the particular State from which the offender came, or usually resides; after which it shall be deemed scandalous for any officer to associate with him." Armstrong obviously did not want his name to be associated with any such business. Winthrop, *Military Law and Precedents*, 974.

[808] Resignation notice, March 3, 1793, PJA. Armstrong's formal resignation apparently referred to the army's reorganization into the United States Legion in March 1792.

Regardless of having signed the certificate mandated by Wilkinson that he had been satisfied with the proceedings of the court, Armstrong wrote to the secretary of war two days later, apprising Knox of his resignation. Accusing Wilkinson of conducting the affair that had been governed by arbitrary measures, he hoped that the secretary would suspend his judgment until he had heard from Wayne, to whom he was also writing. He felt it his duty as an "honest man and citizen" who valued his reputation and "the Rights of every person" to have his case heard through an impartial inquiry that would reveal the cause of his resignation and would also investigate the loss of old army officers from the Legion. He further explained that both his resignation and the certificate he was forced to sign were extorted from him "by an oppressive hand of power calculated to injure my character & to wound the feelings of my friends."[809]

Wilkinson wrote Wayne a few days later, relating his version of the circumstances surrounding Armstrong's resignation.

> After urging every difficulty & delay, to Embarrass the Court, and to perplex & to injure the Service, in the Moment that proofs were depending to convict him unequivocally of every thing base & infamous, He supplicated leave to resign His Commission, and altho opposed to His request, I yielded to the interposition of several members of the Court & to consideration of regard for the Interests of the Service which had been put to hazard, by the Convention of officers which the occasion had rendered necessary, and if the trial had proceeded, the delay which would necessarily have insued, might have produced the most injurious consequences to the Public and to the Army. I therefore accepted his resignation on the 3rd Inst., under circumstances which rendered His name infamous, dissolved the Court, and discharged Him from service on the 4th.[810]

---

[809] Armstrong to Knox, March 5, 1793, PJA.

[810] Wilkinson to Wayne, March 9, 1793, Wayne papers, XXV: 69 in Cochran notebooks, PJA.

Court-martial proceedings were halted with Armstrong's resignation. The sudden turn of events leaves this question: why would Armstrong, who only one week before had been boldly resolute in his defense, suddenly give in to the powers aligned against him? The answer may lie in the captain's next letter to Wayne to which he attached numerous copies of correspondence relating to his trial. Armstrong explained that he realized that nothing short of close confinement would have awaited him if he again pleaded for time to collect his witnesses. Without his witnesses, he had no case. Wilkinson had used every method available to prejudice the court against him. Under those circumstances, he saw resignation as his only option.

Perhaps more importantly, Wilkinson apparently resorted to blackmail. Armstrong informed Wayne of his recent marriage and told of the threat that Wilkinson had held over him. The day preceding Armstrong's resignation, Wilkinson had crafted a plan designed not only to "wound the feelings" of his friends but also to "disparage my companion." What threat Wilkinson could have made that involved his young bride Tabitha or possibly her father, Judge Goforth, one can only surmise. Wilkinson more than likely had exhumed some dark fact regarding Armstrong's past during his years on the frontier with which to extort the captain's resignation and had possibly used his time at Fort Hamilton to do so. Had Armstrong, not unlike other officers of the time, had mistresses or relations with female camp followers during his years in the West? Armstrong indicated that had he been single, his misfortune would have been confined only to himself.

Armstrong assured Wayne that he had no desire to continue serving under a man as deceitful as Wilkinson. In a comment that was surely not lost on the commander, he also questioned the brigadier general's motives for attempting to rid his immediate command of officers who had previously served and fought under Wayne. In a following letter, Armstrong requested an investigation into Wilkinson's conduct on the prosecution governed by "Passion and Malice" rather than principles of duty. He would send documents relative to the trial proceedings with Dr. Allison who was expected to travel to Legion headquarters in a few days and asked the general to suspend his opinion relative to its outcome until he received this detailed account.[811]

---

[811] Armstrong to Wayne, March 10, 1793, PJA; Armstrong to Wayne, March 16, 1793, Wayne papers, XXV: 87 in Cochran notebooks, PJA.

As Armstrong began preparing his case to present to Wayne, he carefully copied and stitched together sixteen documents relating to his trial, also requesting the general's help in procuring a copy of the court-martial proceedings since his initial request for one had been refused. He reiterated his reluctance to leave the service, but no consideration would induce him to serve under a man as "void of feeling principle and humanity" as Wilkinson. He would, however, cheerfully lead one more company under Wayne's command. Again questioning Wilkinson's motives for attempting to rid the army of officers who had served previously with Wayne, he added that Wilkinson was a man of "desperate fortune and perhaps conceives these officers possess too much virtue to join in the execution of some plans he may have in view . . . he is an artful designing [illegible] man & is pushing to obtain the command of the Army." If Wayne had been previously oblivious to Wilkinson's command designs, Armstrong certainly gave him much to consider.[812]

His detailed letter of March 23 unfortunately delayed, Armstrong sent his packet off to Wayne on April 2 on an express boat going up to Legionville. In an accompanying note, he reiterated his request for a court of inquiry and his desire to be of service in the coming campaign, offering "those services that experience, knowledge of the woods and of the Enemy may contribute to promote public good and give ample Satisfaction to my Superiors."[813]

Matters came to a close on May 12 when Wayne, having brought the Legion westward and now encamped downriver from Fort Washington at the location he had dubbed "Hobson's Choice," responded to Armstrong in a letter that the latter later chose to publish in the Cincinnati newspaper, *Centinel of the Northwest Territory*. Although expressing his sincere regret over the loss of an officer known for his bravery and experience, the general

---

[812] Armstrong to Wayne, March 23, 1793, PJA. According to Article 24 of the 1786 appendix to the Articles of War, Armstrong was entitled to a copy of the proceedings against him, which he had apparently not received. Original documentation was to be sent to the secretary of war.

[813] Armstrong to Wayne, April 2, 1793, PJA; Armstrong had apparently wanted Dr. Allison to take the packet to Wayne, an arrangement that would allow the surgeon to fill Wayne in on the entire saga. Unfortunately, Allison ended up not traveling upriver, and Armstrong had to send his missive via express boat some ten days later at a time when decisions made by Wayne and Knox would have been crucial.

explained that Armstrong's resignation had precluded any further military investigation into his case, but since the captain had indicated an interest in participating in another campaign added, "Query could you or would you undertake to raise a corps of mounted volunteers for a given period?"[814]

Armstrong received his letter the following week and immediately replied to Wayne, acknowledging his regret in learning that the matter of his resignation was now closed. Asking to see him on the following Monday, he would then reply to the general's request regarding the raising of a troop of mounted riflemen.[815]

Armstrong did not accept the general's offer. Perhaps he had held out for reinstatement into the regular army in which he could serve directly under its commander, but after seventeen years of army life, Armstrong's days of active duty were at an end.

The trial and subsequent resignation of Capt. John Armstrong represented only a minor blip in the military career of James Wilkinson. Whether or not Armstrong's ouster from the officer corps was purposely designed to rid the army of potential Wayne supporters, Wilkinson had seized on a moment of Armstrong's indiscretion. The captain's resistance reignited Wilkinson's life-long intolerance to criticism or to any perceived slight of character and conveniently provided the excuse for him to manipulate conditions within his immediate command to his favor. His handling of the case forced Armstrong to turn to his archrival for assistance, setting into motion yet another incident calculated to enhance his position against his perceived foe. Armstrong became an early pawn in his quest to unseat Wayne.

The irony is that in ridding himself of Armstrong, Wilkinson lost an officer who could have been of service not only to the army but also to him. Armstrong was a career man; he knew no other trade. Until his arrest, he gave no indication that he had immediate interest in leaving the army. In all likelihood, he would have proven an objective and faithful subordinate to Wilkinson, the foundation for which had been laid prior to his arrest. Instead, Wilkinson exceeded his authority, issuing directives that were clearly contrary to both the spirit and the letter of the laws of military justice of the day that, as a minimum, included undue command influence

---

[814] Wayne to Armstrong, May 12, 1793, Wayne papers, XXVI: 79, Cochran notebooks, PJA.

[815] Armstrong to Wayne, May 19, 1793, PJA.

over the jury, denial of the accused to be present at the depositions of witnesses, overruling decisions made by the court in the defendant's favor, framing questionable charges, and presumably making heavy-handed threats to exact statements from Armstrong in order to keep his own reputation from being sullied. Additionally, Armstrong's trial undoubtedly alerted Wayne to his second-in-command's intentions, providing a basis for his interpretation of events to follow.

In a letter sent from Greenville the following spring, Maj. Gen. Anthony Wayne apprised Armstrong that at the time of his resignation, he would have been considered as having assumed the rank of major as of November 27, 1792, filling Erkuries Beatty's vacancy. The question spurred by the memorial issued earlier by Cushing and other former Second Regiment officers had been answered by Washington in Armstrong's favor. His commission was contingent, however, upon his acquittal from his arrest. Thomas Cushing assumed the rank of major on March 3, 1793, the day of Armstrong's resignation. Wilkinson had achieved one more milestone in his attempt to undermine Wayne.[816]

---

[816] Knox to Washington, February 18, and Washington to Knox, February 19, 1793, http://founders.archives.gov. Armstrong's biographer, Charles Cochran, believed that word of Washington's approval of Armstrong's status as the ranking captain and next in line for promotion could have reached Wilkinson by the time Armstrong was forced to resign on March 3. While possible, the timing would have been tight. Cochran to Gayle Thornbrough, PJA; Wayne to Armstrong, May 15, 1794, "Letter of General Anthony Wayne to John Armstrong, Esq.," *PMHB* 28, no. 3 (1904), 382–83.

EPILOGUE

Life and War's Next Chapter

John Armstrong's transition from military to civilian life was not a smooth one. His hopes for a court of inquiry were dashed by the receipt of Wayne's letter; continuing in the army was not an option, and he had to figure out what new direction his life would take. Circumstances might have been different had he returned East, but choosing to settle in Columbia in the shadow of Fort Washington complicated matters. With the army encamped nearby at Hobson's Choice, the area was now home to friends and foes alike. Pro-Wilkinson loyalists were not content to let Armstrong's upstart trial defense and open criticism of his commander and the court-martial's judge advocate go unchallenged. In September, he wrote Wayne that his "enimies and late persecutors" were preparing a civil suit against him alleging embezzlement related to shortage of forage during his command and again requested the general's help in procuring a copy of his court-martial proceedings in order to obtain copies of depositions by witnesses attesting to his innocence in that matter.[817]

Just how far this case proceeded is unknown, but shortly after writing Wayne, Armstrong found himself in improved civil, legal, and financial straits that no doubt brightened his spirits. In October, he was appointed to the positions of justice of the peace for Hamilton County and judge of the Court of Common Pleas by territorial governor Arthur St. Clair.

---

[817] Armstrong to Wayne, September 3, 1793, from Wayne Papers, XXVIII: 124, 125 and from the Simon Gratz Collection, in Cochran notebooks, PJA.

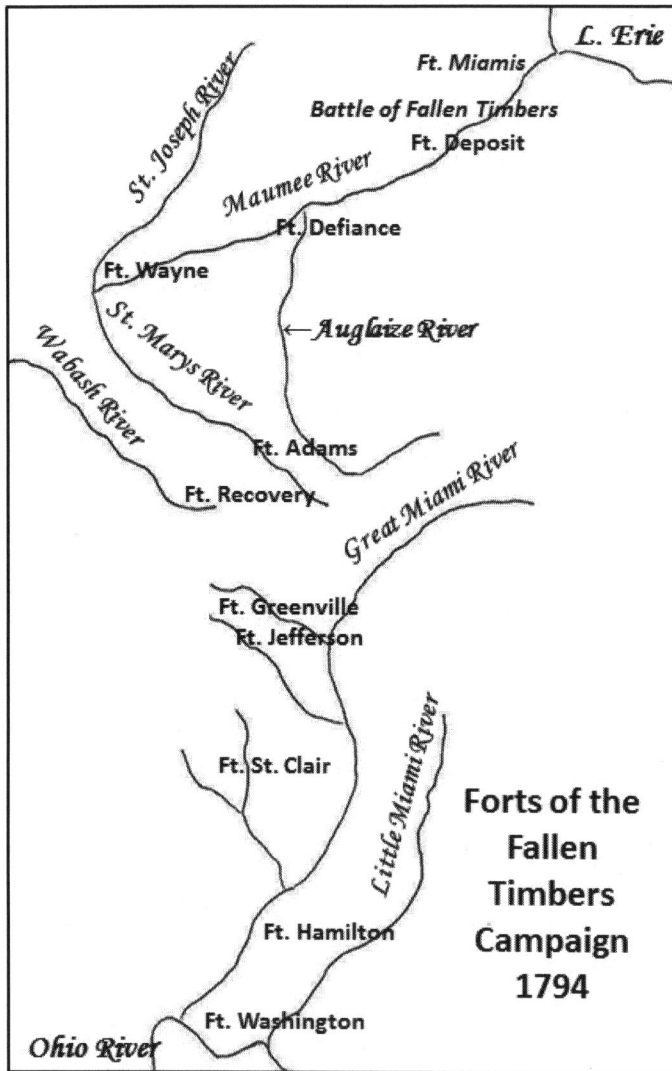

Forts of the Fallen Timbers Campaign 1794

Map labels: L. Erie, Ft. Miamis, Battle of Fallen Timbers, Ft. Deposit, St. Joseph River, Maumee River, Ft. Defiance, Ft. Wayne, St. Marys River, Auglaize River, Wabash River, Ft. Adams, Ft. Recovery, Great Miami River, Ft. Greenville, Ft. Jefferson, Ft. St. Clair, Little Miami River, Ft. Hamilton, Ft. Washington, Ohio River

It apparently paid to have influential in-laws and to be on good terms with others well placed in civilian circles.[818]

The Legion departed its Ohio River encampment on October 7, 1793, having finally been given the go-ahead by the administration following a final unsuccessful attempt by commissioners to obtain a peace treaty with the confederated Indian nations. A week later, the army had marched

---

[818] Smith, *SCP*, II: 323–24.

six miles past Fort Jefferson, stopping at that point to construct Fort Greenville (originally Fort Greene Ville), named in honor of Wayne's friend Maj. Gen. Nathanael Greene, and to winter there before advancing toward Indian strongholds on the Maumee River.

During the long winter marked with outbreaks of smallpox and influenza, Wayne gathered a force of about three hundred soldiers and on Christmas Eve arrived at the scene of St. Clair's defeat. There, along with burying some five hundred remains and recovering abandoned artillery, they constructed a new outpost, appropriately named Fort Recovery.[819]

Armstrong was not averse to taking revenge on his old nemesis Maj. Thomas Cushing when the opportunity arose. When the major found himself at Fort Washington in February 1794, Armstrong filed suit against him on charges of defamation of character for the sum of $1,000 plus another $60, most likely to cover court costs. When writing Wayne to inform him of the arrest, Armstrong explained that he had hoped to avoid conflict with his personal enemies but conceded that "the disposition of some men is such that were they in heaven they would there seek some object to gratify their ill nature upon." Armstrong reported that charges against Cushing could be covered by bail and that the major would be free to reassume his duties at Greenville and return to Cincinnati for his court date later in the year. Cushing, however, felt that he could not afford the amount of bail specified by the court and wrote Wayne that he, therefore, had to remain in Cincinnati.[820]

Armstrong kept Wayne apprised of Cincinnati gossip and news. In the same letter in which he had described the circumstances of Cushing's arrest, Armstrong warned the general of "characters under your command, and I fear one near your person, who are placed as spies on your conduct." He related his efforts to discern the author of a scurrilous letter penned at Greenville that had made its way to a Cincinnati newspaper but returned unpublished by the printer, as well as another appearing in the latest edition

---

[819] Gaff, *Bayonets in the Wilderness*, 182–85.

[820] Order of Judge William Goforth to Sheriff D. C. Orcutt, February 22, 1794, and Cushing to Wayne, March 8, 1794, Wayne Papers, XXXIII: 48–49; Armstrong to Wayne, April 13, 1794, Wayne Papers, XXXIV: 11 in Cochran notebooks, PJA. Armstrong apparently filed a second suit against Cushing for $1,500 for "trespass" on the case. Joseph Strong to John Pratt, May 14, 1794, John Pratt papers, Connecticut State Library in Cochran notebooks, PJA. Strong noted that "it will be a fiery trial and perhaps Johnny will get burnt."

of the paper. Armstrong was later able to inform Wayne of confirmed reports identifying Cushing as the author of the second letter. He had also discovered that Wilkinson had somehow learned of the contents of his own letter of April 13.[821]

Whether prompted by Cushing's annoying presence in Cincinnati and the major's leaking of poison-pen letters to the local newspaper or whether triggered by the necessity to clear his name, Armstrong wrote a lengthy letter to the editor of the *Centinel of the Northwestern Territory* on August 30, 1794, calling upon his detractors to come forward with public accusations so that any allegations of his past conduct could be settled in court once and for all. To build his case in the public's eye, he included copies of Wayne's letter expressing regret over his resignation and Wilkinson's commendation of his performance as commandant of Fort Hamilton, as well as recently taken depositions from former soldiers in Armstrong's company.[822]

The military campaign had begun by the time Armstrong's letters were published. It had already been a long year for Anthony Wayne. What was to have been a winter encampment at Greenville had stretched into summer, and the wait was not easy for the impatient general. Wilkinson and Wayne continued superficial niceties toward each other, but privately, Wilkinson schemed while Wayne grew ever more suspicious of him and his associates. In a private letter to Knox in November 1793, he noted the pattern of discord within the officer ranks. "The same baneful leaven which has been and is yet fermenting in the Atlantic states has also been fermenting in this Legion, from the moment of my first landing at Hobson's Choice." He continued, "The most visible and acting person is a Major Cushing, who is a very artful and seditious man. There is Capt Guion, not far behind but with less art." Alan D. Gaff notes that Wayne held Cushing and Guion

---

[821] Kohn and others note Wilkinson's hand in the evolution of a "whispering campaign" in Cincinnati to the effect that Congress had lost confidence in Wayne's leadership and attribute Wilkinson as the author of the unpublished letter. Kohn, *Eagle and Sword*, 181; Armstrong to Wayne, April 13, 1794, PJA; Wayne to Armstrong, Wayne Papers, XXXIX: 37 and Armstrong to Wayne, June 18, 1794, Wayne Papers, XXXVI: 19 in Cochran notebooks, PJA. See also William Maxwell, ed., *Centinel of the Northwestern Territory* on April 12, May 17, June 7, and June 14, 1794, https://news.google.com/newspapers?nid=0IG13jR3yJEC.

[822] *Centinel*, August 30, 1794.

particularly responsible for fomenting dissatisfaction within the officer ranks on the question of leave, blaming the pair for encouraging junior officers to submit their resignations when denied furloughs.[823]

★

Wayne's plans called for departure from Greenville in the spring. Forced initially with keeping troops at Hobson's Choice for five months for authorization to begin his march northward and with the additional wait at Greenville during the long winter and into the spring, Wayne had to deal with the problems of maintaining discipline and training for the bored, unpaid troops. As Wayne's frustration grew, he became more irritable and ill-tempered; officers aligned with one or the other general argued among themselves, and perceived slights of personal honor resulted in duels. John Armstrong's younger brother, Lt. Hamilton Armstrong, was not immune to the practice. Whatever his feud was with Lt. William Diven, the younger Armstrong ended up with a shot entering his cheek near his nose and passing out behind his ear. His wounds, fortunately, were not fatal; and he was promoted to captain shortly thereafter, leading the Second Battalion of the First Sublegion at Fallen Timbers.[824]

Wayne began to question events surrounding the operation itself. As early as October 23, 1793, while the army encamped at Greenville, he wrote to Knox, citing the failure of contractors Elliott and Williams to provide required provisions at Fort Jefferson. Wayne could not afford to repeat the logistical failure that had crippled St. Clair's expedition, and the contractors' inability to stockpile rations to support the army as it progressed northward could lead to disaster. The general became suspicious to the point where he considered the contractors' operation itself as one intended to undermine the Legion's mission and to cause the army to retreat for lack of supplies. His assumption was correct, and he eventually discovered that Wilkinson was behind the delay. Wayne was ill with gout, at times too incapacitated to supervise the contractors, and had to rely on Wilkinson's reports concerning their progress in delivering supplies. The contractors became irritated by Wayne's demands, but Wilkinson's surrogates assured them that the brigadier general would soon assume

---

[823] Gaff, *Bayonets*, 181.

[824] Joseph Strong to John Pratt, May 14, 1794, Pratt papers, Connecticut State Library in Cochran notebook, PJA.

command and that their job would become easier when they took orders from him alone. Secretly urging the contractors to delay the delivery of vital stores and meanwhile assuring Wayne that they could not move faster due to poor road and transport conditions, Wilkinson effectively slowed down their flow. In his ongoing determination to discredit Wayne in the eyes of the War Department, he essentially was attempting to sabotage the plan to launch an attack in the spring of 1794 when warmer weather would afford adequate forage for horses and livestock. Delaying the operation might subject Wayne and the Legion to the risk of another disaster as complete as that which had crushed Harmar and St. Clair.[825]

Wayne was no fool, nor did he lack friends. Although initially without proof of Wilkinson's collusion with the contractors, he remained wary of his second-in-command. In addition to being apprised by Armstrong of rumors in Cincinnati, he received warnings from others loyal to him. Cornet William Blue wrote him in January 1794 from the dragoon camp in Kentucky of hearing about a conspiracy among Wilkinson's officers, as well as an astounding report from a Philadelphia merchant that a movement was afoot by some senators in Philadelphia to impeach Wayne at the request of Wilkinson "on charges of Peculation Speculation Fraud &c." Wayne took steps to uncover the cause behind the contractors' poor performance and directed deputy quartermaster Maj. John Belli to organize a network of sources to provide intelligence on such activities in Kentucky. Although it took several valuable months to solve the supply problem, Wayne eventually hit upon this solution: Quartermaster James O'Hara was to take charge of the contractors' operation and make required deliveries at their expense. Not surprisingly by the end of May, the general reported that his gambit had been successful and that the contractors had delivered the promised supplies. The prospect of facing financial ruin more than likely prompted the frightened duo into action. Wayne's biographer Harry Emerson Wildes speculates that by this time, Wilkinson, believing that Wayne's plans had been sufficiently sabotaged for a timely campaign, loosened the hold he had placed on the contractors.[826]

To counteract any actions his adversaries might take in Philadelphia, Wayne commissioned Wilkinson's counterpart on the command staff, Brig.

[825] Wayne to Knox, October 23, 1793 in Knopf, *AWNIA*, 278; Wildes, *Anthony Wayne, Trouble Shooter*, 400–01.

[826] Gaff, *Bayonets*, 181; Wildes, *Anthony Wayne, Trouble Shooter*, 402.

Gen. Thomas Posey, to call on Congress and the administration while on leave in order to contradict any misrepresentations or exaggerated accounts that might be circulating in the capital. Wayne's ally, Kentucky politician and Wilkinson rival Maj. Gen. Charles Scott, was in Philadelphia at the time the controversy erupted and also met with Washington and Knox. The secretary of war's letter of March 31, 1794, to Wayne revealed how well Posey and Scott had served their friend. The administration had the highest confidence in the general.[827]

When Scott arrived with Kentucky horsemen for the campaign in July, an unhappy Wilkinson had to make room for his rival, whom he labeled a "fool, a scoundrel, and a poltroon." Scott had been tapped to assume command of the army in the event that Wayne became incapacitated, a victory for Wayne and an irritant to Wilkinson's easily bruised ego. Other circumstances also worked in Wayne's favor. Thomas Cushing did not return to the Legion until September 11 after the the critical battle at Fallen Timbers. Wayne spared himself from having to deal directly with the major, effectively sidelining him for the remainder of the operation. As the next ranking officer, Cushing would have commanded the First Sublegion, but Wayne sent him instead to Fort Defiance, an intermediary garrison built during the army's advance toward Fallen Timbers, to serve as second-in-command to another major, Thomas Hunt. Wayne had earlier managed to sideline the other member of the trio, Isaac Guion, by sending him down the Ohio River to build a new post at the site of old Fort Massac. Following an altercation with the Cincinnati sheriff involving the official's attempt to arrest his mistress, Guion defied an order of Maj. Thomas Doyle and allowed her to accompany him downriver. When she was discovered at Fort Steuben, Doyle ordered Guion's arrest, and Wayne subsequently turned the captain over to civil authorities in Cincinnati.[828]

When Wilkinson realized that his part in the contractor scandal had been uncovered, he responded defensively by writing to Knox, demanding him to order Wayne to hold a court of inquiry to put down rumors he had attempted to undermine the supply system. He made the mistake, however, of addressing the secretary of war through a private letter rather

---

[827] Gaff, *Bayonets*, 178, 180–81, 204–05, 238; Wayne to Knox, May 7, 1794, *AWNIA*, 324–25. See also Wildes, *Anthony Wayne, Trouble Shooter*, 402–07.

[828] Gaff, *Bayonets*, 215–17, 340. Randolph, "A Precise Journal of General Wayne's Last Campaign," *Proceedings of the American Antiquarian Society* (October 1954), 293.

than submitting a formal request. Knox chose to delay any action, arguing that an investigation would disrupt the army on the eve of battle. By this time, the administration was fully aware of Wilkinson's ongoing efforts to discredit Wayne. A June 25, 1794, edition of a Philadelphia newspaper, the *Gazette of the United States*, included a scathing attack on Wayne. "Stubborn Facts," written anonymously but widely believed to have been penned by Wilkinson, was then republished in other eastern newspapers. The administration refuted the letter by publishing a rebuttal on July 19, 1794, by "A Friend to Truth," which included letters from Knox and Charles Scott, and let the matter rest.[829]

★

The Legion's protracted wait to venture northward came to an abrupt end on June 30, 1794, when a strike was made near Fort Recovery by some 2,000 Wyandots, Delawares, Shawnees, Miamis, and Weas. Led by Little Turtle, Blue Jacket, and Simon Girty, the combined force initially attacked a supply train outside the fort. Its defenders, although suffering heavy casualties, managed not only to hold on during the two-day siege but also to effect the retreat of their assailants' forces. Among the dead, however, was Armstrong's former company officer, Capt. Asa Hartshorne.[830]

The campaign was now on. The Legion departed Greenville on July 28, 1794, reaching deserted Maumee River settlements on August 8 and stopping there to build Fort Defiance. On August 15, the force set out to the northeast, stopping three days later to construct a rude holding area dubbed "Fort Deposit." Leaving baggage and roughly 100 men to guard equipment and stores, Wayne and the Legion headed toward Fort Miamis, the British stronghold near present-day Toledo, where roughly 1,100 Ottawa, Wyandot, Shawnee, Miami, Delaware along with lesser numbers of Ojibwe, Potawatomi, Mingo, Mohawk warriors, and approximately

---

[829] Kohn, *Eagle and Sword*, 181, attributes the letter to Wilkinson. Gaff, *Bayonets*, 203–04 ascribes it to Lt. James Glenn, described by the *Martinsburg Gazette*'s editor as "a gentleman from General Wayne's camp, who may be depended upon." John Fenno, ed., *Gazette of the United States & Daily Advertiser*, June 25 and July 19, 1794, https://chroniclingamerica.loc.gov/lccn/sn84026271/1794-06-25/ed-1/seq-2/ https://chroniclingamerica.loc.gov/lccn/sn84026271/1794-07-19/ed-1/seq-2/.

[830] Jacobs, *The Beginning of the U.S. Army*, 168–70.

70 Canadians awaited its arrival. Despite their amassed numbers, at the crucial time of the Legion's arrival, only a core of about 400 tribesmen and 60 Canadians were in the immediate area to provide resistance to the advancing troops. Scouts had concluded that no attack would take place that day, and the core of the defenders had retreated to the rear to get their first meal in the past twenty-four hours. Subsequently, the approximately 1,000 Legionnaires attacked a force of less than 500, and the decisive battle at Fallen Timbers was over in forty-five minutes. Wayne then turned the Legion westward toward Fort Defiance to await food and supplies before marching onward to establish a stronghold at Kekionga. Arriving at the confluence of the St. Marys, St. Joseph, and Maumee Rivers on September 17, he spent a little over a month at the outpost that became Fort Wayne before departing for Greenville. By November 2, 1794, the campaign was over; and the treaty process could begin.

The alliance was broken. The confederation nations, now realizing their folly in trusting those who had incited them to war, understood their limited options. The British, always willing to goad them to action, would not support them as allies in battle. When warriors had fled to the Fort Miamis garrison for refuge during the Battle of Fallen Timbers, they found the gates of the blockhouse slammed in their faces.[831]

★

Having been apprised by Knox of Wilkinson's prior demands for a court of inquiry in December 1794, Wayne was even more alert to the brigadier's machinations and effectively managed to sideline him during peace talks and boundary negotiations at Greenville. He also had the opportunity to interview deserter Robert Newman whose story mirrors that of a modern-day spy novel. According to Newman, he was contacted by unknown men at Greenville prior to the beginning of the Fallen Timbers campaign and instructed to deliver a letter to British agent Alexander McKee at the Miami villages on the Maumee River. Following his stay there, he managed to return to the army and, finding himself under arrest, disclosed details of his time with the British. While at the villages, he met Indian agent Mathew Elliott whose brother Robert Elliott was the "Elliott" of the contractor firm "Elliott and Williams," about whom Wayne already had

---

[831] Jacobs, *The Beginning of the U.S. Army*, 172–75.

grave suspicions. Newman claimed to have gleaned positive information regarding collusion between Wilkinson and the contractors to slow the delivery of provisions. Newman's account was hard to believe, but parts of his story rang true with Wayne. He was convinced that Wilkinson was in correspondence with the British and "Democrats" in Kentucky to dismember the union.[832]

His diplomatic duties completed upon the signing of the Treaty of Greenville on August 3, 1795, Wayne traveled to Philadelphia to oversee the treaty's ratification and to lobby Congress for maintaining the size of the army. Before departing Fort Washington in December, he issued specific instructions to Wilkinson, severely circumscribing his power.[833]

The general was met upon his arrival in Philadelphia on February 6, 1796, with a resounding hero's welcome by its citizens and an appreciative reception by civic and governmental leaders, the magnitude of which could not have been lost on Wilkinson. Upon completing his business there, Wayne returned west to supervise the transition of British posts into American hands, an action now required by the ratification of the Jay Treaty, adding to the far-flung array of garrisons already under the army's command. Back at Greenville, he relieved Wilkinson of his duties and granted him permission to travel east. Although he long before had confirmed knowledge of Wilkinson's treachery, little did he realize the full extent of his second-in-command's intentions.[834]

Wilkinson had been busy launching savage attacks on his commander, writing influential friends and condemning Wayne's leadership within

---

[832] Whether Newman was working for Wilkinson or sent off by Wayne himself to uncover Wilkinson's collusion with the British is debated by biographers. Historians cite correspondence regarding Newman in papers of both British agent Alexander McKee and Lt. Governor John Graves, as well as that of Wayne to Knox and Pickering, May 7, 1794, through January 29, 1795. See Timothy M. Rusche, "Treachery within the United States Army," *Pennsylvania History: A Journal of Mid-Atlantic Studies* 65, no. 4 (1998), 478–91; *AWNIA*, 322–84, Linklater, *An Artist in Treason*, 142–43, and Jacobs, *Tarnished Warrior*, 155–56.

[833] Knox to Wayne, December 5, 1794, *AWNIA*, 364–65. Wilkinson immediately issued a formal notice that conditions within the command had changed with Wayne's departure. Jacobs, *The Beginning of the U.S. Army*, 181–84.

[834] Knox to Wayne, December 5, 1794, and Wayne to Knox, January 29, 1795, AWNIA, 364, 368–369, 383; Linklater, *An Artist in Treason*, 154.

the battle itself while belittling its successful outcome. According to his estimate, victory was due simply to the inferior numbers and "injudicious conduct of the enemy." Wayne was "a liar, a drunkard, a Fool, the associate of the lowest order of society, & the companion of their vices, of desperate fortune, my rancorous enemy, a coward, a Hypocrite, and the contempt of every man of sense and virtue." Wilkinson had kept a personal journal of the campaign and was also associated with another more critical account of the operation. Written anonymously, "From Greenville to Fallen Timbers" is undoubtedly a product of the pro-Wilkinson faction and is believed to have been written either by Wilkinson himself or dictated to a clerk. It chronicled not only the progress of the Legion but also described instances of Wilkinson's advice being disregarded by Wayne. Wilkinson no doubt planned to use its contents as ammunition in any future legal battle with Wayne. Once in Philadelphia, he planned either to sustain or withdraw the charges he had earlier preferred against him, as well as to prevent any investigation of his own questionable conduct. Jacobs notes that talk of his dealings with the Spanish government and Robert Newman's implication of Wilkinson in the delay of supply deliveries to the Legion was arousing suspicion. Above all, he needed official assistance in his efforts to best Wayne.[835]

Realizing that the administration would never replace Wayne after his widely acclaimed military victory and treaty with the Indian nations, Wilkinson decided to pursue a different route by threatening to take his case to Congress over the heads of Washington and Knox. The timing was poor for the administration's handling of Wilkinson's charges, and it procrastinated in dealing with a potential procedural nightmare. A new presidential administration would soon come in, and the current defense organization was in the process of change. Congress had abolished the Legion since the country was now officially "at peace." Washington consulted his cabinet for a solution. In a tortured review of the Constitution and the Articles of War, the attorney general ruled that Wayne could be tried if the president, as commander-in-chief, so ordered, but the issue was rendered moot. On his way to establish winter quarters at Pittsburgh,

---

[835] Wilkinson to Innes, December 1794 in Linklater, *An Artist in Treason*, 140–41; Jacobs, *The Beginning of the U.S. Army*, 190–91. See Dwight L. Smith, ed., *From Green Ville to Fallen Timbers: A Journal of the Wayne Campaign* (Indianapolis: Indiana Historical Society, 1952). Gaff, *Bayonets*, 389n attributes the journal to Wilkinson's direct or indirect authorship.

Wayne suffered another of his recurring attacks of gout. This was followed by fever and intestinal pains, and he died at Presque Isle, present-day Erie, Pennsylvania, on December 15, 1796. After five years of bitterness and recrimination, fate had intervened to allow James Wilkinson his victory over Wayne.[836]

★

By the time of Wayne's death, John Armstrong had made a new life for himself. No doubt Tabitha was happy to remain near her parents and siblings, and the size of Armstrong's extended family increased with the arrival of the McAdams family in Columbia. Armstrong had opened a mercantile business, announcing the arrival of merchandise and terms of sale in early editions of the *Centinel of the Northwestern Territory*. In 1795, he went into partnership with John Smith, an ordained Baptist minister with many outside interests: farmer, entrepreneur, eventual territorial delegate, and US senator. The two apparently set up shop within Armstrong's house, but the partnership was dissolved six months later due to "divers [*sic*] controversies and disputes" between Armstrong and Smith.[837]

Tabitha and John celebrated the birth of Ann on December 11, 1793. With clockwork regularity, they welcomed a total of ten children until their final son, John Hildreth Armstrong, was born on April 5, 1809. Armstrong continued to purchase land locally and to invest in stock and Pennsylvania real estate through Francis Johnston, adding to the acreage he owned in Northumberland County, as well as what he had purchased from his soldiers throughout the years. By 1796, the assessed value of his Columbia property was $1,522, making him the ninth-largest landholder

---

[836] The Articles of War contained no provision for trying a commanding general since only he possessed the power to convene military courts. Furthermore, any officer who sat in judgment would be a subordinate, thereby jeopardizing his career if he rendered a guilty verdict. Kohn, *Eagle and Sword*, 187; Linklater, *Artist in Treason*, 161.

[837] *Centinel*, November 16, 1793, and April 5, 1794. See also indenture between Armstrong and Smith dated September 5, 1795 and agreement for dissolving the partnership, March 15, 1796, PJA. McAdams's name appears on the Columbia Township tax list of 1796. See Daniel Reeder, Assessor, "A Return for Columbia Township," *Quarterly Publication of Historical and Philosophical Society of Ohio* 14, no. 2–3 (1918–1919): 6.

in that jurisdiction. To add to his income as farmer, merchant, and civil servant, he conducted a side business selling fruit trees, and was well known in the area for successfully propagating seedlings sent to him from the East.[838]

Armstrong also supplied the army with feed for its horses. In the fall of 1797, he apparently sold a significant amount of corn to the garrison at Fort Washington. The transaction ended unsatisfactorily as indicated by the heated and exhausting exchange of letters some months later between Armstrong and the officer ordering the shipment, Capt. William Henry Harrison. The future president of the United States complained that he had paid a premium price for corn so bad that the horses wouldn't eat it. When Armstrong heard from friends that Harrison had aired his dissatisfaction to others regarding the sale, he fired off an indignant letter demanding apology. Never one to take slights of honor lightly, he wrote, "I am informed that you have been industriously imployed in defaming my character having in a public assembly declared I was a knave and Raskal, that I had cheated you in the measurement of corn. Reports of this kind false and unfounded as they are may have a tendency to injure my character and at the same time add nothing to yours."[839]

Harrison responded that it was not the quantity but the quality he objected to, and he felt justified in criticizing the transaction until he became convinced that Armstrong was unaware of the quality that he had sold. Their correspondence continued until Harrison tried to beg off by stating that he was tired of the issue, that he had already spent too much time addressing Armstrong's complaints, and that he would not respond again to the latter's demands.

---

[838] Reeder, "A Return for Columbia Township," 7–16. Of 282 individuals assessed for taxes that year, only 13 had valuation of more than $1,000. Armstrong was known for his success in planting fruit trees in the vicinity of garrisons during his time in the army and appeared to have a significant business supplying saplings from his farm in Columbia, as well as those of his mother-in-law, Catherine Goforth, and the widow of his business associate, Samuel Armstrong. Virginius C. Hall, "The Genesis of an Orchard," *OHPSB* 7, no. 2 (1949): 87–89. See also Charles Theodore Greve, *Centennial History of Cincinnati and Representative Citizens* (Chicago: Biographical Publishing Company, 1904), I: 411.

[839] Armstrong to Harrison, July 16, 1798; Harrison to Armstrong, September 18, 1797, PJA.

Armstrong refused to drop the issue, and their exchange grew more heated, both utilizing words and phrases common at the time in regard to offenses against personal honor. Armstrong wrote Harrison,

> ... I have the right to expect that you will recall those invectives and use the same industry in contradicting that ill natured and unjust report that you did in giving it circulation. If you do not I shall seek some mode of punishing you if it should be by speaking of you both at home and abroad in the same way you have done of me and I have not determined that the business shall end there.[840]

Not to back down, Harrison replied that once it was clear to him that Armstrong was unaware of the quality of corn that had been delivered, he would be happy to apologize, "but if you prefer a shorter mode of vindication you may rest assured that you shall not be disappointed." The implied challenge to a duel apparently was ignored, and the issue appears to have been diffused by the fact the sale was now ten months past and Harrison was no longer in the army. The fact that by this time both men were then serving concurrently in the Ohio territorial government makes the incident even more interesting. Harrison served as secretary of the territory from June 1798 to December 1799, joining Armstrong who had been appointed as treasurer by Governor St. Clair in September 1796 and served until 1803 when Ohio achieved statehood.[841]

Armstrong's duties as the first treasurer of the Northwest Territory were significant. At the time of his appointment in 1796, he might have conducted the business of the office in Cincinnati, but in 1800 the territorial government was formally established approximately 85 miles east to Chillicothe. As treasurer, he accounted for financial assets received

---

[840] Armstrong to Harrison July 16, 1798

[841] Armstrong to Harrison, July 16 and July 28, 1798; Harrison to Armstrong, July 26 and August 8, 1798, PJA.
Official document denoting Armstrong's appointment, September 13, 1796, PJA. Cayton, *Frontier Indiana*, 175. The affair may have been exaggerated by Armstrong's perception of Harrison's regard for him. Harrison's father-in-law was John Cleve Symmes who had earlier indicated his dislike for Armstrong's heavy-handedness in dealing with settlers within his purchase areas. See Bond, *The Correspondence of John Cleves Symmes*, 149, 161

by the territory, distributed funds for warrants and certificates drawn by the state auditor, collected revenue, and reported regularly to the territorial legislature about the state of its accounts. The position required a bond of securities payable to the government for $20,000 and yielded him an annual salary of $400.00. Armstrong undoubtedly spent a considerable time away from home during the latter years of his appointment. [842]

★

A description of Columbia is given in the *Journal of a Tour in Unsettled Parts of North America in 1796 & 1797* by Englishman Francis Baily. The visitor described Armstrong's business partner John Smith's log house, which was apparently typical of those in the town. In the writer's opinion, far from the degree of refinement and comfort one might expect in more civilized parts of the country, the house nevertheless bore marks of industry and cleanliness, adjoining a farm of several acres, composed chiefly of profitable meadowland. His warehouse was near the waterside, consisting of one room featuring European-manufactured articles that were in demand. Baily noted that two or three other stores of the same kind were in Columbia, and merchants could expect a 100 percent profit on goods sold. The settlement was laid out on a regular plan but did not appear to be flourishing. It lay on low ground and the river often overflowed.[843]

Hamilton County became the hotbed of the Ohio statehood movement. No sooner had the victory at Fallen Timbers occurred than talk of statehood began in earnest. Judge Goforth was chairman of the Hamilton County Committee of Correspondence in 1797, worked to gather support for statehood from other jurisdictions within the territory, and was elected as a representative from Hamilton County to the House of Representatives of the First Territorial Legislature that convened in February 1799. The majority good Democratic-Republicans, their designs did not necessarily coincide with those of the territory's Federalist governor, Arthur St. Clair, who initially opposed statehood.[844]

---

[842] Northwest Territory, *Laws of the Territory Northwest of the River Ohio: Including the Laws of the Governor and Judges, The Maxwell Codes and the Laws of the Three Session of the Territorial Legislature 1791-1802* (Cincinnati: 1833), 231-233.

[843] Francis Baily, *Journal of a Tour in Unsettled Parts of North America in 1796 & 1797* (London: Baily Brothers, 1856), 195–202.

[844] Correspondence between Armstrong and William Wells indicates that

Although he wasted little time settling into civilian life, Armstrong's ego festered over the manner in which his departure from the army took place. He evinced no regret in not having to serve under a commander like Wilkinson, but continued to seek clarification regarding his rank and the pay due at his resignation. Armstrong became influential in local militia activities and politics. In August 1797, he received an appointment as lieutenant colonel of the First Regiment, Hamilton County militia and on September 23, 1797, was appointed lieutenant colonel commandant of the Second Regiment. Still serving in 1804, he was considered for the position of brigadier general of the First Brigade. When Congress authorized a temporary increase in the army in April 1808 in response to the threat of war with Great Britain, Armstrong wrote Secretary of War Henry Dearborn that should the government seek to increase the army's size through raising units in Ohio, he would volunteer to command a regiment.[845]

★

The long-awaited congressional resolution of December 7, 1795, that defined borders for future states within Northwest Territory presented Armstrong with the opportunity to enter into land speculation on a large

---

although Armstrong was appointed by Federalist St. Clair, he was clearly aligned with the Democratic Republican party and pleased with the outcome of the 1800 presidential election of Thomas Jefferson. Wells to Armstrong, January 23, 1801, PJA. See Downes and Lindley, *Frontier Ohio*, 177–200 for a detailed account of the conflicting interests of Congress, St. Clair, and leaders of Hamilton County, Marietta, and Chillicothe from 1795-1801; Fred J. Milligan, *Ohio's Founding Fathers* (Lincoln: iUniverse, Inc., 2003), 61–63.

[845] Armstrong is often referred to as "Colonel," the rank held during his command of the militia. Armstrong did not hold, at least initially, the top spot in the Hamilton County militia. The position of colonel was held by prominent Columbia resident Oliver Spencer. Armstrong, along with his brother-in-law John Stites Gano, held subordinate positions of lieutenant colonel in the organization. See Armstrong's notebooks and August 22, 1797, Commission, PJA; Richard C. Knopf, *Transcription of the Executive Journal of the Northwest Territory*, I: 547 at www.ohiohistory.org/ onlinedoc,northwest/exjournal; John Gano, "Major General John Gano to Governor Edward Tiffin, August 20, 1804," *QPHPSO* 15, nos. 1–2, (1920): 17–18; Armstrong to Dearborn, May 9, 1808, PJA.

scale. He had long eyed the land surrounding Fort Hamilton as choice property for settlement, advertising the prospect of sale as early as April 1794 in the *Centinel of the Northwestern Territory*. While having to wait to act on that project, he explored others. In December 1796, he and Abraham Shepherd jointly purchased lands lying between the Scioto and Miami Rivers. The next year, Armstrong formed a partnership with Hamilton County resident William Wells to reconnoiter lands in the area designated to settle claims of Revolutionary War veterans. Utilizing their knowledge of choice lands, the pair offered to serve as agents for those attempting to locate acreage, to attend to the drawing of lots, and to ensure the proper registration of land warrants and completion of other necessary paperwork in return for one-eighth of the land negotiated or a monetary compensation. The Wells-Armstrong partnership later included Cincinnatian Israel Ludlow. [846]

Armstrong had long been drawn to lands farther down the Ohio River that had been part of "Clark's Grant," awarded to veterans of Virginia's Illinois Regiment during the Revolutionary War. They were primarily in what was to become Clark County, Indiana. He became well acquainted with the richness of the land during the time he spent at Fort Steuben and even then had considered obtaining property there. As early as 1788, he had set his sights on the holdings of Capt. Richard McCarty who was killed before the war's end in 1781. Armstrong had agreed to act as middleman to dispose of property that McCarty held in Illinois and purchased other pieces for himself and his brother Hamilton in Indiana. Purchase or disposal of all McCarty's holdings took years to accomplish. Negotiations with his widow in Canada and his dealings with the family's attorneys eventually spanned decades and multiple generations on both the McCarty and Armstrong sides. Delays were precipitated by a multitude of factors: deferral of legislation authorizing land sales, an officially declared war, tense governmental relationships with Britain that impeded correspondence to and from Canada, and court decisions determining pre-Revolution ownership of land in Illinois. Armstrong's mission to the Mississippi in 1790 was no doubt filled with efforts to research titles to

[846] *Centinel*, April 12, 1794; articles of agreement between Abraham Shepard and John Armstrong, December 15, 1796, between William Wells and John Armstrong, October 17, 1797, Armstrong, Wells and Ludlow, December 13, 1800, PJA; Downes and Lindley, *Frontier Ohio*, 84.

McCarty's holdings and most likely were the focus of later journeys in the late 1790s and early 1800s.

By the end of 1804, Armstrong began to make serious plans for his future and that of his growing family. He then owned "Spring Hill" on land next to "Armstrong's Station," the blockhouse he and his men had built that had served as an outpost of Fort Steuben during his assignment there. Originally part of Clark's Grant and perched high above the Ohio, it afforded a panoramic view of Grassy Flats, a point at which the river was fordable that had been a site for Indian crossings to and from Kentucky. His manager, brother-in-law William Plaskett, oversaw tenancy of the property that eventually supported a small settlement.[847]

Four years later, Armstrong realized another business and life goal, creating his own township. Armstrong had purchased acreage along the Ohio River not far from Spring Hill. With his on-site partner Plaskett, he laid out plans for the settlement that became Bethlehem, Indiana. Advertising lots for sale in June 1809, he reserved many for himself and his heirs.[848]

The draft of an informative letter written in response to that of his brother James in June 1810 reveals much about the status of Armstrong's finances as well as updates on the family of his sister Nancy McAdams. The only document in Armstrong's papers that proved his brother James was not only alive in 1810, had a family, was apparently financially sound, it unfortunately did not indicate James's place of residence or refer to his activities. In his letter, John sought to gain James's authorization to withdraw from any potential claim for property owned by brother Hamilton who had died in 1801, explaining that although his brother had never married, he

---

[847] Announcement of sale, July 1804; receipt for acreage, August 15, 1804, PJA; William Plaskett married Jemima Goforth, Tabitha Goforth's younger sister. References to correspondence with Joseph Perrault, family attorney to McCarty's widow, that appear in Armstrong's papers are too numerous to cite. For information concerning Captain McCarty, see G. Malcolm Lewis, "Richard McCarty," in *Dictionary of Canadian Biography*, vol. 4, *1771–1800; Lewis Collins, History of Kentucky* (Covington: Collins & Co., 1878), II: 17.

[848] Advertisement, June 17, 1809, in Armstrong papers, PJA. The township of Bethlehem lies within Hunterdon County, New Jersey. Cochran's research notes that the Plaskett family also began their time in the American colonies in Hunterdon County, so the christening of the town "Bethlehem" appears logical on several counts. Cochran notebooks, PJA.

had two "natural" children and that any inheritance should rightfully be transferred to them despite their lack of status as legal heirs. Armstrong indicated his pleasure that James was doing well financially and that his own finances were sound and any debt he carried could be settled easily.[849]

★

By October 1810, Armstrong's health had begun to deteriorate. In a letter to business associate Joseph Hemphill, he confided that he was barely able to ride ten miles due to what he described as "rheumatism in the small of my back" following his trip to Louisville the previous December and that he might be unable to leave his farm again. His outlook regarding the future appeared to change dramatically as he observed his own limitations; the settling of old debts and resolution of property sales began in earnest. To complicate matters, a significant amount of acerage was held jointly with William Wells and his deceased partner, Israel Ludlow. In a cash-strapped economy based on down payments and indenture agreements between buyers and sellers, he had the unpleasant task of calling in payment from men who had purchased property from him. He could no longer accept parcels of land as payment. Additionally, he had to settle his own payments due on property previously purchased.[850]

Armstrong had accumulated a significant amount of land, and looking ever westward may earlier have considered adding to his holdings. Whether for business or to satisfy his wanderlust, he again travelled to the Mississippi in September 1808, prior to which he left a memorandum itemizing his individual and joint land ownership. Of the total acreage included in partnerships with Wells and Ludlow, he claimed 5,590 acres in his own name. Additionally, he owned 15,333 acres in Pennsylvania, Ohio, and the Indiana Territory plus miscellaneous lots in Northumberland County, Pennsylvania; Bethlehem, Indiana; and along the Mississippi, totaling 20,923 acres.[851]

---

[849] John Armstrong to James Armstrong, June 22, 1810, PJA.

[850] John Armstrong to Joseph Hemphill, October 17, 1810, PJA. No task could have been more distasteful to Armstrong than having to collect money owed him by his longtime mentor, Francis Johnston, himself bereft of funds, brother officers having died owing him large sums of money. Johnston to Armstrong, May 20, 1811, PJA.

[851] Memorandum of John Armstrong, September 24, 1808, PJA.

An indication that Armstrong's health had deteriorated further appears in a letter to John Kerr on March 21, 1812. Kerr was seeking a price quote for land in which he was interested. Armstrong's fifteen-year-old son, William Goforth Armstrong, penned the response, informing Kerr that the elder Armstrong was too ill to enter into negotiations at the time. John had apparently suffered a stroke, and the younger Armstrong had begun to act as his father's personal secretary.[852]

His son's help in handling his business and correspondence was not Armstrong's only source of assistance at the time. Ohio was a "free" state in that the selling and purchasing of slaves was prohibited. It was, however, common practice for them to be leased from their owners in slaveholding states under the guise of indentured servants, many with dates of freedom specified in a written agreement. Proximity to Kentucky made a fertile field for such practices. Under such an agreement, George Painter, brought to Ohio in 1807 when he was eleven years old, would serve the Armstrong family until he was twenty-eight years of age, at which time his freedom was stipulated.[853]

---

[852] John Kerr to Armstrong, March 7, 1812, and William G. Armstrong to Kerr, March 21, 1812. In a letter to old military associate Maj. Isaac Craig on February 17, 1813, Armstrong commented that he'd been in a "helpless state" for three years and could not write, stand, or walk but could still "retain my thinking faculties," PJA.

[853] Benjamin Anderson to Armstrong, March 20, 1807, PJA. Terms of the agreement were apparently carried out. Painter's marriage to Lucy Kirtley in 1827 was recorded in the Clark County Registry of Marriages, 1820–1828, vol. B, 196. According to John's granddaughter Eliza Armstrong, George took care of the elderly Armstrong's personal needs. Painter apparently continued to work for the family after the expiration of his indenture. In an interview with Charles F. Cochran, Ms. Eliza quipped that she thought that her father William G. Armstrong thought more of him than of her. Cochran interview notes, undated, PJA. Armstrong had also apparently leased a female slave from Kentuckian Richard C. Anderson for an unknown period of time in 1806, perhaps to help Tabitha with her children and to assist in household chores during Armstrong's many absences. Richard C Anderson to Armstrong, May 16, 1806, PJA. Armstrong's father-in-law Judge Goforth was adamantly opposed to slavery. In a speech to the Columbian Patriotic Society on the twentieth anniversary of the country's founding, Goforth expressed his hope that "slavery be extirpated from the face of the earth . . . and may all the sons of Adam learn to do as they would be done to." Armstrong may have been

In May 1814, Armstrong's correspondence began to originate from Clark County, Indiana, indicating that he, Tabitha, and conceivably the younger children had moved to Spring Hill. Life could not have been easy for Tabitha who left her two married daughters Nancy and Catherine in the familiar surroundings of Columbia along with her widowed mother and nearby sister Mary Gano. In her letter to Tabitha, Mary alludes to Armstrong's temperament as being of an "inconsistent and contrary" nature," adding "his conduct is thought by all to be more than human nature ought or can bare."

Indeed, Armstrong did not seem to go quietly into that good night. On a scrap of paper found in the Cincinnati Historical Library dated March 25, 1814, son Thomas Armstrong wrote for his father: "Col. Armstrong in conversation with Thos. Armstrong observed that some people wish to deprive him from doing business stating he was insane, but said he to T. Armstrong let them look at some deeds I executed on the sale of Col. Anderson's land."[854]

The end came two years later in the early morning hours of Sunday, February 4, 1816. At sixty-one years of age, he was preceded in death by many comrades through wars, illness, and old age, and would be accompanied in later years by family and friends-in-arms whose time on earth was drawing to a close. Younger brother Hamilton had died fifteen years earlier, and sister Nancy and brother-in-law John McAdams were not to survive much past his own death.

John Armstrong had founded an American dynasty. His eight surviving children went on to produce a lineage from which hundreds of Americans now claim ancestry. As for Tabitha, she managed to shock her older children by marrying minister William Lockhart three years after Armstrong's death, moving with him to Bethlehem with her six youngest children and hopefully enjoying a happy marriage of twenty-four years until his death in 1843.[855]

★

---

inclined to minimize his use of these "indentured servants" during his father-in-law's lifetime. Goforth's speech, July 4, 1796, PJA.

[854] Mary Goforth Gano to Tabitha Armstrong, July 31, 1814, PJA; statement by Thomas Armstrong, March 25, 1814, in Cincinnati Historical Library and Archives, MSS VP 1322.

[855] Pension file 10202, Armstrong, John, Revolutionary War, ancestry.com,

Thomas and Jane Hamilton Armstrong's three sons, James, John, and Hamilton all found their calling in military service. James's talents, recognized early following his enlistment in Pennsylvania's Second Regiment, led to commissioning and the eventual rank of captain. He distinguished himself as the bravest of many brave cavalry officers in Lee's Legion and, like his brother, served to the war's end. He chose not to return to Pennsylvania, following instead officers of his former unit in settling in the postwar South. Like John, he later commanded military units, first the Second Troop of Volunteer Light Dragoons in Richmond County and later Georgia's Hundred Horse in 1794 when the federal government responded to deteriorating conditions with the Creek nation. His later military position was that of major in the 5th Regiment, a unit that was authorized in 1799 but never mustered when an anticipated war with France never materialized.[856]

Brother Hamilton too found his way in the military but through a different path. Remaining in Northumberland County, his service in militia and Ranger units placed him on the front line of brutal conflict in western Pennsylvania for seven long years. Joining John in the Ohio territory sometime around 1787 or 1788, he paid his dues in the First Regiment by assuming the duties of an unofficial subaltern for about two years before being commissioned to fill a vacancy following Harmar's expedition in 1790, serving until his resignation 1797. Apparently lacking his brother's stern reserve, he was possibly an alcoholic. He was injured in a duel in 1794 and brought up on charges filed by his company commander and fellow officers three times over a two-year span prior to and following Wayne's campaign. Regardless, he continued to accompany the army after his resignation, possibly as a contractor or with the quartermaster department, dying in his quarters at Fort Wayne in 1801. Adding to his

Series: M804, Roll 75, Image 694; https://www.ancestry.com/imageviewer/collections/1995/images/MIUSA1775D_134641-00693?usePUB=true&_phsrc=rUg119&_phstart=successSource&usePUBJs=true&pId=1833;
Letter from Ann Armstrong Morten to William Goforth Armstrong, December 7, 1819, expressing surprise and concern over her mother's marriage, PJA; The death of John Gano Armstrong, 1800-1808, resulted from an accidental musket shot; Thomas Pool Armstrong (1) was born in 1802 and died unexpectedly four months later. Genealogy notes, PJA.

[856] Gordon Burns Smith, *History of the Georgia Militia 1783–1861, vol. 4, The Companies* (Milledgeville: Boyd Publishing Company, 2000), 109, 134.

life's mystery was his relationship with the mother of his two children whom he never married.[857]

In many ways, John Armstrong's life story reflected a pattern typical of other immigrant families. His parents abandoned the land they had known in order to carve out a living in a country that promised, in the long run, a better way of life for their offspring. Their children reaped the rewards of their leap of faith. Thomas Armstrong never realized great fortune in America; he was never wealthy but at least died financially solvent. John Armstrong's story may have differed somewhat from those of other immigrants' children, however, in that he knew of his mother's lineage of Irish gentry and seemingly spent a lifetime trying to recapture the respectability it implied. Armstrong, without the benefit of family wealth or extensive education, found that opportunity in the army, rising to the class of "gentleman" afforded him as an officer. He paid his dues during the seventeen strenuous years he served the institution that afforded him that distinction, and his endeavors in later years echoed that quest. A gentleman's status followed him as public official and militia regimental commander. Gentlemen owned property, and he followed the lead of others of his generation to gain wealth through possessing vast amounts of land, eventually creating his own town named after the place of his birth. He married the judge's daughter, fathered ten children, and in the end died at Spring Hill, a small settlement he founded, surrounded by the gentlemanly trappings of books and other fine possessions that denoted early nineteenth-century refinement.[858]

Undeniably American, he nevertheless held true to his original Ulster Scots and Armstrong roots. Remarkably tall for the times and physically strong, he was not afraid to hold his ground when challenged nor to speak his mind when it mattered. Like other Scots-Irish who served in countless

---

[857] *SCP*, II: 188–89; C. M. Burton, "General Wayne's Orderly Book," *Michigan Pioneer and Historical Society* 34 (1905), 478; PAW, XXXIV: 117, L: 88; Wayne MSS, Courts-Martial supplement 1793–1795, 154–55 in Cochran notebooks, PJA.

[858] Estate inventory indicated a sizable library that included books on medicine, geography, the law, morality, history and commentary, bookkeeping, and farming, as well as French and English dictionaries, contemporary magazines, and the Bible. Household possessions included breakfast and dining tables, multiple desks, sets of china, silver cups, ivory-handled knives and forks, as well as a backgammon set. Inventory labeled "1816," PJA.

numbers in the Revolution, he was loyal to the authority of his military "clan" leader in the system imposed by army structure. Nevertheless, perceived slights to his character did not go unchallenged. Like his Scots-Irish brothers, he was not hesitant to utilize the legal system to right a personal wrong. In later years, as leader of his own family clan, he purchased land for his younger brother while including him in his own army career and kept the extended family together through moves from Pennsylvania to Ohio. And in patterns typical of Scots-Irish migration, he kept his eye on the western horizon when seeking a place to settle permanently.[859]

The young John Armstrong appeared destined to spend his life bound to his father's hardscrabble farm, but war intervened. Military service set him on a track that led in a far different direction. He served seven long years in the Revolutionary War itself, endured winter encampments, and fought in hazardous skirmishes and bloody battles while experiencing the close comradery of his brothers in arms, and spent subsequent years at lonely territorial outposts dealing with threats of Indian attacks and the actions of bored and dissatisfied soldiers while assuming responsibility for their overall safety and welfare. He saw the bloody ravages of war and witnessed the loss of his soldiers and his friends. Later making solitary exploration of America's rivers, forests, and prairies; engaging in business, farming, and public service; assuming the risks as well as the profits in land speculation; and overseeing his growing family, John Armstrong led a life he could not have envisioned as a boy who had once helped his father scratch out a meager living in the Pennsylvania woods.

★

A lone obelisk marks John Armstrong's grave. It is worn and gouged by the ravages of time and weather and stands amid a hayfield at what was once Spring Hill high above the Ohio River. It represents a stark tribute to a man who interacted with many of the best-known miliary men of his time—Washington, Knox, Lafayette, and Wayne, and others less well-known like St. Clair, Harmar, and the odious Wilkinson—many of whom were influential in founding a new nation at a time the country and the world were much smaller. Two hundred years later, his is not a household

<hr>

[859] Armstrong and Cochran notebooks, PJA.

name nor are those of most of his comrades with whom he served in the young nation's first army. In the history of the United States, this brief era is all but forgotten, but without men like him who served on the wild and often dangerous frontier, the story of the fledgling nation's development might have been written quite differently.

Appendix 1

Wilkinson, 1796–1825

An officer renowned for never having won
a battle or lost a court-martial.
—Robert Leckie[860]

Following the unexpected good fortune provided by the death of Anthony Wayne in December 1796, James Wilkinson, whose primary mission in Philadelphia had been to continue his efforts to discredit his commander, lingered in the city to cultivate influential government officials and to attend John Adams's presidential inauguration before returning to the Ohio territory. Denied promotion to major general through the army's reorganization, he was nevertheless its ranking officer and on him devolved the task of overseeing the management of human and material resources in garrisons that stretched from the lower Ohio River to the Great Lakes.

Wilkinson now became even more aware of his exposed status as a Spanish agent. In October 1797, Thomas Power, a known courier for the New Orleans government, appeared in Detroit at the time when Wilkinson was inspecting the recently acquired British garrison at Mackinac. To allay suspicion, the general ordered Power under house arrest until his return. When the two men met, Power disclosed an unlikely plot requiring Wilkinson's assistance in seizing Fort Massac as a prelude to calling for

---

[860] Robert Leckie, *The Wars of America*, vol. 1, *From 1600 to 1900* (New York: HarperCollins Publishers, 1992), 235.

Kentucky's independence and establishing an independent republic of the Mississippi. Wilkinson flatly rejected the proposal. James Ripley Jacobs surmises that Wilkinson might then have wanted out of the profitable deal he had struck with Spain but didn't want to sever his ties completely. During the four years since receiving his army commission, Spain had remitted $25,000 to Wilkinson for information, most of which was fictitious. Accordingly, he had Power removed from US territory by military escort; but by doing so, Power was safe from detainment by authorities along the way. Wilkinson entrusted Power with a letter to Governor Carondelet in which he asked for $640 the New Orleans government still owed him. Holding out a carrot to future business, he inferred that opportunities might arise for renewing their relationship at a future time and that in his capacity as commander of US forces, he would keep Britain from invading Spanish territory from the north.[861]

Territorial and boundary disputes between the government and the Indian confederation within the Ohio Territory at least nominally settled, the focus of the army's attention drifted to the Southwest upon areas bounded by the lower Ohio and Mississippi Rivers. In June 1798, Wilkinson headed to Fort Adams, forty miles south of Natchez, to assist Winthrop Sargent, governor of the newly organized Mississippi territory ceded to the United States through ratification of the Pinckney's Treaty in 1796. There he renewed contact with Don Manuel Gayoso de Lemos, governor of Louisiana who succeeded Carondelet, and moved his family into the governor's former home in Natchez. During the quasiwar with France in 1799, George Washington and Alexander Hamilton were appointed the army's commanding officers, and Wilkinson was summoned to the capital to meet with them, returning again the following year after the crisis had abated. While there, he regaled future president Thomas Jefferson with details of the West. Following the two-step transfer of Spanish territory west of the Mississippi to France and subsequently to the United States, Wilkinson, as commanding general of the United States Army, was also appointed governor of the Louisiana territory in St. Louis in 1805, serving there until replaced by Meriwether Lewis in 1807.[862]

---

[861] Linklater, An Artist in Treason, 164-65; Jacobs, The Beginning of the U.S. Army, 204. See Jacobs, Tarnished Warrior), 152, 164–66 and American State Papers, 1789–1838, Miscellaneous, II: 105–09.

[862] Jacobs, The Beginning of the U.S. Army, 232–41, 310, 325.

Wilkinson hungered to reembrace his role as a Spanish spy and the money that would go with it. Upon meeting with Vicente Folch, governor of West Florida in 1804, he prepared a document outlining the long-term strategy that Spain should pursue following the Louisiana Purchase and also revealed one of Jefferson's most vital secrets—the proposed expedition of Meriwether Lewis and William Clark to explore a route to the Pacific—and stressed the importance of it being stopped by force. He also recommended fortifying the Florida and Texas frontiers to prevent American incursions and land seizure and noted the necessity of averting any exploration of the Red and Arkansas Rivers. Impressed by this information, the military governor of Spanish Louisiana, the Marqués de Casa Calvo, granted him $12,000 and a permit to export 1,600 barrels of flour annually to Havana.[863]

Wilkinson's run of good luck was about to end. The patterns of duplicity and the enemies he had made throughout his careers in business, politics, and the military were soon to catch up with him. His complicity in what would become known as the Burr conspiracy marked the beginning of his downfall. From its beginning, Burr's plan was nebulous, with objectives either to invade Spanish Mexico to achieve its independence or to effect the secession of western states and territories, possibly Kentucky, Tennessee, Ohio, and parts of Georgia and the Carolinas, in order to form a separate country by aligning with Britain in order to receive necessary funds and support. Wilkinson first met with the vice president clandestinely in 1804, later corresponding with him through encrypted letters. He apparently had Burr's confidence in the plan, but Jacobs notes that Wilkinson in all likelihood did not relish the idea of treason in the hope of being a secondary figure in a new state of illegitimate birth but rather thought he could enhance his reputation as American patriot through capitalizing on Burr's scheme. He would magnify the danger to his country and then step forth as its savior.[864]

---

[863] Linklater, *An Artist in Treason*, 206–08. Linklater notes that at least three attempts by an armed Spanish patrol of two hundred men were sent out to kill or capture Lewis and Clark's party. Had they succeeded, the history of Western exploration would have been delayed for a generation, with far-reaching consequences including the unopposed expansion of British settlement throughout Oregon.

[864] Linklater, *An Artist in Treason*, 215, 218, 221; Jacobs, *The Beginnings of the U.S. Army*, 337; Jacobs, *Tarnished Warrior*, 221–23.

When Burr notified Wilkinson of his advance down the Ohio with a projected force of 500 to 1,000 men that would be accumulated en route, the general wrote Jefferson about Burr's plan, inflating the number of men who were to rendezvous at New Orleans where a fleet would take them to seize Vera Cruz. He informed the president that he would meet this threat to the nation by thwarting the embarkation of Burr's men. Wilkinson then sent a messenger to the viceroy of Mexico, presenting a bill of $110,000 for saving the country from invasion, but his bold attempt to benefit financially through this means yielded nothing.[865]

Wilkinson entered New Orleans on November 25, 1806. Wanting its inhabitants to believe that the mob would soon be at their gates to overturn the government and ransack the city, he launched actions that came back to haunt him, arresting those who might know too much about his own involvement in the scheme, flaunting the local judiciary, and in essence establishing a military coup. In the end, Burr's plan fizzled. He gathered few volunteers as he ventured down the Ohio. Along the way, his mission was delayed by his appearance in two courts, but grand juries failed to bring charges. He wisely abandoned his deluded followers and fled, only to be apprehended in Alabama in February 1807. At the trial that followed, however, the jury failed to convict him of treason.

Burr's reputation was ruined, but Wilkinson's testimony at the trial was enough to raise suspicion about his own activities. His unsavory connection with the Spanish government was always in the undercurrent of conversation, and his recent acts of high-handedness in New Orleans roused formidable congressional enemies and put the Jefferson administration on the spot. John Randolph, foreman of the Burr grand jury and member of Congress, pushed for congressional resolutions in December 1807 and January 1808, requesting the president to appoint a special commission to inquire into the general's conduct and for the chief executive to turn over any documentation it had relating to Wilkinson's relationship with Spain. Jefferson complied only half-heartedly, noting that some records had burned in the War Office fire of 1800. In attempts to head off the current scandal, Wilkinson requested a military court of inquiry that convened in January 1808, and following six months of testimony and deliberation by the tribunal, he was exonerated. Linklater notes, however, that the board's decision would not have come as a surprise since it consisted of three

---

[865] Jacobs, *The Beginning of the U.S. Army*, 337–38.

officers of lesser rank who were not only in tight spots regarding their past and future relationships with the general but who were also Wilkinson allies. Col. Thomas H. Cushing served on the court as did another friend, Jonathan Williams, superintendent of West Point.[866]

Wilkinson subjected himself to yet more controversy upon his return to New Orleans in April 1809. He had made bitter enemies in the city during the Burr debacle. It was, however, his decision concerning the location of his new headquarters that proved his downfall. New Orleans was not satisfactory for the army, and his men were in bad shape. One-third of his NCOs and privates were too ill to serve, and the force of 1,733 sick and demoralized men had few remedies available for their recovery. Wilkinson was authorized to move, and Secretary of War William Eustis encouraged the general to locate upriver toward Natchez. Wilkinson instead opted to relocate his men to land below New Orleans, close enough to the city to keep track of his detractors and to enjoy the company of his friends. The move proved catastrophic. After his men cleared the site, rain created a quagmire of mud and filth. Soldiers had no shade to escape the heat, flies, and mosquitoes. With scarce supplies and provisions, poor food, and threadbare clothes, soldiers died a wretched death. Eustis ordered Wilkinson to move his men to high ground upriver to Fort Adams on June 22, 1809, but the general did not do so until three months later. Many died along the way.[867]

The disaster that was the product of Wilkinson's troop relocation had now given his enemies in the House of Representatives more ammunition in their pending investigation of his dealings with Burr and his alleged Spanish intrigue. Despite a mass of data, however, the House took no punitive measures against him, but because Wilkinson was now an embarrassment to the administration, Secretary of War Eustis ordered him to appear before

---

[866] Jacobs, *Tarnished Warrior*, 240–44; Linklater, *Artist in Treason*, 276–80. See also Annals of Congress Debate and Proceedings 1789–1824, 10th Congress, December 31, 1807–January 13, 1808, 1445, 1460. Among the advocates for congressional inquiry was Daniel Clark, who had been a clerk to the senior Daniel Clark when the elder entered into early business dealings with Wilkinson and was now an influential merchant in the city and congressional representative from New Orleans. In 1809, he published *Proofs of the Corruption of Gen. James Wilkinson and of His Connexion with Aaron Burr, with a Full Refutation of his Slanderous Allegations in Relation to the Character of the Principal Witness against Him* (Philadelphia: Wm. Hall Jr. and Geo. W. Pierie, 1809).

[867] Jacobs, *The Beginning of the U.S. Army*, 345–53.

a court-martial panel in 1811. Evidence was sketchy. Burr's acquittal made a weak case to convict Wilkinson of wrongdoing even if he was to be considered an accomplice, and other charges were tied up in ambiguous orders that could not be proven. Wilkinson again escaped sanction, found not guilty on February 1812 in present-day Frederick, Maryland, on all counts.[868]

Granted new life by the court, Wilkinson learned on his return to New Orleans in July 1812 that war had been declared with England the previous month. He strengthened the city's defenses and gained the surrender of Mobile in April 1813. Four months later, he was transferred to the northern front of the conflict in New York, a move that afforded an appropriately higher rank. After serving over twenty years as a brigadier general, he had finally been promoted.

Wilkinson's command was a disaster. He was often ill, the operation was plagued by logistical and supply problems, and he was frequently second-guessed by then secretary of war John Armstrong Jr., who chose to micromanage decision-making while at the front. Wilkinson was ultimately to assume responsibility for the failure of American troops in the St. Lawrence River area of conflict and the disastrous retreat of his sick and demoralized men that November. Jacobs notes that the general at last had been given the chance to demonstrate able leadership but had failed. Hoping to enhance his military reputation, he instead had irretrievably ruined it. The public, alarmed by the condition of its men who suffered not only from defeat, but also the effects of the cold and illness, as well as lack of provisions, food, and cold-weather clothing, pressed the War Department for his dismissal. On April 12, 1814, he was relieved of his command.[869]

Wilkinson now faced yet another court-martial, this time held in New York in January 1815 on indictments arising solely from events on the northern frontier. While most charges were of a purely military character, other allegations included scandalous drunkenness and willful lying. Wilkinson pleaded not guilty to all charges. Poorly phrased and lacking specification, the indictments were extremely difficult to prove, and once again, Wilkinson was found not guilty.[870]

Congress reorganized the army upon the war's end. The act of March 3, 1815, reduced its size to 10,000 men to be commanded by two major

---

[868] Ibid., *The Beginning of the U.S. Army*, 354–55.
[869] Jacobs, *Tarnished Warrior*, 277-305
[870] Ibid., 308–11.

---

generals and four brigadier generals; only 39 of approximately 216 serving field officers would remain in service. Older officers were unceremoniously tossed aside with only a three-month salary payout for their long and honorable service. Wilkinson was among them.[871]

Wilkinson set about writing his memoirs to clear his name of all aspersions cast upon his performance and character throughout the entirety of his military career. *Memoirs of My Own Times*, completed in 1817, provided 2,000 pages that interpreted events from the author's perspective. Fortunately for him, sales were good, at least temporarily boosting his perpetually depleted financial situation.[872]

Wilkinson returned to New Orleans, his friends, and to his young second wife and children, but also to one-time associates he had wronged. Gen. John Adair, Kentucky politician who had made known his interest in attaining Mexican lands, had been in New Orleans when Wilkinson swept into the city during his show of force in 1806 and had been unceremoniously arrested. Adair subsequently sued Wilkinson for his mistreatment in the episode. When the court announced its verdict in favor of the plaintiff, Wilkinson could not pay the judgment levied against him and faced debtor's prison. Only friends saved him from this fate.[873]

Wilkinson eventually turned his eyes toward Mexico. In March 1822, he sailed for Vera Cruz and ventured onward to Mexico City. He had envisioned measures through which he hoped to be paid, holding out hope that he might also receive a Texas land grant. He was sixty-eight years old and in poor health. Opium offered little relief. When he died on December 28, 1825, friends sought to have him buried with military honors, but such rites were not permitted in Mexico. Instead, his remains were interred in a newly made grave. They, along with those of others, were later gathered up and indiscriminately buried in a common vault. There they remain today, beneath the floor of the Church of the Archangel San Miguel.[874]

---

[871] Ibid., 314–15.

[872] Jacobs, *Tarnished Warrior*, 316–19; James Wilkinson, *Memoirs of My Own Times*, vols. 1–3.

[873] Anne Biddle Wilkinson died in February 1807 of tuberculosis. Wilkinson subsequently married Celestine Laveau Trudeau, young daughter of Louisiana's surveyor general and one of the city's leading citizens. Linklater, *An Artist in Treason*, 253, 285.

[874] Jacobs, *Tarnished Warrior*, 329–40.

Appendix 2

Standing Army vs. Militia
throughout U.S. History

"What, sir, is the use of a militia? It is to prevent
the establishment of a standing army, the bane of
liberty. ...Whenever Governments mean to invade the rights
and liberties of the people, they always attempt to destroy
the militia, in order to raise an army upon their ruins."
–Elbridge Gerry, Fifth Vice President
of the United States[875]

Readers of this book might wonder why there was so much resistance after the Revolution to creating a permanent peacetime military force. As has been amply demonstrated, the regular force that was raised in 1784 and slightly expanded in 1791 was far too small to control settlement in the Northwest Territory, to adequately man its garrisons, to prevent attacks by the Native American tribes on settlements on both sides of the Ohio River, or to prevent retaliation by the settlers who often took their revenge on innocent tribesmen, much less conduct a major offensive operation in the tangled wilderness of the Ohio Territory. The government's continued refusal to provide adequate pay to recruit good soldiers, and even to pay them

---

[875] Florida Debate over the Second Amendment, August 17, 1789, The James Madison Library and Information Center, https://madisonbrigade.com/e_gerry.htm

after joining, caused the army to be manned at far less than its authorized strength. This forced both Josiah Harmar and Arthur St. Clair to rely on largely untrained and undisciplined militia augmentees, and this in turn resulted in the twin disasters at Kekionga in 1790 and the Wabash in 1791.

The creation the Legion of the United States and Wayne's victory at Fallen Timbers in 1794 ought to have silenced those who had long opposed a permanent military force, but it did not. For the better part of the 19th century, the nation was content to rely on a very small permanent force that had to be substantially augmented with militia and volunteers in the War of 1812, the Mexican War, the Civil War, and the Spanish-American War. Not until the 20th century and after the Second World War did the nation come to accept a large standing army in peacetime.

The reason for this state of affairs was based on two components: First, it was far cheaper in peacetime for the nation to rely on militia forces rather than to pay for an expensive regular force. Secondly, militia proponents asserted that a permanent standing army was a threat to liberty. The reason for this ideological fixation about a standing army is deeply rooted in the political culture of England, an island nation that discovered it needed not to rely on a large army to defend its interests. The victory over the Spanish Armada in 1588 convinced many in England that national survival required a strong navy rather than an expensive land force. This view was reinforced by the English Civil War that culminated in the military dictatorships of Oliver Cromwell and King James II and ultimately led to the Glorious Revolution of 1688 and subsequent passage of an English Bill of Rights. Signed into law the following year by co-regents William and Mary, the bill outlined specific constitutional and civil rights, ultimately giving Parliament power over the monarchy by determining among other things that "raising or keeping a standing army within the kingdom in time of peace, unless it be with consent of Parliament, is against law." The Quartering Act and the Boston Massacre provided local rallying points in the thirteen colonies to demonstrate that a standing army was not just a distant threat, but it was a tangible local entity that threatened the liberty of innocent people. These examples were front and center in the minds of many members of the Second Continental Congress on June 14, 1775, when it approved the choice of George Washington to command the militia forces then blockading the British Army in Boston, thereafter known as the Continental Army.[876]

---

[876] "English Bill of Rights (1689)," *The Founders' Constitution*, eds. Philip B.

Washington and his senior subordinates quickly realized the necessity of creating a professional military force to fight the British Army rather than to use unreliable militia units recruited for short terms of service and controlled by thirteen colonial governments. This quickly became a source of friction between one faction in Congress who feared the dangers of a standing army and another who agreed with Washington that without one the Revolution would be lost. This friction continued until the end of the Revolution—and well beyond. Those who opposed the notion of a standing army during and after the Revolution were called by a variety of names—"True Whigs," Anti-Nationalists, Anti-Federalists, and, when political parties eventually made their appearance in America, Democratic-Republicans. Elbridge Gerry of Massachusetts, who is quoted above, was perhaps the leading exemplar of this view in the 1787 debates over the Constitution.[877]

In the spring of 1783, with victory within sight, George Washington was urged by Alexander Hamilton, then a member of Congress, to forward his views to that body on a standing peacetime military establishment for the new nation. Envisioning a force capable of defending the new nation's territory and citizens, protecting commerce and trade, and opening the newly acquired lands west of the Appalachian Mountains, the commander-in-chief of the Continental Army sent this response on 2 May 1783:

Kurland and Ralph Lerner (Chicago, IL: University of Chicago Press, 1987).

[877] The "true whigs" are from Benjamin Rush's taxonomy of the five classes of whigs—those motivated by power, resentment, self-interest, love of military life, and love of country. Only the last form was considered to be free from naked self-interest and militarism. To them, the militia was superior to a standing army, patriotism was superior to self-interest, and sacrifice was a virtue to be embraced during the Revolution. Anti-Nationalists and Anti-Federalists preferred a weak federal government like that under the Articles of Confederation and were generally opposed to the Constitution of 1787 for giving too much power to federal government and too little to state governments. The two sides eventually coalesced into two political parties, the Federalists under Alexander Hamilton and John Adams and the Democratic-Republicans under Thomas Jefferson and James Madison. Rush's letter is found in L.H. Butterfield, ed., *Letters of Benjamin Rush, vol. 1, 1761-1762*, (Princeton NJ: Princeton University Press, 1951), 152-153.

A Peace Establishment for the United States of America may in my opinion be classed under four different heads Vizt: First. A regular and standing force, for Garrisoning West Point and such other Posts upon our Northern, Western, and Southern Frontiers, as shall be deemed necessary to awe the Indians, protect our Trade, prevent the encroachment of our Neighbours of Canada and the Florida's, and guard us at least from surprizes; Also for security of our Magazines. Secondly. A well organized Militia; upon a Plan that will pervade all the States, and introduce similarity in their Establishment Manoeuvres, Exercise and Arms. Thirdly. Establishing Arsenals of all kinds of Military Stores. Fourthly. Accademies, one or more for the Instruction of the Art Military; particularly those Branches of it which respect Engineering and Artillery, which are highly essential, and the knowledge of which, is most difficult to obtain. Also Manufactories of some kinds of Military Stores.[878]

Washington estimated that such a force would require 2,631 uniformed regulars and more if a single regiment proved inadequate to patrol both the newly acquired Northwest Territory and the southern frontiers of Georgia. The congressional deliberations on this issue took more than a full year, and on June 2, 1784, Congress finally decided not to decide the issue. It terminated the service of all remaining Continental Army regulars except for eighty men to guard stores at West Point and Fort Pitt. The next day, before it adjourned for the year, it merely recommended that four states— New York, Pennsylvania, Connecticut, and New Jersey—raise a force of about 700 men to safeguard the country's interests in the west. Thus was sown the seeds of the 1790 and 1791 disasters in the Northwest Territory.[879]

The 1792 congressional authorization for the Legion of the United States more than doubled the size of the army, and although the key to Anthony Wayne's victory at Fallen Timbers, it still lacked several other

---

[878] George Washington, "Sentiments on a Peace Establishment," http://webdoc. sub.gwdg.de/ebook/p/2005/CMH_2/www.army.mil/cmh-pg/books/revwar/ ss/peacedoc.htm

[879] A good analysis of the factional disputes over the creation of peacetime military establishment in the decade after the Revolution is by Palmer, *1794: America, Its Army, and the Birth of the Nation*, 241- 248.

vital elements of national defense: coastal fortifications to protect key harbors, a corps of engineers and artillerists, a military academy, a navy, and arsenals to manufacture and store arms. Astonishingly, in the first six months of 1794, all of this was passed into law by Congress, but the continuing fear of a large standing army led to the defeat of a motion to authorize an army of 10,000 men. By 1796, the Legion had been disbanded and replaced by a force of four regiments of infantry regulars. At long last, Washington's original 1783 vision had finally been brought to fruition.[880]

The four-regiment army did not last long. Under the Jefferson administration, it was cut back to just two regiments, the same size it had been under St. Clair. Jefferson had only a brief chance to test his convictions about a strong militia and a small standing army, for war clouds were gathering once more. The United States almost began a second war with England when the British warship *Leopard* attacked the American *Chesapeake* in 1807. This act of British aggression caused Congress to add five regular infantry regiments in 1808, the 3rd through the 7th, and also to constitute a Regiment of Riflemen. When the United States declared war on Great Britain in June 1812, the size of the Army was 6,686 men. As indicated in Table 1, it reached its greatest strength of 38,186 men in 1814, relying on militia and volunteers to provide 83 percent of its strength. The performance of militia units in that war, however, frequently matched that experienced by Harmar and St. Clair, the most egregious example being at the Battle of Bladensburg in August 1814 when 500 regulars and 6,500 militia broke and fled from a smaller British force, opening the way for the burning of the White House and the Capitol Building in Washington, D.C.

Nevertheless, the same model was used for the Mexican War, the Civil War, and the Spanish-American War, in which a relatively small peacetime army had to be augmented by militia and volunteers to provide for respectively 82 percent, 98 percent, and 87 percent of the highest strength in each conflict. Battle performance was greatly improved in all three wars, not particularly because of any improvements in militia organization or training, but by the presence of a cadre of trained professional officers turned out by the United States Military Academy at West Point, which had been founded in 1802.

This situation was repeated in World Wars I and II and the Korean War in the first half of the 20th century, but an adequate comparison of

---

[880] Ibid. 243-246.

expanded regular army strength and volunteer components cannot be made between nineteenth century wars and larger twentieth century conflicts. In the early years of the century, a major organizational change to the traditional militia system was mandated. In 1903, the Dick Act required the states to divide their militias into two sections, recommending the title "National Guard" for the section formerly known as the organized militia, and "Reserve Militia" for all others. Next, Congress passed the National Defense Act of 1916, which required the use of the term "National Guard" for state militias and further regulated them. Lastly, the 1933 National Guard Mobilization Act finalized the split between the National Guard and the traditional state militias by designating volunteer components as state National Guards and the National Guard of the United States, i.e., the Army Reserve, mandating that all federally funded soldiers take a dual enlistment/commission and thus enter both the state National Guard and the National Guard of the United States.

With a far better trained and federally regulated National Guard and Reserves to replace the 19th century militia system, the U.S. Army was able to more quickly mobilize and field large troop formations than had formerly been the case. In World War I, a regular Army of 108,399 in 1916 expanded into a force of 2,395,742 within two years; in World War II, a regular Army of 189,839 in 1939 expanded into a force of 8,266,373 by 1944; and in the Korean War, a regular force of 593,167 in 1950 expanded three-fold to 1,596,419 by 1952. In all three cases, entire divisions of relatively well-trained men were available almost instantly through the National Guard system.

All subsequent wars—Vietnam, the 1991 Gulf War, and the post-911 wars in Afghanistan and Iraq were fought almost exclusively with regular forces with no mobilization of either National Guard or Reserve divisions, although smaller units of each component tasked with force-support missions rotated for relatively short tours of duty in all four conflicts.

Although there is today almost complete acceptance of the need for a capable standing peacetime military force to protect the nation's interests around the globe, the old friction between truer and lesser whigs occasionally continues to raise its head. This time it is again reflected in the two political parties' traditional support of the federal budget: the Democratic Party usually wants to spend less on national defense in order to spend more on social and welfare needs while the Republican Party usually takes the opposite view.

Table 1[881]

Year	U.S. Pop.	Military Strength	Army	Navy	Marines	Army/1M Pop.
1790	3,929,214	718	718	0	0	1.82
1810	7,239,881	11,554	5,956	4,875	523	1,215.6

Highest Army strength in War of 1812 was in 1814—38,186: 83% militia/volunteers (6,686 regular soldiers in 1812)

1840	17,063,353	21,516	11,319	8,275	1,269	1,507.5

Highest Army strength in Mexican War was in 1848—47,319: 82% militia/volunteers (8,509 regular soldiers in 1845)

1860	31,443,321	27,958	16,215	9,942	1,801	1,939.2

Highest Army strength in Civil War was in 1865—1,000,692: 98% militia/volunteers (16,215 regular soldiers in 1860)

1890	62,979,766	38,665	27,373	9,248	2,047	2,300.8

Highest Army strength in Spanish-American War was in 1898—209,715: 87% militia/volunteers (27,855 regular soldiers in 1897)

---

[881] Population figures from U.S. Census Bureau, https://census-charts.com/Population/pop-us-1790-2000.html; All military figures are from *Department of Defense, Selected Manpower Statistics, Fiscal Year 1996*, prepared by Washington Headquarters Service Directorate for Information Operations and Reports, https://apps.dtic.mil/sti/pdfs/ADA324807.pdf.

Notes

Sources frequently cited have been identified
by the following abbreviations:

ASP-Indian Affairs	Congress of the United States, *American State Papers, 1789-1838, Indian Affairs*
ASP-Military Affairs	Congress of the United States, *American State Papers 1789–1838, Military Affairs*
AWNIA	Knopf, Richard C., *Anthony Wayne, A Name in Arms*
Centinel	Maxwell, William, ed., *Centinel of the Northwest Territory*
CM	Cist, Charles, *Cincinnati Miscellany or Antiquities of the West*
OAHQ	Ohio State Archaeological and Historical Society, *Ohio Archaeological and Historical Quarterly*
OHPSB	Historical and Philosophical Society of Ohio, *Ohio Historical and Philosophical Society Bulletin*
OOTW	Thornbrough, Gayle, ed., *Outpost on the Wabash 1787-1791*
PA	*Pennsylvania Archives, Published Series*
PAW	Anthony Wayne Papers, Historical Society of Pennsylvania, Philadelphia, Pennsylvania
PGW/RWS	Crackle, Theodore J., ed., *Papers of George Washington, Revolutionary War Series*

PJA   John Armstrong Papers, Indiana Historical
               Society, Indianapolis, Indiana

PMHB   Historical Society of Pennsylvania, *Pennsylvania*
               Magazine of History and Biography

QPHPSO   Historical and Philosophical Society of Ohio,
               Quarterly Publication of the Historical and
               Philosophical Society of Ohio

SCP   Smith, William Henry, ed., *The St. Clair Papers:*
               The Life and Public Services of Arthur St. Clair

WGW   Fitzpatrick, John C., ed., *The Writings of George*
               Washington from the Original Manuscript Sources

BIBLIOGRAPHY

Primary Sources

Unpublished

John Armstrong Papers, William H. Smith Memorial Library, Indiana Historical Society, Indianapolis, Indiana.

Armstrong, Thomas. March 25, 1814. Cincinnati Historical Library and Archives, Cincinnati, Ohio, MSS VP 1322.

Clark County Registry of Marriages, 1820–1828, vol. B. George Painter and Lucy Kirtley, 24 May 1827. 196.

Founders Online. National Historical Publications and Records Commission (NHPRC). http://founders.archives.gov.

Hunterdon County New Jersey Records Management Office, Flemington, New Jersey.

New Jersey State Archives Manuscript Collection, 1680s-1970s. New Jersey State Archives, Box 1-41, Folder 4-1. Accessed through *U.S. Census Reconstructed Records, 1660-1820.* https://www.ancestry.com/search/collections/catalog/?title=%E2%80%9CU.S.%20Census%20Reconstructed%20Records,%201660-1820%22.

Northumberland County Courthouse Documents, Office of the Register and Recorder, Sunbury, Pennsylvania Northumberland County Book of Wills, vol. 1:25.

Northumberland County Book of Deeds, vols. B and D.

Papers of the War Department 1784–1800, Roy Rosenzweig Center for History and New Media. George Mason University, Fairfax, Virginia. https://wardepartmentpapers.org/s/home/ page/home.

Pension file 10202, Armstrong, John, Revolutionary War, ancestry. com, Series: M804, Roll 75, Image 690-718. Accessed April 1, 2012. https://www.ancestry.com/discoveryui-content/view/1833:1995?tid=&pid=&queryId=9e1fa51cd1d 3e4adc0978de875ff4c3e&_phsrc_=rUg119&_phstart=successSource.

Public Records of Northern Ireland. *Abercorn Papers.* Groves Manuscripts T808/6134. https://www.proni.gov.uk/introduction_abercorn_ d623.pdf.

Anthony Wayne Papers, Historical Society of Pennsylvania, Philadelphia, Pennsylvania.

Published

Adams, John. *The Letters of John and Abigail Adams.* New York: Penguin Books, 2012.

Baily, Francis. *Journal of a Tour in Unsettled Parts of North America in 1796 & 1797.* London: Baily Brothers, 1856.

Bain, Joseph, ed. *The Border Papers: Calendar of Letters and Papers Relating to the Affairs of the Borders of England and Scotland,* vol. 1. Edinburgh: H. M. General Register House, 1894.

Beatty, Erkuries. "Diary of Major Erkuries Beatty, Paymaster of the Western Army, May 15, 1786 to June 5, 1787." *Magazine of American History* 1 (1877): 175–179, 235–243, 309–315, 380–384, 432–438.

Bond, Beverly W. Jr., ed. *The Correspondence of John Cleves Symmes.* New York: Macmillan Company, 1926.

———. "Memoirs of Benjamin Van Cleve." *Quarterly Publication of the Historical and Philosophical Society of Ohio* 27, nos. 1 and 2 (1922): 7–71.

Boyd, Julian P., ed. *The Susquehanna Company Papers, vol. 4, 1770-1772.* Wilkes-Barre: Wyoming Historical & Geological Society, 1922.

Burton, C. M., ed. "General Wayne's Orderly Book." *Michigan Pioneer and Historical Society* 34 (1905): 341–501.

Cist, Charles. *The Cincinnati Miscellany or Antiquities of the West.* Vol. 1. Cincinnati: Caleb Clark Printer, 1845.

———. *The Cincinnati Miscellany or Antiquities of the West.* Vol. 2. Cincinnati: Caleb Clark Printer, 1846.

Clark, Daniel. *Proofs of the Corruption of Gen. James Wilkinson and of the Connexion with Aaron Burr: With a Full Refutation of his Slanderous*

Allegations in Relation to the Character of the Principal Witness Against Him. Philadelphia: Wm. Hall Jr. and Geo. W. Pierie, 1809.

Congress of the United States. *American State Papers, 1789-1838, Indian Affairs.* Vol. 1. Washington: Gales and Seaton, 1832.

———. *American State Papers, 1789-1838, Military Affairs.* Vol. 1. Washington: Gales and Seaton, 1832.

———. *American State Papers, 1789-1838, Miscellaneous.* Vol. 2. Washington: Gales and Seaton, 1834.

Crackle, Theodore J., ed. *Papers of George Washington, Revolutionary War Series.* Vols. 14, 15, 20, 24. Charlottesville: University of Virginia Press, 2004.

Denny, Ebenezer. *Military Journal of Major Ebenezer Denny, an Officer in the Revolutionary and Indian Wars.* Philadelphia: J. B. Lippincott and Company, 1859.

Fenno, John, ed. *The Gazette of the United States and Daily Advertiser,* June 25. https://chroniclingamerica.loc.gov/lccn/sn84026271/1794-06-25/ed-1/seq-2/.

———. *The Gazette of the United States and Daily Advertiser,* July 19, 1794. https://chroniclingamerica.loc.gov/lccn/sn84026271/1794-07-19/ed-1/seq-2/.

Fitzpatrick, John C., ed. *Journals of the Continental Congress 1774-1789.* Vol. 30. Washington, D.C.: U.S. Government Printing Office, 1934.

———. *The Writings of George Washington from the Original Manuscript Sources.* Vol. 27. Washington, D.C.: Government Printing Office, 1938.

Gano, John. "Major General John S. Gano to Governor Edward Tiffin, August 20, 1804." *Quarterly Publication of the Historical and Philosophical Society of Ohio* 15, nos. 1–2 (1920): 17–18.

Goodman, Alfred Thomas, ed. *Papers Relating to the First White Settlers In Ohio.* Cleveland: Western Reserve Historical Society, 1871.

Hamilton, Alexander. "Letter from Alexander Hamilton to Elias Boudinot, July 5, 1778." *Founders Online.* https://founders.archives.gov/?q=%20Author%3A%22Hamilton%2C%20Alexander%22&s=1111311111&r=198.

Hildreth, S. P., "Journal of Joseph Buell." *Pioneer History: Being an Account of the First Examinations of the Ohio Valley, and the Early Settlement of the Northwest Territory.* New York: H. W. Derby & Co., 1848.

Holmberg, James J., ed. *Dear Brother: Letters of William to Jonathan Clark.* New Haven: Yale University Press, 2002.

Honeyman, A. Van Doren, ed. *Documents Relating to the Colonial History of the State of New Jersey, First Series*, vol. 32: *Calendar of New Jersey Wills, Administrations, Etc.*, vol. 3, *1751-1760.* Somerville, New Jersey: The Unionist-Gazette Association, Printers, 1929.

Knopf, Richard C. *Anthony Wayne, A Name in Arms.* Pittsburgh: University of Pittsburgh Press, 1960.

———. *The Harmar Papers from the Clements Library Ann Arbor, Michigan.* Columbus: Anthony Wayne Parkway Board, 1954.

———. *Transcription of the Executive Journal of the Northwest Territory*, 1: 547. www.ohiohistory.org/onlinedoc/northwest/exjournal/0547.cfm. Accessed 3/23/2012.

Lacey, John. "Memoirs of Brigadier-General John Lacey, of Philadelphia." *The Pennsylvania Magazine of History and Biography* 26, no.1 (1902): 101–11.

Library of Congress. Annals of Congress Debate and Proceedings 1789-1824, 10th Congress, December 31, 1807–January 13, 1808. https://memory.loc.gov/cgibin/ampage?collId=llac&fileName=017/llac017.db&recNum=752.

Maxwell, William, ed. *Centinel of the Northwestern Territory*, vols. 1 and 2. Cincinnati: Ohio. https://news.google.com/newspapers?nid=0IGl3jR3yJEC.

May, John. *Notes on Journals and Letters of Colonel John May of Boston Relative to Two Trips to the Ohio Company in 1788 and '89.* Cincinnati: Robert Clarke Company, 1873.

Martin, Joseph Plumb. *Private Yankee Doodle.* Edited by George F. Scheer. Little, Brown and Company, 1962.

McCrea, Kenneth D. *Pennsylvania Land Applications*, vol. 2, *New Purchase Applications 1769-1773.* Philadelphia: Genealogical Society of Pennsylvania, 2003.

McHenry, James. "The Battle of Monmouth, Described by Dr. James McHenry, Secretary to General Washington." *Magazine of American History: With Notes and Queries* 3 (1897): 355–63.

Michigan Pioneer and Historical Society. *Historical Collections.* Vol. 24. Lansing: Robert Smith & Company, 1895.

———. *Historical Collections.* Vol. 34. Lansing: Wynkoop Hallenbeck Crawford Company, 1905.

Miner, Charles. *History of Wyoming in a Series of Letters from Charles Miner to his Son, William Penn Miner, Esq*. Philadelphia: J. Crissy, 1845.

Minutes of the Supreme Executive Council of Pennsylvania, Vol. 14. Harrisburg: Theodore Fenn and Company, 1853.

Mittelberger, Gottlieb. *Journey to Pennsylvania in the Year 1750 and Return to Germany in the Year 1754*. Translated by Carl Theodore Eben. Philadelphia: John Joseph McVey, 1898.

Newman, Samuel. "Captain Newman's Original Journal of St. Clair's Campaign." *Wisconsin Magazine of History* 2, no. 1 (1918): 44–73. Accessed March 20, 2021. http://www.jstor.org/stable/4630127.

Northwest Territory. *Laws of the Territory Northwest of the River Ohio: Including the Laws of the Governor and Judges, The Maxwell Codes and the Laws of the Three Session of the Territorial Legislature 1791-1802*. Cincinnati:1833.

Pennsylvania Archives, Published Series

Hazard, Samuel, ed. *Pennsylvania Archives*. Series 1, vol. 10. Philadelphia: Joseph Severns and Company, 1854.

———. *Pennsylvania Archives*. Series 1, vol. 11. Philadelphia: Joseph Severns and Company, 1855.

Egle, William Henry, MD. *Pennsylvania Archives*, Series 2, vol. 18. Harrisburg: E. K. Meyers, State Printer, 1893.

———. *Pennsylvania Archives*. Series 3, vol. 19. Harrisburg: Wm. Stanley Ray, State Printer, 1897.

Montgomery, Thomas Lynch, ed. *Pennsylvania Archives*, Series 5, vols. 2 and 4. Harrisburg: Harrisburg Publishing Company, 1906.

———. *Pennsylvania Archives*, Series 6, vol. 3. Harrisburg: Harrisburg Publishing Company, 1907.

Powell, G. H., ed. *Memoirs of Robert Carey Earl of Monmouth*. London: Alexander Moring, 1905.

Quaife, M. M., ed. *A Narrative of Life on the Old Frontier; Henry Hay's Journal from Detroit to the Mississippi River*. Madison: State Historical Society of Wisconsin, 1915.

Randolph. "A Precise Journal of General Wayne's Last Campaign." *Proceedings of the American Antiquarian Society* (October 1954): 273–302. https://www.americanantiquarian.org/aasproceedings?page=41.

Reeder, Daniel. "A Return for Columbia Township." *Quarterly Publication of Historical and Philosophical Society of Ohio* 14, no. 2–3 (1919): 3–16.

Reeves, John B. "Extracts from the Letter-Books of Lieutenant Enos Reeves, of the Pennsylvania Line." *Pennsylvania Magazine of History and Biography* 21, no. 1 (1897): 72–85.

Sargent, Winthrop. "Winthrop Sargent's Diary While with General Arthur St. Clair's Expedition Against the Indians." *Ohio Archaeological and Historical Quarterly* 33, no. 2 (1924): 237–273.

Shaw, John Robert. *A Narrative of the Life and Travels of John Robert Shaw, the Well-digger, Now a Resident of Lexington, Kentucky.* Lexington: Daniel Bradford, 1807.

Smith, Dwight. *From Green Ville to Fallen Timbers: A Journal of the Wayne Campaign.* Indianapolis: Indiana Historical Society, 1952.

Smith, William Henry, ed. *The St. Clair Papers: The Life and Public Services of Arthur St. Clair.* Vols. 1 and 2. Cincinnati: Robert Clarke & Company, 1882.

Shepherd, William R., ed. "Papers Bearing on James Wilkinson's Relations with Spain, 1787-1816." *American Historical Review* 9, no. 4 (1904): 748–766. Accessed March 21, 2021. https://www.jstor.org/stable/1834098.

St. Clair, Arthur. *A Narrative of the Manner in which the Campaign Against the Indians, in the Year One Thousand Seven Hundred and Ninety-one, Was Conducted, Under the Command of Major General St. Clair.* Philadelphia: Jane Aitken, 1812.

Thwaites, Reuben Gold, ed. *Original Journals of the Lewis and Clark Expedition, 1804-1806,* 7. New York: Dodd, Mead, and Company, 1904.

Thornbrough, Gayle, ed. *Outpost on the Wabash 1787-1791.* Indianapolis: Indiana Historical Society Publications, 1957.

Tilden, John Bell. "Extracts from the Journal of Lieutenant John Bell Tilden, Second Pennsylvania Line, 1781-1782." *Pennsylvania Magazine of History and Biography* 19, no. 2 (1895): 208-233.

Waldo, Albigence. "Valley Forge, 1777-1778. Diary of Surgeon Albigence Waldo, of the Connecticut Line." *Pennsylvania Magazine of History and Biography* 21, no.3 (1897): 299-323.

Wayne, Anthony. "General Wayne's Orderly Book." In *Michigan Pioneer and Historical Collections* 34, Lansing: Michigan Pioneer and Historical Society, 1905.

————. "Letter of General Anthony Wayne to John Armstrong, Esq." *Pennsylvania Magazine of History and Biography* 28, no. 3 (1904): 382-83.

Wilkinson, James. *Memoirs of My Own Times*, Vols. 1-3. Philadelphia: Abraham Small, 1816.

Wilson, Frazer E. *Journal of Capt. Daniel Bradley: An Epic of the Ohio Frontier.* Greenville, Ohio: Frank H. Jobes & Son, 1935. http://oldnorthwestindianwar.blogspot.com/p/daniel-bradley-was-not-militiaman-he.html.

Secondary Sources

Books

Agnew, Daniel. *Fort McIntosh: Its Times and Men With a Historical Sketch of the French and British Claims in the Northwest, and Their Meeting in Arms at the Head of the Ohio, and the Indian Incursions and Outrages in Western Pennsylvania and the Ohio Territory.* Pittsburgh: Myers, Shinkle and Company, 1893.

Ambrose, Stephen E. *Undaunted Courage, Meriwether Lewis, Thomas Jefferson, and the Opening of the American West.* New York: Simon and Schuster, 1996.

Amory, Thomas C. *The Military Services and Public Life of Major General John Sullivan.* Boston: Wiggin and Lunt, 1968.

Armstrong, James Lewis. *Chronicles of the Armstrongs.* Jamaica, New York: The Marion Press, 1902.

Armstrong, Robert Bruce. *The History of Liddesdale, Eskdale, Ewesdale, Wauchopedale and the Debateable Land*, Part 1. Edinburgh: David Douglas, 1883.

Baird, Lewis C. *Baird's History of Clark County, Indiana.* Indianapolis: B.F. Bowen, 1909.

Bell, Herbert C. *History of Northumberland County, Pennsylvania.* Chicago: Brown, Runk, and Company, 1891.

Bill, Alfred Hoyt. *Campaign of Princeton, 1776-1777.* Princeton: Princeton University Press, 1948.

Brown, Daniel T. *Westering River, Westering Trail: A History of St. Charles County, Missouri to 1849.* St. Charles, Missouri: St. Charles Historical Society, 2006.

Burd, Frank E. "Education, 1964." In *The First 300 Years of Hunterdon County 1714-2014*. Flemington: Hunterdon County Cultural & Heritage Commission, 2014.

Cayton, Andrew, R. L. *Frontier Indiana*. Bloomington: Indiana University Press, 1996.

Chambers, George. *A Tribute to the Principles, Virtues, Habits and Public Usefulness of the Irish and Scotch Early Settlers of Pennsylvania*. Chambersburg: M. A. Foltz, printer, 1871.

Chernow, Ron. *George Washington: A Life*. New York: The Penguin Press, 2010.

———. *Alexander Hamilton*. New York: Penguin Books, 2004.

Churchill, Winston S. *The New World*. New York: Dorset Press, 1956.

Cleves, Freeman. *Old Tippecanoe: William Henry Harrison and His Time*. New York: Charles Scribner's Sons, 1939.

Cochran, Charles F. *Seven Generations of the Ancestry of Captain Abram Piatt Andrew*. Washington, D.C.: National Publishing Company, 1924.

Coffman, Edward M. *The Old Army: A Portrait of the American Army in Peacetime, 1784-1898*. New York: Oxford University Press, 1986.

Collins, Lewis. *History of Kentucky*, vol 2. Covington: Collins & Co., 1878.

Cruikshank, Ernest. *The Story of Butler's Rangers and the Settlement of Niagara*. Welland, Ontario: Tribune Printing House, 1893.

Cunningham, John T. *The Uncertain Revolution: Washington and the Continental Army at Morristown*. West Creek, NJ: Cormorant Publishing, 2007.

Cuvier Press Club. *Cincinnati "The Queen City" Newspaper Reference Book*. Cincinnati, 1914.

Dandridge, Danske. *American Prisoners of the Revolution*. Baltimore: Genealogical Publication Co., 1967.

Dickson, B. Homer. *The Border or Riding Clans Followed by a History of the Clan Dickson*. Albany: Joel Munsell's Sons, 1889.

Dickson, R. J. *Ulster Emigration to Colonial America, 1718-1775*. Belfast: Ulster Historical Foundation, 1966.

Dillon, John B. *Oddities of Colonial Legislation in America*. Indianapolis: Robert Douglass, Publisher, 1879.

Dobson, David. *Ships from Ireland to Early America 1623-1850*, Vols. 1 and 2. Baltimore: Genealogical Publishing Company, Inc., 2004.

Downes, Randolph C. *Council Fires on the Upper Ohio, until 1795*. Pittsburgh: University of Pittsburgh Press, 1940.

Downes, Randolph C. and Harlow Lindley. *Frontier Ohio, 1788-1803.* Columbus: The Ohio State Archaeological and Historical Society, 1935.

Dundas, Rev. E. T. *The History of Donagheady Parish.* Omagh: Tyrone Constitution, n. d.

Dwyer, William M. *The Day is Ours! November 1776-January 1777: An Inside View of the Battles of Trenton and Princeton.* New York: The Viking Press, 1983.

Eckert, Allan W. *A Sorrow in Our Heart: The Life of Tecumseh.* New York: Bantam Books, 1993.

Ellis, Joseph. *American Creation.* New York: Vintage Books, 2007.

Fischer, David Hackett. *Albion's Seed: Four British Folkways in America.* New York: Oxford University Press, 1989.

———.*Washington's Crossing.* New York: Oxford University Press, 2002.

Fleming, Thomas. *Washington's Secret War: The Hidden History of Valley Forge.* New York: Smithsonian Books, 2005.

Foster, R. F., *Modern Ireland: 1600-1972.* London: Penguin Books, 1988.

Fraser, George MacDonald. *The Steel Bonnets: The Story of Anglo-Scottish Border Reiver.* New York: The Akadine Press, 2001.

Gaff, Alan D. *Bayonets in the Wilderness: Anthony Wayne's Legion in the Old Northwest.* Norman: University of Oklahoma Press, 2004.

Ganoe, William Addleman. *The History of the United States Army.* Ashton, Maryland: Eric Lundberg, 1964.

Garden, Alexander. *Anecdotes of the American Revolution* II. Charleston: A.E. Miller, 1828.

Gayerré, Charles. History of Louisiana, vol. 5. The Spanish Domination. New York: Wm. J. Widdleton. 1867. https://penelope.uchicago.edu/Thayer/E/Gazetteer/Places/America/ United States/Louisiana/Texts/GAYHLA/home.html.

Gearhart, Heber G. "Northumberland County Troops in the Continental Line." *Northumberland County in the Revolution.* Edited by Charles F. Snyder, 27-66. Northumberland County Historical Society, 1932.

Gnichtel, Frederick W. *The Trenton Decree of 1782 and the Pennamite War.* Trenton: The Trenton Historical Society, 1920.

Golway, Terry. *Washington's General: Nathanael Greene and the Triumph of the American Revolution.* New York: Henry Holt and Company, 2005.

Graydon, Alexander. *Memoirs of His Own Time and Reminiscences of the Men and Events of the Revolution.* New York: Lindsay and Blakiston, 1846.

Graymont, Barbara. "Joseph Brant." In *Dictionary of Canadian Biography,* vol. 5, *1801–1820.*
Toronto: University of Toronto Press, 1983.

Greve, Charles Theodore. *Centennial History of Cincinnati and Representative Citizens,* Vol. 1. Chicago: Biographical Publishing Company, 1904.

Guthman, William H. *March to Massacre: A History of the First Seven Years of the United States Army 1784-1791.* New York: McGraw-Hill, 1970.

Hanna, Charles A. *The Scotch-Irish or The Scot in North Britain, North Ireland, and North America.* Vols. 1 and 2. New York: G. P. Putnam's Sons, 1902.

Harrison, John. *The Scot in Ulster: Sketch of the History of the Scottish Population of Ulster.* Edinburgh: William Blackwood and Sons, 1888.

Harvey, Oscar Jewell. *A History of Wilkes-Barre, Luzerne County, Pennsylvania.* Vol. 2. Wilkes-Barre: Raeder Press, 1909.

Harvey, Oscar Jewell and Ernest Gray Smith. *A History of Wilkes-Barre, Luzerne County, Pennsylvania,* Vol. 3. Wilkes-Barre: Raeder Press, 1927.

Heinl, Robert Debs, Jr., ed. *Dictionary of Military and Naval Quotations.* Annapolis: United States Naval Institute, 1966.

Heitman, Francis B. *Historical Register and Dictionary of the United States Army,* Vol. 1. Washington: Government Printing Office, 1902.

———. *Historical Register of Officers of the Continental Army during the War of the Revolution, April, 1775 to December 1783.* Washington, D.C.: Rare Book Shop Publishing Company, Inc., 1914.

Hill, Roscoe R. *Descriptive Catalogue of the Documents of the United States in the Papeles Procedentes de Cuba deposited in the Archivo General de Indias at Seville,* Issue 234. Washington, D. C.: Carnegie Institution of Washington, 1916.

History of Cincinnati and Hamilton County, Ohio: Their Past and Present, Cincinnati: S. B. Nelson & Co., 1894.

Horsman, Reginald. *Expansion and the American Indian Policy 1783-1812.* Norman: University of Oklahoma Press, 1967.

Huber, John Parker. *General Josiah Harmar's Command: Military Policy in the Old Northwest, 1784-1791.* PhD dissertation. University of Michigan-Ann Arbor, 1968.

Jacobs, James Ripley. *The Beginnings of the U.S. Army 1783-1812*. Princeton, Princeton University Press, 1947.

———. *Tarnished Warrior*. New York: The McMillan Company, 1938.

James, Alton James. "Some Phases of the History of the Northwest, 1783-1786." In *Proceedings of the Mississippi Valley Historical Association for the Year 1913-1914*. Vol. 7. Edited by Benjamin F. Shambaugh. Cedar Rapids: The Torch Press, 1914.

Johnston, Henry P. *The Storming of Stony Point*. New York: James T. White and Co., 1900.

———. *The Yorktown Campaign and the Surrender of Cornwallis*. Freeport NY: Books for Libraries Press, 1881; reprinted 1971.

Knapp, H. S. *History of the Maumee Valley: Commencing with the Occupation by the French in 1680 to Which is Added Sketches of Some of its Moral and Material Resources as They Exist in 1782*. Toledo: Blade Mammoth Printing and Publication House, 1872.

Knouff, Gregory T. *The Soldier's Revolution: Pennsylvania in Arms and the Forging of Early American Identity*. University Park, PA: Pennsylvania State University Press, 2004.

Kohn, Richard H. *Eagle and Sword: The Beginnings of the Military Establishment in America*. New York: The Free Press, 1975.

Krieger, Brian. *Power Struggle in the Old Northwest: Why the United States Won and the Indians Lost the Indian War, 1786-1795*. MA thesis, North Carolina State University, 2008.

Leckie, Robert. *The Wars of America*, vol. 1, *From 1600 to 1900*. New York: HarperCollins Publishers, 1992.

Lecky, Alexander G. *In the Days of the Laggan Presbytery*. Belfast: Davidson and McCormack, 1908.

Lecky, William Edward Hartpole. *A History of Ireland in the Eighteenth Century*, Vol. 1. London: Longmans, Green, and Company, 1913.

Lewis, G. Malcom. "Richard McCarty." In *Dictionary of Canadian Biography*, vol. 4 *(1771-1800)*. http://www.biographi.ca/en/bio/mccarty_richard_4E.html.

Leyburn, James G. *The Scotch-Irish: A Social History*. Chapel Hill: University of North Carolina Press, 1962.

Linklater, Andro. *An Artist in Treason: The Extraordinary Double Life of General James Wilkinson*. New York: Walker Publishing Company, 2009.

Lockhart, Paul. *The Drillmaster of Valley Forge: The Baron De Steuben and the Making of the American Army*. New York: Harper Collins, 2008.

Lytle, Richard M. *Soldiers of the First American Army, 1791*. Lanham, Maryland: Scarecrow Press, 2004.

Martin, David G. *The Philadelphia Campaign, June 1777-July 1778*. Cambridge, MA: De Capo Books, 1993.

Mathews, Alfred. *Ohio and Her Western Reserve*. New York: D. Appleton and Company, 1902.

Mayer, Holly A. *Belonging to the Army: Camp Followers and Community during the American Revolution*. Columbia: University of South Carolina Press, 1996.

McBride, James. *Pioneer Biography: Sketches of Some of the Early Settlers of Butler County, Ohio*. Vol. 1. Cincinnati, Robert Clarke & Company, 1869.

McClung, John A. *Sketches of Western Adventure: Containing an Account of the Most Interesting Incidents Connected with the Settlement of the West, from 1775 to 1794*. Dayton: L. F. Claflin and Company, 1854.

McGuire, Thomas J. *The Philadelphia Campaign*, vol. 1, *Brandywine and the Fall of Philadelphia*. Mechanicsburg, PA: Stackpole Books, 2006.

———. *The Philadelphia Campaign*, vol. 2, *Germantown and Roads to Valley Forge*. Mechanicsburg PA: Stackpole Books, 2007.

Meginness, J. F. *Otzinachson, or A History of the West Branch Valley of the Susquehanna*. Philadelphia: Henry B. Ashmead, 1857.

Milligan, Fred J. *Ohio's Founding Fathers*. Lincoln: iUniverse Inc., 2003.

Moffat, Alistair. *The Borders: A History of the Borders From Earliest Times*. Edinburgh: Birlinn, Limited, 2002.

Morrison, Leonard A. *Rambles in Europe: In Ireland, Scotland, England, Belgium, Germany, Switzerland, and France*. Boston: Cupples, Upham, and Company, n.d.

Mott, George S. *The First Century of Hunterdon County, State of New Jersey*. Flemington: E. Vosseller, 1878.

Moyer, Paul B. *Wild Yankees: The Struggle for Independence Along Pennsylvania's Revolutionary Frontier*. Ithaca: Cornell University, 2007.

Murry, David. *History of Education in New Jersey*. Washington: Government Printing Office, 1899.

Miles, Nelson A. *Report of the Lieutenant-General Commanding the Army in Seven Parts*, part 1. Washington: Government Printing Office, 1900.

Nasatir, A.P. *Before Lewis and Clark: Documents Illustrating the History of the Missouri, 1785-1804*. Norman: University of Oklahoma Press, 1952.

Neagles, James, C. *Summer Soldiers: A Survey and Index of Revolutionary War Courts-martial*. Salt Lake City: Ancestry Inc., 1986.

O'Brien, Michael J. *The McCarthys in Early American History*. New York: Dodd, Mead, and Company, 1921.

O'Shaughnessy, Andrew Jackson. *The Men Who Lost America: British Leadership, the American Revolution, and the Fate of the Empire*. New Haven: Yale University Press, 2013.

Palmer, Dave R. *1794: America, Its Army, and the Birth of the Nation*. Novato, CA: Presidio Press, 1994.

Pennsylvania Historical Society. *The Fort Augusta Story*, Official Publication of the Fort Augusta Bicentennial Celebration, 1956.

Perry, James M. *Arrogant Armies, Great Military Disasters and the Generals Behind Them*. New York, John Wiley and Sons, 1996.

Presbyterian Historical Society of Ireland. *The Story of the Presbyterians in Ulster: Pocket History and Heritage Trail*. Belfast: Presbyterian Historical Society of Ireland, n.d. www.presbyterianhistoryireland.com.

Prucha, Francis Paul. *The Sword of the Republic: The United States Army on the Frontier 1783-1846*. Lincoln: University of Nebraska Press, 1969.

Quinn, Dermot. *The Irish in New Jersey: Four Centuries of American Life*. New Brunswick: Rutgers University Press, 2004.

Rafert, Stewart. *The Miami Indians of Indiana: A Persistent People 1656-1994*. Indiana Historical Society, 1996.

Reid, James Seaton. *History of the Presbyterian Church in Ireland, Comprising the Civil History of the Province of Ulster, from the Accession of James the First*. Vol. 1. London: Whittaker and Co. 1853.

Robb, Graham. *The Debatable Land: The Lost World Between Scotland and England*. New York: W. W. Norton & Company, 2018.

Roosevelt, Theodore. *The Winning of the West*, vol. 3, *The Founding of the Trans-Alleghany Commonwealths, 1784-1790*. New York: G. P. Putnam's Sons, 1894.

———. *The Winning of the West*, part 4, *The Indian Wars, 1784-1787: Franklin, Kentucky, Ohio, and Tennessee*. New York: The Current Literature Publishing Company, 1905.

———. *The Winning of the West*, part 5. *St. Clair and Wayne*. New York: The Current Literature Publishing Company, 1905.

Roulston, William J. *Parishes of Leckpatrick and Dunnalong: Their Place in History*. Letterkenny: Browne Printers, 2000.

———. *Researching Scots-Irish Ancestors*. Belfast: Ulster Historical Foundation, 2005.

———. *Three Centuries of Life in a Tyrone Parish: A History of Donagheady, 1600-1900*. Letterkenny: Strabane History Society, 2010.

Rutherford, Reverend John. *Donagheady Presbyterian Churches and Parish*. Belfast: McCaw, Stevenson & Orr, Ltd., 1953.

Scott, Walter, Esc. *The Border Antiquities of England and Scotland; Comprising Specimens of Architecture and Sculpture and other Vestiges*. Vol. 1. London: Longman, Hurst, Rees, Orme, and Brown et al., 1814.

———. *The Minstrelsy of the Scottish Border*, Vol. 1. Edinburgh: Robert Cadell, 1849.

Schellhammer, Michael. *George Washington and the Final British Campaign for the Hudson River, 1779*. Jefferson NC and London: McFarland and Company, 2012.

Shepherd, William R. *Guide to the Materials for the History of the United States in Spanish Archives*. Washington, D.C.: Carnegie Institution of Washington, 1907.

Shreve, Royal Ornan. *The Finished Scoundrel: General James Wilkinson, Sometime Commander-in-chief of the Army of the United States, Who Made Intrigue a Trade and Treason a Profession*. Indianapolis: Bobs-Merrill Company, 1933.

Slocum, Charles Elihu. *The Ohio Country Between the Years 1783 and 1815*. New York: G. P. Putnam's Sons, 1910.

Smith, Gordon Burns. *History of the Georgia Militia 1783-1861*, vol. 4, *The Companies*. Milledgeville: Boyd Publishing Company, 2000.

Smout, T.C. *A History of the Scottish People, 1560-1830*. London: William Collins Sons & Co., Ltd, 1969.

Snell, James P. *History of Hunterdon and Somerset Counties, New Jersey, with Illustrations and Biographical Sketches of its Prominent Men and Pioneers*. Philadelphia: Everts & Peck, 1881.

Stewart, Stanley. *A History of Donagheady Presbyterian Church*. Bready, Strabane: Donagheady Presbyterian Church, 2005.

Stille, Charles J. *Major General Anthony Wayne and the Pennsylvania Line in the Continental Army*. Philadelphia: J. B. Lippincott, 1893.

Stryker, William Scudder. *The Battles of Trenton and Princeton*. Boston: Houghton, Mifflin, & Co., 1898.

Sword, Wiley. *President Washington's Indian War: The Struggle for the Old Northwest, 1790-1795*. Norman: University of Oklahoma Press, 1985.

Trussell, John B. B. *The Pennsylvania Line: Regimental Organization and Operations, 1775-1783*. Harrisburg: Pennsylvania Historical and Museum Commission, 1993.

Ulster-Scots Community Network. *Londonderry 400: Plantation of the Walled City*. Belfast: Ulster-Scots Community Network. n.d. http://www.ulster-scots.com/uploads/Londonderry400.pdf.

Valentine, Alan. *Lord Stirling: Colonial Gentleman and General in Washington's Army*. New York: Oxford Press, 1969.

Van Doren, Carl. *Mutiny in January*. New York: The Viking Press, 1943.

Ward, Christopher. *The War of the Revolution*, vol. 1. New York: The MacMillan Company, 1952.

Watson, Godfrey. *The Border Reivers*. London: Robert Hale & Company, 1974.

Samuel Watson, ed. *Warfare in the USA, 1784-1861*. Burlington: Ashgate Publishing Company, 2005.

Webb, James. *Born Fighting: How the Scots-Irish Shaped America*, New York: Broadway Books, 2004.

White, Richard. *The Middle Ground: Indians, Empires, and Republics in the Great Lakes Region, 1650-1815*. New York: Cambridge University Press, 1991.

Wildes, Harry Emerson. *Anthony Wayne: Trouble Shooter of the American Revolution*. Westport, Connecticut: Greenwood Press, 1941.

Williams, Glenn F. *Year of the Hangman: George Washington's Campaign Against the Iroquois*. Yardley, Pennsylvania: Westholme Publishing, LLC, 2005.

Williams, Samuel Cole. *History of the Lost State of Franklin*. New York: The Press of the Pioneers, 1933.

Williamson, C. W. *History of Western Ohio and Auglaize County*. Columbus: W. M. Linn & Sons, 1905.

Wingate, Christopher W. *Military Professionalism and the Early American Officer Corps 1789-1796*. Fort Leavenworth: Combat Studies Institute Press, 2013.

Winthrop, William. *Military Law and Precedents*, 2nd ed. Washington: Government Printing Office, 1920. https://www.loc.gov/rr/frd/Military_Law/pdf/ML_precedents.pdf.

Periodicals and Newspapers

Beatty, Joseph M., Jr. "Letters of the Four Beatty Brothers of the Continental Army, 1774-1794." *Pennsylvania Magazine of History and Biography* 44, no. 3 (1920): 193–263.

Booraem, Hendrick V. "William Henry Harrison Comes to Cincinnati." *Queen City Heritage* 43, no. 3 (1987): 3–22.

Bradford, John, ed. *Kentucky Gazette*, May 26, 1792. http://kdlkyvl.org.

Brown, Alan. "The Role of the Army in Western Settlement Josiah Harmar's Command, 1785-1790." *Pennsylvania Magazine of History and Biography* 93, no. 2 (1969): 161–178.

Caldwell, Norman W. "The Frontier Army Officer 1790-1814." *Mid-America* 37, no. 2 (1955): 101–28.

Carson, Hampton L. "Washington at Valley Forge." *Pennsylvania Magazine of History and Biography* 43, no. 2 (1919): 97–116.

Dailey, John E. "Ohio Lands and Survey Systems." *The American Surveyor* 1, no. 7, December (2004). https://archive.amerisurv.com/PDF/TheAmericanSurveyor FabricOf SurveyingOhio December2004.pdf.

Dailey, Rubin, ed, "A Sleeping Hero." *National Democrat*, January 2, 1885.

Graham, Lewis E. "Fort McIntosh." *Western Pennsylvania Magazine* 15, no. 2 (1932): 93–120. https://journals.psu.edu/wph/article/view/1575/1423.

Hall, Virginius C. "The Genesis of an Orchard." *Ohio Historical and Philosophical Society Bulletin*, no. 7 (1949): 87–89.

Historical Society of Pennsylvania. "Roster of the Officers of the 'Legion of the United States Commanded by Major General Anthony Wayne'." *Pennsylvania Magazine of History and Biography* 16, no. 4 (1893): 423–429.

Knopf, Richard C. "Crime and Punishment in the Legion, 1792-1793." *Bulletin of History and Philosophy Society of Ohio* 14, no. 3 (1956): 232–38.

Knouff, Gregory T. "An Arduous Service: The Pennsylvania Backcountry Soldiers' Revolution." *Pennsylvania History* 61, no. 1 (1994): 45–74.

Kohn, Richard H. "General Wilkinson's Vendetta with General Wayne: Politics and Command in the American Army, 1791-1796." *The Filson Club History Quarterly* 45 (1971): 361–372. https://filsonhistorical.org/publication-pdf/general-wilkinsons-vendetta-with-general-wayne-politics-and-command-in-the-american-army-1791-1796/.

Mahon, John K. "Pennsylvania and the Beginnings of the Regular Army." *Pennsylvania History* 21, no. 1 (1954): 33-44. https://journals.psu.edu/phj/article/view/22323/22092.

McMichael, James. "Diary of Lieutenant James McMichael, of the Pennsylvania Line, 1776-1778." *Pennsylvania Magazine of History and Biography* 16, no. 2 (1892): 129–159.

Meek, Basil. "General Harmar's Expedition." *Ohio Archaeological and Historical Quarterly* 20, no. 1 (1911): 74–108.

Nicholson, Bradley J. "Courts-Martial in the Legion Army: American Military Law in the Early Republic, 1792-1796." *Military Law Review* 144 (1994): 77–109.

Ousterhout, Anne M. "Frontier Vengeance: Connecticut Yankees vs. the Pennamites in the Wyoming Valley." *Pennsylvania History* 62, no. 3 (1995): 330-363. https://journals.psu.edu/phj/article/view/25244/25013

Rothensteiner, John. "Paul de Saint Pierre: The First German-American Priest of the West." *The Catholic Historical Review* 5, nos. 2 and 3 (1919): 195–222. http://www.jstor.org/stable/ 25011636.

Roulston, William. "Evolution of the Abercorn Estate in Northwest Ulster, 1610-1703," *Familia 1999: Ulster Genealogical Review,* no. 15 (1999): 54–67.

Rusche, Timothy M. "Treachery within the United States Army." *Pennsylvania History: A Journal of Mid-Atlantic Studies* 65, no. 4 (1998): 478-491. Accessed March 24, 2021. http://www.jstor.org/stable/27774142.

Sergeant R———. "The Battle of Princeton." *Pennsylvania Magazine of History and Biography* 20, no. 4 (1896): 515–519.

Savelle, Max. "The Founding of New Madrid, Missouri." *Mississippi Valley Historical Review* 19, no. 1 (1932): 30–56. Accessed March 25, 2021. http://www.jstor.org/stable/1896649.

Shepherd, William R., ed. "Papers Bearing on James Wilkinson's Relations with Spain, 1787-1816." *American Historical Review* 9, no. 4 (1904): 748–66. https://www.jstor.org/stable/ 1834098.

———. "Wilkinson and the Beginnings of the Spanish Conspiracy." *American Historical Review* 9, no.3 (1904): 490–506. http://penelope.uchicago.edu/Thayer/E/Journals/AHR/9/3/Wilkinson and the Beginnings of the Spanish Conspiracy*.html.

Skelton, William B. "Social Roots of the American Military Profession: The Officer Corps of America's First Peacetime Army, 1784-1789." *Journal of Military History* 54, no. 4 (1990): 435–452.

Storm, Colton. "Lieutenant John Armstrong's Map of the Illinois River, 1790." *Journal of the Illinois State Historical Society (1908-1984)* 37, no.1 (1944): 48–55. Accessed March 25, 2021. https://www.jstor.org/stable/40188085.

———. "Lieutenant Armstrong's Expedition to the Missouri River, 1790." *Mid America: An Historical Review* 25, no. 3 (1943): 180–188.

Trask, Roger R. "Pennsylvania and the Albany Congress, 1754," *Pennsylvania History: A Journal of Mid-Atlantic Studies* 27, no.3 (1960): 273–290.

Warner, Michael S. "General Josiah Harmar's Campaign Reconsidered: How the Americans Lost the Battle of Kekionga." *Indiana Magazine of History* 83, no. 1 (1987): 43–64. Accessed March 18, 2021. http://www.jstor.org/stable/27791042.

Whitaker, Arthur Preston. "James Wilkinson's First Descent to New Orleans in 1787." *Hispanic American Historical Review* 8, no. 1 (1928): 82–97. http://penelope.uchicago.edu/Thayer/E/ Journals/HAHR/8/1/Wilkinsons First Descent to New Orleans in 1787*.html.

Wilson, Frazer, ed. "Harmar's Campaign." *Ohio Archaeological and Historical Quarterly 19*, no. 4 (1910): 393–96.

Wokeck, Marianne S. "Irish Immigration to the Delaware Valley before the American Revolution." *Proceedings of the Royal Irish Academy. Section C: Archaeology, Celtic Studies, History, Linguistics, Literature* 96C, no. 5 (1996): 103-35. Accessed March 18, 2021. http://www.jstor.org/stable/25516172.

"Roster of the Officers of the 'Legion of the United States' Commanded by Major General Anthony Wayne." *Pennsylvania Magazine of History and Biography* 16, no. 4 (1893): 423–429.

"Itinerary of the Pennsylvania Line from Pennsylvania to South Carolina, 1781-1782." *Pennsylvania Magazine of History and Biography* 36, no. 3 (1912): 273–92.

Websites and Blogs

Abbott, Tim. "Elias Dayton's Account of the Battle of Germantown." *Walking the Berkshires*. Last modified October 4, 2012. http://greensleeves.typepad.com/berkshires.

Armstrong, Bob. "The Armstrongs: Pictish Warriors." Last modified February 23, 2015. https://www.armstrongclan.info/pictish-warriors.html.

Bready Ancestry. "Poll Book for the Parish of Donagheady c. 1662" and "Hearth Money Rolls." Accessed August 7, 2015. http://www.breadyancestry.com.

Burleigh, H. H. "The Blockhouse at Bergen Wood," Address given March 3, 1965. United Empire of Loyalist's Association of Canada. Accessed March 25, 2021. http://www.uelac.org/PDF/ The-Block-House-in-Bergen-Wood.pdf.

Genealogy Trails. "Members of the Pennsylvania Society of the Cincinnati, The Order in Which They subscribed, in December, 1783." http://genealogytrails.com/main/societyofthe cincinnati.html#PENN.

Sherman, William Thomas. "Lee's Legion Remembered: Profiles of the 2nd Partisan Corps as taken from Alexander Garden's *Anecdotes* (1822 & 1828 eds.)" Last modified
November 20, 2018. https://archive.org/stream/LeesLegionRemembered.

U.S. Army Corps of Engineers. "Geomorphology Study of the Middle Mississippi River." Last modified December 2005. http://www.mvsc.usace.army.mil/arec/Documents/ Geomorphology/Geomorphology Study of The Middle Mississippi River.pdf.

INDEX

A

Adair, John, 398, 398n776, 454
Adams, John, 80, 106, 448
Albany Congress of 1754, *54, 59*
alcohol, 114, 191
Alexander, William (Lord Sterling), 342
Allison, Richard, 392, 399–400, 400n779, 401, 419, 420n812, 420
American Army, 269, 324, 339–40
American Revolution, mythology of the, 93
Americans, 77, 105n186, 109, 118, 120, 129, 145, 155, 163, 190–91, 196–97, 205, 211, 257, 271
Anderson, Benjamin, 312, 442
Anderson, Richard C., 312, 442n851
Anne (queen of England), 34
Antes, Henry, 133, 137
Armstrong, Anna Magdalena Kreutzer, 49
Armstrong, Hamilton, 126, 140n258, 141, 220–21, 427, 439–40, 443–44
Armstrong, James, 67, 77, 102, 107, 127, 233, 347, 440

Armstrong, Jane Hamilton, 28–29, 42, 47–49
Armstrong, John, xiii–xv, 11–13, 27–31, 46–47, 72–73, 96, 109–10, 112–13, 116–17, 119–21, 124–28, 137–41, 165, 281–82, 390–91
Armstrong, John, Jr., 139n255, 141, 143
Armstrong, Johnnie of Gilnockie, 21, 21n38, 21
Armstrong, Kinmont Willie, 11n20
Armstrong, Mary, 126–27, 127n227
Armstrong, Tabitha Goforth, 402–3, 403n784, 440, 442
Armstrong, Thomas, 42–44, 46–47, 49–51, 51n98, 54n102, 58, 60, 62, 62n115, 66, 126, 318, 444–45
Armstrong, William Goforth, 402, 442
Armstrong family, 13, 18, 20–22, 28–30, 37, 42–44, 67, 101, 442
Arnold, Benedict, 114, 336–37, 341, 364
Articles of War, xiii, 170, 184, 384, 405, 407, 409n792, 411, 414, 415n801, 433, 434n835

Asheton, Joseph, 196, 221, 221n416, 269, 365, 399–400
Aupaumut, Hendrick, 370, 389n759

B

Baily, Francis, 437
Battle of Bergen Blockhouse, 113
Battle of Brandywine, 84–85, 87–88, 91
Battle of Fallen Timbers, 431
Battle of Germantown, 87
Battle of Green Spring, 119
Battle of Monmouth Courthouse, 100
Battle of Princeton, 101, 125
Battle of Short Hills, 78, 83
Battle of Stony Point, 108–9
Battle of Trenton, 77, 341
Battle of Wyoming, 129
Beatty, Erkuries, 112, 178, 183, 187–88, 231, 399–400
Belli, John, 366, 386, 428
Big Bottom, 282–84
Blue Jacket (Shawnee war chief), 241, 252, 271, 282, 430
Board of the Treasury, 181, 183
Board of War, 69, 343–45
Borderers, 5–10, 16–17, 19, 31
Border Marches, 13–14, 18–19
Border Reivers, 10–11
Borders, 3, 5–7, 10, 13, 18–21
Braddock, Edward, 55, 251, 275
Brady, John, 68, 84
Brant, Joseph, 203–5, 210–11, 293, 319, 388, 473
Britain, 5, 64, 93, 129, 147, 149, 155–57, 190, 196, 249, 449–50
British Army, 83, 87, 89, 91, 99, 102, 146, 185, 207, 457
British people, 66, 72–77, 82, 90, 97–98, 100–101, 105, 113–15, 119–21, 155, 204–5, 249–50, 291–92, 369–70, 431–32
Brodhead, Daniel, 97–98, 123
Brown, Patrick, 214
Brownstown, 203, 205, 208
Buell, Joseph, 185
Burr, Aaron, 339, 451–52
Burr conspiracy, 450
Butler, John, 128
Butler, Richard, 116–17, 133, 156, 173, 273, 285, 298, 300–303, 306, 308, 310, 314–16
Butler, Thomas, 315, 318, 365
Butler, Zebulon, 128–29, 133

C

Cadwalader, John, 70, 73
Cahokia (Illinois), 196, 224, 227, 231–32
Carleton, Guy (Lord Dorchester), 292
Carmichael, John, 18, 401
Carondelet, 381–82
Catholics, 32, 34–35, 38
cattle, 4, 6–7, 16, 22–23, 57, 81, 113, 180, 193–94, 252, 255–56, 310, 346, 376
Chadds Ford (Pennsylvania), 81–82
Charles I (king of England), 24–25, 27, 30–31, 59
Charles II (king of England), 30–31, 59
Charleston (South Carolina), 79, 121–22, 125, 349
Cherokees, 194, 202, 235, 348, 359, 388
Chickasaws, 194, 312
Chippewas, 152, 157, 205, 208, 252, 314
Choctaws, 348
Christie, John, 132–33, 137
churches, 2, 8, 22, 30, 34, 39, 45, 53
Churchill, Winston, 24, 26
Church of England, 24, 30

Hamilton, Michael, 27–28, 47–48

Hamilton County, 320, 437, 439

Hamtramck, John, 168–69, 182, 194, 205, 214–16, 222, 240–41, 243, 246, 258–59, 319

Hardin, John, 200–201, 248, 260–61, 263–64, 266–67, 270–71, 273, 278, 371

Harmar, Josiah, 144, 149–50, 154, 158–62, 168, 174, 181–82, 193–96, 213, 215–19, 243–44, 246–49, 266–67, 270–73, 275–81
army of, 168, 251, 257, 277
expedition of, 256n483, 267, 271, 277, 360

Harrison, William Henry, 403, 403n784, 435–36

Hartshorne, Asa, 236, 264, 335, 394

Hay, Henry, 253, 468

Hay, Samuel, 107

Heart, Jonathan, 167–68, 172–73, 176, 286, 315, 365

Hector, Francisco Louis (Baron de Carondelet), 381

Henderson, William, 122–23, 137

Hewitt, Thomas, 139

Hobson's Choice, 420, 423, 426–27

Hodgdon, Samuel, 287, 301, 303

Howe, William, 78–79, 81–88, 98, 116

Hudson River, 78–79, 102–3, 105–6, 108, 110

Hunt, Abner, 282

Hunterdon County, 43–44, 50–52, 54

Hutchins, Thomas, 168

I

Illinois River, 230, 232

Indians, 56–57, 172–73, 179–80, 191–93, 196–97, 199–202, 205, 215, 238–39, 249–51, 256–58, 263–67, 269–70, 314–16, 370–71

hostile, 161, 216, 220, 259

Indians, Wabash, 197, 239–41

Innes, Harry, 235, 355n696

Ireland, xiv, 2, 20–22, 24–25, 27, 31–32, 36–40, 42, 46, 57

Irish people, 22–23, 27, 38, 40, 45, 179

Irish Rebellion of 1641, *41n78*

Irvin, Thomas, 263, 308n590

J

James II (king of England), 32

James VI of Scotland/James I of England, 18

Jockey Hollow, 110, 112, 114

Johnston, Francis, 114, 116, 222, 302, 373, 397, 401n780, 434, 441

K

Kaskaskia, 196, 224, 226–28, 230–31, 234–35, 359

Kekionga, 241, 252, 253n477, 261, 267–68, 273, 276, 278, 431

Kentuckians, 195, 197, 200, 214–15, 218–19, 236, 248, 269, 290, 336n657, 350, 352, 362

Kentucky, 148, 154, 160, 165, 189, 198, 219, 235–36, 238, 243, 251, 254, 347, 353–54, 356–59

Kerr, John, 442

Kersey, William, 217, 319

Kickapoos, 99, 190, 205, 209, 252

Kingsbury, Jacob, 282

Kings Ferry, 102, 105

Kingwood, 44–45, 49, 53

Kirke, Percy, 33

Kirkwood, Robert, 296n568

Knox, Henry, 183–84, 218–20, 225, 237–39, 242–44, 248–50, 272–73, 275–76, 284, 293–95, 297–300, 324–25, 327–28, 369–72, 389

L

La Cassagne, Michael, 381, 383
Lafayette, Marquies de, 80, 97–100, 117–19, 125, 149, 446
Lancaster, 85, 93, 122–24, 128, 153, 287, 349
Land Ordinance of 1787, 198, 348
Laud, William, 24
Lee, Arthur, 154, 156–57
Lee, Charles, 99, 190, 205, 209, 252
Lee, Henry ("Light Horse Harry"), 104, 107, 159, 361, 363
Lee's Legion, 104n185, 127, 363, 444
Leges Marchiarum, 15
Legion of the United States, 413–14, 418, 424, 430, 433
Legionville, 367, 377, 391, 399, 401, 420
Le Gris (Miami chief), 252
Lewis and Clark Expedition, 225, 227, 469
Liddesdale, 11, 13, 19, 21
Little Turtle (Miami war chief), 251, 253, 256, 260, 262, 269, 271, 274, 290, 314–15, 331, 388, 430
Logan, Benjamin, 197–98, 201
Logan, James, 41, 41n78
Londonderry/Derry, 29, 32
   siege of, 34–36
Louisville, 166–67, 173, 187, 359, 441
Lowden, John, 65–66
Lower Sandusky, council at, 155
Luce, Francis, 217
Ludlow, Israel, 300, 415, 439, 441
Ludlow's Station, 301–3, 328
Luzerne County, 142

M

Marks, Hastings, 386
Marshall, Thomas, 361

Martin, Joseph Plumb, 89, 89n158, 89, 100, 102–3, 112
Martin, Robert, 136, 139, 141
Mascoutens, 190
Maumee River, 243, 252, 267, 269, 291, 370–71
Mawhood, Charles, 73
Maxwell, William, 81, 426
May, John, 251
May, William, 310, 370
McAdams, John, 60, 62, 62n115, 126, 443
McAdams, Nancy (Ann) Armstrong, 440
McCarty, Richard, 227n425, 439
McCurdy, William, 153, 178n331
McDowell, Nathan, 208
McGary, Hugh, 197–98, 200
McHenry, James, 100
McKean, Thomas, 136
McKee, Alexander, 155, 205, 292, 388–89
McLane, Allen, 96–98, 102–3, 108, 125
McMillan, James, 268
Mead, David, 136, 139
Meigs, Return J., Jr., 256n484
Mercer, Hugh, 72–73
Mifflin, Thomas, 69, 149
Miller, Catherine (Red Headed Nance), 318n620
Mingos, 252, 371
Miró, Esteban, 352
Mississippi, 56, 156, 224–27, 232–33, 235, 338, 347, 351, 356–57, 439, 441, 449
Mississippi River, 55, 156, 196, 232, 232n434, 347
Missouri, 227, 229–30
Missouri River, 231
Mohawks, 59, 156, 173, 211, 252

392–401, 403, 405–13, 415–16, 418–21, 426–30, 432–34, 448–54

William of Orange (king of England), 32

Williamsburg, 118–19

Wilson, Elizabeth Armstrong, 127

Winnebagos, 252

Woolens Act of 1699, 36

Wyandots, 152, 162–64, 202, 204–5, 212, 252, 314, 388, 430

Wyllys, John, 185, 185n346, 214, 221n416, 268–70

Wyoming, 61, 133, 138–39, 141–42, 223

Wyoming Massacre, 129

Wyoming Valley, 58–61, 130, 142–44, 146

Y

Yankees, 61–62, 128, 131, 134, 138, 140–41

Yorktown, 120

Z

Ziegler, David, 167, 381n742

Made in the USA
Middletown, DE
26 November 2022

16102279R00302